# CAMERA & CRAFT

## Titles in *The Digital Imaging Masters Series*:

*Power, Speed & Automation with Adobe Photoshop*
by Geoff Scott and Jeff Tranberry

*Color Management & Quality Output: Working with Color from Camera to Display to Print*
by Tom P. Ashe

*Camera & Craft: Learning the Technical Art of Digital Photography*
by Andy Batt, Candace Dobro and Jodie Steen

## Praise for the series:

Sounds like as close to a dream team as one could get without having to resort to spiritual means. I mean if you could get Ansel Adams to do a section on black and white and landscape—great, but that would require a séance. For the talent living, this is a dream team.

*—Robert Barnett, QBToo (formerly PC-Review Online)*

We loved our old Time/Life series of photography books. Time for an update. This series could become iconic.

*—Anne Pfeiffer, Instructor*

I think that Katrin Eismann's skill in curriculum development is reflected in the approach. I like the approach a lot; I would find it to be a valuable resource and would expect to turn to the texts often for advice.

*—Mark Lewis, SUNY Empire State College*

I think there is a good balance of technical vs. creative.

*—Carol Tipping, FRPS EFIAP*

I think many of the books on the market are software driven, whereas this series is developed to support the photography industry. There is a world of difference between explaining a feature of a software package and explaining how to get an important photography task accomplished through a software tool.

*—Douglas Barkey, The Art Institute of Pittsburgh*

The School of Visual Arts Master of Professional Studies in Digital Photography is an intensive one-year degree program that is offered as an on-campus/summer residency or an online/summer residency program that seamlessly blends the most current technical and aesthetic aspects of contemporary photographic image-making. The program meets the needs of professional photographers and photographic educators who want to advance their skills in digital image capture, image processing and high-quality output to remain competitive in a variety of image-making and related fields. Graduates work as commercial, fashion, fine-art, and editorial photographers; retouchers; studio managers; and higher education staff and faculty.

*—Masters in Digital Photography Program Information*
*http://www.sva.edu/digitalphoto*
*Contact: mpsphoto@sva.edu*

# CAMERA & CRAFT

## LEARNING THE TECHNICAL ART OF DIGITAL PHOTOGRAPHY

**Andy Batt, Candace Dobro and Jodie Steen**

SERIES EDITOR KATRIN EISMANN

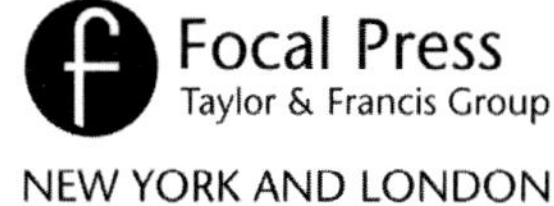

NEW YORK AND LONDON

First published 2015
by Focal Press
70 Blanchard Road, Suite 402, Burlington, MA 01803

Simultaneously published in the UK
by Focal Press
2 Park Square, Milton Park, Abingdon, Oxon OX14 4RN

*Focal Press is an imprint of the Taylor & Francis Group, an informa business*



Series Editor: Katrin Eismann
Series Developmental Editor: Candace Dobro



*Library of Congress Cataloging in Publication Data*
Batt, Andy.
Camera & craft: learning the technical art of digital photography/Andy Batt, Candace Dobro, and Jodie Steen.
pages cm. — (Digital imaging masters series)
Includes bibliographical references and index.
1. Photography—Digital techniques. 2. Photography—Technique. I. Dobro, Candace. II. Steen, Jodie. III. Title. IV. Title: Camera and craft.
TR267.B365 2015
771.3—dc23
2014016171

ISBN: 978-0-415-81012-8 (pbk)
ISBN: 978-0-203-79239-1 (ebk)

Typeset in Trade Gothic, Helvetica Neue and Optima
by Florence Production Ltd, Stoodleigh, Devon, UK

www.focalpress.com/cw/digitalimagingmasters

# Dedication

## Andy

On December 8, 1988 I received one of the best birthday presents an eager young photographer could get. It wasn't a new camera, or a 100-foot spool of TRI-X—it was a three-volume set of Ansel Adams' *The Camera, The Negative and The Print.*[1] This was a gift from Mom and Dad—Kay and Dave. They believed in my fervent desire to become a photographer so much that they bought me these important books. I still have them on my bookshelf. They have been referred to *many* times during the writing of this book. My parents also believed in my dream enough to give me four years at RIT to study photography, and then never said "stop" in my pursuit of making photography a career.

Dad is a retired Navy man, educator and career counselor. Mom was a toxicologist, microbiologist and ketchup tester; she worked in the frog lab and with electron microscopes. She was a singer, pianist and organist. She always made me look words up in the dictionary. From them I was given the tools and support that allowed me to become a photographer and—as of this book an author. Thank you Mom and Dad, for everything.

Mom passed away in 2012, so I am dedicating this book to her.

## Candace

To My Jeffrey: for doing the laundry, tolerating my broken clock, supporting every endeavor I ever embarked upon and loving me as I am . . . and for being a science guy who understands that the most important truths are expressed through the arts.

## Jodie

To Joshua—for looking after the little ones while I taught or wrote late into the night, for loving photography and for loving me, for being officially the handiest guy I know, and mostly for supporting every crazy idea I ever had.

## Note

1 Adams, Ansel, *The Negative: The New Ansel Adams Photography Series/ Book 2* (Boston: A New Graphic Society Book, Little, Brown and Company, 1981).

# Contents

# Foreword

> ***Photography is the easiest thing to make, and one of the hardest things to make well.***
>
> ***—Jerry Saltz***

Knowing how each Photoshop slider or camera setting works does not create compelling images. On a similar note, having great ideas without mastering the skills to realize them will also produce unsatisfying results. To produce outstanding images, you must be dedicated to craft, vision and creativity. Being an artist is simultaneously exhilarating, challenging, frightening, pleasurable, difficult—and rewarding.

With this book, you are privy to the real-world knowledge of many talented, creative and smart photographers. I had the privilege of meeting Andy Batt, Candace Dobro and Jodie Steen in outstanding educational environments. Andy and I graduated from the Rochester Institute of Technology in the early 1990s, just as digital technology was starting to impact photography. Back then, Andy was the one wearing Chucks before they were totally cool. He lived in the studios and darkrooms as he experimented with techniques to uniquely express his vision. Now, a quarter of a century later, Andy's footwear may have changed, but one thing remains the same: He is obsessively dedicated to researching the latest technology, experimenting in the studio and delving into exhibits, music and movies that inspire him.

Andy takes being up to date very seriously, and when he taught in the School of Visual Arts Masters in Digital Photography program, he insisted that his students learn the technical aspects of photography—and, more importantly, that they create compelling images. For Andy, a seemingly banal technical exercise such as an exposure bracket or a color temperature test is an ideal opportunity to make strong photographs. He's a true believer that with every image you make today, you're learning to make better images for tomorrow.

I met Candace when she was a student in the inaugural year of the online version of the SVA Masters in Digital Photography program. It required tenacity and focus to negotiate the uncharted territory of a new online program, and Candace approached the endeavor with an open mind and generous smile, always bringing solutions and suggestions to improve the quality of the classes for everyone involved. She is an experienced editor who knows how to maintain each writer's voice, and is patient, tenacious and detail-oriented—thus making her an ideal partner to guide and harness Andy's intensive focus and busy professional schedule.

The overall concept for this book is based on the "Digital Materials and Processes" class that Jodie Steen developed and taught for the inaugural year of the SVA MPS Digital Photography online program. Jodie is the consummate professional and brings her expertise in workflow, color management and professional problem-solving to these pages.

*Camera & Craft* is much more than a regurgitation of assumed rules and oft-repeated factoids. It is based on critical thinking and will encourage you to understand and apply digital tools and techniques in the essential service of making better images. To enrich your experience, Andy and Candace have called on a wide variety of professional experts—from commercial, portrait, editorial and fine art photography—to generously share their experience, understanding and images.

As photographers, we're responsible for the work we produce and put out in the world. The images we create say more than "I was here" or "This is a model I photographed." They also represent how we perceive the world—and the people—we photograph. It's critical to understand that how we photograph something or someone both captures and reflects our understanding of the subject; it can also influence the viewer's understanding of it. Andy, Candace and Jodie will guide you on your journey from being an image-taker to an image-creator.

You are in good hands.

Katrin Eismann
Series Editor, January 2014

# Acknowledgments

This book originated with the great "Digital Materials and Processes" class Jodie Steen developed with Tom Ashe in the program that Katrin Eismann built at the School of Visual Arts (SVA). Thanks to them for their trailblazing work, the questions they answered and the collaboration they offered.

Erika Velasquez tested every exercise in this book to be sure they worked without a hitch. She also provided many sample photographs to help explain the point of an exercise, even if you don't go through the steps yourself. Erika was one of Andy's best students at SVA—and she was a valuable member of our team. We're delighted to introduce her work. Thanks, Erika!

Many talented others helped as well—and we stand on their shoulders: David Eubank, Eric Meola, Collin Murphy, Jamie Vitale, Charles Luce, Michael Tapes, Michael Jones, Anthony Georgis, Ken Kobre, Meg Storey, Howard LeVant, Seth Resnick, Jamie Spritzer, Peter Krogh, Rick Hatmaker and Carrie Atkins. Thanks especially to Tom Hassler for his expertise and for tech-editing us through the tricky patches.

Until writing this book, we underestimated the importance of the behind-the-scenes support that makes any such project possible! We sincerely thank all the staff at Focal Press, Taylor & Francis Group (our publisher); Studio B, our agent; and the School of Visual Arts, our artistic and educational community. A special shout out to our team at Focal Press: Kimberly Duncan-Mooney, whose impeccable suggestions greatly improved our content; Alison Duncan, who patiently guided us through the manuscript process; Denise Power, our production editor; Jennifer Wise (awesome copy editing!); Florence Production for doing our typesetting; Jonathan Merrett, our proofreader and Matt Willis, cover designer, who designed the beautiful The Digital Imaging Masters Series.

Because we didn't want you to hear the lone sound of our voices or see only the photos we created, Andy asked his colleagues to lend theirs. This project has grown into an amazing collaboration with a group of photographers and experts who generously added their voices to the mix; it's a *big-ass* list! Our photographers are: Holly Andres, Carli Davidson, Kim Campbell, Stewart Cohen, Jeff Conley, Bruce Ely, Craig Ferroggiaro, Toni Greaves and Sol Neelman. Our other experts are: Jim Christian, Rachel Jerome Ferraro, Tom Ashe and Therese Gietler. Thanks, too, to all the fine people in our photographs for allowing us the privilege of photographing them.

## Andy

I co-wrote this book with Candace Dobro riding shotgun. She and I hammered out the basic shape and structure over five days and late nights of Bourbon and Turkish spiced chicken. She acted as my sounding board, my co-author, my editor and my prototypical reader. Candace made me explain everything clearly, and then go back and do it again with half as many words. And then make it interesting to read. And then take out things that seemed important at the time, but didn't add to the whole. Without Candace's guidance, you'd be opening up a much drier, longer book. So send her a note to say thanks.

Jodie Steen was our in-house tech expert, charged with making sure that everything we wrote is technically correct. She provided another valuable set of eyes on every chapter and also kicked ass with some great material in our *Color* chapter. Jodie's expertise in Color Management and Art Reproduction was incredibly valuable.

There are so many words of thanks that need to be said for this book—but the lion's share goes straight to my wife, Therese. Without her care, love and support you wouldn't be reading this page, let alone this book. Everybody stop reading now; this is just for her:

*Hey T—I love you. Without you, I wouldn't have survived any of this. I owe you one forever.*

## Candace

Andy is very modest. Not only is he an ace photographer, but he also understands equipment, physics, computers, software and music—and probably loads of other things I don't know about. Besides all that, he can cook, *and* he makes a mean cup of coffee! Most important, Andy is one of the nicest guys I've ever had the pleasure of working with. He's collaborative, irreverent, generous, responsible, inventive and wickedly smart. If you're looking for a photographer, you should hire him. You won't be sorry. Now that we're finished writing the book, I know I'm going to miss working with him. Perhaps we'll write a sequel . . .

It all began with Jodie's class. I'd like to thank her for teaching it so well, sharing her expertise and keeping us honest as we bashed out these chapters one by one.

Enormous thanks to all the photographers and teachers in the world, specifically: Katrin Eismann and Tom Ashe, who have supported so many of us so well; Nieves Gruneiro for her impeccable advice in all things photographic and for her friendship; Charles Luce, who makes physics clearer than should ever be possible; Tom Sternal, for inspiring thousands of students at Muhlenberg College; and the many generous and gifted teachers at the School of Visual Arts, County College of Morris, the Visual Arts Center of NJ and Peter's Valley. Thanks especially to Michele Reichstein, Carrie Dobro and Mark Ciglar for helping me take the leap!

Heartfelt thanks to the people who matter most: my husband and true love, Jeff (*res ipsa loquitur*); our cherished daughters, Sarah and Dolyn Dobro, who give me hope that the world will be okay (at least for a while); my soul mates Leslie Shaw, Amy Sunshine and Roby Weinreich and my network of family and friends—especially my parents, Jean and Norman DeSouza and Barbara and Murray Dobro and my Aunt, Eileen Brown. You all make it worth the ride.

## Jodie

My sincere gratitude goes to Andy Batt for working enthusiastically on this project. Andy had a vision for this book: Not only did he want to dispense useful information, but he also wanted to offer insight into the working photographer's thoughts, work and habits. The result is a wondrous blend of technical knowledge and first-hand insights. Thank you, Andy, for approaching the material in a new way.

I first met Candace when she was a student in the first class I taught at SVA in the online MPS Digital Photography program. She was inquisitive and thoughtful in her approach and dedicated to honing her craft. It has been an enormous pleasure to work with her on this project, and I am indebted to her for tirelessly refining the work. Thank you.

All of this began with Katrin Eismann, who approached me to develop the online MPS Digital Photography program at SVA. She helped me through writing fifteen courses and creating countless videos and screencasts, and generously offered her guidance and support along the way. I am proud to see the seed of what was created for the MPS program turned into something so much bigger—that will reach so many—and this would not have been possible without her.

A sincere thank you to my family: To my husband, Joshua, for your unending love and support—there is no one else I'd rather be going through this journey with than you. To my babies, Honor and Arden, who were born during this process—you are my greatest creation of all. And to my parents—your love and support mean the world to me.

# Preface

## Andy

To get started, here's a glimpse into the who, what, where and why of this book. First off, the who: I'm Andy Batt and I'm a photographer. In high school, an art teacher (who must have seen something in me that I didn't) pushed an SLR into my hands. That simple action propelled me through four years at Rochester Institute of Technology (RIT) to study photography, even though I had no idea what it meant to be a photographer. I thought I would just figure it out. I was supposed to be an electrical engineer, but had a moment of clarity when I realized I could pursue something I liked, not just something that seemed like a good career. I've spent my entire career learning and plan to continue doing so—if you look hard enough, there are always rabbit holes to go down.

I've never done anything but photography. That might be foolish, because it's tough to make a living that way, but when it's good—when I've got a fantastic project in my hands and am surrounded by great people—it doesn't get any better. I love that photography has allowed me to be the tech geek I am and the artist I want to be.

A few years ago, my colleagues and fellow RIT graduates Katrin Eismann (Editor of this book series) and Tom Ashe approached me in a dark alley, held me at knifepoint and forced me (just kidding) to take a job teaching in their groundbreaking online Masters of Professional Studies in Digital Photography (MPS DP) program at the School of Visual Arts (SVA). (Katrin is Chair and Tom is Associate Chair of the program.)

I found myself teaching a crash course in photography in one far-too-short semester.[1] My students were widely varied, lived in many different time zones and had a broad-ranging array of equipment, skills and backgrounds. Teaching that class made me reach way back to the memory of my classes at RIT. I needed to root around in the dark and unearth all types of things I learned—or should've learned—so I could explain them to my students. I wanted to take all the abstract material and connect it to the craft of photography, and I wanted my students to learn the technical stuff so they could apply it and become better artists.

This book has grown from those roots. I hope you'll find it to be a little different than the other instructional books you've read, and that after reading it, you'll come out on the other side with a foundation you can build upon. *Camera & Craft* isn't meant to be an encyclopedia, a software book or a camera manual. It's meant to be a conversation about the technical aspects and ideas that power creative photography.

With this book, I share my experience as a successful photo geek and commercial artist. My mission is to help you become a stronger photographer.

### On Being a Professional

I'm a member of American Society of Media Photographers (ASMP) and American Photographic Artists (APA)[2] and believe in the value of professional photography. Photographers—along with professionals in many other fields— have felt a seismic change in the work world. The perceived dollar value of photography has been going down, while the use of photography has been skyrocketing, in both consumer and commercial arenas. There are more photographers than there are careers/jobs/clients to support them. Although this may have always been true, it feels more visceral now than ever before.

My hope is to help educate up-and-coming photographers about what it takes to be good at this profession. If you want to get the jobs, you need to have the skills that set you apart from the pack; the more professional you are at your craft, the better chance you'll have at a successful career.

## Candace

When I walked into Katrin Eismann's office in 2008 to find out whether I should apply to the MPS DP program, Katrin asked me what I saw myself doing in five years. "I'm a good photographer," I said, "but I'm not the next Avedon. What I *am* really good at is understanding both the artistic and administrative worlds, so I see myself landing somewhere between the two." Her eyes lit up.

I ended up enrolling in the inaugural year of the Online/Low-Residency version of the master's program—at age 52—and loved it. Near graduation time, Katrin pulled me aside. "I'm building a book series on the program and I don't have time to manage the project. Would you like to help?" . . . Yes!

Since then, I've been Developmental Editor for *The Digital Imaging Masters Series* and the online classes in the Masters in Digital Photography program at SVA. This involves shaping and editing the material for the books and classes so it's clear, relevant, well organized and fun to read, while maintaining the voice of the author. I get paid to encourage and help smart, talented authors/teachers so they can share their experience with their students—and you, their readers. Nice work, if you can get it!

Enter Andy Batt. Andy taught "Digital Materials and Processes" in the MPS DP program from 2011–2013. He wanted to write a book (this book) based on his class, but needed a partner in crime. I was (happily) elected to co-author it with him and Jodie Steen, who developed the course (and was my most excellent teacher—thank you very much!).

As the book developed, we realized we'd fallen into a prolonged teacher–student conversation, so we went with it. Consider me your representative: Andy spoke; I listened, questioned, probed. Andy clarified; I was happy. I hope you will be, too.

The book we wrote is the one we thought you'd want to read. It explores the minds of working photographers and shares their experiences. Andy starts off each conversation, and his many generous colleagues and friends join right in. All of us have the same goal: to help you become a better, more informed photographer.

## Jodie

I came to New York City, just after completing my undergrad at Syracuse University, to pursue a career in photography. I began as a freelance assistant, a job I was not particularly good at. Luckily, the digital revolution was solidly underway in the early 2000s, and I had the good fortune of working with photographer Jack Reznicki. He was an early adopter of digital and encouraged me to pursue a career in technology. I was fascinated by digital photography, by seeing photography reborn in a whole new form; I had found my niche. I went on to work as a full-time tech at Foto Care, where it was my task to support all things digital—computers, digital backs, printers, scanners and color management. It was exhilarating, and I felt like I was being paid to gain an education that I could not buy.

Shortly after, I did my share of freelance digital tech work, which was my most favorite job I've ever had. It was a thrill working on large photo sets with talented photographers and crews. All the while I continued to shoot, first on my own, then with my husband and partner, Joshua.

In 2005 I launched 127 Productions, Inc., a color management consulting firm. Over the years, this has grown larger than I ever dreamed, and I feel lucky to work with interesting clients that challenge me to do great work.

When I accepted the offer to teach the first Digital Photography MPS course for SVA, under the direction of Katrin Eismann, I had no idea what I was in for! Katrin guided me through course development, writing and teaching my first class. I treasure the relationships I built with the students, especially Candace Dobro, who was an integral part of this book. I had the pleasure of meeting Andy as he entered the MPS program as an instructor.

The content we have worked to create is a synergy of ideas, and my greatest hope is that it gives you insight into the craft of photography, and that it inspires you to make pictures.

## Notes

1 Teaching is very hard work. I now sympathize with every professor I ever had in college.

2 American Society of Media Photographers (http://asmp.org/) and American Photographic Artists (http://www.apanational.com/).

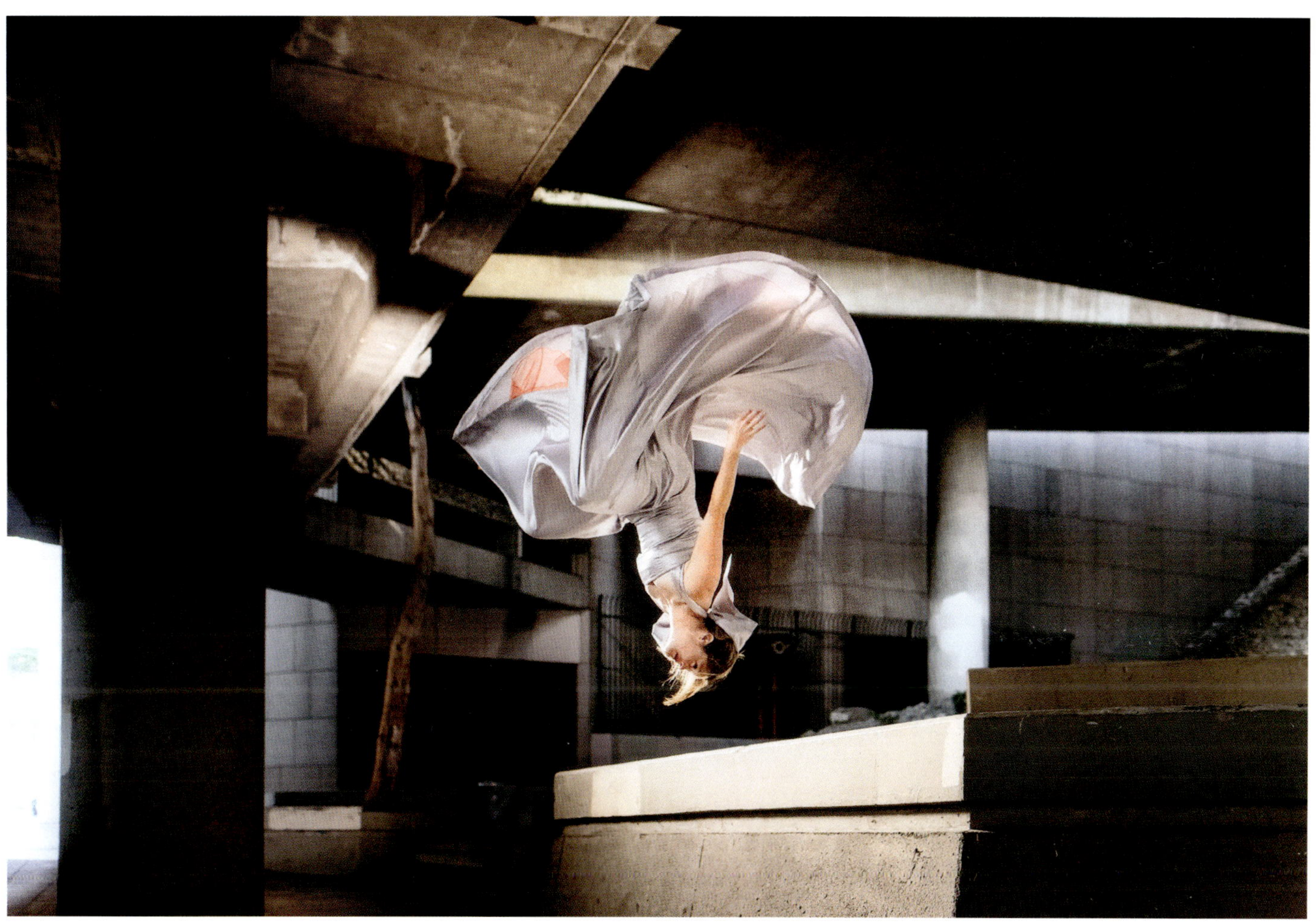

**FIGURE I.1**
IMAGE © ANDY BATT, *LUCI ROMBERG, PROM DRESS UNDER THE BRIDGE*, 2009.

# INTRODUCTION: OUR PHOTO EXPERTS

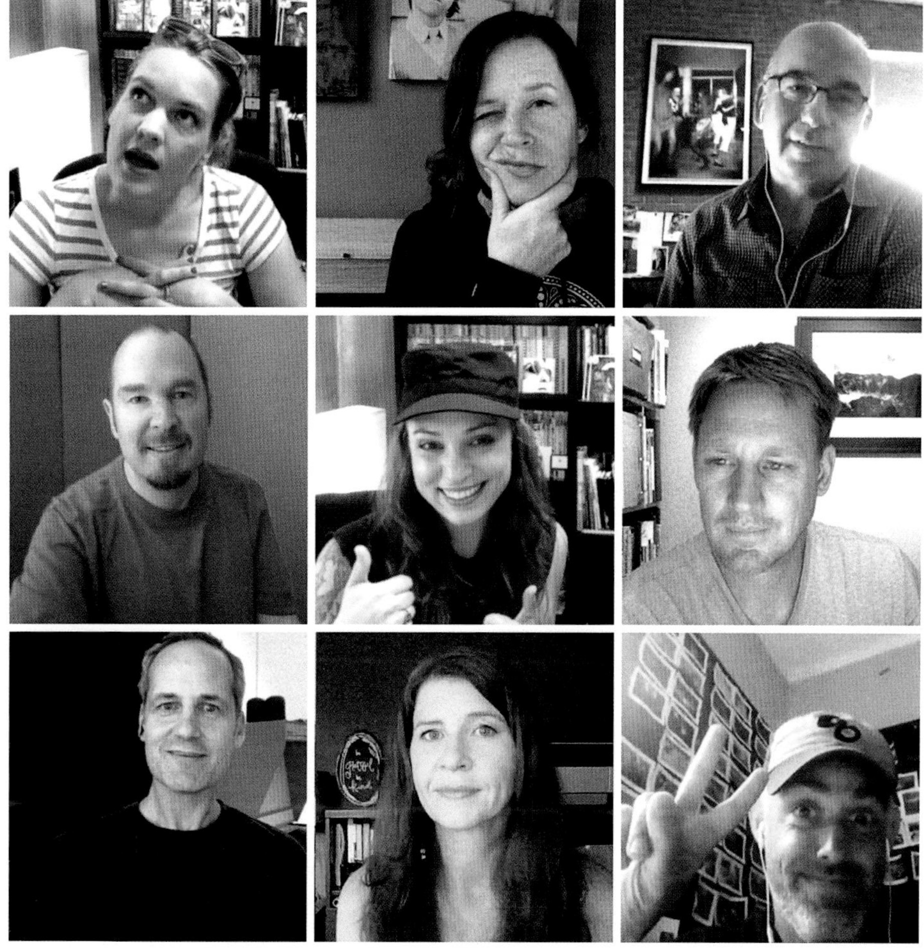

**FIGURE I.2**
Our photo experts are very smart and charming people! (Top row, left to right: Holly Andres, Kim Campbell, Stewart Cohen. Middle Row: Jeff Conley, Carli Davidson, Bruce Ely. Bottom row: Craig Ferroggiaro, Toni Greaves, Sol Neelman.)
IMAGE GRID © ANDY BATT AND CANDACE DOBRO, *PHOTO EXPERTS ON SKYPE: EXPERIENCE + KNOWLEDGE!*, 2013.

---

Did you ever wish you could get inside the heads of your favorite photographers to understand how they think? We have, too. That's why we invited nine working photographers, of all different genres, to talk with us about creating successful imagery.

Together, we go beyond the basics, delving into the how and why of photographic principles. We believe that the goal of good photography is to produce art—not necessarily "Art" with a capital A, but art in which you create an image to the best of your ability.

We also believe that the more you understand photo technology and equipment, the more you'll open up aesthetically.

To this end, these pages include explanations, conversations and exercises to help you understand and explore your tools, plus plenty of imagery to illustrate the ideas and techniques discussed.

We begin with the basics in *Chapter 1, Prerequisite: Photo 101*, so that the subsequent chapters make sense to anyone unaccustomed to working with manual camera controls. After that, we explore looking through the viewfinder, managing digital workflow, considering lens work and sensor technology and discussing specific strategies to control exposure and color. We draw to a close by considering the natural arc of jobs—from pre-production to the actual shoot and file delivery—and wind up with a selection of imagery and some excellent advice from each of our photo experts.

Before meeting the experts, here's an idea of some questions they'll address in the pages that follow:

- What do they consider when they look through the viewfinder?
- What are their workflow protocols?
- Which lenses do they choose, and why?
- What do they know about sensor technology that makes their images look so good?
- How do they nail their exposures?
- Which tools do they use to control color?
- How do they prepare for a job?
- What have they learned about working with models, producers and crew?
- When do they use retouchers?
- What are some things they've learned about working with clients?

We had the pleasure of conducting Skype interviews with nine talented colleagues who shared their many years of experience as professional photographers. Not only do we greatly respect their work, but we also value their generous and open contribution of knowledge and experience to the photo community.

The work and the information they shared is scattered throughout the book, so you'll be hearing from our experts on every subject we explore. If you can't wait to see more examples of their imagery, then turn ahead to *Chapter 9, Guest Photographers: Photos and Advice*, where you can learn more about the way they approach their practice. In the meantime, by way of introduction—and inspiration—here are some stories about how they became photographers . . .

---

## Holly Andres

### *Fine Art and Editorial Photographer*

My undergrad degree is in painting and drawing. I studied photo and video in graduate school and studied film at the Northwest Film Center after that. It was then that I considered the potential for freezing a single film still and using photography—in dialog with cinema—as a way of conveying a particular narrative. I wanted the viewer to be more interactive and think about what might have happened before or after the shot.

I'd taught at the college level since completing my MFA at Portland State University in 2004, and a couple years ago decided that I wanted to broaden my scope in photography. I have a pretty firm foundation in fine art photography and have been repped by some renowned galleries in New York, Atlanta, LA, San Francisco and Portland. I'd been told that my fine art photography, specifically, might have some commercial application.

I was ready for a career, so two years ago I compiled a commercial book and started peddling it around. Right off the bat, people were intrigued with it; none of the work was made for a client or a commercial application. I signed on with a photo agent, Hello Artists, and for the last two years I have been shooting commercially, primarily editorial work. My very first job was a week-long project at Rockaway Beach for *The New York Times Magazine,* and I've shot for them several times since. I think my ability to capture a creative, narrative portrait lends itself in particular to editorial subjects.

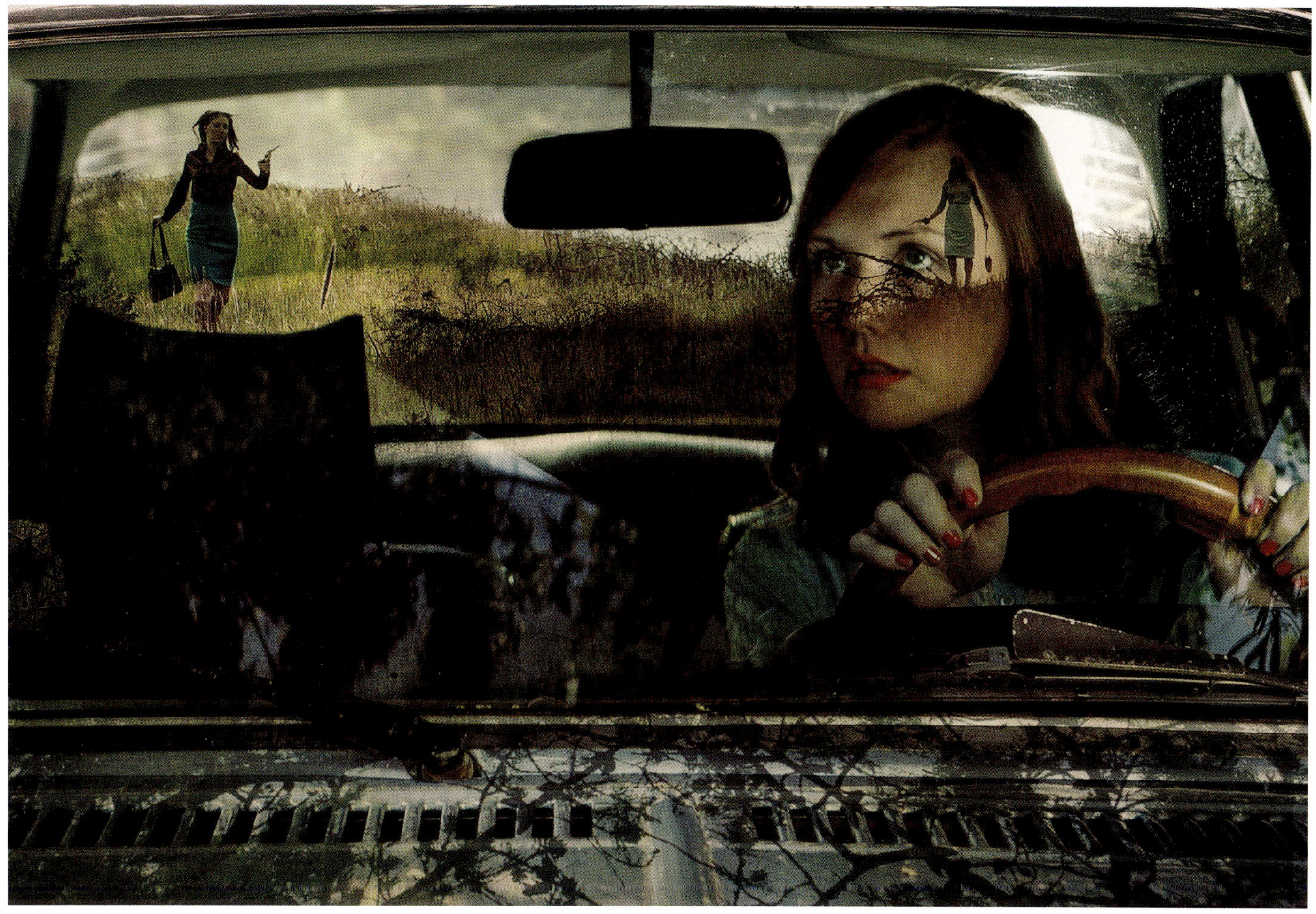

**FIGURE I.3**
With this shot, Holly was loosely influenced by the rear-view projections commonly used in the driving sequences of classic films and attempted to simultaneously show two conflicting moments in time within the same frame.
IMAGE © HOLLY ANDRES, *GUNFIGHT*, 2012.

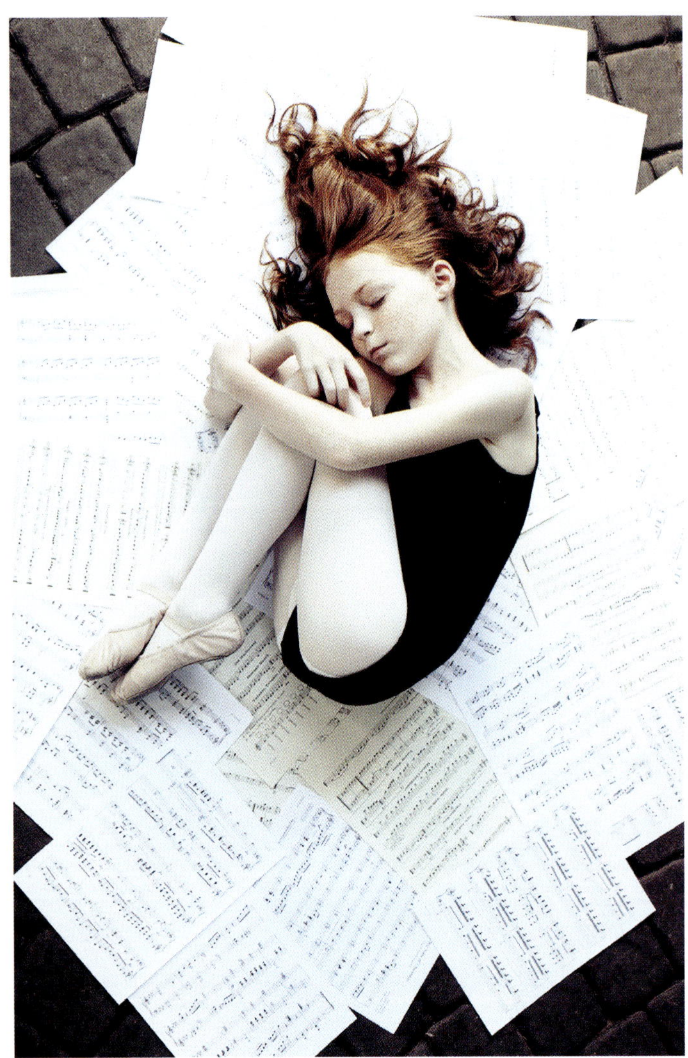

**FIGURE I.4** Kim likes to work with kids between the ages of 5 and 12, because they have so little inhibition. She'll say, "Hey, let's try this," and lay out props that could go with the theme or mood—then let them handpick some so they have an investment in the project.
IMAGE © KIM CAMPBELL, *DREAMER*, 2012.

# Kim Campbell

## *Portrait Photographer*[1]

I have a Master's degree in Art Therapy and worked in that field for a couple of years. I became a photographer when, due to life circumstances, I couldn't work as a therapist any longer. My husband, Francisco Salgado, was a photographer who taught at local colleges, and he essentially gave me a backup career. It actually turned out to be a very positive thing for me; I enjoy it immensely.

I became a photographer in '97. I learned about photography by taking his classes and from assisting him, but then one day he handed me the camera and told me that I needed to go for it and try a photo session on my own. After that he often joked, "She never gave the camera back!"

My husband and I each come from a fine art background, so we didn't go the traditional portrait-photographer training route. We just created pictures that moved us or interested us, which was a different approach into the portrait-photography field. I think that's one of the reasons we've had such a good niche. Our photos are recognizable because we create something that looks unique. Each one stands by itself.

## Stewart Cohen

### *Director/Photographer*

I came up through the still-photography world and have been working at it for 25-ish years. I got a BA, not a photo degree, and was a photo assistant for a few years. I did it the old-school way of coming up through the ranks, then started my own business in the late 80s; I've been doing it ever since. That's the short story.

I didn't want to be a photographer until midway through my sophomore year in college. I took electives in photography and loved it. Right before Thanksgiving of that year, my professor told me that I'd be good at whatever I wanted to do, but not to do photography, as I didn't have the talent—so that made me decide that I *was* going to do it.

I didn't come from much, so I knew I had to make a living, which played heavily on me when I started out. Back then, the big photographers were shooting a lot of annual reports; they were getting to travel all over the world, and I wanted to travel and meet a lot of people. So I worked for a few very successful photographers, did annual reports and got to go around the world quickly a couple of times in my early 20s. That gave me a taste for travel and staying in nice hotels; I was hooked on that whole lifestyle.

I started doing work on my own and building a career. One of the guys I worked for early on sold pictures as stock photography, so I placed my pictures at a stock house to make extra money. That grew over the years to become very important for my business. People would pay a lot more money for stock photos back then.

I knocked on a lot of doors. I still knock on doors, shoot a lot of pictures and knock on more doors. Over time, I developed relationships and started to build a staff. I had my first full-time assistant about two years after I started. There are six or seven of us here now.

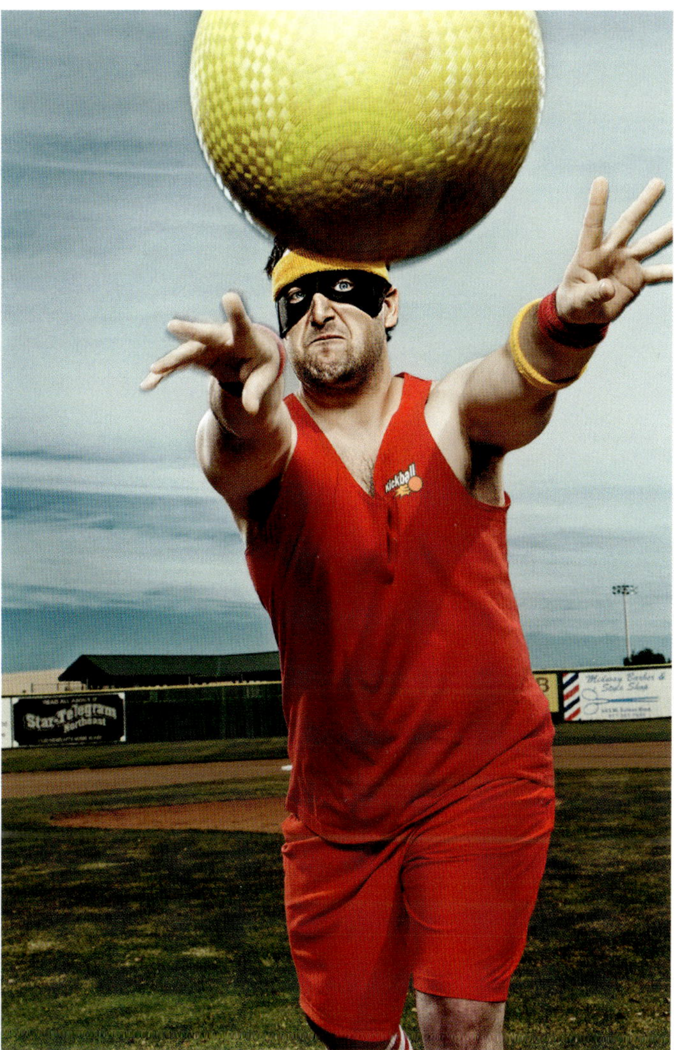


**FIGURE I.5** Stewart shot this image as part of a campaign for Mike's Hard Lemonade®. IMAGE © STEWART COHEN, *KICKBALL*, 2012.

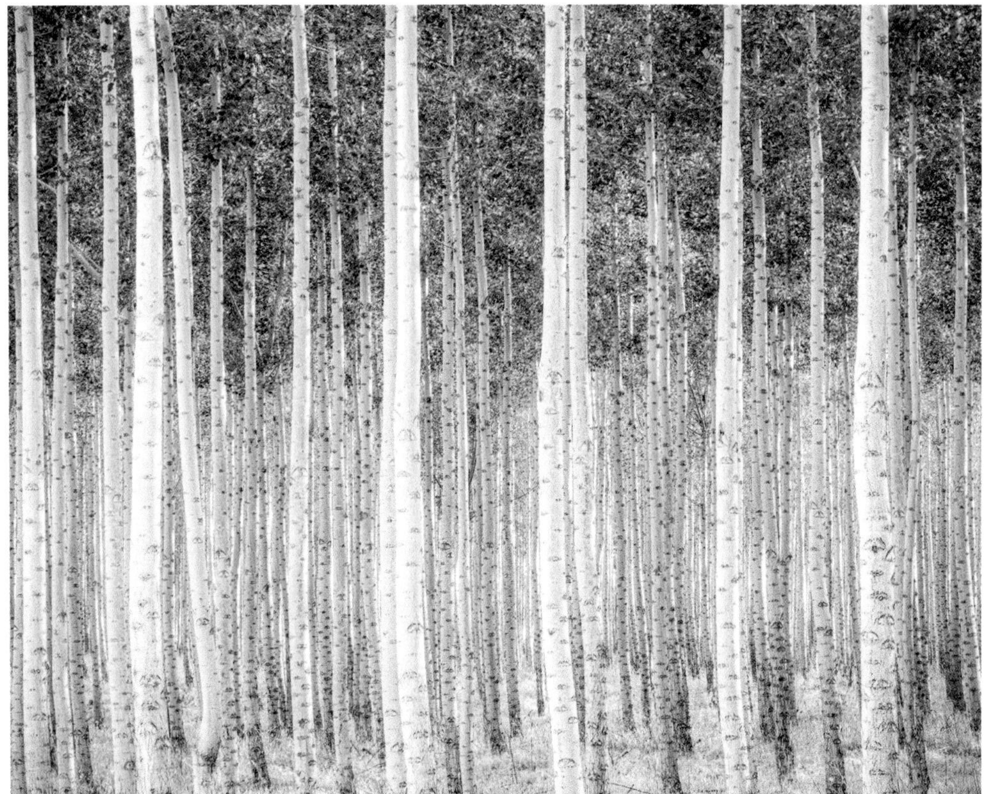

**FIGURE I.6**
For Jeff, being amongst these trees is simultaneously serene, meditative and enormously grand—like a cathedral. When he made this photograph, the light seemed to be dancing around, reflecting off the white tree trunks. He used a 200mm telephoto lens to compress the scene and accentuate the feeling that the trees were stacked, as in a mosaic. IMAGE © JEFF CONLEY, *POPLAR GROVE, DUSK*, 2010.

## Jeff Conley

### *Landscape and Nature Photographer*

I've been working as a professional photographer for twenty years. The physicality of the photograph—getting an image back to the print form—is important to me. I'm represented by a few galleries and eke out a living that way, selling my prints.

As a longtime film shooter, I now work almost exclusively with digital capture, and love it, absolutely love it! I can't get rid of the Hasselblad, but haven't exposed a frame of film in a few years. I make digital photographs, and on the desktop convert the color capture into black-and-white images. I sometimes put a correction curve on them or correct for spots on the sensor—that kind of thing. Although I'm not opposed to working with a heavy hand in Photoshop, it's not something I typically do, since I tend to have a representative vision of nature and landscapes.

After creating a finished file, I FTP it to BowHaus[2] in Los Angeles. In a week or so, they send me (by FedEx) a 4 × 5 inch LVT[3] film negative. These negatives can be enlarged optically and are very beautiful. I take the negatives into the darkroom—which is right next door to my office—and pop them into the enlarger to make traditional photographic prints, the old-school wet chemical process.

It's nice to take the digital file to a negative. I still feel very gratified working in the darkroom, because I appreciate the connection to the print and the physicality of the negative. There's a strong appeal to having that physical negative, because I don't have to worry about hard-drive failures or any of the other calamitous events that can degrade your images. I'm still worried about storing my negatives. I keep meaning to get a fireproof negative safe . . .

That's more or less the way I work. It's kind of quaint, isn't it?

**FIGURE I.7**
*SHAKE* is a series of fun portraits of dogs shaking, jowls flapping and fur flying. It captures images of dogs transformed by the simple action of shaking off water.
IMAGE © CARLI DAVIDSON, *SHAKE KaDee 1*—FROM THE *SHAKE* SERIES, 2012.

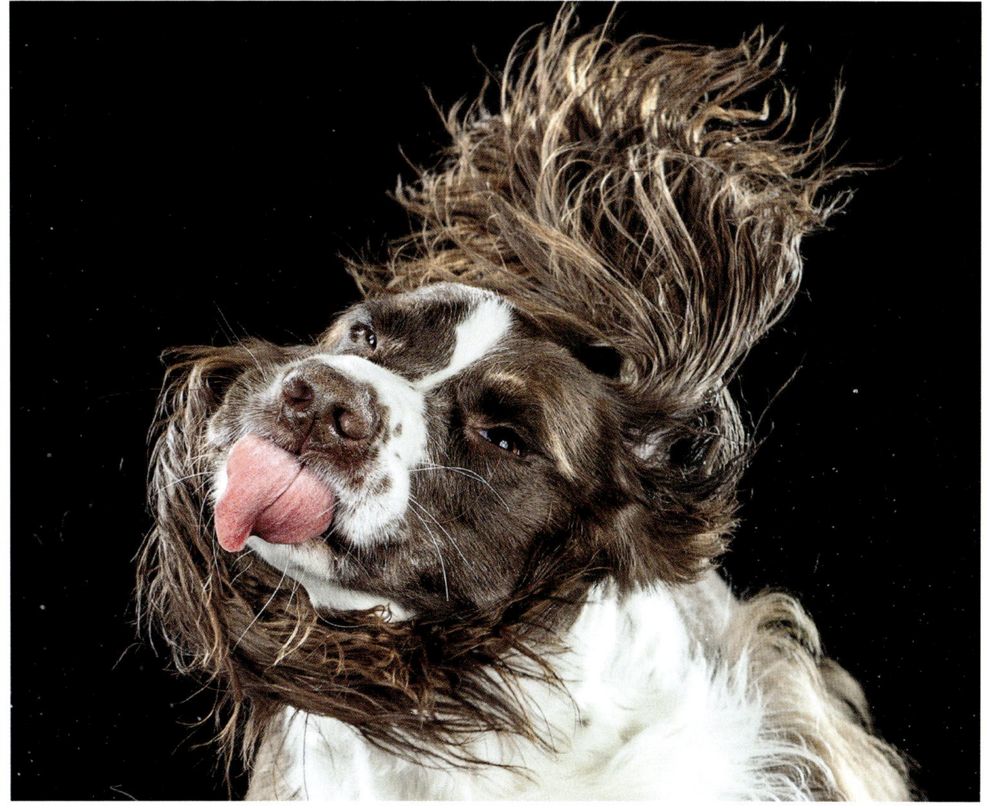

## Carli Davidson

### *Animal Photographer*

I'm a photographer who works with animals. I've been a little obsessed with animals my entire life, so it naturally flowed into my art. I started working at nature reserves when I was old enough to legally work, so I've worked with animals a lot longer than I've been a photographer—even though I did take a lot of bad pictures of dogs in dresses when I was six.

I dabbled in photography for a long time, working as an assistant in high school and as a retoucher. My dad was in advertising, so I had a lot of access to stuff like that. I was fascinated by it, but didn't know I wanted to do it professionally. When I moved to Portland, I got a job at the zoo, worked there a while and got into a car accident. My doctor told me to take some time off and I decided to go back to photography till I got strong enough to go back to the zoo.

I started a studio, figuring I'd do commissions shooting people's pets and see what happened, but I'm not very good at the business end of things. I began obsessing over projects that I thought might be fascinating. The first one was on dogs that were disabled. I'd approach special-needs pets' owners I saw walking their dogs around town and say, "Hey, can I take portraits of your animals?"

I did a couple other projects, and then *SHAKE*[4] happened; *SHAKE* blew up! The project got my name everywhere and I started getting more commercial work and licensing. It opened up a lot of opportunities for me.

When I was in high school, I was the worst kid. I got kicked out in the ninth grade for various reasons and was placed into an alternative program. The program was inside one of the public high schools, and they had a photography darkroom right behind the room that my class was in. I asked if I could take a mainstream art class and they said okay.

I was really excited about this photography class. We have a lot of artists in our family. I was always taking pictures and drawing when I was a kid, and for the first time in my educational experience, I was excited about taking a class or being in school.

I remember making my first print and being totally overwhelmed by watching the image exposed on the paper. That positive experience kept me going back for more: I wanted to learn; I wanted to roll my own film; I wanted to go out to shoot. I went to graveyards and took pictures of my friends—very "Goth." I lived that experience, and I was fascinated.

I credit photography with keeping me in school, and with giving me something to feel proud of. It helped me gain a sense of confidence and curiosity in my education. And that's how I got into photography.

## Bruce Ely

### *Newspaper Photojournalist*

Photography was a hobby of my father's; he had a little darkroom in the kitchen pantry. I photographed for the high-school yearbook and enjoyed it, but when I got to college, I thought, "I'm going to study accounting." I don't know why I decided to do that, but I did. So for two years I studied accounting, and towards the end of college I worked at a photo portrait studio. I really didn't like portrait photography. It just wasn't my thing—I didn't like posing people.

When I was studying accounting at Spokane Falls Community

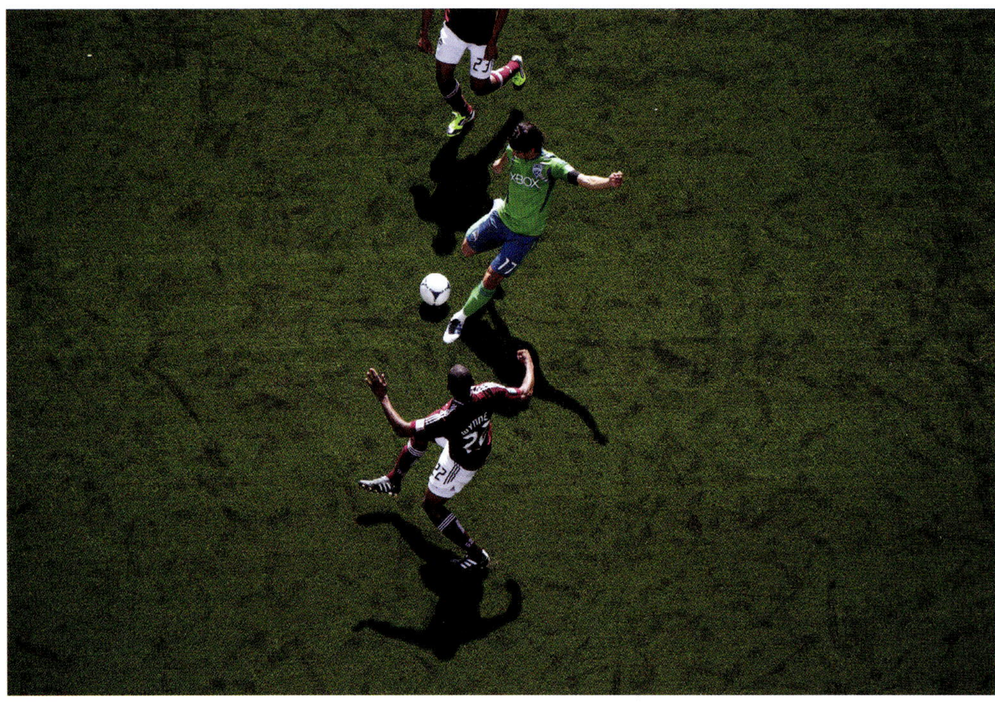

**FIGURE I.8** Seattle, Washington, April 14, 2012: The Seattle Sounders defeat the Colorado Rapids at CenturyLink Field. IMAGE © BRUCE ELY, *SEATTLE SOUNDERS*, FOR *ESPN THE MAGAZINE*, 2012.

College, I ran into a *Spokesman-Review* photographer at a basketball game. I thought, "That's cool, that would be a fun job." I had never considered that you could make money as a photographer in ways besides shooting proms and portraits.

I asked him where was a good place to go to school and he told me to go to the University of Montana. So at the end of that quarter, I transferred, switched careers and ended up going there for journalism. It worked out great; I loved going to school there. My first job was in Evansville, Indiana, and then I got the job at *The Oregonian;* I've been there since 2000.

***Candace Dobro:*** **Are you sad you didn't become an accountant?**

***Bruce Ely:*** My bank account is sad, but I'm not sure I would have enjoyed that kind of work. I don't regret my choice because of the places I've gone—and because the things I've seen were incredible. I wouldn't trade that for a big paycheck.

## Craig Ferroggiaro

### *Photographer/Retoucher*

***Craig Ferroggiaro:*** I started off with this brilliant idea that I was going to be a professional photographer—I just did it on my own, no

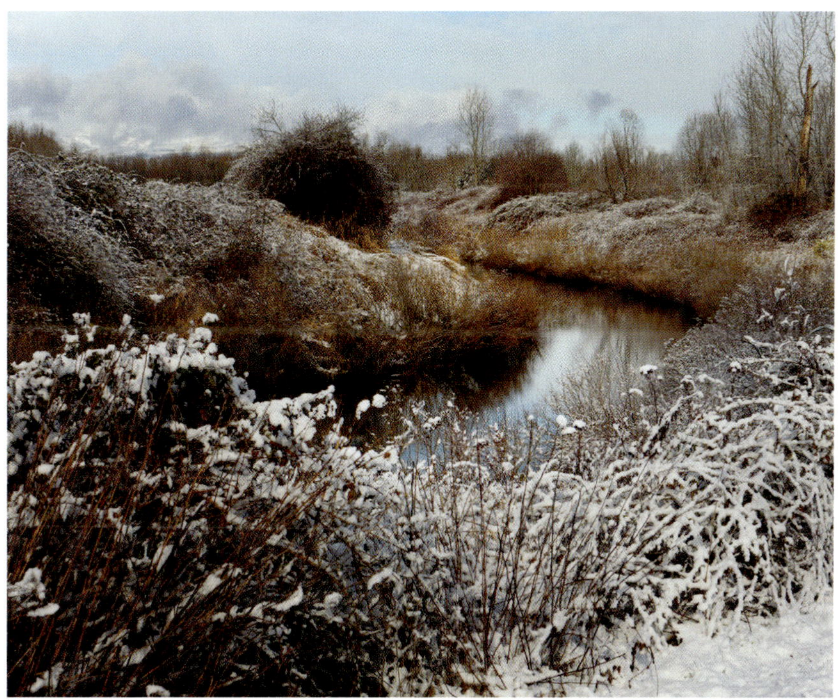

**FIGURE I.9** Craig always tries to balance the technical and the artistic in his landscape work and says, "We all tend to gravitate towards one or the other, but achieving both is a good goal to have."
IMAGE © CRAIG FERROGGIARO, *LIGHT DUSTING, SAUVIE ISLAND,* 2011.

school, no anything. Somehow, I made it for about two years without starving.

Eventually I got hungry, got a job and got into printing. I'm a third-generation lithographer, so I grew up around loupes and light tables. When I got a job for a prepress place in San Francisco, it was very entry level—just making proofs—but I loved the whole environment. I loved walking in and seeing all the strippers' faces being lit from the illuminated tables underneath.

***Andy Batt:* You'll have to define what a stripper is!**

***CF:*** I always like to tell people I was a stripper at one point in time; it's a good icebreaker. A stripper basically did what people do now in InDesign: They set up copy and images on a page—except at that time, they did it all manually, with film. I would make prints from four-color CMYK film; there were two or three different methods of making proofs. There was also a new technology called Scitex.

***Candace Dobro:* Wow, I worked for a color separator back in the day, and they had a Scitex studio! It was like rocket science. The area was refrigerated and the people wore gloves; it was incredible.**

***AB:* Scitex was a verb before Photoshop was.**

***CF:*** Yes, it was. Scitex was an Israeli company with great technicians that would come in straight from Israel and work on the machines, which had about four megabytes of RAM. Each pixel would load in; it was crazy stuff. One night I wandered into Scitex, the cold room; it was air-conditioned underneath and they had an elevated floor. The machinery was so hot they had to air-condition the whole place. So I walked in and there was an image on the screen. I pressed the "from this area to this area" control and was able to put an eyeball in the middle of a model's head. It was such a mind-blowing experience!

***CD:* And thus, a retoucher was born . . .**

***CF:*** That's it; that was the beginning. I said, "I've got to do this." It was the equivalent of the first time I ever looked through a 35mm lens and could focus on objects. I didn't even have film; I just walked around—for two or three days—just focusing on different stuff. I was probably 13 years old.

***CD:* That is such a good story; I love the way you got into this! What happened after you discovered that's what you wanted to do, because you didn't end up as a Scitex operator, right?**

***CF:*** Actually, I did. I pursued it and learned. I had an eye for it from my photography days and I was always doing art. The owners of the company were very open to giving people opportunities, so I would try out things. I eventually got to work on a Scitex machine some years later and was doing the equivalent of stripping, which is assembling all of the layouts. Some years later Apple got it together and made a big enough, strong enough machine so that the transition to Macintosh started happening. After that, retouching took off for me.

So, I have a background in printing and a huge knowledge of CMYK—plus everything that goes on in there and what people need for printing. At the same time, I have a sense of what a photographer would want; it makes a pretty good combination for a retoucher.

## Toni Greaves

### *Documentary Photographer/Photojournalist*

I describe myself as a documentary photographer, because I have a preference towards long-term storytelling—but I often do assignment work for publications, magazines, newspapers, etc., along with shooting for commercial clients. In these cases, I'll typically shoot from an hour to a day, but it can vary greatly. Most of what I do is within a storytelling realm, and for the most part with natural situations. I also do environmental portraiture, which is a little bit different.

I'm currently working on my first book, which is about a long-term project I began in early 2008. The book will be titled *Radical Love* and will be published by Chronicle Books, Fall 2015.

I studied at the International Center of Photography (ICP) in New York City. They have a one-year program in Documentary Photography and Photojournalism. I already had plenty of education as part of my design career (on top of a degree in journalism before that), so I didn't feel the need to go back and spend four more years

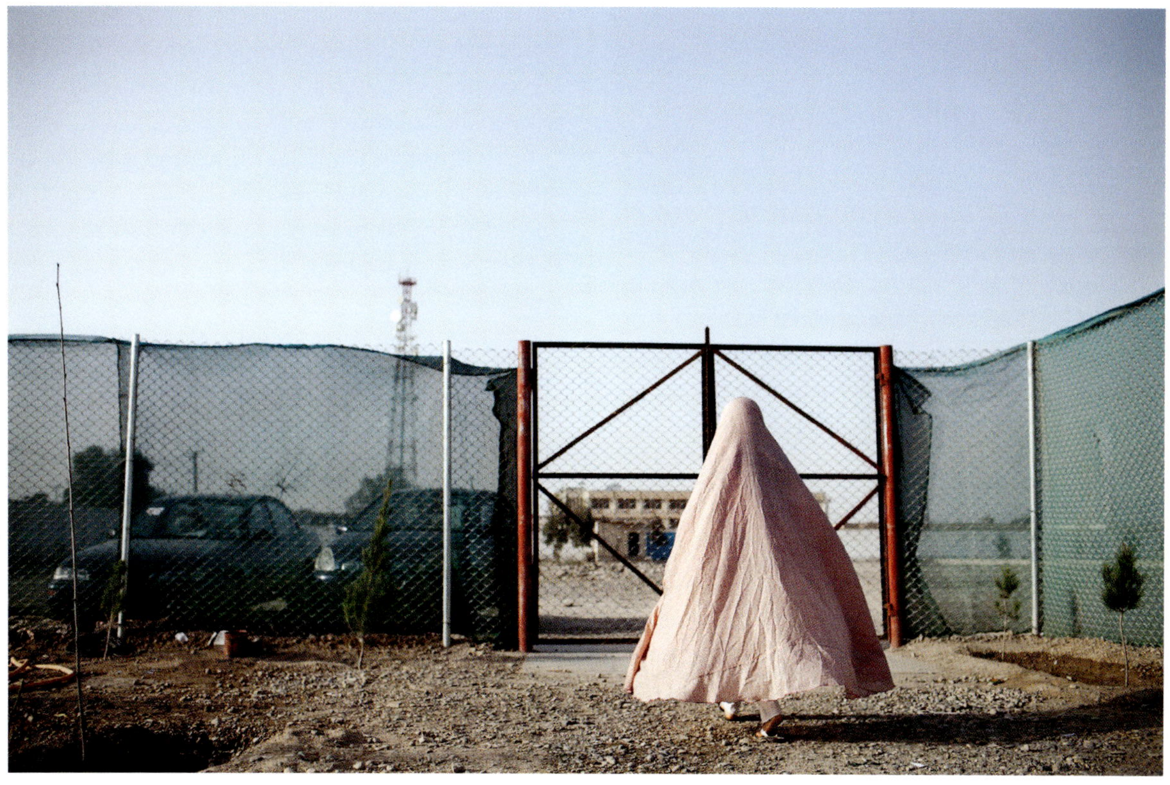

**FIGURE I.10** Less than a year after opening, this vocational training center for women had 900 enrolled students studying English, computer skills, tailoring, embroidery and calligraphy. Education is a new opportunity for many of these women, and they're excited about the chance to learn and improve their lives.
IMAGE BY TONI GREAVES FOR MERCY CORPS, *EDUCATION AGAINST ALL ODDS, AFGHANISTAN: LEAVING SCHOOL FOR THE DAY*, 2012.

in school. I wanted something immersive and intensive. The one-year program at the ICP turned out to be more intense and harder work than my Master's degree in Visual Communication Design. It was really transformative for me; the ICP is a great school!

I've been doing this as a career for six years, but I had being doing photography for a long time before being formally trained in it. I had a career in design before shifting to photography; I worked in the design industry for fourteen years, coming through the path of being a graphic designer, art director and creative director. I had done photography on the side though, just for fun, for at least ten years before leaving my other career.

Even when I was 18, I was doing some photography. It's been scattered a little bit throughout my life. When I worked as a creative director, I took leave from my job to spend six weeks living with a tribe in Kenya to document a rite-of-passage ceremony. I've always been in a visual arts career; visual acuity, and art in many forms, has been a thread throughout my life.

One of the things I enjoy about this kind of work is building relationships with subjects. I really enjoy meeting people I might not have had the chance to know before, and finding depth in the work that I'm doing.

## Sol Neelman

### *Commercial, Editorial and "Weird Sports" Photographer*

***Sol Neelman***: I'm a recovering newspaper photographer who has freelanced for six years and counting. I do advertising commercial work—and a little editorial work, which doesn't pay very well, so I don't seek it out. In my free time, I use whatever resources I can muster to pay for traveling and photographing Weird Sports around the world. I've published one book already, *Weird Sports,* and am working on my next book, cleverly titled *Weird Sports 2.*

***Andy Batt:* Going back to the dawn of time . . . how did you get started in photography?**

***SN:*** I took a class in photography in eighth grade—the only real photography class I've ever taken. My yearbook instructor, Gary Sehorn, who was awesome, taught it. I actually think about him a lot when it comes to the lessons he taught.

He taught me the basic stuff about photography; I was the photo editor of my high-school yearbook. I liked the access, being off the clock, the irregular schedule. I was especially shy, and photography allowed me to be more obnoxious and outgoing and engaging—and to meet people.

I went to the University of Oregon to study journalism, but they didn't have a photo program, so I focused on broadcast journalism. I would sweat profusely whenever I was on camera; it was miserable. When I graduated, I worked at retail jobs in Portland. I ended up photographing for a suburban community newspaper for free.

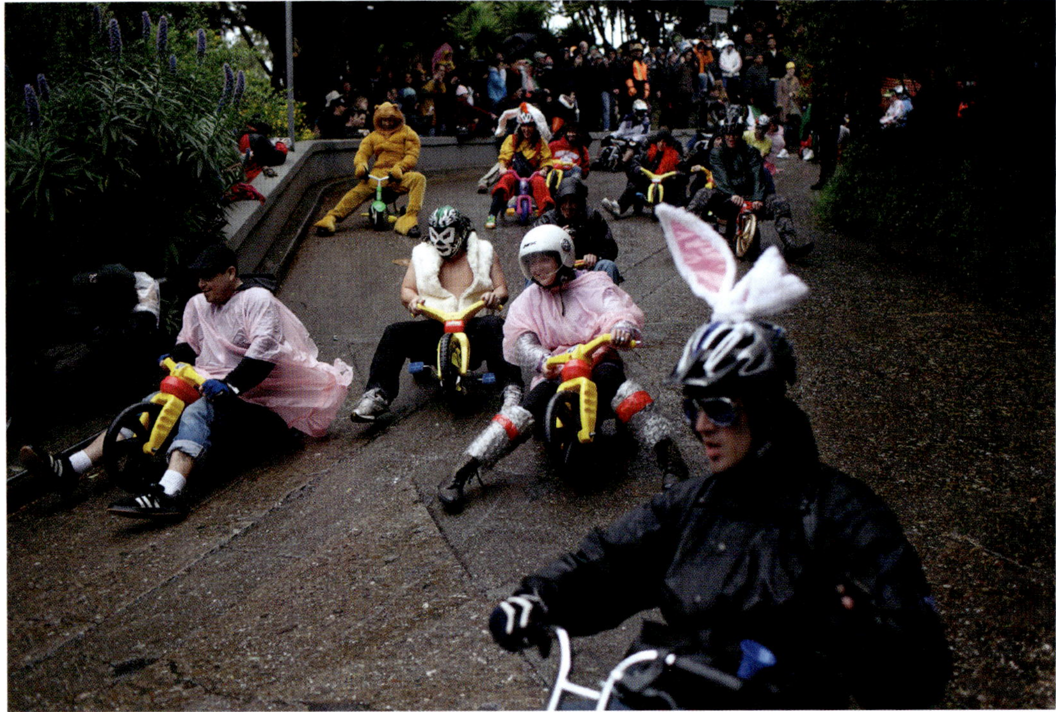

**FIGURE I.11** Despite severe congestion and slick road conditions, weaving through San Francisco traffic has never been more fun than at the annual Bring Your Own Big Wheel race.
IMAGE © SOL NEELMAN, *BIG WHEEL RACING,* PRINTED IN *THE NEW YORK TIMES,* 2012.

While I was there, I photographed Zakira, a refugee from Sarajevo, in 1995–1996, and she said, "I am going back, war is over—you want to photograph my family?" So I quit my job at Citizens Photo and went with a hundred rolls of film to Bosnia for a couple of weeks, photographing Zakira, who reunited with her family.

I was at the Old Town Turkish Market in Sarajevo, writing to my best friend in Oregon: "I love it here, I wish I could find a way to stay," and ten minutes later was offered a job by an American humanitarian who was the Head of Mission for an NGO. He had seen my cameras and said, "I need a photographer; do you want a job?" That literally happened. I said, "Yeah, sure," and ended up working for the largest NGO in Bosnia for six months as a result.

***AB:* What made you leave that path to shoot a little bit of everything, including Weird Sports?**

***SN:*** Newspapers are very literal beasts. I wasn't happy working at a newspaper; I didn't feel creatively challenged or motivated. Newspapers were already starting to tank, so although it was a hard decision to leave in the short term, I knew that in the long term I wasn't going to retire as a newspaper photographer. I had saved some money and moved from Eugene to Portland—and have been trying to figure it out ever since.

***AB:* Did Weird Sports come out of an assignment?**

***SN:*** No, it came from talking to people in the industry who encouraged me to do what I love to do and from shooting behind-the-scenes sports stories for a column that Bruce Ely created. That changed the way I looked at photography, because we were doing it for ourselves. Making pictures for the paper was a challenge, because I was trying to please *them* instead of myself.

After I found out in 2005 that Roller Derby was happening again, I drove up to Seattle a couple of times to shoot their league. I had a great time; it reminded me why I love photography . . . and that was the start of Weird Sports.

## About *Camera & Craft*

We set out to open a conversation about making photographs, and you'll find that we don't cover all things within that encyclopedic realm. Instead, we recommend books and online sources throughout the chapters—and in the *Bibliography*, as well. We hope you'll use these assets to deepen your knowledge and fill in any blank spots.

If you'd like to practice some of the principles and techniques in this book, keep an eye out for invitations to *Try This at Home.* The full step-by-step exercises are on our companion website: **www.focalpress.com/cw/digitalimagingmasters**.

Although we use Adobe Photoshop Lightroom, OS X and Canon DSLRs for most of the examples in this book, we wrote it so you can easily apply the ideas using any camera, computer or software.

Most of the interviews for this book were recorded during Skype conversations and then transcribed. All interviews have been edited and condensed for readability.

## Notes

1 Kim and her husband, Francisco Salgado, operate Campbell Salgado Studio in Portland, Oregon, www.campbellsalgado.com.

2 Bowhaus, www.bowhaus.com.

3 LVT stands for Light Valve Technology, originally created by Kodak.

4 *SHAKE,* Carli Davidson, Carli Davidson Photography, www.carlidavidsonphotography.com.

# PREREQUISITE PHOTO 101

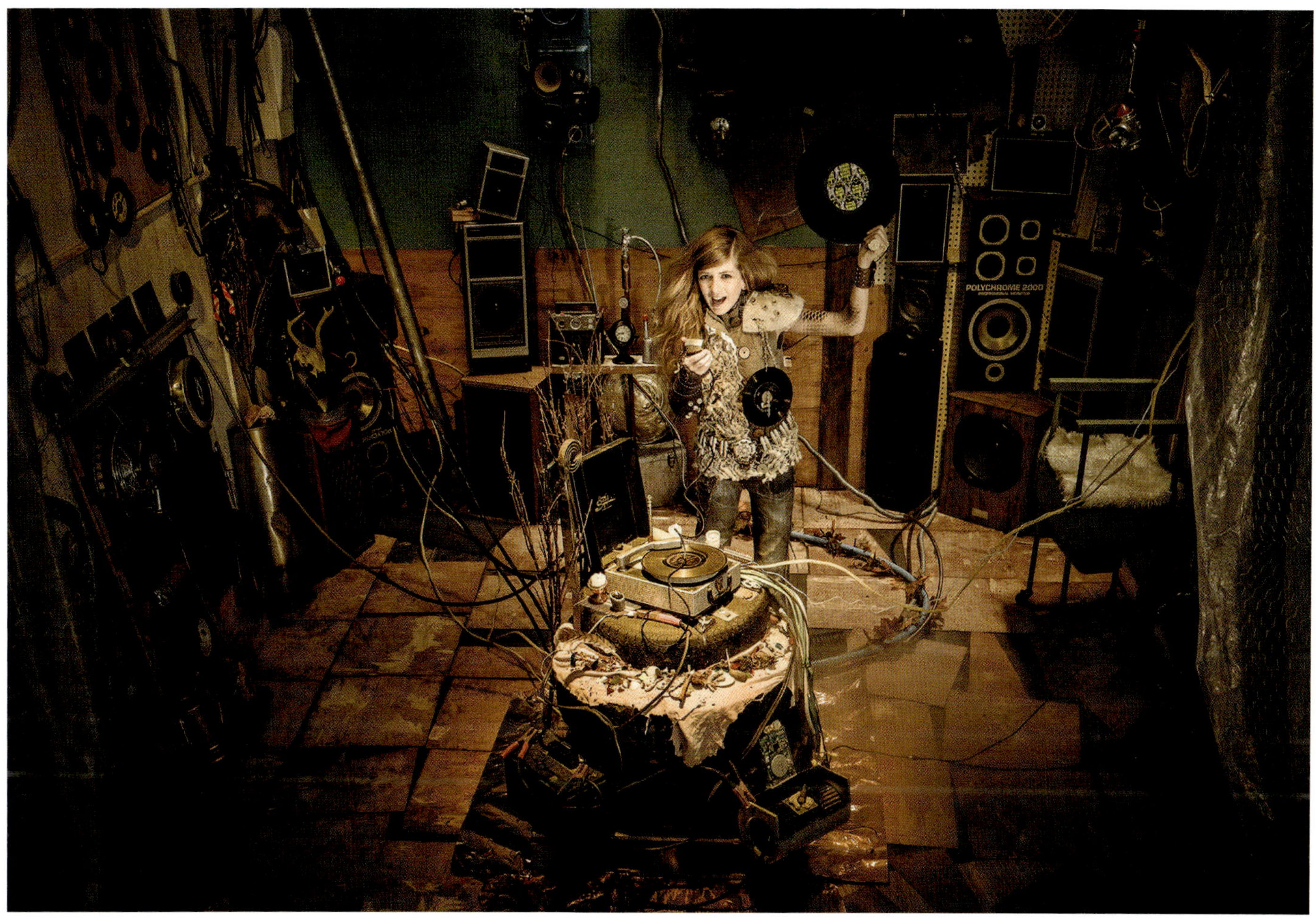


**FIGURE 1.1**
IMAGE © ANDY BATT, *THE RECORD KEEPER,* 2008.

In this chapter, we take a broad look at some essential camera skills—controlling time, focus, exposure, and color—that will allow you to pick up any camera and put it to work. If you already have these skills down cold, then feel free to skim over the chapter, stopping to read the topics you want to review. *Note:* There are some great tips in *Overcoming LCD Variables* and *Setting a Brightness Level for Your Camera* towards the end of the chapter, so be sure to check them out.

## The Camera Is Not a Photographer—You Are

Cameras are smart and capable, but there's one thing they are not: photographers. *We're* the photographers, and to create the photos we really want to make, we have to understand our cameras and take control of them. That's the point of this book—to give you control.

Digital photography is a curious thing. Because it's easy to point, shoot and end up with good images, many of us approach our cameras as though they're mysterious magic boxes we don't need to understand. They're pretty good at taking photos, so we take them for granted. To become an adept photographer, you need to open the "magic box" and understand what goes on inside of it. When you learn take full control of your tools—by controlling time, focus, composition, aperture, shutter speed, exposure and composition—you'll improve your artwork.

This book occupies the territory between seeing the camera as a magic box and *knowing* it as a tool for making art. We'll share our way of doing things and show you some ways that other photographers work. We'll give you a strong foundation in camera work and explore everything from exposure and digital workflow strategies to working with a crew and deciding when to hire a retoucher. Along the way, we'll work in a practical manner, experimenting and questioning the photographic process so that you can pick up any camera and use it creatively.

> *I try to keep things fairly straightforward, since one of the challenges is just how many options there are every step of the way, from cameras to lens choices—and everything down the line to the infinite possibilities when working in Photoshop. If you can keep things somewhat simple and consistent, you get to a point where you anticipate what your images are going to look like. That anticipatory process is vital to my photography.*
>
> *—Jeff Conley*

## Philosophy: Put It on Manual

It may seem like an antiquated idea to use manual controls at a time when cameras can be re-focused in post-production and we can apply retro-style photo filters to our snapshots with our smartphones. With access to smart autofocus systems, color analysis, facial recognition, and specialty modes for just about anything we might photograph—and countless other innovations—we can create good images without knowing much of anything about photography.

But if you want to make images that have a life longer than five seconds online, if you want to be in control of your process and create images with meaning, ideas and story, then it's time to take control of your camera and put it on Manual Mode. Only you can determine what your goal is in any given situation. Your camera doesn't know whether you want your sunny scene to be captured as a silhouette against a blue sky or as a backlit portrait against a blown-out white sky. *You* are the only one who knows how you want an image to turn out and which techniques you'll apply to achieve that goal. The reason to work manually is to create the photographs you want to take.

"Put It on Manual" is an imperative; it's also a metaphor. When you choose "M" on your camera, you are in charge. You choose your shutter speed, F-stop and white balance. You choose whether to use shallow depth of field (DoF) or deep focus. You decide how to expose your images: dark and moody or bright and sunny. You adjust your shutter speed to add motion blur or stop the action. You determine how your lens choice will affect the image. These decisions speak directly to the kind of story your photo will tell.

## FEATURED PHOTOGRAPH

### Randy Leonard Portrait

Andy shot this photo of Randy Leonard (**Figure 1.2A**) for *Portland Monthly* magazine. Leonard is a retired politician and fire commissioner for Portland, Oregon. The creation of this portrait exemplifies the "Put It on Manual" concept. By controlling all aspects of the camera work, subject and lighting, Andy made deliberate choices that crafted the final image.

***Andy:*** The decision-making process began with the knowledge that the magazine was going to run the image as a full page, 8.5 × 11 inches. Shallow DoF works great at that size. If the same image were printed small (**Figure 1.2B**), it wouldn't reveal the qualities that make it work.

I used an 85mm lens on a full-frame camera[1] for this shot, because it's a clean, neutral lens that does a nice job of portraying subjects without distortion or heavy compression. It performs very well when the aperture is wide open ("WFO," in the trade, for wide-freakin' open), and even better slightly stopped down. I've tested this lens for accuracy and distortion and use it frequently, so I'm confident of how it will perform during a job. I made the choice to use *f*/2.8 so that the shallow DoF would focus the viewers' attention on Randy's eyes and help them see him in a unique way (**Figure 1.2C**).

Because the goal was to emphasize Randy's eyes, I kept the lighting and background simple. I wanted a shallow focus and planned on taking advantage of my camera's clean high-ISO speed so I could shoot at a wide-open F-stop and high shutter speed. This meant I could use a single continuous light source instead of a strobe. I shot in my studio with an 800-watt HMI[2] in a strip soft box positioned over the camera, with a silver card below the camera. With this setup, I could photograph quickly and concentrate on working with my subject to get a range of interesting looks.

Simplicity is a big part of this photo's appeal. I wanted the viewer to make an immediate connection with Leonard's eyes, so all of my technical choices reflected that. I call this the Sushi Principle: With Nigiri sushi, there is only the fish, the rice, the seaweed—and maybe some wasabi. With so few elements, each one needs to be right. The same thing applies to photography. When an image has only a few elements, each one needs to be as perfect as you can make it.

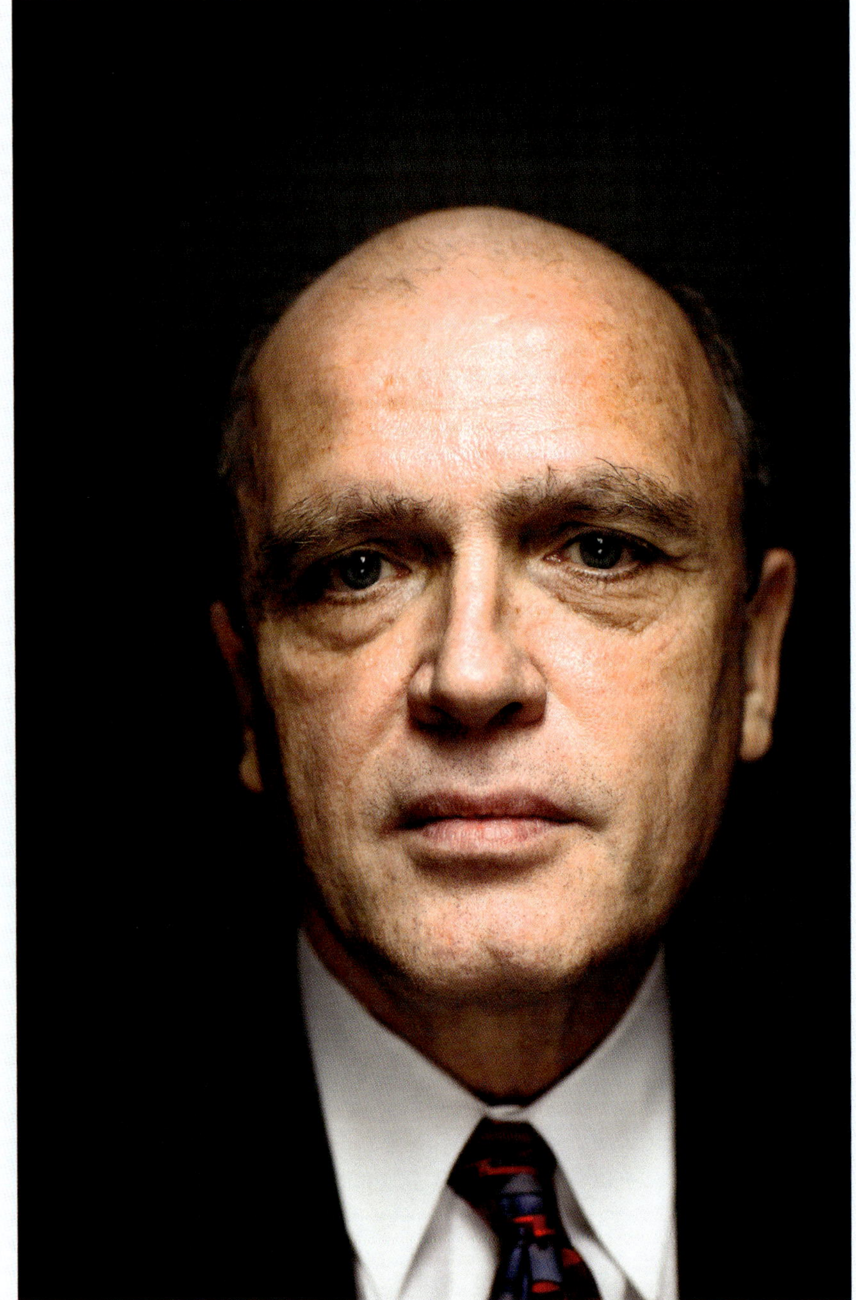

**FIGURE 1.2A**

Andy always tries to implement the "Put It on Manual" idea. For this photograph it meant thinking about how the final image would be reproduced and making a deliberate aperture choice to produce a shallow depth of field.

IMAGE © ANDY BATT, *RANDY LEONARD* FOR *PORTLAND MONTHLY* MAGAZINE, 2012.

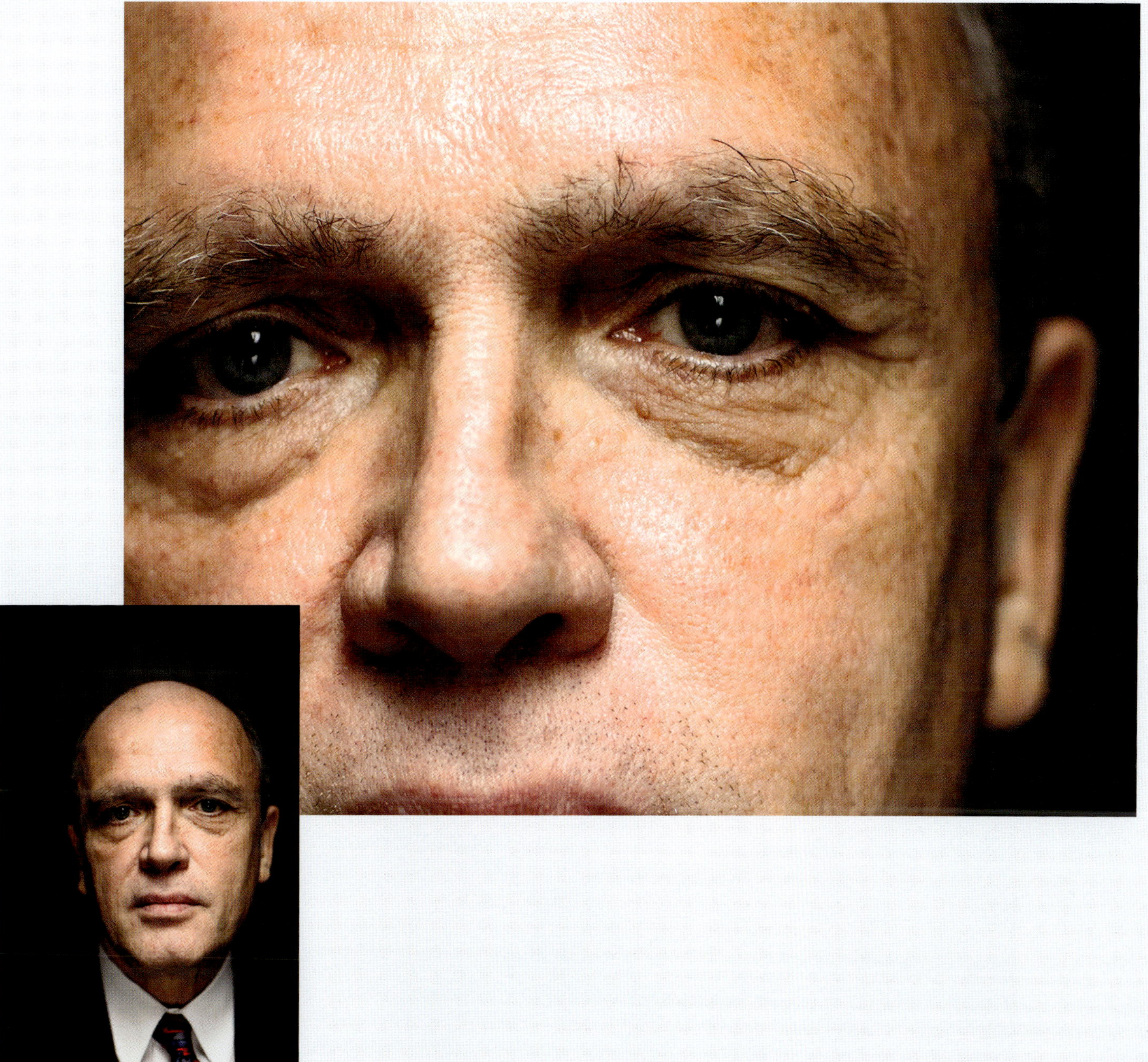

**FIGURE 1.2B**
It's important to know what size your images will be displayed at. The shallow DoF in the portrait isn't apparent at this much smaller size.
IMAGE © ANDY BATT, *DETAIL 1, RANDY LEONARD*, 2012.

**FIGURE 1.2C**
In this crop, check out the difference in focus between the eye and the ear. It's a subtle, but important, difference in the look of the final image.
IMAGE © ANDY BATT, *DETAIL 2, RANDY LEONARD*, 2012.

## Working in Front of the Camera

We refer to the term "working in front of the camera" as making the deliberate technical choices that will affect the aesthetics of an image. When you approach photography in a deliberate way, as Andy did with the Randy Leonard portrait, you make conscious choices about your camera settings, instead of allowing the camera to make them for you. Most of these choices have nothing to do with the specific model and brand of camera you use—and everything to do with using technique and knowledge to tell your story. To craft images, you manipulate four basic choices in photography, all of which are independent of camera type: exposure, time, focus and framing. Whether you're using a Canon EOS 6D or a Hasselblad H5D, you involve all four of these elements.[3]

> *My camera is my passport into other worlds. That's one of the things that I love about this realm of documentary photography: I can get access to pretty much anything I want to photograph. The camera is the tool I use—the camera is how I communicate stories.*
>
> *—Toni Greaves*

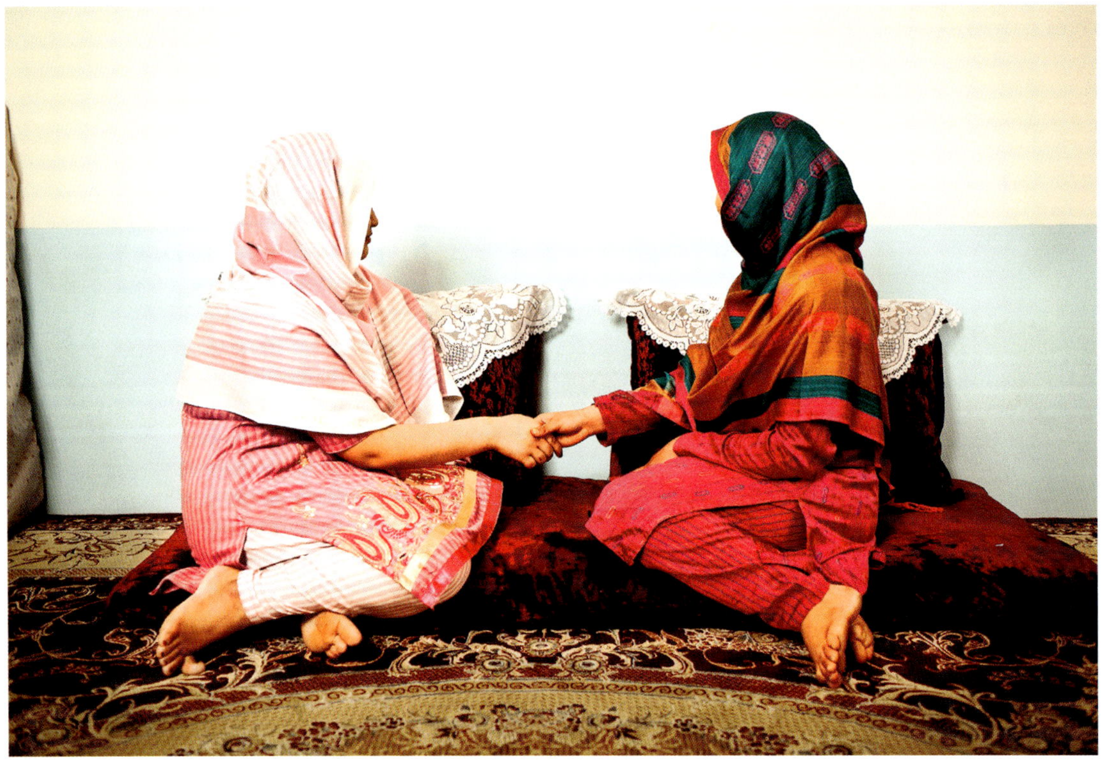

**FIGURE 1.3** Toni's camera is her tool for telling meaningful stories. In this shot, Fatima (left) takes a computer class at Mercy Corps' vocational training center for women. IMAGE BY TONI GREAVES FOR MERCY CORPS, *EDUCATION AGAINST ALL ODDS, AFGHANISTAN: FATIMA AND ZAHRA*, 2012.

## Manual Mode Isn't Pretty—At First

Once you put your camera on Manual, it will no longer make the decisions for you; and at first, your images will probably get worse. Taking control is a learning experience, which means it's sure to entail frustrations like bad exposures and unintentionally blurry shots. With practice, you'll learn what decisions you need to make and when to make them.

This book isn't a manual that will explain exactly which buttons to push on your specific camera. For that, you can buy one of the many excellent, independently written guidebooks that describe in detail which settings to use on the exact camera you own.[4] These books are excellent references and very handy to have—especially if you want to know something specific or need a "get out of jail free" card when things go wrong.

In *Camera & Craft*, we'll help you accomplish more with less. Later on, you can reintroduce any features you like—once you understand how they work and which decisions they make on your behalf. A good rule of thumb is: If a setting seems like magic, then turn it off until it no longer does.

> *In* Camera & Craft*, we'll help you accomplish more with less. The rule of thumb? If a setting seems like magic, then turn it off until it no longer does.*

### Your Images Will Get Better—a Lot Better

The whole point of learning the technical side of photography is to create interesting and artistic imagery. Once you take control—of your process, your camera, the light, image processing and even hard-drive backups—you'll have more time to spend on the content and meaning of your work, whether you shoot landscapes, fashion editorials or food photography.

### Manual Mode Defeats Program Mode!

Program Mode[5] is a sort of artificial intelligence[6] for your camera. Its job is to make sure that the shutter and ISO speeds are fast enough for you to handhold your camera (and prevent blurring) and that the F-stop is deep enough to hold focus.

Your Program Mode might also have the ability to recognize faces, colors and situations and cross-reference that knowledge with a database of test situations. If so, then it can make some fairly intuitive guesses with all that information: It might be able to figure out that your subject's face is more important than the sky behind it and that you'd rather have a higher ISO (with more noise and less blur) than a slower shutter speed (with less noise and more blur).

With Program Mode, these choices are guesses, since your camera has no way of knowing that you'd like to expose the scene to be moody and dark or that you'd prefer a little motion blur. Program Mode tries to make the best photo possible, based on a guess. Your goal is to be a much better photographer than that.

#### What's Left?

Here's what you'll have left after you shut off all the automatic controls and decide not to use any of the bells and whistles:

- *ISO Speed Control:* You control the light sensitivity of the camera.
- *Shutter Speed:* You control time and light.
- *Aperture Size (F-stop):* You control focus and light.

#### Turn the Dial!

The first thing you need to do is to literally turn the dial, push the button or use the touchscreen to put your camera into Manual Mode. Congratulations; you've just defeated the automatic choices, turned off the helpful modes and maybe earned a little respect from your camera!

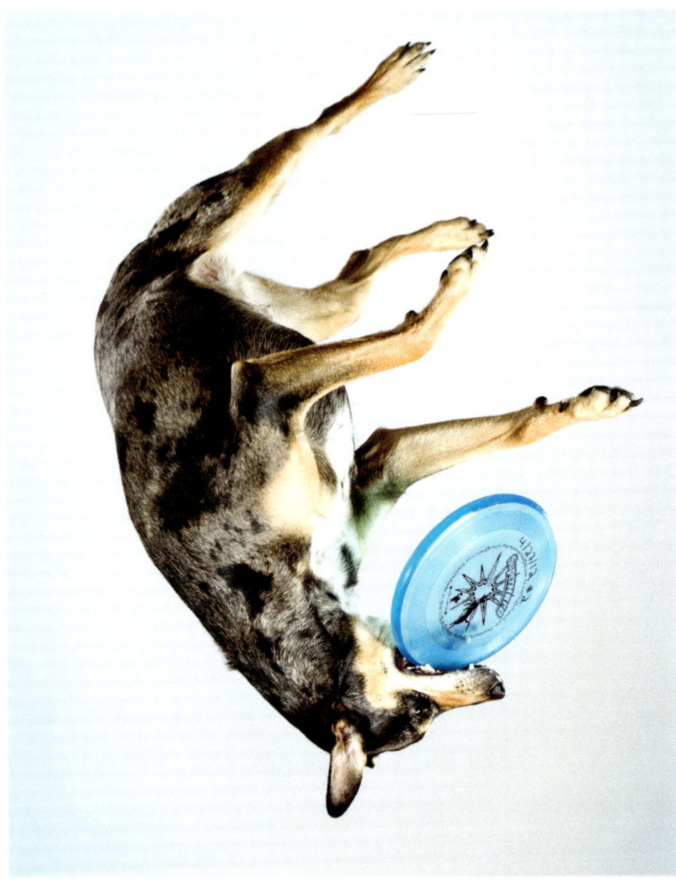

**FIGURE 1.4** Carli captures animals in motion at high speed and says, "It's pretty imperative that I know my gear well . . . if I spent time figuring out how to set my camera and lights, then I wouldn't be able to focus on getting the animals to do what I want them to do. When you don't have your gear nailed down, it can kill the creative energy of a shoot."
IMAGE © CARLI DAVIDSON, *FETCH 2*, 2012.

*When I have an idea, I know how to execute it, because I know my tools. With the images from the SHAKE series, or with any of the imagery that I do, I'm capturing a moment that's happening at high speed. It's pretty imperative that I know my gear well so I can communicate the idea I'm having. If I spent time figuring out how to set my camera and lights, then I wouldn't be able to focus on getting the animals to do what I want them to do. It frees you up to know your gear; it makes the gear itself secondary to the concept.*

*—Carli Davidson*

## Exposure Basics: Shutter Speed, F-Stop and ISO

If you're venturing off Program Mode for the first time, don't be nervous; we're about to walk you through the basics. The main job of a camera is to capture an image, and to do that, it needs to control the amount of light—or exposure—that gets to the lens on its way to the sensor.

Program Mode is like a smart light meter that takes complete control of the components that determine exposure. *When we manually set exposure in our cameras, we always select a combination of shutter speed, F-stop and ISO.* We achieve good exposures when we skillfully manipulate all three components.

What do we mean when we say "good exposure"? In *Chapter 6*, we'll get to the gritty technical explanation, but for now, we're referring to images that hold detail (tones, textures and information) in the shadows, midtones and highlights. We're also referring to images that interpret your scene as you intended.

### 1/3- or 1/2-Stops?

Some cameras give you an option to work in 1/3- or 1/2-stop increments. We recommend working in 1/3-stop increments, which gives you more control over your exposure. You'll find this setting buried in your menu system. If your camera is set to the 1/2-stop setting, you'll end up with a slightly different scale of F-stops and shutter speeds. For the 1/3-stop setting, you'll have: ***f*/2.8 > *f*/3.2 > *f*/3.5 > *f*/4.0 and 1/250th > 1/320th > 1/400th > 1/500th**. For the 1/2-stop setting, you'll have ***f*/2.8 > *f*/3.3 > *f*/4.0 and 1/250th to 1/350th to 1/500th**.

## Creative Decisions

When you make deliberate changes to any of the three basic settings, you also manipulate time, focus and quality. These creative decisions are at the heart of every photographer's camerawork, and no matter how big the projects are or how famous photographers become, the images they create rely on these same, basic choices. One of the most satisfying things about photographing over a long period of time is that you eventually understand how a camera sees—and that once you reach that point, you can manipulate it to create images as you see them.

These concepts can be applied to any photographic endeavor, from fine art imagery to sports photography. For some projects, such as a catalog shoot, the story might be incredibly simple: "That sweater is a nice shade of red and it looks soft and warm." Your client will love it if you can visually communicate those qualities about the sweater they're trying to sell. Other projects get more complex. For an editorial project, you might need to illustrate just how powerful a person is and what unique abilities have helped him or her to excel. The idea is to make deliberate choices—before you click the shutter—about the images you want to take and what you want to communicate.

*You've got to be at the top of your game to make a living at photography. Finding your own voice is really the key. My husband and I come from a fine art background, so we created pictures that moved or interested us, which was a different approach in the portrait-photography field. Our photos are recognizable because we create something that looks unique.*

*—Kim Campbell*

## Creating Images Your Way

- Think about controlling *shutter speed* as a way of manipulating time and dramatically altering how your camera sees the world. A super-fast shutter can freeze action and a slow one can add motion blur, neither of which you can see with your naked eye.
- By altering the *F-stop*, you control an image's depth of field (DoF). In this way, you can select how and where the focus will fall on your subject. Smaller-diameter apertures (e.g., *f*/16) give you a deeper field of focus and larger-diameter apertures (e.g., *f*/2.8) give you a shallower field of focus.
- Your ability to alter *ISO* speed is subtler. The rule is to use the slowest speed possible (the lowest number) that enables you to use the shutter speed and F-stop you want. The slower the ISO, the less noise there will be in your image. *Noise* is the catchall term we apply to all types of unwanted artifacts, but its basic description is blotches of color that aren't actually in the scene you photographed. (We'll get into more detail about noise and testing in *Chapter 5*.)

## Measure of Light

There's a common photo term called a *stop* that we use to indicate a unit measure of light. Shutter speeds, F-stops and ISO speeds can each be changed in stops of exposure. A stop is the same unit amount, whether it's the shutter, F-stop or ISO speed that alters it. For example, if we slow down the shutter speed by a whole stop (which lets more light in), then we can close down the aperture (which lets less light in) a whole stop—and end up with the same exposure value we had before making those changes. The change in shutter speed and aperture would have other effects on the image, but the amount of light being passed on to the camera's sensor would be the same.

Let's say we set an exposure by selecting a combination shutter speed of 1/125th (of a second), an aperture of *f*/8 and an ISO of 400. If this exposure were 2 stops too dark, we could add more light by slowing down the shutter speed by a whole stop to 1/60th to let in 1 stop more and changing the aperture value to *f*/5.6, which would let in another stop more. The new exposure of 1/60th at *f*/5.6 would increase the overall exposure by 2 stops.

We can also make adjustments in smaller amounts: Depending on our camera setup, we can work in 1/4-, 1/3-, or 1/2-stops. For example, from *f*/5.6, we can increase our exposure by 1/3-stop by opening the aperture value to *f*/5.0—this is the same value as *f*/4.0 + 2/3-stop. **Figures 1.5A and 1.5B** show you the relationships between shutter speed, F-stop and ISO.

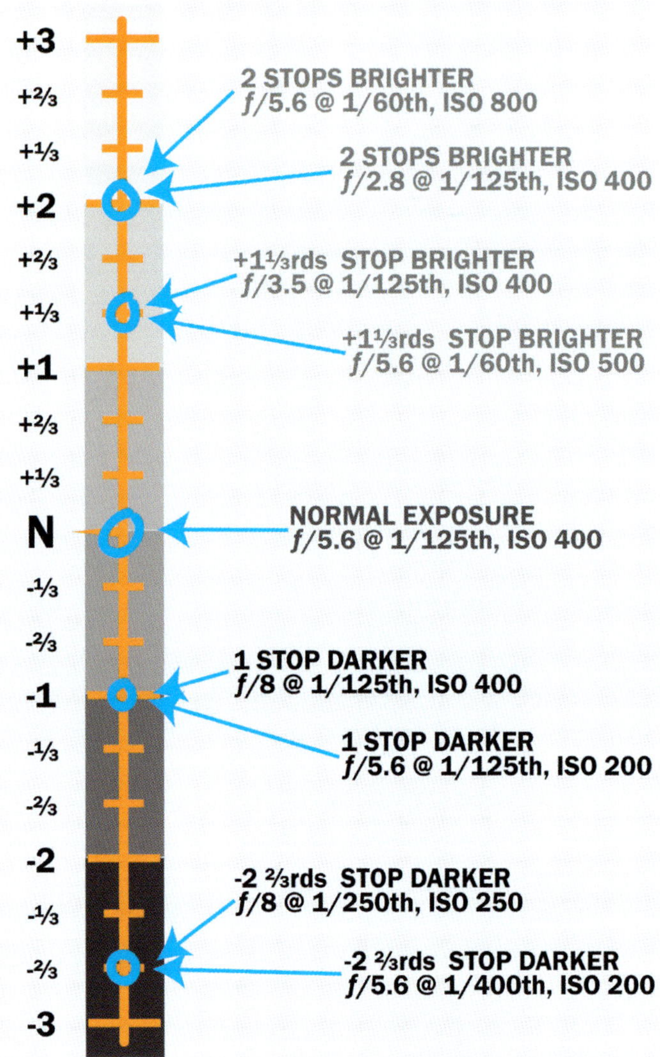


**FIGURE 1.5A** We established a good, "normal," exposure of *f*/5.6, 1/125th at ISO 400. From there, we plotted out how to *brighten* the exposure by +1 1/3–stops and by +2 stops. We also plotted out two *darker* exposures: –1 stop and –2 2/3–stops. You'll notice that for each of these alternate exposures, we mapped out two possible exposure settings that would yield the same increase or decrease in exposure.

With the three variables of aperture, shutter speed and ISO speed, it's possible to have many combinations that give the same ultimate exposure value. All you need to do is adjust one setting brighter or darker, and then compensate for it with one or both of the other settings.

ILLUSTRATION © ANDY BATT, *EXPOSURE VALUES*, 2013.

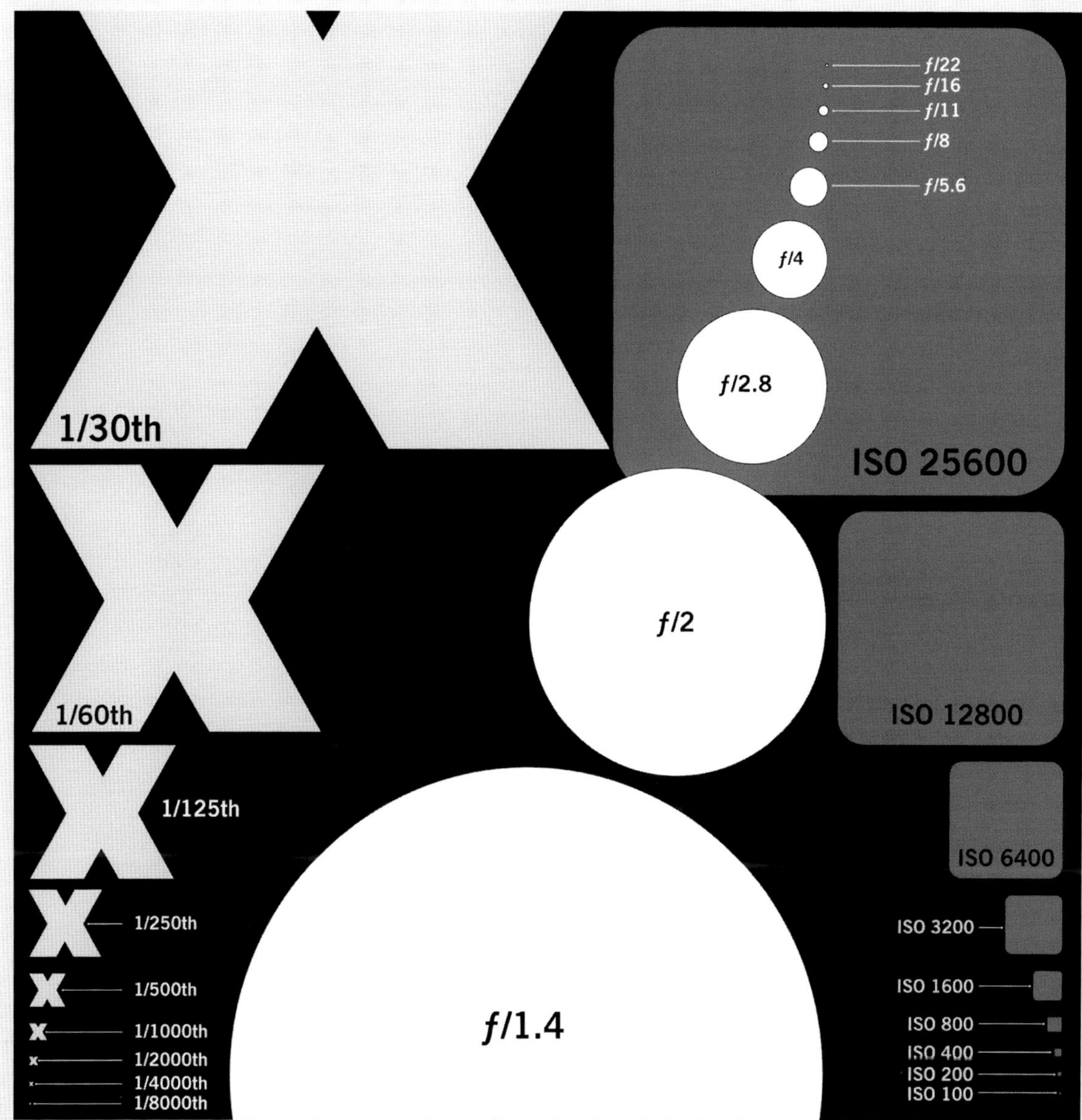


**FIGURE 1.5B**

To give you a sense of how these three exposure settings work, Andy created this chart to illustrate how each exposure value—shutter speed, F-stop and ISO speed—relates. It's mapped out in full stops of light: The larger the icon, the more light the camera takes in. Shutter speeds are represented by *X*s; apertures (F-stops) are represented by circles and ISO speeds are represented by squares. Since a 1-stop increase equals double the amount of light, and a 1-stop decrease equals half the amount of light, each icon is 50% smaller than the next larger one—or 200% larger then the next smaller one.

ILLUSTRATION © ANDY BATT, *EXPOSURE VALUES IN WHOLE STOPS*, 2013.

## FEATURED PHOTOGRAPH

### Parkour Artists Brian Orosco and Tyson Cecka

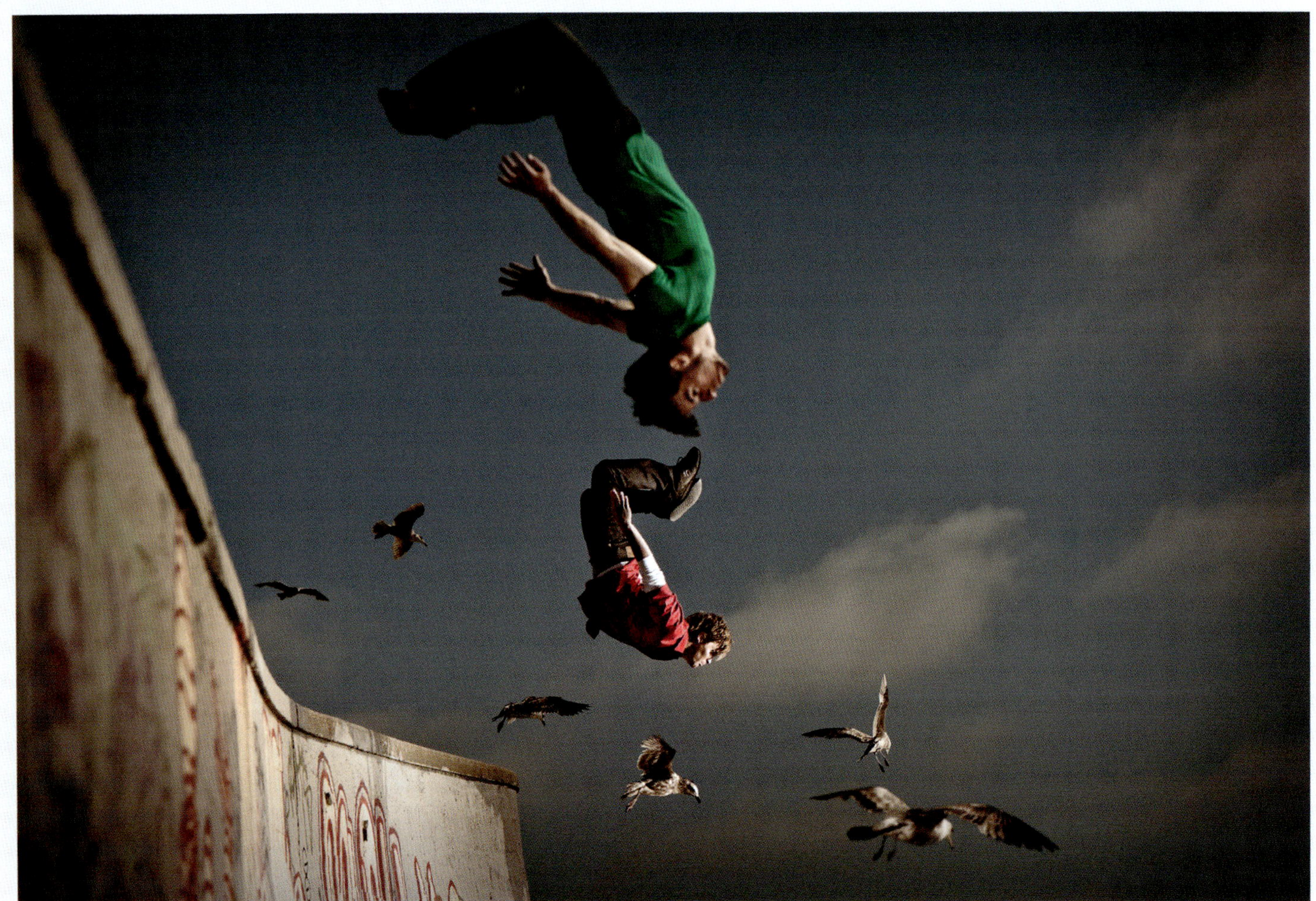

**FIGURE 1.6A** Working in–camera is always a goal for Andy. The only things that aren't 100% real in this image are a few of the seagulls. Everything else resulted from technique, equipment and good teamwork.
IMAGE © ANDY BATT, *PARKOUR ARTISTS BRIAN OROSCO AND TYSON CECKA, SAN FRANCISCO, CA,* 2009.

Andy created this photo (**Figure 1.6A**) during a portfolio shoot at San Francisco's Ocean Beach. The two Parkour artists, Brian Orosco and Tyson Cecka, brought him to one of their favorite locations because the sand that gathers at the base of the wall is soft and makes a great landing spot.

***Andy:*** Brian said that this location lets them pull off some great moves; I was excited to find a place to create those impossible moments of flight. My goal was to stop time and to show an amazing, gravity-defying image.

To accomplish this, I used a Canon EOS-1Ds Mark III camera at 1/8000th of a second, and a strobe—with a Profoto Pro 7b Battery Operated Power Pack—to add some punch and the feeling of late-afternoon sunlight. At the time, the 1Ds MIII was my lead camera; it's built for professionals and has a great sensor and autofocus system. The Profoto Pro 7b is an industry standard for portable powerful battery-powered strobe lights. The strobe head was set with a simple seven-inch silver reflector and aimed from camera right, directly where Brian and Tyson would be as they flew through the air. I used a PocketWizard TT5 and TT1 to wirelessly trigger the strobe pack. The TT models have a unique mode that allows for syncing at a much faster shutter speed than is typical for a DSLR, in this case, at 1/8000th instead of 1/250th of a second.

I always try to capture "real" images in-camera. If I can't, then I happily turn to the magic of Photoshop—but always with a purpose. When it's necessary to build an image in Photoshop, I want it to be for a reason I determined on the shoot or prior to it. For the Parkour shoot, I really wanted to capture the artists in the air and didn't want to assemble a composite image in post.

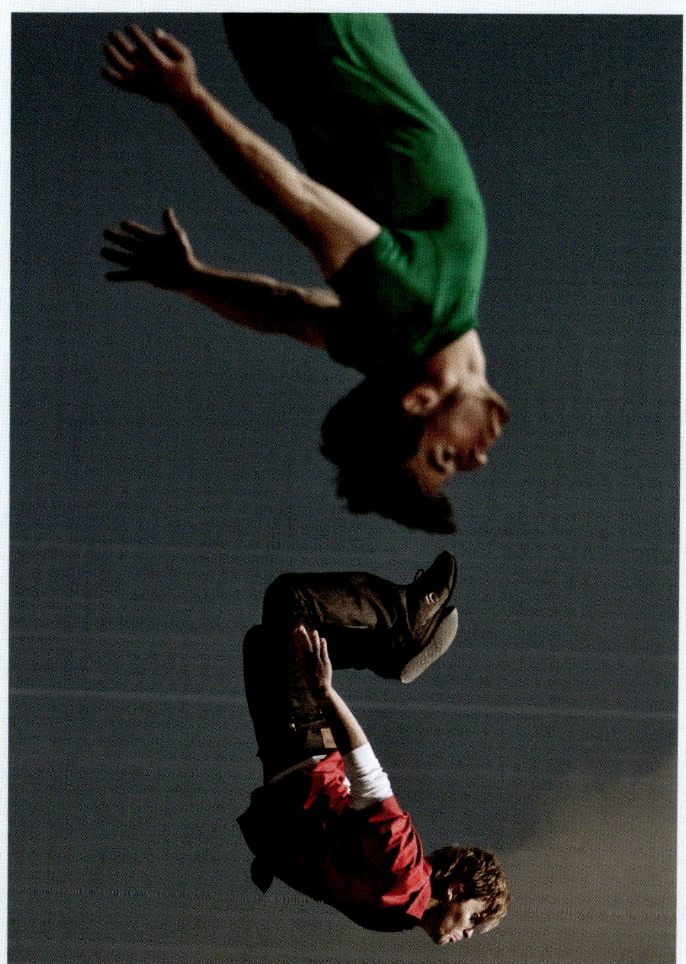

**FIGURE 1.6B** Notice the difference in focus between the two subjects. This subtlety is real, and it isn't from Photoshop.

IMAGE DETAIL © ANDY BATT, *PARKOUR ARTISTS BRIAN OROSCO AND TYSON CECKA, SAN FRANCISCO, CA,* 2009.

Brian, Tyson and I worked out the timing together so we would get the perfect shot: They're both in the air—no Photoshop required. Take a look at the inset detail (**Figure 1.6B**), where you can see the difference in focus between Brian (in the back) and Tyson (in the front). The presence of Tyson in soft focus adds a sense of depth, which would be absent if I had built the image in post. I've seen amazing Photoshop techniques, but in my opinion, the artificiality of creating effects like this in post-production is always trumped by the ability to create it "inside" the camera.

There's some secret retouching in this image: the birds. While shooting, the seagulls were flying into the shot, which was a great addition to the image. Not only were there two men defying gravity, but also they were actually flying with the birds! Unfortunately, those birds were never in the perfect place in any of our best shots. My producer, Therese, suggested that we grab some background plates[7] of just the birds, which we easily accomplished by throwing a bunch of corn chips in the air. (Brilliant, right? There's more to successful photography than mere technological skill!) Once in post, I added a few more seagulls to contribute to the sense of flight. That fits my definition of working in front of the camera, since I photographed the birds at the same spot I was shooting and because we knew ahead of time that adding birds in post would be part of the final art.

## Controlling Time

The shutter has a range of 55 different speeds[8], starting at 1/8000th of a second and ending at 30 seconds. Once you take control of your shutter speed, you can bend time and reshape the world. It's important to understand the difference between how our eye-brain combo and our cameras "see." We "see" time at about 1/30th of a second, which is approximately how long it takes us to look at the world and then refresh. Events that take place at higher speeds tend to blend together in such a way that we don't notice the separate events.

***Once you take control of your shutter speed, you can bend time and reshape the world.***

### Shutters: Controlling Exposure

Although we regulate exposure with many settings, options and tools, the shutter is one of the most fundamental controls of all. By using a fast shutter speed, we can immobilize our subjects and freeze them in place—perhaps revealing unseen behaviors, or perhaps just making sure that the moment is sharp and easy to read. Or, we can head in the other direction by slowing down exposure times so our subjects blur and soften or by moving the camera itself to create motion where there is none.

Sometimes we use shutter control to remove a problem, whether it's finding the limit of how slow a speed we can use while shooting handheld[9] or compensating for a telephoto lens that magnifies not only the subject, but also the effects of camera-shake.

### Inner Workings: Shutter Mechanics

There are two main ideas when it comes to shutter mechanics: moving gap and the rapid aperture, i.e., the focal-plane curtain shutter and the leaf-aperture shutter.

DSLRs are focal-plane cameras; by pressing the shutter release, two moving blades are put into action. The first uncovers the sensor and the second follows a precise amount of time afterwards, covering up the sensor. That precise amount of time is your shutter speed. If you're working at 1/250th or slower,[10] the entire surface of the shutter will be exposed all at once. If you increase that speed, there will be a small, but significant change: The entire surface of the sensor won't

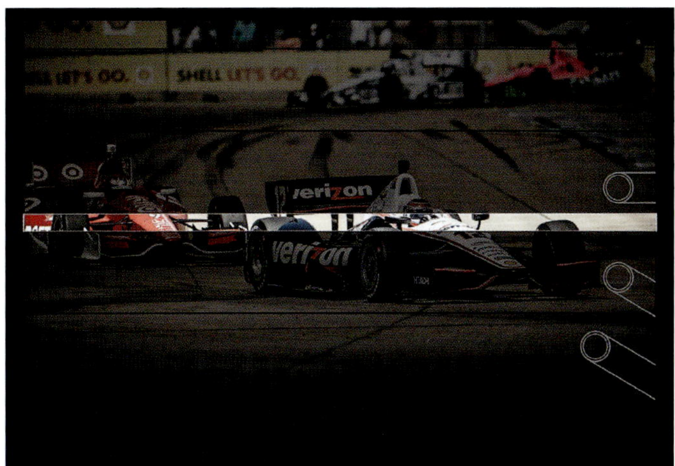


**FIGURE 1.7A** Fast Shutter: With most cameras, shutter speeds higher than 1/250th are accomplished by moving a gap (between the leading and trailer edge of the shutter blades) rapidly across the sensor. This exposes the sensor incrementally, instead of all at once.
IMAGE © ANDY BATT, *GAP BETWEEN BLADES OF A FOCAL-PLANE CURTAIN SHUTTER,* 2013.

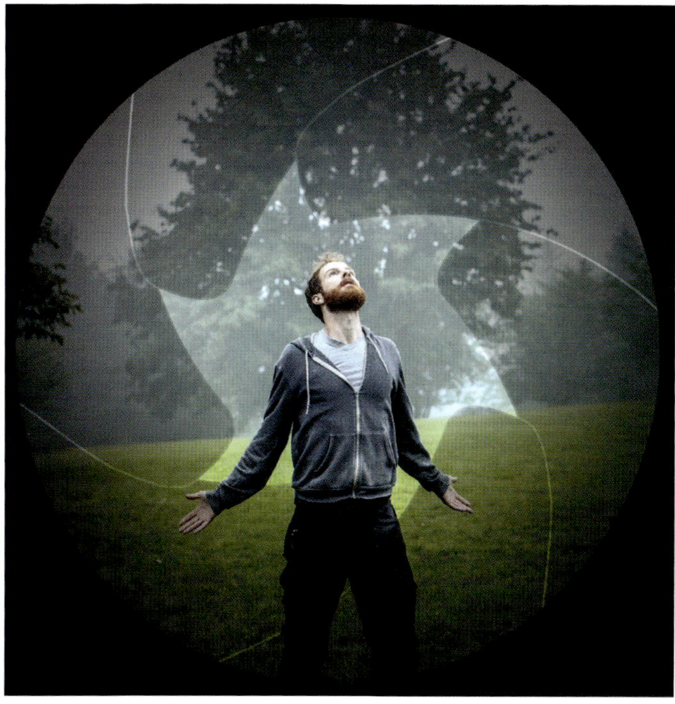

**FIGURE 1.7B** A leaf shutter works in a similar fashion to a lens aperture: It's a circular shape and opens and closes rapidly. Unlike a focal-plane curtain shutter, the entire surface of a leaf sensor is illuminated at the same time, even at high shutter speeds.
IMAGE © ANDY BATT, *VIEW OF AN OPEN LEAF-APERTURE SHUTTER,* 2013.

be exposed all at once. The physical size of the gap between the first and second blades will now be smaller than the sensor, so the image will be exposed as that gap passes over the sensor (**Figure 1.7A**).

If you have a medium-format camera, there's a good chance it uses a leaf shutter (**Figure 1.7B**). The shutter release causes a closed aperture to open and then close; the amount of time between the open and closed states is the shutter speed. This has the benefit of exposing the entire sensor for *any* shutter speed. The downside is that most leaf shutters top out at around 1/1600th, much slower than the top DSLR speeds of 1/8000th.[11]

The mechanical nature of the leaf shutter design creates its own limitation. At slower speeds, the shutter opens, stays open for the time required and then shuts. At high speeds, the shutter begins to vignette; the center of the lens is exposed for the entire time, but the edges are not given the same amount of time as the center, so less light is let in at the edges. This effect might be more pronounced at larger F-stop values. At smaller F-stops, the image is already constrained by the aperture, so the leaf shutter should expose evenly.

One more type of shutter, the *global shutter,* essentially turns the sensor on and off for whatever duration the shutter speed is set to, and the sensor acts as its own shutter. This type is found in a variety of cameras, from point-and-shoots to smartphone and high-end cinema cameras.

### Fluorescent Curiosity

Find an old warehouse that's lit with ancient fluorescent lights and *manually* set your camera to an exposure faster than 1/30th.[12] Now take a series of photos. From photo to photo you'll see either a change in brightness, color or both—or you'll see the effect as a rolling band that goes through the image. That's because this type of light changes color and brightness at a speed that our eyes can't detect.

## Shutter Revelations

Eadweard Muybridge's famous photographic experiment in 1877 proved that at a full gallop, a horse lifts all four legs off the ground at the same time. Before that time, it was thought that a horse maintained contact with the ground at all times. Muybridge employed a new photographic technique to reveal an action that previously had been hidden from the naked eye, as Naomi Rosenblum explains in *A World History of Photography* (1997: 249):

> *This experiment initiated a collaboration, beginning in 1887, between [Leland] Stanford and Muybridge with the goal of providing visual information about animal movement . . . the animals were photographed as they moved in front of a calibrated backdrop, tripping specially designed, electrically operated shutters of 12 cameras equipped with Dallmeyer stereographic lenses at one-thousandth of a second. News of the sensational photographs that resulted—photographs that documented what the human eye had never registered—appeared in the California press in 1877 . . .*

Cameras are able to slow down time so we can experience a world that we can't observe with our naked eyes (**Figure 1.8**). By slowing—or dragging—the camera's shutter, time can be slowed down. Think of it as layering time: Every moment the shutter is open builds on top of the previous moment and adds something to the image. You can use this layering effect to subtly add a hint of motion—or you can use it in a more obvious way to draw out the lines of a body in motion (**Figure 1.9**).

## Camera Gear and Setup: Bruce Ely

***Andy Batt:* Tell us about the camera gear you use.**

***Bruce Ely***: The newspaper supplies most of my camera gear. I'm issued two cameras (a Canon EOS-1D Mark IV and a Mark II N) and a variety of lenses (16–35mm, 24–70mm, 70–200mm and 300mm). I would be very skeptical of ever buying used gear from a photojournalist, mine included. The nature of the daily photojournalism grind just doesn't leave gear in very good condition. That's the beauty of the job, though. The gear gets used—nearly every day, rain or shine.

***AB:* Is there a piece of gear or a specific technique that's important to your work?**

***BE***: One simple technique is to separate the focus control of the camera from the shutter button. Most advanced camera systems enable this by allowing you to assign a button on the back of the camera to start the AF [autofocus] function. This setup allows you to have more control. I separate metering from focusing, which lets me use different focusing techniques to track moving subjects more easily.

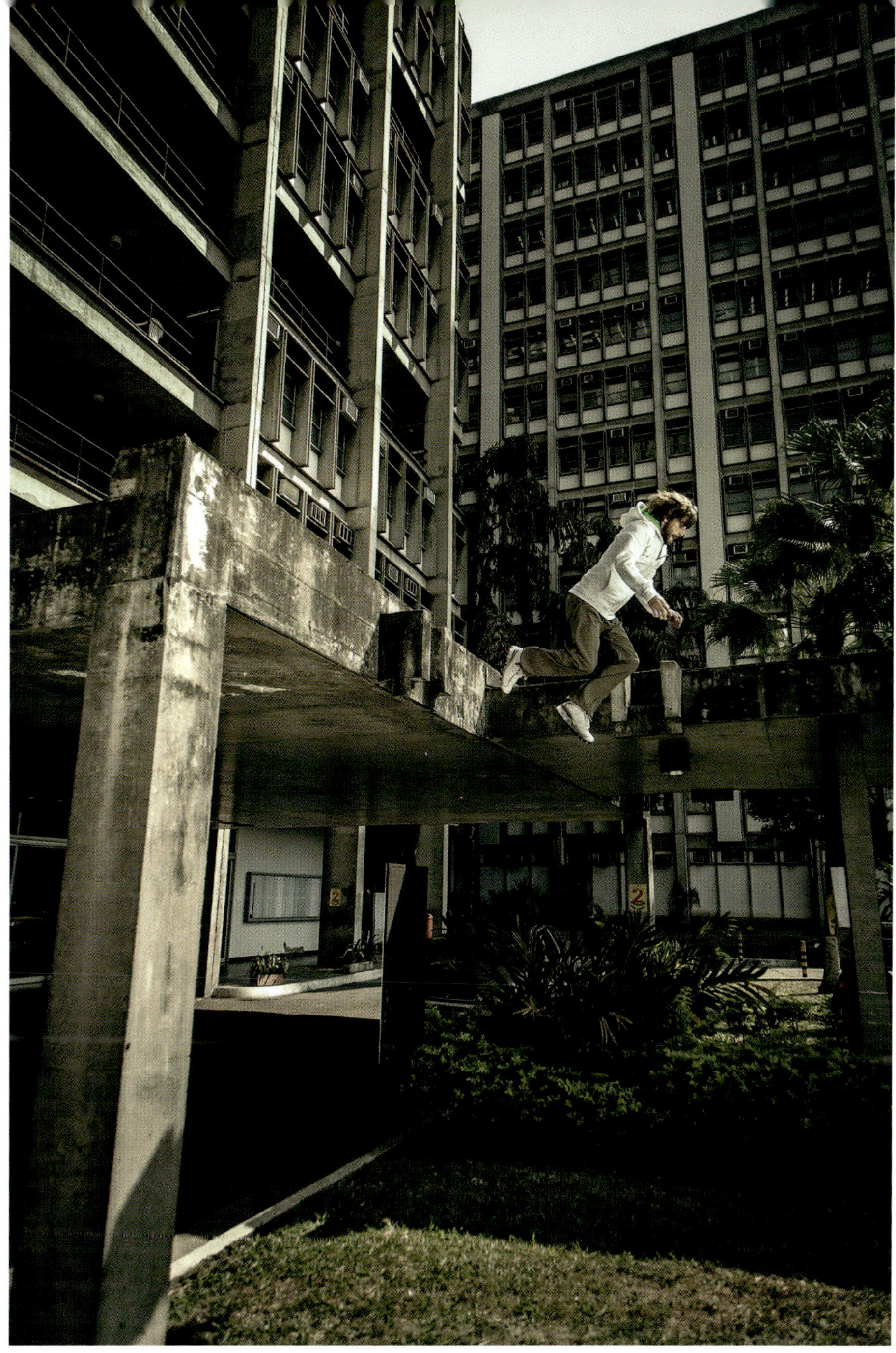

**FIGURE 1.8** Andy photographed an athletic apparel project in Rio de Janeiro, where he had the luck to work with an amazing Parkour artist. In this shot, the athlete jumped from the top of the covered walkway and landed safely with a tuck and roll. Andy loves this shot because the subject's position is very surreal. He says, "I set the camera to 1/2000th of a second and pre–focused the lens to make sure the subject would be sharp. I didn't want a sense of motion here; I wanted him to look like he's floating." It's an amazing thing to hold in your hands, a tool that can stop time.
IMAGE © ANDY BATT, *PARKOUR IN RIO DE JANEIRO, BRAZIL*, 2006.

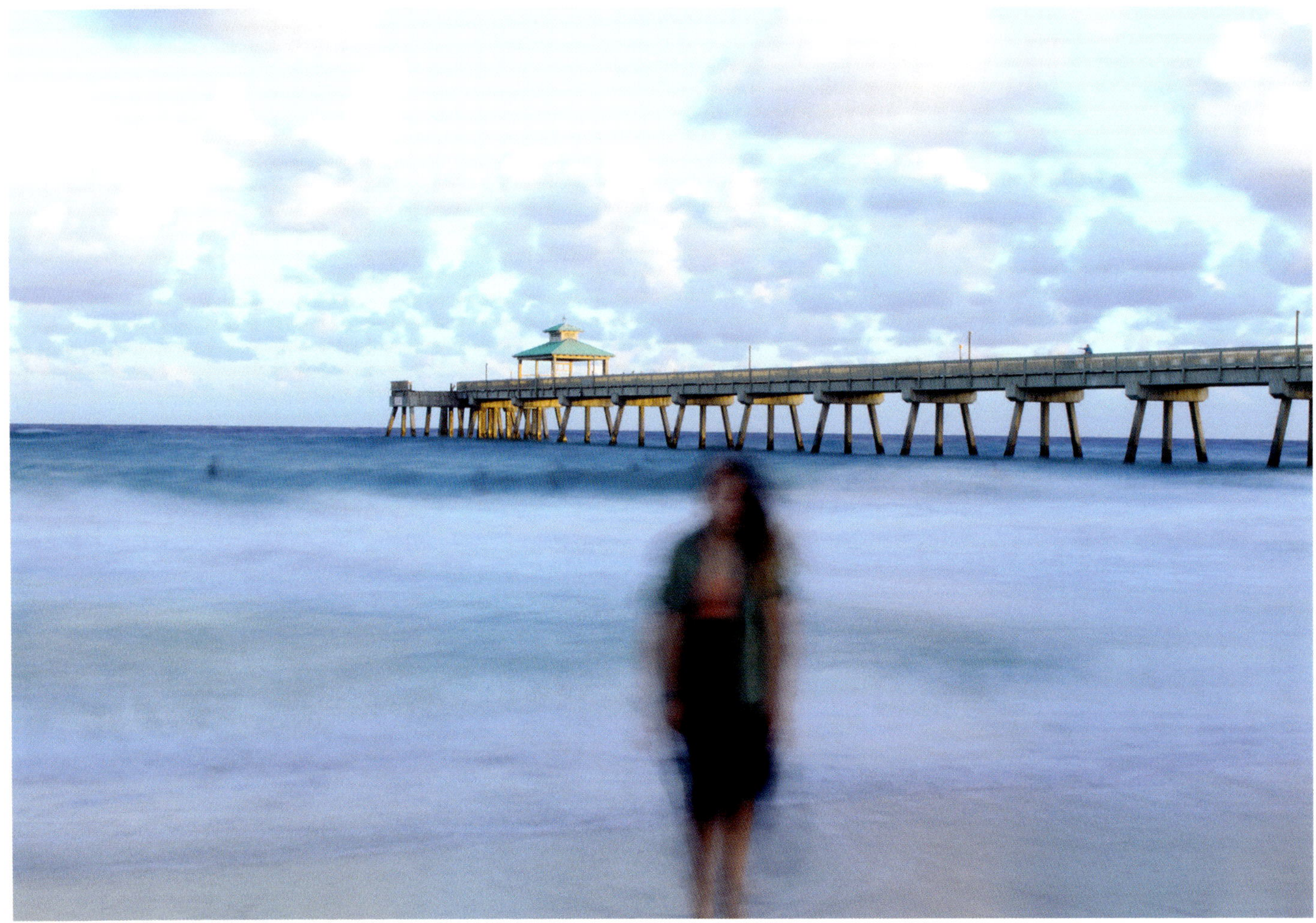

**FIGURE 1.9** It took a lot of trial and error to get this shot. "I set out to capture motion in the water and the subject to reveal something that wasn't easily seen," Erika says. "If the shutter speed was too long, the model simply disappeared. She needed to keep up a swaying movement for her image to register."

Using a tripod, Erika ended up using a four-second shutter speed to add blur to the surf. The pier remains sharp, providing a contrast in focus with the main subject. While our eyes are drawn to the clarity of the pier, our brains respond to the girl. We know that she's the subject, but we're puzzled that she's blurry. This is a great photograph, because it draws us to it like a puzzle—we want to figure out what's going on.

IMAGE © ERIKA VELASQUEZ, *FLORIDA PIER WITH BLURRY GIRL*, 2012.

# TRY THIS AT HOME

## Instant Apocalypse Technique

**For step-by-step instructions, go to: www.focalpress.com/cw/digitalimagingmasters**

Try slowing your shutter speed way down to remove moving objects from your image.

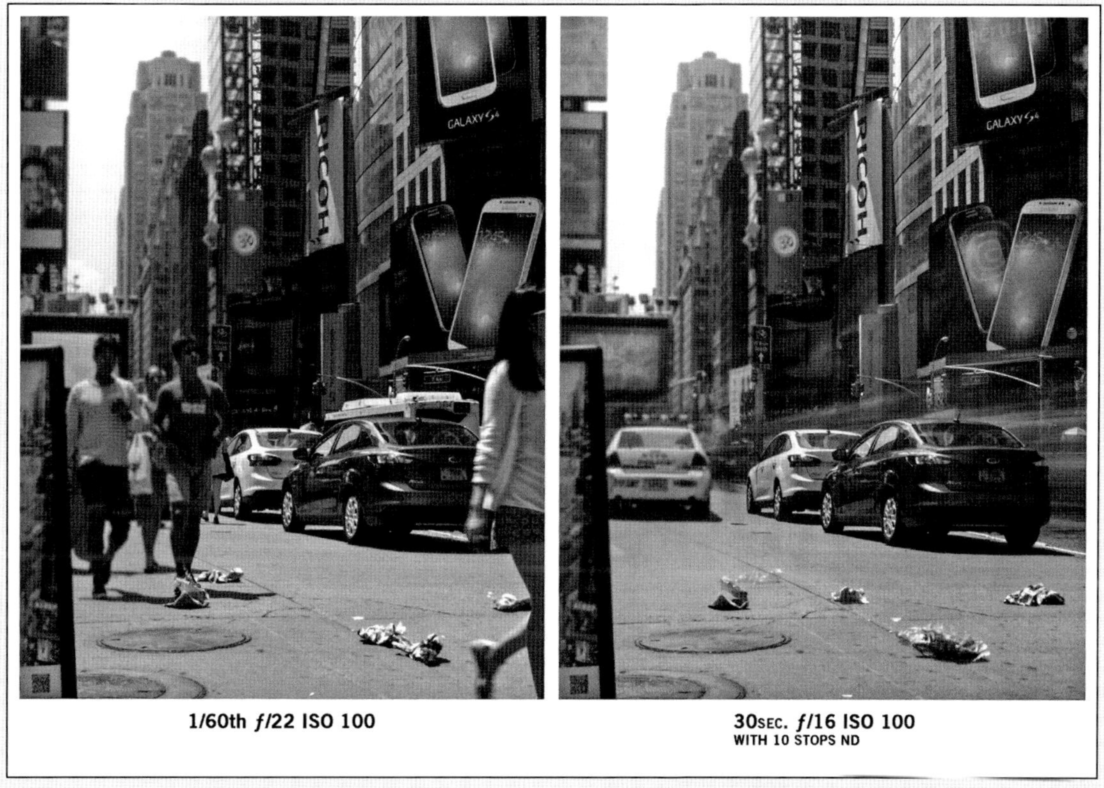


**FIGURE 1.10** Here's a way to empty a city street in the middle of the day. The image on the left was taken just before the image on the right. Erika shot this long exposure by setting her camera on a tripod; putting it on Manual Mode; adding a heavy Neutral Density filter to the lens; and using ISO 100, *f*/16 and a 30–second exposure. Any people that moved through the scene during the exposure simply vanished: They weren't in the same place long enough to be recorded in the image.
IMAGE © ERIKA VELASQUEZ, *EMPTY THE STREETS*, 2013.

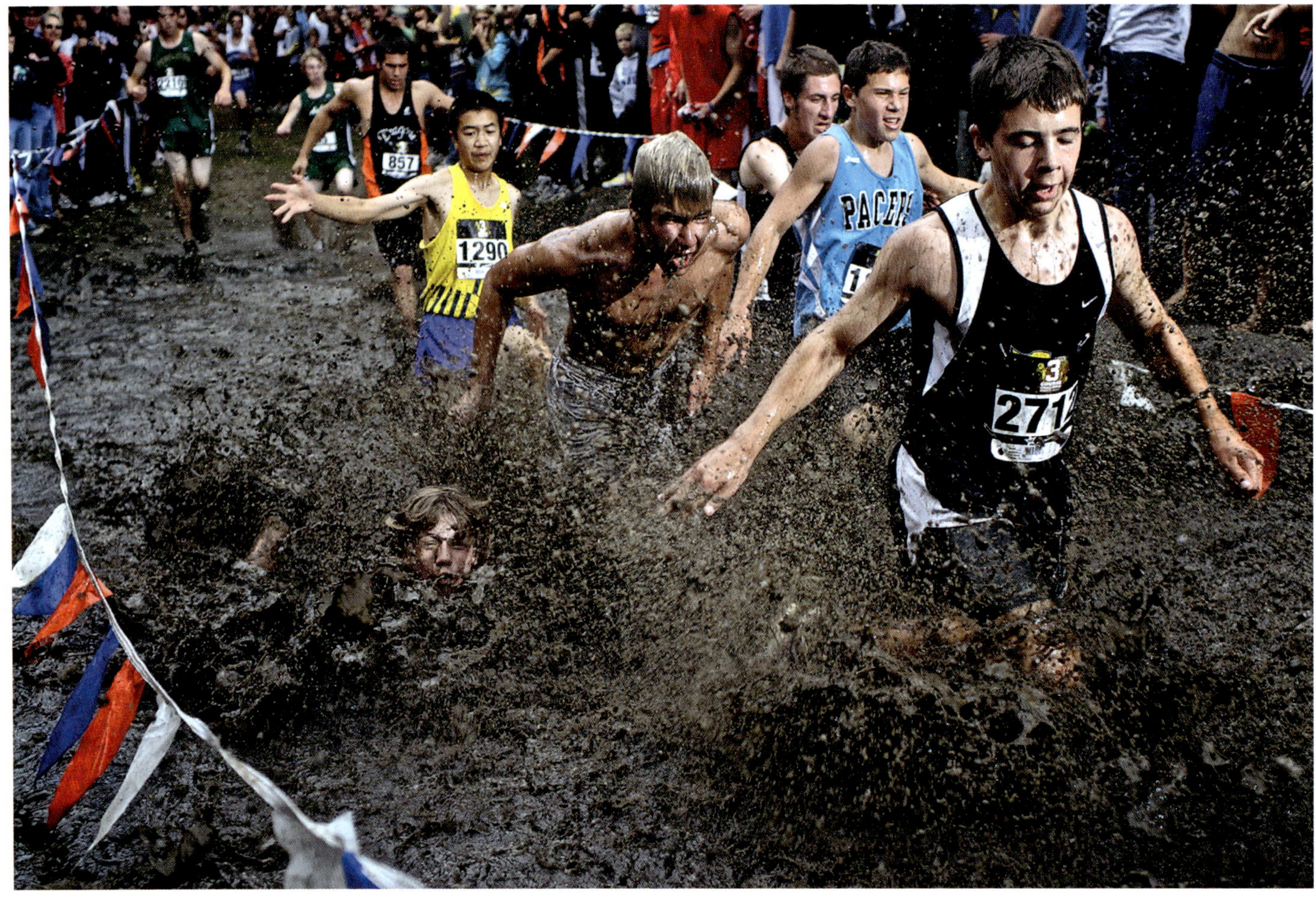


**FIGURE 1.11** Bruce says he'd be very skeptical of ever buying used gear from a photojournalist, himself included. "The nature of the daily photojournalism grind just doesn't leave gear in very good condition."
IMAGE BY BRUCE ELY, *3–COURSE CHALLENGE CROSS–COUNTRY MEET AT SEASIDE, OREGON*, © AND COURTESY OF *THE OREGONIAN*, 2009.

---

***AB:* How about exposure? What tools and techniques do you use to make a correctly exposed image?**

***BE:*** While this seems like a simple question, it really depends on the situation. I work mostly in environments where I have no control over lighting. Finding nice light is a skill that's important to photojournalists. Sometimes I'll position myself at the location where the light is working well and just patiently wait for something to happen in that spot.

My camera setups change often. For the most part, I shoot in fully Manual Exposure Mode. I'll keep an eye on the in-camera meter and adjust on the fly. In situations where the lighting is rapidly and unexpectedly changing, I'll shoot in Aperture Priority Mode while rolling the Exposure Compensation dial accordingly. I often use up to four different camera models, and the LCD screens are vastly different on each of them, so they're unreliable for judging exposure. The histogram is a great tool for confirming that my exposures are where I need them.

## Learning to Focus Like a Camera

Our eyes and brains sample many different points of focus almost simultaneously and take in a wide view that includes information from our peripheral vision. We combine all that information to create our vision, and our brains respond almost instantaneously. They allow us to concentrate on what's in front of us, putting everything we see in focus, no matter where we look.

Our cameras can't focus in the same way our eyes and brains do. Specific lens/camera combinations can create markedly different fields of view and can make us aware of what we're focusing on. For instance, when we choose a wide-angle lens, we create a broad view of the world that complements or exceeds our own peripheral vision—and when we choose a narrow-angle lens, we create a restricted crop of the scene in front of us.

When we make choices about aperture, we also make choices about the stories we tell. Since the aperture controls the amount of light and the range of focus in our images, we always need to consider both factors when choosing the F-stop. If we choose *f*/22, then we'll have a small opening and a substantial increase in depth of field that approaches the way our eyes perceive a scene. If, at the other end of the spectrum, we choose *f*/2.8, then we'll have a large opening with a shallow focus that reveals how differently (from our eyes and brains) our lenses can interpret a scene.

The image in **Figure 1.12A** is very different from what Andy saw with his eyes. "Even looking through the viewfinder," Andy recalls, "I was getting a very different look. The shallow focus wasn't revealed until I had the image up on my monitor. Due to having experience with my lens at *f*/1.4 and being very critical about where I focused, I was able to make this image the way I wanted it."

### Putting the Settings to Work

If your assignment were to photograph a runner during the last hours of daylight, you would need to make some decisions about your camera setup. You'd want to choose a lens that gave you the look you wanted, a fast enough shutter to freeze the runner's motion and the right combination of ISO and F-stop to let you make a decisive DoF choice.

***Andy:*** I would use a full-frame DSLR for this type of job and probably grab my 70–200mm lens, for its flexibility. Runners' bodies don't move all that quickly, but their hands and feet swing much faster, and you need 1/1000th of a second or faster to freeze them. I'd shoot at *f*/4, since that would give me a little more DoF, and I like to work one stop in from the widest aperture (with this lens, it's *f*/2.8), since it's a little sharper overall and corrects any minor lens-curvature issues.

In my runner image (**Figure 1.13**) I was shooting at 1/2000th, *f*/4 at ISO 640. If the light had dropped a stop, I probably would have stolen a little bit from each setting, i.e., I'd have opened up a third to *f*/3.5, slowed down a third to 1/1600th, and gotten another third from by bumping up to ISO 800. If the light values continued to drop, I'd stop the shutter at 1/1000th and probably keep increasing the ISO.

### The Visual Difference Between Stops

Have you ever wondered why you would purchase an *f*/1.2 lens over an *f*/2.8 lens? The reason is because "faster" lenses give you more creative options.

One of the key differences between the faster *f*/1.2 lens and the slower *f*/2.8 lens is that at the super-wide end of the aperture scale, there's an enormous visual (and aesthetic) difference in focus between stops. For example, at *f*/2.0, you have *significantly* less DoF then at *f*/2.8. At midrange apertures—between *f*/8 and *f*/11—the visual difference is much more subtle.

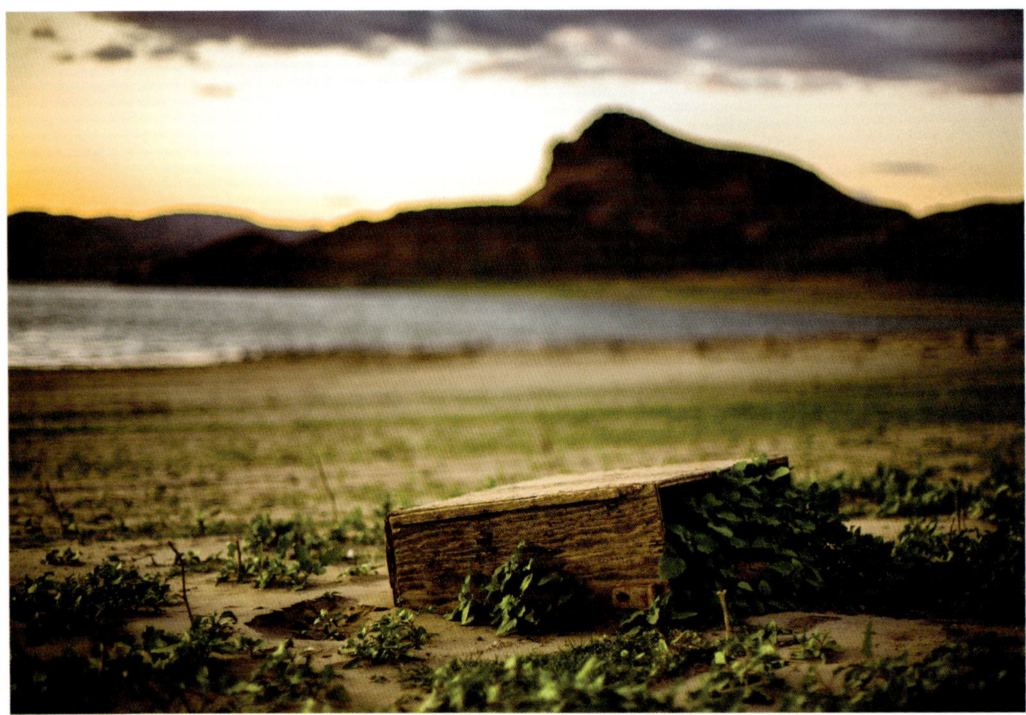

**FIGURE 1.12A** Andy deliberately photographed this scene so that it's different from a traditional landscape. He opened the aperture on his 50mm lens to its maximum value of *f*/1.4. This choice caused distortions and falloff that brought attention to the half-buried box and created the dreamlike background Andy was looking for.
IMAGE © ANDY BATT, *DRIFTWOOD BOX, EASTERN OREGON, OWHYEE RIVER*, 2008.

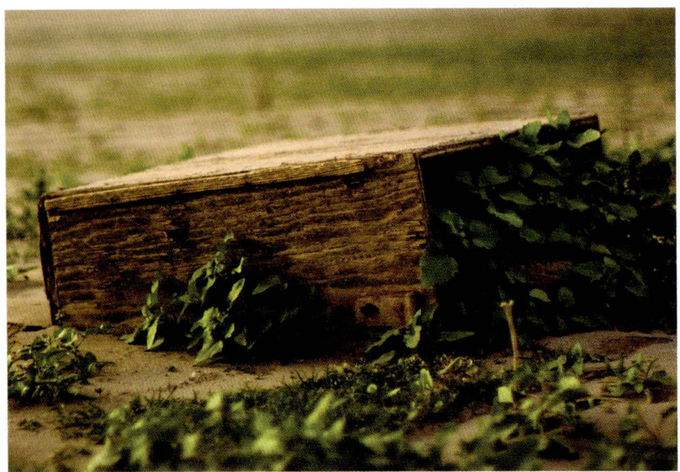

**FIGURE 1.12B**
IMAGE DETAIL © ANDY BATT, *DRIFTWOOD BOX, EASTERN OREGON, OWHYEE RIVER*, 2008.

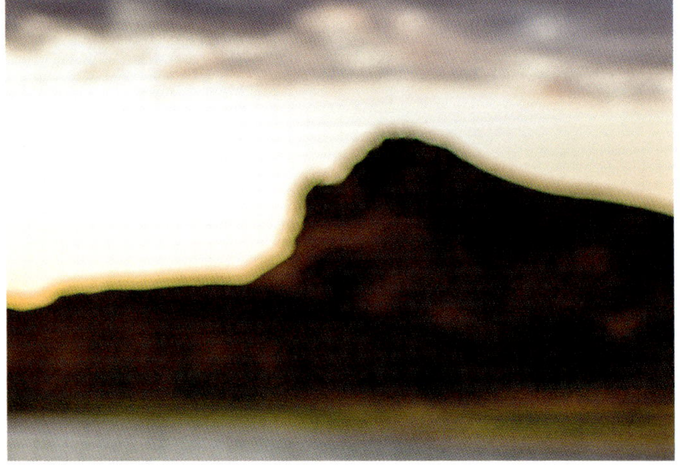

**FIGURE 1.12C**
IMAGE DETAIL © ANDY BATT, *DRIFTWOOD BOX, EASTERN OREGON, OWHYEE RIVER*, 2008.

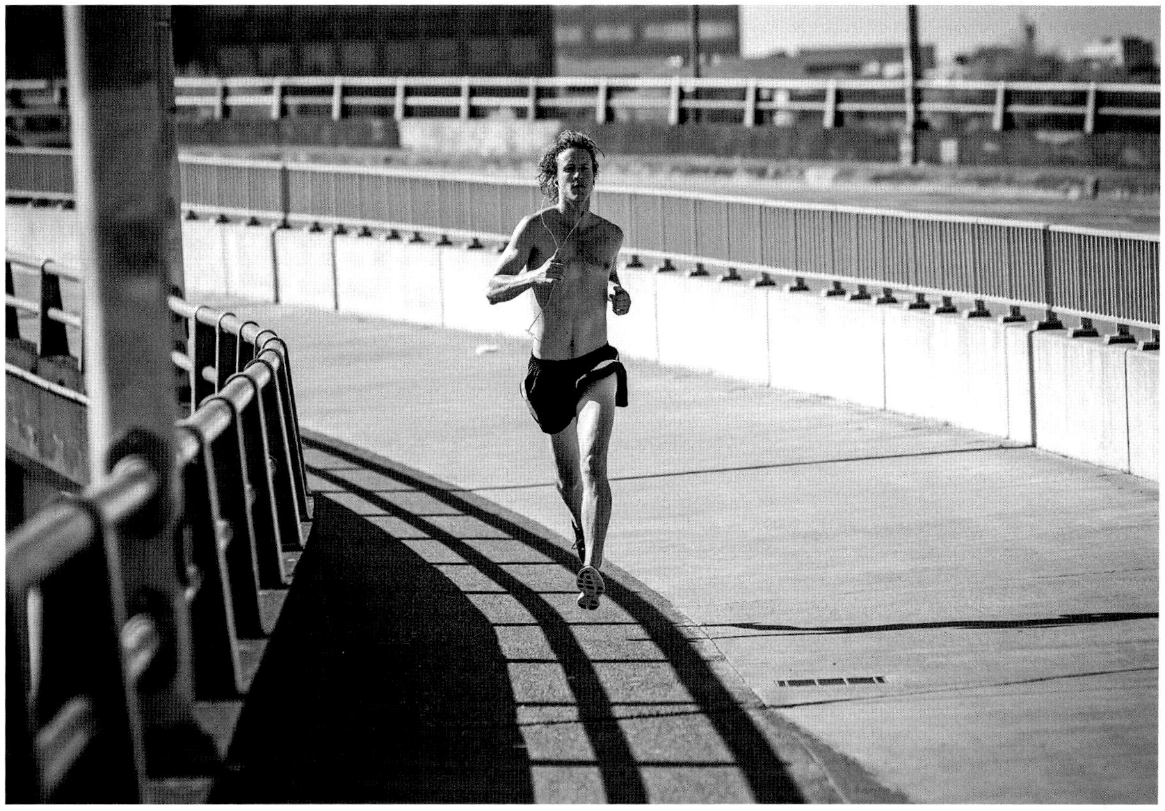

**FIGURE 1.13** Andy shot this runner during the last hours of daylight at 1/2000th, *f*/4.0 at ISO 640 with a 70–200mm lens. His choice of lens and aperture shaped the look of the image, which he shot for a Monster Cable® sports earbuds campaign.
IMAGE © ANDY BATT, *BRIDGE RUNNER*, 2012.

With this kind of shot, there's a limit to how slow you can take the shutter, because at a certain point you're making a different picture than the one you intended. Experience and testing with this camera have shown me that you can push some pretty high-ISO values and get very usable pictures. The trick is to understand that at higher ISO values, you'll have to do more work in post to remove the noise and preserve details.

## Depth of Field (DoF)

DoF is a measure of how much "focus" an image has. With greater (deeper) DoF, a broader area is in focus; with less (shallower) DoF, the zone of focus can be limited to a very narrow area. For instance, in a close-up portrait with shallow DoF, the eye might be in focus, while the ear is not. Different lenses have different DoF capabilities. A good rule of thumb is that for the same F-stop value, a wide-angle lens will have greater DoF than a telephoto lens.

## TRY THIS AT HOME

### Change the Story with Focus

**For step-by-step instructions, go to: www.focalpress.com/cw/digitalimagingmasters**

Try shamelessly manipulating one scene by shooting at both the widest and smallest apertures on your lens; you'll end up with two distinctly different photographs.

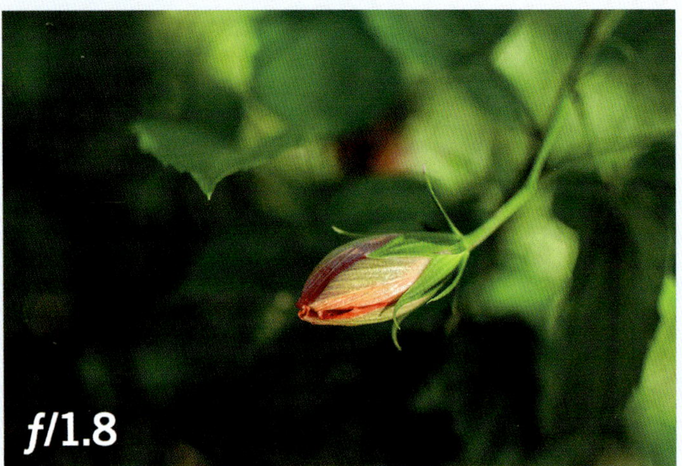


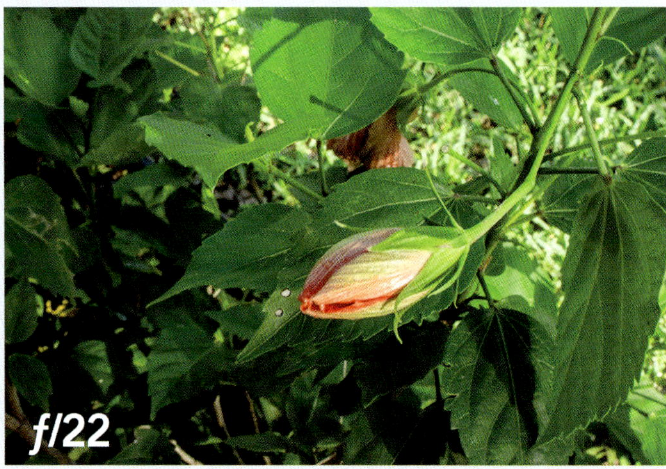


**FIGURE 1.14** These two shots were taken with the same exposure and focus, but with different F–stops. Your DoF choice shapes the stories you tell.
IMAGE © ERIKA VELASQUEZ, *ROSEBUD*, 2013.

## Taking Control: Metering and Histograms

Part of being a photographer is taking control of exposure. To a camera, a scene is just a sea of tonal values, but to you, it's a story you want to tell and a feeling you want to express. When we talk about good exposure, we mean two parallel ideas: capturing the best data possible to process out the highest-quality image and capturing the scene the way you see it, to tell the story you want to tell. A dark, underexposed image feels moody or dangerous; a bright and slightly overexposed image feels high-tech or clean; and soft light at a normal exposure subtly recedes behind the subjects.

One of the best ways we know of improving your exposure skills is to work in Manual Mode as often as possible. It's a great motivator for learning, because if you don't take control over your exposure in Manual Mode, then the camera won't do anything about it, and you'll end up with badly exposed images.

Practicing this discipline will help you make stronger connections between your settings (cause) and your photos (effect). To shoot manually, you'll need to take charge of the shutter speed, aperture and ISO, using those tools to create good exposures (**Figures 1.15 and 1.16**). If you want to achieve good exposures, you'll also need to understand the relationship among the light meter, the histogram (on both the LCD and in Lightroom) and the values in your image.

***When you control exposure, you control your craft.***

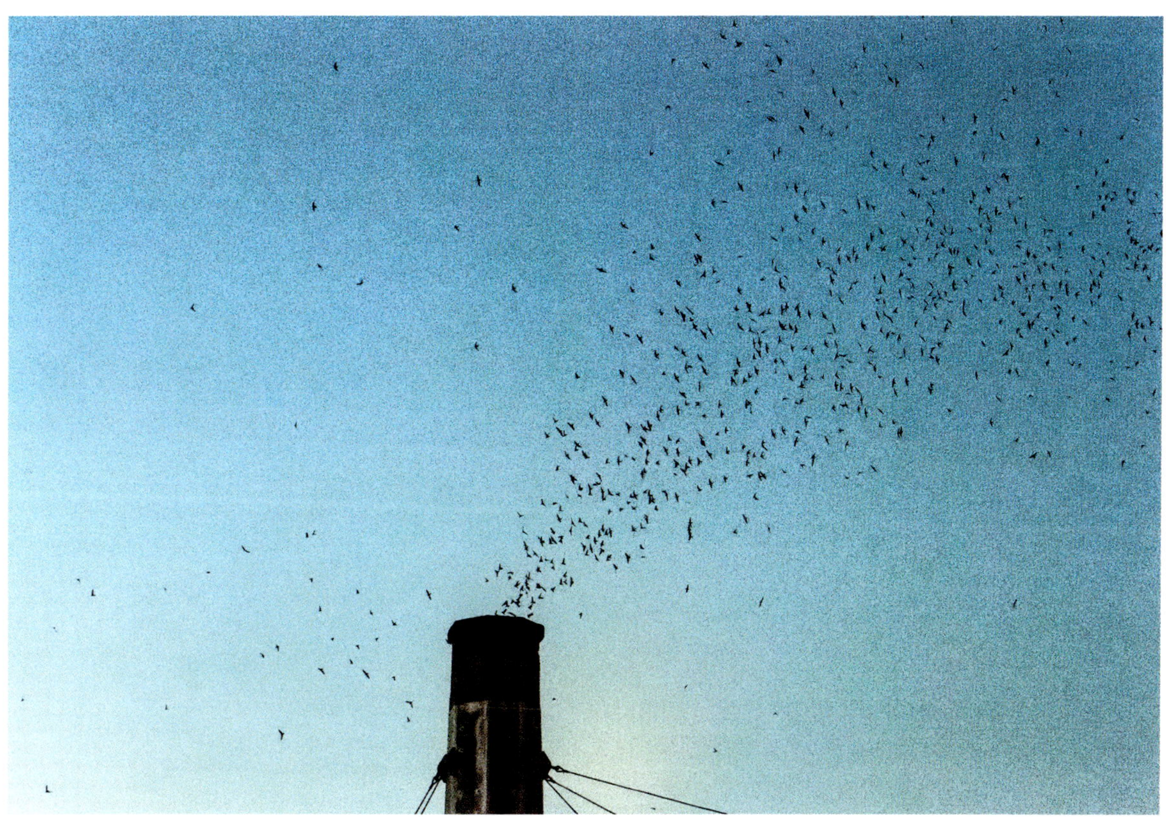

**FIGURE 1.15** This image presented a challenging situation that needed manual metering. The sun was going down. Andy needed to set a 1/1250th shutter speed in order to freeze the swifts in flight, and he wanted to hold *f*/5.6, so that enough of the birds would be in the zone of focus. He says, "Wanting both of these values meant I needed to shoot at ISO 10,000. I used Manual Mode, because although I was filling my frame with sky, my subjects were tiny, rapidly flying dark shapes. Manual let me lock in my exposure and get the shot."
IMAGE © ANDY BATT, *VAUX SWIFTS, CHAPMAN SCHOOL*, 2013.

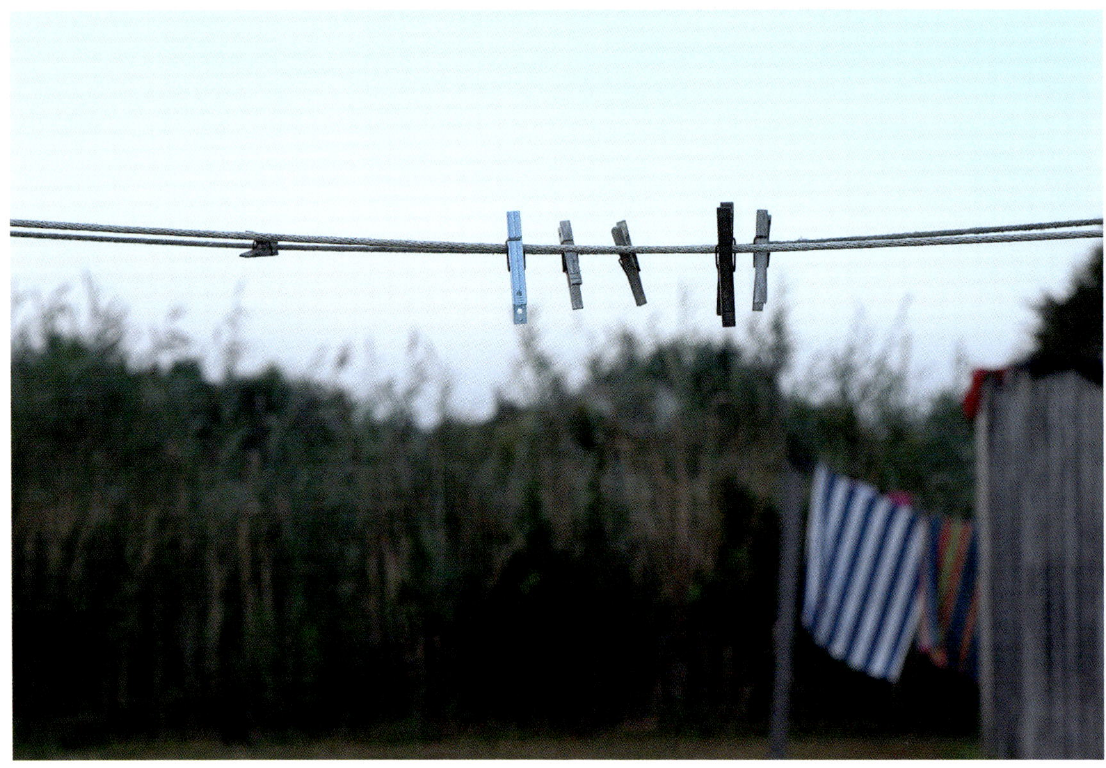

**FIGURE 1.16** For this shot, Candace wanted to draw attention to the clothespins, an iconic reminder of lazy summer days on Cape Cod. It can be tricky to find the right exposure at dusk, when the sky is still relatively bright and subjects on the ground have already begun to recede into shadow. To assure that the clothespins—the most important part of the composition—were properly exposed, Candace used Manual Mode and spot-metered on the blue one (her favorite), checking the camera's monitor to make sure the sky wasn't blown out and the shadows on the ground maintained detail. This image was shot at 1/60th of a second at *f*/8.
IMAGE © CANDACE DOBRO, *CAPE CLOTHESLINE*, 2013.

---

*Everything in photography is a rabbit hole. You might think you've gotten to a certain level where a subject is closed and there's no new information—but every time I get there, I'll read an article, see a photograph or just talk to somebody and it'll hit me: "Wow, I've never thought of it like that," and that's exciting to me. You can dive down a rabbit hole with any of these topics. The lessons and ideas might become subtler as you go along, but they're out there. I'm still learning about exposure—I think I'll always be learning.*

*—Andy Batt*

## Metering In-Camera

Your light meter and histogram are the two most effective tools you have in your camera bag for determining exposure—apart from your own experience (the best tool of all!). Your in-camera light meter is a way to measure exposure *before* you shoot, and your in-camera histogram is a way to check your data *after* you shoot. Your camera offers different metering mode options, but they all rely on your understanding of what the meter is telling you about the scene in your viewfinder. Mastering this skill is deceptive: Your goal is to be able to quickly take a meter reading and make a purposeful decision to either accept or make changes to the exposure settings—without having to interrupt your image-making process.

The in-camera meter is a simple tool that's designed to be read at a glance. **Figure 1.17** shows an illustration of one; yours might look different, but the essentials will be the same. When the indicator (the square to the right of the mark) lines up with the center mark, you have what the camera considers to be a normal exposure. If you use Program, Aperture Priority or Shutter Priority Mode, the meter should consistently hit that mark. If you dial in over- or under-exposure compensation, or choose auto-bracketing, you'll see that the square lands at marks above and below the center mark.

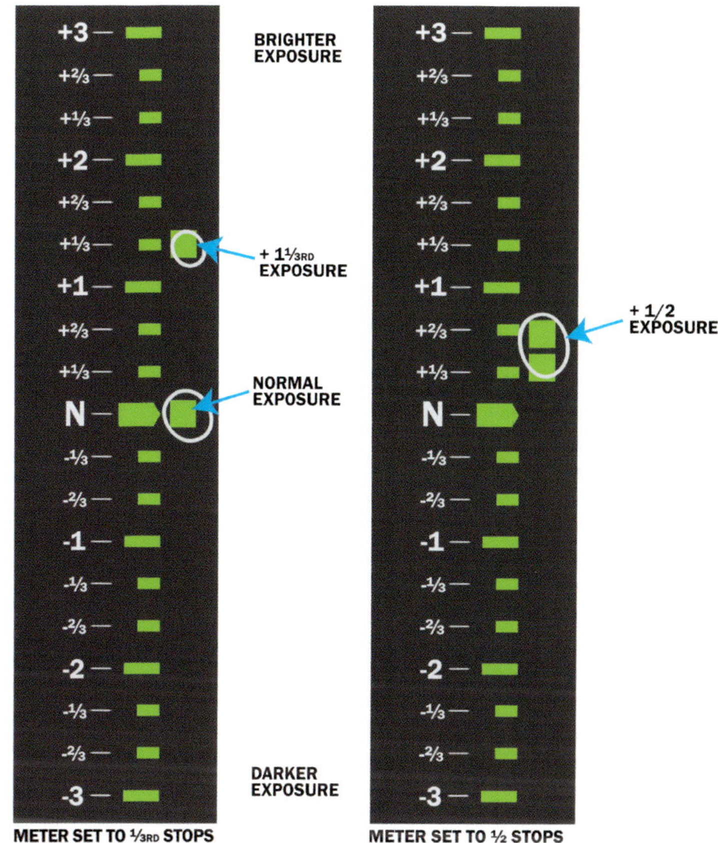


**FIGURE 1.17** Your camera's built-in meter probably looks something like these illustrations, which are based on Canon's meter view. Normal exposure is right in the middle, with brighter exposures going up and darker ones going down. The meter has whole and 1/3-stop marks. If you're using an automatic mode, the meter's indicator should be at center, since its goal is to give you what it considers a "normal" exposure at all times.

In Manual Mode, the indicator will move around, depending on how you've dialed in the exposure settings. On the scale at left, you'll see a second square indicating what the exposure readout would be if you were 1 1/3-stop brighter than what the camera considered to be a normal reading.

Some cameras can be set to 1/2-stop increments. The scale at right shows the meter set to 1/2-stop mode. The indicator changes from a single square to a double square when it's at a 1/2-stop interval between whole stops. With the 1/2-stop setting, you end up with a slightly different scale of F-stops and shutter speeds: ***f*/2.8 > *f*/3.3 > *f*/4.0 and 1/250th > 1/350th > 1/500th**.

ILLUSTRATION © ANDY BATT, *IN-CAMERA METERING*, 2013.

## Give It a Try

Pick up your camera right now and put it on Manual. An easy first step in Manual-Mode photography is just to accomplish what the automatic controls do: Get the indicator right at the normal mark.

Frame up a shot of anything and set your F-stop, shutter speed and ISO to get your meter to the normal mark. Now, turn around in your environment while looking through your viewfinder and watch the indicator bounce up and down. The meter reacts to any change in light levels, but it also reacts to bright and dark objects in the same way. For any place you point your camera, you can adjust your settings to get back to that normal mark.

Next, try to find a dark object and a bright object[13] that are near each other. You could use a sheet of white paper or a black t-shirt if there's nothing else around. When you frame up the shot of the bright object, adjust your meter to get to the normal mark. Then recompose on the dark object and see the meter change; the object is too dark and the meter is telling you that you need to open up your exposure! The light in the room hasn't changed, so why did the meter change? Because the meter in your camera reacts to the information you put in front of it. A bright white chair causes more light to go into the camera, and a black velvet painting causes less light to go into the camera.

So . . . which is the right exposure? With Program Mode, the camera automatically decided to darken the bright objects and lighten the dark ones—but now you want to make the decisions. This is your first big step towards taking control: You recognize that your in-camera meter is reacting to the brightness of the objects you put in front of it. In *Chapter 6,* we'll dive into this issue in depth.

***For now, think about exposure in two ways:***

- Exposure is determined by the brightness of objects in front of the camera that reflect light.
- Exposure can also be determined by the light that falls onto those objects, instead of being reflected from them.

***Andy Batt:*** **How much do you trust the back of the camera to give you an accurate image?**

***Carli Davidson:*** I trust it to let me know that my exposures are within a very acceptable range, so I can tweak the exposures in post. Generally I haven't had to tweak anything more than a quarter stop, because I know how my camera and lights work in my studio—I know what I'm getting.

## Which Is the "Right" Exposure?

Take a look at **Figure 1.18A**. It shows three variations of a portrait that Andy shot. These images were all taken within a short period of time, without any changes to the light values. Andy kept the aperture and ISO consistent, but changed the shutter speed—from 1/13th to 1/40th, then to 1/200th, between shots. **Figure 1.18B** shows the back-of-the-camera versions of the images in Figure 1.18A. These are brightness histograms, which combine all three color channels to give an overall look at the data values of the exposures. Can you tell which one of these exposures is correct? Which histogram is the right one? The answer is that all three images are interesting—and each one has a slightly different story. As you look at them individually, see how you react to the story being told.

***Andy***: In the darkest image, the imagination of the viewer can fill in the shadows. In the brightest image, you get a lot more visual information about the place where the subject is standing. For myself, I think the darkest version is the most interesting—and correct—one. In all three versions, I did make sure there was enough data in the image for keeping a good skin tone.

## What Your Camera's Histogram Wants You to Know

We like to think of the in-camera histogram as a way to take a meter reading after we take the shot. It's full of valuable information that can help us understand how all the different areas in the scene are exposing. In order to take advantage of all that data and info, we need to know what it's telling us (**Figure 1.19**).

To read a histogram effectively, the biggest idea to grasp is that there isn't one universal, perfect histogram that we're all trying to achieve. Every photo you've ever taken is unique in some way—and so is its histogram. Within each of the unique data patterns, there are five basics areas: shadow tones, 3/4 tones, midtones, 1/4 tones and highlights. These correspond to the five divisions you see in most histograms. When we're working, we generally reduce the idea down

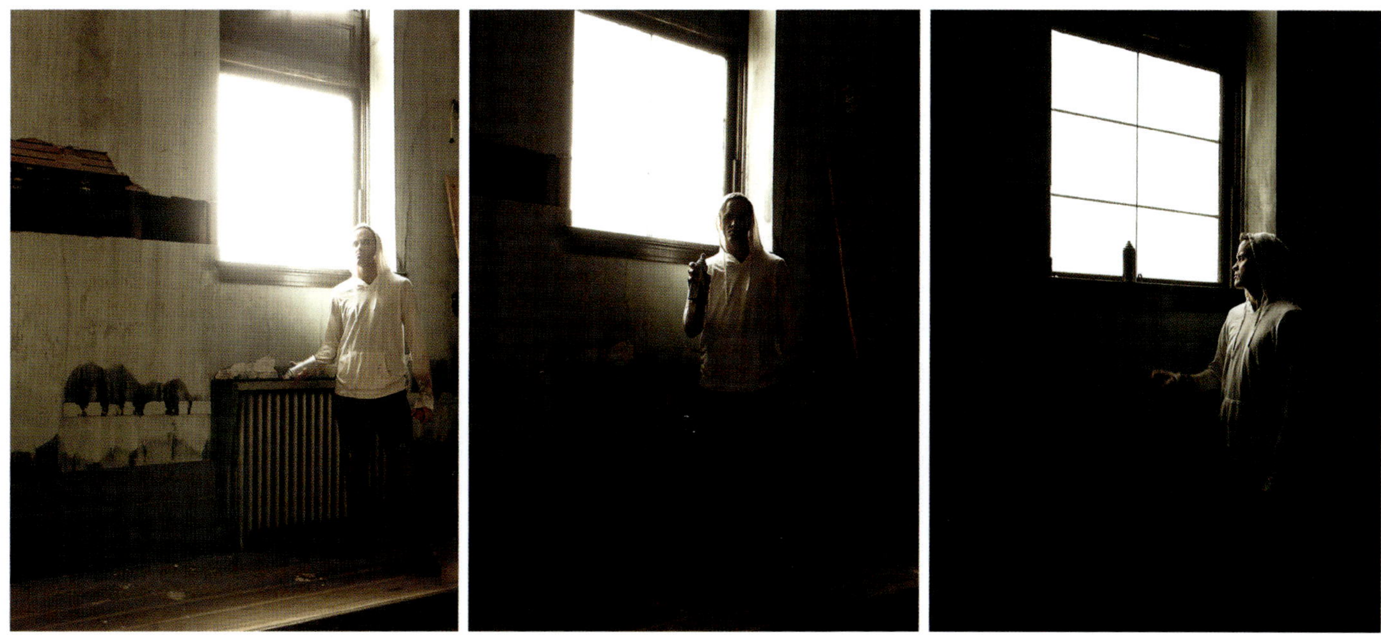

**FIGURE 1.18A** Three different exposures yielded three different photos. The question is: which one is the right or "good" exposure? From left to right: shutter speed settings of 1/13th, 1/40th and 1/200th of a second, all shot under the same lighting conditions at *f*/5.0, ISO 800. The "good" exposure is the one that creates the story the photographer wants to tell. In this case, Andy preferred the darkest image, since it matched the mood of the character being photographed.
IMAGE © ANDY BATT, *ACTOR MICHAEL FETTERS*, FROM THE FILM *THE LAST GARDEN*, 2011.

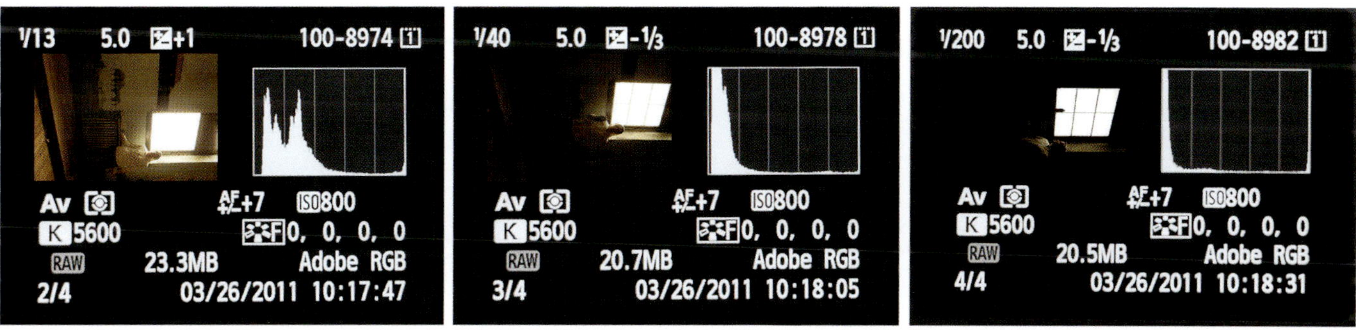


**FIGURE 1.18B** Here are the images from Figure 1.18A as they look on the back of the camera. We're interested in how the histograms of the images look, since we use them to help us judge exposure. These are brightness histograms, which combine all three color channels to give an overall reading of light values.

On the vertical scale, the histograms measure the volume of information (the number of pixels), and on the horizontal scale, the histogram represents the image's progression from black (far left) to white (far right). The trick is in knowing that the histogram is only *part* of the puzzle. Without any other information, we would say the best looking histogram is the left-hand image—but the image on the right is the one that best represented the photographer's vision.
IMAGE © ANDY BATT, *BACK-OF-THE-CAMERA BRIGHTNESS HISTOGRAMS*, 2013.

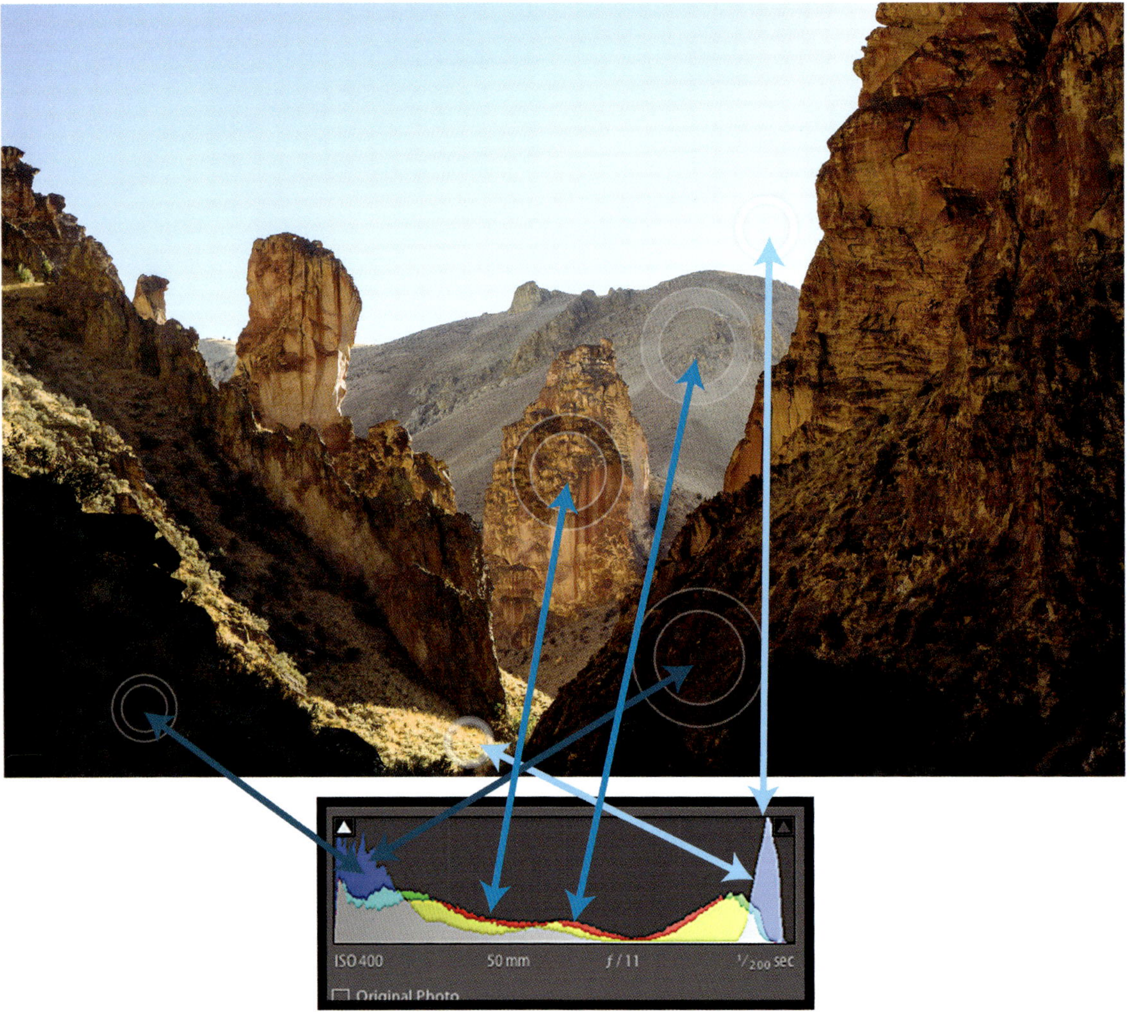


**FIGURE 1.19** Andy linked the areas in this image to points on their Lightroom histogram, to give you an idea of how they correspond. He says, "One of the most challenging and useful things to learn is to connect the histogram data to the image you just made. It's easy to get hung up worrying whether the data is too far to the left or right, when all you're doing is seeing the data by itself."

The key is to never look at just the histogram. Try to understand the scene you've photographed: Are there a lot of dark objects that should be rendered as dark in the image? If so, then you'll have a lot of data on the left side of the histogram. If you don't have many midtoned objects, then the data in the middle will be minimal. And pay attention to any spikes in the image: They can change the vertical scale of your image and make significant parts of the image seem insignificant in the histogram. To take this idea to the next level, start trying to see the world in front of your camera and make those connections before you even take the picture.

IMAGE © ANDY BATT, *LAKE OWYHEE CANYON*, 2013.

to these broad strokes: shadow tones, midtones and highlights. Take a look at **Figure 1.20A** to see how these tones look in a basic histogram.

Histogram 1 could be a photograph of a black cat sitting on a black couch in a room with a black carpet. The majority of the image is darker tones, so the majority of your data ends up on the left side of the histogram. Histogram 2 could be a photograph of a room with gray wallpaper, a gray wingback chair and a gray cat. All the data is in the middle. What about Histogram 3? It could be a photograph of a white cat sitting on a . . . you get the idea. All that data is right where you'd expect it, pushed over to the right side.

Each histogram is directly connected to what the scene itself looks like. If we were photographing a faithful reproduction of that

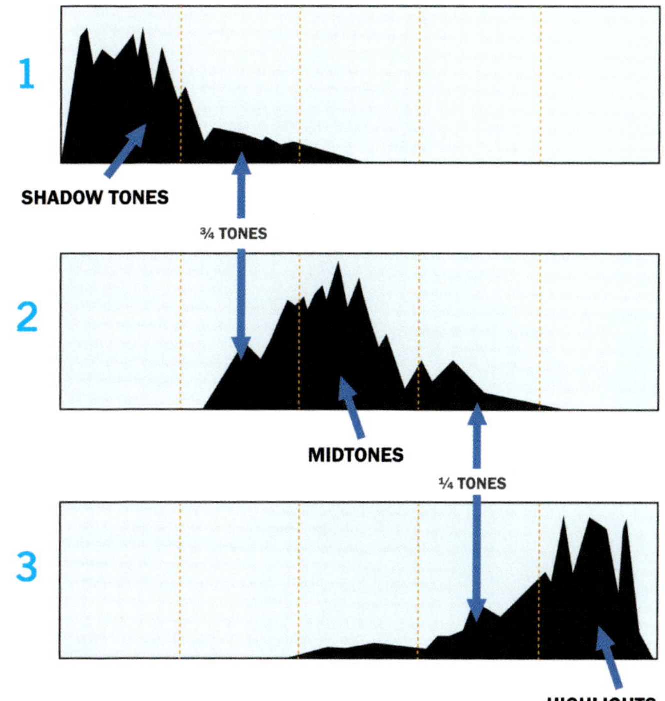


**FIGURE 1.20A** Your image histogram can be shown as brightness values, three separate color values (RGB) or as an overlay of all three, as Lightroom does in this illustration. Here, we've created three different brightness histograms that show the data for three different scenes: Histogram 1 is a low-key image with lots of dark-tone objects in it; Histogram 2 is a low-contrast image, with nothing but midtones; and Histogram 3 is a high-key image, made up of objects with bright values. All three histograms can be considered "good," since they accurately represent their respective scenes.
ILLUSTRATION © ANDY BATT, *HISTOGRAM BASICS I*, 2013.

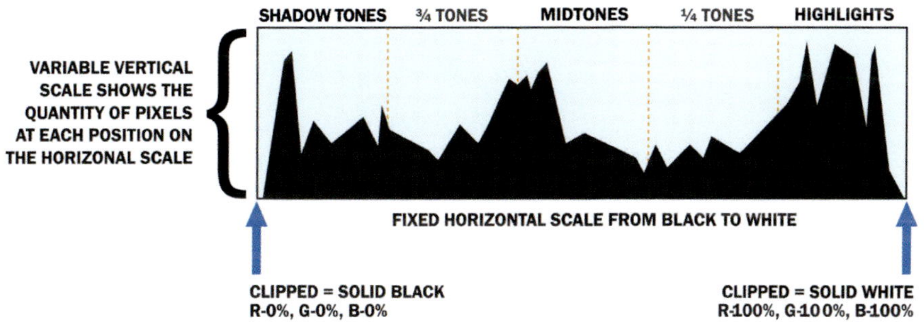


**FIGURE 1.20B** The horizontal scale is fixed and stretches from solid black on the left edge to solid white on the right edge. The vertical scale is trickier: For every point on the horizontal scale, the vertical scale shows you how many pixels exist in the image at that tonal value; think of it as a volume meter. The tricky bit is that it's a variable scale—if you have a particularly large volume of a single tone, it would show up as a tall spike. The vertical axis would be automatically scaled to fit that tall spike, and all the other graphed data would shrink. It's not changing the data, it's just changing the way it's being shown.
ILLUSTRATION © ANDY BATT, *HISTOGRAM BASICS II*, 2013.

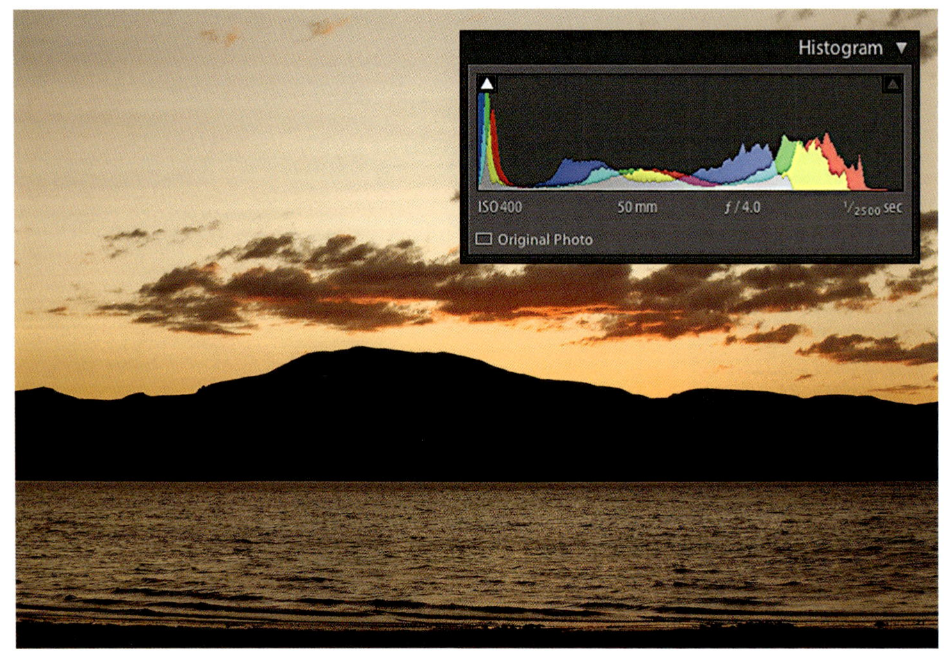


**FIGURE 1.21A**
IMAGE © ANDY BATT, *LAKE OWYHEE RIVER*, 2013.

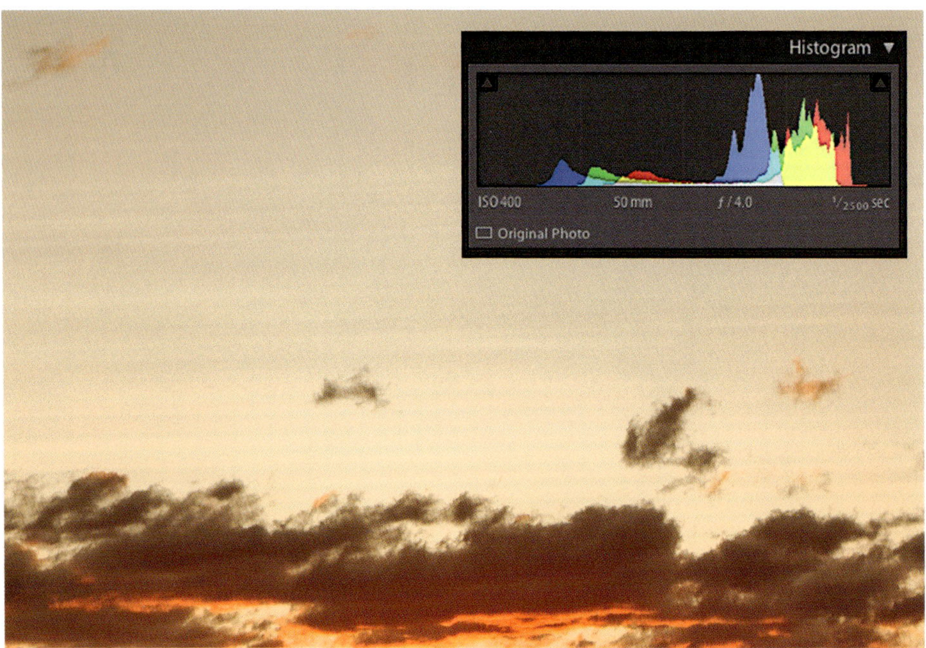


**FIGURE 1.21B**
IMAGE © ANDY BATT, *LAKE OWYHEE RIVER—DETAIL*, 2013.

white room, we'd want Histogram 3. If, instead, the photo of the white room resulted in Histogram 1 or 2, we'd know we were underexposing, since all the data is over in the shadow tones or midtones, respectively. A histogram can only show us how the data from the image is represented; it can't tell us if it's a good exposure. *We* need to be the ones to connect the idea of good exposure to the histogram.

**Figure 1.20B** breaks down the layout of the histogram data. On the vertical scale, the histogram measures the volume of information—the number of pixels—while the horizontal scale represents the image's progression from shadow tones (far left) and midtones (middle) to highlight tones (far right).

The vertical axis is a variable scale. It's been automatically scaled up or down, on an image-by-image basis, determined by the volume of pixel data. What does that really mean? Take a look at **Figure 1.21A** to see this in action. In the full image, you can see a spike on the left-hand side of the histogram—that comes from the dark hillside silhouette. The data in the right side of the histogram is much "shorter" in comparison.

Now look at the histogram of the cropped-in detail (**Figure 1.21B**). The spike on the left side of the histogram is gone, because the hillside was cropped out,[14] and values on the right side of the histogram are now shown much "taller." Other than cropping the image, nothing changed about the actual image data. These dynamic histograms exist to give us more flexibility in viewing our image data, and can be found in both your camera and post-processing histograms. The problem is that from shot to shot, you're not comparing data on the same scale. Once you know this, the histogram gets a lot less mysterious.

> ***The key to using a histogram effectively is to understand that there isn't one universal, perfect histogram that we all try to achieve. If you looked at every photo you've ever taken, you would find that each one has a unique histogram.***

## Rules of Thumb for Evaluating Histograms

1. If the data is pushed "over" on the right side (off the scale), then the highlights are being clipped. That means some part of the image will be rendered as pure white, without any tonal information. This is generally something you try to avoid, unless you're trying to do it deliberately—for example, if you wanted a white background to blow out completely.
2. If the data is pushed "over" on the left side (off the scale), then the shadow details are being clipped. That means some part of the image will be rendered as black, without any tonal information. Again, you probably want to avoid this, unless you have a specific idea in mind that requires pure black.
3. The vertical scale of data is a variable; it can shift from image to image.
4. There is no perfect histogram. The data is directly connected to the scene you're photographing and the intent you have in capturing it.

## The LCD Lies

Once you get it under control, the LCD screen is a valuable tool—but there's a good chance it's been lying to you and giving you false information. Your camera's LCD screen is a hugely subjective device. It can give you bad information that leads to bad pictures. Here's why: Looking at a photo on your LCD indoors in a dark room or outside in the bright sun are two entirely different viewing conditions. The relative brightness of your environment changes how you actually see the image on your camera. In a dark room, your image might look great on screen, because it's super bright. If you move the camera outside on a sunny day, that same image will probably look too dark. Screen brightness is another factor. When your screen is turned way up or way down, it also changes how you see the exposure.

## Overcoming LCD Variables

If you base the quality of your "good exposure" on the way the image looks on your LCD screen, then you could be under- or over-exposing. How do we overcome these variables? We already have two tools we can use: metering and the histogram, neither of which is affected by viewing conditions. If we see that there's a good histogram and the meter confirms a good exposure setting, then the likelihood that an image is underexposed goes way down, even if it looks that way on screen.

> ***The reason in-camera histograms are so valuable is that they remain exactly the same, no matter what the viewing conditions.***

### Viewing Conditions

Another easy way to make the LCD more reliable is to remove the environmental variable by taking control of your viewing conditions. You could use a DSLR-specific LCD loupe, which is used to block out light from the screen (**Figure 1.22**). These loupes also apply a slight magnification to the image, and on high-resolution screens, you can use them to check focus. You could also recreate an old-school technique: the dark cloth. Taken straight out of view-camera photography, this is a very simple idea of covering the camera and your head with a black cloth. At the risk of looking slightly silly, it blocks out the ambient light really well and has the advantage of being cheap. You can stash a piece of black fabric in your camera bag or use a jacket, towel, blanket or whatever you have lying around.

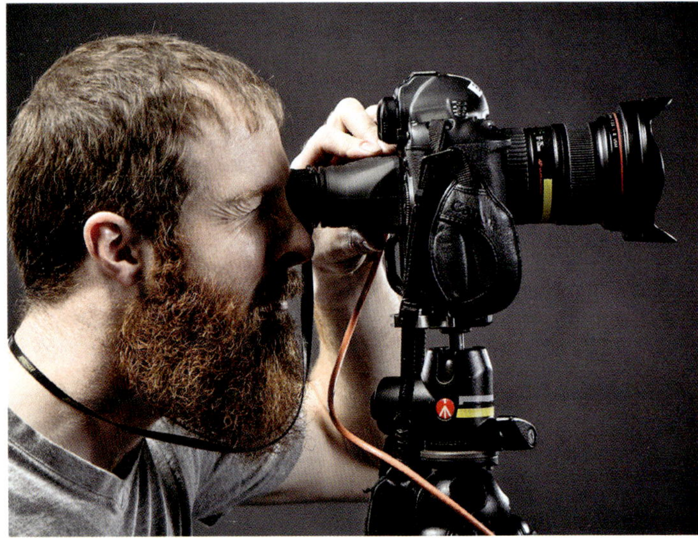

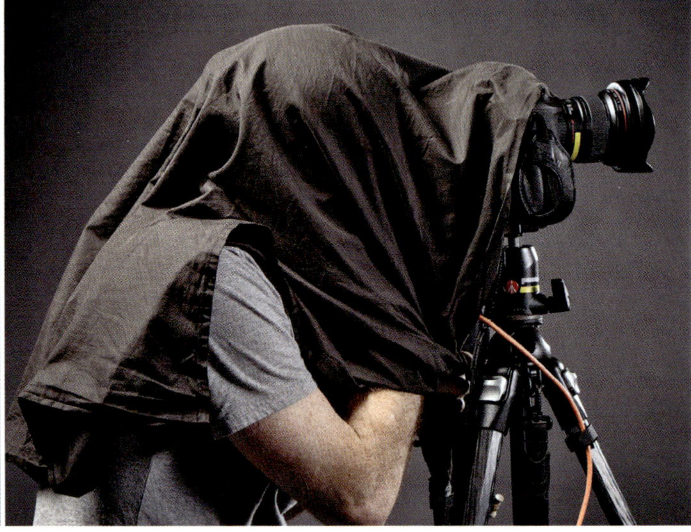

**FIGURE 1.22** Using a camera loupe or dark cloth allows you to remove the ambient light and create a consistent environment in which to view your camera's LCD screen. That way, you can judge your images without being affected by the lighting in the locations where you work.
IMAGES © ANDY BATT, *CAMERA LOUPE AND DARK CLOTH*, 2013.

### Brightness Level

The last key to getting the LCD under control is to set a brightness level for your camera. In combination with a loupe or dark cloth, this helps lock out the variations that can give you a false idea of your exposure. You can go down two roads with this idea: one simple and one complicated. The simple route is to leave the screen at its default setting (usually right in the middle) and get used to working with it there. With time and experience, you'll know how the LCD relates to the actual image. The complicated route relies on a few factors that we'll discuss in *Chapters 6* and *7*: having a color-managed and profiled monitor in a neutral viewing environment—and setting your camera's Picture Style[15] to "Neutral."

## White Balance = Color Control

Controlling color is an important part of the "Put it On Manual" philosophy, and the white balance (WB) setting is the camera's center of color control.

You can set WB manually (through the WB icons or by entering a color temperature value) or automatically (with the Automatic White Balance (AWB) setting). Since the image's white balance information is just metadata that's embedded into the raw file,[16] it doesn't change the raw data itself. That means you can endlessly alter the WB of the image without worrying about compromising image quality. For instance, if by mistake you leave the WB set to "Tungsten" while you're shooting in daylight, then you can simply switch the setting to "Daylight" in Lightroom when you process the image, and it will be the same as if you had chosen that setting in-camera. If you'd like, you can apply your creative brain to the WB setting, purposefully making the image cooler or warmer than it actually was when you took the photo.

While AWB can do a great job of removing colorcasts, it can also unintentionally remove the mood from a cool-morning or warm-afternoon scene. AWB has no knowledge of your sensitive artistic soul; it simply wants to render everything as accurately and neutrally as possible. Since you're shooting raw, you might ask, "Why shouldn't I just set the camera to AWB, since I can change it to anything I want when I'm processing out the image?" Take a look at the following list for some answers . . .

### Setting a Brightness Level for Your Camera: The Simple Version

1. Take a photo with a broad variety of tones and colors that avoids clipping on either side of the histogram.
2. Download the image to your computer, and then put the media card back in your camera.
3. Bring up the image on your computer (in Lightroom, or whatever raw processor you use). Use the default settings for the image. Don't make any changes.
4. Bring up the image on your camera and grab your loupe or dark cloth.
5. Adjust the brightness of the camera's LCD screen until it's as close a match to the image on the computer monitor as you can get it.
6. Once you have the brightness value where you like it, promise yourself never to adjust it! Just keep using the loupe or dark cloth to standardize your viewing conditions. If your images still feel overly dark or bright, repeat this process with a variety of images until you find a value that works.

### Great Reasons to Control Your Own White Balance, Instead of Using AWB

- *To help you think creatively about color at the moment of shooting:* Instead of reacting to your images when you get back to your computer, react while you're shooting them. Look at your scene and decide if making it a little warmer, cooler or more neutral would be an improvement.

## TRY THIS AT HOME

### The Silhouette Portrait Experiment

**For step-by-step instructions, go to: www.focalpress.com/cw/digitalimagingmasters**

For this test, you'll deliberately put yourself into a situation where the meter is wrong and the histograms are weird. With your light source—the window—behind your subject, you'll make three very different portraits.

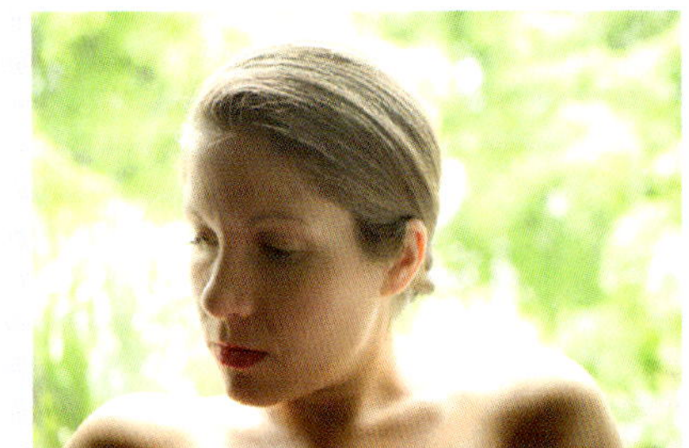

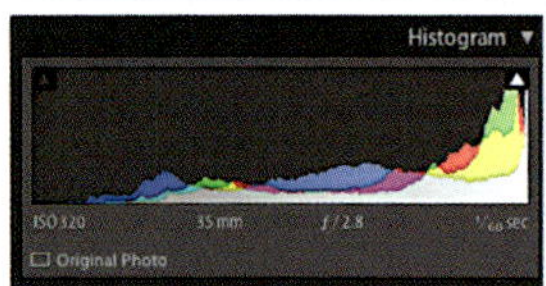


***f*/2.8 @ 1/60th, ISO 320**
**METERED FOR FACE**

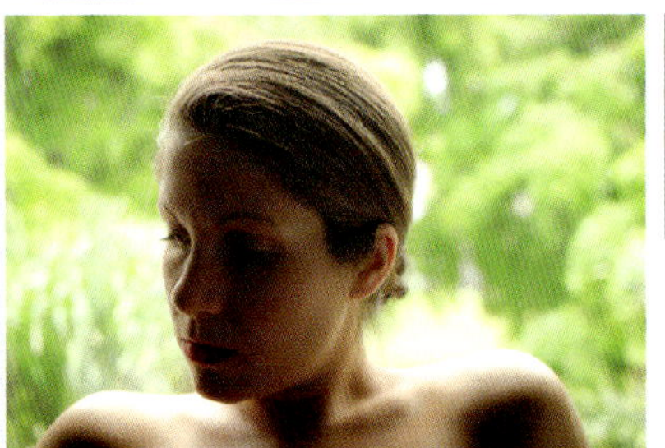

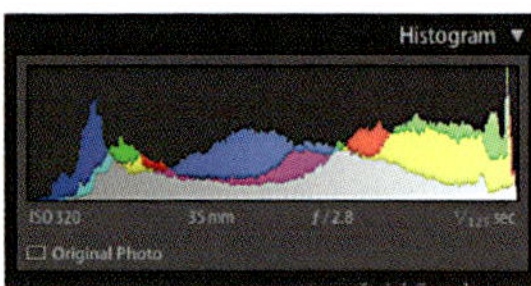


***f*/2.8 @ 1/125th, ISO 320**
**METERED FOR FACE AND BACKGROUNI**

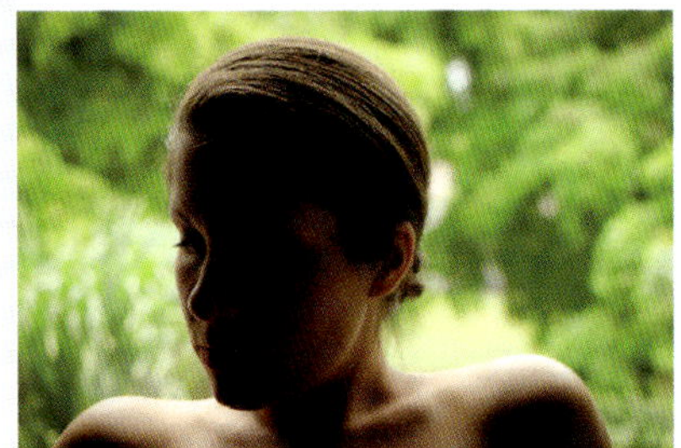

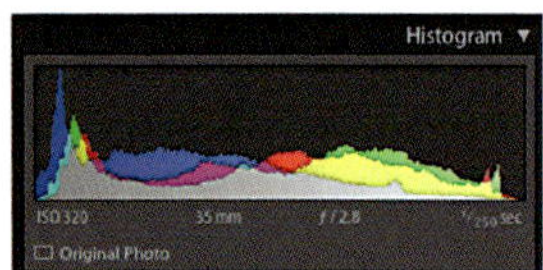


***f*/2.8 @ 1/250th, ISO 320**
**METERED FOR BACKGROUND**

**FIGURE 1.23** By using three different metering techniques for the same scene, Erika created three distinctly different portraits. Examine each histogram and the way their corresponding tones are rendered. For the top image, the meter reading was taken of just the face of the subject. For the center image, the meter reading covered both the subject and the background, averaging them together. For the bottom image, the subject left the frame so a meter reading could be taken of only the background. Depending on what kind of story you're interested in telling, you could select any of these and have it be "correct."
IMAGE © ERIKA VELASQUEZ, *WINDOW PORTRAIT*, 2013.

- *To learn more about the light around you:* When you select your own WB setting, you have to pay attention to the quality of light around. You'll be more in tune with your photographs if you're aware of the time of day and the type and color of the light source.
- *To experiment with drastic shifts in color:* When you open your raw images in Lightroom, you'll have already begun the process of crafting a final image.

## Setting White Balance In-Camera

### WB 101

Grab your camera and find the WB menu. For quick access, you can program your camera so that WB appears in the "My Settings" menu.[17] For starters, select an option based on the light source that illuminates your scene. The icons that most cameras use can be a little inscrutable, so we made a quick guide (**Figure 1.24A**) to help you decipher them.

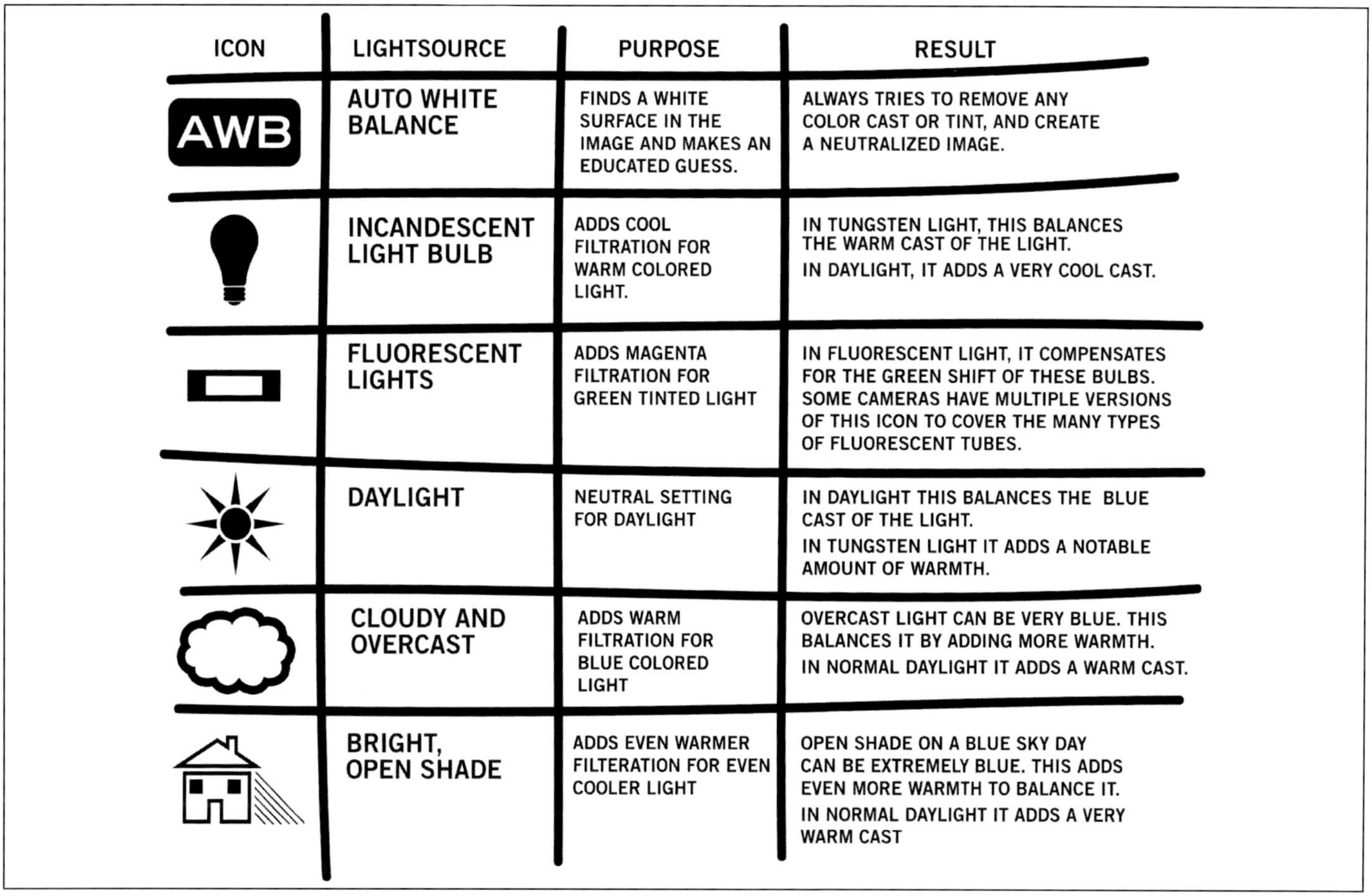

| ICON | LIGHTSOURCE | PURPOSE | RESULT |
|---|---|---|---|
| AWB | AUTO WHITE BALANCE | FINDS A WHITE SURFACE IN THE IMAGE AND MAKES AN EDUCATED GUESS. | ALWAYS TRIES TO REMOVE ANY COLOR CAST OR TINT, AND CREATE A NEUTRALIZED IMAGE. |
| | INCANDESCENT LIGHT BULB | ADDS COOL FILTRATION FOR WARM COLORED LIGHT. | IN TUNGSTEN LIGHT, THIS BALANCES THE WARM CAST OF THE LIGHT.<br>IN DAYLIGHT, IT ADDS A VERY COOL CAST. |
| | FLUORESCENT LIGHTS | ADDS MAGENTA FILTRATION FOR GREEN TINTED LIGHT | IN FLUORESCENT LIGHT, IT COMPENSATES FOR THE GREEN SHIFT OF THESE BULBS. SOME CAMERAS HAVE MULTIPLE VERSIONS OF THIS ICON TO COVER THE MANY TYPES OF FLUORESCENT TUBES. |
| | DAYLIGHT | NEUTRAL SETTING FOR DAYLIGHT | IN DAYLIGHT THIS BALANCES THE BLUE CAST OF THE LIGHT.<br>IN TUNGSTEN LIGHT IT ADDS A NOTABLE AMOUNT OF WARMTH. |
| | CLOUDY AND OVERCAST | ADDS WARM FILTRATION FOR BLUE COLORED LIGHT | OVERCAST LIGHT CAN BE VERY BLUE. THIS BALANCES IT BY ADDING MORE WARMTH.<br>IN NORMAL DAYLIGHT IT ADDS A WARM CAST. |
| | BRIGHT, OPEN SHADE | ADDS EVEN WARMER FILTERATION FOR EVEN COOLER LIGHT | OPEN SHADE ON A BLUE SKY DAY CAN BE EXTREMELY BLUE. THIS ADDS EVEN MORE WARMTH TO BALANCE IT.<br>IN NORMAL DAYLIGHT IT ADDS A VERY WARM CAST |

**FIGURE 1.24A** Wouldn't it be great if all the camera manufacturers got together and hired a good interface designer to come up with a better set of white balance icons? The icons are a lot more useful when you understand what they mean! This chart should help take the guesswork out of interpreting them.
ILLUSTRATION © ANDY BATT, *WHITE BALANCE (WB) ICON CHART*, 2013.

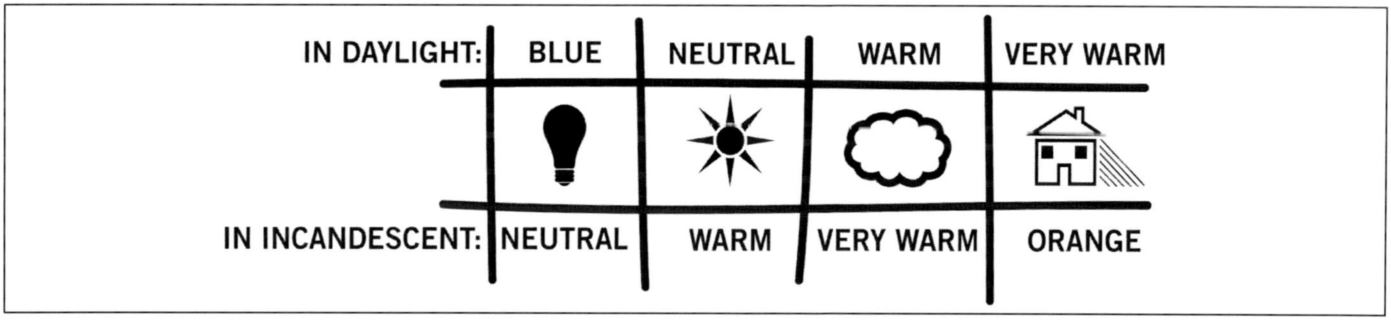

| | | | | |
|---|---|---|---|---|
| IN DAYLIGHT: | BLUE | NEUTRAL | WARM | VERY WARM |
| | | | | |
| IN INCANDESCENT: | NEUTRAL | WARM | VERY WARM | ORANGE |

**FIGURE 1.24B** Here's a quick guide to shifting your color balance. The top row lists the effect, from cool to warm, of four different icons when you're shooting in regular daylight. The bottom row lists the effect of the same icons when you're shooting in incandescent light (tungsten bulbs).
ILLUSTRATION © ANDY BATT, *CHOOSING A WHITE BALANCE ICON FOR EFFECT*, 2013.

## Manual WB

Depending on the light source in your scene, white tones may take on color shifts and end up being warm, cool, green or magenta, instead of neutral. When we set WB manually, we're essentially telling the camera what kind of light we're taking the photograph in. The camera applies some fancy mathematics (algorithms) to calculate any existing color bias and then creates a shift to get rid of it, encoding all of this information into the raw file. When you process the raw file, the data is decoded and the image is adjusted accordingly.

Keep in mind that the camera applies WB adjustments to your entire image, not only the white parts, which means that it controls the warm-to-cool color balance and the green-to-magenta tint of every part of your photographs.

By selecting a particular icon, you're essentially performing an AWB yourself. When you decide which setting to use, you'll gain experience of lighting conditions, instead of taking it for granted that AWB will do it for you. There's no risk in trying: You can always adjust the color balance later if you get it wrong.

### WB: The Next Level

Sure, you can use the "correct" setting for the light you are in, but what happens when you deliberately set the wrong icon? Try moving the color in a warm or cool direction to change the story of your image. We made a quick cheat sheet (**Figure 1.24B**) to help you shift your colors. In *Chapter 7*, we'll dive into higher-level white balance settings using the Kelvin scale, neutral cards and click balancing.

***I often choose the wrong setting intentionally. Selecting the "cloudy" icon when I'm in regular daylight adds nice warmth to the images. By doing this instead of choosing AWB, I make decisions about color while I'm making the image. It's a deliberate way of determining how I want a scene to look in the final photograph. This method is especially useful when I know a retoucher will be processing my raw files, since it gives them a heads-up about my intention.***

***—Andy Batt***

## Any Camera

One of our goals is to guide you to the point where you can pick up any camera and be able to start working. Every camera shares the same key basics: shutter speed, aperture, ISO, in-camera light meter, histogram and white balance—so when you master these skills, you'll be able to put any camera to work.

The companion to this notion is that it's also important to work with your own, specific camera. When you're familiar with your camera's buttons, dials and menu systems, you won't have to fumble for settings. This will smooth out your whole process and make a big difference in the way you work. Once you master the key basics, you'll have the foundation to understand and take advantage of customizations and options—and you'll be able to determine which ones are useful and which ones aren't.

***Photography is a very technical art; when we practice it thoughtfully, we treat our cameras as tools—and not magic boxes.***

## TRY THIS AT HOME

### Make the Wrong WB Choice

**For step-by-step instructions, go to: www.focalpress.com/cw/digitalimagingmasters**

To experience the creative power of making a 100% wrong decision on purpose, try this white balance exercise.

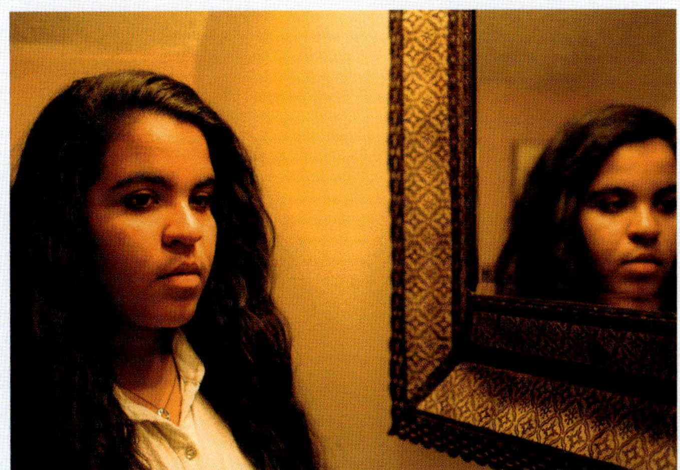

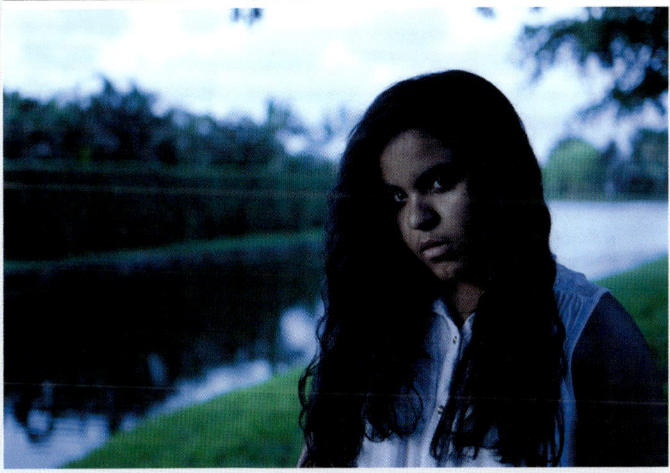

**FIGURE 1.25** Erika took these two images by deliberately choosing the wrong WB setting. For the top image, which was lit by tungsten light, she chose the Daylight icon in-camera. The image is very warm, because the warm filtration is usually used to balance out the cooler color temperature of daylight. The bottom image is very blue, because the Tungsten icon was chosen for this scene, although it was shot in daylight. This setting is normally used to add a cooling filter to balance out warm tungsten light sources. Both are interesting portraits, and very different in meaning than they would have been if the light sources had been neutral and the colorcasts had been removed. IMAGE © ERIKA VELASQUEZ, *THE WRONG WHITE BALANCE ON PURPOSE*, 2013.

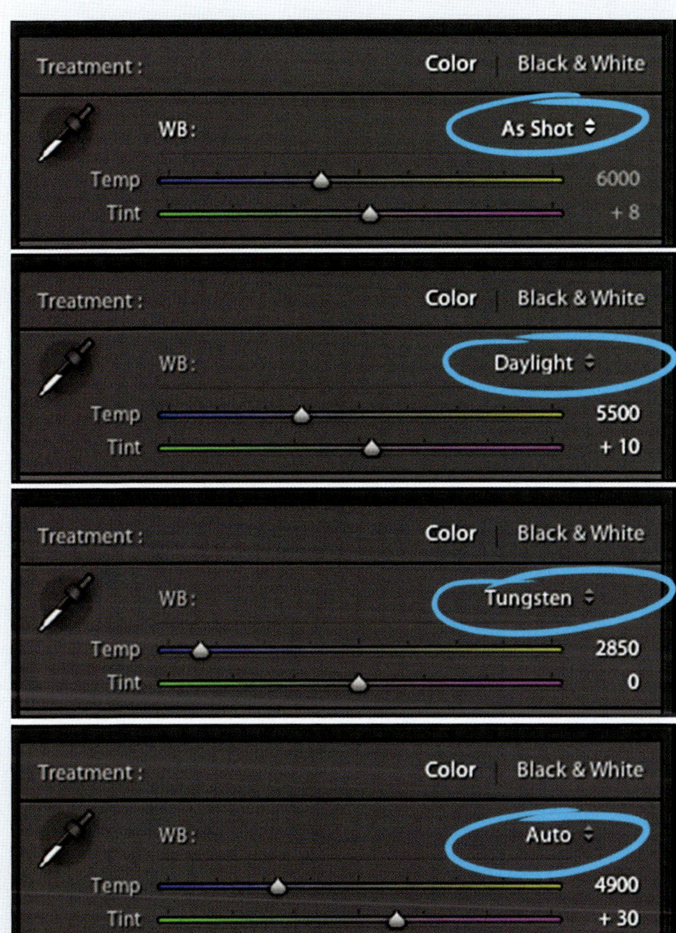


**FIGURE 1.26** Lightroom has a number of controls for adjusting the color balance of an image. The quickest ones to grasp are the presets, which are available in the blue-circled menus. Other applications have a very similar menu system. Here, you can see the same choices that you have in-camera. By choosing a different WB setting in Lightroom, you dynamically alter the raw file data, much the same way you would by choosing a different icon in-camera. SCREENSHOT © ANDY BATT, *LIGHTROOM'S WHITE BALANCE ADJUSTMENT PANEL*, 2013.

# EXPLORATIONS

## What Do You Like About the Photos You Take?

You'll find one of these "Explorations" at the end of each chapter. They're meant to further your own discovery of a concept we investigated along the way. This first one will help you understand what type of images appeal to you—and why.

***Step One: Find Three Images***

Find three images that you've taken within the last year. Any type of subject matter is fine, but it's important that the images really resonate for you. They should transcend "nice" composition or the simple capture of a moment and inspire you to keep coming back to them because they're personally rewarding. Note: You can also follow up this personal Exploration by repeating it, using images that were taken by other photographers whose work you admire.

***Step Two: Spend Time with the Images***

If the images are on screen, then open them into an application that allows you to hide everything else, leaving only the image. (Adobe Photoshop, Adobe Photoshop Lightroom and Apple Preview all have this capability.) If you're looking at prints, then place them onto a neutral background and use good, even lighting. Look at each image individually and identify the elements listed below. You may want to write down the list of elements so that you can reference them as we move through the Exploration.[18]

***Step Three: Consider (but don't limit yourself to) the following:***

- *Focus:* Is the focus very shallow or deep?
- *Blur:* Is the image tack sharp or soft and blurred?
- *Complexity:* Is the image minimal, or does it contain many intense elements?
- *Composition:* Is it symmetrical, asymmetrical, chaotic or balanced?
- *Expression:* Are you drawn to the people in the image? Do their faces communicate a specific thought?
- *Movement:* Is an activity occurring?
- *Light:* Is the quality of light unique? Is it warm, cool, hard or soft?

***Step Four: Observe***

Your next step is to focus on your most strongly felt observations. Open each image again and identify what about the image holds your attention. Make a specific choice about the most interesting quality, and if it's not possible to winnow it down to one, then figure out which two factors work in combination to become the most interesting quality. Make a note of this for each image.

***Step Five: Evaluate***

Now look at all three images together with your notes. Are there any common elements that interested you in the three images? There might be a trend in your work that engages you. For each image, try to describe in technical terms what created the interest. For example, if the most interesting thing about an image is the stopped action (like the Parkour image in this chapter), then how did you and/or the camera achieve that quality? If there is a very narrow focus (like the Randy Leonard image), then what created it? Don't worry if you can't explain exactly what's going on technically; it's enough to know that some process or tool was at work behind the aesthetics. You'll learn more throughout this book about the technical side of the equation.

***A Sample Exploration***

To illustrate the Exploration, Candace selected three of her favorite images (**Figures 1.27–1.29**).

***Andy:*** The first thing I notice is that each image contains a key detail that is a bright highlight. Then I see on two of the images that there are large portions of dark tones that create contrast against the highlights. The images have a fairly wide tonal range, so the challenge was to find the correct exposure that would

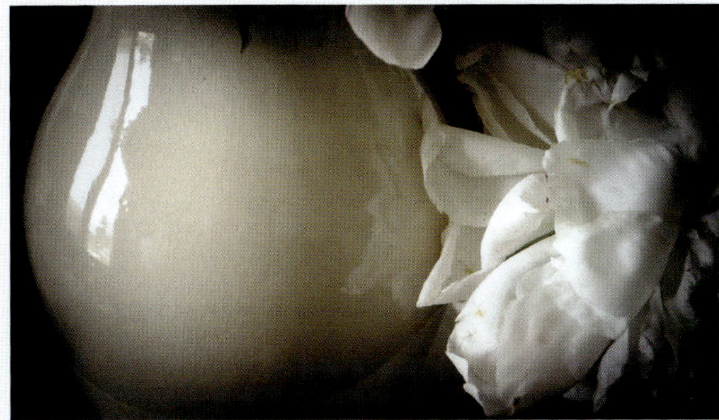

IMAGE © CANDACE DOBRO, *PEONY*, 2012.

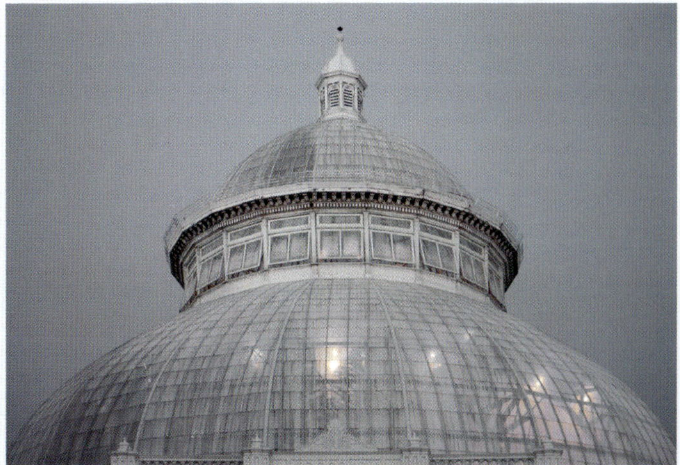

IMAGE © CANDACE DOBRO, *DOME (THE NEW YORK BOTANICAL GARDEN)*, THE BRONX, NY, 2012.

hold texture in the highlight detail and keep the shadow detail from blocking up to solid black.

***Candace:*** Yes! Since I often shoot low-light scenes with a full tonal range, there's a constant juggle to balance the ISO, F-stop and shutter speed. The goal is always to arrive at the best exposure for maintaining detail in the highlights and shadows, while keeping noise to a minimum. It's really helpful to state that as a personal mantra.

## Goal

The goal of this Exploration is to make connections between the aesthetics of an image and the technical skills used to create them. When you complete it, you'll have created an interesting learning tool: a specific understanding of what draws you to your favorite imagery and how you created it. You can easily repeat this idea with different types of images. You may find that different themes emerge from your portrait work than from your landscape work. You might find that all of your images share the same characteristics, yet use different techniques, or that you identified a single technique that yields a variety of qualities you like. You can use this kind of exploration throughout your career to refine your look and discover new ideas.

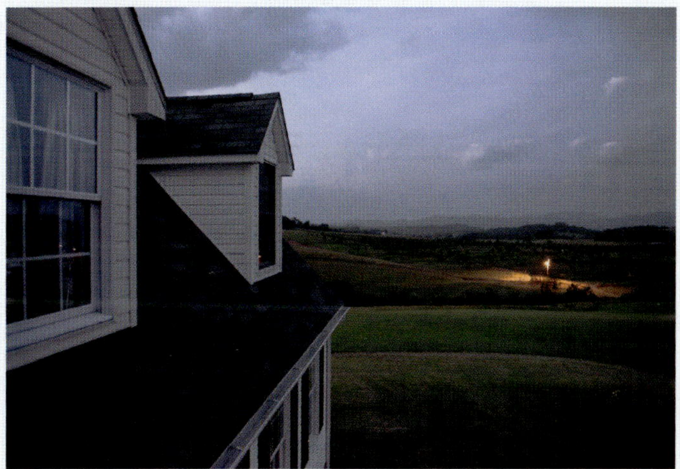

IMAGE © CANDACE DOBRO, *BLACKSMITH INN*, NATURAL BRIDGE, VA, 2012.

**FIGURES 1.27–1.29** Candace selected these three images for the Exploration. Since each one contains a fairly wide tonal range, it was important to set exposures that would maintain detail in both the highlights and shadows.

## Notes

1 A full-frame camera uses a sensor that's approximately the same size as a 35mm film negative: 24mm × 36mm. Photographers use this as a general reference, even though there are many different sensor sizes in modern cameras. Sensor size has a direct effect on DoF and lens choice.

2 In case you were wondering, HMI stands for Hydrargyrum Medium-arc Iodide.

3 Focal Press author Angela Faris-Belt has a great book titled *The Elements of Photography: Understanding and Creating Sophisticated Images,* which we love. It's full of great ideas and expands on this theme.

4 You could also read the manual that came packaged with your camera, but we find that most photographers toss those into their camera bags without ever reading them. They're a bit on the dry side, and sometimes feel like they were written in a secret engineer's language, but they do contain a ton of useful information.

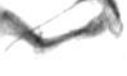

5 In some circles, it's called PHD mode: Push Here, Dummy. We all use this mode from time to time (cocktail party snapshots are much easier with PHD mode).

6 The relative level of artificial intelligence in your camera is going to vary—you might have one with a planet-sized brain capable of tracking a single person through a crowd, or you might have one that can't tell the difference between a smiley face sticker and your daughter. Check the manual to see which type you have.

7 Background plates are photos that are taken to provide additional source material from which to retouch. It's standard practice these days to shoot plates to provide a clean background—without action or subjects. The term "plates" comes from the motion picture industry, during a time when photographs were made to project onto a background and provide a scenic image behind the actors.

8 This number refers to a camera set to 1/3-stop increments. Your camera may be set to 1/2-stop increments, or even 1/4-stop increments: It's time to dig out that dusty camera manual and see what your options are!

9 A good starting place is 1/X, where X is the focal length of the lens. We say it's only a starting place, because it doesn't take into account all of the plus and minus factors. (Plus factors: you have an image-stabilized lens, Popeye biceps of steel, are using a monopod or have an ultra-light lens. Minus factors: the lens is heavy, you have wiggly biceps like Olive Oyl, the lens is a super-super-telephoto, or it's crazy windy outside.) You'll need to spend some time testing to see what you can get away with.

10 This amount of time depends on your camera; each one may be slightly different.

11 There have been faster shutter speeds on production cameras, but 1/8000th is the current norm.

12 You might have to experiment with shutter speeds to capture the effect with your particular camera.

13 Be sure not to use a source of light like a window or light bulb; you want an object that's reflecting light, not emitting it.

14 Lightroom dynamically rebuilds the histogram based on whatever is inside of the crop tool.

15 Different camera brands use different terms for this: Nikon calls it "Picture Control." This feature helps remove any unnecessary saturation or contrast boosts the camera might apply.

16 To find out more about shooting raw, turn to "Raw All the Way" in *Chapter 3: Your Digital Skeleton.*

17 Most cameras have customizable menus for stashing favorite settings. Dig through the camera manual to find yours.

18 Some of us are word people and some of us aren't. You don't have to keep a proper journal while you go through this book, but we do suggest using a system to keep track of your work while you carry out the Explorations and experiments in it. We use a variety of digital and paper-based tools for note taking: A Moleskine® notebook and a Cloud-based application, like Evernote, are a great combination.

Two

# IT'S YOUR VIEWFINDER: INTERVIEWS WITH THE PROS

The viewfinder (whether it's optical, an LCD screen or live-view on your computer) isn't merely a technology tool; it's also the way you see the world when you're composing photographs. Through it, your eyes are grafted directly to your camera so that you can actively take control of your image making.

Although the viewfinder has plenty of information built into it—such as the shot count, exposure settings, various warnings, focus indicators and your light meter—it is, at its heart, a cropping tool that can edit the world into a two-dimensional photograph. It's the link between you and your camera.

In a way, everything else, including lens effects, raw image data, color balance, etc., connects back to the viewfinder, because that's where you decide to press the shutter button and engage all the other moving parts. It's no surprise that photographers feel strongly about this connection, as you'll find out from the interviews that follow.

> *Photographing over and over again for so long, you start realizing what separates a good image from a great one. There's also, of course, a great degree of self-criticism that photographers are steeped in that pushes us to be concerned about these things. There's a shot I love and keep looking at . . . but [sigh], I have to go back to the dunes on a full super-moon at 3:00 in the morning to capture it again, because the dune line's broken and it's driving me completely insane! If you look at the frame of the image, down over by the corner, it's super-dark, so you can barely notice it—but I notice it!*
>
> *—Carli Davidson, Animal Photographer*

## Andy Batt

### *Co-Author of Camera & Craft and Professional Photographer*

***Candace Dobro:* What do you think about when you look through your viewfinder?**

***Andy Batt:*** The viewfinder is my most visceral connection to my photographs. It's deceptively simple; there's so much more than just making sure your subject is in the frame. I look through the camera at my subjects, and they look through the camera back at me. I experience the world as it's presented to me via the lens and the borders of the frame. Seeing through the viewfinder is definitely a skill that needs to be learned and practiced.

***CD:* What's the difference between merely pointing the camera at your subject and *really* seeing what you're looking at?**

***AB:*** Your viewfinder is a communications tool; you should be very purposeful and decisive with it. It's a framing device, a way to decide what you're going to keep and what you're going to discard. You use the viewfinder as a cropping tool to include or exclude things and to create relationships between people and objects. It's how you frame an image to show that you meant every bit of it (**Figure 2.1**).

***CD:* In addition to framing the shot, your viewfinder shows you all types of data. What's your process of working through it all?**

***AB:*** It depends on the kind of photography I'm doing at the moment. If it's a commercial project, I've probably done a lot of metering and other work outside the viewfinder, like checking the histogram, using my light meter to calculate and making decisions based on the data. I'll use the in-camera information in the viewfinder to confirm that what I meant to do is consistent with what I am doing.

If you don't purposefully apply yourself to seeing that information, it's easy to stop paying attention to it—and that can get you in trouble. Having at least a peripheral awareness of all that information is important.

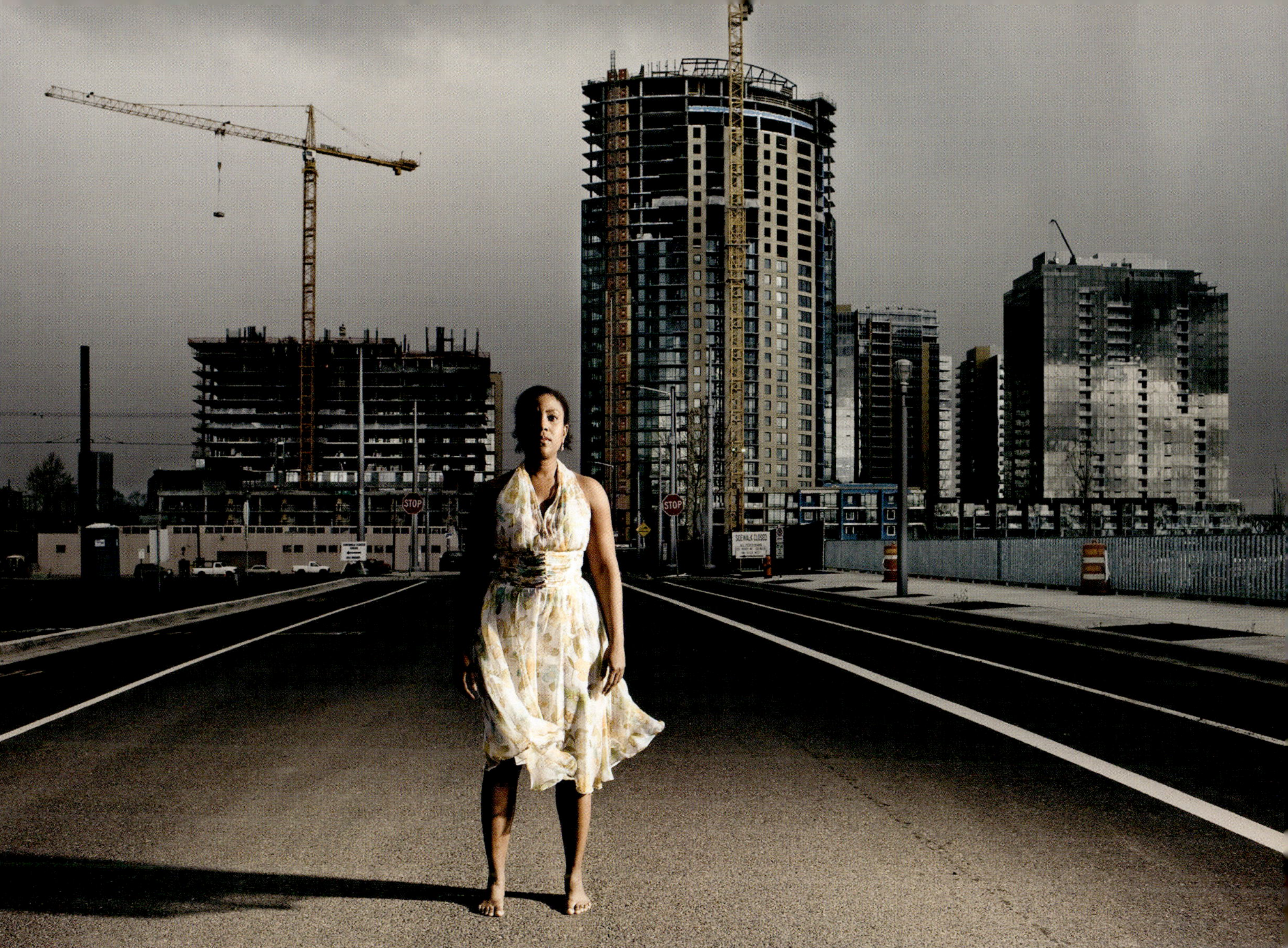


**FIGURE 2.1** Andy made this poster image for the Sojourn Theatre company. With all the perspective lines and vertical elements, it required careful composition work. IMAGE © ANDY BATT, *SOJOURN THEATRE: BUILT*, 2008.

When I'm street shooting, being connected to that information is even more important. It's how I can quickly assess the light and the exposure and be aware of the kind of image I'm creating with focus and time. That way, I can shoot without having to constantly chimp[1] the back of the screen.

***CD:*** **Did you experience this when you were starting out?**

***AB:*** There's always been something special to me about looking through the viewfinder—it's part of what I really like about photography. Actually going out and taking pictures is still a thrill for me. Just being able to experience the world through the camera is energizing; it's always been that way for me.

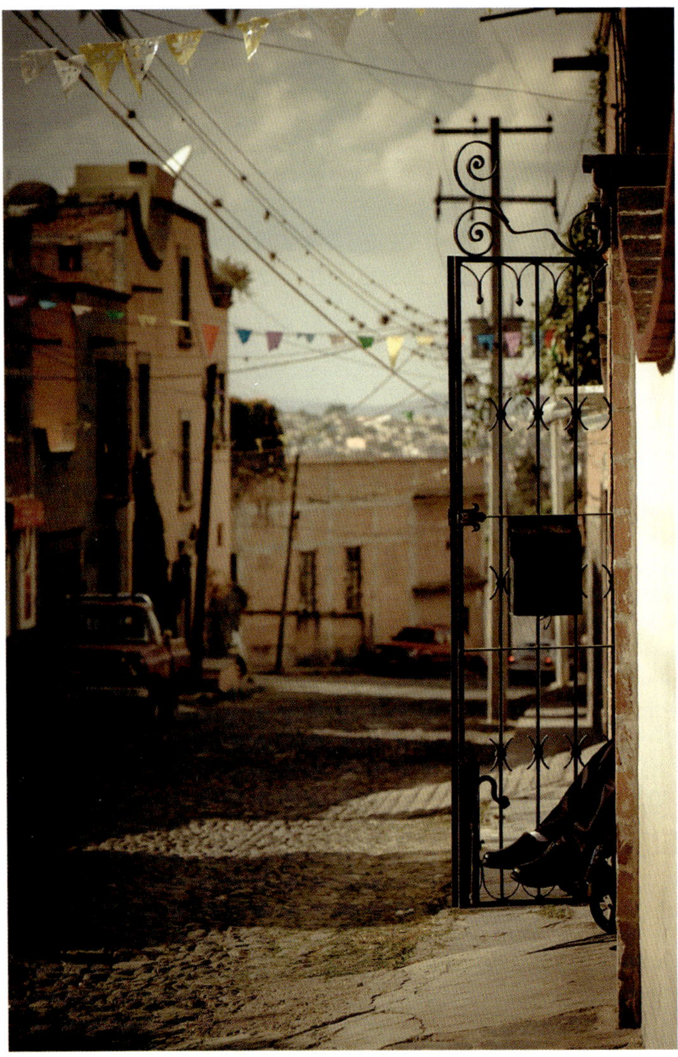

**FIGURE 2.2** Andy is obsessed with patterns, lines and shapes when he composes. This shot has strong vertical elements, such as the gate that lines up with the telephone pole. It also has perspective lines, from the power lines and the street receding diagonally. The feet in the wheelchair are the main subject. It's a good image for thinking differently about composition and being deliberate with all areas in the image, not just the center.
IMAGE © ANDY BATT, *SAN MIGUEL—WAITING*, 2005.

***CD:*** **When you're framing an image, what tools do you use and what ideas help you to compose?**

***AB:*** "Tools" is a good word. I think of everything at my disposal as tools in my toolbox: the viewfinder, shutter speeds, lenses, etc. They're all tools that let me craft my work.

I don't like the idea of "rules." I prefer guidelines, knowledge and information; the minute you call them rules, I feel like they're boxing me in—and not in a way that leads to creativity.

The biggest idea I keep in mind when I look through the viewfinder is that I'm 100% responsible for 100% of the view. The person looking at the photograph will assume that anything I put in it was meant to be there, so I try to be extremely aware of everything that's in the frame (**Figure 2.2**).

***CD:*** **How is seeing through your camera different than seeing with your naked eyes?**

***AB:*** When I take in a scene with my eyes, I see the person I'm there to photograph—along with everything else that's going on around me. By putting a specific lens on your camera and looking through it, you change everything about the way you experience your world. With my camera I can choose what to include along with my subject, and what to leave out—I'm able to tell a story (**Figure 2.3**).

***CD:*** **Had someone else taken a picture of the same scene, they could have made an entirely different choice with a very different result.**

***AB:*** Right. If you put twenty photographers in the same scene and give them creative freedom, they'll take twenty different pictures. Each of us interprets scenes by making choices—the camera is just a tool; it's not creative by itself.

***CD:*** **What's the best thing you've ever learned about composition—from other artists or mentors, or just from experience?**

***AB:*** One of my advertising photo teachers at RIT,[2] Howard Levant, told me always to set up the camera before adding lights and props, picking angles, etc. That simple idea has really stuck with me. You create a lot more work for yourself when you try to figure out how a

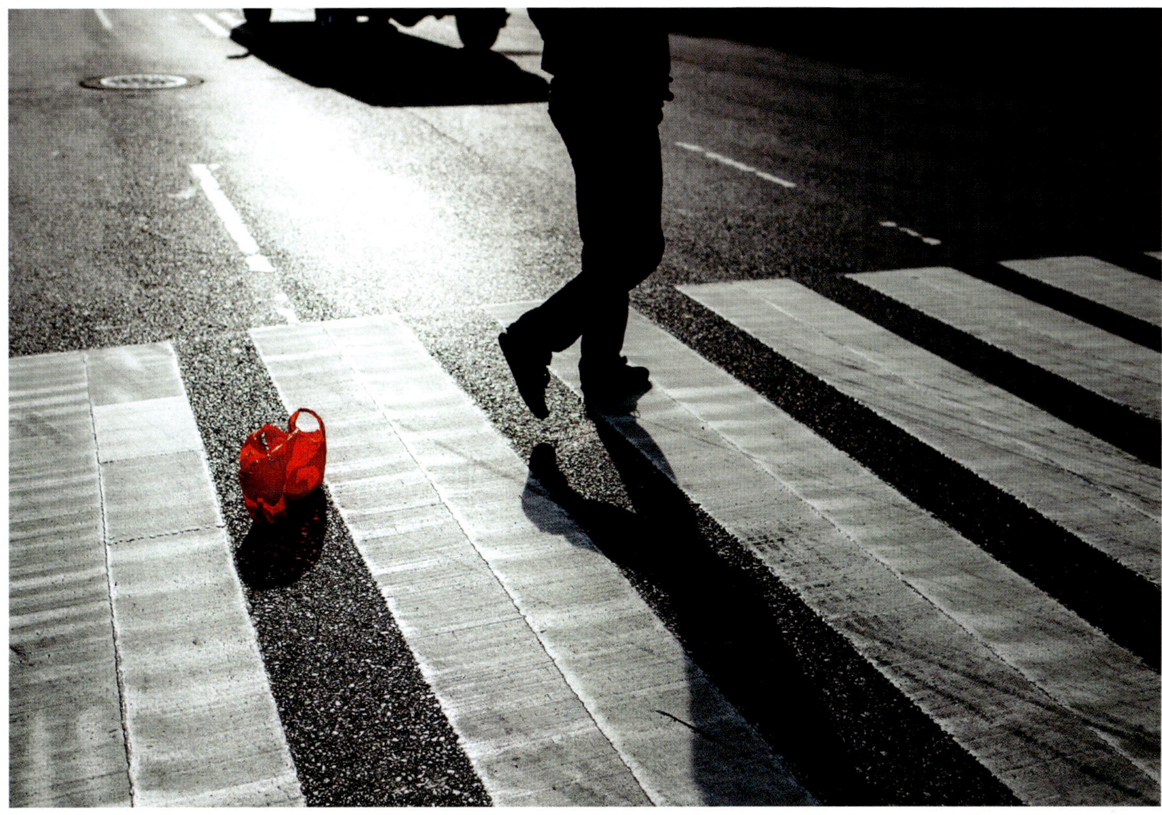

**FIGURE 2.3** Being a photographer is about creating a relationship among the elements in your scene. Every time Andy's in NYC, he sees these red plastic bags, and he keeps photographing them. This image is a story about shapes, lines and textures—everything is there to support that red bag.
IMAGE © ANDY BATT, *RED BAG,* 2010.

photograph will look without first being informed by the way the camera sees a scene.

Jay Maisel has a gift for stopping you in your tracks and making you think about what you do in a fresh way. One of my favorite things I learned from him was to recognize that there are places where you know a good photograph can be made—because there's beautiful light, an interesting shape or something that speaks to you about the particular environment. His advice is to stop moving for a while. Eventually, something will happen in this incredible spot—and there will be your photograph.

***CD:* Have you experienced this?**

***AB:*** When I'm out shooting for myself, I'll find light that's special or a spot that's interesting. I'll plant myself and wait for something to happen. Every now and then I'm rewarded and something happens (**Figure 2.4**). You never know if it'll end up being art with a capital

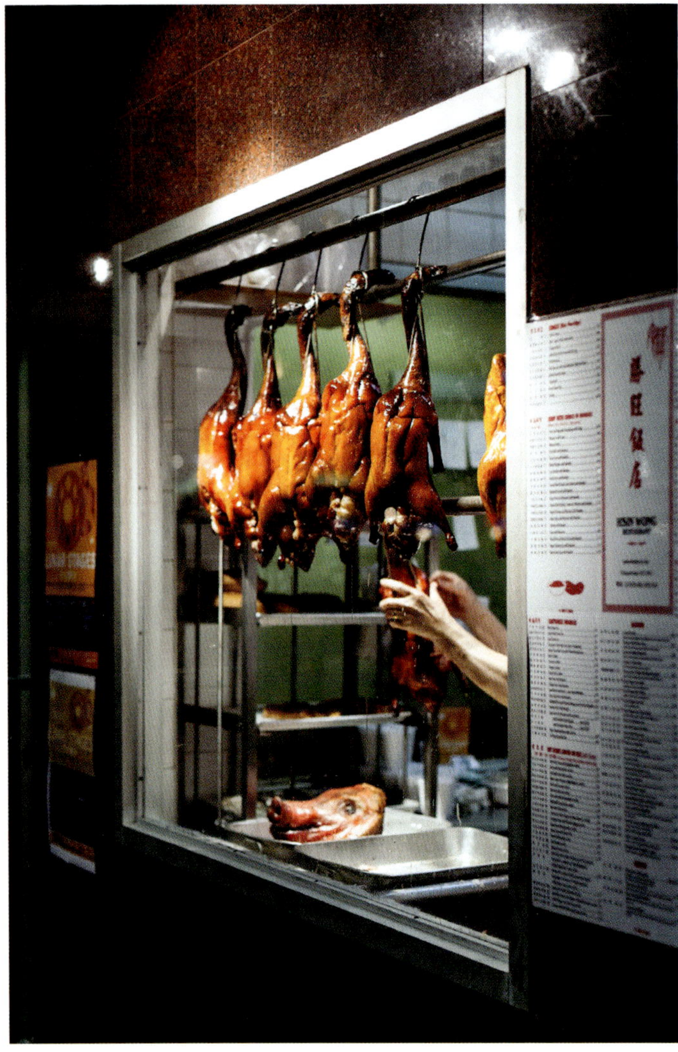

**FIGURE 2.4** The windows into Chinese restaurant kitchens in NYC fascinate Andy. He says, "This shot became a photo for me when the hands reached up to grab the duck. Without the hands, it's just another shop window, but with the addition of the unknown hand, a story emerges."
IMAGE © ANDY BATT, *DUCK WITH HANDS*, 2006.

"A," but it's a nice way to practice. It makes you feel a little less frantic.

***CD:* That's always good. Do you have any more words of wisdom to share with our readers?**

***AB:*** I encourage anyone who's serious about photography to use the viewfinder with more purpose. Don't be passive with it; be aware and decisive and use it actively.

## Framing with Purpose

- **Consider 100% of the frame**
  The center is important—but the rest of the image is just as important. Take the time to consider your entire frame.
- **Check the edges and corners**
  Look for accidental triangles or odd bits that stick into the frame. Decide to get rid of them, or else find a purposeful way to include them.
- **Watch out for tangents**
  Learn to see when the edges of graphic shapes touch. Make a choice about whether the edges touch, overlap or have a distinct separation.
- **Words**
  Including a word in an image means you want your viewer to read it. Your decision to either include or remove any words hinges on that idea.
- **Wait for it**
  If you find interesting light, a captivating pattern, or just something unique that intrigues you—but the photo isn't there—then wait for it.
- **Turn around**
  Always look behind you, even if you have a good shot in front of you. Sometimes the better photo is at your back.

## Stewart Cohen

*Director/Photographer*

***Andy Batt:*** **What kind of photographer are you?**

***Stewart Cohen:*** The reason I got into photography was to travel and meet people, so I'm a photographer who's inspired by locations. I become inspired by a little shaft of light that might dance across glass; that's the kind of thing I capitalize on. Some of my best shots are reactions to environmental cues. I admire guys that create everything virtually; I'm just not that way. It suits me to be on location.

***AB:*** **On the project I just wrapped, we had to shoot football players against a white background so we could then put them into backgrounds we had already shot.**

***SC:*** Yeah, we do that too, and there's nothing wrong with that. I just . . .

***AB:*** **It's just not as much fun.**

***SC:*** Yeah, exactly—and I'm in this for the fun.

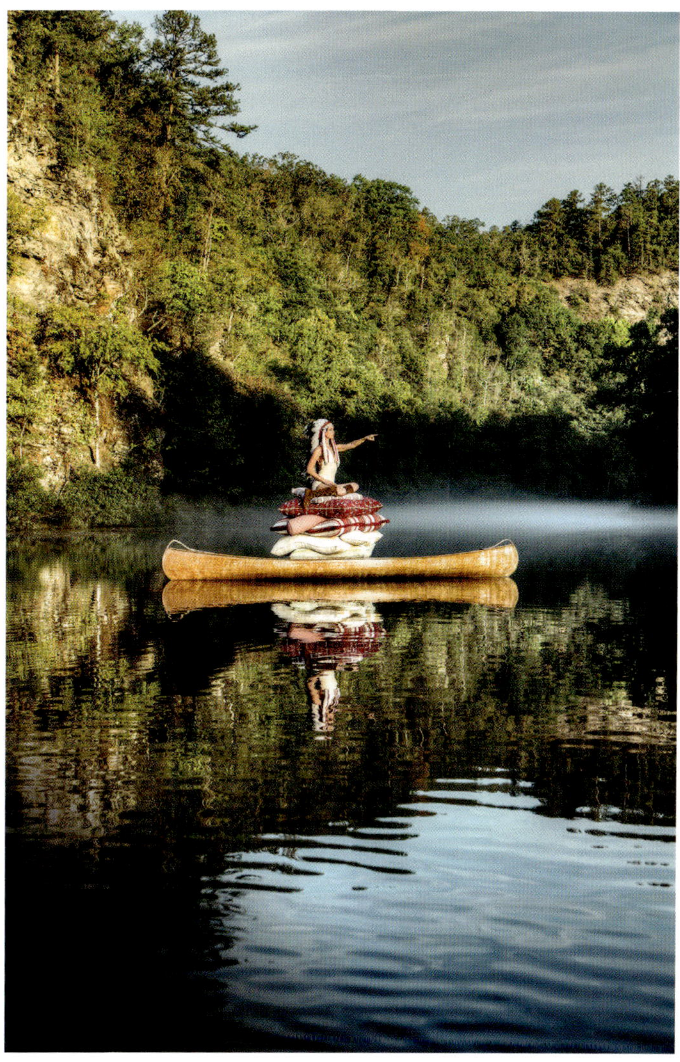

**FIGURE 2.5** Stewart is inspired by locations. This image appeared on the cover of a brochure for Perennials® Fabrics.
IMAGE © STEWART COHEN, *CAMP WANNA GET AWAY*, BROKEN BOW, OK, 2012.

## Toni Greaves

*Documentary Photographer/Photojournalist*

***Andy Batt:*** **Toni, how do you think the viewfinder affects your work?**

***Toni Greaves:*** I see and compose in multiple ways. Because I'm thinking about storytelling, I don't go in with the expectation that I have to capture a picture of this one situation, and, "Here's how I want to frame it." I'm constantly assessing the entire situation around me, because maybe that one situation is taking more time and something is happening over there that's going to go away—in which case I'll move, do the other thing and then come back to finish what I had been doing.

***AB:*** **Talk to us about the integrity of building an un-cropped image.**

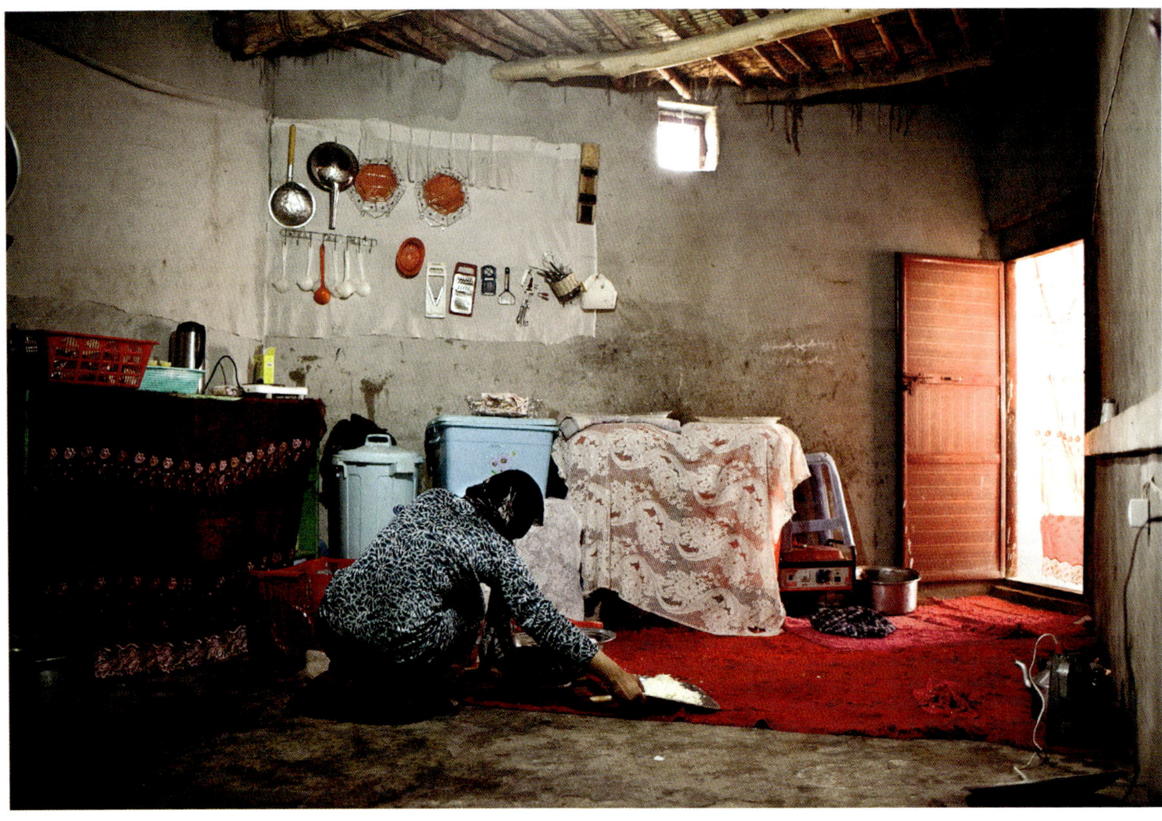

**FIGURE 2.6** One of Toni's greatest skills is to make her subjects feel comfortable so they can behave naturally. She makes herself "invisible," and often, they don't even realize she's there.
IMAGE BY TONI GREAVES FOR MERCY CORPS, *EDUCATION AGAINST ALL ODDS, AFGHANISTAN: SHAMSIYA*, 2012.

***TG:*** I'm quite a purist about the fact that I'm composing everything in-camera. I very rarely rely on cropping. Maybe this is part of being experienced; earlier on I may have cropped, because I wasn't composing quite as well, but now I don't do it. Like Henri Cartier-Bresson, I'm always looking for the exact moment, the magic of it all when you have a beautiful composition and bring the moment into it.

***Candace Dobro:* Can you take us into your head when you get that magical feeling as you look through the viewfinder?**

***TG:*** It's like the way the lens—especially in low light—is always finding focus; I'm constantly assessing what's happening. There's a picture I took of a young woman in Afghanistan serving rice onto a plate, and it's in a kitchen (**Figure 2.6**). What's happening in the frame tells the story. Things on the wall give a sense of place. We're learning about her environment; we know she's in a kitchen; we can tell that they're not a wealthy family and that they lead a very simple life.

***CD:* Were you thinking about this while you were looking through the viewfinder?**

***TG:*** I innately know all of this, but here's the thing: I shot that photo, but I also shot a range of other pictures of the same situation. I shot images that were closer; I shot pictures of her hands with the rice. In the process of putting a story together, you choose images based on comparisons with other images that you're using. The reason why that image is in the portfolio on my website is that it's stronger than other images from the same scene.

For a documentary photographer, the world exists as a variety of scenarios. In every scenario there's a multiplicity of things I capture in order to have the option—later on, when putting a story together—to have the pieces to be able to tell it. Often I shoot work that ends up being used in both print and multimedia. When shooting for multimedia, I need to find micro-scenarios within a situation—so you might see her washing the vegetables and then see her cutting them up, then serving them. This allows the multimedia people to put together a narrative.

***CD:* Tell us more about the way you build a narrative. If I were in a comparable situation, I might get a portrait of the subject with all of her stuff and then get a picture of the details in her environment, because they're fascinating. Is that similar to the way you work?**

***TG:*** If I have the luxury of time in that sort of situation, I might start out photographing—things on the wall, the bowl, the food—while the subjects are in the room working, so they get used to my presence and the sound of the camera, and they become more comfortable. When I start homing in on them being in the photos, there's an ease about it. I make an effort to never break the situation, since my role is to help the person be as comfortable as possible with me—to the point where I can "disappear." I've been told that I'm very good at this and that that's why I do well with documentary photography. It's about people not realizing you're there. Of course they know that you're there, but they're able to get back into their realm and sort of ignore you.

> *My role is to help the person be as comfortable as possible with me—to the point where I can "disappear." It's about people not realizing you're there. Of course they know that you're there, but they're able to get back into their realm and sort of ignore you.*
>
> *—Toni Greaves*

## Jeff Conley

*Landscape and Nature Photographer*

***Andy Batt:* What makes you feel connected to your camera? Do you use any compositional rules or ideas when you create your work?**

***Jeff Conley:*** Looking through the camera is vital in terms of composition, because ultimately, deciding what not to show is as important as what you *do* show. With respect to landscape or nature photography, I try to communicate the essence of where I am and what's outside the periphery of the scene. I look through the camera a lot, make adjustments and get closer or further back from the scene. I prefer not to use a zoom lens, and I take a lot of time forming the composition.

***Candace Dobro:* How long?**

***JC:*** It depends on the scene and what kind of access I have. I have no problem cropping later if I need to—for example, if I have limited access on the edge of a bluff. I can spend an hour or so at a place, waiting for the light to change and making adjustments to my perspective, but that's not necessarily the norm.

***AB:* Do you lock yourself down when you know you've got the shot—or do you take a couple of shots, look at them and then decide it would be better a hundred yards over to the left?**

***JC:*** When you look at your images after the fact, you can see the evolution. You'll make a photograph based on your initial reaction, then slowly refine the perspective and point of view and switch lenses.

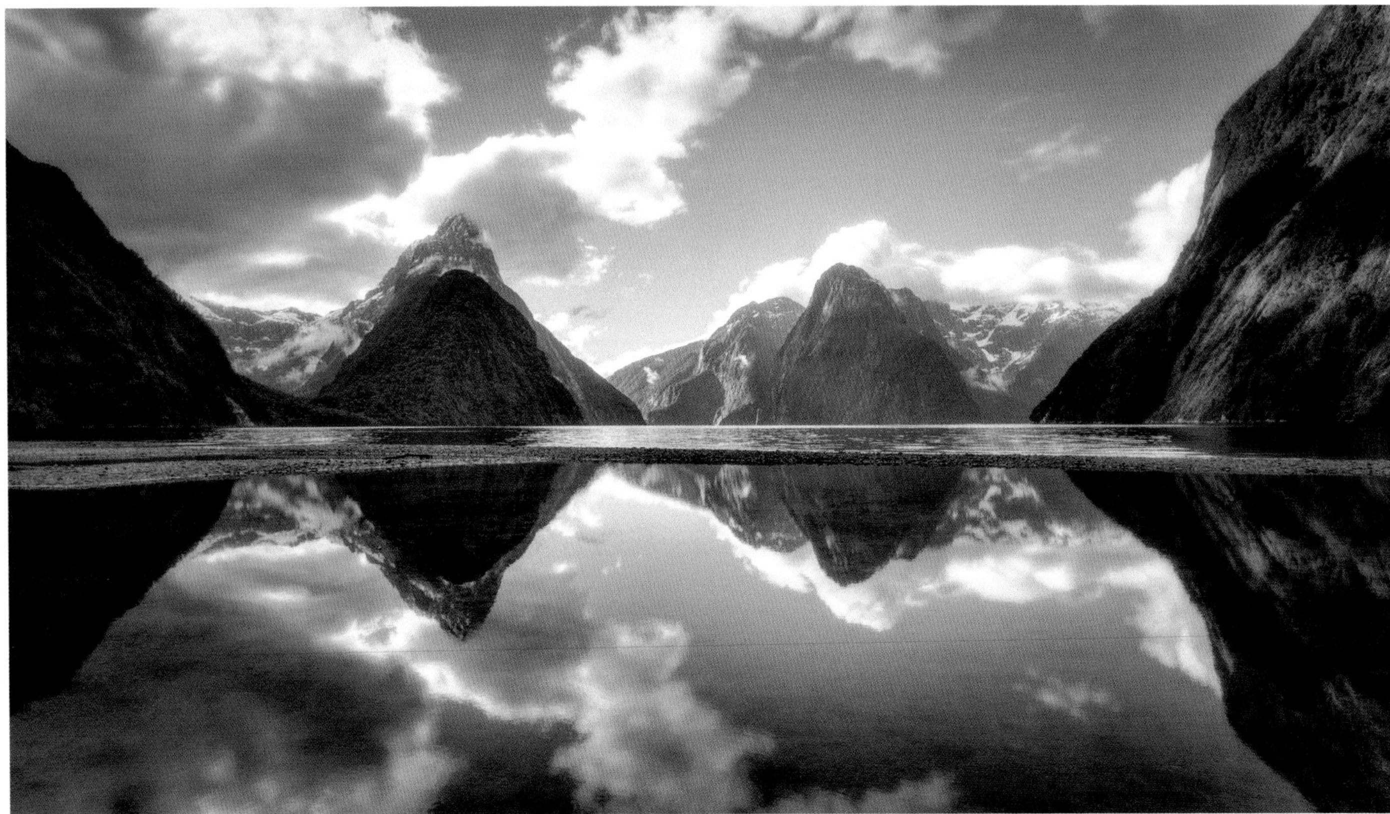

**FIGURE 2.7** This photograph was made at Milford Sound in Fiordland National Park on the South Island of New Zealand. Jeff arrived at the Sound before sunrise, anticipating the possibility of wonderful morning lighting—but instead found a dull, gray fog shrouding it, so he hiked back to his camper van, ate some soup and went to sleep. He explored the area and spent the day waiting for the lighting conditions to improve. Fortunately, in late afternoon the skies cleared to reveal the enormity of the place. By stitching together two images, Jeff essentially expanded the field of view of his 24mm lens, which helped convey the vastness of the place.
IMAGE © JEFF CONLEY, *FIORDLAND, DUSK, NEW ZEALAND*, 2011.

It evolves and rolls, one image to the next. Shooting with stitched-together images is harder to pre-visualize. I can see the essence of what I want to capture, but I have to get much more beyond the edge of the scene to make it all work. There's definitely a slow evolution towards progress (**Figure 2.7**).

I'm an old-school, zone-system guy, so I continually look at things in terms of maintaining a consistent approach. I think that idea carries over fairly seamlessly into the digital realm. I walk around with the tripod swung over my shoulder with my camera backpack, so I'm not really working all that differently from when I was exclusively shooting film, to be perfectly frank.

***AB*: So your camera is still on a tripod and you approach your camera work in the same way?**

*JC:* Yes—recently I've been working with a pan head—made by Nodal Ninja[3]—for stitching together images around the nodal point. I've been working on these ultra high-resolution files, which is very cool. I can walk around with this very small camera body, but essentially pack into it the potential resolution of an 11 × 14 view-camera and film. It's pretty phenomenal. It's logistically challenging to work with: a static scene is important, your depth of field can become problematic, lighting can change, so there are a lot of technical hurdles to deal with. I couldn't have done this with film—it's an approach only attainable through digital capture.

> *When you look at your sequence of images after the fact, you can see an evolution. You'll make a photograph based on your initial reaction, then slowly refine the perspective and point of view and switch lenses. It evolves and rolls, one image to the next.*
>
> *—Jeff Conley*

***CD:* It's interesting to look at a photographer's un-edited work to see the frames that lead up to a final shot. You start with an idea of what you want to capture, and as you shoot and look at the feedback from your camera, you decide you don't quite have it, so you keep adjusting and shooting until you get what you're after. Do you usually know when you've captured what you want?**

*JC:* Yeah, I think you know when it doesn't feel quite right—and when the image is resolved. It certainly helps that you can go back and review on site and evaluate where you are. You can look at the histogram, you can take a look at critical focus—you can do so much more digitally than you ever could with film.

## Sol Neelman

### *Commercial/Editorial/Weird Sports Photographer*

***Candace Dobro:* Do you ever have a picture in your mind of what you want to capture, *before* you look through the viewfinder?**

***Sol Neelman:*** My memory is horrible, and it serves as something of an advantage. I try to go with a fresh slate to every shoot. I just want to capture something I haven't seen before. I have no idea what to imagine.

There are definitely moments where you take a picture and think, "I got it!" and you do a little dance around. I actually called Bruce Ely once when we were working on a column together. I was photographing some kids in Eastern Oregon who were shoveling snow off the track so they could start track practice. I told him, "Dude, I got it, I got it! Dude, you don't understand what I got right now; this is awesome!" and it was good. It was that unique frame—and it wasn't something I had anticipated.

***CD:* Do you think your photographs are successful because you're excited about every moment, because you capture the thing as it happens—without planning or having a preconceived idea of what you're after?**

***SN:*** To be honest, I'm not that good at staging stuff, but I am really good at reacting to things. I think that's what I offer.

***Andy Batt:* As you react to what's going on, what kinds of decisions are you making?**

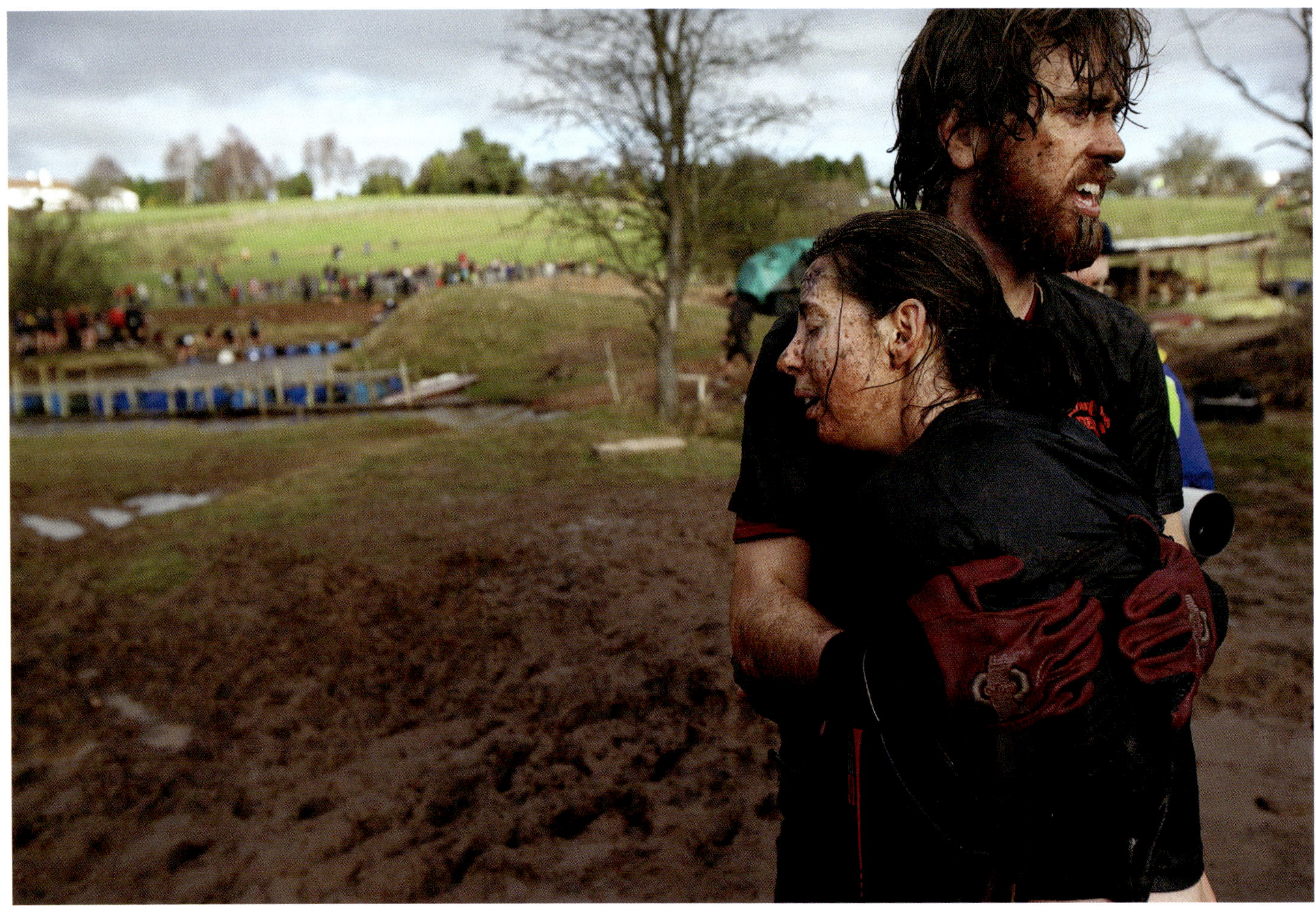

**FIGURE 2.8** Through experience, Sol has become comfortable going up to people and asking if he can photograph them. This shot was taken at the end of January 2014 at Tough Guy™,[4] a cross–country run followed by an assault course. Running the course involves risking cuts, scrapes, burns, dehydration, hypothermia, acrophobia, claustrophobia, sprains, twists, joint dislocation and broken bones.
IMAGE © SOL NEELMAN, *TOUGH GUY*, 2008.

***SN:*** My journalistic background has taught me to assess a situation and react on the fly. I can compensate for whatever's happening, even if it's to befriend someone so I can get closer to them—so I can be in someone's personal zone to make a picture that's intimate (**Figure 2.8**). I think that's part of taking a lot of pictures and becoming more comfortable with yourself and your boundaries. It's being able to go up to people to say, "Hey, my name is Sol and I'm taking photographs of this event, do you mind if I photograph you?" There once was a younger Sol who wouldn't do that, who was scared to do that—but I've been doing this long enough that I feel more comfortable now.

## Kim Campbell

*Portrait Photographer*

***Andy Batt:*** **What happens when you pick up a camera and put it up to your eye?**

***Kim Campbell:*** When I approach a photo, I'm fairly calm, but there's a little butterfly in me, because I don't know what I'm going to create. I like that edge in my experience. With my portrait photography, I have a good idea of the backgrounds I'm going to use, and what kinds of things I might do with the family or a kid, but I still wait for it to unfold when the personalities come in front of my lens (**Figure 2.9**).

I'm a real watcher. I put the camera up to my eye. I watch; I wait. Because my face is covered, they can't react to it, and I really want to connect to them—so I do a lot of talking and have a photo assistant smiling at them from behind me.

With portrait photography, I can photograph everything from a baby to a family of twenty people, and when I add more and more people into a photo shoot, my eye is constantly scanning everything that's happening. In a matter of seconds, I'm looking for body positioning that looks awkward or hair covering faces. I'm composing the subjects and looking at lighting. I'm quickly taking sample shots so I know what is and isn't working. There are a lot of things actively going on in my mind as I look through the camera. Nobody realizes all of these things are happening—except perhaps another photographer.

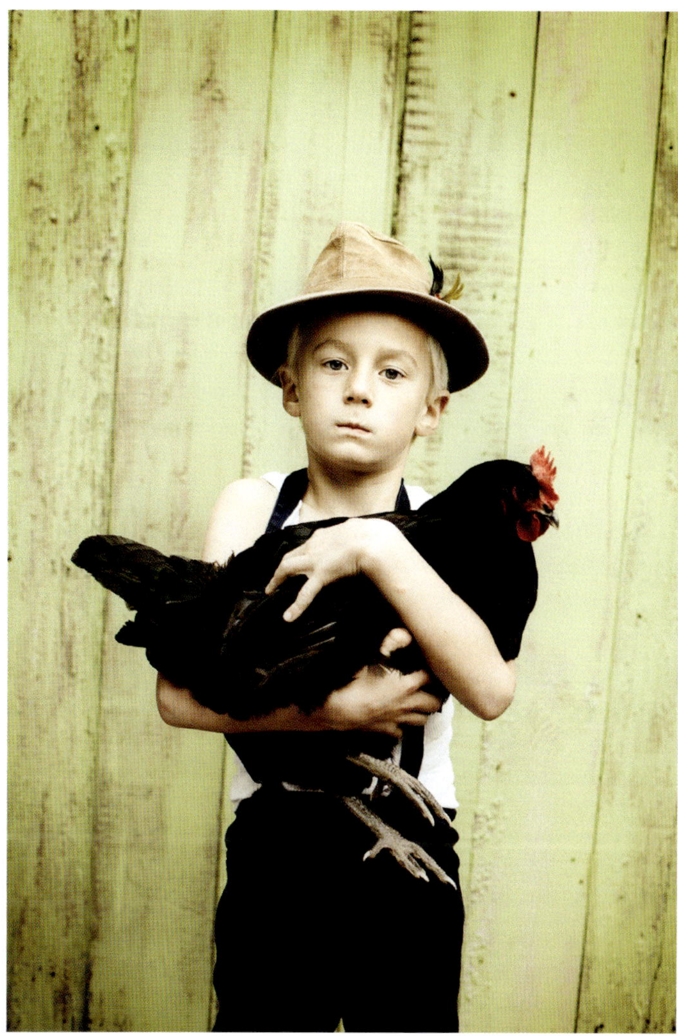

**FIGURE 2.9** Putting folks at ease is one of the best skills a photographer can develop when working with people. For Kim, "Creating a non–threatening and enjoyable environment is key. I never reprimand or 'parent' children in my session. I'll redirect them or change gears if something I'm doing doesn't work."
IMAGE © KIM CAMPBELL, *EL GALLO,* 2010.

***AB:*** **Is it different when you're shooting fine art photography?**

***KC:*** My fine artwork unfolds differently; I have some loose concepts and don't always know what's going to happen—until I get my subjects dressed in their costuming and in position with lighting I like. Then we'll start collaborating about how they might express themselves through body positioning. As I shoot, I review images to know if I need to stay with it or can move on.

Often, you'll just know when you've got that one great shot. That's one of the brilliant things about shooting digitally. With film, you had to trust your gut and measure everything correctly. With digital, you still need to do the same things to get a good shot, but you can assess as you go along, which is really different. I really do prefer digital capture to film.

> *When I approach a photo, I'm fairly calm, but there's a little butterfly in me, because I don't know what I'm going to create. I like that edge in my experience.*
> *—Kim Campbell*

***AB:*** **Do you use the viewfinder as a tool for composition?**

***KC:*** I do, but it's something I don't really think about; it's so second nature to me. The right composition can make portraits ho-hum or artistic. In my portrait work, the sets are fifteen feet wide at most, so sometimes there are limits to my compositions. I make them work by moving people around, looking to create interesting compositions. Often, I think of grouping people like musical notes on a page. Because I photograph anywhere from five to ten sessions a week, I do different things all the time to keep my photography interesting.

***Candace Dobro:*** **You mentioned that you talk to your subjects when you're behind the camera. How do you get them to behave naturally, so they're comfortable?**

***KC:*** As soon as they walk in the door, I try to get them to have fun. I give people a lot of direction, because I personally don't like it if somebody points a camera at me and doesn't tell me what they expect. I tell people that I'm happy to give them suggestions of what to do—but I'll also capture anything they just do naturally.

My desire to become intimate with my photo subjects quickly means I need to make them comfortable sharing their stories—and it usually helps that I share some of mine, too. I photograph them when they're laughing and telling jokes. I give them a lot of cues to keep the session moving and fun—like asking a family to give mom and dad a big hug at the same time. As soon as I see attention is slipping, I change it up. We may change clothes, backgrounds, or simply take a break. When children are squirrely, I'll tell them to run around. My husband likes to tease me and say I'm bossy—but I think I'm directorial.

***CD:*** **So many of the choices depend on the way you communicate with your subject; setting the right tone makes all the difference.**

***KC:*** Right, I'm always thinking about making it easy and enjoyable for them. Being sincere, kind and friendly seems to put most people at ease.

## Bruce Ely

### *Newspaper Photojournalist*

***Andy Batt:*** **As a photojournalist, how do you think the viewfinder influences the way you experience the world through your camera?**

***Bruce Ely:*** I find that the process of looking through the camera is a big barrier in my job. The writers at the paper often have a microphone so they can record their conversations. They're standing with a microphone in the guy's face and they have an ability to form a relationship with their subject way quicker than I can, because I've got this big thing [the camera] in front of my face. It can slow down the process of building a relationship with a subject.

If I go into a strange situation, I won't look through the camera. I'll sit there and talk; we'll have a conversation. They get comfortable. I get comfortable. In the back of my mind, I'm brainstorming about what picture I want to end up getting—looking at the surroundings wondering, "Where can we take this picture?" The point is that looking through the viewfinder can be an obstacle in the process of getting the pictures you want.

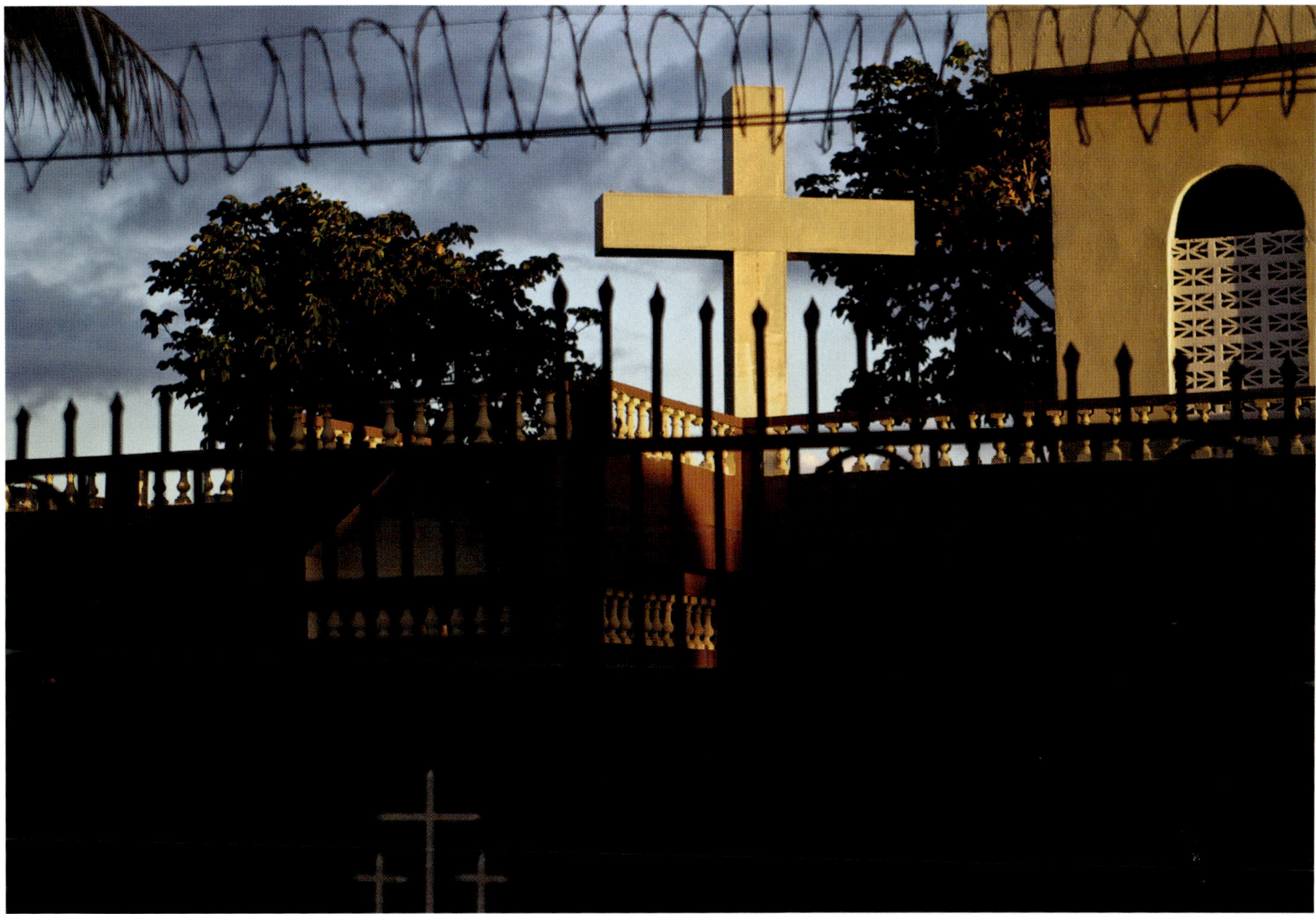

**FIGURE 2.10** Nearly a year after the devastating earthquake, Haitians in remote areas set up clinics to battle rising cases of cholera.
IMAGE BY BRUCE ELY, *HAITI EARTHQUAKE*, © AND COURTESY OF *THE OREGONIAN*, 2010.

***Candace Dobro:* Can you describe what it's like for you once you *have* established a relationship with your subject?**

***BE:*** I don't know that I'm able to describe it compositionally; I point the camera so that it looks right and feels good. It's just natural.

***CD:* Do you move or pan a little bit to find the sweet spot you want to capture?**

***BE:*** For me, a lot of that's done before I look through the camera. I guess there's a little moving around to make sure the things line up the way I want them to (**Figure 2.10**). When you point a camera at people, they get really self-conscious—or they start showing off for you, which is equally as bad.

I just keep pointing the camera at them, and finally they get to the point where they're bored of thinking about being uncomfortable or showing off, and they start to act normal. I didn't figure this out for a long time, but it takes my being comfortable to make it work—and I love doing it now.

***CD:* Did your pictures improve once you were comfortable?**

***BE:*** Yeah, absolutely. I just stick with it and wait until they get over whatever they're dealing with, as opposed to giving up on it. You have to get people to act like themselves, because nothing genuine happens when people are self-conscious. If you can get to the point where they just forget about you—then that's successful.

> *I just keep pointing the camera at them, and finally they get to the point where they're bored of thinking about being uncomfortable or showing off, and they start to act normal. I didn't figure this out for a long time, but it takes my being comfortable to make it work—and I love doing it now.*
>
> *—Bruce Ely*

## Holly Andres

*Fine Art and Editorial Photographer*

***Andy Batt:* Tell us about the way you create work—how you see and how the viewfinder relates to your vision.**

***Holly Andres:*** I hope to create—with the camera—the thing that's in my mind's eye. Often I have a really specific image in my mind and may even create a storyboard for it, which I then try to capture photographically. Inevitably, there's a degree of grief between what I've captured and how it departs from the vision that was in my mind. Usually, it takes me a few days to adjust.

When I shoot, I'm almost always thinking about the post phase: How am I going to merge two different plates, different exposures and different subjects in post? That phase is also creative, because I have images and materials and start to think about how I can finesse my composition. How can I better emphasize certain subjects or create something that (at least at my skill level) I wasn't able to accomplish exclusively in the shooting phase?

***AB:* It sounds like you take as much control as you can during the shooting phase.**

***HA:*** Yes, very much so. My compositions are formal and are influenced by the way people paint. I learned to pay a lot of attention to the negative space surrounding the positive form (**Figure 2.11**). My goal as an artist is to have the same amount of control over an implied narrative, art direction, colors, textures, patterns and lighting—and then to wait for and capture those ungoverned, less-directed moments. There's some real magic where the two collide.

> *I almost always shoot with a tripod so that I can be conscious of every area within the frame. Then I think of ways of using the camera to reveal the way the natural eye can't see.*
>
> *—Holly Andres*

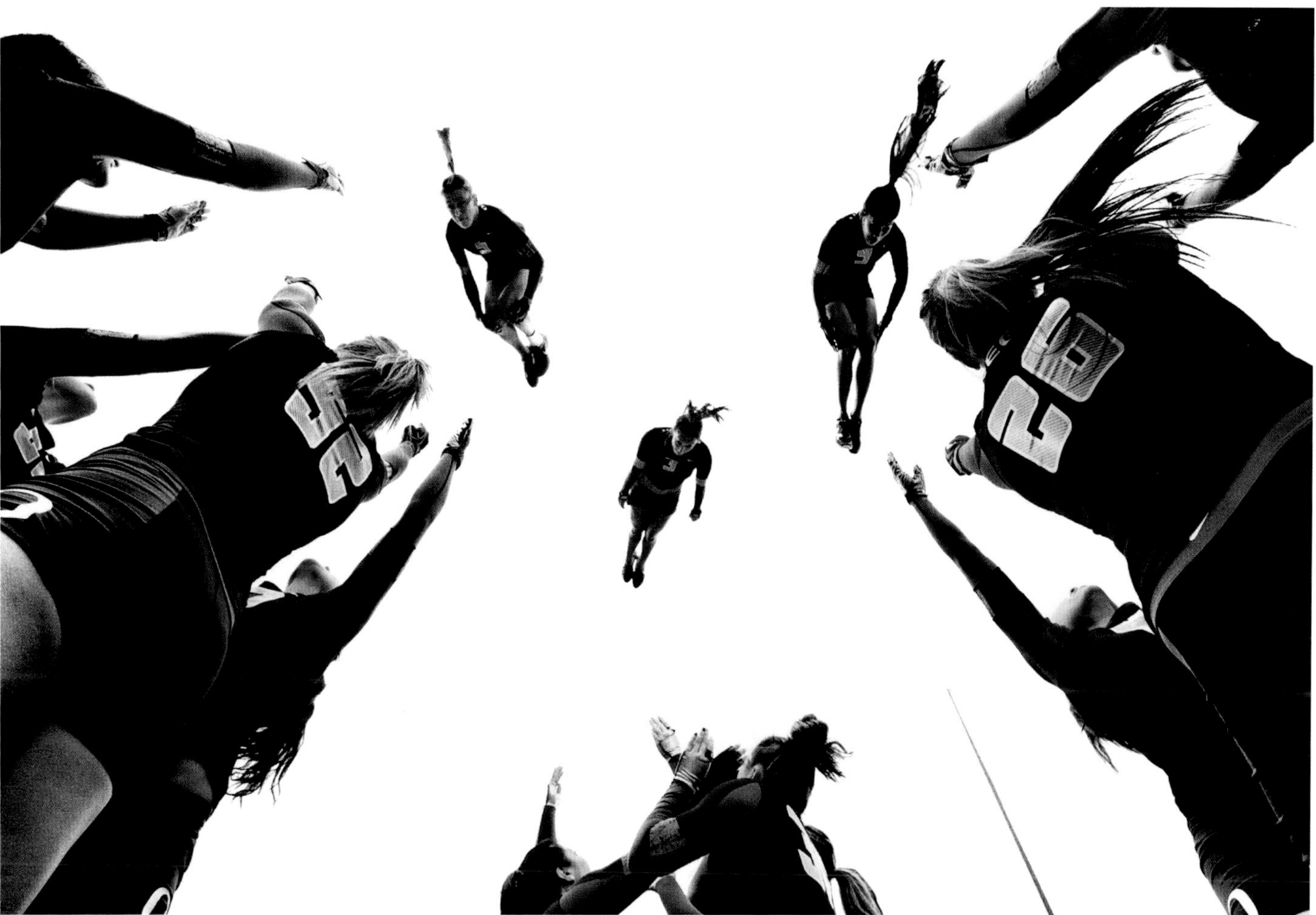

**FIGURE 2.11** Holly pays a lot of attention to the negative spaces in her compositions. With this shot, the unconventional perspective allowed her to create a more dramatic, heroic and graphic image for an article that discussed legitimizing cheerleading as a serious sport.
IMAGE © HOLLY ANDRES, *CHEER FACTOR: CHEERLEADING AND TITLE IX*, FOR *TIME* MAGAZINE, 2012.

***AB:*** **A big part of a photo shoot is getting everything ready so things can happen—being prepared so you can let go of everything else. The camera is merely a tool; it's what you do with it that's important.**

***HA:*** I usually spend a lot of time dialing in my composition. I don't want to make a total generalization, since every project is different, but I almost always shoot with a tripod so I can be conscious of every area within the frame. Then I think of ways I can use the camera to reveal the way the natural eye can't see. One of my devices is to capture and freeze movement. Recently, I've been doing some double-exposure transparencies as well.

***AB:*** **Describe the process between the time you pull your camera out of the bag and the moment when you lock it down and know the composition.**

***HA:*** If I were to walk into a space, I would probably have the experience and wherewithal to frame a compelling enough composition, and maybe insert a person into it. There's a pretty interesting phenomenon: It's a combination between doing what I have to do to get the shot and the camera becoming a buffer to the external world.

***Candace Dobro:*** **Does that buffer ever get you in trouble?**

***HA:*** When I shot the *Time* magazine cheerleading photographs (**Figure 2.11**), I was literally lying with my head on the grass right next to the feet of the cheerleaders who were hurling bodies up in the air. It was a pretty dangerous and compromising position. I knew I had to get the shot, and for some reason, when I'm behind my camera I don't have the same degree of fear that I might have in other situations.

I recently photographed a bunch of cheetahs, and I guess that when a cheetah is ready to attack, it will scratch the ground. There were people behind me with big rakes (like bigger cheetah paws), and they were going to scratch the ground if the cheetah got angry. I wasn't scared, because I was behind my camera. There's something about it that feels like a shield or bubble.

***AB:*** **When you're shooting, it's only about what you're looking at; you feel a little like Superman, a little invulnerable. It might even be dangerous—I know exactly what you're talking about.**

***HA***: It could probably get me into some trouble. Maybe I had a little bit too much confidence in those situations.

***CD:*** **The viewfinder is a powerful thing.**

***HA:*** Yes, it is.

## See What's Happening

No matter what kind of work you do as a photographer—capturing cheetahs, mud wrestlers or small children wearing animal masks—you use some kind of viewfinder. It's a defining concept; what we decide to include (and crop out) are some of the most fundamental decisions we can make.

### Photo Expert Goals for Improving Your Viewfinder Skills

- **Work with your subjects to help them relax.**
  If you want to engage with them, have a conversation before you take a single image, and keep the energy positive.
- **Be purposeful with the negative space that surrounds your subject.**
- **Don't rely on the zoom lens.**
  Instead, use your feet to move around and try different compositions.
- **Evolve your image.**
  While you shoot, keep refining your idea.
- **Try to capture something you haven't seen before.**
- **Assess your work as you shoot.**
  When you know you've "got the shot," move on and try something new.

## EXPLORATIONS

### Building Relationships

Your viewfinder is an editing tool, a way to decide what you're going to keep and what you're going to discard. If you put two people into a frame, you give them a relationship. If you combine objects in a frame, you create a pattern.

### Your Mission

Head out and make a series of photographs that explores the idea of framing relationships—a "relationship" is the deliberate inclusion of two or more subjects in the same frame to create a story. You can do this Exploration as street photography, or by constructing a fictional narrative (**Figure 2.12**).

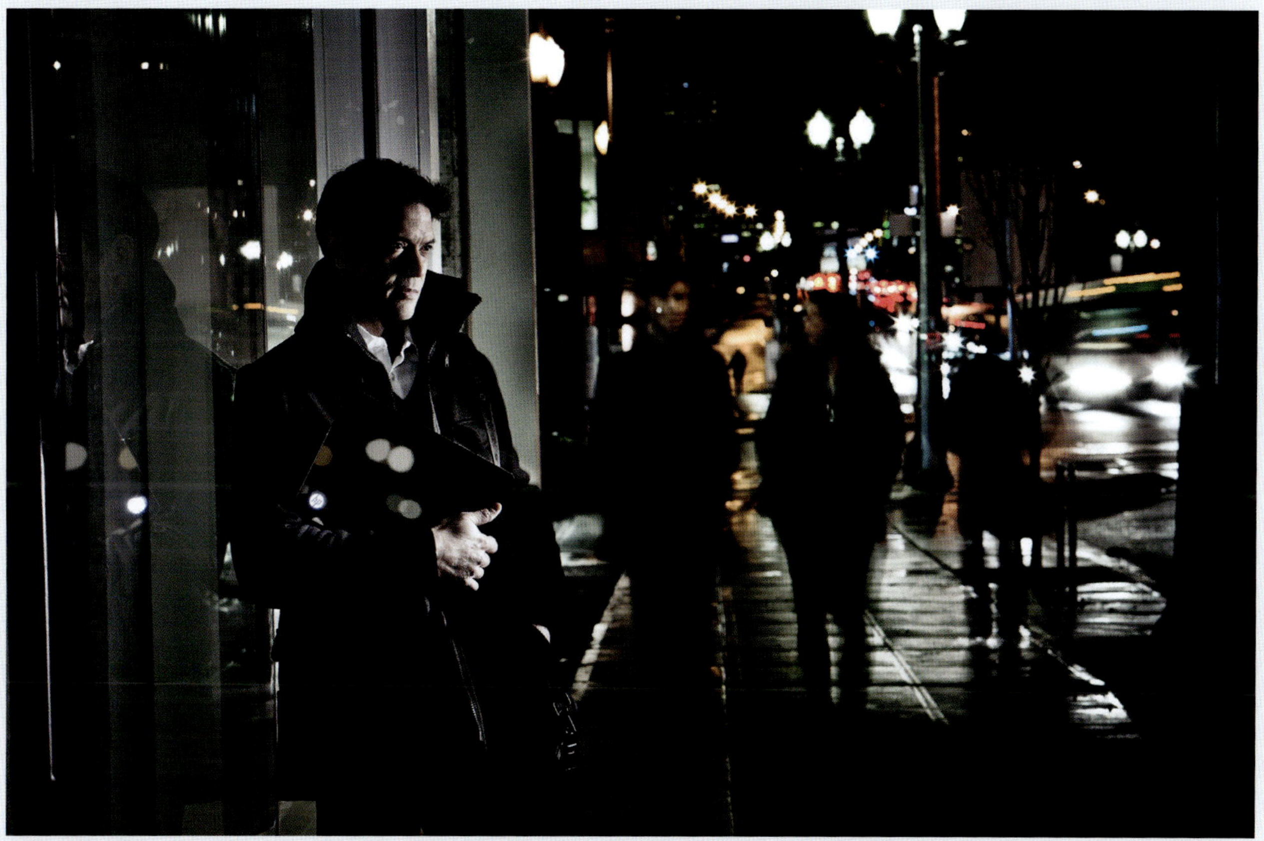

**FIGURE 2.12** Andy and his team created this film noire image for HP. The idea was to fill the frame and have activity behind the mysterious stranger to form a fictional narrative. (All the people in the shot are models.) Without the figures in the background, this photo would tell a totally different story.
IMAGE © ANDY BATT, *RAINY NIGHT*, 2009.

Look for ways to connect your subjects:

1. Can you accomplish this with style? Clothing? Actions?
2. How do your subjects relate to their environment?
3. How does your choice of lens, angle and framing alter the story idea?
4. Are there graphic relationships at work? Can you find patterns of repeated shapes?
5. Are there words in the image? How do they change the meaning of the image?

The goal is to develop your use of the viewfinder as a framing tool—so concentrate on making deliberate choices about the story you want to tell.

## Notes

1 Chimping: obsessively reviewing your images (on the camera's LCD screen) as you take them.

2 Rochester Institute of Technology, www.rit.edu.

3 Nodal Ninja, www.nodalninja.com.

4 Tough Guy™, www.toughguy.co.uk.

Three

# YOUR DIGITAL SKELETON

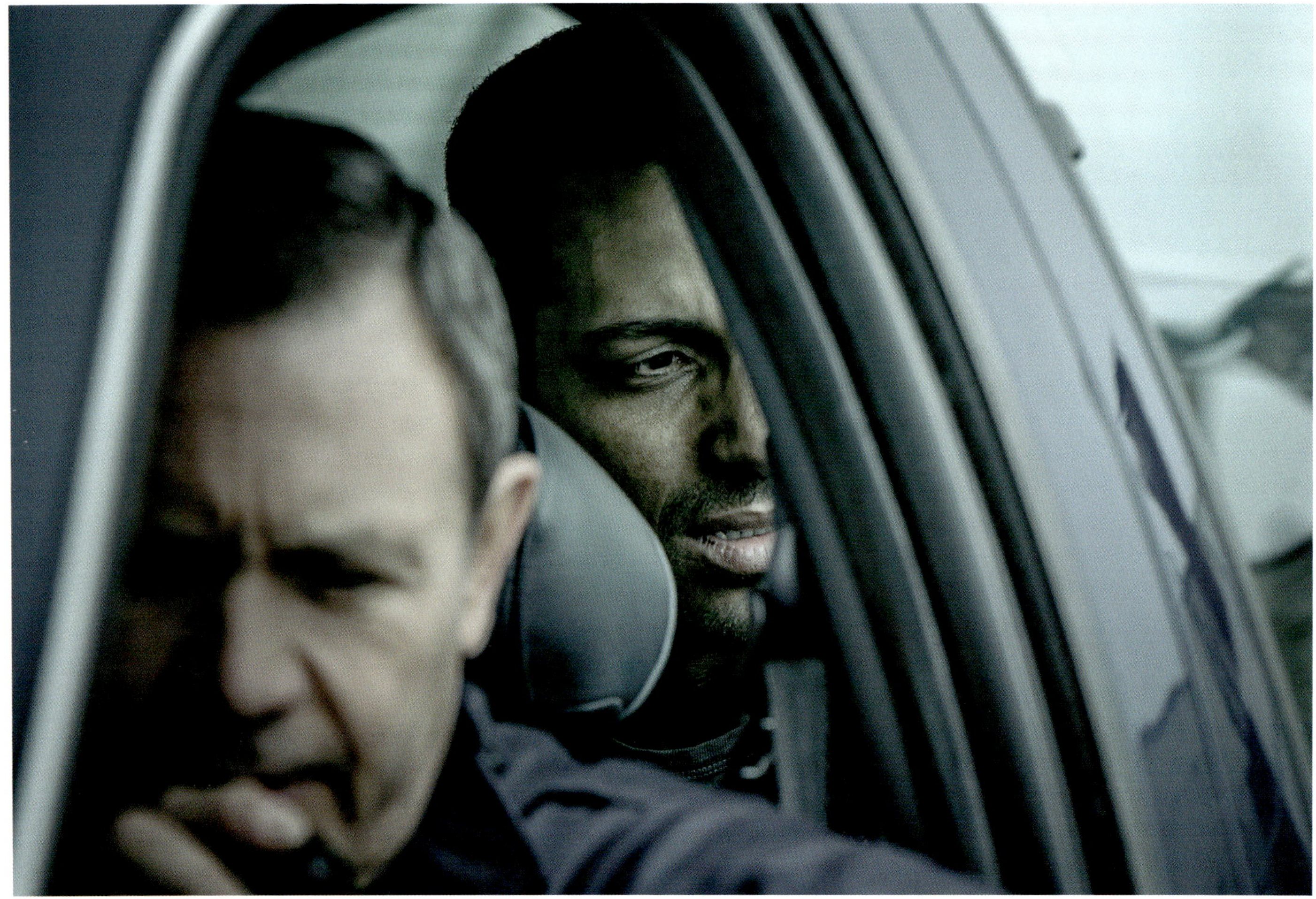

**FIGURE 3.1** For this project, Andy and his team created a thirty-second stop-motion TV spot using still cameras. Andy says, "We shot five scenes—with two cameras covering each scene—using intervalometers to shoot one frame per second. We shot 24,473 raw files over two days, just under 300GB. From there, we needed to find the best sequences and export them out as animation frames. The production timeline was very short on this project; without a solid workflow, we would never have been able to keep track of all the different options and quickly deliver the final images to the editor who put the TV spot together."
IMAGE © ANDY BATT, *CHARLIE'S STORY—UNITED WAY*, 2012.

When it comes to digital image workflow, there are three types of photographers: the ones who don't know they have problems, the ones who don't want to know they have problems and the ones who have found solutions to their problems. Workflow isn't something that occurs naturally; it's something you have to actively develop—and although it can be intimidating, it doesn't need to be. In this chapter, we're going to talk with our experts and give you some solid ideas you can put to work right away.

## What Is Digital Workflow?

You could write an entire tome about this subject.[1] For this book, we're taking a foundational approach by examining the bones of your digital system. We'll talk about the process of moving raw images off your camera over to your computer, adding information to them, changing the filenames and making sure everything is safely backed up. This will all be done using a *consistent methodology,* or workflow. The basic parts of this system are: external hard drives, media cards, card readers, image cataloging software (Lightroom, Aperture, etc.) and backup software. The only other thing you'll need is a plan.

# Raw All the Way

Much of image workflow deals with file management, so let's establish some basics about raw files. If you already work in the raw format and want to skip ahead to the next section, *To DNG or Not to DNG*, then go for it; otherwise, join us for a quick section on why you're going to shoot nothing but raw files from now on.

## Setting Your Camera

Begin by diving into your camera's menu until you find the Image Quality setting; then set it to "raw." Voilà! You've just made a huge leap forward in quality, control and your ability to work in your digital darkroom—and you won't regret it! Raw files give you pure data that's captured by the sensor and is minimally processed on the camera's part. A raw file is captured at the sensor's full size and is delivered to you without any quality or size settings.[2] In the JPEG world, *quality* refers to how much compression is used: the more compression, the lower the image quality. Raw files have no quality setting, since they simply comprise the original raw data.

## The Raw Processor

Open any raw-processing application and check out the options for adjusting exposure, color, contrast, lens corrections, etc.—the list goes on and on. The biggest benefit of these features is that they enable your raw files to be infinitely variable and changeable; nothing is permanent, and you pay no penalties for tweaking and adjusting the way your image looks. Nothing gets locked down until you process it out into another format.[3] This is referred to as *parametric image editing*—although we usually just say processing. We'll get into more detail about how the data is captured and how raw files are processed in *Chapter 5.*

## Raw File Types and Metadata Basics

If you own more than one brand of camera, you've probably noticed that each brand creates images in its own format (**Figure 3.2A**). Canon

| | |
|---|---|
| NIKON | .NEF |
| CANON | .CR2 |
| FUJI | .RAF |
| PENTAX | .PEF |
| OLYMPUS | .ORF |
| HASSELBLAD | .3FR |
| PHASE ONE | .IIQ |
| LEICA | .DNG |
| LEAF | .MOS |
| SAMSUNG | .SRW |
| PANASONIC | .RAW |
| SONY | .ARW |

**FIGURE 3.2A** Every raw file gets tagged with a three-character filename extension that identifies the type of camera it came from and that it's a raw file.
ILLUSTRATION © ANDY BATT, *RAW FILE TYPES BY MANUFACTURER,* 2013.

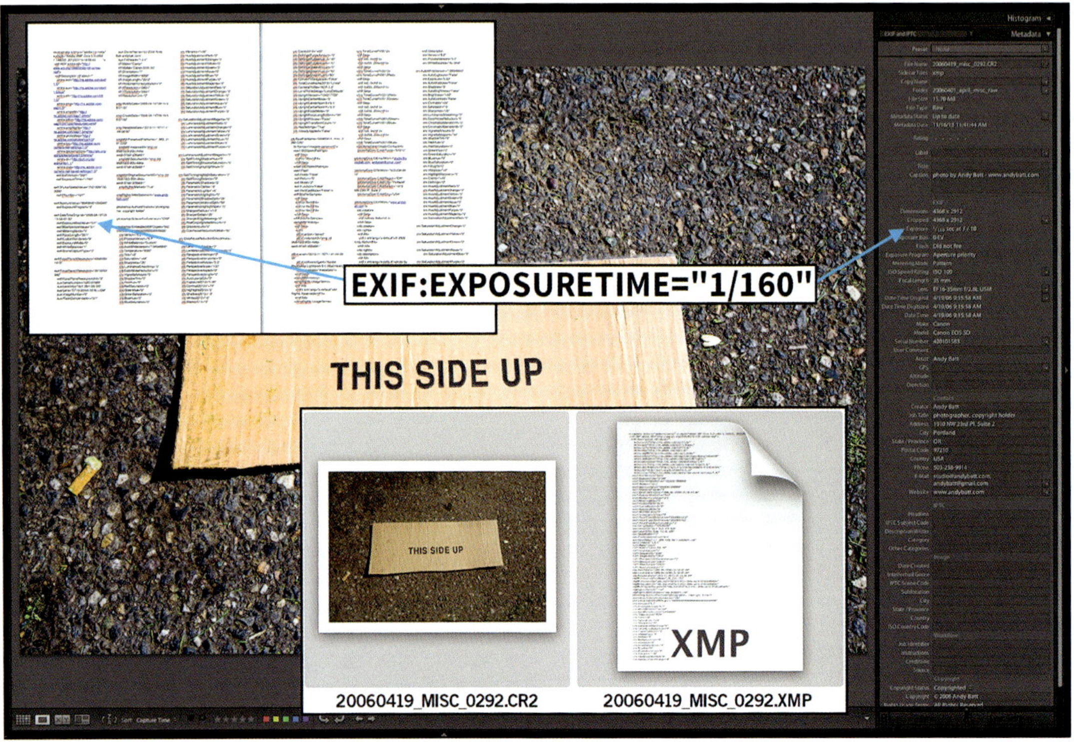


**FIGURE 3.2B** The camera embeds metadata into the raw files. A raw processor reads that information, adds its own metadata (ratings, processing instructions, etc.) and creates an XMP sidecar file that is stored next to the raw file. Applications like Lightroom also store this information inside their own database. These applications never write data into the original file.
SCREENSHOT © ANDY BATT, *RAW FILE AND METADATA*, 2013.

raw files will be named something like "_DXA_1452.cr2," while Nikon raw files will be named something like "DSC2134.NEF." Depending on the type of software you use, you might see some companion files, such as "_DXA_1452.XMP" or "DSC2134.XMP," sitting next to the raw files. (More about XMP files in a minute.)

Every raw file gets tagged with a three-character filename extension—such as *.cr2*—that identifies the type of camera it came from and that it's a raw file. Any program that recognizes raw file types will recognize these extensions[4] and know they're dealing with original camera raw files. All the other information about your image—from camera type to the time you shot the image—is handled by the metadata stored inside of the raw file (**Figure 3.2B**).

## Metadata

Metadata is simply data about data. It covers a huge range of topics, such as camera settings, lens information, your personal information, shoot location and GPS coordinates. Some of it is embedded inside the camera's original file and is generally called EXIF[5] data. The camera creates EXIF data automatically.

Another type of metadata is IPTC[6] data. You generate this information, which includes your name, keywords, model's name, etc. A few bits of information—such as your name and copyright—can be entered on your camera. The remaining information needs to be added using software, after you've shot the images.

Your camera embeds the original metadata into the raw file. Everything else can be found in one of three places: the sidecar XMP file; the internal, hidden database of the program you're using (e.g., Lightroom or Aperture); or the DNG file (more about this in a bit). These three alternate locations are used to protect the original camera raw file. They exist so we don't have to risk damaging the image by reaching inside that file to make changes.

The XMP sidecar is created automatically any time you use Adobe Bridge to work on raw files or tell an application, such as Lightroom, to create them. XMP files allow you to transfer additional metadata between different applications.[7] What do you need to do with them? Nothing! Just leave them alone and don't delete them.

## Why Shoot Raw?

- **Variable white balance**
  This allows you to control how warm, neutral or cool an image is.
- **Better image quality**
  Your computer is better at processing your images than your camera is.
- **More tonal range**
  Those "blinky" camera warnings alerting you that you're overexposing an image are usually wrong. Your raw-processing software is a more accurate way to judge over- and under-exposure.
- **More flexibility**
  You can adjust the look of your images infinitely and can always reset the image for a clean start.

If you only work with a single catalog and never switch applications, you might never have a reason to work with XMP files. Applications like Lightroom store all of that metadata inside the catalog file, safely and automatically.

## To DNG or Not to DNG

What is that mysterious DNG file type? It shows up in the list of original camera raw files as the native format for Leica cameras, and if you've ever used Lightroom to import your raw files, you may have noticed the "Copy as DNG" option. In the Export dialog—the same place you create TIFF or JPEG files—there's an option to process your images out as DNGs. Can these actually be used as an original native format, an import format and an output format—a miracle product capable of curing all ills? Surely it's snake oil? No, friends, this is the real deal!

The DNG file format was created by Adobe and is based around a very simple concept: to create an open standard for storing raw image data, support for all current metadata, expansion for any future metadata and space for any (current or future proprietary) "secret sauce" that the camera manufacturer wants to keep out of sight. With DNGs, Adobe has created a better archival format.[8] If you shoot DNG originals or archive in DNG format, you take a real step forward in safeguarding your archive into the future, since you won't have to rely on the survival of proprietary image formats. DNG is also a champ (**Figure 3.3**) when it comes to metadata: It has the equivalent of an internal XMP file that's buffered from the original raw data, so that writing information into a DNG never puts your image data at risk.

***Candace Dobro:*** **Why is DNG such a useful format?**

***Andy Batt:*** As a capture format, DNG is like the Holy Grail—it's an ideal format that's sought after by photographers. If you don't use DNGs and a manufacturer goes out of business, you won't be able to count on them to provide up-to-date software to process your archived raw files.

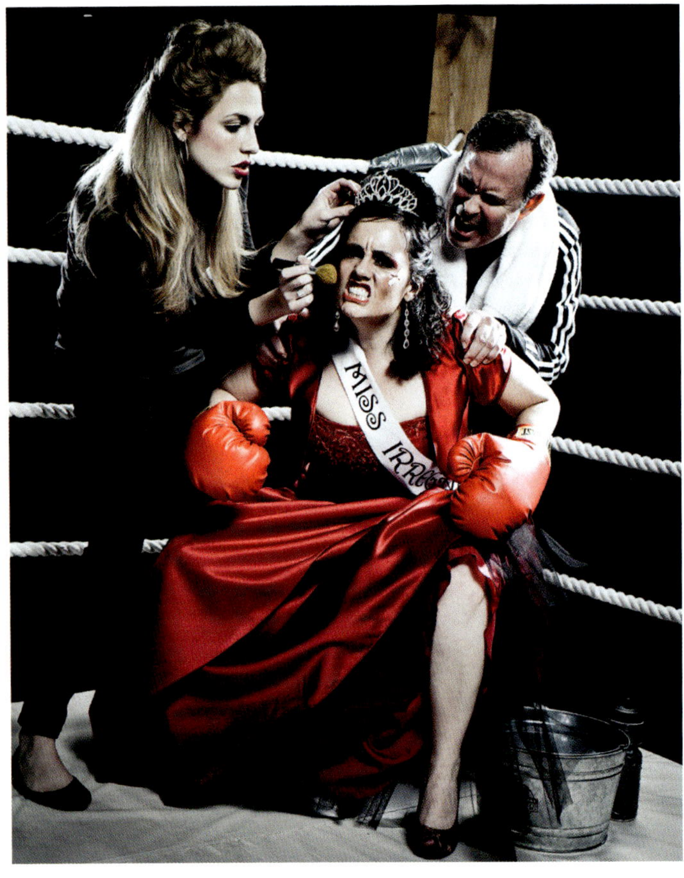


**FIGURE 3.3**
The DNG format is a champ. It's a universal format that doesn't rely on the manufacturer's support. DNGs preserve all your image data and metadata and also encode and protect your processing instructions—your image's look and feel—as long as you open it into a compatible raw processor.
IMAGE © ANDY BATT, *MISS IRREGARDLESS*, 2011.

A few notable companies—like Ricoh, Pentax and Leica—have already adopted DNG as a native or optional file format. This open standard benefits the photographer and anyone who makes raw-processing software. If all the camera manufacturers would give us the option to shoot DNG files, then we'd avoid problems with archiving our images.

***CD:* How can you use DNGs in your workflow?**

***AB:*** DNG files are interesting, because they can be used in different ways: as camera-original raw files, by converting to them when you import or as a final file of sorts (if you export to DNG after processing the original raw format in a program like Lightroom).

At my studio, we use DNG as a "transport format" when we need to deliver raw files to a retoucher or a client. I can embed my metadata and processing instructions into DNGs, so when a client opens them in Photoshop, Photoshop will read and use all the tweaks I've made in Lightroom.

## Andy's Time Comparison Test

I shot 248 files with my Canon EOS-1DX onto a SanDisk 32GB Extreme Pro CF card. That's a 160MB/s, UDMA 7 card; it's very fast. I used a SanDisk USB3 card reader, Lightroom 5, and downloaded the files to my Thunderbolt-connected RAID 50,[9] which is also very fast. I chose a straight import: There was no renaming or additional backup, and I used embedded JPEGs for previews. Each test was done exactly the same way.

- **Copy as CR2 original**
  1 minute, 3.34 seconds. Each image took .26 seconds to transfer.
- **Copy as DNG**
  5 minutes, 12.38 seconds. Each image took 1.25 seconds to transfer.

For a project that has 8,000 images, it would take 168 minutes (2.8 hours) to download and convert to DNG. To ingest the original format, it would take only 35 minutes. It comes down to scale: If you're working with hundreds of images, then converting to DNG on import isn't going to have that big an effect on you. Once you get up to working with thousands of images, though, those extra seconds pile up.

***CD:* You don't use the "Copy as DNG" function on import?**

***AB:*** The only thing stopping me at this point is the time penalty, because when converting to DNG, it takes more time to ingest images. We deal with such large quantities of images that we have to seriously question anything that adds time to the process.

***CD:* What software can read DNG files?**

***AB:*** Photo Ninja, Aperture, Lightroom and Photoshop. It's an open standard, so many programs support it.

***CD:* If you send a camera-original raw file with an XMP sidecar to the client, is it the same as sending them DNGs?**

***AB:*** When you send a raw file with an XMP sidecar, you're asking the client to be responsible for two files instead of one. You don't know which system they're going to use to manage the data, which software they're going to use to move it around and who's going to have access to it. If someone throws out those XMP files, most of your metadata will disappear.

***CD:* Is this one of the reasons why you rarely send raw files to a client, and why you tend to send TIFFs instead?**

***AB:*** I'd much rather send a processed TIFF to a client, because it's been processed with my look and feel and has my metadata *hardcoded* inside it. If I need to deliver a raw file, I'll send a DNG—but there needs to be a compelling reason for a client to have it. You give up control when you send a raw file out.

# Media Card Management

With just about any camera system, you capture your images directly to some kind of flash memory card; CF, SD and Micro SD are the most common ones. These durable cards are the workhorses of the capture process—saving, transferring and being formatted over and over during their lifetime. Your images are at their most fragile when they exist in only one place. Until you've downloaded and backed them up, your entire shoot (and all the time, effort and money that went into it) depends on your media cards. One of the simplest, yet most important things you can do—besides not dropping them in the mud or running them through the washing machine[10]—is to create a media card workflow.

***Candace Dobro:* Do you use a specific methodology for handling media cards?**

***Andy Batt:*** We have two different systems, depending on how complicated the project is and how many assistants I have.

## The Easy System

***AB:*** The easy system uses a Think Tank® card wallet with ten CF-card slots. We've determined three different positions for the CF media: label facing down, label facing up and the card turned sideways. If the card is *facing down*, that means it's ready to be shot. It can then go into the camera, where it gets formatted immediately.

***CD:* You want to format it in your camera, not in your computer, right?**

***AB:*** Right. The camera is a computer. You always want a fresh format from the camera you're shooting with. Next, you shoot your pictures and put the card back into the wallet with the label side *facing up*—this means that the card is shot and needs to be downloaded. As you shoot, you work through your cards sequentially. You also go through sequentially when you ingest the cards. After each card has been imported it goes back into the wallet *sideways*. This means the card was downloaded, but not backed up. The card is your backup until your hard drive has been backed up.

***CD:* Then what?**

***AB:*** We make our backup to a pair of hard drives, so we have two copies of all the images. Once we have a verified backup, we'll put the card back into the wallet with the label facing down.

## The More Complicated System

***CD:* What's the other, not-so-easy system?**

***AB:*** I use a more complicated system when I have multiple cameras and assistants. They have a few different colored rolls of paper tape and a log sheet to keep track of the cards. A color-coded piece of tape goes across the "business" end of the card, so it can't be loaded back into the camera. My assistants label each card with the name of the camera and the next number in the card sequence.

For example, if I've shot six cards on Camera A, the next card gets labeled "Camera A, Card 7." This is logged with the ID number of the CF card. Once the card is downloaded it gets a different color tape indicating that it's waiting for backup. Once the backups are made, the tape gets removed and the card is ready to go. It's a more complicated system—but when we're shooting multiple cameras on a complex project it's vital.

***CD:* This way, you're able to track all your cameras, right?**

***AB:*** Yes—when my DIT [Digital Imaging Technician] receives a card, he knows which camera it came from. It would be downloaded into the Camera A folder and renamed with the camera ID as part of the new filename. We do this for good organization and as an insurance policy. Occasionally, if we're working with two identical cameras, we might have two different images with the exact same name. Separate ingestion folders keep them from overlapping. If we catch this during the shoot, then we can reset the camera-assigned filename; otherwise, we'll modify it during renaming.

***CD:* So many things to think of.**

***AB:*** When you're shooting a complicated multi-camera job and it all works—that's when you know you have a good system!

## Squeaky Clean Media Card Workflow

You'll need a set of sequentially labeled media cards and some kind of card case or wallet. Make sure to capture your project over different cards. That way, if there's a problem with one of the memory cards, it won't affect the entire job.

1. **Card Prep**: All cards go into the card wallet sequentially, with the same side up and in the same orientation.
2. **Camera Prep**: The beginning of a photo shoot is a good time to reset the camera's file numbers.
3. **Format**: Load the first media card into your camera and hit the "Play" button, just to make sure you haven't picked up a card that needs to be downloaded. Next, format it.[11] This will empty the card so you can start fresh. If you'll need to quickly load cards, then you can format them ahead of time—but only do this with the camera you're shooting with. Be sure not to format cards in a Nikon and then put them into a Canon!
4. **Shoot**: Fill the card with images and put it back into your card wallet upside down. This indicates that the card has been shot and that you should not use it again.
5. **Ingest**: Sequentially download your media cards. After downloading each one, put it back into the card wallet upside down and turn it sideways. This indicates that you haven't backed it up yet.
6. **Backup**: Make sure you have two copies of the images on two separate hard drives (at least one should be external).
7. **Refresh**: Now you can flip all those cards right-side up. They're ready for use again.

**Bonus**: If you can't download and check your images on set, always shoot a few images onto a second memory card—you can go even further and use a second camera for extra protection.

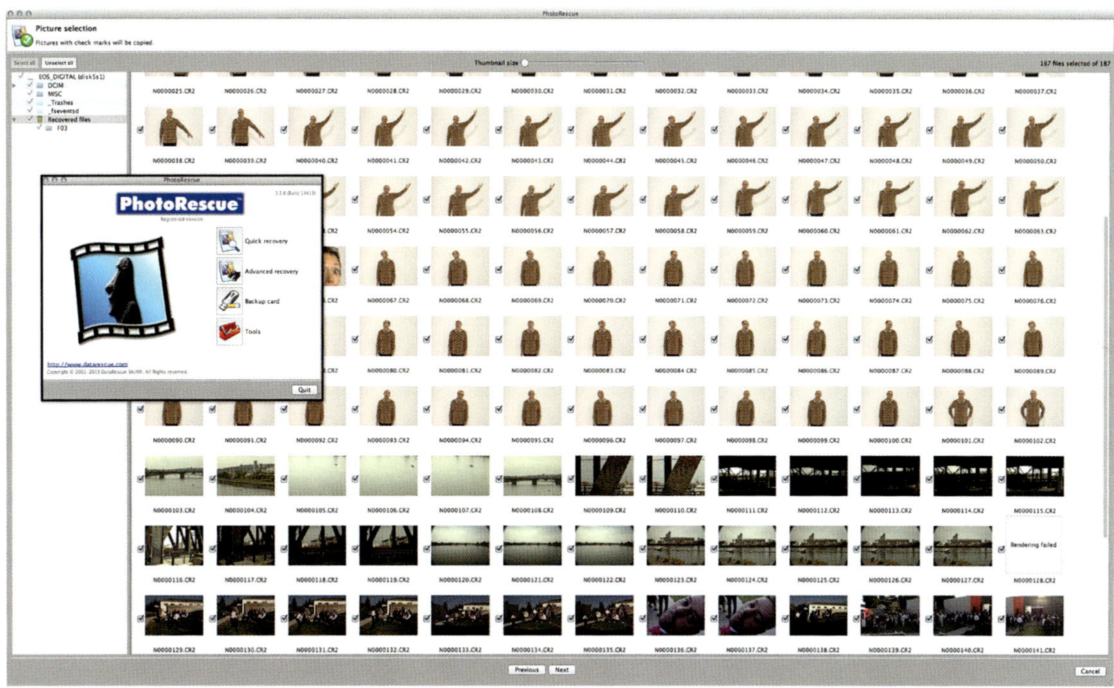

**FIGURE 3.4** Andy formatted a 4GB card in his camera and then opened it up with PhotoRescue. It found images from at least five different sessions, which means the card had been formatted at least five times. The images were all easily recoverable and usable. The formatting step doesn't destroy image data; destruction only occurs when new images are saved on top of old ones.
SCREENSHOT © ANDY BATT, *PHOTORESCUE*, 2013.

## Save Me!

Media cards can throw an occasional error—due to malfunction, removal while the camera is still "on," or just from gremlins.[12] Usually, you won't be aware of an error until the download stage. At this point, the card won't download at all; it will stop partway through or your images will show up scrambled. Sometimes you might accidentally format a card that hasn't been downloaded yet!

In any of these cases, good media recovery software can save your bacon. Andy has been using PhotoRescue[13] for years (**Figure 3.4**). There are other applications to do the job, but this one has proven itself over and over again where others have failed.

On those incredibly rare occasions when you format a card when you shouldn't have, there's good news: Most cameras simply create a new "map" (file directory) and just forget about the image locations. When you format that media card, you wipe out the map that keeps track of the location where all those images are stored—but the images are still there. If you don't realize this until after you take some photos on the card, you'll lose some of the original images, but you should be able to recover most of them with image-recovery software.

## Card Recovery

Try these techniques for a media card that won't download, gives you corrupt images or was accidentally formatted:

1. **Change the hardware**
   Try a different card reader, cable or computer; sometimes, the problem is with a bad piece of hardware.
2. **Recovery software**
   Try PhotoRescue (or the camera manufacturer's recovery utility). Your images are probably still on the card, and this will find them for you.
3. **+1 Photo**
   Try putting the card back into the camera and confirm that you can see the images there. Now shoot an additional image—this adds more information to the file directory, which occasionally "fixes" it.
4. **Cable download**
   Put the media card back into the camera and connect the camera to your computer via cable. Use the manufacturer's software—or anything else that's capable of connecting to the camera—to download the images.

### FEATURED INTERVIEW

## Rachel Jerome Ferraro

*Photographer and Educator*

***Andy Batt:*** **Tell us about the work you do.**

***Rachel Jerome Ferraro:*** I teach commercial photography at RIT. I still freelance as much as possible, but transitioned to teaching after 18 years as a commercial photographer in NYC.

***AB:*** **What does workflow mean to you, and can you describe what that covers?**

***RJF:*** For me, it covers the process of handling image files from start to finish. My starting point would be file organization; otherwise, the cart goes before the horse. A well-organized system for file handling will establish a great foundation for housing images. From there, we can capture and ingest files, optimize them, output them and back them up.

***AB:*** **When do you think a photographer needs to learn workflow?**

***RJF:*** There seems to be a critical point where someone loses information, creates a big organizational mess or becomes extremely frustrated. A photographer should nail down a workflow before this happens. Anyone who takes photos (which is everyone, right?) would benefit from the basics of a good workflow, especially for organization and backup.

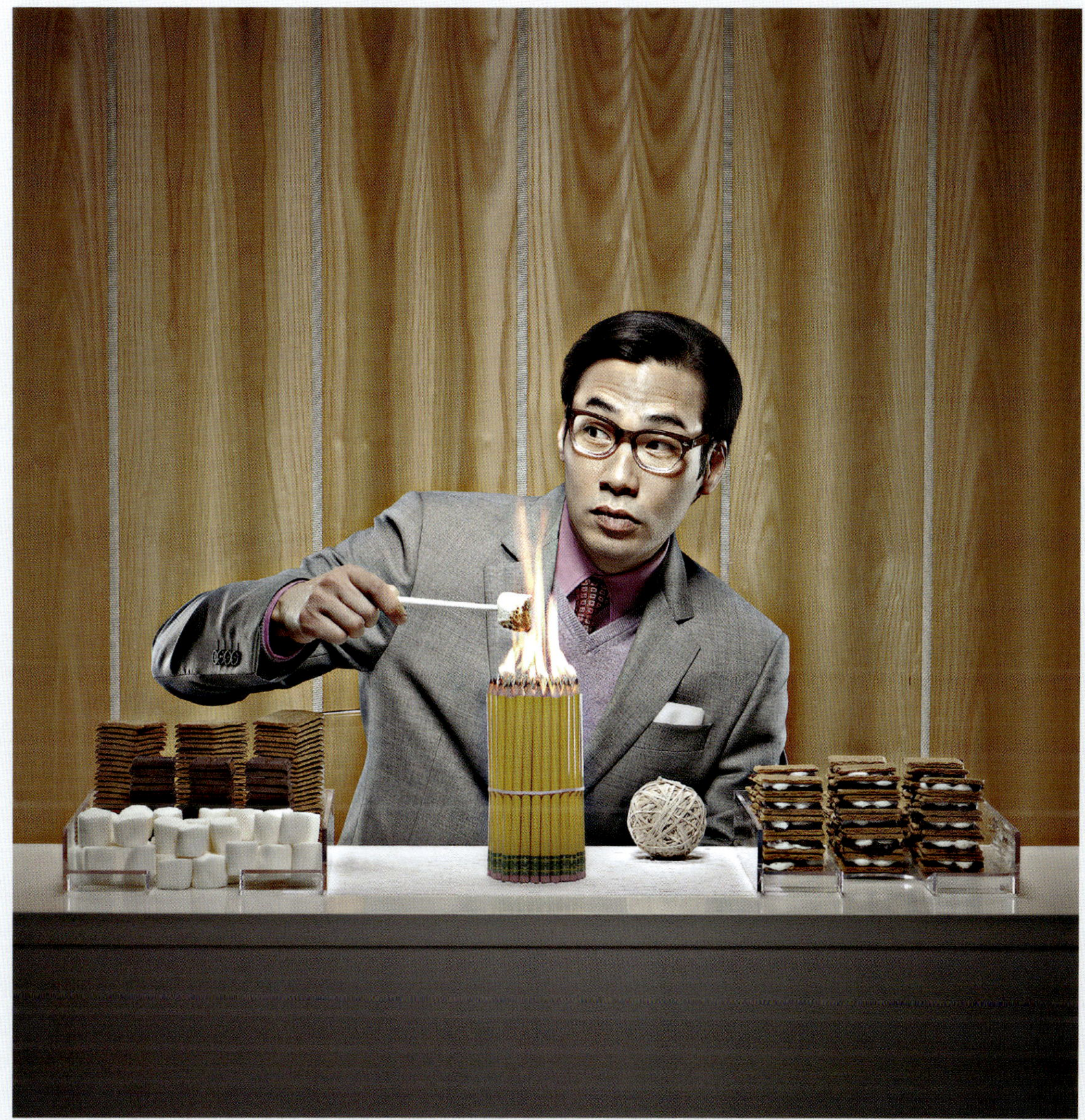

**FIGURE 3.5**

Rachel created this conceptual image for *Deliver*, the trade magazine for the US Postal Service. It was produced as a series of 3–D mailers, each containing a tasty s'more[14] for its lucky recipient.

IMAGE © RACHEL JEROME FERRARO, *S'MORES*, FOR *DELIVER* MAGAZINE, 2010.

***AB:*** **What are the key ideas everyone needs to address in their workflow—what does a good workflow cover?**

***RJF:*** All the best practices seem to be geared towards maximizing image quality and protecting yourself from data loss—as well as minimizing wasted time and preventing frustration. Users ultimately reach their comfort zone, where everything is in its place and functions well for their needs. For a volume shooter, this may mean ample storage and quick editing of multiple images; whereas for an advertising shooter, it may entail faster performance with large files. In an ideal world, we would all be able to afford abundant storage capacities, lightning-fast everything, etc. The reality is that we prioritize the things that are most important to the way we work.

***AB:*** **What happens if you implement a bad workflow?**

***RJF:*** Chaos ensues!

## Bad Workflow = Bad Things

- **Bad names**
  If there is no consistent naming convention for files, there will probably be instances of overwriting files—and much time-consuming confusion. ("Oh wow. I have six files named IMG_042 . . . I should have named things by date and maybe even by subject, like 20130812–01 or 20130812-Cats-01.")
- **Backups**
  File backup is where I think people take the most risks. The obvious danger here is data loss. Whether it's minimal or catastrophic, it's always painful. Buying data storage isn't the most fun way to spend money, but it's absolutely necessary.
- **Time wasting**
  Anything that wastes time or causes frustration for the user is not ideal.

***AB:*** **Do you think there's one "Holy Grail" for workflow? Is there one method that works for everyone, or is there a need for multiple types of workflows?**

***RJF:*** No. As much as I love the idea of standardization, even my own workflow varies sometimes.

***AB:*** **How can photographers who are less techie—work more by instinct and are looser with their approach—implement a successful workflow? It can be an intimidating subject.**

***RJF:*** Definitely intimidating. There is so much techie stuff out there that I'd advise diving in at the depth you're most comfortable. The implementation of a structured workflow usually comes to mind just after a hard lesson is learned. So, at least with my students, I emphasize a good naming convention of files and folders. It's a huge task to do this retroactively, but extremely beneficial. Also of primary importance is having at least one backup, preferably offsite. As with most tasks, if photographers practice these things from the beginning, it's much easier than if they change course after habits are established. So I encourage starting as soon as possible!

***AB:*** **What are your main concerns with ingesting media cards?**

***RJF:*** My primary concern would be that all files arrive at their destination without corruption. My secondary concern would be time. If I only have one card to download, I'll import directly to Lightroom. If I have more, which is usually the case, I'll use ImageIngesterPro,[15] with the same presets for all my settings. I have a standard USB/UDMA card reader, although there are faster options available. I always check the transfer log and visually check thumbnails before moving forward. ImageIngester is fantastic for lots of things, like automating tasks and working with multiple cards, especially for those who archive during ingestion.

***AB:*** **Do you ever use an ingestion tool with a checksum[16] feature?**

***RJF:*** I prefer to convert to DNG upon import, which has a built-in checksum.

## Good Workflow = Good Things

- **Good naming**
  Consistently use naming conventions and folder organization.
- **Organization**
  Consistently use catalog-based software, especially for high-volume shooting.
- **Parametric**
  Use a parametric[17] editing tool (like Lightroom) for raw captures and optimized image editing.
- **Hardware optimization**
  You need sufficient storage and processing power to do your work.
- **Proper color management**
  This is vital for image capture, editing and output and includes using a calibrated and profiled monitor.
- **Good metadata practices**
  Embed copyright, contact information, keywords and other IPTC data.
- **Data safety**
  Get into the habit of good backing up and archiving practices.

***AB:*** **Do you apply any metadata or keywords at this stage?**

***RJF:*** I have a basic metadata preset with copyright and contact information, which is a good starting point. After this, I'll enter any other project-specific information that can be applied.

***AB:*** **Do you have any tips on handling media cards, i.e., formatting, deleting, handling, protocols, etc.?**

***RJF:*** After viewing rendered previews, I'll trash the files from the card, but I won't format the card right away. I usually format it right before I shoot it again. This might be categorized as a superstition of sorts, but it may come in handy for that one time everything goes down—except for the cards. Otherwise, I do the standard protocols of flipping the shot card over in the card wallet and trying not to put them in my pockets or run them through the laundry (although this has happened).

***AB:*** **Tell us how you use the DNG format in your workflow.**

***RJF:*** I convert all of my DSLR files to DNG upon import. Again, many folks archive their proprietary raw files first, but for me, the redundancy is too much of a data space-hog.

***AB:*** **When do you rename? Where do you store the images?**

***RJF:*** I rename upon ingestion. I have several large parent-folders that correspond to large catalogs, and the subfolders and filenames all include dates, plus a one-word description. I find that's the best way to ensure I have unique filenames.

***AB:*** **What software do you use for all of this? Do you work with a single catalog, or do you create them "per project"?**

***RJF:*** Lightroom is my go-to catalog software. I'm somewhere in between the one-vs.-many catalog practice. I have one for personal stuff, one for jobs and one for teaching. These umbrellas are unique to each user, but I make the distinction, because I'd never have to cross-reference files among these three catalogs.

The reason to have the big catalogs is so you can easily search everything under that one umbrella. I use lots of "Collections" and "Smart Collections" to group images, and prefer this to closing and opening catalogs and importing multiple times. There are instances where I'll keep a devoted catalog to a project, because of speed or client viewing, but it'll ultimately get merged with a larger parent-catalog.

***AB:*** **What about alternative software? What else do you use besides Lightroom?**

***RJF:*** I use Capture One[18] with Phase files or when I'm shooting tethered. I've used Aperture, which has a pretty intuitive interface and [easy] learning curve, but I ended up missing some of my

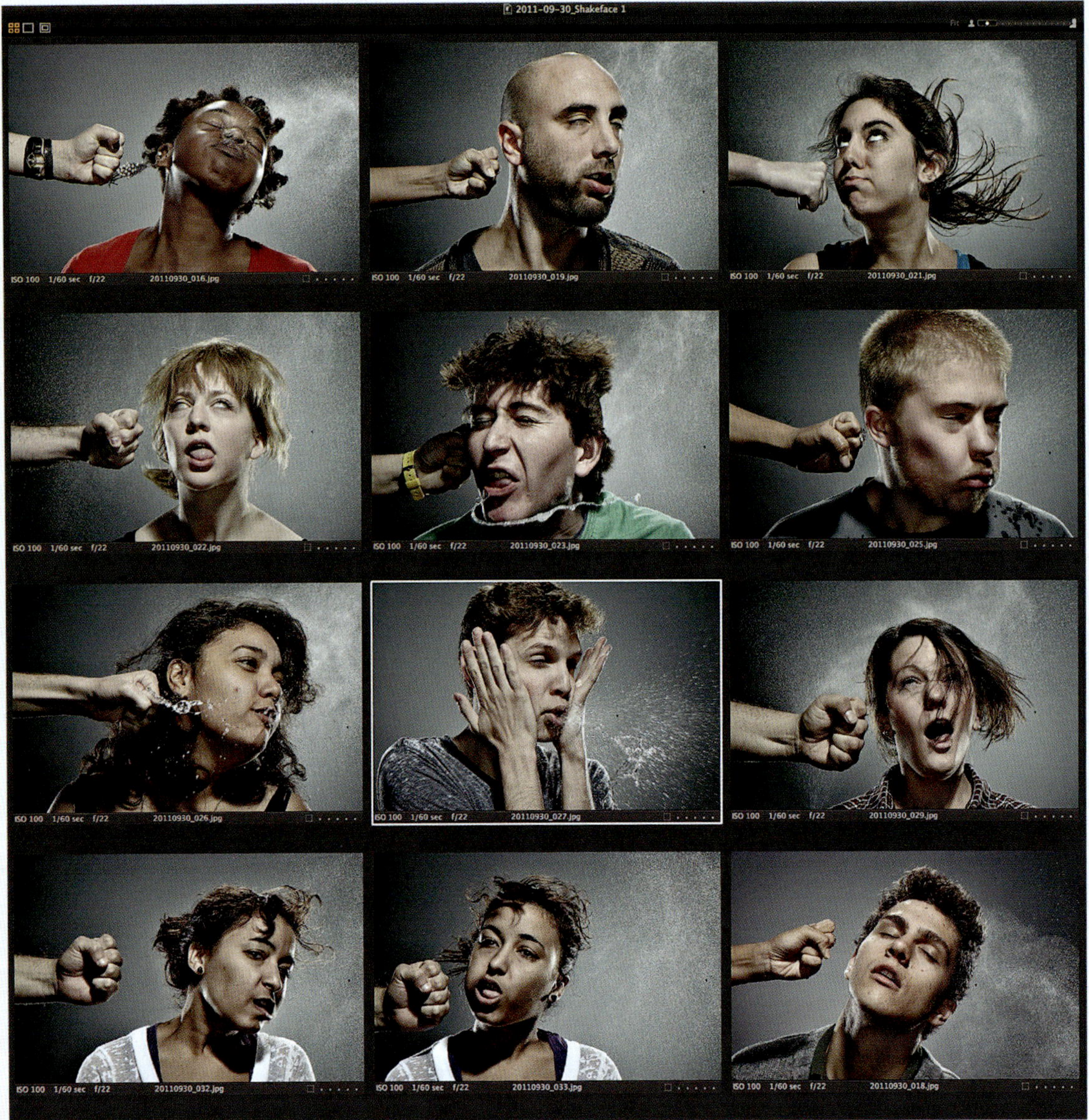


**FIGURE 3.6A**
Lightroom is Rachel's go–to catalog software. Her starting point is file organization, which establishes a great foundation for housing images; from there, she captures and ingests files, optimizes them, outputs them and backs them up.
IMAGES © RACHEL JEROME FERRARO, 2011.

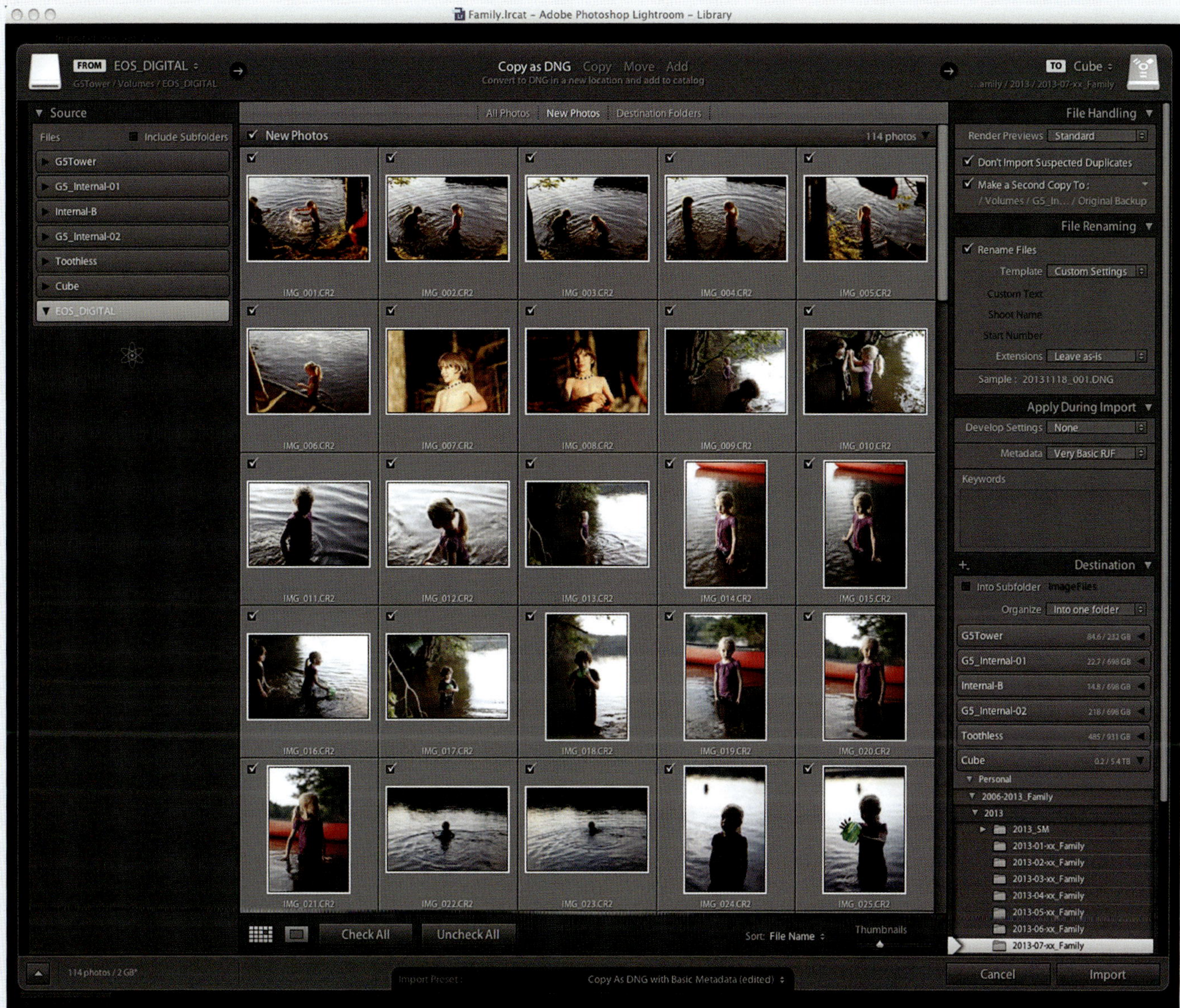


**FIGURE 3.6B**
Rachel converts all of her DSLR files to DNG upon import.
SCREENSHOT © RACHEL JEROME FERRARO, *INGESTING IMAGES*, 2011.

favorite features—like Lens Correction, Upright (for perspective correction) and Smart Previews. PhotoMechanic19 is the standout for keywording, captioning and quickly judging sharpness, which makes sense for most photojournalists.

***AB:* Once your initial set of images is downloaded, renamed and in a catalog, what do you do next?**

***RJF:*** I do an initial selection by rating or rejecting images and adding more keywords. (I rely heavily on Smart Collections generated by keywords, since that information can be saved with the file). The Develop process can be simple or complex at this point, but I'll start by optimizing in Lightroom. Most of my conceptual images take a trip to Photoshop after I optimize them, for compositing or intricate masking. Images that don't require these things can be handed over to a retoucher or client as an exported TIFF.

***AB:* When do you make your first backup?**

***RJF:*** Does a mirrored RAID count? My image files are duplicated automatically, via disk-mirroring on a LaCie[20] Cube. This drive is automatically backed up to an offsite server once a week, or manually if I need to back up more often.

***AB:* When you deliver files, do you stick with your naming system, or do you adopt the client's system?**

***RJF:*** I stick with my naming system, unless directed to do otherwise. If I do need to rename a file or two according to a client's delivery needs, I'll make virtual copies with a Copy Name, so that the file can easily be linked to the original. The exception to this would be when we're shooting tethered according to a client's specific naming convention, when I'll abandon my convention altogether and store the files according to date.

***AB:* When is a job "done"? Do you take any specific steps (cleanup, preparation for archiving, etc.) to wrap up the workflow?**

***RJ:*** I've just recently begun to delete my rejects after a second pass, if time allows. File sizes and catalog sizes are too big (for me) to skip that kind of housekeeping. Before archiving, I'll break up the archive folders into Blu-Ray-sized chunks, if necessary.

***AB:* After you've delivered a project, how do you archive it?**

***RJF:*** I have an internal Blu-Ray writer (in addition to the third backup of the working file). It isn't ideal to break up the image files on a large shoot, but it's the best method I've come up with before going to some other media. I archive my edited catalog with DNG image files. This might raise a red flag with folks who like to archive their virgin files, but I have a risk tolerance here, since I'm pushing the buttons myself. If I had a team of assistants, my workflow would include virgin file archiving.

***AB:* How do you work with hard drives? They're the backbone of so many things in image workflow.**

***RJF:*** My primary working drive is a mirrored RAID, which backs up to an offsite server. On location, I'll shoot/ingest to my internal drive and run ChronoSync[21] in the background to a LaCie Rugged drive (or two). I like flash drives if I need to deliver up to 64GB of files, but most often I deliver a handful of files via FTP. I also have a few legacy drives I spin up periodically, because even though I've migrated from them, they still work.

***AB:* One problematic thing about workflow for many up-and-coming photographers is the cost of hard drives, so they skimp and keep everything stuck on their laptops. Can you motivate them to adopt safer habits?**

***RJF:*** Thankfully, we can get 2TB hard drives for around $100, and the speed tradeoff on those is well worth it, for peace of mind. With data storage, the climate has never been more affordable, so it's a good time to be on the entry level. Granted, there will be an upgrade or two in their future, but it's no longer an overwhelmingly expensive way to start.

## The Importance of Image Workflow

***Candace Dobro:* How would you persuade photographers who aren't interested in workflow that it's important?**

***Andy Batt:*** I'd use math: Count the number of photos you took last year and the amount of space they took up (in gigs). Next, multiply that by five to figure out how many images you might shoot over the next five years, if you kept shooting at the same pace. Consider that as your photographic practice changes, you could theoretically double the volume of images you shoot each year. We're talking about a lot of images to keep track of! I just did a quick survey of my hard-drive kingdom, and I've got probably 18TB of images. They're all types of raw files, TIFFs, etc.—but just for comparison, if they were all 23MB raw files, that would be 820,624 images to manage. That would be sheer chaos if I didn't have some kind of system. As it is, it's managed chaos.

***CD:* In what specific ways can a good workflow help us keep track of all our images? Where does it begin?**

***AB:*** Image workflow isn't exciting, but it is incredibly important. It's like performing routine maintenance on your car: As long as you do it regularly, your car will keep running. If you ignore it and don't do your maintenance, the car will stop working. Ignoring workflow and just going with the default settings is the same as never changing your oil or checking your tires. Bad things will happen.

***CD:* What *is* the default behavior?**

***AB:*** The default behavior kicks in when you turn on your software and allow its pre-programmed settings to take control. The problem with this is that you aren't in control. The default behaviors themselves might not necessarily be bad choices, but if you don't understand them, you can end up in a bad spot.

I'll give you a "for instance." On a Mac, the default behavior for many photo programs is to download all of your images into the "Pictures" folder inside the "Home" folder. That's what happens when you let your operating system manage your images for you. I want to be in control of where my images are stored. If you don't know where your software is putting your images, how can you be sure that everything has been managed correctly?

***CD:* Folder hierarchy and organization are incredibly important!**

***AB:*** Yes, if you know where your files are supposed to be, it's easy to stay on top of them. In my studio, there's a lot of back-and-forth activity with clients and retouchers. A project can get complex with multiple copies of the raw files, "Work in Progress" (WIP) Photoshop files and final client-ready TIFFs. My image workflow keeps that all under control.

### A Year's Worth of Images

Take an average DNG file size of 23MB. Let's say that for a day's work we shoot 1,000 images, and that we shoot seven days in a month. In one year that's 84,000 images and almost 2TB of data.

- **1 File**: *23MB*
- **1 Shooting day**: 1,000 images = 23GB
- **1 Year of photography** (84 shooting days): 84,000 images = 1932GB or 1.89TB

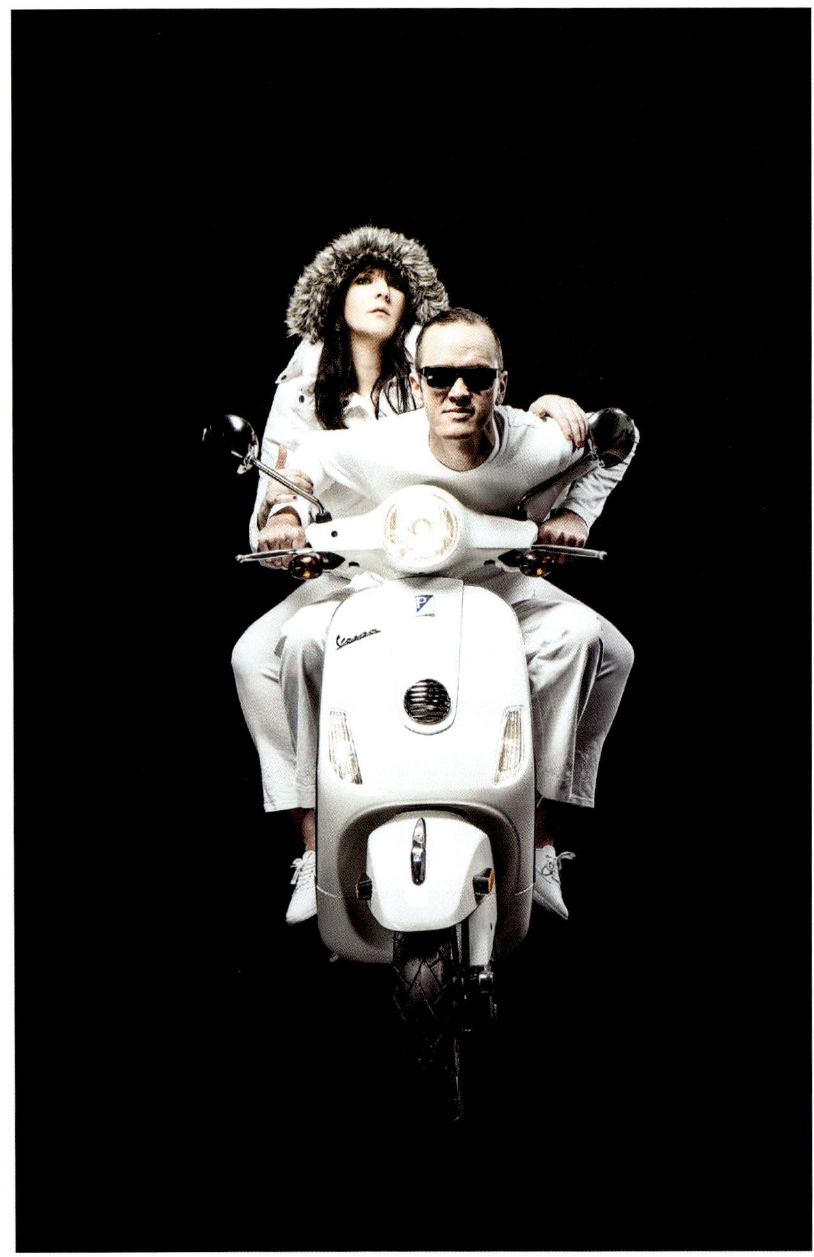

**FIGURE 3.7** Practicing good workflow is like performing routine maintenance on a scooter. As long as you do it regularly, your scooter will keep on running, but if you don't . . . bad things will happen.
IMAGE © ANDY BATT, *THE ACES—GOING PLACES*, 2013.

## Renaming

***Candace Dobro:* Renaming your images is a big part of image workflow. How do you handle renaming in your workflow?**

***Andy Batt:*** Renaming is a simple idea with large ramifications. The names we give our folders, raw files and processed images are all important. A good naming convention helps you find, sort and work with your images on any computer system, with any specific application. You need to have a standard naming convention that will apply to all the files and folders across your archive.

I've been using my system for a long time now, and it's proven itself to be a workhorse. The four biggest ideas to keep in mind when you're putting together a system are: flexibility, repeatability, simplicity and teachability. If you can satisfy those four elements, then any system you come up with should work well. That last term is more important than you might think. If you can teach a workflow successfully to someone, you have a good one.

My naming system extracts the shoot date from the raw files' metadata and puts it at the front, adds a couple of keywords in the middle and re-uses the original camera filename at the end for sequencing. You can use just about any imaging software that handles ingestion and organization tasks to do this.

***CD:* I use a similar method. For me, the ultimate goal is to have my files line up in a row and be neat, orderly and findable. I put the year first (20140125_CapeCod_DSC4103), because I don't want my Januarys from 2014 to be next to the Januarys from 2015—as they would be if I put the month first. When I look at my file hierarchy, I know exactly what's there, and it's very easy to track something down, even outside of Lightroom.**

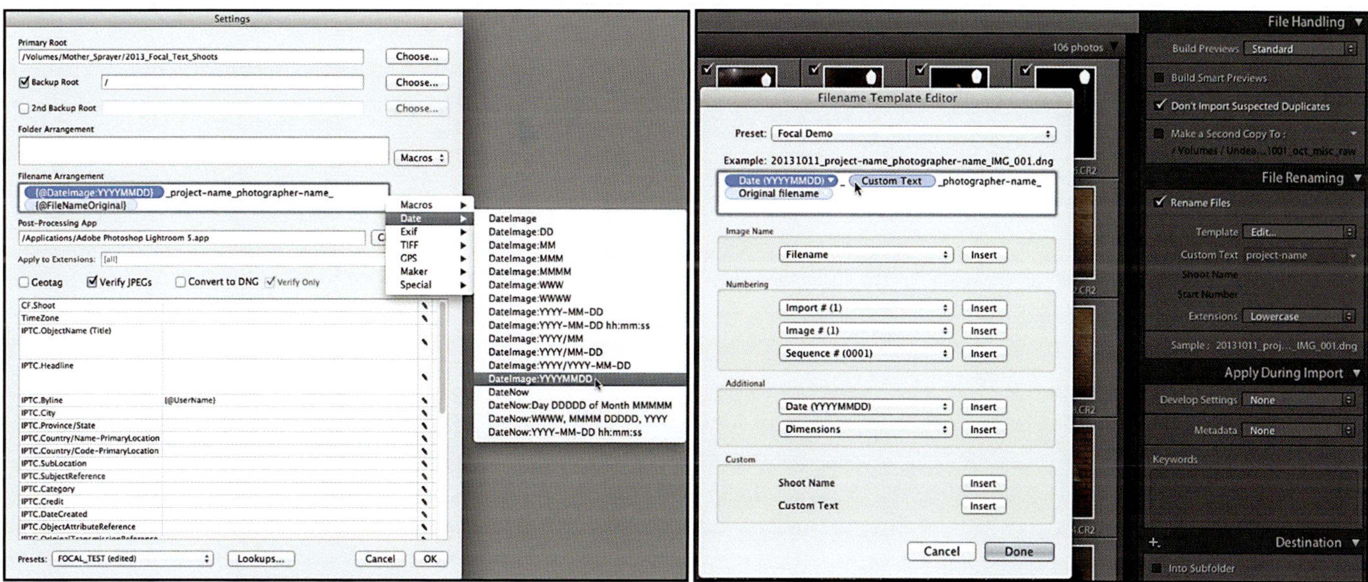


**FIGURE 3.8**
Ingestamatic and Lightroom are two different applications we use for renaming on ingesting. Both operate using "tokens" (placeholders) that allow you to create automatic routines that pull information from metadata—such as the shoot date—and incorporate it into the new filename. Ingestamatic has more intensive capabilities and works independent of your raw processor. Lightroom's tool is built in, and while it has fewer options, it's more streamlined.
SCREENSHOT © ANDY BATT, *CUSTOMIZED NAMING*, 2013.

***AB:*** That's a good point—the method you choose affects the way your library of images will show up on your computer. Some photographers use hierarchical naming, with a master folder for each regular client and different date-name project folders inside of it, so their library sorts alphabetically. There's nothing wrong with that, it just doesn't work for me. The trick is to consider the long-term ramifications of any system you adopt. Ask yourself how well organized it's going to be after five or ten years' worth of projects. How well will it hold up when it's handling hundreds of thousands of images?

***CD:* Can a naming system be too complicated?**

***AB:*** You can definitely cram too much information into a naming system. There is a limit to the number of characters you can put in a filename, but more importantly, the more complicated you make a system, the harder it is to keep using it over the long haul.

***CD:* You mentioned using keywords in the filename . . .**

***AB:*** Without using a keyword in the filename, you have a harder time knowing what project the image belongs to. Your images start with filenames that your camera provides, e.g., _DXA0150.CR2. Unless you open the image or look at the metadata, you can't tell much about the file from that name. By placing a breadcrumb of information—a keyword—in the filename, you can help yourself ID that image. We always choose something related to the job. For a project photographing NFL players sponsored by Verizon, our filenames look like this: **20130823_Verizon_NFL_playername_IMG4432.CR2**.

With a filename like this, I can tell at a glance when the photo was taken, the project it was for, and which NFL player we photographed. Your own name can be a useful keyword also, because it identifies the file as yours, so when the image leaves your hands, everyone else can recognize whose image it is. A good naming convention will add a few chunks of useful information to the name. You *can* stick with the original filenames, but if you do, you'll have two big issues to overcome: name repetition and rollover problems.

***CD:* Is there anything to avoid when renaming files and folders?**

***AB:*** The Mac OS will let you use anything as a filename, but other software can get really confused by certain characters. You never want to use characters like the dollar sign, slash or period, because in some operating systems, they can be interpreted as instructions. This might do bad things in your applications or be rejected and not work at all. You don't really want to use anything but underscores and hyphens.

***CD:* What do you do when a client requests a different naming scheme at the beginning of a project?**

***AB:*** Some clients have very specific file-naming requirements. I do my best to explain to them why that's a bad idea, but some clients are going to rename the files (no matter what I say), because they've been using the same internal naming convention for twenty years. In cases like this, the best thing to do is to come up with a compromise, because they're going to change my filenames anyway, and we might as well

## Name Repetition Problems—and Solutions

By default, every time you manually reset your camera's naming system, it starts at "0001," (e.g., _DXA0001.CR2) and you create another set of images with the same names. We want to avoid having multiple images with the same name, because that's just asking for trouble. You might delete one set thinking you had duplicated the same images! You can run into a similar problem when shooting with two identical cameras on the same project. By using the default naming system used by each camera, you could end up with two different images that are both named, for example, IMG_0089.NEF.

To resolve the naming-repetition problem, you need to develop a renaming convention using your ingestion software. By adding a date and keyword in front of the camera-assigned filename, you can establish a new, never-to-be-repeated filename. It's a little like giving your images a unique serial number. If you have two identical cameras, you can change the original camera filename via the camera's menu system.[22]

be in control of the way it ends up. We find a way to work with our clients; communication is an important part of successfully managing this element of the process.

I had a client who always uses "RM" or "RF" (for Rights Managed or Royalty Free), underscore and the photographer's initials to start all their filenames. We talked and came up with a compromise: **RM_AB_20130504_projectname_DXA4219.CR2**. We named our project *folder* the way we usually name it.

***CD:* So you compromised, rather than risking the possibility of having to change the name along the way—because once the client changes the filename, you won't be able to identify the files they're referring to.**

***AB:*** Right. If they come back to me in a year and want to access the original files, it will be difficult to find them if they threw out our filenames and switched them to match their own internal system—because nothing will match anymore. We've had clients who wanted to use absurd, long strings of product UPC codes as filenames. We showed them that we could put the UPC codes in as keywords and how they could find them in Adobe Bridge. That allowed us to stick with our naming style, and also gave them a better solution.

## The Master Folder Standard

***CD:* You shoot thousands of images per project and share multiple versions of your files with clients, art directors, retouchers, etc. Do you have a method for organizing all the files that relate to a project?**

***AB:*** To keep things nicely organized for client work, we create a master project folder (**Figure 3.9A**) that contains all the images and data related to a project. This includes image catalogs, raw image files, layered PSDs and flattened TIFFs—anything at all. There are two tasks at hand: to carry the naming convention from file naming over to the folder naming and to organize the hard drive that the master folder lives in.

***CD:* Details, please!**

### Rollover Naming Problems—and Solutions

After shooting a number of projects, your camera's file naming can easily reach something like IMG_9800.NEF. If you create 350 new images, you'll end up with a "rollover" problem: Images from IMG_9800.NEF through IMG_9999.NEF will occur chronologically before images IMG_0001.NEF through IMG_0150.NEF. When you sort your images by name, they won't match the shoot order. If you sort them by time, they'll be in the correct sequence, but the numbers will appear out of order. This can cause confusion, especially on bigger or multi-camera projects.

*There are two options to resolve this problem*:

1. Reset the camera's filename manually each time you begin a project, and then rename on import, preserving the original sequence number.
2. Rename the files on ingestion with a new sequence number.

In either case, ingest your media cards in the order they were shot, renaming as you go—or ingest all of the media cards without renaming, sort the images by shoot time and rename them all at once.

### Filenames: Good and Bad

- Good filename:
  **20141101_elite-client_bob-robertson_IMG4458.DNG**
- Bad filename:
  **20141101.E1|TE-(1!EnT_B()B-r()8e|2T$0|\|_I|\/|94458.DnG**

***AB:*** This part is easy. Since I did all the hard work when I named the files, all I have to do is carry over the same exact structure, with one exception: Swap out the sequence number (or camera-assigned original filename) for an ID word. In this case, for the top-level folder, I use the word "master": **20141101_elite-client_bob-robertson_master**.

If I'm working on a multi-day shoot, I keep everything contained inside a single master folder that's named for the first day of photography. Inside of this folder, I create as many subfolders as I need. If the project needs to be organized by separate days, scenes or shot numbers, I can customize as needed (**Figures 3.9A and 3.9B**). By using this simple step, you can assure that anything related to a project shares the same name.

I keep a separate Lightroom catalog of all the personal work I shoot. There are 121,450 images in it right now. The raw files are all organized into their own folders, separated by date. Anything shot in April 2010 will be in the folder **20100401_april_misc_raw**. I've been using this method for years, as a way of collecting and organizing my personal files.

## Make It So: The Key to Naming

When creating a naming convention and ingestion workflow, ask yourself these three questions:

1. Is it flexible enough to accommodate a variety of projects?
2. Is it easily repeatable—can I use it without a complex cheat sheet?
3. Is it simple enough teach to someone else?

Once you decide on a system, write it down in a short step-by-step guide. Not only will this force you to carefully consider your process, but it will also result in a valuable guide. You can hand it over to assistants/interns/digital techs—so they'll know exactly how you like things done.

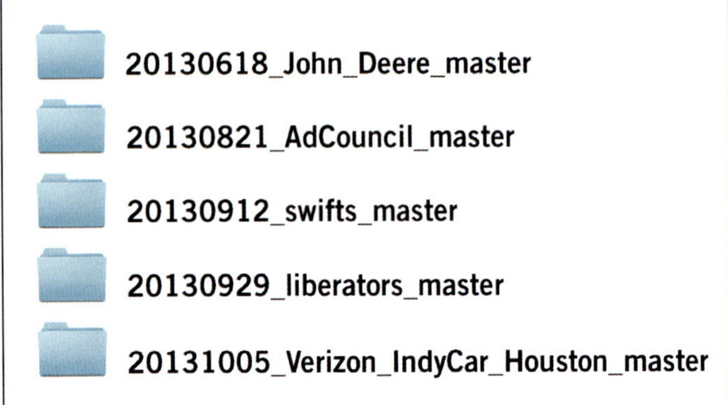


**FIGURE 3.9A** Here's a section of Andy's master folder list. When you use the YYYYMMDD format as your naming convention, files line up in an intuitive way. If you use a MMDDYYYY format instead, the files will be categorized by month, then year, which can be confusing when you're trying to locate an image chronologically. SCREENSHOT © ANDY BATT, *MASTER FOLDER*, 2013.

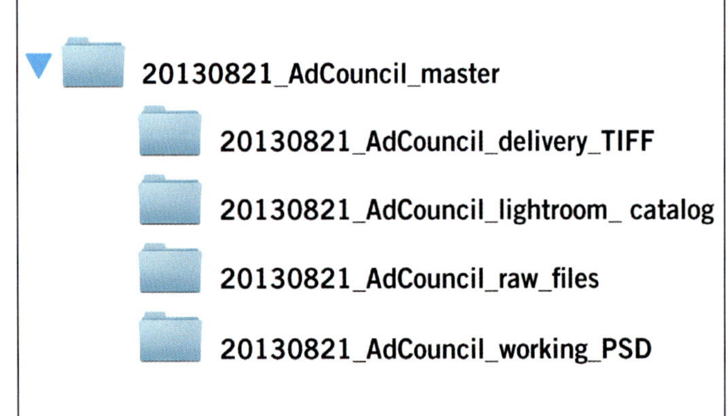


**FIGURE 3.9B**
This screenshot shows what's inside Andy's **20130821_AdCouncil_master** folder. Notice that he uses the same naming convention across an entire project. That way all of the folders, images and support files are associated—and easy to find. SCREENSHOT © ANDY BATT, *FOLDER STRUCTURE*, 2013.

## Ingestion and File Naming: Stewart Cohen

***Andy Batt:* As a commercial shooter, you have thousands and thousands of files to organize and store. How do you deal with all of them?**

***Stewart Cohen:*** Our workflow came about organically. With our first digital camera, we had to figure out a new workflow—where we were going to archive the files and how we were going to edit, tag and deliver them.

We still learn new things when new guys come to work here, since they come from different places and might throw some new ideas at us. We've hired freelance DITs on multiple occasions, thinking they may bring something new to the party, but at the end of the day they all agree that our system is great. It's built for speed. We developed it to do the work we need it to do: Get images from the camera into the computer—renamed with the IPTC metadata added—then on to edit and delivery.

***AB:* What kind of naming scheme do you use, and how far does it go back?**

**SC:** Every project starting from around 1985 uses the same naming scheme.

***AB:* Did you go back to retroactively apply this naming scheme?**

**SC:** No, we just continued using my original naming system. When I started out, my job number was the year—plus 101. That's how my career started. So my first job number was 85–101. Then the jobs continued, but the years changed. Now we're at 2136511. So the images would be named **2136511_0000 filename**. The image files get sequentially renamed on ingest. Before we deliver files, we organize them and put them into folders. It's pretty simple stuff—you've just got to find something that works for you, and then keep it.

***AB:* Sticking with it is probably the most important thing about having a system. Does this method make it easier to find specific images?**

**SC:** Our job numbers are the same as our filenames, so if we're looking for job 2136511, we can go back into our software and find out that

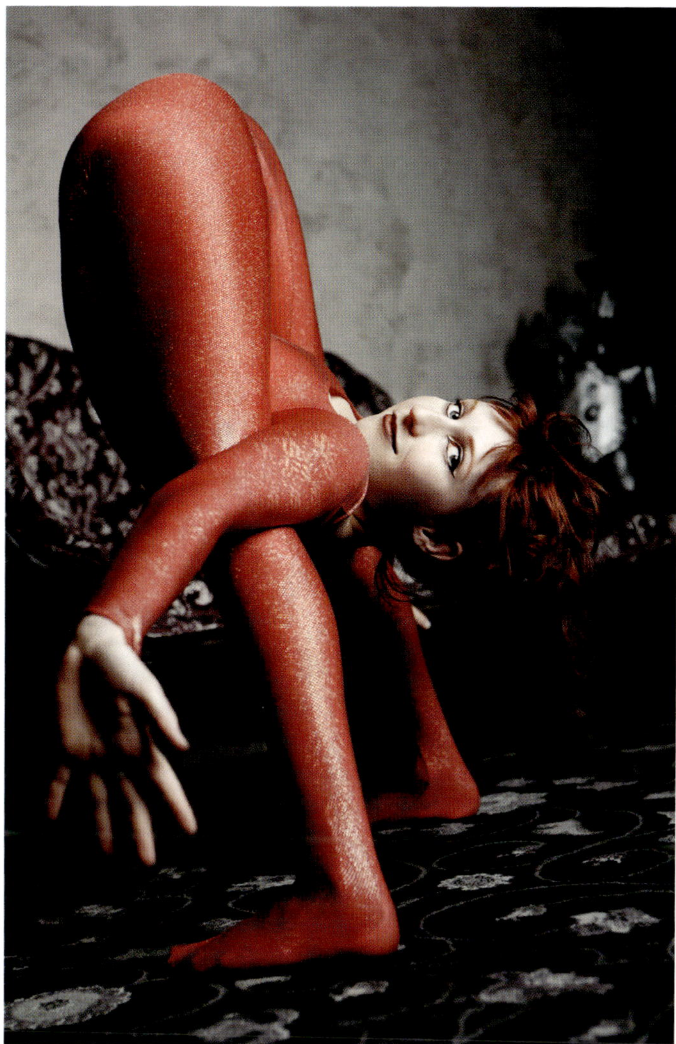

**FIGURE 3.10** Stewart captured this shot as part of a personal project titled "Chuck's People." He manages a multi-terabyte image archive and has been using a naming system that extends back to his pre-digital projects. The system has proved flexible enough (visual pun intended) to keep on working over the years.
IMAGE © STEWART COHEN, *BENDABLE BONNIE*, LOS ANGELES, CA, 2005.

the job was for client X; all the information is attached to it. Everything is tagged back to the job number. I also create a job number every month for the personal, non-job-related material I shoot.

The job number is labeled on our RAID. The name will include the job number and client name. If it's a job for Saatchi and Saatchi, for instance, the name will be **job number_client code_project-title**, e.g., **2136511_xxxx_SSX_Job Name**. That job number is assigned when the estimate becomes a job, and the job number will travel all the way through to delivery and archiving. Every file that relates to the job—scouting pictures and receipts, for instance—will have that job number attached to it.

## Backing Up and Archiving

***Candace Dobro:*** **What are your backup and archiving methods?**

***Andy Batt:*** Backing up and archiving are two sides of the same coin. From a workflow standpoint, the main difference is at what point in the overall workflow you create them. Backups occur when a project is active, while archiving is done when the project has been delivered to the client and everything is wrapped up.

You can make this process as complicated as you want to, but at its simplest, you just need a few hard drives and good backup software. A setup for backing up will cost you a few hundred dollars to implement, but that's pocket change compared to the expense of losing your image library.

***CD:*** **Can you describe your backup workflow on a typical job?**

***AB:*** On a project, my DIT will ingest the image files to the laptop (Copy 1). The files will immediately get backed up onto a portable RAID mirror (Copy 2) and then immediately get backed up onto another portable drive (Copy 3). These are verified backups using ChronoSync (backup software), so we know the data is safe. At the end of the shoot, I'll take one of the drives; my DIT (Digital Imaging Technician) will also take one. The laptop copy will be saved on his laptop until I'm able to transfer the project to my RAID at the studio.

***CD:*** **What about just using a RAID, since it mirrors the data?**

***AB:*** We use RAIDs, and they're great, but you run a risk when you depend on just a RAID.

***CD:*** **Why?**

***AB:*** You're always operating in the "what if" mode with your backups: You want to avoid fire, theft, loss, etc. If you have two copies in two separate locations—even if it's just in two different backpacks—you increase the odds that the same bad thing won't happen to both of them. If you just use a RAID and somebody spills iced tea on it, you'll lose *both* copies. Mirrored RAIDs protect you against drive failure, but not against the loss of the RAID from a fire or theft.

***CD:*** **How often do you back up a project?**

***AB:*** We back up at ingestion and then again periodically throughout the project—anytime we make a significant change, such as ingesting new images or making selects for the client. We use ChronoSync to back up the entire project folder so that our raw files, the Lightroom catalog and any sample files are identical on each drive.

***CD:*** **It sounds as though backing up is a continual process for you.**

***AB:*** Yes, it's a frequent and constant activity that takes place throughout the process of working on a project. The backups keep occurring until the project is over. Then we move to archiving it. Before I archive the project, I make sure I've gone through the files, checking them for proper naming, etc., and I do any necessary cleanup. I ask myself whether in five years I'll be upset because I left a big mess.

***CD:*** **For practical purposes, how is archiving different than backing up?**

***AB:*** The main difference is in the way the files are going to be used. I'm not going to access archived projects the same way I access active ones. My working drives are reused; we pack them up and take them with us on projects. My archive drives live at home and at the studio, are labeled differently and have a different purpose.

When archiving, I still make sure I have three copies: My first copy goes onto a working archive on a RAID tower. Then I copy the

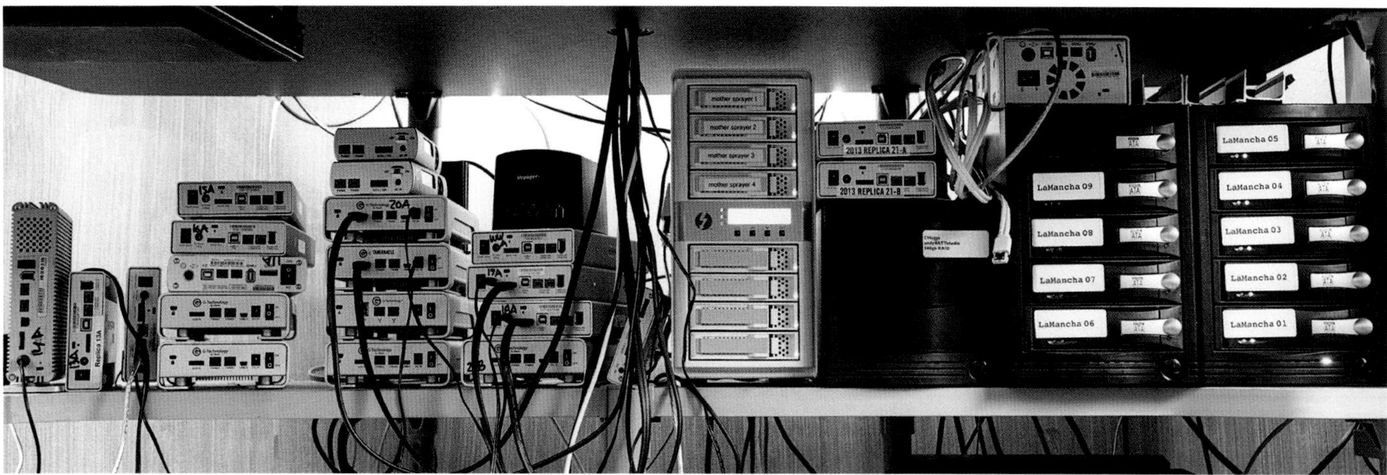


**FIGURE 3.11** Andy is like the rest of us; he just has a couple more hard drives. It might look confusing (okay, it does look confusing), but really, everything shown in this picture is a known quantity.
IMAGE © ANDY BATT, *CONTROLLED CHAOS*, 2013.

project to two separate archive drives. One of them goes into storage here at the studio and the other goes into storage at my house. That's not as good as sending one drive across the country, but at least the two drives are physically separated in two different places in Portland. I think it's worth mentioning that my archive drives are still just regular drives; I don't use proprietary hardware or software solutions for them.

***CD:*** **Do you use any Cloud-based storage?**

***AB:*** I use some Cloud-based storage, but not for archiving—yet. I'm waiting for the cost of a truly high-speed connection (one where I can quickly transfer 100GB of data) to come down. Drive space in the Cloud is fairly cheap, and it's getting cheaper. I think we're almost at a breakpoint where using it might be more efficient. I'm concerned about solely using the Cloud, because if the company goes out of business, I could lose access to my archive—maybe for good.

***CD:*** **What type of hardware do you use for your backups and archives?**

***AB:*** At the moment, we happen to be changing over hardware and the way we handle hard drives.

***CD:*** **What's your current hardware setup?**

***AB:*** Our immediate on-set backup is a matched pair of WiebeTech[23] portable RAID mirrors that use swappable laptop-size hard drives. Using RAIDS, we get the immediate safety of two copies with one backup. By using two of them, we have insurance—and since the drives are swappable and cheap, we can keep buying new ones as needed.

Our working drives are a pair of matched 2TB 7200RPM external drives. The projects get offloaded to these; one goes offsite and one gets left at the studio.

Our working RAID is a Thunderbolt RAID tower. Now we have a 9TB RAID Level 50, which is a super-safe, fast and redundant system. All active projects get offloaded to this, and it's where all processing and editing take place. Only four of the eight bays are filled right now, so I can expand the total size by another 9TB. For a while, I won't need to take anything off this tower, so it's also going to function as a working archive.

***CD:*** **You just can't spill coffee on it.**

***AB:*** Someday there will be an ultimate, sealed RAID that I can spill coffee on. I can depend on my RAID to protect me against drive failure. If you depend on a single drive, such as your laptop drive, then you're risking everything, because that drive will fail; it's a guarantee. The RAID is proof against a single drive taking down an archive.

A drive has mechanical parts, so with use and age, it will fail. Some people think they can solve this problem by using Solid-State Drives (SSDs), since they have no moving parts. The problem with SSDs is that they have electronic parts, and as electricity courses through their veins, it wears on their circuits. Over time, through heat and usage, the SSDs start developing faults. They're smart, so they'll map out the faults, but then they'll have a little bit less space and will be a little bit slower. This problem will repeat over and over until the SSD is not as fast as it used to be, and at some point, it'll just stop working.

***CD:*** **Drat! I thought SSDs were safe.**

## Your Drives Will Fail

Your hard drive is going to fail. The companies that build hard drives know it; now you know it, too. A hard drive has a limited mechanical life. Each drive has an average lifespan that the manufacturer calculates by performing simulated aging on a given drive and then extrapolating an average "Mean Time Between Failures" (Scheier, 2007). Even an SSD will eventually fail. Although they contain no mechanical parts, the movement of electrons through the circuits takes its toll (Mearian, 2013).

So how do you deal with drive mortality? By using a solid backup plan. If you follow the Rule of Three (read on for details), you'll be protected. When your backup plan is ready for your drive to fail, you will be, too.

***AB:*** The good news is that you'll probably finish using the drive before it dies.

***CD:*** **How do you set up ChronoSync?**

***AB:*** I use it to protect myself against my own stupidity. Any decent backup software will do a good job of this. I build my backup routines in ChronoSync, always setting it to verify and log any errors. Verification is an important thing; if you just drag and copy using the Mac OS Finder, it won't do anything other than compare file sizes and dates. Good software uses check summing to guarantee that the files are identical on the "inside." ChronoSync also does data comparison. It reads the source and destination folders and only copies over the files that have changed or are new, which is much faster in the long run than using the OS.

I run ChronoSync in "Mirror" mode and select "Move to Archive." The goal is to make the second drive look like exactly like the first. Anything that has been deleted from the first drive gets stashed in a new folder called "Archived Items," which protects me (from myself!) by hanging on to any deleted files. I prefer to run this manually.

***CD:*** **Why don't you put ChronoSync on automatic?**

***AB:*** Because I like to be in control of its behavior. For a while I ran it automatically, but that didn't work for me; I kept forgetting to boot up the right drives before leaving the office. I have so many hard drives and there's a lot of wear and tear if they're all running. In the summer, the heat can be intense.

***CD:*** **I don't do work at the same intensity that you do, so I automatically back up my files with SuperDuper![24] while I'm sleeping. It's very reassuring to know that my system is backing up on a regular basis.**

***AB:*** That's fine—as long as you check on it. You don't want to get a message that says, "Hey, we found a problem with your backup so we didn't do anything. Two weeks ago. And we're waiting for you to tell us what you want us to do."

***CD:*** **I get a daily message that reports whether the backup was successful or not.**

***AB:*** That's good. You want to always check in with automatic routines. Most of the backup software can also send you text or email messages; some software supports remote login, too.

## Back It Up—the Verified Rule of Three

***CD:*** **There are many types of backup storage—from self-managing standalone RAID towers that plug into your network with a full web interface to the humble portable bus-powered drive.[25] There are also many software options you can use, ranging from dragging-and-dropping (using the computer's operating system) to complex automatic systems that duplicate your files and keep a cache of older versions in case you need to go back in time. What are your thoughts on the various options?**

***AB:*** With any of these options, it comes down to the "Verified Rule of Three": Your images aren't safe until you have three copies of them—one of which is stored offsite—and know that those copies were made with software that verified their integrity. It doesn't matter whether you store images in the Cloud, on Blu-Ray discs or on hard drives. Be careful of using CDRs and DVDRs as backup media: In the short term they work fine, but the Library of Congress has tested them under simulated long-term conditions and found that they can fail (Shahani, Manns & Youket, 2005).

You can modify this rule by using the "Rule of Two," where your working copy is kept on a RAID 5 (or a Mirror, RAID 50, etc.—any RAID that incorporates redundancy) and you keep an offsite copy. The RAID will verify your data and protect you from drive failure, but not from user error.

***CD:*** **What about over the long term—what do we do about storage technologies that haven't been invented yet?**

***AB:*** You're talking about migration! If you're building an archive that you want to hang on to for a long time (as a legacy library for your heirs to inherit), you'll need to keep moving your data. You don't need to migrate your files onto every new storage media that comes out, but you do need to be aware of shifting storage standards. For a long time, tape backup was the standard for big companies—and it's still an option used today because it's cheap and reliable—but it's not easy to implement, and it's proprietary. Right now everybody is saying "Cloud, Cloud!" It seems like a good idea, but the Cloud's not the standard, yet.

For now, keeping your archive on hard drives is fine—with a big BUT. You can't depend on the 500MB drive you bought fifteen years ago (that was formatted with OS9) to be able to spin up and connect to your brand new Mac. A good maintenance plan is to spin up old hard drives and keep checking them—and to move your files to bigger and faster drives.

### The "Back-It-Up-Quick" Guide

- **What gets backed up**
  Your Master Project Folder, containing your raw files, processed files and catalog files—plus anything else related to the project.
- **When it gets backed up**
  Often! After you initially download and rename images, after an editing session and after processing out your final files . . . after making any significant change.
- **Where it gets backed up**
  Follow the Verified Rule of Three and keep a copy on three separate media. At least one should be stored offsite, and you get bonus points for using a mirrored RAID as one of the three.
- **How it gets backed up**
  We highly recommend using backup software that does verification—not the operating system.

# The Simply Paranoid DNG + Lightroom Workflow

Are you über-protective of your data and want the benefits of DNG? Then have we got a workflow for you! Yes, it's over the top, it's redundant and it's going to take time to implement—but your data will be protected from file corruption, theft, earthquake and fire! All it takes is nine steps (and some software and a few hard drives).

## What You'll Need

- **A media card reader**
- **Ingestion and catalog software**: We like Lightroom.
- **Backup software**: We like ChronoSync.[26]
- **Nine hard drives**: Labeled "Safety Drive A," "Safety Drive B," "Working Drive A," "Working Drive B," "Offsite Drive A," "Offsite Drive B," "Archive Drive A," "Archive Drive B" and "Archive Drive C." The safety, working and offsite drives can be smaller, less expensive drives. Ideally, they'll be sized to match the number and size of typical projects you're likely to work on concurrently. The archive drives should be as large as you can afford; multiple TB-sized ones (i.e., ≥2TB) would be best.
- **Optional**: Cloud storage, RAID

## Step One: Ingest Original Camera Files

Use any ingestion software to download your original raw files with a media card reader.

1. Don't rename your files or add any metadata at this stage.
2. Create a folder titled with the shoot date, keyword and the word "virgin_files," e.g., **YYYYMMDD_job-keyword_lastname_virgin_files**.
3. Ingest these to Safety Drive A. This is a short-term backup of your virgin camera-original files.

## Step Two: Safety Backup

Make an immediate, verified backup of your virgin files, using backup software.

1. Use "Mirror" mode to make an exact copy of the original.
2. Use "Data Verification" to make sure the backup is safe.
3. Make this backup on Safety Drive B. When you're finished, unplug it and put it in your office closet.

## Step Three: Create DNGs and Rename Your Files

Create a new Lightroom catalog and new DNG versions of your image files. While the images are being ingested, you'll automatically build preview images from the raw data as a visual check that there are no problems.

1. On Working Drive A, create a master folder and name it with the shoot date, keyword and the word "master": **YYYYMMDD_job-keyword_lastname_master**.
2. Inside of the master folder, create a DNG folder titled **YYYYMMDD_job-keyword_lastname_DNG**.
3. Inside the master folder, create a new Lightroom catalog, titled **YYYYMMDD_job-keyword_lastname_lightroom**.
4. Open up the new catalog and go to "Catalog Settings" to change the standard image preview size to 1,024 pixels.
5. Choose "Copy as DNG" and select the DNG folder you just created.
6. Use the upper left "From" button to find your images on Safety Drive A. In the top-middle, choose "Copy as DNG." In the upper right, use the "To" button, select "Other Destination . . ." and find the empty DNG folder you just created.
7. Change the "Build Previews" selection to "Standard."
8. In the Import Images dialog, set up your file renaming. We recommend this format: **YYYYMMDD_job-keyword_lastname_ORIGINAL-FILENAME**.
9. Enter basic metadata about yourself and the project.[27] Hit the "Import" button once it's done. Repeat the process for any remaining media cards.

After the all images are imported, wait for the progress bar to finish Building Standard Previews. If any of your preview images are corrupt or there was some kind of glitch, then try re-ingesting those specific files, a different card reader or different cables. If that doesn't work, then see the "Save Me" section earlier in this chapter.

### Step Four: Working Backup

Using your backup software, make an immediate backup of your new master folder onto Working Drive B.

1. Use Mirror mode to make an exact copy of the original.
2. Use Data Verification to make sure the backup is safe.

### Step Five: Editing Phase

A lot happens in the editing phase, and it all takes place in the Lightroom catalog on Working Drive A. In "Catalog Settings," uncheck the box (in the Metadata section) for "Automatically write changes into XMP." This speeds up your work by not forcing Lightroom to constantly save information outside the catalog.

1. Add keywords or other metadata.
2. Rate your images using Stars and Colors.
3. Organize your images using Collections.
4. Choose your "selects" and apply styles to your images.
5. After an editing session, select all the images in the catalog and choose "Save Metadata to Files" under the Metadata pull-down menu. This writes into the DNG file all of the information you just worked on.
6. Any time you make a significant change, run your backup software to update the copies on Working Drive B.

### Step Six: Offsite Backup

Now create Offsite Drive A and Offsite Drive B for offsite storage. The goal is to always rotate one of these drives somewhere besides your office—former salt mines are a good location.

Back up the master folder from Working Drive A to Offsite Drive A and take it off site.

1. The next day, back up the master folder from Working Drive A to Offsite Drive B.
2. Take Offsite Drive B home and swap it with Offsite Drive A.
3. Decide on an interval—perhaps weekly—and keep repeating this step until you're ready to archive the project.

### Step Seven—Optional: Duplicate Your Selects

Once you've chosen and processed your final images, store copies of the DNG and TIFF files on a server so they're available for quick access.

- **Local Option**: Make a copy to a standalone RAID mirror. The RAID gives you protection against drive failure.
- **Cloud Option**: Make a copy to any Cloud-based online storage. This will give you access from anywhere and keeps your critical files permanently offsite.
- **Travel Option**: Copy them to a USB3 flash drive or a bus-powered SSD to keep with you.

### Step Eight: Archive the Project

Once your project is finished, you'll archive it. We recommend using large multiple TB-sized drives for your archive, since they will contain multiple projects.

1. Make a verified backup of the master project folder from Working Drive A to Archive Drive A.
2. Make a verified backup of the master project folder from Archive Drive A to Archive Drives B and C.
3. Take Archive Drive B offsite. As you archive additional projects, rotate it with Archive Drive C.

### Step Nine: Blank the Workhorses

Once you have completely *and* utterly confirmed that your archive drives contain your entire project, it's time to erase it from the Safety, Working and Offsite drives—and prepare them for the next project.

1. Confirm your projects are on the archive drives.
2. Confirm it again.

3. Delete all related project folders from the Safety, Working and Offsite drives.

Is this system crazy? Yes. In fact, it's way over the top! Consider, though, the cost of losing a project, accidentally formatting a media card before downloading it or having your archive destroyed by fire or theft. Suddenly it's looking a little less crazy, isn't it?

# Digital Workflow

## Bruce Ely

***Andy Batt*: What digital workflow does *The Oregonian* use?**

***Bruce Ely:*** They use a system called "Merlin,"[28] and it's all keyworded.

***AB:* How do you interact with Merlin?**

***BE:*** The latest system is that we're in the field, we shoot, we download the images to our computer and then we upload. We're asked for a JPEG, usually full-sized, and then we FTP it to the server. That server is watched and copies over to Merlin, which I believe is a redundant system, so those pictures are well taken care of. Anything published in the paper goes into the system.

***Candace Dobro:* When do the files get processed?**

***BE:*** In the field, the photographers do the processing—in their cars, or wherever. We crop them and do a basic tone. We recently learned that Merlin will soon be the only way we're going to save pictures that are deemed publishable; the rest of them will go into the garbage.

Unlike Andy, I don't own any images I shoot for the newspaper; they own everything. I have an interest in keeping images I like, because I want to put them in my portfolio, keep a little scrapbook, whatever. I store these images separately for myself, and with the rest of them, I just do what they ask.

***CD:* So the unpublished images get deleted?**

***BE:*** Yeah, it was too expensive to store them.

***CD:* We're talking about many files. How many jobs do you shoot in a typical day?**

***BE:*** I shoot less than the typical *Oregonian* photographer, because I travel more frequently, which takes a lot of time. I shoot one to two assignments a day, but some people average three a day.

***AB:* Do you have an organizational system for your personal work?**

***BE:*** It's all date-based, and I separate the stuff I shot for work. I use **YYYYMMDD**—for example, "**20130706**." In Aperture, I have Smart Folders that look at the year—so I can quickly look at the 2013 folder and then type in "Christmas," or another keyword. I keep my keywording basic, just names, the people that are in the picture and then subjects, like "Christmas."

***AB:* How much metadata do you add to an image, and are you responsible for the captions?**

***BE:*** There are probably a dozen fields to fill out, mostly in templates. I'm responsible for the *accuracy* of the information in the caption. They're often rewritten.

***AB:* How do you back up your personal work at home?**

***BE:*** It's probably not as safe as I'd like it to be, but it is a pretty good system. I have a RAID setup—one of the LaCies. It has two bays in it, and they're mirrored.

***AB:* Then you have one RAID system that gives you two drives. Is everything on there?**

***BE:*** A year and a half ago, I made a copy of that RAID and stored it at my office, but that was a year and a half ago. I should do it again, because it's a year and a half's worth of stuff. The old data is totally safe, but I'm not very good at keeping up with that complex a backup system.

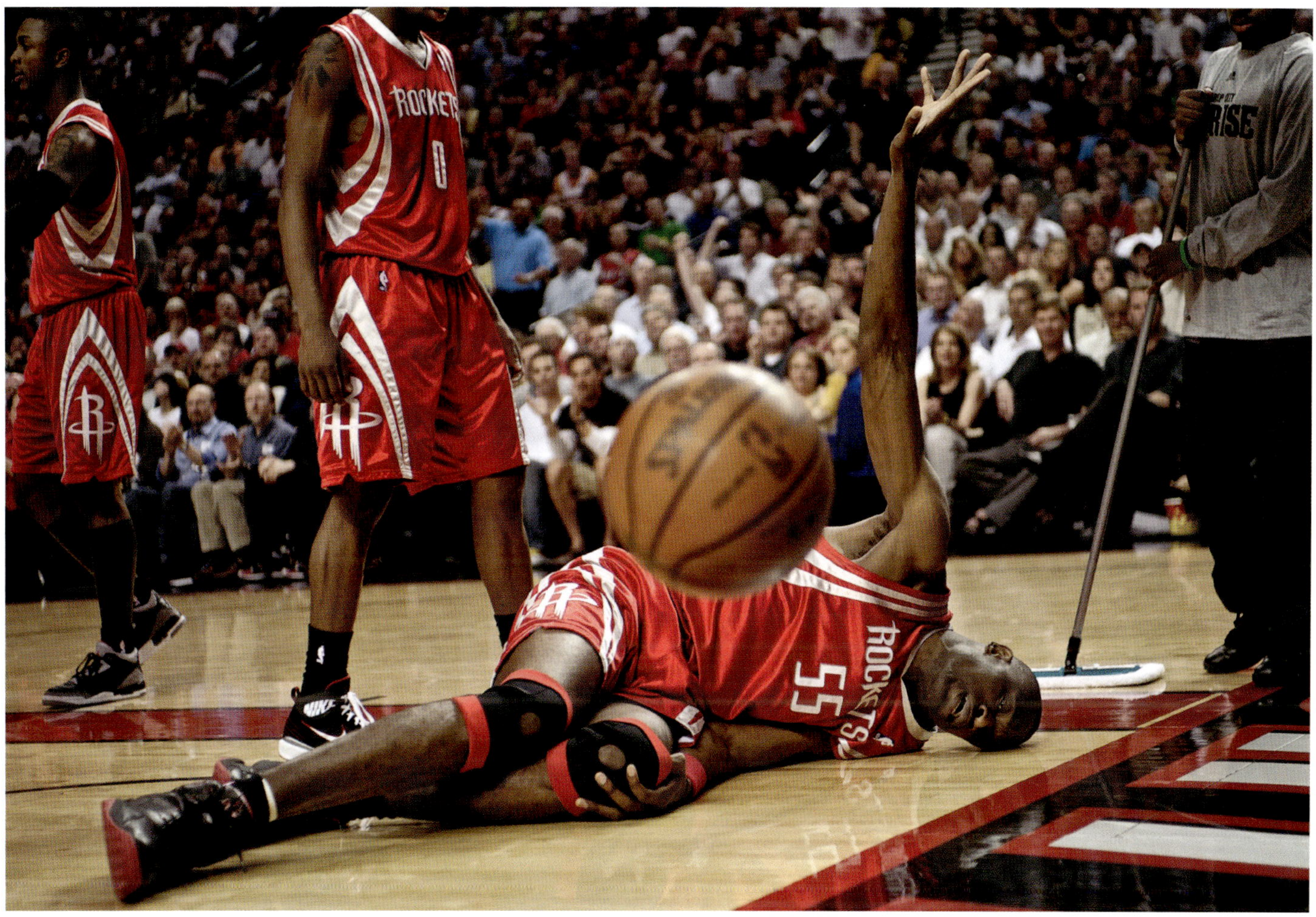


**FIGURE 3.12**
Houston's Dikembe Mutombo is injured as the Portland Trail Blazers face the Houston Rockets in Game 2 of the NBA playoffs on Tuesday, April 21, 2009 in Portland, Oregon at the Rose Garden.
IMAGE BY BRUCE ELY, *DIKEMBE MUTOMBO—GAME 2, 2009 PLAYOFFS,* © AND COURTESY OF *THE OREGONIAN*, 2009.

***AB:* Have you ever had a problem with image storage—something that changed the way you work?**

***BE:*** I shot a time lapse of a building being torn down and built across the street from *The Oregonian*—and thinking back on it, it's amazing that it worked at all, considering what I'm about to tell you. It was a two-year time lapse with multiple cameras. About every three months, I'd pull the card off the main camera, which was up the whole time, and download them.

I kept the files all in one place—in an Aperture library. At one point, I realized I had no idea where six months' worth of originals went. The master files had been deleted, and it was my fault. Thankfully, the Aperture library had built previews, and those preview images were plenty big for the project, so I was able to use them—and it worked. I got lucky.

***AB:* What did you do differently afterwards?**

***BE:*** I had been using a system where I would put the pictures in as "Referenced" files. As a result of that incident, I changed to "Managed" files, so now I can't get my hands on them.

***AB:* That's an interesting way to keep your work safe.**

***BE:*** On my laptop, day-to-day, I use "Managed," which hides the pictures internally to the program. I can delete them, but Aperture gives you big warning signs like, "Are you sure you want to do this? That would be stupid." Once I move the files to the hard drive for archiving, I make them "Referenced," because ten years from now, when Aperture disappears and some other program comes along, I don't want to have to figure out how to get those files out. When I put them in as "Referenced," they sit in folders with appropriate names. So I use both "Referenced" and "Managed" in my workflow.

***AB:* What a great example of creating a workflow to fit an individual style.**

## Toni Greaves

***Andy Batt:* You do many long-term projects, which makes me think about your process of downloading images, making them safe and keeping them stored and organized. You must have thousands and thousands of image files; what steps do you take to avoid chaos—and keep them in a usable form?**

***Toni Greaves:*** I have everything in Lightroom catalogs by year and keep separate catalogs for each project. For example, I will remember shooting a story in 2009, then I go to the "2009" folder and find the folder that's labeled **20090714_the name of the thing**.

I began shooting a project in India in 2009, so the Lightroom catalog was set up in 2009. When I started shooting the same subject again in 2012 and 2013, I moved that catalog into my folder for those years as they happened. Maybe people do it by having everything in a catalog for the year, but this way just makes sense to me.

***Candace Dobro:* You have more than one catalog?**

***TG:*** Yes. I need to be able to take that catalog from the India project, put it on my 1TB portable G-Tech[29] drive and take it with me when I return to India. My project on the nuns, for which I've had a lot of publicity, is always on my portable drive—as well as the other drives—because I'll often get requests for it when I'm on the other side of the world. In fact, I even have my main images from that collection stored in PhotoShelter.[30] When I shoot assignment work, though, I generally deliver the photos via PhotoShelter, which allows me to retrieve those images anywhere I am.

***AB:* When you're traveling and working on a project, do you wait until you get back to the hotel to download your images? How do you make sure your images are safe—so that if your laptop crashes, you don't lose a project?**

***TG:*** I don't keep any of my files on my laptop; I keep them on external hard drives. I usually carry two small hard drives (1TB or 750GB) and use one as my master and the second as a backup. Generally, at the end of each evening, I download files to the catalog.

If I'm staying overnight in a situation where I'm photographing, I don't do it then. I tend to be out shooting for a day or two and get immersed in things, then go back to the hostel or hotel where I'm staying. Then I'll have a day where I'm just sorting through the images. It helps me get a bit of space and clarity about the work, too. I never download on the fly, because it would take me away from the situation where I need to be. It's also not good for me to carry around a laptop and open it in front of people in some situations, because it wouldn't be safe—and sometimes, it's just not appropriate.

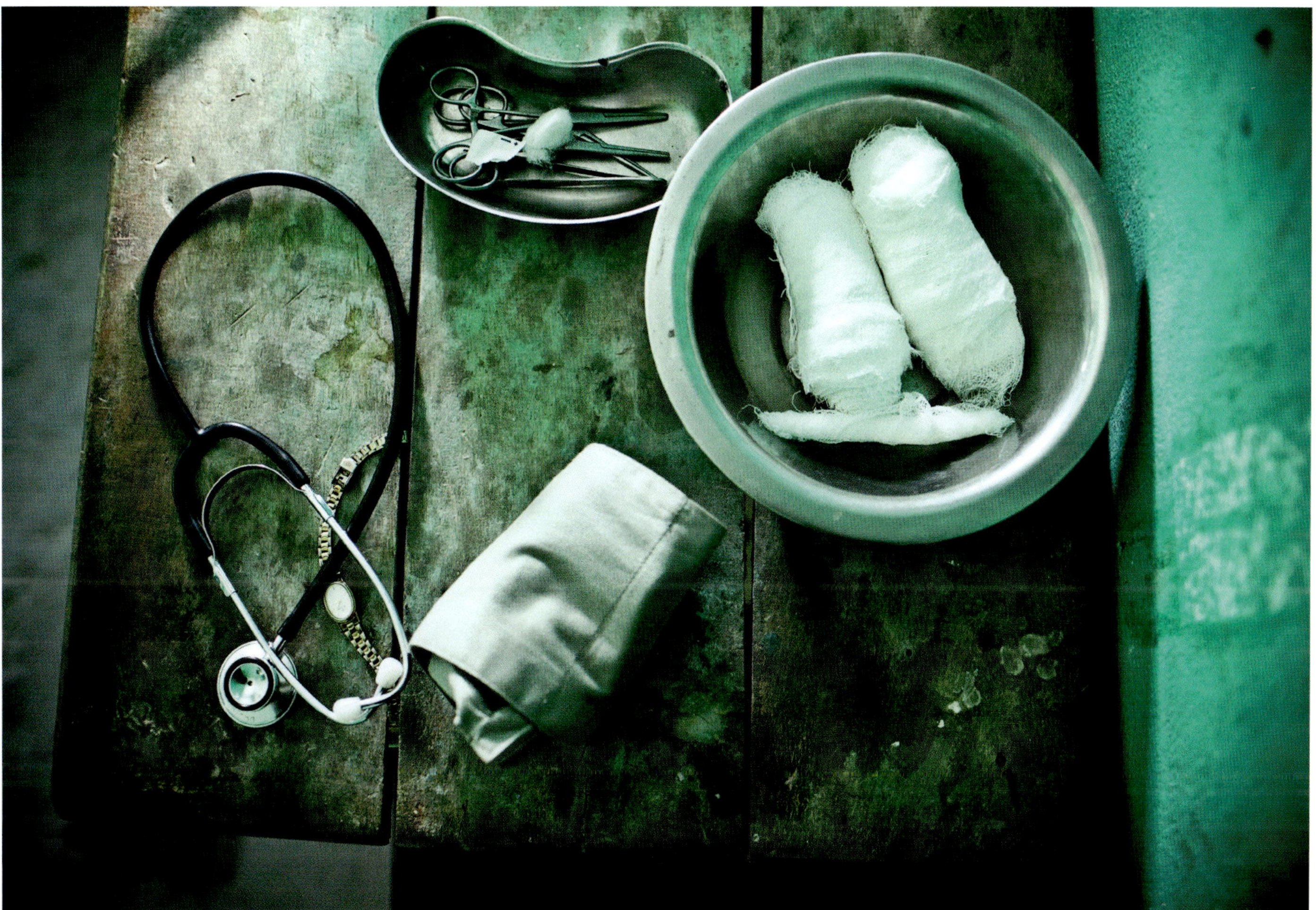

**FIGURE 3.13** The local sub–health post for Dikha Village has very basic facilities for health care, and no doctor. A hospital with one doctor is a five–hour walk away. IMAGE BY TONI GREAVES/GETTY IMAGES, *BIRTH IN RURAL NEPAL, THE MOST DANGEROUS DAY: BIRTH SUPPLIES, VILLAGE CLINIC,* © BILL & MELINDA GATES FOUNDATION, 2009.

## Sol Neelman

***Andy Batt:*** **Here's a scenario: You're out in a muddy field on a shoot, and you know you'll be making about 4,000 pictures in one day. How do you handle that?**

***Sol Neelman:*** Generally, I have enough compact flash cards to cover my entire shoot, so I'm not worried about downloading on the spot. (I download my images onto my laptop in an emergency, if I need to clean cards.[31]) When I'm out in the field, all I worry about is taking pictures. I'll go back to the hotel or home, download images onto my laptop and (if I'm smart) I'll back them up to an external hard drive that I pack separately in my suitcase.

I use PhotoMechanic to edit and tag images. I'll do a quick run through and delete anything I think I'll never, ever use. I might email select images to a client—or to magazines to say, "Hey, I just shot this Chuck Wagon Race, are you interested in these images?" I'll come

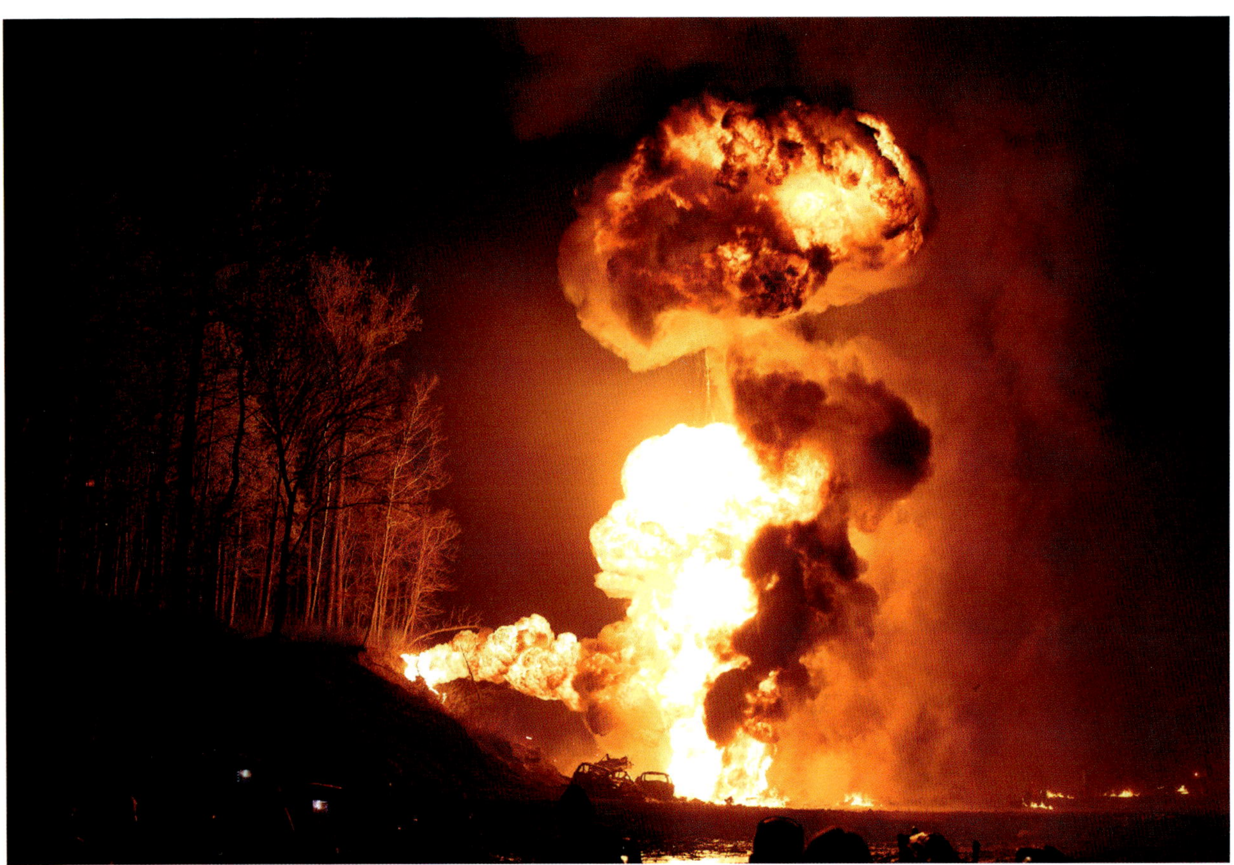

**FIGURE 3.14** Twice a year, gun lovers gather in rural Kentucky for a Machine Gun Shoot.[32] "The goal of the target practice," Sol says, "is to blow stuff up." IMAGE © SOL NEELMAN, *MACHINE GUN SHOOT*, 2011.

home, dump them onto my 3TB hard drive (which is marked for the year) and back that up to an external tower. Then I'll make a third copy. Right now, my third copy is in my basement, but after the year is over, I'll send it off to my friend in Montana—so I am officially archival. If something happens to my home, there's an offsite copy of all my images. It's super-cheap to do all this stuff now, and I sleep a lot better knowing that if my computer crashes, I haven't lost my career's work.

***AB:* Is there a consistent way you name your files?**

***SN:*** Yes. I have one hard drive dedicated for each year, and when I adjust images, I include in the metadata a basic title like "Electric Run."[33] If I'm shooting with a friend, I might add, "with Erika Schultz," plus the location and my name, copyright, etc. to the metadata. I'll dump that into a folder with a name that includes the date and a general title. Then I'll use PhotoMechanic to rename all my images with the date, the name of the shoot and a numerical sequence.

If I were doing corporate headshots for a bank, then I'd probably use a more creative title or a better file system, but since I may only shoot the Electric Run once in my lifetime, it's easy for me to find it using this method. The Mac makes it simple to search the database for things I've shot before.

## Kim Campbell

***Andy Batt:* Can you walk us through your studio's process of dealing with images?**

***Kim Campbell:*** We photograph digitally and shoot raw images onto a compact flash card. Next, we upload the card onto a server and into a folder called "INCOMING," with the client's full name on the folder—and an additional folder within that, with the session date. That means it needs to be processed, and my husband, Francisco, will begin taking care of them. He renames those images, puts them into Lightroom and edits them. He'll apply some color and exposure balancing and essentially make them a little prettier. Then he outputs them back into a folder within the dated session folder labeled "jpg-lr."

Every client folder is stored in an alphabetical archive for each year—by last name. For our clients who come back over the years, all of their sessions are really easy to find.

***Candace Dobro*: Do you make sure all of your photos have your copyright and contact information embedded?**

***KC:*** I do, especially for anything that's going out on the web. I'll also watermark most of our work, so it's easily identifiable.

***AB:* How do you name them, and do you use the same naming style for all projects?**

***KC:*** We do use the same naming style—we use last names. We put the session number into the filename, too, which has really been helpful, because we have clients who come repeatedly over the years. It's so nice to be able to identify whether it's their first, second or fourth session. A client's file will be labeled: **last name_S (for session) session number_frame number**.

***AB:* So it would be something like Smith_S1_5678.CR2?**

***KC:*** Yep. Those photos go into their dated session folder. All the raw files are in a folder called "raw." If we've photographed JPEGs as well, they'll go into a folder entitled "jpg." After being processed and edited, they're imported into ProSelect,[34] which is selling software. Have you heard of it?

***AB:* No, tell us about it.**

***KC:*** It's a sales tool for portrait photographers. You load your client's photos into it and create an album. Then you can quickly create a slideshow set to music to show to your clients. It's especially nice that, as you're going through the photos later, you can knock them into different categories—such as "Happy," "Neutral" or "Dislike"—so if people like a photo, you can accept it with an easy keystroke. You get rid of any they don't like by putting them in the "Dislike" category, and you can compare multiple photos on the screen. We can show clients what their pictures look like on a sample wall in different arrangements—or on the wall of their own home, if they've sent us a digital photo of their wall. It's a really effective sales tool.

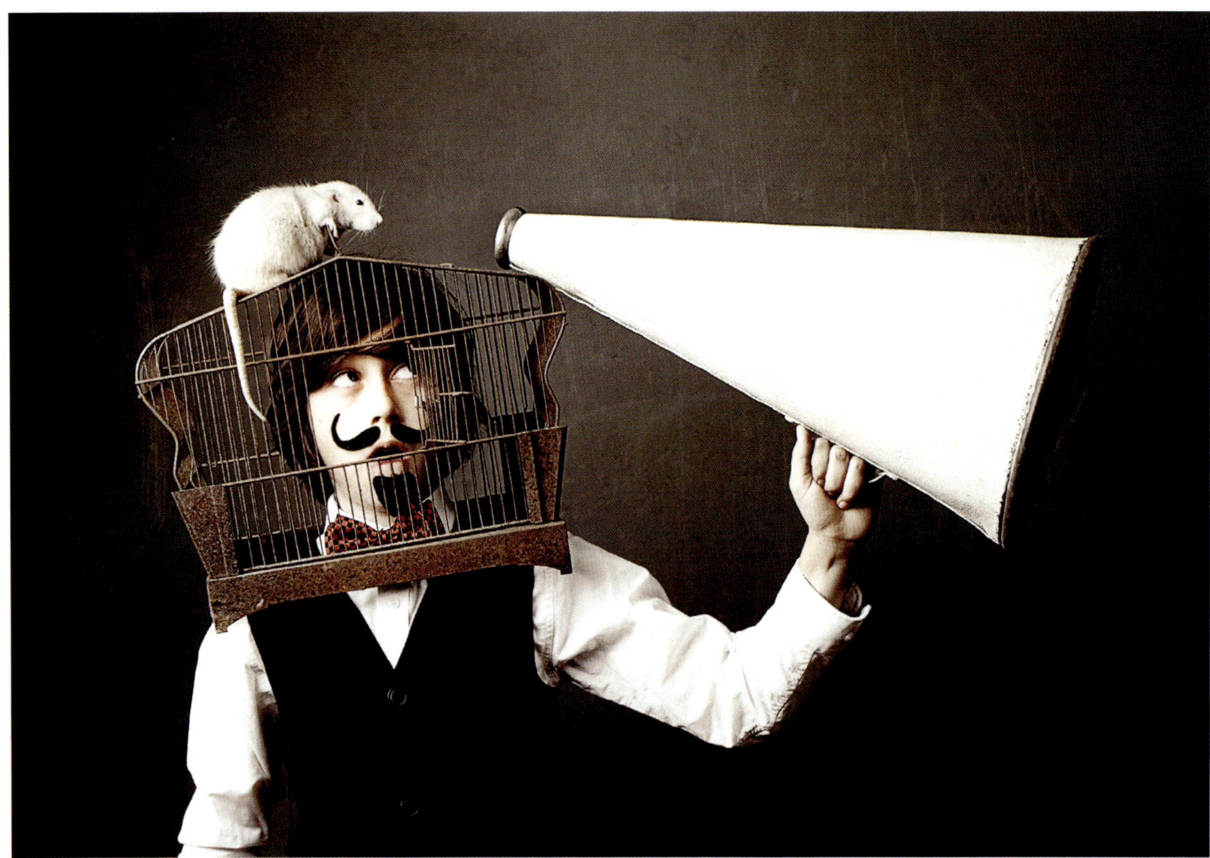

**FIGURE 3.15**
Kids are a great inspiration for Kim. She says, "Staying calm and light-hearted to ease stress and anxiety in my little—and big—clients is a number-one goal."
IMAGE © KIM CAMPBELL, *HELLO*, 2012.

***AB:* Do you create an album for each customer? Where does it get stored?**

***KC:*** It's a one-off—we have one ProSelect sales album for each client. This album is stored within the dated session folder in a folder entitled "orders," with any invoice PDFs that we've created. Our salesperson physically prints an order form for the client to take home. She also generates one for our in-house retoucher that has thumbnails (for cropping), quantity and the sizes the photos are ordered in.

***CD:* That sounds efficient.**

***KC:*** When we switched to digital, we had Tyler Havener at Resonant Media help us set up our system correctly from the beginning. Our whole system—however many hundreds of thousands of pictures we've taken—is really well organized, and that's been great. He also set up our servers, archive and our processing workflow for retouching. There are certain keystrokes for creating filters that look very film-like and for adding subtle Gaussian blurs and sharpening back the eyes. There are loads of built-in tools that really speed up the workflow. My photo retoucher also does work for another photographer, who doesn't have these custom actions set up, and she says it takes her a long time to achieve the same effects that she gets with us.

***CD:* How does your retoucher fit into the workflow?**

***KC:*** After a sale occurs for a final print, our in-house retoucher gets involved in taking the raw file and transforming it into a striking image. When our retoucher is going through her workflow, she'll begin by moving the client's folder to a main folder called "Production." She'll create several folders that are part of our workflow.

We keep all the client's data within that one named and dated folder, so any work someone does is in there and we can find it again. The photo retoucher saves everything—finished files she prints from and any digital files that are going to the client—in the folder called "output-ready." At that point, she's put the size and quantity into the filename. For example, at the end of **Smith_S1_5678.tif**, we'll put **Q** (for quantity) **2–5x7**. The whole name would be: **Smith_S1_5678_Q2–5x7.tif.**

***CD:* When you archive, do you save all the sizes?**

***KC:*** We save anything that we print from. (There are few extra steps in between, so if the retouching wasn't quite right, our retoucher can go back to a certain stage, but those are deleted once the client picks up the order.) We keep the raw files, the output-ready files and any of the client's orders.

***CD:* Smart; if a client wants to order more, they can. How is all of this stored?**

***KC:*** I don't even know how many terabytes we have in storage, but we do have quite a big server, plus we have backup storage drives—and there are duplicate copies of those. We rotate our backup drives every two weeks. That's a whole other ball game; I don't know exactly how much space we have on those, but I do know that we try to back up *every*thing.

My own personal computer always has two hard drives attached: one for all of my documents and photos (so my machine works faster, because I'm not storing those on my computer) and one for the Time Machine[35] drive. I swap out the Time Machine drive every couple of weeks, so I have two Time Machine drives saved at all times. We're really conscientious about not losing stuff.

***CD:* It sounds like you do all the things that people know they should do—but often don't. That's admirable.**

***KC:*** Well, we haven't had any huge losses, but we have had a couple of scares where somebody accidentally deleted a whole client folder off of the server—and once you delete something off the server, it disappears. Lucky for us, we had a backup drive to turn to.

***CD:* Is the server the only place where your files live, or do you have another way of backing up?**

***KC:*** We have the backup drives that back up the server. If somebody accidentally deletes something off the server, then we have to go back using software called Retrospect[36]—which is almost like Time Machine, but for the server. We need to know right when it happens, though, because people keep working, and then we have to go back—so we'd lose their work. We don't like to do that very often.

***CD:* Are all your archive files on the server, too, or at some point do you take them off and store them away for posterity?**

***KC:*** They're all still connected. We have them on separate hard drives. What we ended up doing, which is a good tip, is to store the archive per year. We have one main archive that goes up to 2009; it has four years in it. After that, we started splitting it off. Now we have an archive for 2010, 2011 and 2012. Once you know what year the session was, you just go to that archive.

***CD:* Do you use Lightroom (or another application) to keep track of your data, so you can search throughout all your files?**

***KC:*** No. We use the Finder on our Mac to find things. They're not keyworded, so files are only searchable by client name. That's why we name all the files.

***CD:* So that every file has the client name embedded into it.**

***KC:*** Right, and those get uploaded into the sales software. My salesperson sells the photos and outputs an order. Then she saves the digital version (a PDF) in the client file and makes the hardcopy print, which goes onto our retoucher's desk. Our retoucher uses it to retouch the images, and then she prints them. We do this all in-house (unless the images are really large, in which case we send them out) using an Epson 4900 Printer. Our photo retoucher saves everything in an "output-ready" folder for future reference. After the client picks up the order and everything is good, that folder goes into an alphabetized archive for the year. That's where it stays; that's it!

## A Plan

Now that you've heard about several different photographers' digital workflows, you have plenty of ideas for creating a plan. With a minor investment in hard drives, a few key pieces of software and time (to create templates and presets), you can develop a solid image workflow for downloading your raw images quickly, safely and redundantly. Keep in mind that any backup plan needs to be flexible, repeatable, simple and teachable. Remember, that last term is more important than you might think, because if you can write down a step-by-step plan and teach it successfully to someone else, you know your workflow is a good one.

### EXPLORATIONS

### Before and After

Before you began this chapter, you followed some sort of image workflow. It might have been a formal one that echoes the ideas in this chapter, or an informal one that was in place just to get things done.

**Step One: Your Old Workflow**
Write a description of your old image workflow, breaking it down into these areas:

- **Ingestion**: What tools and software did you use to get your images out of your camera and into the computer?
- **Renaming**: What naming style did you use, and when did you apply it?
- **Metadata**: What metadata did you add, and when did you apply it?
- **Folders**: Where did you store your work? How were your folders named and organized?
- **Backups**: What methods and gear did you use for making backups?
- **Archives**: How did you store images for the long term?

**Step Two: Improvements**
Based on your old workflow, write down at least one way of improving each of these areas:

- **Ingestion**
- **Renaming**
- **Metadata**
- **Folders**
- **Backups**
- **Archives**

Combining the successful elements of your old workflow with the improvements you came up with, write out a new, step-by-step workflow. Refer to The Simply Paranoid DNG + Lightroom Workflow if you need an over-the-top example.

**Bonus**: Teach your workflow to a fellow photographer. You'll know very quickly whether it makes sense.

## Notes

1 For a soup-to-nuts guide, we're particularly fond of *Digital Photography Best Practices and Workflow Handbook*, by Patricia Russotti and Richard Anderson.

2 Note that some raw file formats do have a compression-setting option.

3 TIFF, JPEG, PSD, PNG, etc.—any format other than the original raw file. The two exceptions are Photoshop Smart Objects, which embed the raw file, and DNG files, which are considered a universal raw format.

4 Note that "Preview" won't recognize a raw file and that manufacturers' proprietary applications turn a blind eye to anything other than their own file types.

5 Exchangeable image file format.

6 International Press and Telecommunications Council. The IPTC is a group responsible for the standardization of certain kinds of metadata, usually related to describing image content and image creator information.

7 Multiple applications can access and write data into the XMP file. For example, Adobe Bridge could have access and add metadata to an image that was ingested with Lightroom. In cases such as this, you would need to tell Lightroom to read the XMP data from the sidecar file, so it could update its internal database.

8 A note from Jodie Steen: Many people love the DNG format, but there are a lot of photographers out there that haven't adopted it. If you happen to like Capture One Pro, for example, then converting to DNG involves another step, more time and—if you choose to keep the proprietary raw format, too—double the files.

9 RAID stands for Redundant Array of Independent Disks. Think big, fast, safe storage. It's a way of combining individual hard drives together to protect data. The simplest version for safety is the Mirror RAID AKA RAID 1. With this setup, you see a single drive on your computer, but it's really two identical drives. RAID systems get more complex from there, incorporating various strategies that improve speed, allow for replacement drives to be swapped while the RAID is running, etc. Just remember that RAIDs won't protect you from user error!

10 Many photographers have accidentally done both of those things, and have still been able to download their images!

11 Somewhere in your camera's menu system is the "Format" command. Don't confuse it with the "Delete All" command, which is different.

12 Gremlins are responsible for anything that's not your fault. They are small, green and hard to see—but they are all around us.

13 PhotoRescue, DataRescue, www.datarescue.com/photorescue.

14 A *s'more* (shown in **Figure 3.5** stacked unassembled, left, and assembled, right) is a classic American confection that consists of a toasted marshmallow and a piece of chocolate sandwiched between two graham crackers.

15 ImageIngester and Ingestamatic come from independent software developer Marc Rochkind, www.basepath.com.

16 A checksum is a mathematically calculated number: An application can run a calculation on the original and then on the copy. If the data is exact, then the answers to the calculation will be exactly the same. If the data changed even a little bit, it will throw the calculation off and get alarm bells ringing. Calculating a checksum is much faster than examining the data bit by bit, and just as accurate. This all happens "behind the scenes." Currently, there is no way to get any information or perform a checksum manually. It's a trust exercise.

17 Parametric image editing is a term we use for the practice of working on raw files without making permanent changes to them. See *Chapter 5* for more information.

18 Capture One software by Phase One, http://www.phaseone.com/en/Imaging-Software.aspx.

19 Photo Mechanic by Camera Bits, www.camerabits.com.

20 LaCie, www.lacie.com.

21 ChronoSync by Econ Technologies, Inc., http://www.econtechnologies.com/pages/cs/chrono_overview.html.

22 Not all cameras allow custom filenames, so be sure to check your manual.

23 WiebeTech, www.wiebetech.com.

24 SuperDuper!, Shirt Pocket, http://www.shirt-pocket.com/SuperDuper/SuperDuperDescription.html.

25 This is a portable drive that's built around a laptop-sized spinning disk drive or flash memory drive. It draws its power from USB, Firewire or Thunderbolt ports.

26 You can also try SuperDuper!, Shirt Pocket, http://www.shirt-pocket.com/SuperDuper/SuperDuperDescription.html; Super Flexible File Synchronizer, Super Flexible Software Ltd. & Co., http://www.superflexible.com/ftp.htm; or SyncBack, 2BrightSparks, www.2brightsparks.com/syncback/.

27 Or, create a basic metadata template that you can re-use.

28 MerlinOne, www.merlinone.com.

29 G-Technology, a division of HGST, Inc., www.g-technology.com.

30 PhotoShelter, PhotoShelter, Inc., www.photoshelter.com.

31 Cleaning cards – downloading them and putting them back to work.

32 Knob Creek Gun Range, http://www.knobcreekrange.com/events/featured-events/machine-gun-shoot.

33 Electric Run, www.electricrun.com.

34 ProSelect Portrait Studio Software, TimeExposure, http://www.timeexposure.com/portraitstudiosoftware.php.

35 "Time Machine is the built-in backup feature of OS X that works with your Mac and an external drive (sold separately) or AirPort Time Capsule," Apple Inc., http://support.apple.com/kb/ht1427.

36 Retrospect®, Retrospect, Inc., www.retrospect.com–.

# CREATIVE CONTROL: USING YOUR LENS

Your lens is one of the most defining tools there is for crafting images. Both technically and aesthetically, the lens you choose literally shapes the light and expresses itself in your final image. If you change your lens, you'll change the way you create your image; you'll also affect the style of the image itself.

The goal is always to make the best images possible with the gear you have. By understanding the strengths, weaknesses and "personality" of your lenses, you'll be able use them to their full potential. There's a saying that roughly goes "You can make the world's best photo with the world's worst lens—and the world's worst photo with the best lens." Remember that the images you make through the lens are always more important than the lens itself. (Of course, if you're already making good photographs, a nicer lens can potentially make them even better!)

> ***We must come to know intuitively what our lenses and other equipment will do for us, and how to use them . . . the photographer who understands the concepts of lens function will certainly benefit in his work.***
>
> *—Ansel Adams (1980: 43)*

(Humor us and read the quote again; it's the essence of the entire chapter.)

# Each Lens Has Its Own Personality

Your goal is to understand the lens that you're using—how it shapes and changes your subject and what its strengths and weaknesses are. You can make stunning images with a 50mm lens, whether it's a $100 used Nikon *f*/1.8, a $725 version made by Carl Zeiss or a $1,600 Canon L-Series. If the only things we ever looked at were price tags and printed specifications, we might never understand that the used Nikon lens creates beautiful images, evenly sharp and with nice *bokeh*. There's more on bokeh later in the chapter.

With experience, you'll develop instincts about how a lens would look in any situation. These instincts will lead to good habits, like using a 35mm lens for landscape work, since it offers the right combination of a wide view with minimal distortion. Developing those habits means that you'll make decisions based on knowledge and experience. It'll also mean that you know your lens well enough to go against established patterns and achieve great results by using the "wrong" lens for a shot.

There are trends in photography that associate a certain focal-length lens with a style or subject. These are worth understanding, since they're based on real-world practices—but they aren't hard-and-fast rules. Lenses are tools, and it's up to you to know them—and use them—well.

## Your Lens Vs. Your Eyes

The way each of us sees the world is subjective. What we ultimately see is a construction of multiple glances at a scene, focused on numerous points and layered together—with peripheral vision added in. Any lens will be more objective than our eyes and brains, because it's only capable of creating an image inside the camera one way. Depending on the aperture and where it's focused, that image can be altered—but it will always deliver a unique view that's substantially different than the way we perceive the world.

It's easy to see how the ultra-wide, circular view of a *fisheye lens* is different from our vision. When it comes to lenses that are considered "normal,"[1] though, the difference is less obvious. *Normal lenses* seem to leave no trace on the image, and when we look through them or at the resulting images, we feel like we're getting an unvarnished view of the world. Even normal lenses have a slightly different magnification than our eyes, and we'll see a change in focus at all but the deepest F-stops. Even then, a normal lens will crop the rest of the world out, framing the scene and forcing us to see differently.

*Macro lenses* magnify the scene in front of us and show microscopic detail in a larger-than-life way. *Telephoto lenses* bring the faraway near and allow us to see elements that are hidden from the naked eye. *Super wide-angle lenses* shrink the world and capture more of it in a single frame than seems possible.

Lenses can change our experience of the world in more ways than by focal length. By manipulating apertures, we can change what's in and out of focus with any lens. The color and tone of a scene will differ, depending on the type of glass, number of coatings and design of the lens, so that a 50mm lens made by Carl Zeiss will have a separate look from one made by Nikon or Canon. Even shooting into the sun will add flare and lower the contrast, creating an image that's very different from the experience of viewing it in person.

***Andy:*** All of these differences are part of what makes photography exciting. Some science-fiction writers have created worlds where people have artificial eyes that take the place of a camera and can record exactly what they see. That goes against my idea of what's amazing about photography. I don't want to record the entire world in my view; I don't need a 180° view. What I want to do is edit the world (**Figure 4.2**). I want to see only a portion of it and use my tools to create an image that's unlike the one my eyes see.

## FEATURED PHOTOGRAPH

### The Limousine Shot

Sketch comedy group SWEAT hired Andy to create a poster photo for their marketing materials.

***Andy:*** First we did a series of shots in studio. We worked on a set with controlled lighting and did portraits and a group shot—all very nicely lit and styled. Before we started, the group let me know they had hired a Russian limousine for an hour, and that they wanted to get a celebrity-in-the-limo shot. I had a very short amount of time to put this idea together, while we were getting the in-studio shots done. Once the limo pulled into our lot, I had thirty minutes to dial in the lighting and camerawork, leaving thirty more to get the shot.

This was one of those moments where it was important to know—before I began shooting—what my equipment could do and what I could pull off in post-processing. I grabbed a Canon 14mm lens, knowing that I had to make a tiny space work for a group shot involving five people. That super-wide angle lens isn't a cheap one, and even though it was going to have that super-wide feel, I knew I wasn't going to get a lot of distortion or curvature in the corners. I also knew that with the Lens Correction tools in Lightroom, I could tweak the shot to make it slightly less wide-angle looking.

During the shoot, I deliberately placed the members of SWEAT in the sweet spot, where there would be less warping—keeping everyone away from the left and right edges of the frame. The lighting was achieved with two HMI[2] PAR lights, beaming in the windows from behind the subjects, and two Broncolor Lightbars[3] coming in through the car doors. The limo had colored accent lights that added a nightclub feeling, but the intensity of the lights was very low. The shutter would have needed to be extremely slow to capture them—too slow to work effectively handheld with five moving subjects. Since we had limited time to pull this off, I opted to add the color in post-production.

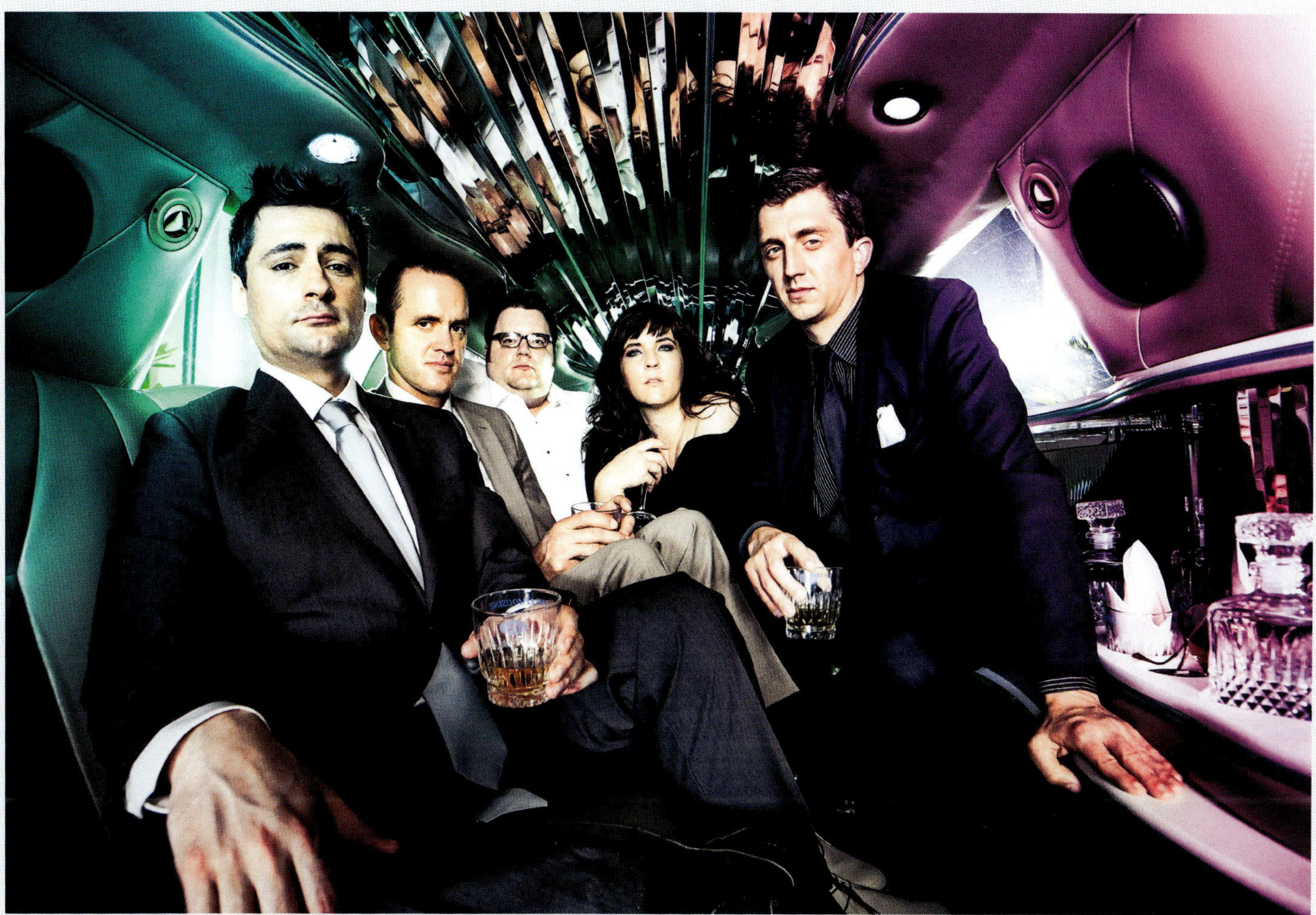

**FIGURE 4.1** Andy used a 14mm super-wide lens to make a tiny space work for a group of five.
IMAGE © ANDY BATT, *SWEAT SKETCH COMEDY GROUP*, 2011.

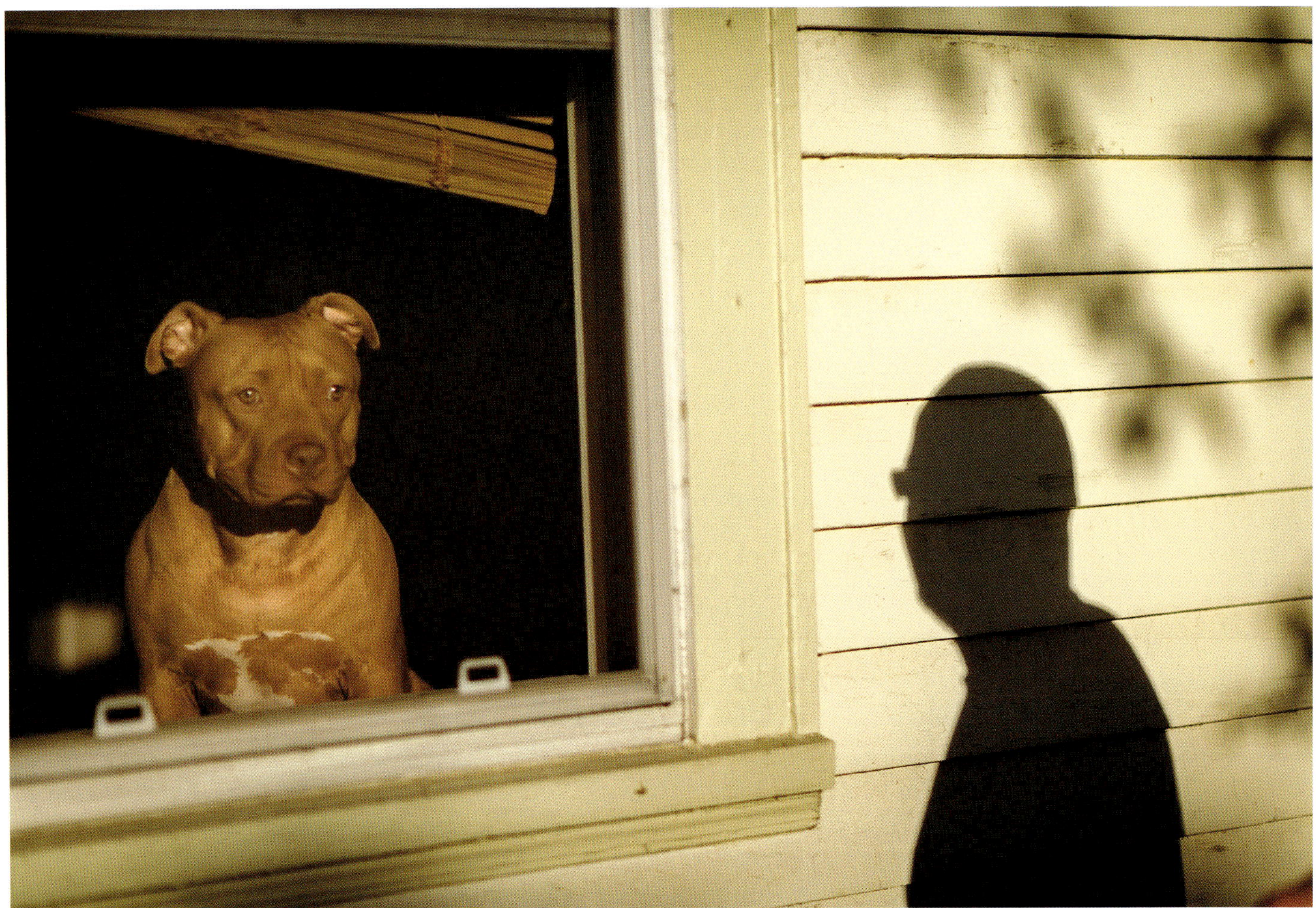

**FIGURE 4.2** The only thing in sharp focus is the texture of the paint in the shadow. Andy says, "If I had shot this image with a greater depth of field, it would have lost many of the qualities that I love about it. There's something painterly about the way Tonka is rendered, and I appreciate the fact that she's out of focus—and that the focus is clearest where the only other 'person' is in the frame." The camera was set at *f*/1.2 with an 85mm lens.
IMAGE © ANDY BATT, *TONKA AND THE SHADOW MAN*, 2005.

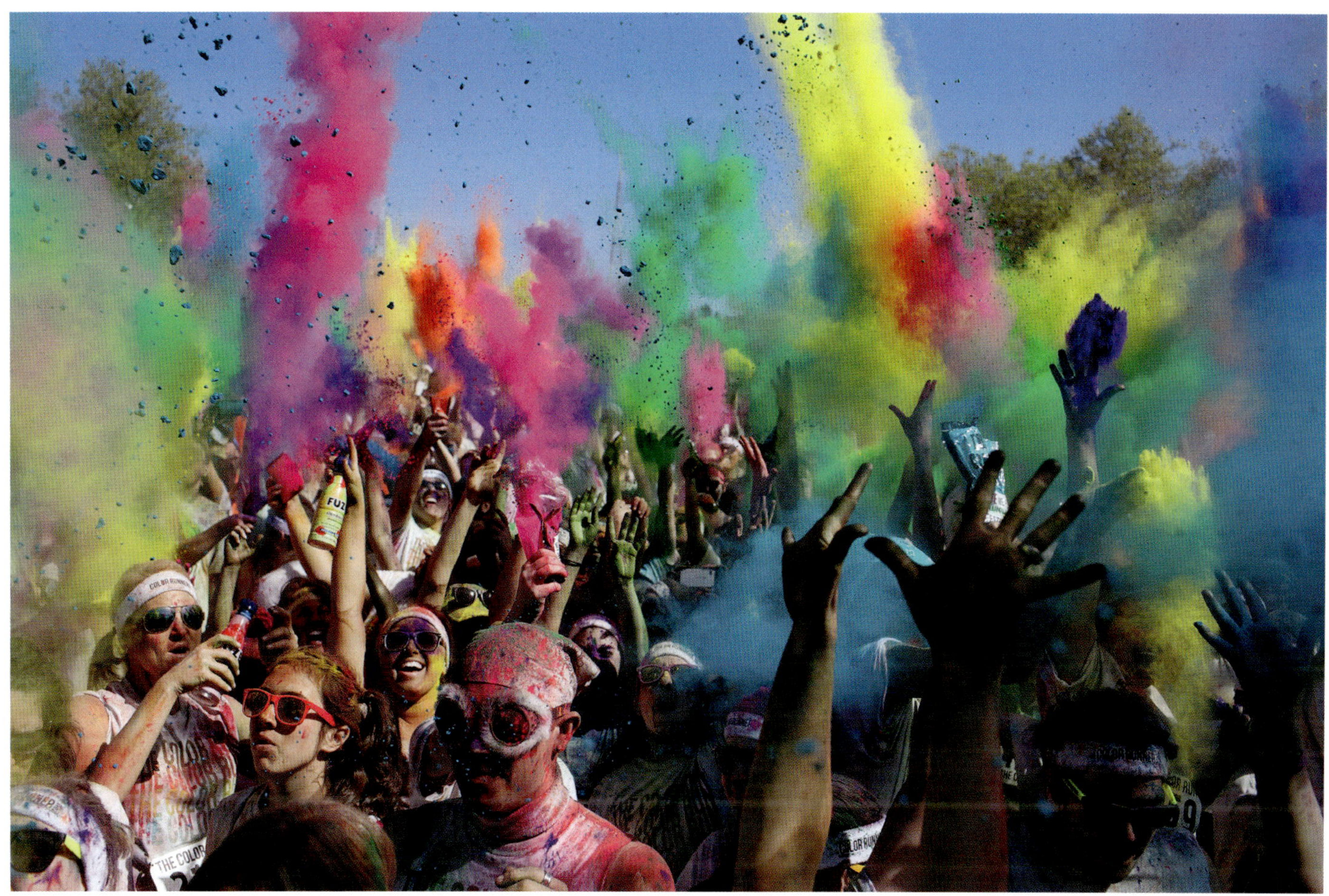

**FIGURE 4.3** The Color Run™[4] more resembles a Hindu Holi festival of color than a 5K fun run. "It's not about the run," said photographer Erika Schultz, Sol's colleague. "I think it's about being a human canvas. Your body becomes art. You become art, a big impressionistic human painting."
IMAGE © SOL NEELMAN, *THE COLOR RUN*, PRINTED IN *MARIE CLAIRE*, 2013.

---

## Travel Gear: Sol Neelman

***Andy Batt:*** **What kind of gear travels with you?**

***Sol Neelman:*** I have my Think Tank® backpack full of gear and am pretty ready to rock and roll at any point. In my bag, there's a Canon 1-DX and a 1-Ds Mark III camera body. I have a 35mm *f*/1.4, a 50mm *f*/1.2 and a 70–200mm *f*/2.8. I also have a 28mm *f*/2 lens that I throw in, but never use. My favorite sports lens is my 35mm 1.4, which no one thinks of when it comes to sports. I'm not trying to make 400mm *f*/2.8 long-glass tight images. I want layers; I want moments; I want a messy picture (**Figure 4.3**).

## Choose Your Lens

### Cartier-Bresson: A Classic, 50mm Prime Lens

Henri Cartier-Bresson, of Magnum Photo fame, shot with a Leica rangefinder and a 50mm lens, because through it, the world looked natural to him; it was a lens that didn't change his perception of the world. The idea of choosing a lens to minimize its effect on your photograph is a powerful one. It's a very deliberate action that we should consider every time we choose a prime lens or set a zoom lens to a particular focal length.

Cartier-Bresson's 50mm is the classic example of a *prime*, or *fixed focal-length lens.* It's the anti-zoom lens, because you have only a single focal length to work with. That might seem like a negative at first, but it's not. When you work with a prime lens, you're forced into developing a good photographic habit: If you want to get closer to your subject, you're required to walk towards it, and if you want to be farther from your subject, you're required to walk away from it. A prime lens is sometimes called a "shoe leather zoom." Using a prime lens makes you an active participant in the process and encourages you to discover new relationships when framing your shots.

By sticking with a single prime lens, you learn about its qualities—what the depth of field looks like in post and which characteristics it lends to your images. Simply put, when you practice for a long time with a prime lens, you become comfortable with it. A prime lens allows you to keep it simple and concentrate on making photographs.

Biographer Pierre Assouline explains how Henri Cartier-Bresson worked with his lenses (2013: 245):

> ***The tools for the job were one or two Leicas, M4 or 3G, their chrome covered with black tape, usually fitted with a 50mm Elmar, the lens that doesn't cheat because it allows the photographer to view the world at eye level. The Cartier-Bresson distance was, of course, never too near or too far. In his bag, although they were rarely used, were a 90mm lens to capture the foreground of landscapes, and a wide-angle 35mm lens. He generally avoided using the former because it distanced him too much from the subject, and the latter because it could jeopardize the balance between forms.***

### Winogrand: A 28mm Wide-Angle Prime Lens

Garry Winogrand, known for his long career as one of the best NYC street photographers, shot much of his work with a 28mm, because it let him work in close proximity to his subjects and gave him the unique angle of view afforded by wide-angle lenses. He used a prime lens in much the same way Cartier-Bresson did—as a fixed point of view that he felt was the correct lens through which to see the world.

> ***Ideally, I wish I had a lens that took in my whole angle of vision, without mechanical distortion—that's the headache with these things. Ideally, that would probably be the most interesting to work with. The 28[mm] is probably where the mechanical distortion is least limiting—much less limiting than a 21. It's closest to the angle of attention. It's pretty close to at least my angle of attention. Probably the 21 is more so, but it's just extremely limiting. You have to use it very carefully.***
>
> ***—Garry Winogrand (Hagen, 1977: 10)***

### What About Zoom Lenses?

Many of us purchased a zoom lens with our first camera. Andy's first one was mounted to a 1980s Pentax SLR. It seemed like a good idea at the time, since it was the equivalent of an entire camera bag full of lenses. The one he bought was probably a 24–150mm "miracle" lens (more about those later in this chapter).

"You get what you pay for" is an economic truth that applies to zoom lenses. The bigger the zoom range, the more design compromises that need to be contended with. Unlike prime lenses, zoom lenses have multiple, moving optical elements. The more elements, the more internal flare there will be; and the more those elements need to move around, the more complicated the design. One of the

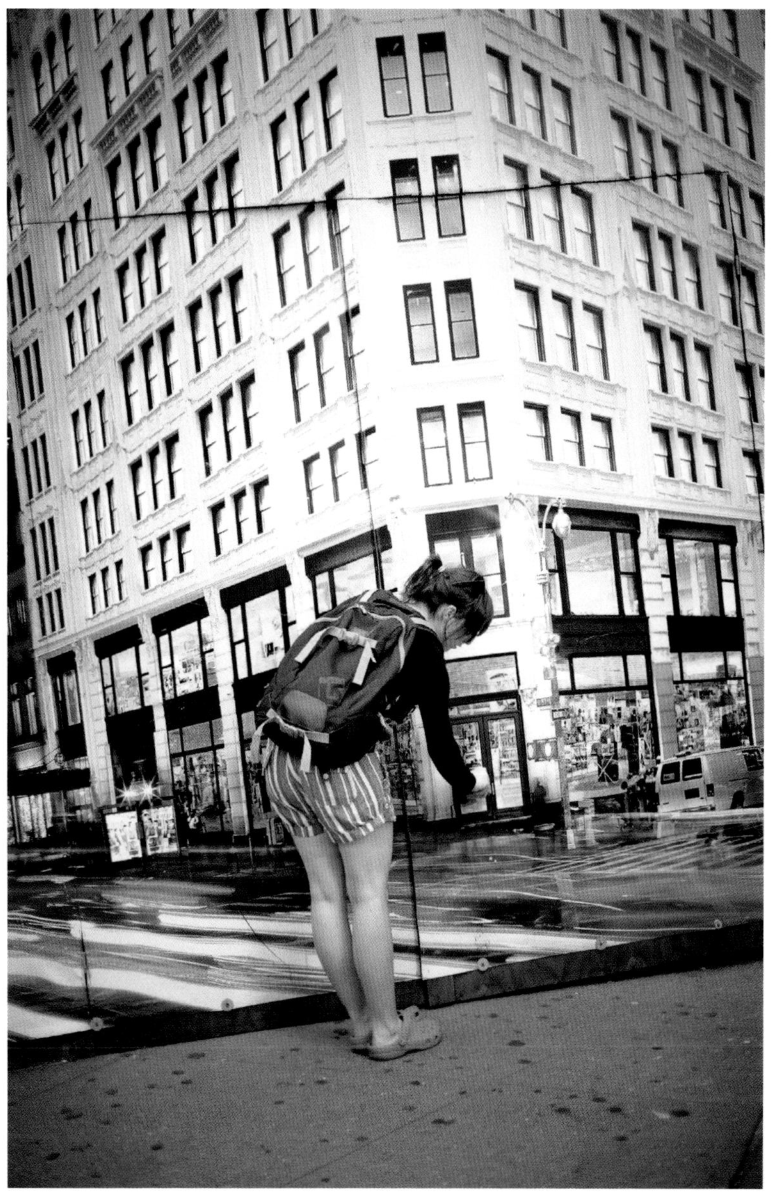

**FIGURE 4.4** Andy has a few different 50mm lenses and says, "For street photography, I prefer the Canon 50mm *f*/1.4. It's an unobtrusive lens that most people don't pay attention to; it's an excellent all-around lens. You can shoot close-ups and wide views just by moving your feet."
IMAGE © ANDY BATT, *NYC—NOT TO SCALE*, 2009.

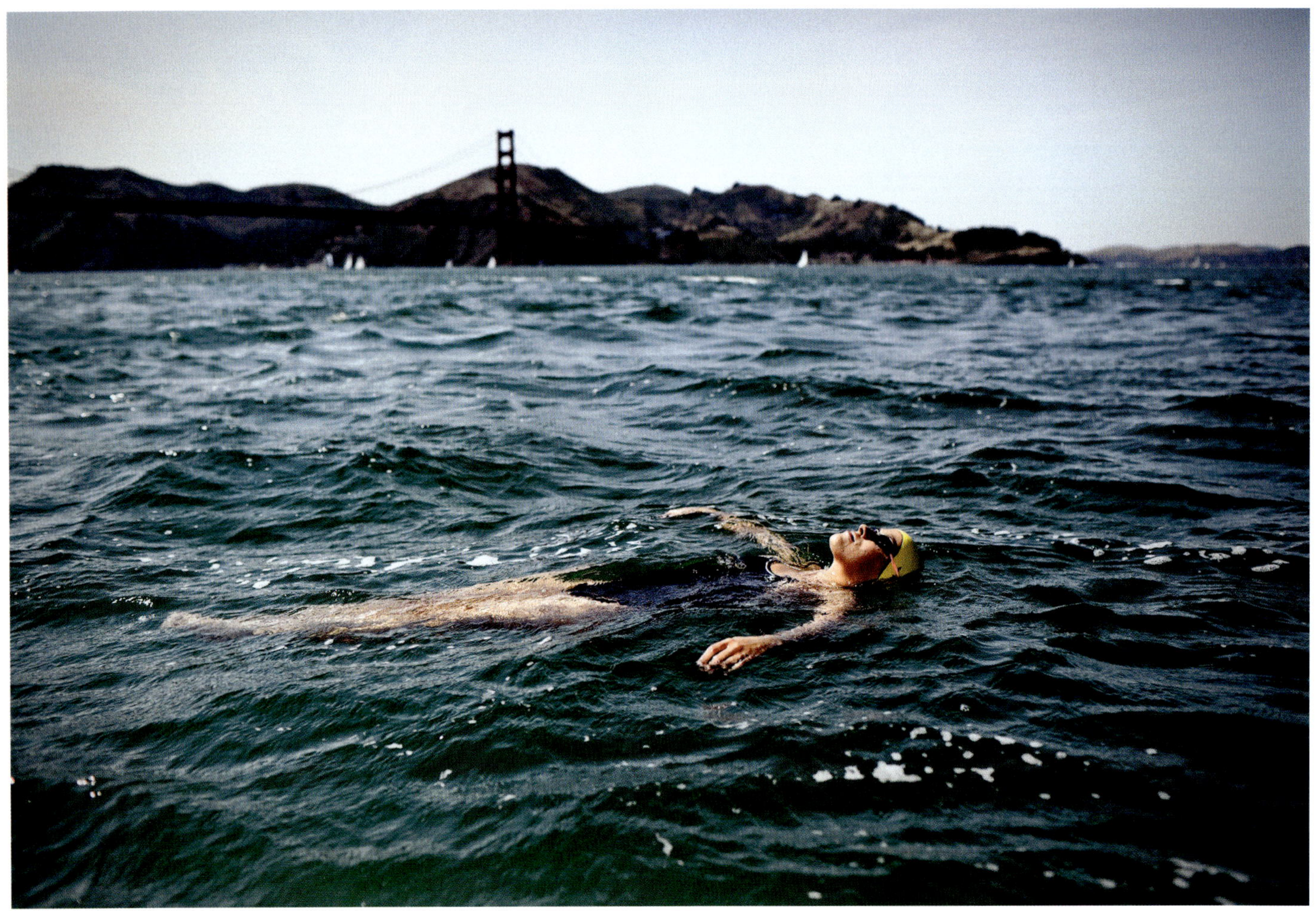

**FIGURE 4.5A** Andy photographed Laurin Weisenthal for *Outside* Magazine. She's an amazing distance swimmer who trains regularly in the cold waters of the San Francisco Bay. Andy hired a photography boat so he could photograph her in the water. He says, "I knew I didn't want to change lenses in an open boat, and I wanted flexibility, so this was a perfect shoot for a zoom lens. I used a 70–200mm lens, since I had control over where the boat would be. It gave me the range to get a wide view—including the bridge—and some tight views of just Laurin's face, at peace in the water (**Figure 4.5B**).
IMAGE © ANDY BATT, *LAURIN WEISENTHAL, SF BAY,* FOR *OUTSIDE* MAGAZINE, 2009.

advantages you get when you buy higher-quality lenses is engineering that overcomes those design compromises.

Working with a quality zoom is like having a bag full of lenses mounted to your camera simultaneously (**Figures 4.5A and 4.5B**). As an added bonus, you can avoid changing lenses, which is a gift when you're working in dusty environments, since every time you change a lens, you risk introducing more dust onto your sensor.[5]

The trick is not to become a lazy zoom photographer. Don't use zoom lenses just so you don't have to move your feet! Instead, treat each focal length as its own unique lens (see *Explorations* at the end of this chapter for details).

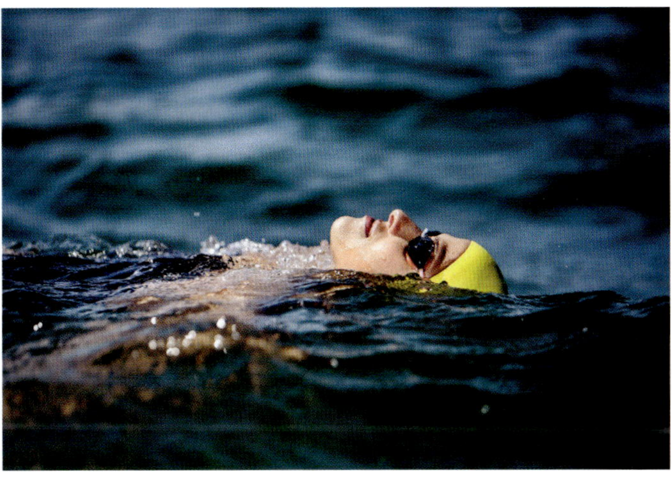

**FIGURE 4.5B** Andy used a zoom lens for this shoot, which gave him the range to capture this tight view, as well as a wide view (**Figure 4.5A**).
IMAGE © ANDY BATT, *LAURIN WEISENTHAL—CLOSE-UP, SF BAY*, FOR *OUTSIDE* MAGAZINE, 2009.

## Zoom Lenses: Eric Meola, *Photographer*

The work of photographer Eric Meola, a gifted master of photography, features a seemingly effortless ability to acknowledge and capture color, shape and moments in time. Eric created a body of work that made extensive use of a zoom lens. That body of work became a book: *India: In Word and Image, Revised, Expanded and Updated.*

Eric frequently carried a Canon EF 100–400mm *f*/4.5–5.6L IS USM push-pull zoom lens[6] on his India shoots. It allowed him to easily carry the equivalent of an entire kit of long-range lenses—and it's an image-stabilized lens,[7] so he could literally jump out of a moving taxi and start shooting handheld at a variety of focal lengths. The photos are stunning, and incredibly sharp.

As Eric described to Andy in an email:

> *I've always been intrigued by the idea of using just one lens, but with zooms that don't mean just one focal length. Just one lens, because when I work in a dusty place like India (where there's so much excitement and so many things happening at once), I want to be able to work very quickly, and yet be able to either pull back and frame a landscape or zoom in for a face.*
>
> *The Canon 100–400mm L lens became my lens of choice when working in India, because it allowed me incredible flexibility—and at the long end, it's the way my mind sees. I tend to crop in-camera, and I also love the way this lens visually compresses the foreground and background together, so the main subject is isolated through selective focus.*
>
> *I like to walk the streets as well as drive around in a car, hopping out when I see something, or—if I'm really intrigued—leaving the driver behind while I walk around. I try as much as possible to blend in, so carrying one body and one lens helps me do that. No bag, maybe a bottle of water . . . in a way, tourists have it "right," and my goal is to attract as little*

***attention as possible, but to have as much flexibility as possible with whatever lens I bring along. So for me, the 100–400mm L has become my favorite lens for quick street shooting.***

## Lens Tips

Every lens has its own personality; with practice, you'll learn the strengths and weaknesses of each particular lens. Eventually, you'll know before you take the picture what the effect will be.

1. **Know your falloff:** When shooting wide open, a lens will usually produce images that are sharp in the center, with increasing softness towards the edges, particularly at the corners.
2. **The sweet aperture:** The middle aperture values—usually *f*/8–*f*/11—will render the sharpest image, with that sharpness running evenly across the lens.
3. **Depth of Field:** The difference in DoF between the same scene taken at *f*/2.0 and at *f*/2.8 is huge. The difference between *f*/5.6 and *f*/11 is much smaller.
4. **DoF in relation:** DoF increases as subject distance increases, focal length decreases and/or aperture size decreases.
5. **F-Stops will vary:** Not all *f*/8s are equal. Two different lenses at the same F-stop can give you different exposures, because an F-stop is a mathematical calculation, not a measured one.
6. **Color shift:** Two lenses with the same focal length, but made by different manufacturers, will have different color and contrast.
7. ***f*/1.2 quality:** You don't always buy an *f*/1.2 lens so you can shoot it wide open. Some people buy ultra-fast lenses because the quality at *f*/2.8 is (usually) better than a similar lens that starts at *f*/2.8.

## Which Is the Right Lens for You?

The answer to this question leads to another question: What type of images do you want to make? Architectural photographers might invest in a set of *Tilt-Shift lenses* that enable them to make perspective corrections at the lens level. Sports photographers will find it vital to have an *image-stabilized telephoto zoom*[8] that performs well at its widest aperture. Portrait photographers will get a lot of use out of a fast 85mm lens; the combination of a *moderate telephoto* and wide aperture can create beautiful portraits.

***Andy:*** I always tell up-and-coming photographers to buy a good-quality 50mm lens. No matter what your budget is or which camera system you have, there's usually a really good 50mm available to suit it. Buy the best one you can afford, and don't be tempted by a zoom lens at the same price. You'll get much better build and optical quality from the 50mm. If you're working with an APS-C sensor camera, you might consider a 35mm instead; the effect will be roughly the same as a 50mm on a full-frame sensor (for details, see the *Angle of View* section later in this chapter).

We all find uses for lenses that are the opposite of our daily tools. Sometimes a different way of seeing can get you out of a rut or give you a unique version of a standard shot. Photographing action sports with a 21mm lens will force you to find locations and angles that are completely different from the ones you would find when shooting with a long lens. Creating an architectural image with a fisheye lens might go against the rules of perpendicular lines and correct perspective, but it just might create a really exciting and different

**FIGURE 4.6**
Ten years ago, this area was burned. Jeff says, "In spite of the devastation, I find burn areas to possess an austere kind of beauty. Under the crisp white of the winter snow, the contrasts are stark and crisp." For this photo, Jeff used a Canon 5D MII and a 300mm telephoto lens to compress the scene.
IMAGE © JEFFREY CONLEY, *ZEN HILLSIDE 1, OREGON CASCADES*, 2009.

image. There's no right or wrong lens—there's only the lens that you have on your camera.

> *I like to use a lens that's faithful to and representative of the scene—and that has minimal distortion. For example, I have never really liked the way ultra-wide lenses depict the landscape, at least for my purposes. Honestly, I think you can do a lot with just about any lens out there. If you're working within the sweet spot of the aperture—shooting at f/8—most lenses are going to be pretty darn sharp. It all depends on what you're trying to do. If you're looking for really wonderful bokeh, then you'll want a super-fast lens. You can't really replicate that through a lens that's limited to a f/5.6 aperture. I'm a little old-school, west-coast style with my photography: I tend to favor a sharp image with a long depth of field* ***(Figure 4.6).***
>
> *—Jeff Conley*

## Which Lens? Shooting the 2004 Olympic Trials

### Bruce Ely and Sol Neelman

***Sol Neelman's Version:*** I've got a Bruce Ely story: We're at the Olympic trials together in 2004, in Sacramento. We are all at the finish line—Maurice Greene is running in the 100 meter, so you can imagine how long that race is going to last. If there were lens rules at the finish line, they'd be to use a 70–200mm or a 300mm lens. Bruce has a 400mm lens on a digital camera with a crop sensor, so it's the equivalent of a 600mm. Later, we're back at the hotel looking at images and Bruce shows me this picture of Maurice Greene sticking his tongue out. It's great, it's in focus and I say, "Why did you shoot that? I would never have shot with that lens! I would never even think to do that—that's stupid!" Bruce says to me, "Whatever—I just thought I would shoot it tight," and I say, "You are nuts." He got a double-truck magazine spread in *ESPN The Magazine* out of that shot.

***Bruce Ely's Version:*** So, I'm at the US Track and Field Championships in Sacramento sitting next to Sol Neelman. We're shooting the Men's 100 Meter—the big event of the meet—and everybody is paying attention to the race. Maurice Green is the big name, and he's in Lane 4 or 5, right in the middle somewhere, and the finish line is full of photographers. All of a sudden they start to race, and Sol turns back and looks at me. He says, "Oh my God, what are you doing?" I say, "What are you talking about?" He says, "You're shooting the finish line with a 400!"—which you know is a very long lens—and we're pretty close to the finish line.

I swing the 400mm for the finish. I figure there are two of us and I see him shooting with what everybody else was shooting with—he was probably using a 200mm. We're a couple of seconds away, so he turns around and shoots. And you know, I shoot and I just follow this guy the whole time. Right as Maurice Green goes across the finish line, he sticks his tongue out and makes this great face.

***Candace Dobro:*** **You got that?**

***BE:*** It was perfectly framed. I know it took a little luck. What I'm talking about is this: If you know you're in a situation where it doesn't really matter whether you screw up, and if you've got that ability to take a chance—then go for it. Why not?

I could have screwed up and not had anything, but it ended up being sent to *ESPN The Magazine,* and it was my first picture, I think, to run in one of the big sports magazines as a double-truck.

***Andy Batt:*** **That goes right back to the idea of mastering your gear so that you can take chances.**

***BE:*** Right; otherwise you sit around and worry about technical stuff. To be a good photographer, there are lots of things you need to think about—beyond your gear.

## TRY THIS AT HOME

### Focal Length Portrait Comparison

**For step-by-step instructions, go to:**
**www.focalpress.com/cw/digitalimagingmasters**

The ability to instinctively choose a lens comes from experience. Try expanding your knowledge by shooting the same subject with each of your lenses, and then comparing the results.

**FIGURE 4.7** You can learn a lot about your lenses by doing a simple portrait test. Andy photographed Sean with a full-frame Canon, using 16–35mm, 50mm, 85mm and 70–200mm lenses. While there's an obvious difference between the 16mm and 200mm lens portraits, many of the other differences are subtler. With the 16mm lens, the magnification is uneven and the perspective is very distorted. Also, the ears appear to recede far from the eyes, while the nose comes far forward. These characteristics lessen as the focal length gets longer and the field of view narrows. At 135mm, the face starts to feel compressed, and at 200mm, it appears even more so.
IMAGE © ANDY BATT, *FOCAL LENGTH PORTRAIT COMPARISON WITH ELEVEN FOCAL LENGTHS*, 2013.

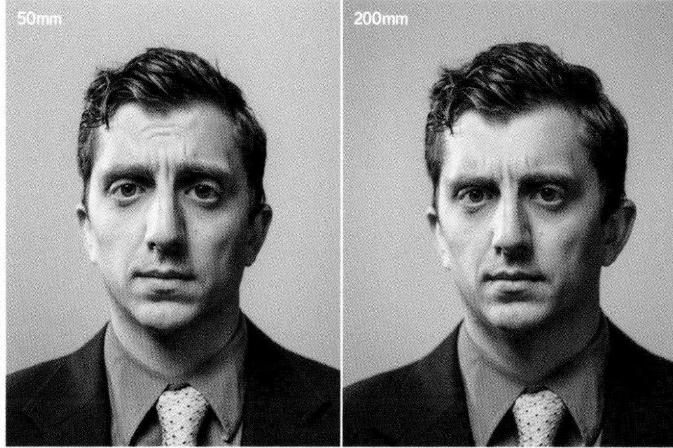


**FIGURE 4.8** There's a distinctive change in the shape of the face as determined by these two lenses. The image on the right was taken with the 200mm lens, while the one on the left was taken with the 50mm lens. There isn't an obvious choice of which one is better. When deciding between the 16mm and the 200mm lenses, the choice is fairly clear—unless you're doing a comic portrait and distortion will help your story. Pay attention to the eyes, nose, ears, chin and cheekbones. In the shot taken with the 200mm lens, the ears and nose appear closer (front to back) than in the one taken with the 50mm lens. In the 50mm-lens portrait, the face looks slightly more oval and the ears seem farther away. Before you decide which image is better, cover up the right side and look at the 50mm-lens portrait alone. Give it enough time so that you forget the other image. Now switch and repeat. With both images showing, the differences might be clear to you, but when you examine each image on its own merits, the choice is tougher.
IMAGE © ANDY BATT, *COMPARING 200MM AND 50MM LENSES*, 2013.

*Note:* The person you're photographing has a lot to do with how a lens works. An individual's facial structure may look better at either end of this spectrum.

## TRY THIS AT HOME

### Move the Background

**For step-by-step instructions, go to: www.focalpress.com/cw/digitalimagingmasters**

With wider lenses, the background appears farther away from your subject, and with longer lenses it appears closer. In addition, each focal length has a different magnification that changes the compression in your scene. Try photographing your subject in an area with a distinctive environment, and see how changing the lens affects the background.

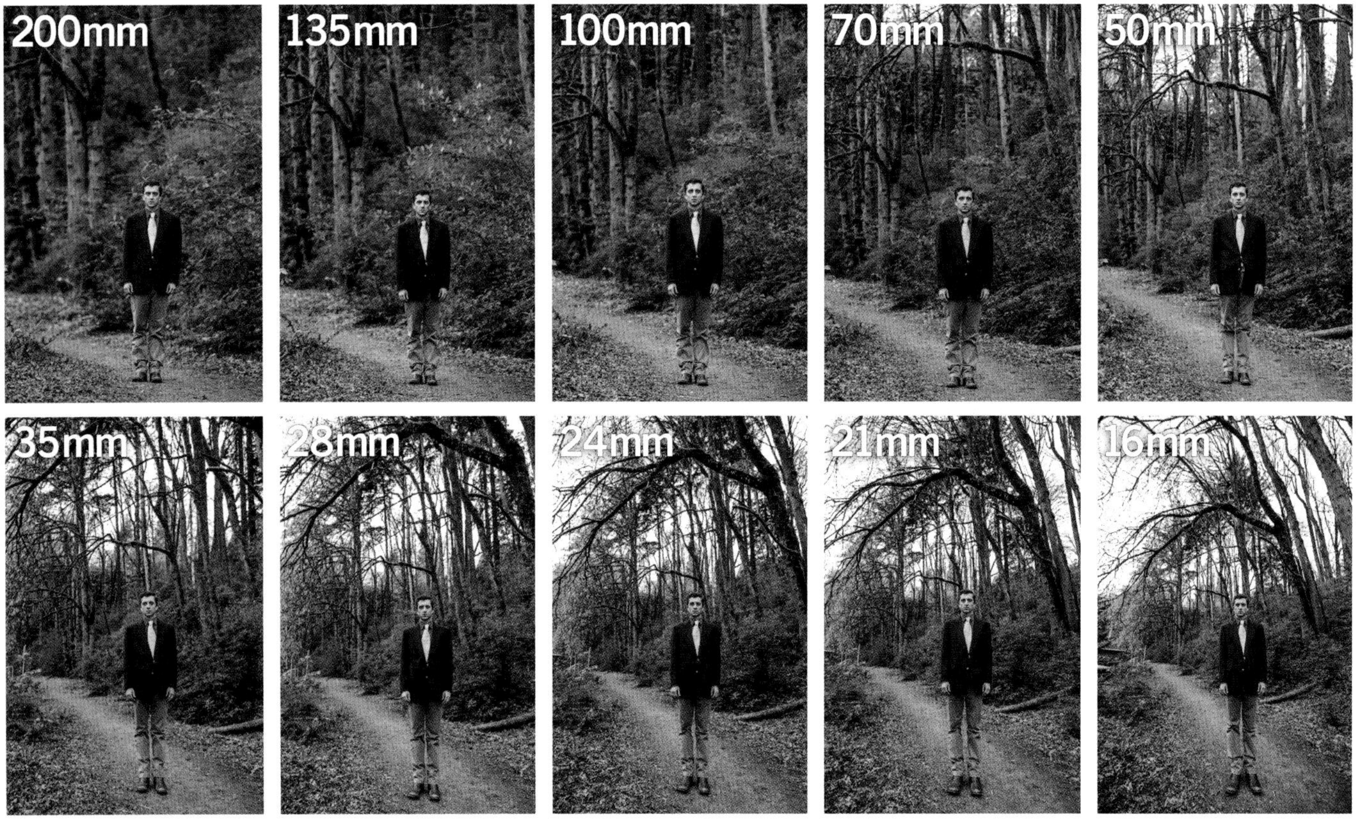

200mm 135mm 100mm 70mm 50mm

35mm 28mm 24mm 21mm 16mm

**FIGURE 4.9** Using a range of lenses, Andy kept Sean at approximately the same size in the viewfinder, by moving the camera and using Sean as a constant. The environment around Sean changes dramatically as the focal length changes. The 16mm (with its wide angle of view) takes in a large portion of the environment and appears to increase the distance between the subject and the trees in the background. It also has the unfortunate effect of distorting the subject, especially around the edges. The 200mm (with its narrow angle of view) shows us a much more cropped view of the background and has the effect of bringing the trees closer to the subject.
IMAGE © ANDY BATT, *COMPRESSION IMAGE GRID WITH TEN FOCAL LENGTHS*, 2013.

# Stuff for the End of Your Lens

With the array of post-processing tools at our disposal, we no longer rely on specialty filters to make color balance adjustments, add warmth to an image or create a graduated sunset effect. There are still a few essential pieces we keep on hand for the end of our lenses.

## Filters

### Skylight Filters: Aka Optical Flats, UV Filters or Clear Glass

Although we do need to protect our lenses' front elements, they're surprisingly tough.[9] For normal day-to-day use, we don't keep these filters on our lenses. The biggest reason is that they add extra surfaces in front of the lens that can cause flare and reflections, which will degrade your image. When we do use them, we treat them like disposable filters to protect a lens from harm—such as flying grit, blowing sand, saltwater (mostly to prevent salt from drying on the lens), etc.

### Polarizers and ND Filters

Polarizing filters interact with light in a unique way. While rays of light bounce around in all directions, polarizing filters allow only a single direction of light to pass through to the lens. The filter absorbs all of the light from any other direction.

The most significant effects of using these filters are a deepening of colors, an elimination (or moderation) of surface glare and a darkening of blue skies. *Polarizing filters are unique; their effects cannot be simulated in post-production.* There's usually quite a bit of light loss

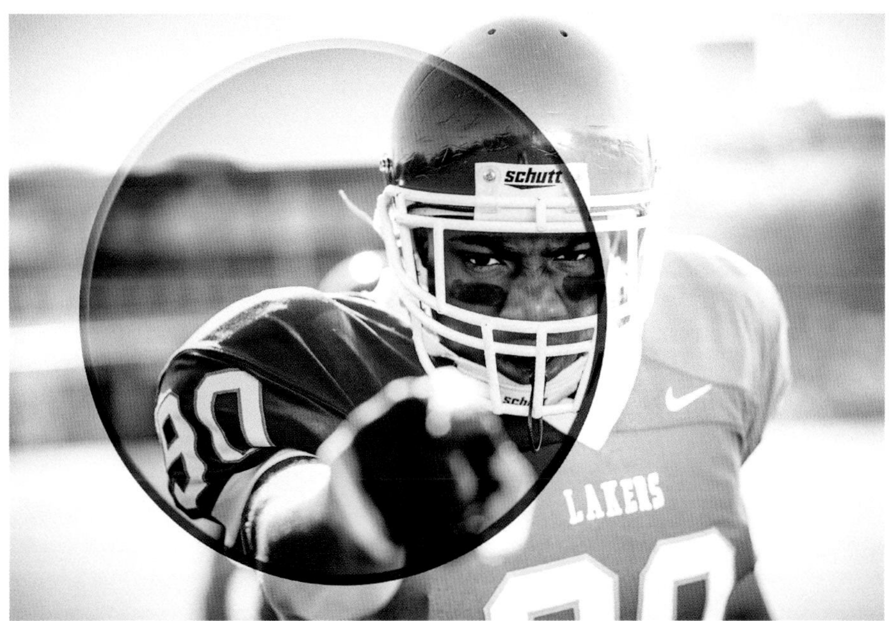


**FIGURE 4.10** One of the reasons to use an ND filter is to force a super-shallow DoF, as in this image, which was shot at *f*/2.5. On a bright sunny day, you might not be able to open up that far without overexposing, even with a fast shutter and low ISO. Adding an ND filter allows you to "lose light" and use a much wider F-stop.
IMAGE © ANDY BATT, *NEUTRAL DENSITY FILTER SIMULATION. IMAGE: GAMEFACE,* 2010.

## FEATURED PHOTOGRAPH

### Using the Wrong Lens for the Right Project

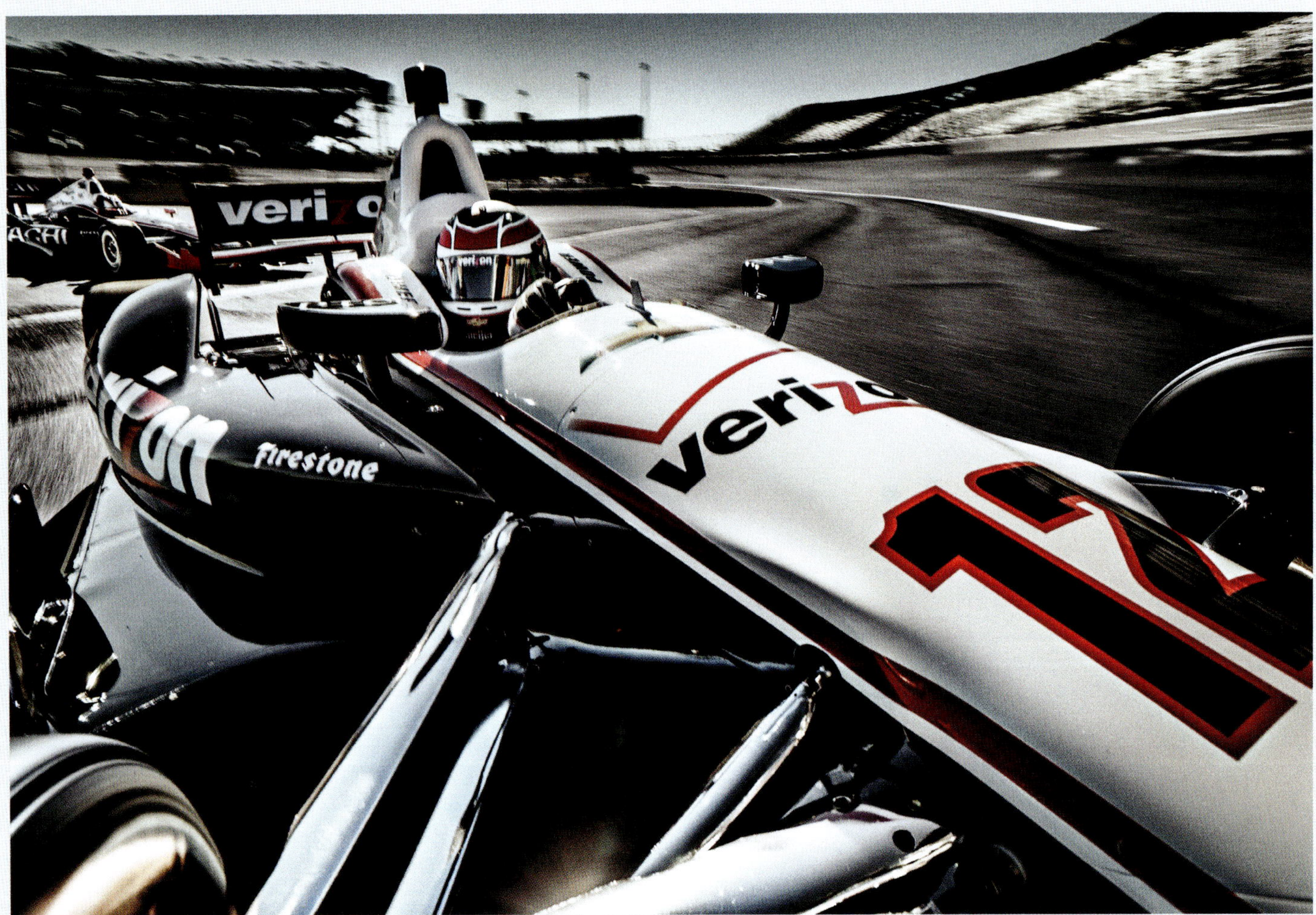


**FIGURE 4.11** This image was captured using a 20mm lens mounted just above the left wheel of the Indy car. Most photographs of Indy car racing are captured with long lenses, since the majority of them are captured during race and training events. For this project, Andy had unlimited access to the cars and track, so he could use the "wrong" lens to get a great shot.
IMAGE © ANDY BATT, *UP CLOSE ON THE VERIZON INDY CAR,* 2013.

Choosing the right lens really depends on your situation. It's important to experiment so you can base your choice on experience. Whenever Andy is told that there's a "right" way to do something, there's a voice in his head asking, "Why? Why is that the right way—what about doing it differently?"

***Andy:*** When it comes to lens choice, I try to listen to that inner voice to see if it knows anything. Sometimes I go with the "right" lens, because sometimes the obvious choice is the right one. I know that my 85mm takes really nice portraits, so unless I can come up with a reason to use something different when I'm taking a portrait, there's a good chance I'll just reach for it. Then there are those times when selecting the wrong lens makes sense.

I was planning a project where I would be photographing Indy[10] racecars in action. One of the classic approaches to photographing these cars is to stake out a corner or angle that has a nice composition and to use a super-telephoto lens to pan with the cars and capture them as they hit the sweet spot in the composition.

You can get some amazing images this way, especially if you work out the timing so you can pan with the car: The roadway and background will blur, and the car will remain sharp. I knew that with this project I had a unique opportunity to work differently, since the cars and drivers were there for the purpose of our shoot. Nobody else was on the track, and I had a blank slate to work on. I thought that by attaching a super wide-angle lens to the car itself, I would get a unique view and a great shot (**Figure 4.11**).

Since I wasn't going to be viewing and reframing the shot, I knew I would need several cameras mounted to the car at the same time, so I would have different angle options to choose from. Once there was a plan, we worked with a rigging crew and the Penske race team to attach bits and pieces of grip hardware onto their multi-million dollar car.

After about eight hours of work on the first day, I finally had an opportunity to head back to the media center, where my DITs were downloading and backing up the images. I felt okay about the shots and had been in radio contact with my DITs to make sure the exposures were all right—but I hadn't had time to go sit in front of the thirty-inch monitors to see the work. It was rewarding to hear my clients oohing and ahhing over the work, but when the Indy car drivers came in and saw the shots—that was amazing. You know you've done good work when you create a shot these guys have never seen before!

with the use of polarizers, about 2 1/2-stops, on average. (For this reason, they can be used as stand-ins for ND filters.) A good polarizer costs quite a bit of money, but is worth the price, since a cheap one will most likely add some unwanted color. You want your polarizer to be nice and neutral.

The purpose of ND (Neutral Density) filters is to reduce exposure without adding any color or effect to the image. They're invisible, except for the effect they have on exposure. ND filters allow you to use wider apertures or slower shutter speeds than your lighting would normally allow (**Figure 4.10**). They're available in a variety of standard densities (1-stop, 2-stop, 3-stop, etc.) or as a variable filter that can be adjusted to different density settings. As with other tools, we also tend to get what we pay for with ND filters. Cheap ones, for example, may add an unwanted colorcast.

## Lens Hoods

The primary purpose of a lens hood is to reduce lens flare. It blocks stray light from falling onto your front element so you can maintain good image contrast and clarity. Lens hoods have a secondary purpose though, which makes them invaluable: They make great bumpers. A lens hood protects the front element of your lens, which is great for those times when you're juggling a cup of coffee, two cameras and a smartphone—and one of your cameras swings just a little too close to a steel gate.

# Technical Control: Understanding Your Lens

## Demystifying the Magic Glass

Your lens is a mechanical and electrical wonder that's crafted from incredibly pure, specially made glass and is filled with coated optical elements. It has an iris of perfectly manufactured aperture blades, miniaturized ultra sonic motors, numerous precision gears and—if it's an image-stabilized lens—tiny gyroscopes.

When you focus a shot, an entire system orchestrates within a fraction of a second to bring your subject into focus. Press the shutter release, and the lens's aperture closes to an exact value, the shutter curtain opens and closes at a precise speed and the aperture returns to its wide-open state. All of this takes place within a microsecond. When you change the focal length of a zoom lens, a mechanical ballet is set in motion to rearrange the optical elements and create an entirely different lens. Lenses perform a sort of magic by allowing you to create a 2-D image out of a 3-D world.

> *Any sufficiently advanced technology is indistinguishable from magic.*
>
> *—Arthur C. Clarke's "Third Law"*

## Nodal Points

Your lens creates an image from the light that falls onto the front surface of the lens. The light comes from the object point, in front of your lens, and passes through the front nodal point. The lens focuses the light at the back focal point, where the sensor is located, to create the image. The rear nodal point of the lens is the location from which the image is projected.

Depending on a lens's design, the actual location of the rear nodal point can vary widely. Using a very simple lens design, the rear nodal point would be towards the back of the lens, in an intuitive location. Modern lens design pulls off some mean optical engineering feats. For example, some telephoto lenses can have their rear nodal point positioned in front of the physical lens. A wide-angle lens might have its rear nodal point behind the physical lens, positioned extremely close to the sensor itself. For zoom lenses, the nodal point will shift as different focal lengths are chosen. Although for most purposes, you don't need to know where the nodal point is, learning lens physics can help you understand your equipment.

## Focal Length

The focal length of a lens is calculated by measuring—while the lens is focused at infinity—the distance from the rear nodal point to the focal plane, where the sensor is located (**Figure 4.12**). Focal length is independent of sensor size and camera format, so a 100mm lens will always have a focal length of 100mm, no matter which camera it's mounted to—a full-frame DSLR, an APS-C or a medium-format camera.

## Angle of View

When we use lens shorthand, e.g., a "wide-angle" lens, we're actually talking about angle of view. The angle of view describes how wide or narrow a scene is when it's projected onto the sensor (**Figure 4.13**). Whereas humans perceive the world at a 180° view, lenses restrict that breadth. For instance, on a full-frame camera, a Canon 14mm lens has only a 114° view and an 800mm lens has approximately a mere 3° view.

Angle of view is usually measured on the diagonal of the focal plane.[11] The diagonal measurement on a full-frame 35mm sensor (24mm × 36mm) is about 43mm. If you use a smaller or larger sensor, you increase or decrease that dimension.

The focal length of a lens never changes, but the angle of view does, depending on the sensor size of the camera it's attached to. For example, if we put a 50mm lens on a full-frame camera, its angle of view is 46°. If we mount that same lens on a smaller APS-C sensor (22mm ×15mm), the shorter diagonal measurement (26mm as

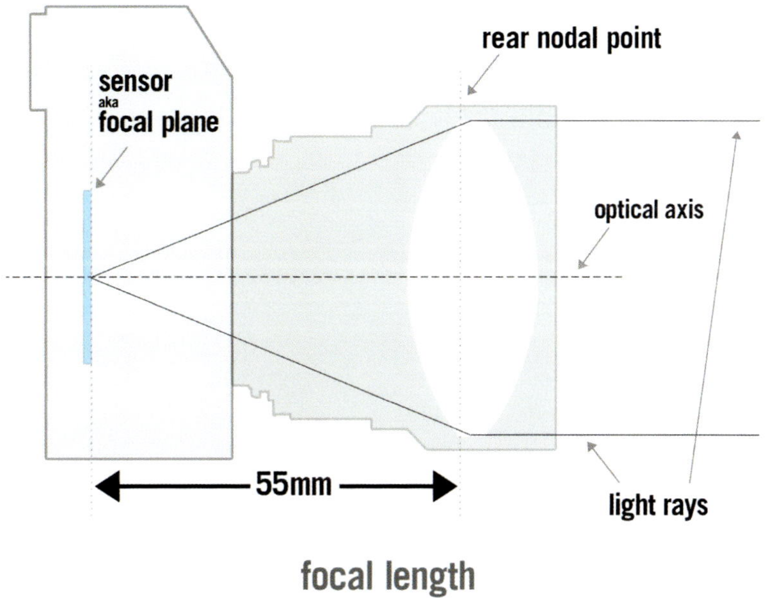


**FIGURE 4.12** The focal length of a lens is calculated by measuring the distance from the rear nodal point to the focal plane (where the sensor is located), while the lens is focused at infinity.
ILLUSTRATION © ANDY BATT, *FOCAL LENGTH,* 2013.

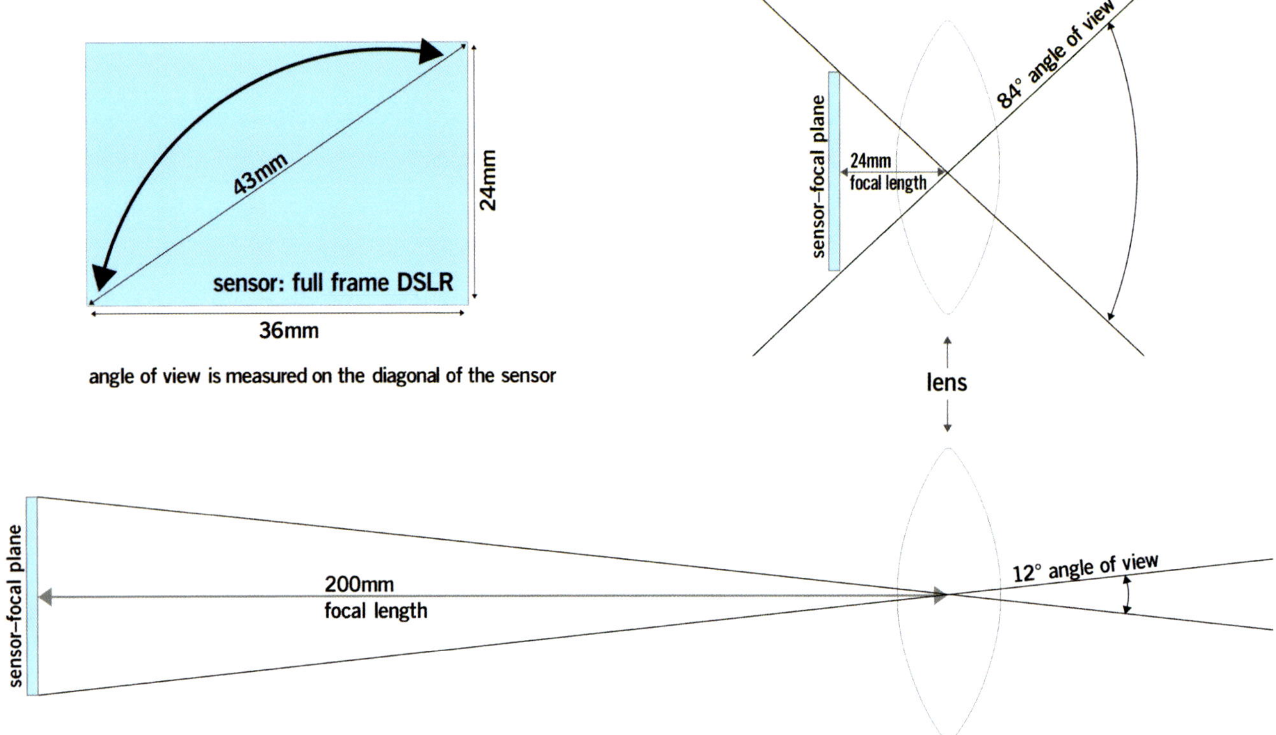


**FIGURE 4.13** We think of our lenses as super-wide, wide, normal, telephoto (or long) and super-telephoto. These terms relate to the lens's angle of view, which describes how much or little of a scene (that's in front of the camera) ends up at the sensor. Given the same lens, a camera with a small sensor will yield a smaller angle of view than a camera with a large sensor.
ILLUSTRATION © ANDY BATT, *ANGLE OF VIEW AND FOCAL LENGTH,* 2013.

compared to 43mm on a full-frame sensor) reduces the angle of view to about 28°. The angle of view for an 85mm lens mounted to a full-frame camera is also 28°, which means that a 50mm lens with an APS-C sensor has the same angle of view as an 85mm lens on a full-frame camera.

## In the Image Circle

Optical lens elements are designed to work together in a combination known as a compound lens. This type of lens has refractive optical elements; they bend light and focus the image onto the sensor plane. The shape and position of the optical elements determine the focal length and angle of view of the lens.

The image that's projected onto your rectangular sensor is circular. We never see a significant portion of that image, because it spills over the sides of sensor. The entire area that's projected is called the image circle. As you shift the focus between infinity and the lens's close-focus distance, the size of the image circle changes. At close-focus distances, the image circle is larger than it is when the focus is at infinity.

At a certain point in the continuum between close-focus distances and infinity, image sharpness and exposure begin to fail at

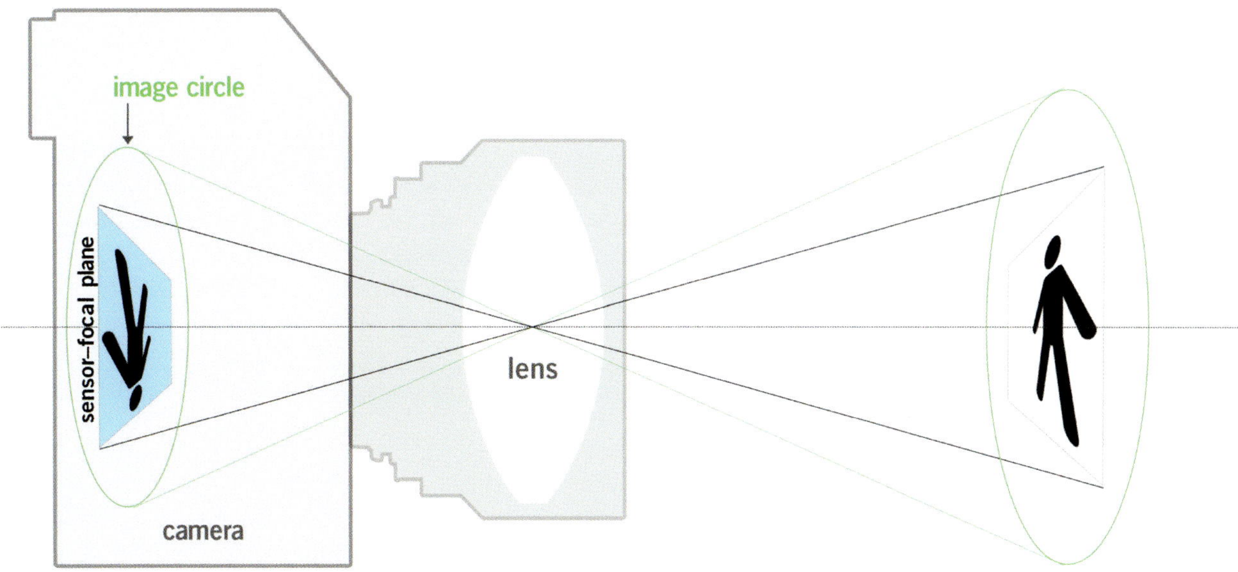


**FIGURE 4.14A** This is a simplified diagram of what takes place inside of your camera. Camera lenses are designed to project a focused image onto your sensor. When the image is projected onto the sensor by the lens, it's flipped upside down.
ILLUSTRATION © ANDY BATT, *THE LENS, SIMPLIFIED,* 2013.

the edges of the image circle. There's an inner area—called the circle of good definition—where the image is even and sharp. The part of the image circle that lands on the sensor lies within this circle. With some cameras and lenses, you can take advantage of the larger image-circle area. You can manipulate a Tilt-Shift lens or a bellow attachment with rise and fall, for instance, to change which part of the circular image lands on the sensor.

Imagine standing inside of a giant camera. A white rectangle is on one side, opposite the lens. The lens projects a circular image that is much larger than the white rectangle—this is the image circle. The portion of the image that we capture is what lands on the white rectangle (**Figures 4.14A and 4.14B**).

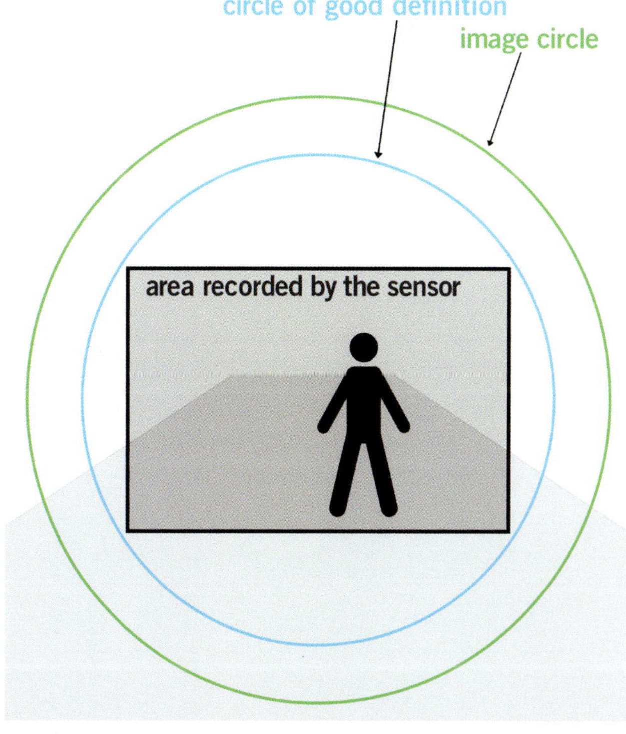


**FIGURE 4.14B** The lens projects a circular image known as the image circle, which is larger than the area captured by the sensor. Inside of the image circle is the circle of good definition—the useable area, where the quality of the lens is consistent.
ILLUSTRATION © ANDY BATT, *IMAGE CIRCLE AND CIRCLE OF GOOD DEFINITION,* 2013.

## Same Lens, Different Results

If we combine two ideas—angle of view and image circle—we can understand how cameras with different-sized sensors can use the same lens, but yield different results (**Figures 4.15 and 4.16**). Let's assume our view is based on a lens that's mounted to a full-frame DSLR.

The full-frame camera (with a sensor size of 36mm × 24mm) has a diagonal of 43mm, while the APS-C camera (with a sensor size of 22mm × 15mm) has a diagonal of 26mm. We can compare these different-sized sensors by dividing the larger diagonal by the smaller one to calculate the *crop factor*. In this case, we divide 43mm by 26mm and arrive at a crop factor of 1.65.

If we want to figure out the approximate field of view of a 50mm lens when it's mounted on the APS-C camera, we multiply 50mm by the crop factor of 1.65 and arrive at 82.5mm. This means that when the 50mm lens is mounted to the APS-C camera, it will have a field of view that acts like 82mm (**Figure 4.16**).

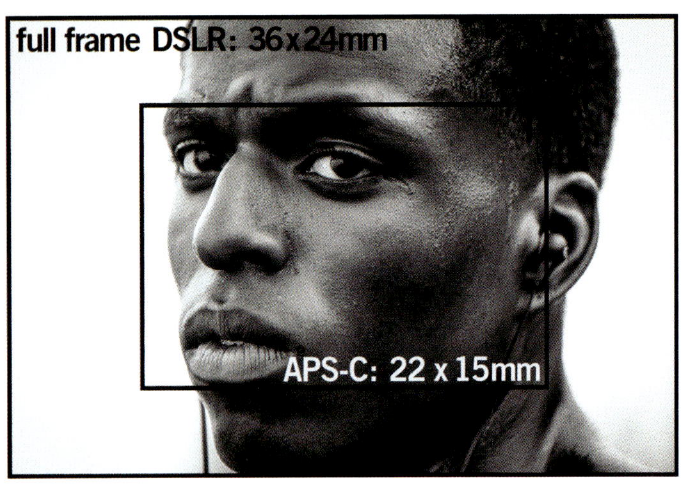


**FIGURE 4.15** This image shows the crop factor from a full-frame 35mm overlaid with an APS-C crop.
IMAGE © ANDY BATT, *AN IMAGE WITH TWO DIFFERENT CROP FACTORS*, 2013.

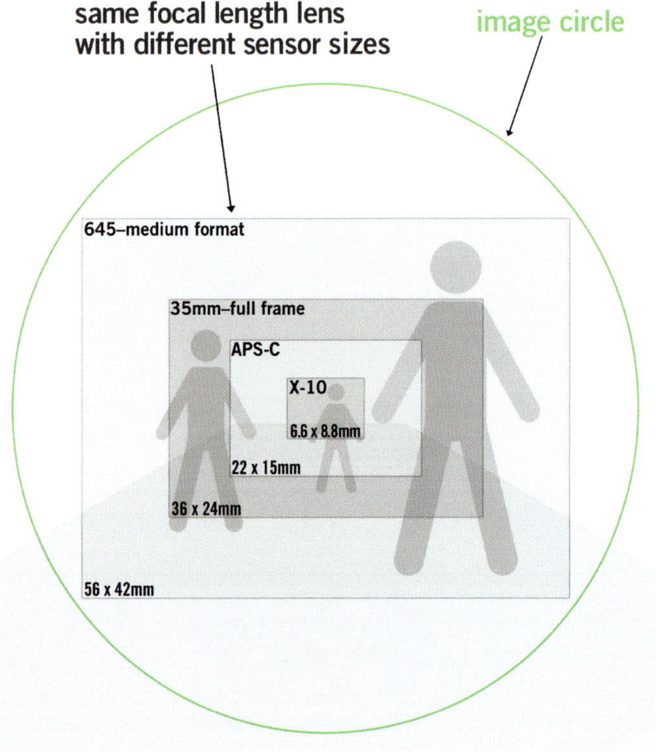


**FIGURE 4.16** The same focal-length lens will result in four different angles of view for four differently sized sensors (as long as the lens has a large enough image circle to cover the 645 medium-format sensor).
ILLUSTRATION © ANDY BATT, *COMPARISON OF SENSOR SIZES*, 2013.

## Focus on the Parts

We photographers are almost obsessive about focus. Is it in focus? Is it sharp? We can even get fixated on areas that are out of focus: Is it out of focus *enough*? What kind of blur is it? Should there be more or less focus overall? Since focus is one of our primary tools for creating photographs, it's useful to understand what we're actually doing when we focus an image.

The *focal plane* (**Figure 4.14A**) is the place where the lens focuses the image. Your camera's sensor lives on the focal plane. When you focus an image, you're moving the optical elements in the lens to bend and shape the light, so that whatever you're focusing on becomes sharp in the resulting image.

A focused image isn't just 2-D; it has depth. There's a narrow zone that extends slightly in front of—and behind—the focal plane, where the image is considered acceptably focused. We call this *depth of field (DoF).* DoF is a variable, and the aperture of your lens has a direct effect on the overall appearance of sharpness in an image: As you decrease the size of the aperture, you increase the DoF, which makes an image look sharper. It accomplishes this by sharpening the appearance of objects in front of and behind the subject you're focused on.

To talk about how DoF works, we need to dig deeper into the idea of apertures, F-stops and T-stops. By casual definition, these terms all mean the same thing, and we often use the terms *aperture* and *F-stop* interchangeably. All three terms refer to the opening that your lens uses to pass rays of light from your subject to the focal plane.

Imagine a lens without any controllable F-stops: It's at its widest setting at all times. The size of the optical elements and lens barrel itself define the aperture of the lens. The entire lens is at work, gathering those rays of light. Now add a variable mechanical gadget to control how big that opening is. It can be opened up all the way, or closed down to a pinhole. By using a formula, we can figure out where to put marks (F-stops) on the aperture control to give us a standardized, repeatable way of controlling the amount of light passing through the lens.

An F-stop is a calculated number that's used to indicate how much light will be passed through the aperture. F-stop is equal to the lens's focal length divided by the dimension of the aperture itself.

For example:

$f/2.8$ = 28mm/10mm
$f/4.0$ = 28mm/7mm

Put another way, for a 28mm lens, the diameter of the actual aperture is 10mm at $f/2.8$ and 7mm at $f/4.0$. (Just do the math.)

A *T-stop* (true stop or transmission stop) is related to the F-stop. The difference is that instead of being calculated, a T-stop is measured and calibrated. By taking into account the differences in lens design and the transmission characteristics of the glass elements, the T-stop delivers a much more precise measure of light to the sensor. Two lenses with the same T-stops will give you the exact same exposure. Two lenses with the same F-stops will give you approximately the same exposure. It's rare to find a still-photography lens[12] marked with T-stops, but it's worth understanding the principle.

## Sharpness Vs. Focus

When you increase your DoF, you're not changing the actual focus of the image, but the perception of focus; you're making the out-of-focus areas in your image *appear* sharper. The more you decrease the size of the aperture, the sharper these areas appear.[13] Actually, the only thing in focus is your subject—the focal plane. When it comes down to looking at an image, we find that the practical difference between actual and perceived focus is minimal. Knowing this does help us understand what's happening with DoF.

## Depth of Field at Work

Take a good look at **Figure 4.17**[14] as we tackle this topic. When we discuss DoF, we always have a near point, a subject point and a far point. For this diagram we put three tiny pinpoints[15] in a staggered row and labeled them "X" for our subject, "Y" for our near point and "Z" for our far point. To keep things simple, the only change between the three cameras is the aperture value. The camera is focused at point X. In the photographs taken by all of the cameras, that pinpoint appears to be the same as it does to the naked eye—tack sharp and distinct.

We set the camera in the top illustration to an aperture value of *f*/2.8, a shallow DoF. The pinpoints of Y and Z (which are the same size as the one at X) are photographed as large, soft-edged circles. On the camera in the middle illustration, we set a value of *f*/8, increasing the DoF. In the photograph, the pinpoints now show up as smaller, more defined circles. The camera in the bottom illustration is set to *f*/22, a major increase in DoF. The X and Y pinpoints now show up in the photograph at about the same size as the X circle, and they appear to be the same sharpness as the subject of the photo.

## Quick Guide: Depth of Field

Here's a list of things to keep in mind when you're working the numbers to your advantage:

- **Shallow DoF**
  Happens at larger-diameter apertures (smaller numbers).

- **Deep DoF**
  Happens at smaller-diameter apertures (larger numbers).

- **Diffraction**
  At the smallest-diameter apertures, you lose overall image sharpness, even with the increase in DoF. Diffraction is simply described as the light bleeding over the edges of the aperture, which decreases the contrast and resolving power of the lens.

- **Equivalent images**
  If you frame up a shot with the same lens on an APS-C camera and a full-frame camera, the smaller sensor camera will have increased DoF at any given F-number, relative to the angle of view.

- **Get shorter**
  As focal lengths shorten, DoF increases.

- **Go longer**
  As your subject distance increases, so does your DoF.

- **One-third/two-thirds rule**
  DoF works in a split: The area in front of your focal point is about one-third the total DoF, while two-thirds remain behind the focal point. Macro photography is a special case, where you're essentially working with such a small zone of focus that the one-third/two-thirds rule doesn't apply. (There are also a few lens designs which don't follow this rule. They aren't too common, but certain Super Angulons are among them—most of the DoF extends to the distance.)

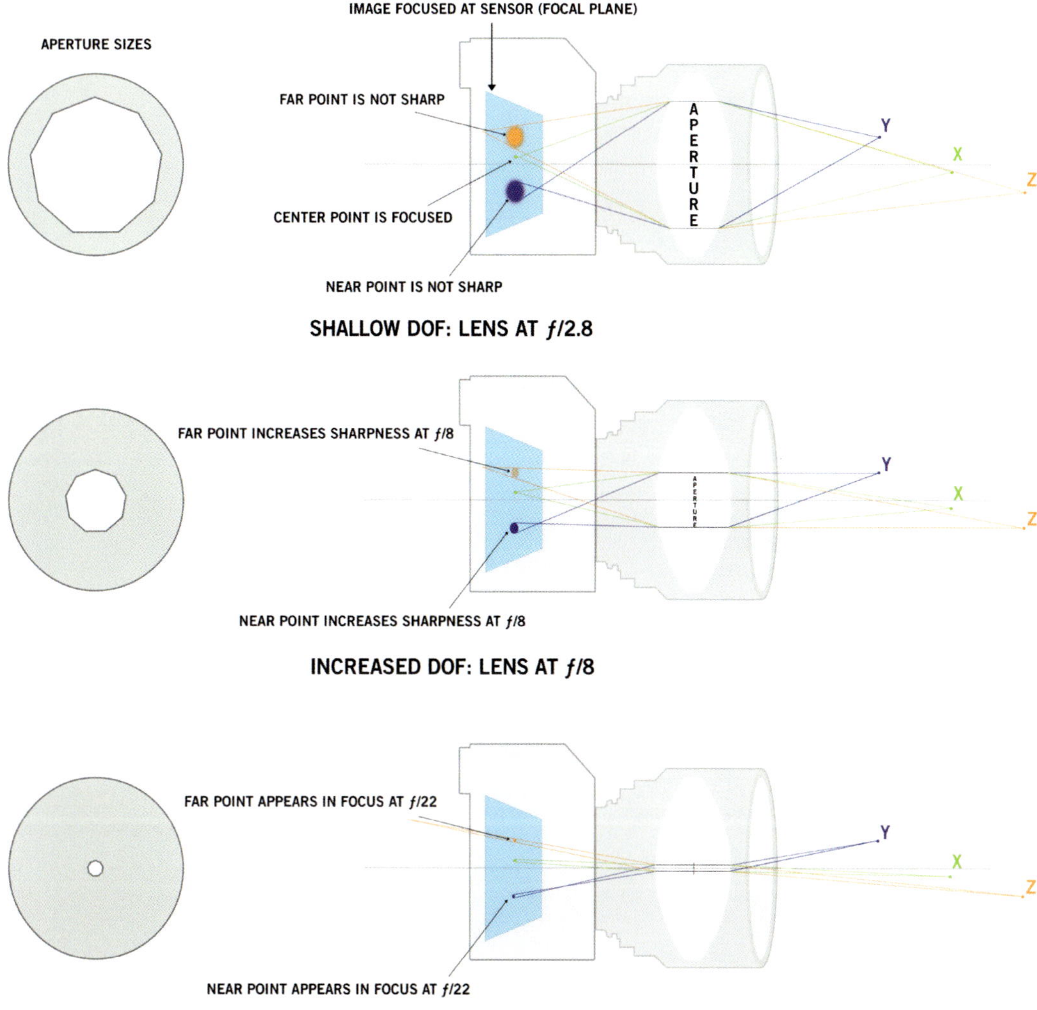


**FIGURE 4.17** In the upper illustration, the aperture is set to *ƒ*/2.8. The lens is focused on point X, so the dot on the subject side and the dot on the sensor are the same size. Y is a point closer to the lens (the near point) and Z is a point further from the lens (the far point). At *ƒ*/2.8, there is very little DoF: The rays of light pass through the lens to render the dots Y and Z as large, out-of-focus circles in the image. Y is focused in front of the sensor and Z is focused behind it.

Now look at the middle illustration, where the aperture is set to *ƒ*/8. Here, the aperture constricts the rays of light so they enter and exit the lens differently than they do in the upper illustration. Everything else is the same, but the circles on the sensor that are created from Y and Z are much smaller here. If you extend this principle to a lens at *ƒ*/22, the circles would be small enough that in the image, dots Y and Z would look practically the same size as dot X.
ILLUSTRATION © ANDY BATT, *DEPTH OF FIELD AND APERTURES,* 2013.

## Bokeh

On the other side of improving focus, you can add more blur to your images. We spend a lot of time caring about the in-focus bits of our photographs, but what about those blurry backgrounds? There's a Japanese word we can use to describe the quality of that blur: *bokeh* (or *boke*). The translations are inexact, but a loose definition is "the flavor and quality of the blur." It's nice to have a word that describes this quality. Bokeh occurs when the background in an image is indistinct. It's a combination of blurry highlights and out-of-focus patterns (**Figure 4.18**).

The focal length of your lens and the shape of your aperture have a lot to do with bokeh. By using a shallow aperture with longer focal lengths, you can drop focus behind your subject. Some wider lenses at fast apertures of *f*/2.0 can also give nice bokeh. With any lens, having a short subject distance will help create bokeh. Conversely, if your subject is twenty feet away at *f*/2.0, you'll have shallow DoF, but no bokeh. The shape of the aperture plays into the shapes created by those out-of-focus highlights: They echo the aperture. A pentagonal aperture will create five-sided highlights, and a nine-bladed aperture will create a much more circular highlight (**Figure 4.19**).

The evaluation of what makes bokeh pleasing is highly subjective; everyone seems to have a different opinion about what constitutes good bokeh and which lenses are the best and the worst at achieving it. What matters most is your opinion.

*Throw these ideas into the mix of lens considerations*:

- Bokeh occurs when the background of your image is out of focus enough to lack definition.
- Fast lenses (with large maximum apertures) and longer focal lengths create more opportunities for bokeh.
- The shape of your aperture influences the shape of the blurry highlights.

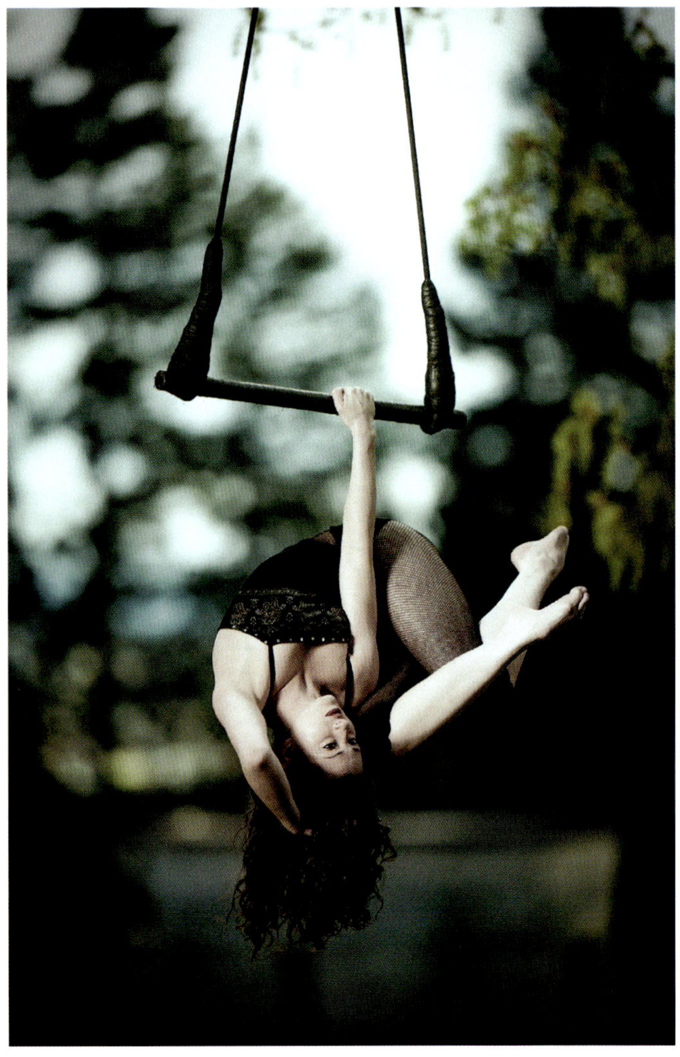

**FIGURE 4.18** Andy took this image at *f*/2.2 with a Canon 200mm lens. When we talk about the quality of blurry areas in the background, we use the term *bokeh*. IMAGE © ANDY BATT, *SY PARRISH*, 2009.

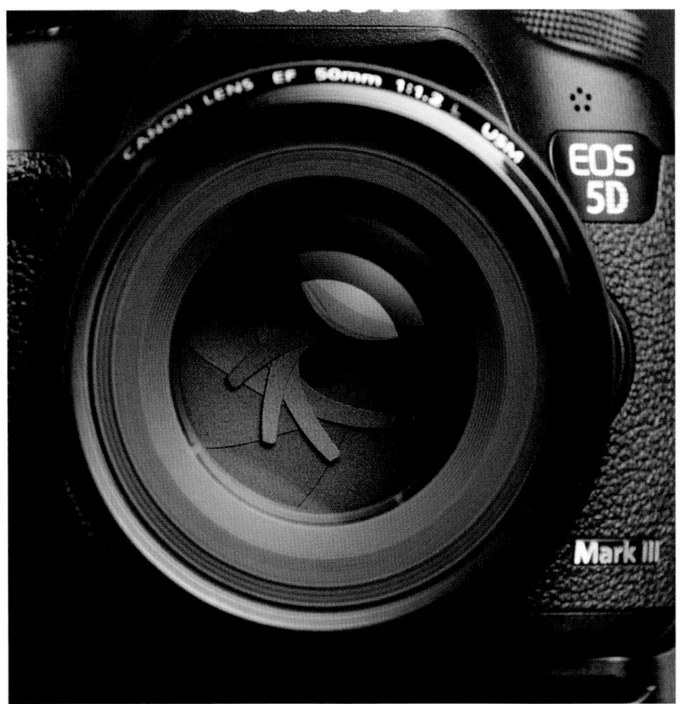


**FIGURE 4.19** The shape created by the aperture blades has a direct effect on the way bokeh is recorded by the sensor. The more blades an aperture contains, the more circular the aperture and the more rounded the bokeh will be.
IMAGE © ANDY BATT, *EIGHT-BLADED APERTURE,* 2013.

## How Good Is Your Depth of Field?

The best, most reliable way to determine if your near and far points are acceptably sharp is to take a photo and examine it on your computer. An actual image incorporates everything that might affect focus, sharpness and image quality—things like flare, high-ISO noise, cheaply made lens elements, etc. Testing is the best way to know, without a doubt, if you're really getting the sharpness you need from the DoF choices you're making.

***Andy:*** There are times when I need to know exactly how good my DoF is—how big of an area is usable and where the edges are. For example, if I'm setting up an action shot where I'm not sure that the autofocus system will be able to track correctly, I'll use zone focusing. This means I'll pick the point where the subject is most likely to be, focus there and tape off the lens focus.

I'll calculate a starting aperture value that I think will give me the DoF I want, and then have my assistants jump out and set up for a test shot. They'll stand at the near and far points of where I'd like the DoF to begin and end, and at the spot where I've focused. I can take a look on the camera's LCD screen, but the only way I'm going to feel 100% comfortable is by downloading the image and checking it out at the pixel level. At that point, I can tweak the focal point and aperture values until I get things dialed in the way I want them (**Figure 4.20**).

## Digital Depth of Field Calculators

Since we aren't always able to download images to check DoF, how can we figure it out on the fly? There are formulas for calculating DoF values, but the odds are against anyone busting out pencil and paper while on a shoot. Older mechanical lenses have DoF scales inscribed onto their barrels, but these are more of a rough guide. Inexpensive autofocus lenses have notoriously bad manual-focus scales and rarely include DoF scales anymore; even high-end lenses rarely include them. You can find more accurate focus and DoF scales if you look at nicely made (manual) mechanical focus lenses, like those made by Zeiss and a few other companies.

For lenses that lack this handy feature (or if you want more accuracy), it's faster and easier to look up your DoF in a chart or use an application—like David Eubank's pCAM Film + Digital Calculator (pCAM for short, **Figure 4.21**)—to calculate it for you. For more on pCAM, try the next exercise.

Remember, even with accurate charts and good software, testing is the best way to be sure that your near and far points are acceptably sharp. Doing a controlled test at home—before you need to go out and shoot—is also a great way to get more experience and value out of your lenses.

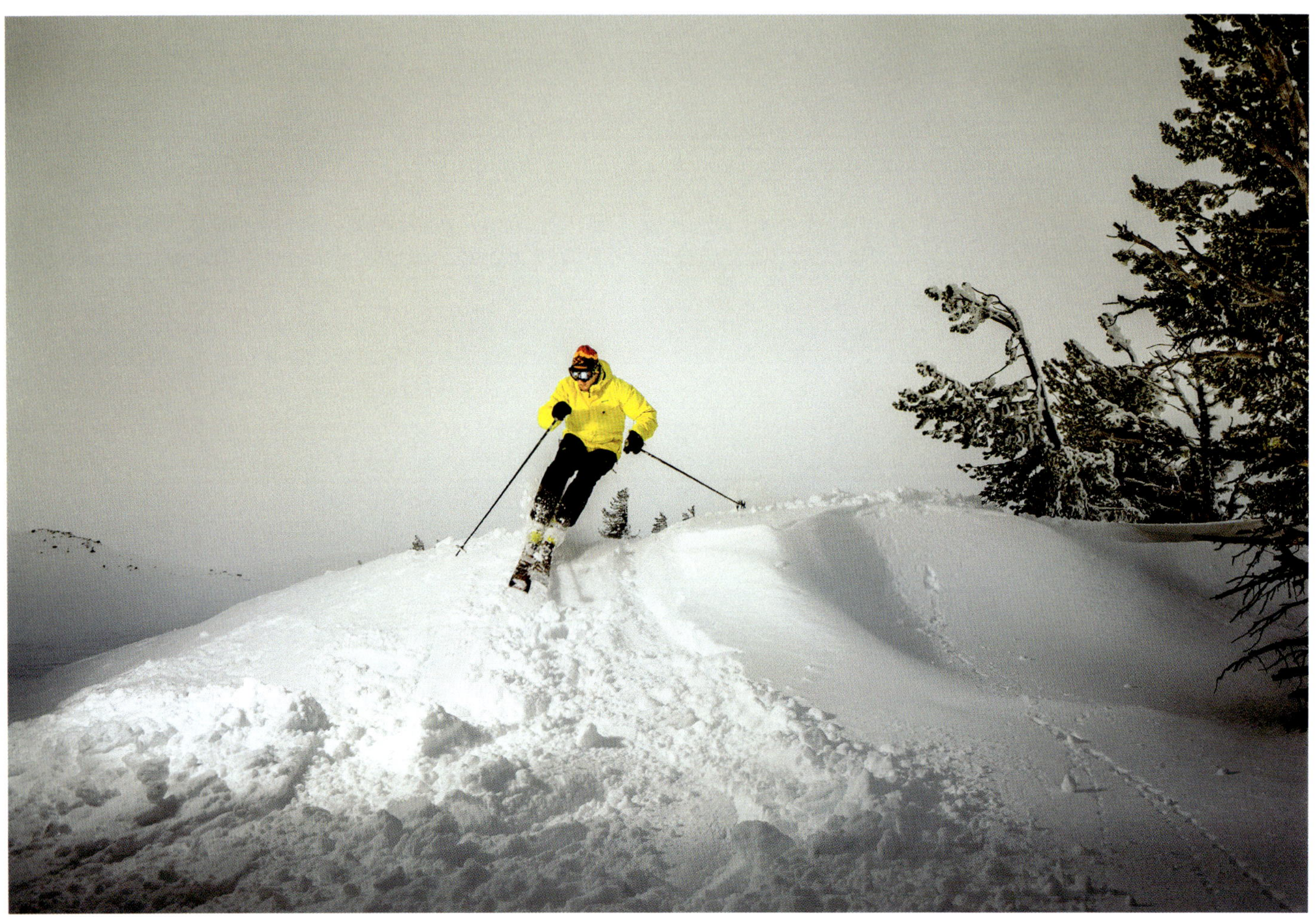

**FIGURE 4.20** Andy tweaks the focal point and aperture values until he gets things dialed in the way he wants them.
IMAGE © ANDY BATT, *DREW BLEDSOE, MT. BACHELOR,* FOR *OUTSIDE* MAGAZINE, 2011.

## TRY THIS AT HOME

### You're Too Damn Close—or—The Fake Band Shot

**For step-by-step instructions, go to:**
**www.focalpress.com/cw/digitalimagingmasters**

This exercise will give you some real DoF experience—with a fake subject. The goal is to help you prepare for those times when you're working by yourself without a computer and need to move quickly.

**Bonus**: You'll learn to work with pCAM, Andy's favorite DoF calculator.

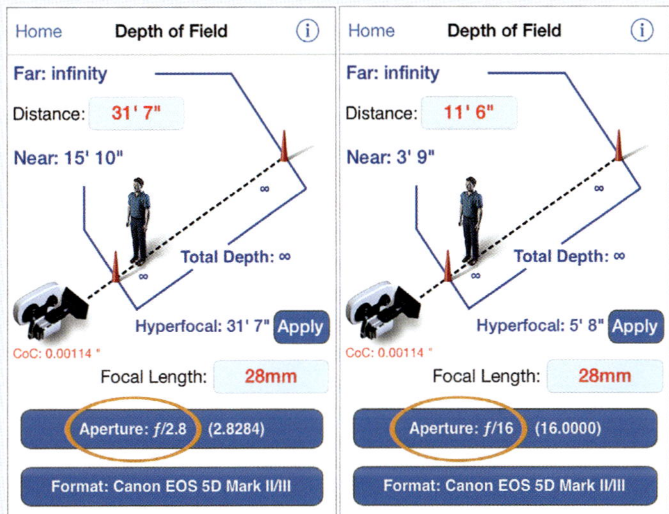


**FIGURE 4.21** Hyperfocal distance calculations can help you create a zone of focus. Here, Andy used pCAM to compare *f*/16 to *f*/2.8 with a 28mm lens on a Canon 5D Mark III.
SCREENSHOT © DAVID EUBANK, *PCAM FILM +DIGITAL CALCULATOR ON iOS*, 2013.

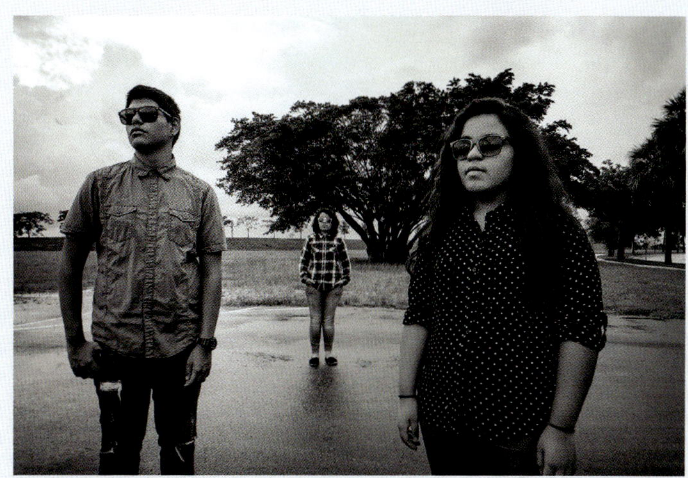

**FIGURE 4.22** By working with different F-stops, and DoF calculators, Erika learned which settings would enable her to hold focus over a large distance—and create her version of *The Band Shot*.
IMAGE © ERIKA VELASQUEZ, *THE BAND SHOT*, 2013.

# Lens Problems and "Miracle" Lenses

## Cheap, Fast, Good

Every time a new lens is developed, the lens designers have to consider focal length, weight, light transmission,[16] the time it takes for design and testing and the selling price. They also have to overcome basic problems, such as distortion, aberrations, color fidelity and accuracy of focus. By the time a commercially manufactured lens ends up in your hands, the designers have already eliminated or minimized these problems to the best of their ability (and their willingness to invest capital).

Generally speaking, you can find reasonably good lenses that are affordable, decently fast, fairly well built and have good optics. Prime lenses, by virtue of being simpler in build, have an edge and give you higher quality for a lower price.

When lenses become more complicated—and, in the case of zoom lenses, cover larger and larger focal lengths—they're susceptible to the "Cheap/Fast/Good" Triangle of Quality (**Figure 4.23**). Using this philosophy, only one or two (never three) elements are possible in any given circumstance, which means you can have a cheap, fast lens or a cheap, good lens, but not a cheap, fast *and* good lens.

"Miracle lenses" are those that claim to deliver all three: a large zoom range, great optics and an incredibly affordable price. Beware the 16mm–300mm zoom lens that weighs eight ounces, is six inches long and can be had for $100. Miracle lenses often embody *some* of the good factors: They can be lightweight, compact in size or have a zoom range—but at the expense of other important factors. A more expensive lens has high-quality optics and coatings, consistent F-stops,[17] quality materials and solid construction. Cheap lenses often exhibit vignetting, color shifts, chromatic aberrations, distortions, corner softness and a level of sharpness that just isn't acceptable. There's a world of build quality between a $12,000 lens and one that costs $500, and another world between the $500 lens and its $120 cousin.

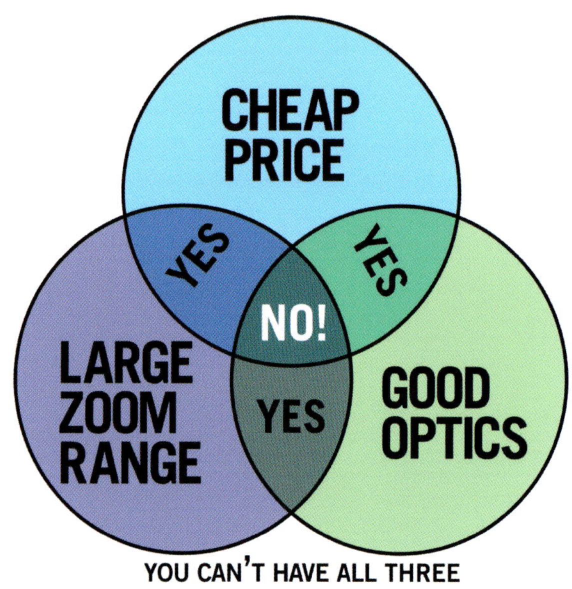


**FIGURE 4.23** This chart illustrates a concept that's useful for explaining many things. When it comes to shopping for a lens, it's not difficult to find a good lens that's also fast (big optical elements with a fast aperture), but it won't be cheap. You'll be able to find a cheap lens that's good (minimal problems with chromatic aberrations and distortion), but doesn't have a fast aperture; and you'll be able to find a fast lens that is cheap, but isn't very good.
ILLUSTRATION © ANDY BATT, *CHEAP/FAST/GOOD—PICK ANY TWO,* 2013.

With any lens, you can take amazing photos. The lens that fits your budget is the right lens for you. Once you understand what your lens can deliver, you'll know more about what you can do with it.

## Lens Choice

### Toni Greaves

***Andy Batt:*** **The image you create depends on the lens you've chosen, because it completely affects what you see. For instance, with some lenses, the view is so much wider than the one you see with your naked eye. How does your lens choice change your experience?**

***Toni Greaves:*** I'm shooting in multiple ways all the time—thinking about getting closer, going wider, backing up, etc. For me, that's all happening with my feet, because I use fixed focal-length lenses. I rarely use zoom lenses, because when I see the image quality, I can tell the difference. I've had very good zoom lenses, but I prefer fixed focal lengths.

***AB:*** **So hang on: You just expressed a technical opinion by making a deliberate choice in your lens work. Tell me more . . .**

***TG:*** The reason why I love prime lenses is that, by learning to shoot entirely with them, my sense of composition is way stronger. If you've got a 35mm lens, you're assessing what's happening within that 35mm frame. You don't have the option to gradually change the lens. I think it's a bit lazy to do it that way. You're going to be a better photographer by being able to move and by innately understanding the framing.

I can look at a picture and say, "Oh, that was shot with a 35mm and somebody cropped it down," because I understand the aspect ratio and the way that a lens sees. With my 35mm, I'll be moving in, backing up and putting myself in different situations (**Figure 4.24**). I'll climb on top of a ladder or on a roof before I'll use a zoom lens to change the frame.

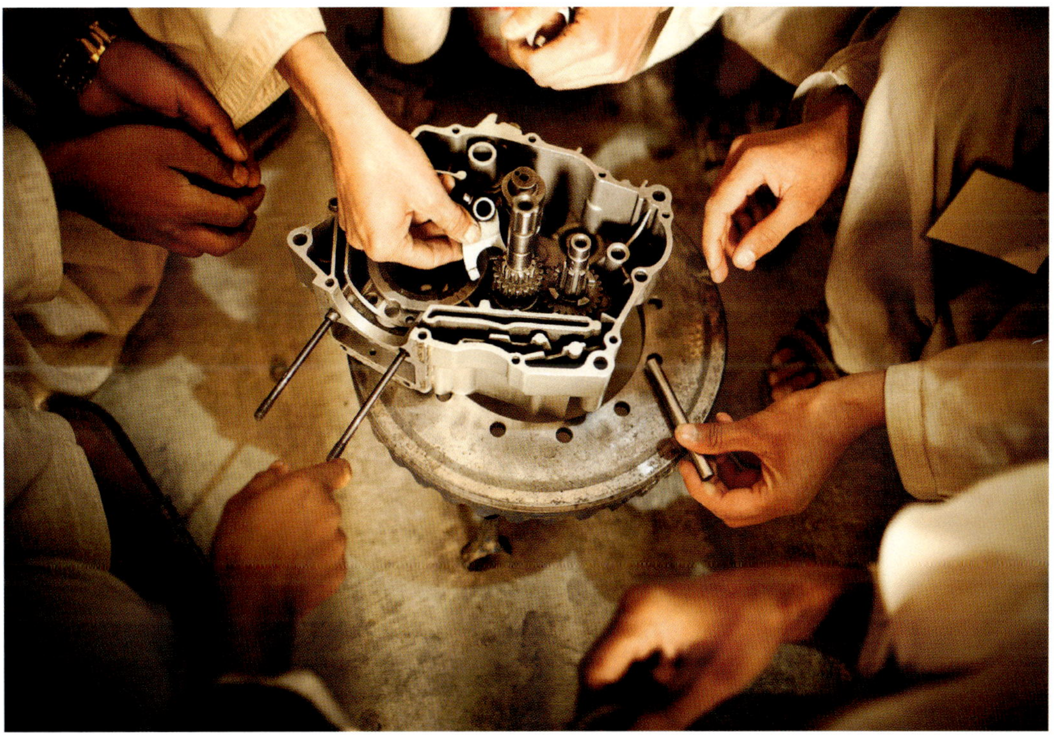

**FIGURE 4.24** For this shot of young men participating in a motorcycle repair class, Toni was able to get in close with her wide-angle lens without intruding upon the action. IMAGE BY TONI GREAVES FOR MERCY CORPS, *OUR SON CHANGING AFGHANISTAN: MOTORCYCLE REPAIR,* 2012.

There have been times when I've used a zoom lens because it's a liability to carry too much stuff. If I have to climb on top of something and do a risky thing, I won't be able to change lenses—so I'll use a zoom lens. [I'll also use one in] situations where my torso is entirely locked in and I'm not allowed to move, such as being in a helicopter. When I have to use a zoom, I actually use it in a manner like a fixed lens.

## Your Lens Might Have a Problem

Most lens problems are corrected in the design stage, but a few flaws will still remain in the finished product. Sometimes the flaws are inherent to the type of lens, and sometimes they're a matter of cost (in design, manufacture and price).

> ***Everything in photography involves compromise. We can never make a perfect lens, but we can make lenses that are optimized for some purpose, taking into account size and cost restrictions. Therefore, lens imperfections are still with us, albeit minimized by advances in computation and materials science.***
>
> ***—Charles S. Johnson, Jr. (2010: 32–33)***

A variety of optical elements are used in lens design, but each element can have side effects, introducing aberrations like image distortion or chromatic aberrations. One of the basic facts of lens design is that you can't use a single optical element to achieve a high-quality image. Adding additional elements to correct the side effects can, in turn, produce more side effects. These inherent flaws of optical transmission have been known since the seventeenth century, and modern lens design is still bound by these limitations. When a lens design becomes final, it's a complex balance of precisely positioned optical elements, all designed to give the best possible image within the parameters of the design.

## Lens Evaluation

The four main areas we want to look at when evaluating the lenses we own (or are thinking about buying) are: sharpness, distortion, chromatic aberration and vignetting. These factors apply to any lens, whether it's a $50 thrift-store special that requires a funky adaptor mount or a $2,500 pro lens.

### Lens Evaluation Overview

- Test to find out which problems your lens has and how severe (or minor) they are.
- Some problems are easily overcome. For instance, a lens that shows problems at *f*/2.0 might not exhibit those problems at *f*/4, and you can add a lens hood to a lens that flares easily.
- Some problems can be fixed in post-processing very simply. Vignetting and minor chromatic aberrations are easily corrected with raw-processing tools.
- Some problems can't be fixed. Once you're aware of them, you can avoid using certain lenses in situations where they'd cause trouble.

### Four Basic Lens Problems

1. **Sharpness**
   Do you have sharp images? Is the sharpness even across the image?
2. **Distortions**
   Do your images create curved lines where they should be straight?
3. **Chromatic aberrations**
   Do your images have red/cyan or yellow/blue fringing?
4. **Vignetting**
   Are your images darker at the edges or corners?

## Diffraction and the Deep Stops

Most lenses have their sharpest focus somewhere in their mid-aperture values—usually around *f*/8. When we stop them all the way down to improve our DoF, we can hit the diffraction wall. Diffraction occurs when light bends around a solid object. In the case of lenses, the light can actually bend around the edges of the aperture blades and diffuse. At narrow apertures, a high percentage of light diffuses in this way, so the image that reaches the sensor is noticeably softened. At wide apertures, the percentage is so small that it's negligible. To reduce or eliminate diffraction, it's a general rule to choose an aperture that's 1–2 stops wider than the narrowest one available.

### Time-Honored Test

The most time-honored DIY method for checking lens sharpness is to test-shoot a sheet of newspaper. By photographing the sheet at each different aperture on your lens and observing the results, you'll be able to tell which aperture value yields the sharpest focus.

> ***Diffraction causes a loss of overall image sharpness. To avoid it, don't use the deepest F-stops. Instead, stick with one that's 1–2 stops down from the smallest available.***

## Curvature of Field and the Shallows

Instead of projecting a flat, evenly sharp image on the sensor (focal plane), some lenses have a curved plane of focus. If your lens has this issue, you might not see it unless you're working with super-shallow apertures, like *f*/2.0 to *f*/0.95, where the DoF is reduced.

An image with this problem would have a sharply focused center (assuming you focused the lens at the center), with corners and edges that fall out of focus. Moving to a deeper aperture will reduce the effect—not by changing the curvature, but by adding DoF.

Knowing the personality of your lens can make a difference. For instance, if you had a lens with severe curvature, such as the potato chip-shaped example in **Figure 4.25**, you could make a choice to embrace the curvature and use it as a stylistic tool—or avoid it by using a deeper F-stop.

### Lens Testing

There are many online resources to help us explore the world's ever-expanding range of photographic equipment. Andy checked in with Dave Etchells, Publisher of SLRgear.com,[18] a lens-testing company that gives photographers a solid resource for researching lenses. He shared this insight:

> ***The plots [on SLRgear.com] should really help people understand that inexpensive lenses can often be as sharp/good as expensive ones, just over a restricted aperture range. One of my goals for SLRgear is to help people understand where the "sweet spots" of their lenses lie, so they can take best advantage of them (as well as to see and understand what they get for their money with more expensive glass).***

## Colored Edges: Chromatic Aberrations

You've probably seen—in areas of high contrast on your images—out-of-registration ripples that are red and cyan or blue and yellow. This occurs when the different wavelengths (colors) of light land at slightly different points in your image. Instead of a single black tree branch, for example, you might see a ripple of red on one side and one of cyan on the other (**Figure 4.26**). The term for this is *lateral chromatic aberration (CA).*

This happens because the different wavelengths are actually being focused at different positions on the focal plane. Think of it as different colors landing slightly to the left and slightly to the right of where they're supposed to be. You'll see it more frequently in the

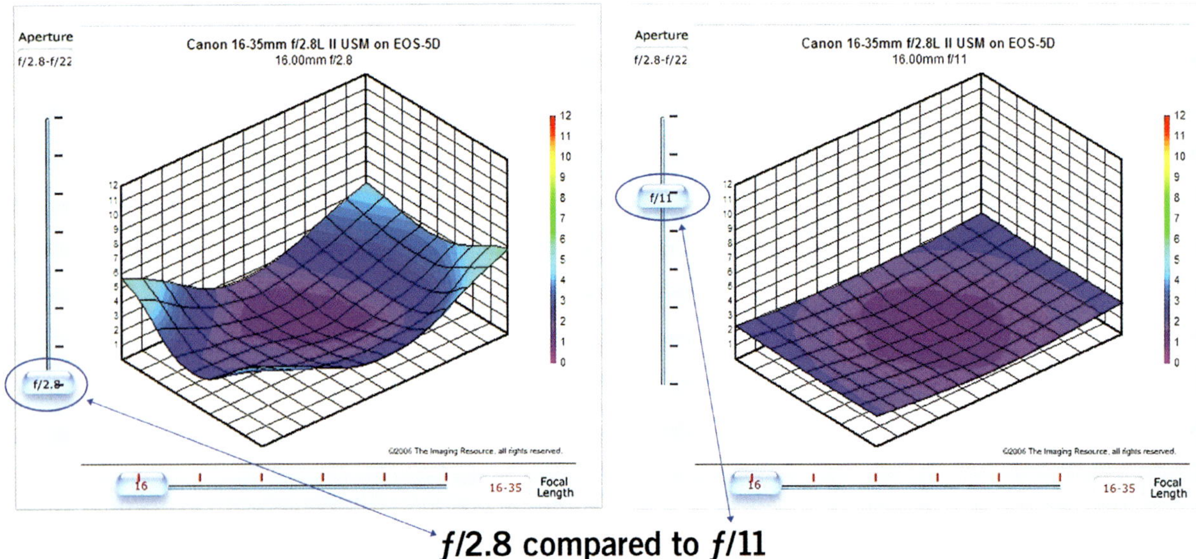


**FIGURE 4.25** This SLRGear.com Blur Chart shows curvature of field for the Canon 16–35mm zoom at *f*/2.8, at 16mm. The center purple area is where the focus is sharp, with quick falloff towards the edges (left image). Once you know that a lens exhibits this behavior, you can choose to use the focus falloff as a creative tool—either by enhancing the shallow DoF at *f*/2.8 or stopping down to *f*/11 to get a flat field of focus (right image).
ILLUSTRATIONS PROVIDED BY SLRGEAR.COM, USED WITH PERMISSION, *CURVATURE OF FIELD AND BLUR CHARTS*, 2013.

---

corners of an image, where the rays of light come in at a steeper angle. You can't improve lateral CA with lens settings, but you can easily reduce or remove it with the CA correction tool found in most raw-processing applications.

*Longitudinal CA*[19] shows up as blurry edges or colored fringing in places where there should be sharp edges. This occurs when the wavelengths arrive out of registration on the lens axis, slightly in front of or behind the focal plane. You can usually improve longitudinal CA by using a smaller F-stop, which increases the DoF. Fringing can also be reduced or removed with the fringe removal tool found in most raw processors.

Chromatic aberrations can show up with any type of lens, but it's generally more of a problem with long focal-length lenses. The magnification rate of these lenses is much higher, so the problems are magnified along with the image. Part of the reason why super-telephoto lenses (like the ones you see at the sidelines of sporting events) have huge glass elements—and cost in the $10,000 range—is to eliminate CA problems.

Worth mentioning here is a related color issue: *purple fringing.* While it appears to resemble CA and is corrected with similar raw-processing tools, purple fringing is actually a sensor problem. We'll cover this topic further in *Chapter 5.*

***Lenses with strong chromatic aberrations can be a problem. To correct out-of-registration colors, you can use the "Remove Chromatic Aberration" checkbox in the Lightroom Lens Correction panel. You can eliminate or reduce color fringing by stopping down—or by using the "Defringe" tool (next to the CA tool in Lightroom).***

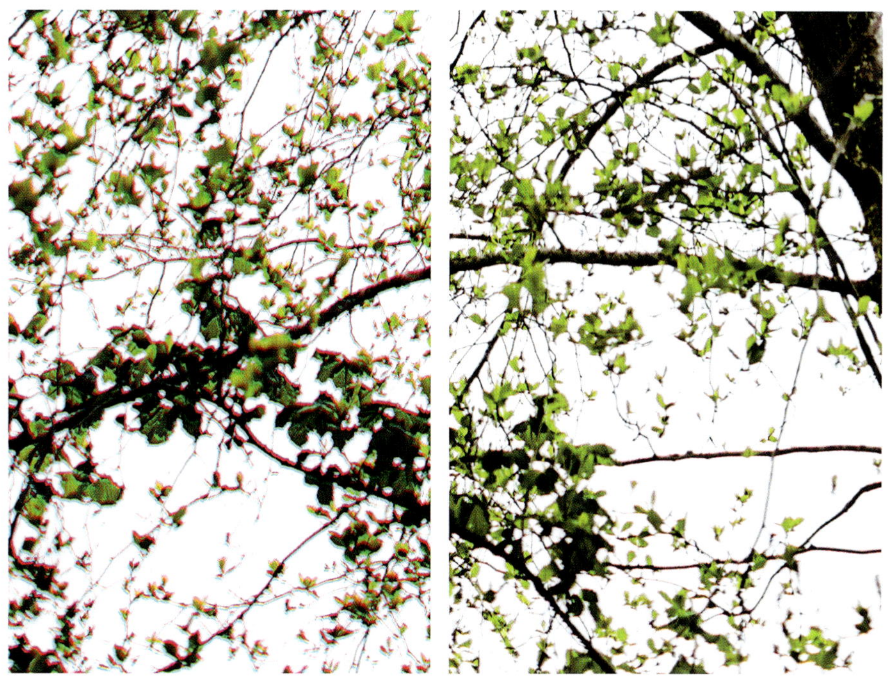

**FIGURE 4.26** Andy selected an image that had some chromatic-aberration issues (left image) and then used Lightroom to correct them (right image). The CA shown here is the lateral type, where different wavelengths (colors) of light are focused slightly out of registration. CA corrections in software allow you to realign the colors. They can go a long way towards fixing images that were created by a lens with bad CA. Always test before you rely on these types of fixes!
IMAGE © ANDY BATT, *CHROMATIC ABERRATION, BEFORE AND AFTER,* 2013.

## Vignetting: Friend and Foe

If you see a gradual darkening of your image around the edges, and it's more pronounced in the corners, then you have vignetting. There are a few reasons why vignetting might appear in your photographs (**Figure 4.27**). Vignetting can shift with focus distance. When your lens is focused at infinity, the image circle it projects is smaller, and more optical or "hard" vignetting will come into play. When you refocus to a closer distance, you increase the size of the image circle, which pushes the vignetting partially or fully outside the image that fills the sensor.

### Correctional Facilities

Your camera might have a feature called "peripheral illumination correction." This is a fancy way of saying it can correct vignetting. By testing their own lenses, camera manufacturers can install a database inside the camera that provides a specific correction for the lens you have. It works great—if you shoot JPEG, since the camera processes the raw file for you. It also works if you use the manufacturer's processing software; the instruction is embedded into the metadata.

Another approach to resolve vignetting is to use the Lens Correction tool within Lightroom (and most other applications). These generally have the ability to read the metadata tag for the lens you're

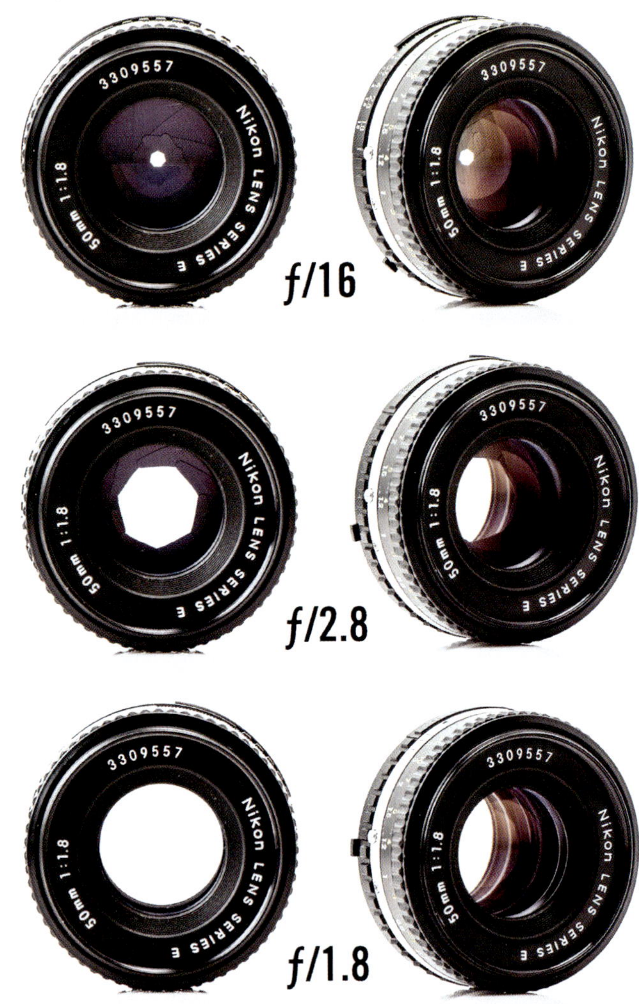


**FIGURE 4.27** When the aperture is wide open, part of it is blocked at the edges by the lens barrel. This can reduce the amount of light that's gathered around the edges of the image. If the darkened area falls inside the part of the image circle that covers the sensor, then you'll get vignetting.
IMAGE © ANDY BATT, *OPTICAL VIGNETTING*, 2013.

using and automatically search their built-in corrections database to see if there's a match. This can be a real advantage when working with third-party lenses—like Zeiss glass—on Canon or Nikon cameras. In the manufacturer's raw-processing applications,[20] though, these third-party lenses wouldn't show up as automatically correctable. If your lens isn't in the database, then you can turn to the full set of manual correction tools. No matter where the vignetting comes from, you can find a processing solution to deal with it.

### Vignetting for Creative Emphasis

Vignetting has long been considered a creative tool and is used to emphasize the subject of an image. You might know it by its alternate name, "edge burning." Many photographers add vignetting in post to an image that doesn't have any. Style is subjective—how little vignetting you add or remove is up to you (**Figure 4.28**).

> ***Vignetting can be "fixed" by using deeper F-stops or using Lens Correction tools in raw file processing. Some photographers consider vignetting to be a desirable quality and add it in post.***

## The Bent Image: Distortion

When you see curved lines where there should be straight ones, you're dealing with distortion. In a perfect lens, the image projected on your sensor will have the same level of magnification across the entire field. Lens distortions are a consequence of uneven magnification in the lens. Many lenses show a change in the magnification, usually towards the edges and corners. The two main types of distortion you'll run into are pincushion and barrel (**Figure 4.29**). *Barrel distortions* curve the lines outward from the center—a result of less magnification at the edges. *Pincushion distortions* curve the lines inward toward the center—because the magnification at the edges increases.

> ***Lens distortions can be fixed in raw file processing—but the image may need to be photographed with a wider view to enable cropping.***

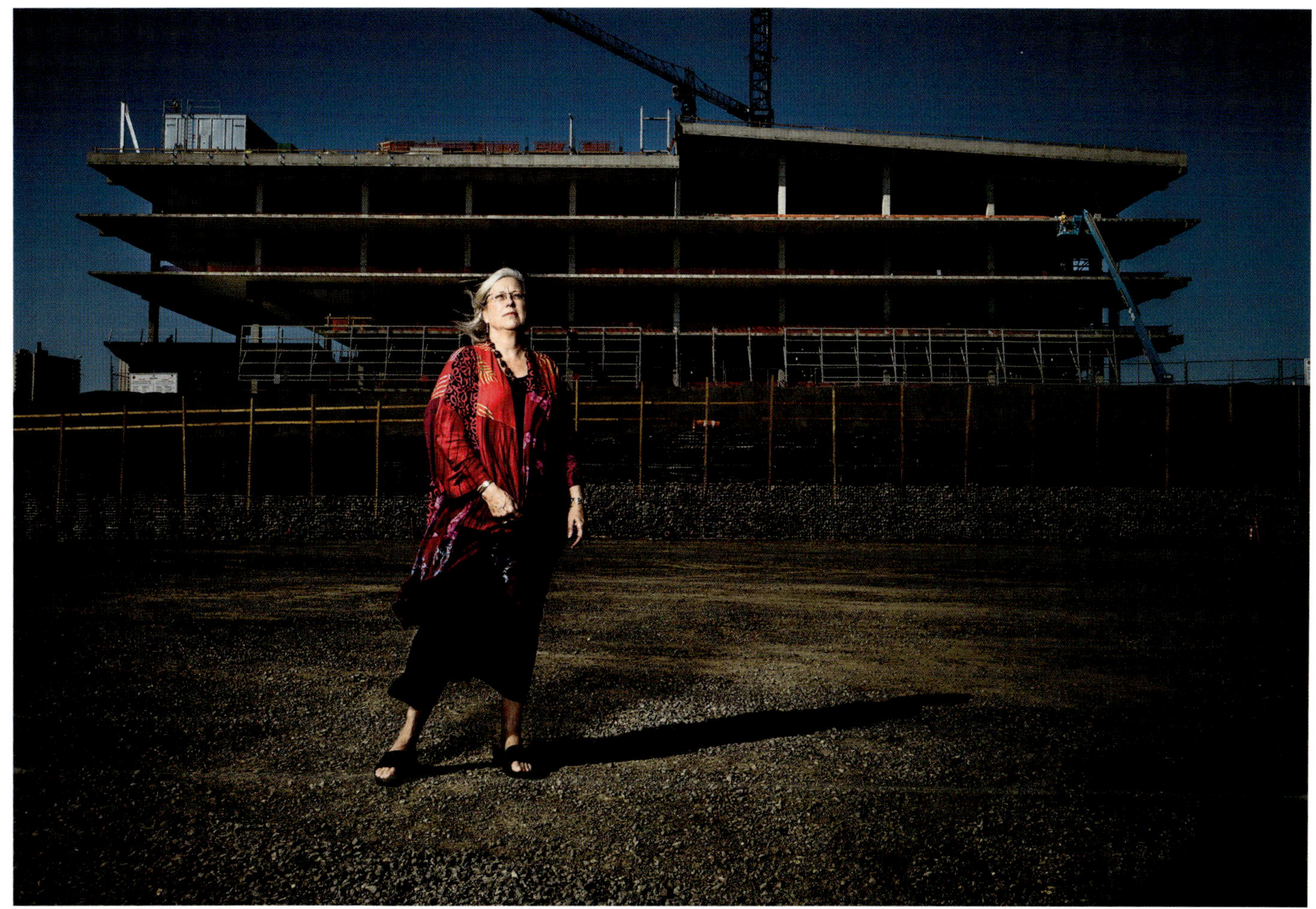

**FIGURE 4.28** Andy used creative vignetting for this environmental portrait to draw attention to his subject.
IMAGE © ANDY BATT, *LISA M. COUSSENS, OHSU,* FOR *PORTLAND MONTHLY* MAGAZINE, 2012.

Any lens can suffer from distortion. It's a good idea to check your zoom lenses, since you might find barrel distortion at their widest focal lengths and pin cushioning at their longest. You can't fix distortion problems at the lens level,[21] but good software solutions can be found in your post-processing application's Lens Correction tool. Distortion doesn't necessarily mean that details are out of focus—you can have a sharp and distorted image. Severe re-shaping of the image might require you to significantly crop into it. If you're aware of the problem ahead of time, then you can move the camera back and shoot a wider view, knowing that you'll need to crop in post.

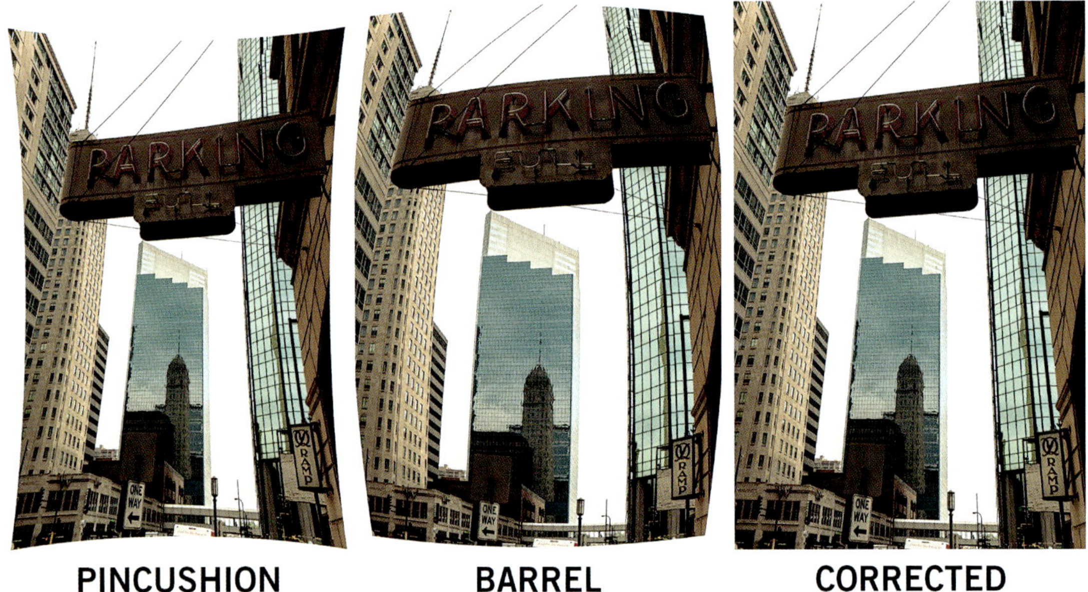


**FIGURE 4.29** Although you can't fix distortion problems at the lens level, you can address the issue with Lens Correction tools in your post-processing application. IMAGES © ANDY BATT, *PINCUSHION AND BARREL DISTORTIONS,* 2013.

## Sometimes Problems Are a Good Thing

We photographers have a problem: We tend to fall in love with things that engineers try to get rid of, like vignettes and distortions. There's something interesting about a lens that has a problem. For the right project, those defects can lend a personality—an organic quality—to the images we create. Sometimes we want to feel the presence of our equipment, rather than having it recede quietly into the background.

With the ever-improving digital sensors, we create raw data—images that don't have a baseline look and feel. Yes, we can choose to *post*-process our images with tools like Red Giant, Nik, Alien Skin or DxO to add a dizzying array of grain, vintage film styles, vignettes, flares, dirt and scratches to our work. If we want to apply style to our images *before processing*, though, our lenses offer us the opportunity.

Here are some recipes: Couple a vintage lens (with its scratches, lack of anti-flare coatings and maybe some mold) to the right adaptor, and then attach it to your six-month-old super-camera. Attach a clear-glass filter—which you sanded on the edges and smeared with Vaseline—on top of your $1,200 lens. Photographers do all types of things in pursuit of adding a unique, intrinsic quality to their photographs.

## Craig Strong

### Inventor of the Lensbaby

One repeatable method for engaging an organic feel (without risking that Vaseline or mold will get into your camera) is to use a Lensbaby. Lensbaby started out as a bendable plastic lens that mounted to your DSLR and has evolved into a sophisticated set of tools. They enable us to go after all sorts of beautiful problems (**Figure 4.30**).

***Andy Batt:*** **What inspired you to create this tool?**

***Craig Strong:*** I came up with the idea for the Lensbaby because I wanted to have a more organic look from images shot with my first DSLR. With early DSLRs, the life that film gave images—even images shot with the best glass—was gone, and my images felt sterile in comparison to what I had captured with film. I was searching for a lens that would fuse the selective focus of a (difficult to use,

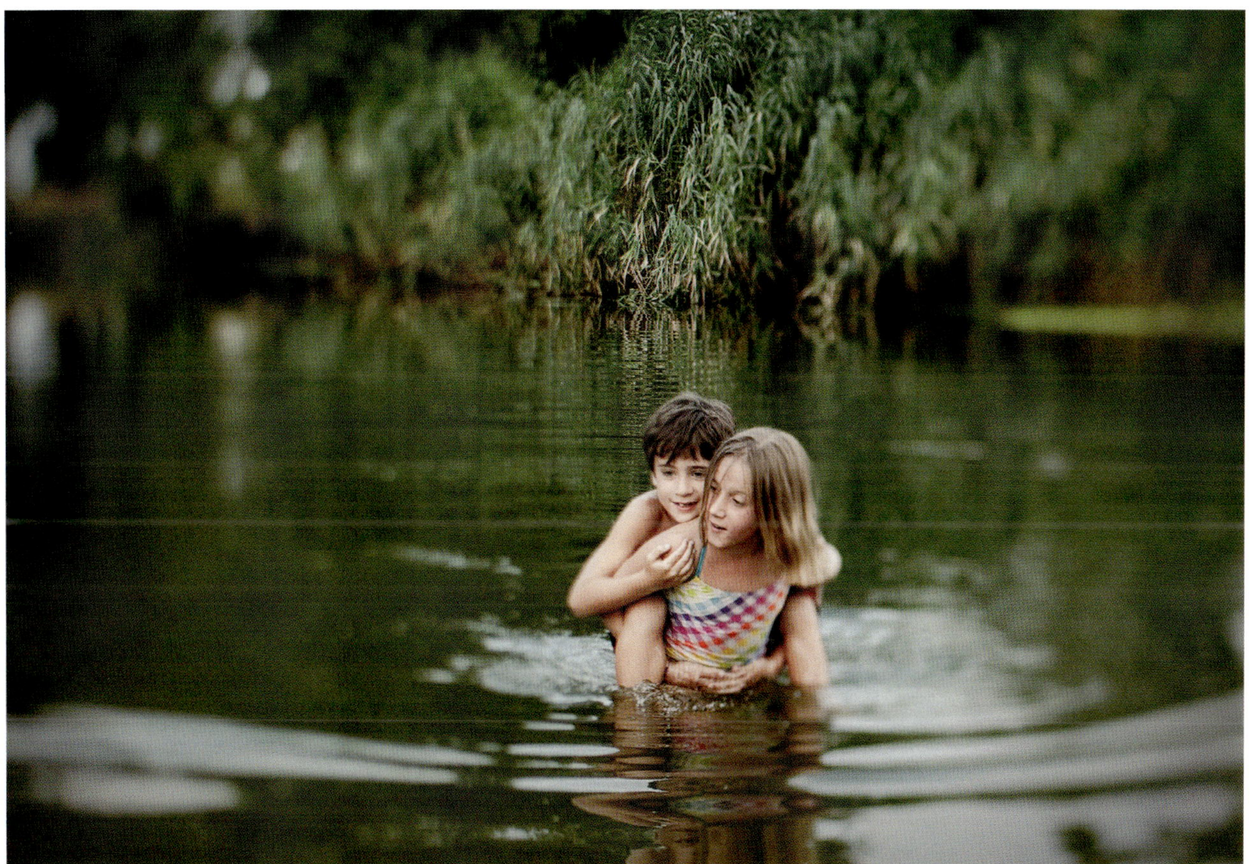

**FIGURE 4.30** This image of the children in the river displays an effect that would be considered a problem in a $1,200 lens, but here it enhances the image. By using a Lensbaby, Craig was able to capture this style in–camera.
IMAGE © CRAIG STRONG, LENSBABY CREATOR, *TILT TRANSFORMER*, 2010.

expensive) Tilt-Shift lens with the more spontaneous, random quality of a Holga.[22]

In my free time, I put anything and everything in front of my DSLR body that would focus light. The first Lensbaby was made with a piece of ShopVac hose (a hardware-store moment of inspiration), a body cap with a hole cut in it, and a 101mm Kodak lens off of my old Speed Graphic camera that had been sitting as an ornament on my bookshelf.

## The Transformative Power of the Lens

The lens is a great leveler; no matter what kind of photographer you are, or what level you're working at, the lens is the thing that shapes your vision. Time, experience and the effort to know your gear are what make good pictures, not the cost of your lens.

Whether it's a used 70–200mm that cost you $500 or a new top-of-the-line lens worth $2,500, all lenses work on the same principles. Yes, there are differences in the extended abilities a high-end lens will offer, but those are trumped by your ability to use the gear you have. These principles are powerful. Your aperture setting selects what's in focus. Your focal length transforms the world, bringing the scene closer to or farther from you. A wide lens increases that distance. These decisions and ideas are at the root level of imagery—and you work with them every time you make a photograph.

---

## Notes

1 For more information on what constitutes a "normal" focal length, see *Angle of View* later in this chapter.

2 HMI (hydrargyrum medium-arc iodide) lights are continuous sources that are daylight balanced.

3 These are really unique strobe lights that have a specific look. They're about three feet long and are shaped like a half-dome of white Plexiglas.

4 The Color Run International, www.thecolorrun.com.

5 There's always going to be dust on your sensor; the key is to keep it at a reasonable level.

6 A push-pull lens relies on the motion of sliding the zoom in and out, as opposed to twisting a ring. This design requires fewer glass elements to make the lens compressible; it can also include a variable aperture, so that as you change the zoom, the maximum diameter aperture shifts. As is true when using fewer glass elements, this is part of the design compromise to make a lighter-weight lens.

7 An image-stabilized lens uses microscopic gyroscopes to balance out the motion of the lens moving when handheld. A good system can allow for handheld shots at very slow shutter speeds.

8 Or a pair of zooms, to cover a longer range of focal lengths: a 70–200mm and 200–400mm would be a great combination.

9 Don't take this as a challenge.

10 Indianapolis 500.

11 You can also measure it on the horizontal and vertical of the focal plane. Some lens specification guides will list all three methods, although the diagonal one is most common.

12 It's more typical to find T-stops on Cine lenses, which are used for making movies.

13 Until you get to a point of diffraction—more on this shortly.

14 Our diagram is based on the one in Ansel Adams's book, *The Camera.* He does a fantastic job of explaining this concept, and we can only hope to come close!

15 Think of these as distant stars in a night sky—easy to see, but incredibly small.

16 Light transmission: How dense are all those glass elements and how much light do they absorb?

17 Some lenses have a variable maximum F-stop that changes as the zoom shifts, i.e., it's an *f*/3.5 lens at one end and a *f*/5.6 at the other. Occasionally, a high-end lens will have this design.

18 SLRgear.com, Digital Camera Reviews, http://www.slrgear.com/reviews/index.php.

19 Longitudinal CA is found almost exclusively in high-speed lenses at very wide apertures.

20 Digital Photo Pro for Canon, and ViewNX for Nikon.

21 It's possible for curvature of field to overlap lens distortion. If that's the case, then changing to a deeper aperture to increase the DoF might help.

22 Holga cameras are low-cost medium-format cameras that take 120mm film. They have a cult following, and images made with them are known for their quirky display of distortions.

## EXPLORATIONS

### Idea #1, The Variable Prime Lens—or Idea #2, The Shoe Leather Zoom

***Gear:*** Your camera, a zoom lens or a prime lens and a piece of tape
***Location:*** Everywhere
***Subjects:*** Everything you see

This Exploration is designed to make you a more active photographer. You can participate with either a zoom lens or with a prime lens. In either case, you're going to move around a lot. The challenge? Using a zoom lens without moving your feet. The method? Treating the zoom lens like it's a prime lens!

#### Idea #1: The Variable Prime Lens

What is a variable prime lens? It's a counterintuitive name, but we think it's a great way to re-label your zoom lens. A prime lens is a fixed focal length, and if you want to change the view, you walk forward or backward. We're asking you to transform your zoom lens into a variable prime with a very high-tech accessory: tape. Choose a focal length, and then tape it in position so you (temporarily) can't zoom to a different focal length.

#### Idea #2: The Shoe Leather Zoom

A shoe leather zoom is the companion idea to a variable prime lens. You might have a bag of lenses—everything from a 14mm to a 300mm—that you drag along with you on every outing. To enable shoe leather zoom mode, you have to do one daring thing: Pick a single prime lens. That's right, you're going to leave the rest behind. It doesn't matter which lens you choose—it will be the right one.

#### *In Practice*

1. Choose Idea #1 or #2, and mount up your lens of choice. If you're using a zoom, then pick a focal length and tape it down. If you're using a shoe leather zoom, leave all your other glass at home.
2. Head out for a day of photography—landscapes, street scenes, whatever you're interested in.
3. Find an initial subject and frame up your best shot. Set your camera to Manual mode and continue to practice good control over shutter speed, aperture, ISO and WB.
4. Once you've nailed down that shot—don't leave! *Walk forward* and find another way of looking at the same scene. Try to maintain the same F-stop.
5. Now *walk backward*, behind the first spot, and find a third shot. Try to maintain the same F-stop.
6. Repeat.

> ***I'm thinking and shooting in multiple ways all the time. I'm thinking about getting closer . . . wider . . . backing up. For me, that all pretty much happens with my feet, so choosing where I stand affects a lot. Almost all the time, it's my feet that function as my zoom lens.***
>
> ***—Toni Greaves***

**Zoom Lens Bonus**: When you're finished with the first shot, change focal lengths and tape a new one down. Find a new shot and go back to Step 3.

***Evaluation***: For each shot you took:

- Look at your initial framing—the first of the series of three. Study your composition: How did the focal length and DoF affect your image?
- Now compare the second and third images in that series. Compared to the first, what about the composition changed?
- How did changing your position change the way focal length and DoF affected the image?
- Which image do you prefer, and why?

# LIGHT BECOMES THE IMAGE

Every time you press the shutter, light is transformed from its original form (waves and particles) into zeroes and ones. In this chapter, we'll examine the way sensors capture images—how your carefully created captures (which contain loads of rich information, from textures and highlights to emotion and decisive moments) become a set of data that's recorded to a memory card. To apply our "technology powers artistry" theme to the subject, we'll explore the way light becomes data and data becomes your image. *Added bonus:* when you understand sensor technology, it's easier to make sound decisions about which camera to buy and when to replace your old one.

# CCD or CMOS: A Two-Party System

The odds are that your camera has either a CCD or a CMOS[1] sensor inside of it. There are other ways of building imaging sensors, but in photography, it comes down to these two heavyweight champions. Each one has strengths and weaknesses, although each successive generation works hard to improve and gain on the other's territory. By carefully considering the sensor technology that sits inside your camera, you'll know how to work with its strengths and how to minimize its weaknesses. When it comes to professional cameras, these two technologies also tend to split along price lines: A professional DSLR is most likely CMOS-based and can run anywhere from $1,000 to $8,000. A professional medium-format digital back is almost always going to be CCD-based and cost between $10,000 and $50,000.

Knowledge is cheap. By understanding what's inside each of these systems, you'll be able to appreciate what inexpensive cameras are capable of and what advantages expensive cameras offer. It's all about matching the camera's capabilities to your needs.

## The Right Camera for the Job

***Candace Dobro:* What do you think about when you're selecting a camera for a particular job?**

***Andy Batt:*** For some projects, the end use drives the camera system. I can rent an 80MP CCD medium-format system[2] to capture a portrait, when I know it'll be printed as a giant two-story poster—especially if the client wants it to be as sharp as possible when somebody walks up to it. For other projects, a technique might drive my choice of camera. To capture intense bursts of fast action, I would use an 18MP DSLR[3] with a high frame rate and a fast autofocus system. If I were going to create an image to be printed as a huge, fine art inkjet, I might go with a 36MP full-frame DSLR.[4] There are plenty of projects where a number of different systems would work. For those times, I look at other factors, such as weight, battery life, lens choices, or post-production workflows.

***CD:* Do you always choose the largest-possible sensor, regardless of the type of job you're working on?**

***AB:*** Some people might argue that larger files are always better, but that's not always true! Just think of the enormous difference between handling 5,000 80MP 480MB files (at 2.29TB!) and 5,000 18MP 20MB files (at 97.65GB). You need to consider your workflow. For example, you'll need to have a good backup structure and allow for the time to back up 2.29TB of images, and you'll need some serious processing power to quickly apply looks and export out JPEGs for a client hard drive. It's all about balancing the needs of the project.

***CD:* Which types of projects would you need those giant files for?**

***AB:*** In advertising, there's a constant need to repurpose images. I'm often asked to shoot so that a single image can be cropped as a square, horizontal *and* vertical—in a variety of sizes and end uses. The images might be used as magazine ads, web banners, double-page spreads, trade-show posters or packaging. An 80MP file allows the client to crop and alter dimensions without needing to upscale[5] the image—since they can be cropped way into the frame and still have plenty of resolution.

## FEATURED PHOTOGRAPH

### Luci Romberg, Wall Runner

Andy chose this image (**Figures 5.1 and 5.2 [right]**) because it was printed out as a huge vinyl inkjet, which illustrates just how much you can accomplish with your camera—if you understand the capability of your equipment and software.

***Andy:*** I went to LA to photograph Luci Romberg; she's an amazing stuntwoman and Parkour artist. We did a bunch of work all over the city, but this image (**Figure 5.1**) is a favorite. It's simple, graphic and has a lot of great story going on. Nothing is Photoshopped—Luci really *can* run sideways on walls! The image was made using strobe light at 1/2500 sec at *f*/2.5.

I used a Canon 1Ds Mark III with a native resolution of 3,744 × 5,616 pixels. At a resolution of 300ppi,[6] that prints out as a 12.48 × 18.72 inch image. It needed to be an eight-foot tall print for an exhibition of my Parkour work at TBWA\Chiat\ Day, an ad agency. The inkjet printer that we printed the full-height image on needed the files to be at 75ppi.[7] We had to "up-rez" the file to 130%—about 97 inches (or 7,314 pixels) on the long side.

The sharpness of the print is pretty amazing—even up close. To give you a sense of scale, I grabbed a snapshot of Luci standing next to it (**Figure 5.2**). To make these prints successfully, it was important to understand that I wasn't comparing their quality to that of an 11 × 14 inch fine art inkjet print. I needed the image to look good on its own terms. Making eight-foot-tall prints from DSLR files is usually met with skepticism—but I knew my equipment, software and files well enough to know that it would work.

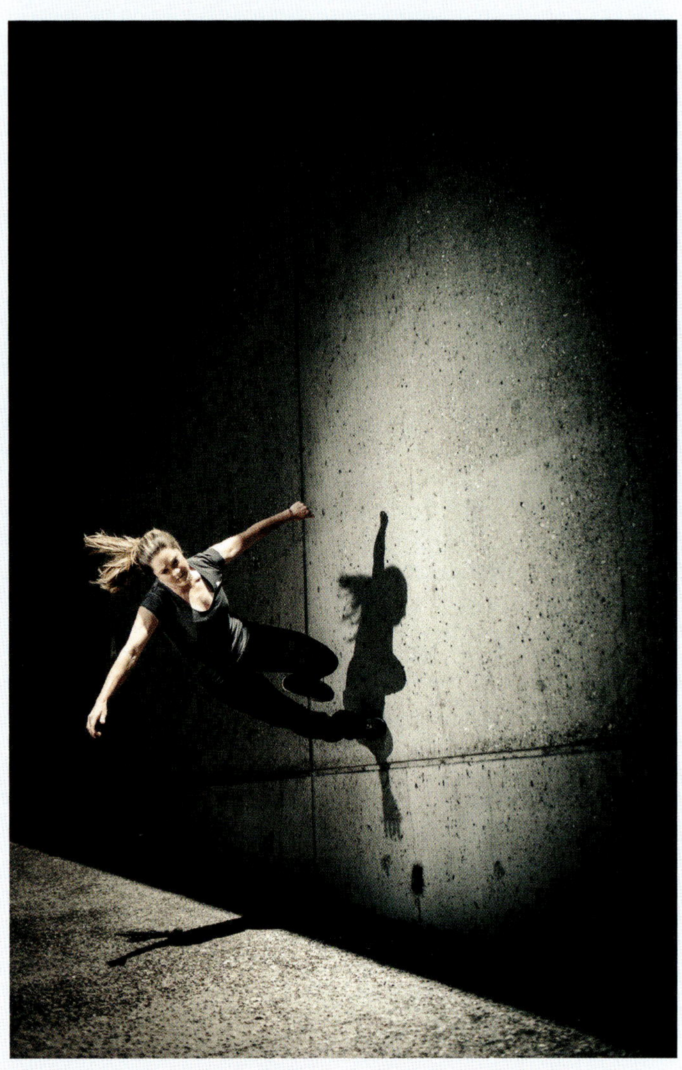

**FIGURE 5.1** Andy photographed Luci in LA with a Canon 1Ds Mark III for a personal project.
IMAGE © ANDY BATT, *LUCI ROMBERG, WALL RUNNER*, 2009.

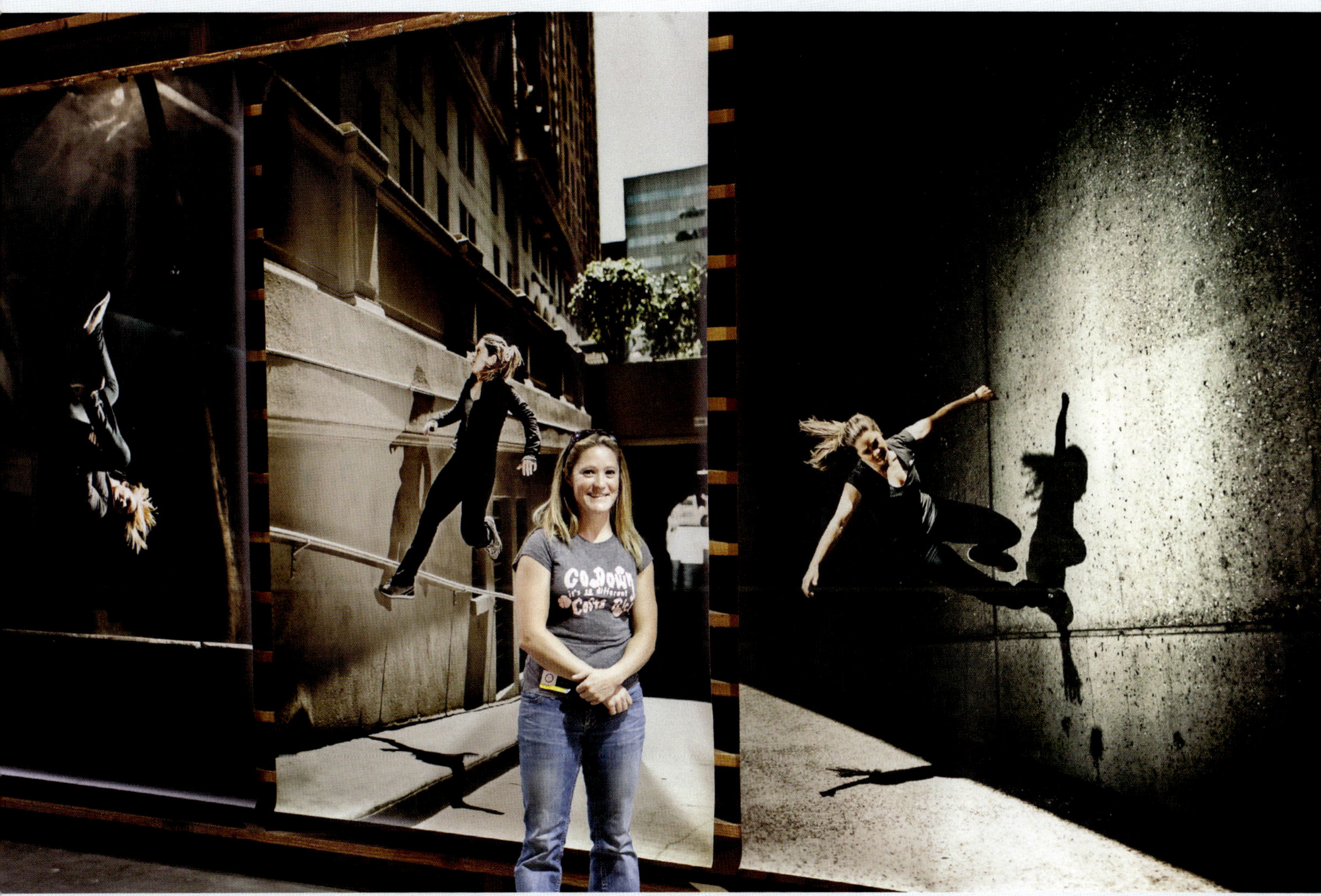

**FIGURE 5.2** The image in **Figure 5.1** was selected for a gallery exhibition of Andy's Parkour work. It was shown as an eight-foot tall print at the offices of TBWA\Chiat\Day in Los Angeles.
IMAGE © ANDY BATT, *LUCI ROMBERG, WALL RUNNER,* 2010.

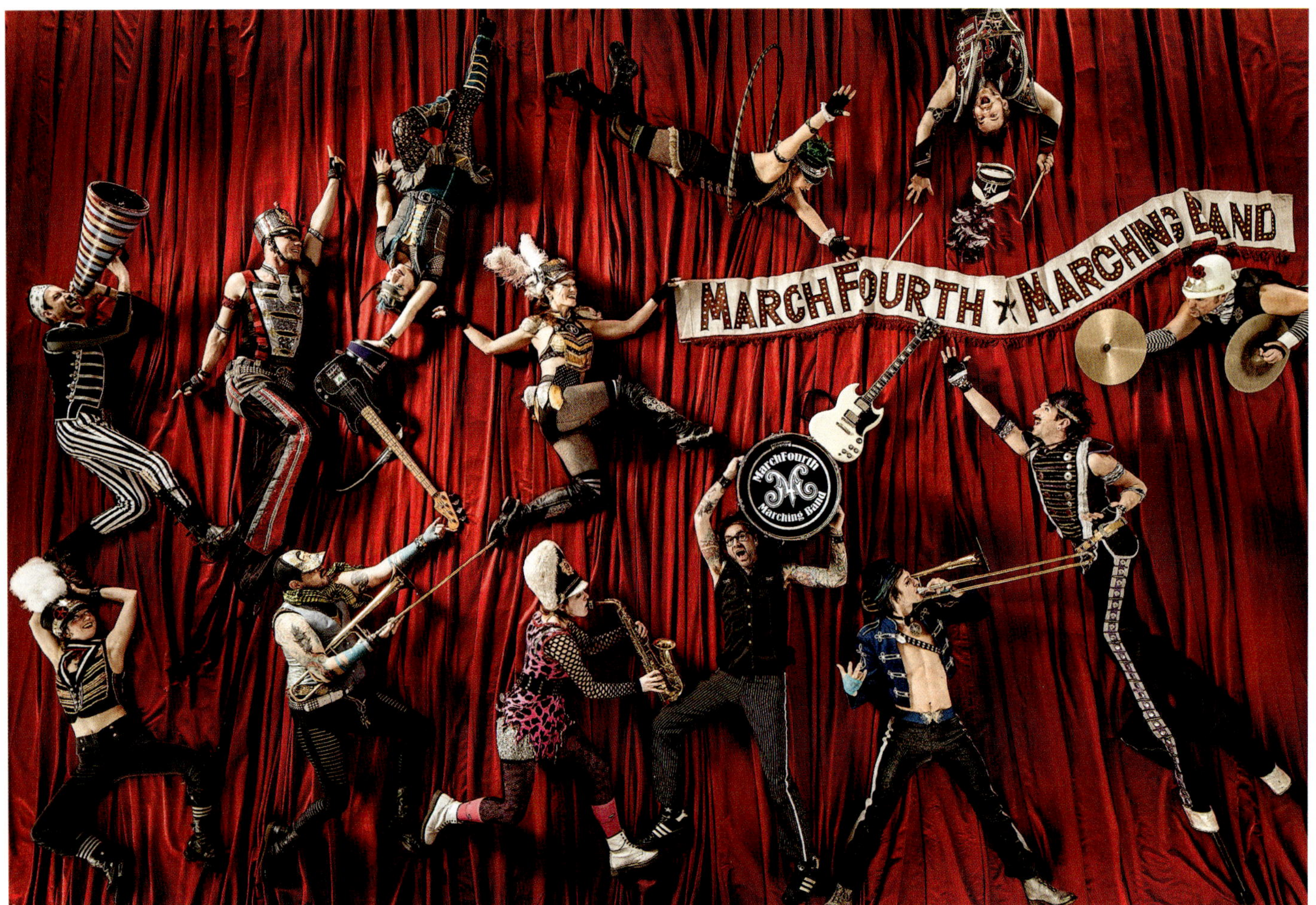


**FIGURE 5.3A** This image was captured with a 36MP Nikon D800 to allow for large print outputs—and to offer flexibility in cropping to fit a double-page magazine spread in *Portland Monthly*.
IMAGE © ANDY BATT, *MARCHFOURTH MARCHING BAND—10TH ANNIVERSARY*, FOR *PORTLAND MONTHLY*, 2013.

I did a shoot for *Portland Monthly* magazine of the MarchFourth Marching Band.[8] They were celebrating their tenth anniversary and the magazine wanted to create a fun double-page image to illustrate it (**Figure 5.3A**). I worked with the Art Director to create a weightless image, with impossible balancing acts and people falling through the shot. In reality, we laid out a giant red curtain and positioned everyone very carefully.

I put a Nikon D800 on a camera jib and had it tethered, so we could operate it remotely and see our shots as we took them. This camera has a native resolution of 36MP—that's 7,360 × 4,912 pixels, or about 24 × 16 inches at 300ppi. That was overkill for the magazine, but I wanted to be able to make a huge print of the shot as well, and the fine detail at 36MP is incredible. It doesn't have the same image quality as a medium-format digital back would offer—it has its own personality—but in terms of resolution, it's definitely a viable solution for huge outputs. Again, that larger file size builds in options for cropping and output (**Figures 5.3A and 5.3B**).

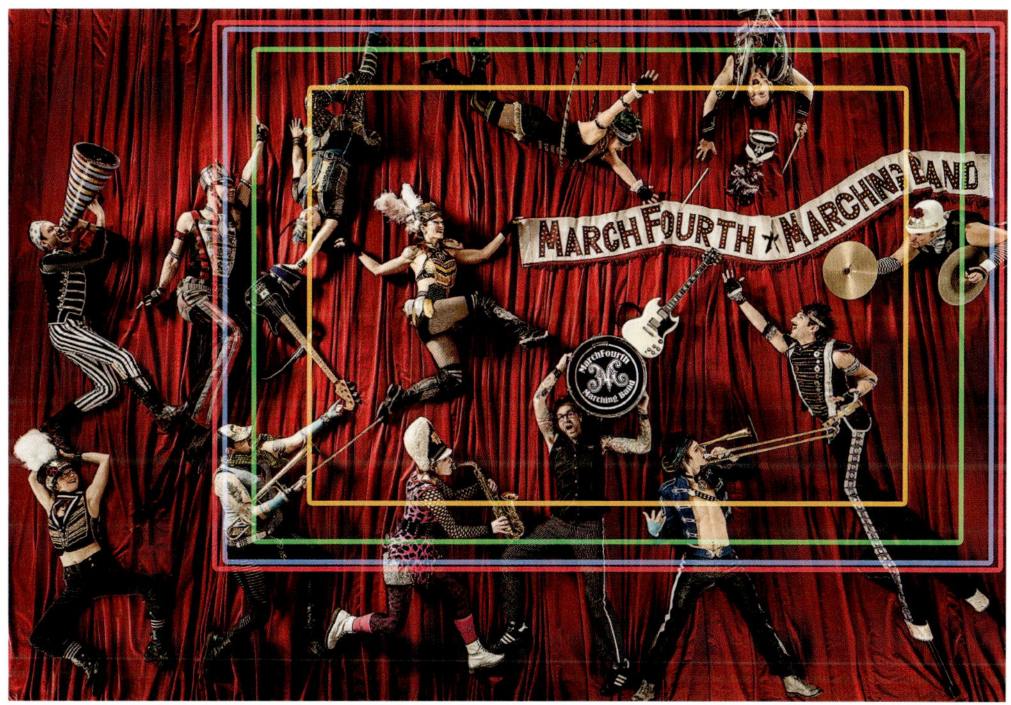


**FIGURE 5.3B** The Nikon D800 has a 36MP sensor—a 7,360 × 4,912 pixel image. At 300ppi, that's a native print size of 16 × 24 inches. To give you a sense of scale, we've overlaid several DSLR resolutions: red = Canon 5D Mark III; blue = Canon 5D Mark II; green = Canon 1Dx; orange = Canon 5D Mark I.
IMAGE © ANDY BATT, *MARCHFOURTH MARCHING BAND—10TH ANNIVERSARY—SENSOR OVERLAY,* 2013.

## The Technology Paradox

There are two certainties regarding your digital camera:

1. Your camera will be "out of date" about eighteen months from its time of release.
2. It will still make the same amazing images it made when it was new.

## Should I Buy a New Camera?

Whenever a new camera comes out, the promise is always there: It's better, because it has more megapixels, improved tonal range or can go to ISO Infinity without noise! Then we go through the routine of wondering if the camera we have now has enough megapixels, if the new ones are that much better, and how much ISO speed we really need.

To confuse matters, point-and-shoot cameras show up that, on paper, appear to have the same specs as our professional cameras and we ask, "How can this $600 camera that fits in my pocket have the same number of pixels as the $1,500 camera I bought eighteen months ago? There has to be a difference, right?"

We need to be able to evaluate our cameras and to key into the real differences in the latest models. The specs aren't the only deciding factor; the most important thing is to understand that the quality of your camera is important *as it relates to the type of photography you do.*

Studio portrait photographers whose work will be printed out up to 11 × 14[9] can easily keep using a camera that's a couple of generations old, has a resolution of around 5,616 × 3,744 pixels (21.1MP) and creates good skin tones. This situation is repeatable and stable; it doesn't require amazingly high ISO or 80MP of resolution (7,760 × 10,328 pixels). The corollary is that new technology would allow those photographers to expand their abilities. With a new camera, they could change from strobes to LED lights and shoot with a high ISO.

In the old days, you knew when you bought a camera that it would be with you for many years. That's because the mechanics and design of its various components—body, lenses, shutters, etc.—were very well established and because scientific advances were applied to film, rather than camera, technology. Today, though, the only way to take advantage of the latest technology is to buy a new camera or digital back, because the most significant improvements occur in sensor technology, rather than film technology.

As much as we might like it to, technology doesn't stand still. Perhaps someday sensor technology will reach a plateau, improvements will be minimal and the incentives to upgrade will be based on other factors. For now, though, we live in a world where sensor technology constantly makes leaps forward. With each generation the designs improve: Sensors pack more pixels onboard, the ISO speeds get higher, tonal ranges get wider, noise gets reduced, fine detail gets finer, color ranges expand . . . and the list goes on.

We all want the most value for our money, which means buying a camera that has the best sensor we can afford and that fits our needs. It's important to balance your needs against the features being offered. There's no point purchasing a camera that has an incredible autofocus (AF) system and allows you to shoot 10 FPS[10] continuously—adding thousands of dollars to the price tag—if the majority of your work is architectural photography. You would be better served finding a higher-resolution sensor that does better with long exposures, shoots 1 FPS and has a terrible AF system.

## Pixel Quality Matters

You frequently hear two things from camera reviews: "The number of megapixels doesn't matter anymore because Camera Company X has higher-quality megapixels which makes this the best camera ever . . ." and "Camera Company Y just released a new camera with 20% more megapixels than their last one, which makes it more hard-core than every other camera out there." How can both of these things be true?

Let's start with a few basics. By increasing the quantity of pixels, you increase the resolution of the file—but increased resolution isn't always the same as increased quality. A megapixel (MP) isn't a single

### It All Comes Down to Pixel Quality, Density and Size

- **Quality**: How good is the information of each pixel?
- **Density**: In a given amount of physical space, how many pixels are packed inside it?
- **Size**: How big is the photosite[11] that created the pixel information?

giant pixel out to destroy Tokyo—it's literally one million individual pixels. The term "pixel" has become the shorthand we use for judging the quality of a camera. We want to know how many pixels a camera has—because more is always better, right? Well, that depends on how good those pixels are and which techniques were used to create them. It's possible to make better images using a camera that has fewer megapixels.

You could design a compact camera to cram 30MP onto its sensor, but to do that, you'd have to take many shortcuts to keep the costs down. The result would be a camera with a high resolution, but poor-quality pixels that are prone to noise, artifacts and errors. If a camera company is going to increase the number of pixels, it also needs to maintain—or increase—their quality. A camera with fewer, but higher-quality, megapixels can produce superior results. A sensor that can gather more light and has minimal errors can create a very high-quality image, and those images can be artificially upscaled to much larger sizes with good reproduction results.

It's also possible to have a high-quality 12MP digital image that can be upscaled to produce a better image than a camera with 24MP and smaller, more error-prone pixels. It's important to know what you're comparing! If you're comparing two generations of professional DSLRs—an older 16MP vs. a new 24MP—then the newer sensor will probably win. If you compare an older 16MP full-frame sensor camera to a newer 24MP point-and-shoot camera with a tiny sensor, then the 16MP full-frame sensor will probably win.

## Analog to Digital: Photons to Pixels

To take a photograph is literally to "write the light." The etymology of the words "photos" and "graphia" can be traced back to Greek, but the modern usage appeared around the 1830s. "Photography" is an old word, but still accurately describes what we do with cameras in a digital age: We use sensors to write an image (made of light) that's projected onto it by the lens. The sensor, along with dedicated image processors, converts that image into binary digital information.

*Light* is a unique substance. It embodies the properties of both waves and particles and has no mass or electric charge. When we're at the pixel level, we treat light as particles—which means photons are involved. *Photons* are the way light energy is carried; think of them as individual packages—or particles—of light. Camera sensors are designed to detect and gather individual photons.

The end product of a camera's sensor is the *pixel*—those square elements in your final image. The image information from every individual pixel is created by gathering groups of photons. When millions and millions of individual pixels are combined in an image, we create an illusion of the real world. The more pixels there are, the bigger the image is and the more detail is reproduced.

**Figure 5.4B** gives us an abstract view of the pixel. The square pixels you see are the literal building blocks of the full-size image. Viewed here at 1,600%, they look like a pointillist image. When the squares become small enough and you combine enough of them, you stop seeing individual points and instead perceive the image as a whole (**Figure 5.4A**). If you use more pixels, the details will be finer and the images will get larger.

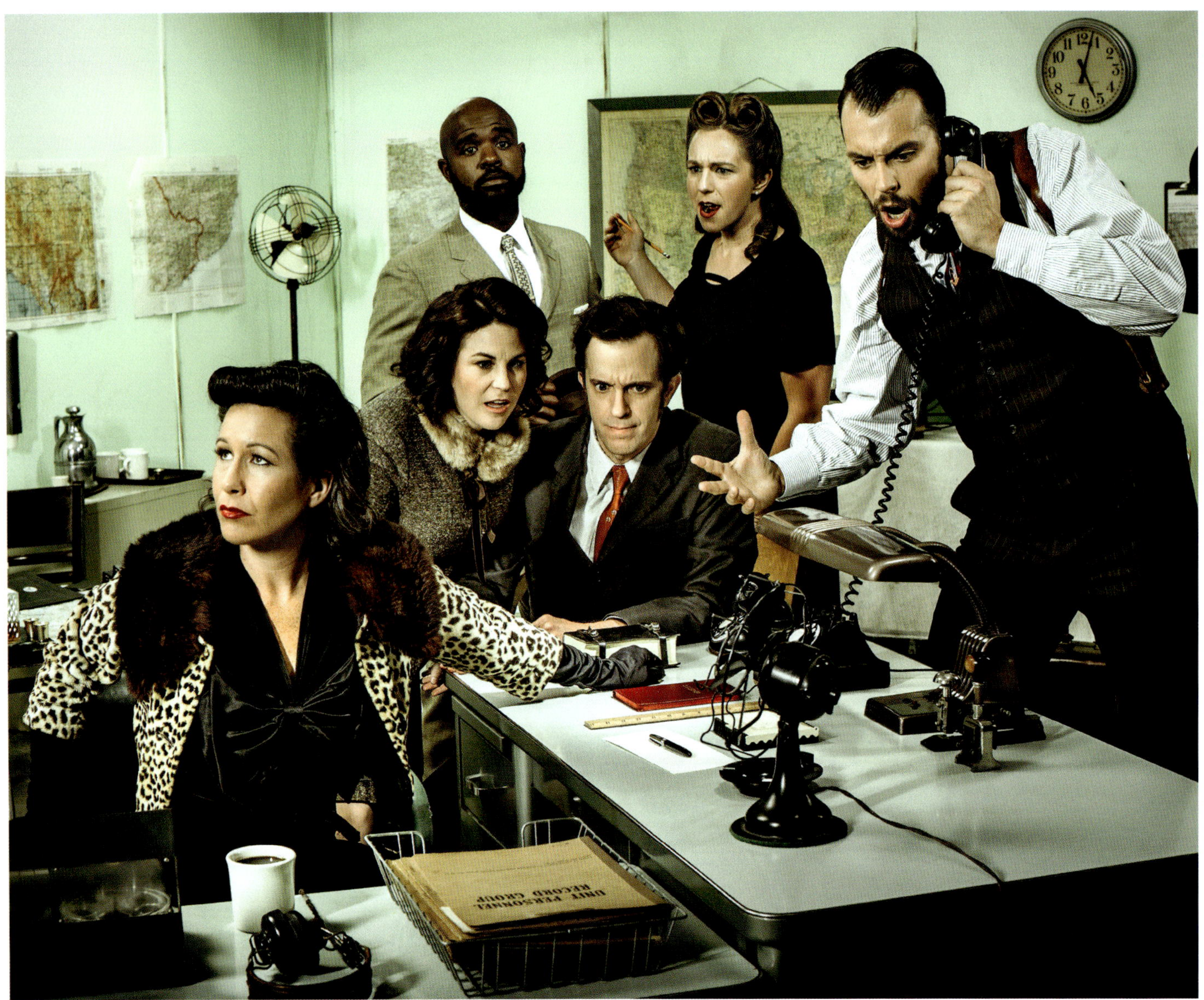

**FIGURE 5.4A** This is the full-size image from which the detail shots (**Figure 5.4B**) were taken. It was captured with a 23.2MP Canon 5D Mark III at 300ppi, which ends up being a 19.2 × 12.8 inch image.
IMAGE © ANDY BATT, *THE IMPROV GROUP, "ADMINISTRATION," TAKING ON THE WORLD, ONE PIXEL AT A TIME,* 2013.

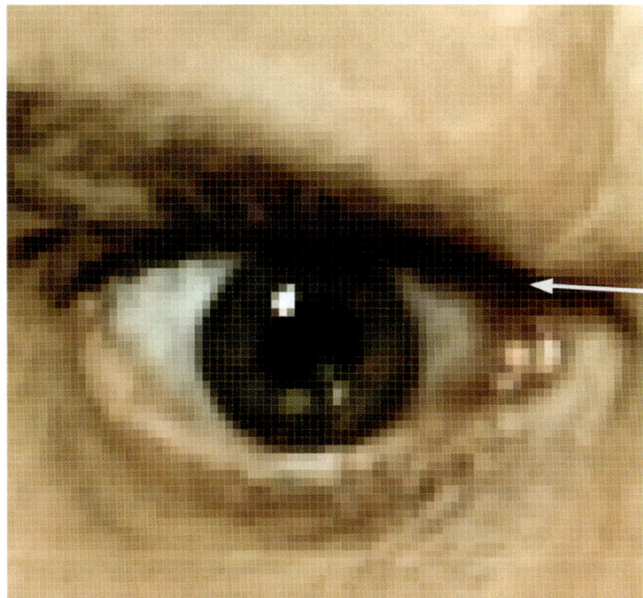

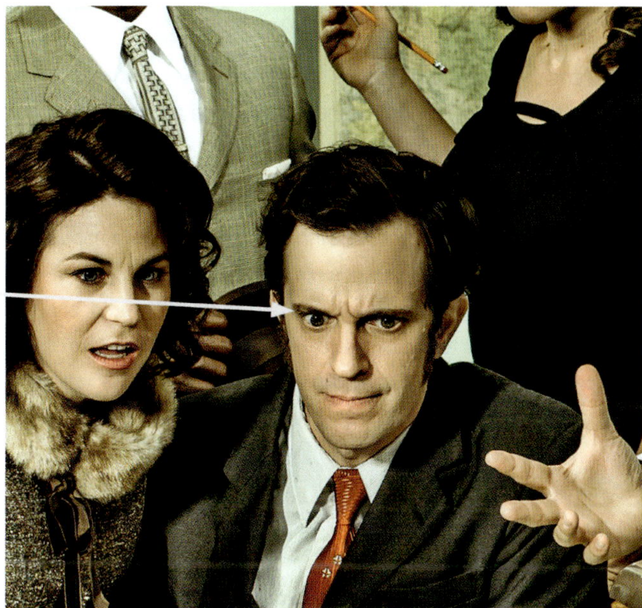

**FIGURE 5.4B** The left image shows a detail of **Figure 5.4A** at 1,600% zoom. It reveals the square pixels that are hidden in this—and every—digital image you work on. The image on the right shows the same "eye" at native print resolution, for context.
IMAGE DETAILS © ANDY BATT, *THE IMPROV GROUP, "ADMINISTRATION," TAKING ON THE WORLD, ONE PIXEL AT A TIME,* 2013.

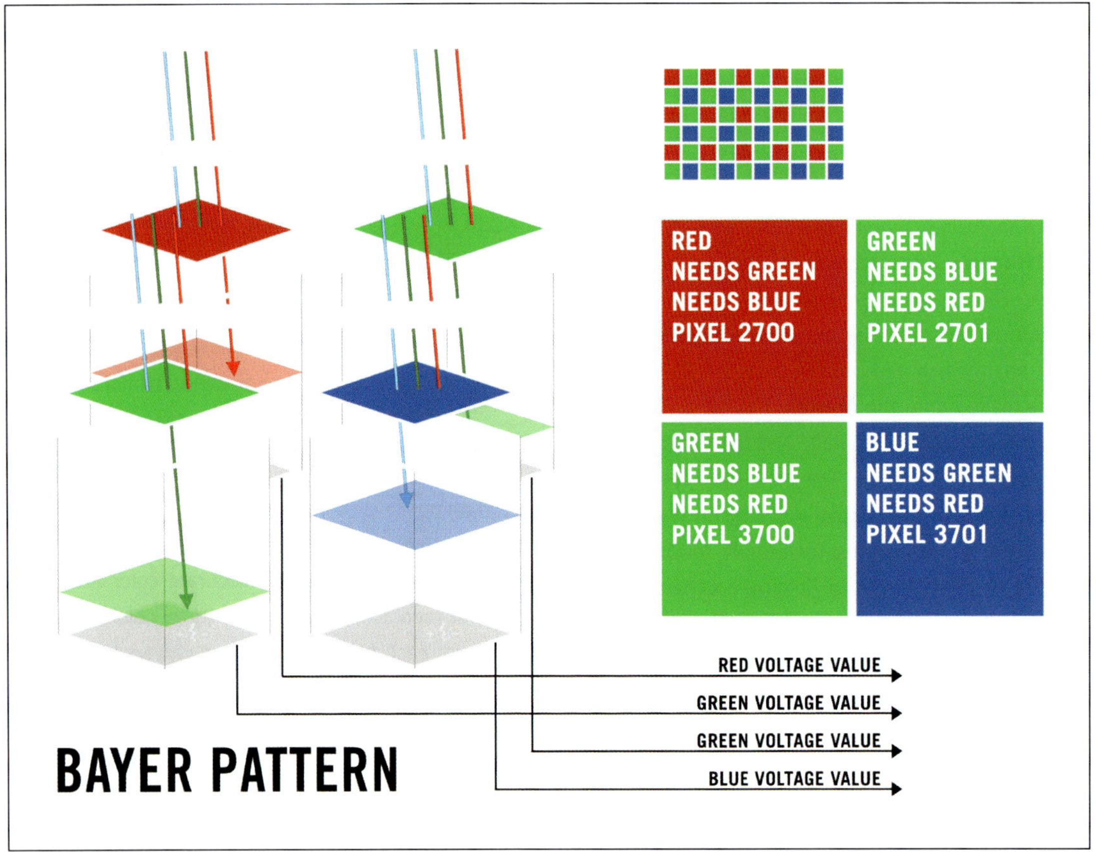


**FIGURE 5.6** If we take four photosites and put a red filter on one, a blue filter on another and green filters on the remaining two, then we have a basic color mosaic called a Bayer pattern. When the RGB brightness values for neighboring pixels are recorded, we can use them to calculate the missing colors for each single, colored pixel. ILLUSTRATION © ANDY BATT, *THE BAYER PATTERN*, 2013.

---

In essence, we capture more green light to get more information about the contrast, tone and brightness of a scene.

To create the missing red and blue information for a particular green photosite, we look at the red and blue photosites that surround it. The red value will be interpolated—or created—by reading the values of the neighboring red pixels and calculating the most likely value for the red channels. This repeats for the missing blue values. This sampling process takes place during the "demosaicing"[13] (guessing) process and occurs for every pixel the sensor records. With a Bayer pattern, all the original information (about one-third of the required data) is recorded at the time of capture, and the demosaicing takes place when the raw file is being processed. Different raw-processing applications use different techniques and algorithms to calculate their guesswork.

## Demosaicing: Before and After

In **Figure 5.7** you can see a full image that was processed normally. It is possible, though, to process your images without demosaicing them, which is a useful way to see what's happening before the demosaicing process is applied. There's a 99.9% chance that you'll never need to process your images in this way—so we did it for you.

By running a raw file through a program called DCRAW, you can convert the raw data into a gray scale image, with each pixel only showing the value recorded. If you compare the detail images in **Figure 5.8,** you'll see the normally processed image at the top row, the DCRAW version in the middle, and a simulated color overlay on the bottom. We did this to give you a visual rendition of the sensor's RGGB layout.

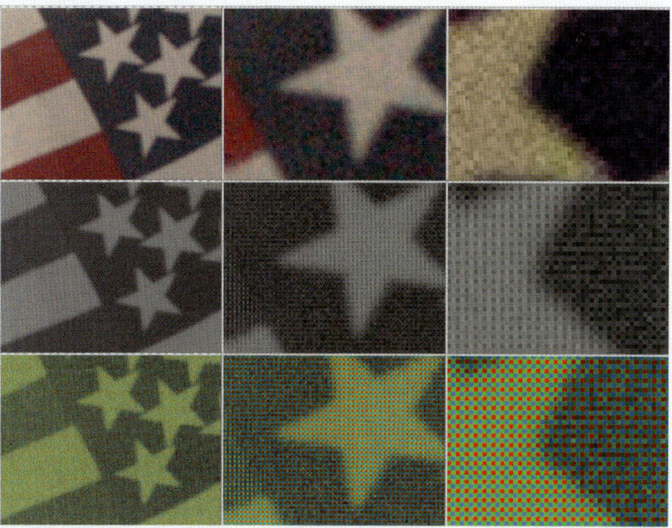

**FIGURE 5.8** The full–frame image (**Figure 5.7**) was processed out of Lightroom with minimal corrections. By using several processing tools, Andy built this grid to show an image detail at three different zoom levels (moving from left to right in each row) to show what's really going on at the pixel level.

*Top row:* Shows the full–color demosaiced image with minimal processing. No noise reduction or sharpening has been applied.

*Middle row:* Shows the version processed through DCRAW—a specialized command–line application for processing raw files that let Andy create an image without demosaicing the file. With this method, he was able to process the image to reveal each pixel's actual value. As a result, we can see the red photosites with their original gray scale brightness values and without interpolation (creation) of the missing green and blue data.

*Bottom row:* Andy overlaid a mosaic pattern on top of the gray scale images from the middle row (in other words, he faked it) to illustrate how the Bayer pattern records pixel values. Remember that photosites only record colored light as a brightness value and that the actual color is applied as part of the demosaicing process.

IMAGE © ANDY BATT, *DETAIL IMAGE: THE BAYER PATTERN IN ACTION, BEFORE AND AFTER DEMOSAICING,* 2013.

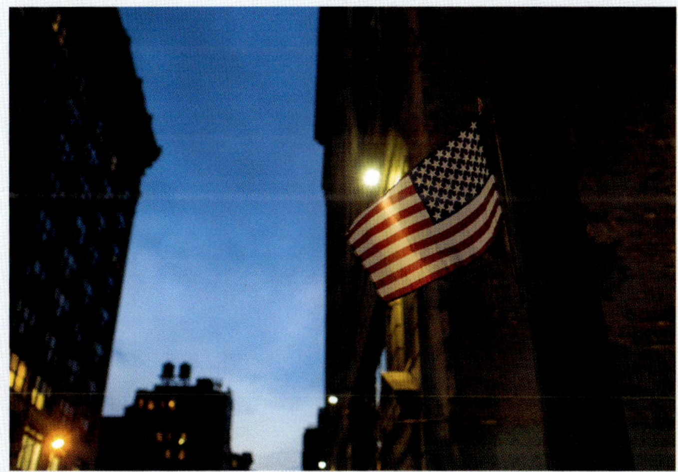

**FIGURE 5.7** This image is part of a loose, ongoing series of American flags. Walking through a NYC street gave Andy this backlit image. He shot it at *f*/2.5, 1/320 sec and ISO 6400.

IMAGE © ANDY BATT, *A NORMALLY PROCESSED IMAGE,* 2013.

Here is Bayer's own description of the way the pattern works (1975: Column 2, Line 64–Column 3, Line 13):

> *. . . three interlaid patterns, (a green-, a red- and a blue-sensitive element pattern) are so arranged that green-sensitive elements (serving to detect luminance) occur at every other array position, with red-sensitive elements alternating with such green-sensitive elements in alternate rows [. . .] blue-sensitive elements alternate with red-sensitive elements to produce a luminance-dominated image sampling having a disproportion in the chrominance samples favoring red over blue. With this arrangement, sampling rates for all three basic color vectors are adjusted respective of the acuity of the human visual system. That is, blue detail, to which the human visual has least resolution, is sampled the least frequently . . . green detail, to which the human visual system is most responsive, is sampled most frequently.*

## The Analog-to-Digital Converter

Your sensor is, in part, an analog device (**Figure 5.9**). The photosites are designed to take particles of light (photons) and convert them into

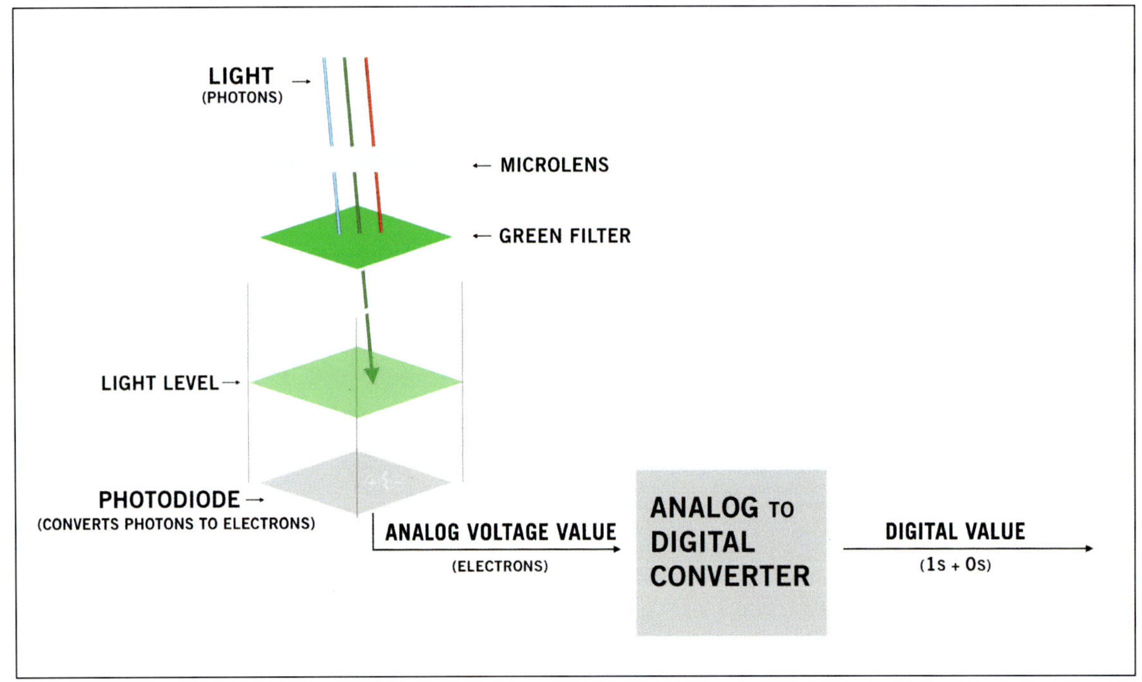


**FIGURE 5.9** This illustration shows the photosite from **Figure 5.6**, with the addition of an Analog-to-Digital Converter, or ADC. The ADC is a dedicated processor that takes all the analog values from the photodiodes (from inside the photosites) and converts them into a digital signal that's a binary code of 0s and 1s. The binary data is what gets recorded to your memory card.
ILLUSTRATION © ANDY BATT, *ANALOG-TO-DIGITAL (ADC) IN THE CHAIN*, 2013.

an analog voltage value (electrons). To exist in digital form, that analog voltage value needs to be converted into a digital one—a *binary code*[14] of 0s and 1s. You can think of your raw image as a giant spreadsheet, with each cell representing a pixel and with a binary value in every cell.

There's a sophisticated supercomputer sitting between your camera's sensor and the memory card. It's called the Analog-to-Digital Converter (ADC or A/D), and it's responsible for turning the electron values into binary code. The ADC doesn't get as much press as its CMOS and CCD cousins, but it's equally responsible for the quality of the pixel—and your final image.

## Put the Needle on the Record: Analog and Digital

To appreciate what the ADC does, it's helpful to understand two essential ideas: digitization of analog signals and bit depth. A vinyl record is a handy analogy for explaining analog signals. Go to your local record store; buy an awesome, limited-edition 180-gram vinyl record from one of your favorite local bands; put it onto your turntable and drop the needle into the groove (**Figure 5.10**).

The sound you'll hear is generated by an analog source. *Analog signals* are continuous, unbroken streams of information. Light is an

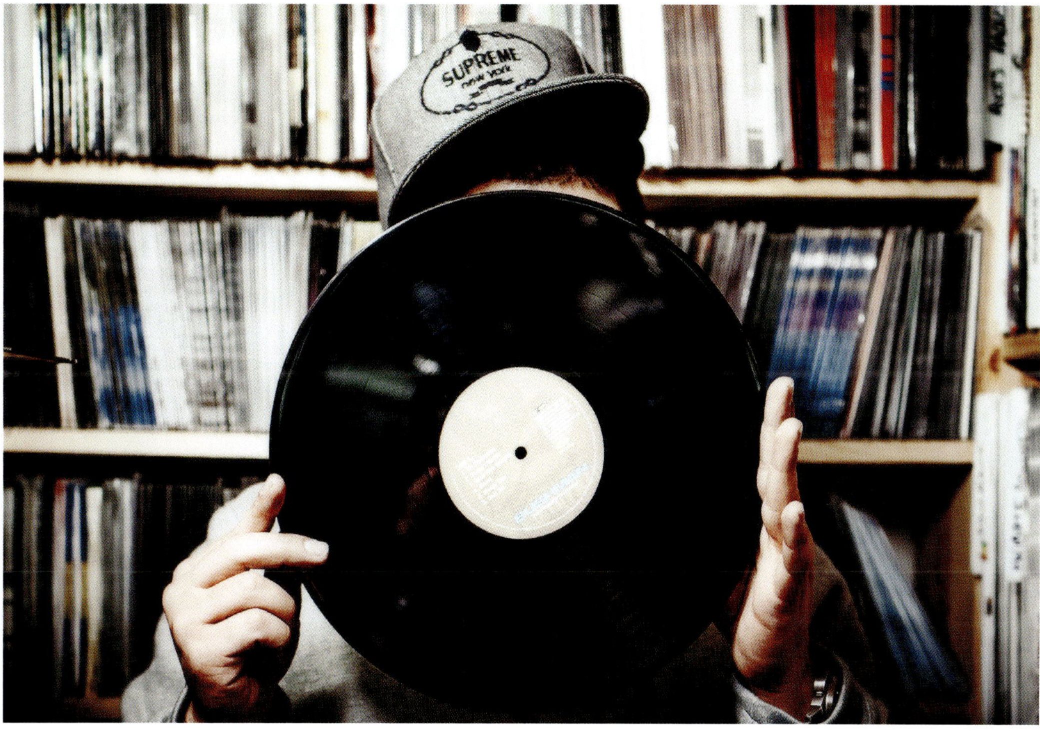


**FIGURE 5.10** A record is a perfect example of an analog signal. A needle is placed in the groove and vibrates in response to the groove's depth and width. These vibrations create a continuous analog signal that's sent to the amplifier, and then to the speakers. Also, vinyl records are just nice to hold.
IMAGE © ANDY BATT, *RECORD STORE*, 2008.

analog signal, and it's still analog when it's converted into an electron value by the photosite. The sound has been generated by the record player's needle vibrating in response to the groove of the record—different depths and widths create different sounds. By running this analog signal through an old-school tube amplifier, the music we hear is a fully analog sound. If we were using a film camera, the light would expose a frame of film, capturing the analog signal on an analog medium.

When the electron values from the photosite run through the ADC, they become a digital signal. If you're using a new stereo,[15] the odds are that it's a solid-state device and that somewhere inside it is a digital amplifier. This circuit digitizes the analog sound and breaks the signal into 0s and 1s, which are amplified. Then the sound is converted back to an analog signal to be sent to your speakers.

When we take an analog signal and convert it to a digital one, we're breaking that continuous stream of information into chunks—into the binary code of 0s and 1s. To do this, we sample the analog signal. If we use a lot of samples, we can create a faithful representation of that original signal. If we use fewer samples, we can still create a version of the original, but it won't sound or look like the original. The more samples we use, the higher its fidelity to the digital version of the original—whether we're dealing with music or images (**Figure 5.11**).

If the ADC uses a high sample rate, or high bit depth, it will represent that analog electron value created by the photosite with high fidelity. This gives us good image detail, tonal range and color range. If the ADC uses a low sample rate, or low bit depth, it will create an image with gaps and loss; the resulting image would look posterized (**Figure 5.12**).

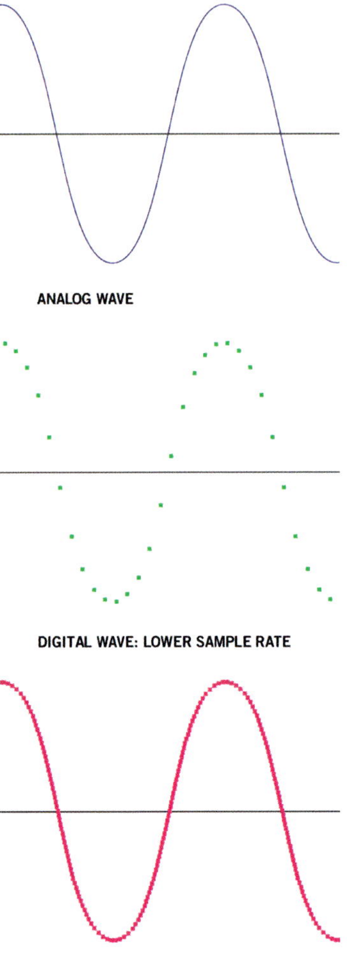


**FIGURE 5.11** The top waveform is a *continuous analog signal*; it's a single connected line that keeps on going. The middle waveform is a digital representation of the original analog signal, but uses very little information to represent it; it's using a low sample rate. The gaps between the samples are places where the original wave wasn't sampled. The middle example doesn't have enough information to recreate the original wave faithfully. The third wave uses a high sample rate; the gaps between each sample are minimal and the signal appears to be the same as the original.

When our ADC creates the raw image file, we want it to use a high sampling rate—or high bit depth—to convert the analog value into a digital one.
ILLUSTRATION © ANDY BATT, *ANALOG AND DIGITAL INFORMATION,* 2013.

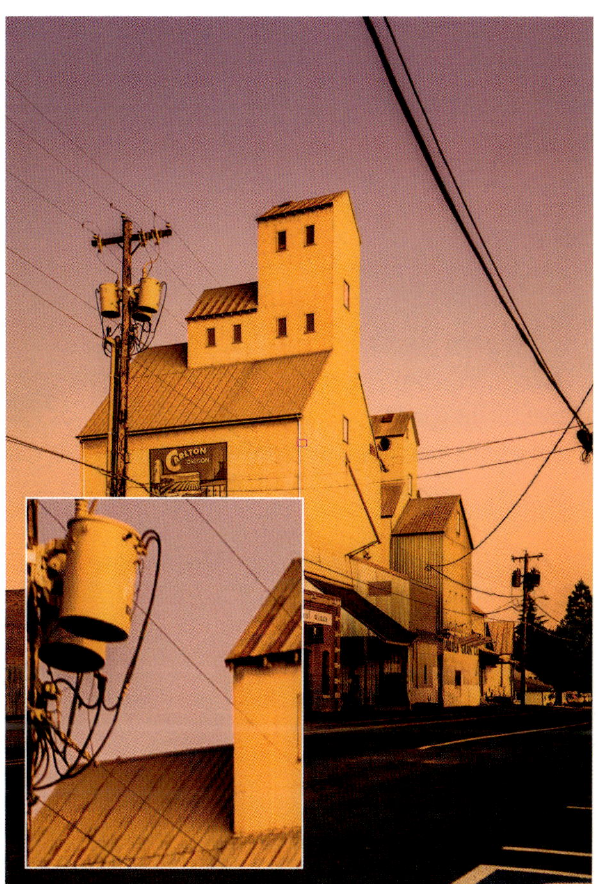


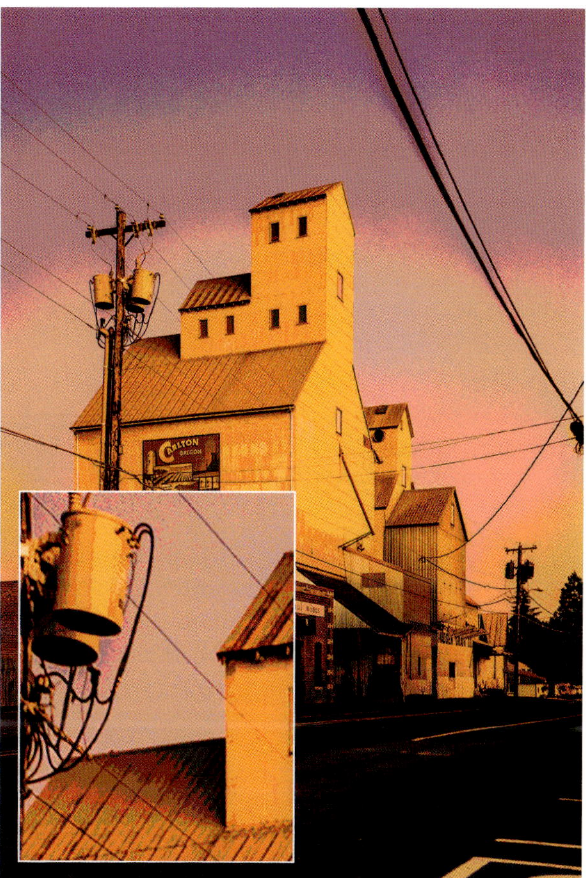


**FIGURE 5.12** The image on the left (a 14–bit digital image from a Canon 1Ds Mark III) is a digital one that's made up of billions of color samples—so many that nothing gives away its digital nature. The version on the right is akin to the middle waveform of **Figure 5.11**; not enough information is used to represent the original image, so we get banding and a loss of detail. Andy simulated this behavior by posterizing the image in Photoshop.

You don't have to worry about controlling this issue, since your camera will output images more like the one on the left, but since this stuff goes on behind the scenes, it's a good idea to understand it.

IMAGE © ANDY BATT, *BIT DEPTH: HIGH– AND LOW–QUALITY SAMPLING*, 2008.

# Bit Depth

You've probably run into the term *bit depth* in camera reviews or when working with Photoshop files. A *bit* is the smallest measure of data and can either be a 0 or a 1 (a binary value). Bit depth tells us how many bits are used to describe a pixel's value. On the extreme lo-fi side, a bit depth of 2 would give a pixel the choice to be either black or white. On the other side of the scale, a bit depth of 16 would give that same pixel value a choice of 281,000,000,000,000 possible colors. More bit depth equals more quality—and takes up more space on your hard drive.

## Pixel Bit Depth

The most common bit depth is 8-bit, where each pixel in the image has one of 16,777,216 possible color values. (Each color channel (RGB) has 256 levels of information and 256 × 256 × 256 = 16,777,216.) With 16-bit files, each color channel can have 65,536 levels of information, so each pixel can have one of 281,000,000,000,000 possible color values (since 65,536 × 65,536 × 65,536 = 281 trillion). You might also see bit depth listed as either 24-bit or 48-bit, which is the exact same thing as 8-bit and 16-bit. It's confusing, but these are just two different ways of labeling the same amount of data in regards to a digital image. (8-bit describes only a single channel of data; if you do the math, then three channels of RGB data equal 24-bits (3 × 8-bits = 24-bits).

## Raw File Bit Depth

Applying this knowledge to raw files, we're interested in the bit depth of the sensor, which is a fixed value that's dependent on the sensor and its supporting circuitry. When we work on raw files inside parametric[16] editing tools like Lightroom or Photo Ninja, we're working with the raw data—at whatever bit depth the sensor captured the image. At this point, we haven't yet put the file into an 8-bit or 16-bit container; that doesn't happen until we output a processed image. With processed images, we make a conscious choice between 8-bit and 16-bit files.

The short version of working with bit depth is that the more samples you have, the closer the digital version will be to the real thing—so, a true 16-bit image will contain much more information than an 8-bit image.

## Camera Bit Depth

Cameras often have a bit depth listed in their specifications. Most cameras output 12-bit or 14-bit files—which translates to 4,096 shades per channel (for 12-bit) and 16,384 shades per channel (for 14-bit). With more data, there should be a higher quality . . . right? Yes, but the quality of the data is also a big factor. The size and design of the photosite—and the supporting electronics—have as much to do with the quality of the image as does bit depth. In general, more bit depth is better, but it's only one of many factors that contribute to image quality.

### Container Size

Bit depth can also be thought of as a container: There are standard containers, such as 8-bit and 16-bit, but what counts is how much data is in each container. A camera could use a 16-bit container, but contain 12-bits of data.

# CCD vs. CMOS: Deep-Geekery

Both CMOS and CCD sensors use photosites to convert light into an analog voltage signal, and both use an ADC to create the digital information. The difference is in the way their electronics are built and how they carry out their tasks. First up are the acronyms.

## The Acronyms

***CMOS*** stands for Complementary Metal Oxide Semiconductor and refers to the technology used to create the sensor. It's also a way to construct a variety of other integrated circuits. Because of this, CMOS sensors can be engineered to accomplish many different tasks all on the same chip.

***CCD*** stands for Charge Coupled Device and refers to the sensor's behavior. The name refers to the elegant way the sensor moves the "charge" of analog voltage information from its simpler photosites through its circuit. This type of photosite design yields better-quality data than a CMOS sensor.

Both types of sensors take in analog information (light rays), use photosites to convert it into an analog value (voltage) and then send it through the ADC to become a digital signal.

## Intelligent or Dumb Photosites

*Think of a CMOS sensor as a series of "intelligent" photosites*, with special circuits integrated into each one. Each photosite acts independently to create its analog voltage value. The problem is that the additional circuitry packed into each photosite creates more heat and leaves less space for the photodiode, opening up more opportunities for noise. Extra noise means more processing of the analog data, which leads to even more opportunity for error.

*A CCD sensor uses simpler photosites in series. Think of them as "dumb" pixels*; their only job is to provide an electron value. When we say "simpler," we mean that for their size, the photodiodes can be bigger and create a higher-quality signal. Groups of photosites work together and send their combined electron values off the sensor without converting the signal. Because of the need for a separate circuit, data gets to the ADC more slowly with a CCD sensor than it does with a CMOS sensor. CCDs, though, have the advantage of capturing the original information faster than CMOSs.

A CCD can actually turn on and off with enough precision to function as an accurate shutter. With this design, most medium-format cameras have a very slow frame rate of one to three frames per second (FPS). With a CMOS sensor, on the other hand, the analog data moves a much shorter distance—and shorter means faster. This enables a high frame-rate camera to operate at 8–15 FPS.

## Blurry Lines and Low-Pass Filters

Another key difference between CCD and CMOS sensors is the use of an anti-aliasing filter, aka a *low-pass filter.*[17] This filter is used to fix problems—such as jagged lines, color artifacting and moiré[18] patterns—that occur from some sensor designs. Adding a low-pass filter right on the surface of the sensor works to eliminate these problems by intentionally and precisely blurring the image (**Figure 5.13**). When done correctly, you trade a small reduction in image sharpness for the elimination of three difficult-to-retouch problems. The small loss of sharpness is mostly compensated with good sharpening techniques in post-processing. The resulting image isn't as sharp as one captured without a low-pass filter, but unless you plan on comparing two cameras shot side by side, it's usually not apparent.

CMOS sensors used to have low-pass filters, while CCDs didn't. Now, though, you'll find CMOS cameras with and without them—and new technologies that allow them to be turned on and off at will.[19] The advantage of not having a low-pass filter is that the images will definitively be sharper, but with CCD digital backs and some CMOS DSLRs that don't have them, it's likely that you'll encounter moiré problems or color artifacting at some point. If the source of the problem is strong enough, you'll have these problems—even with a low-pass filter.

### Color Artifacting

Color artifacting can show up as either fringed or bloomed edges (that are very similar to chromatic aberrations from lens design) or as rainbow-colored noise. This can occur due to the differences in pixel values in the mosaic pattern—especially with specular highlights.

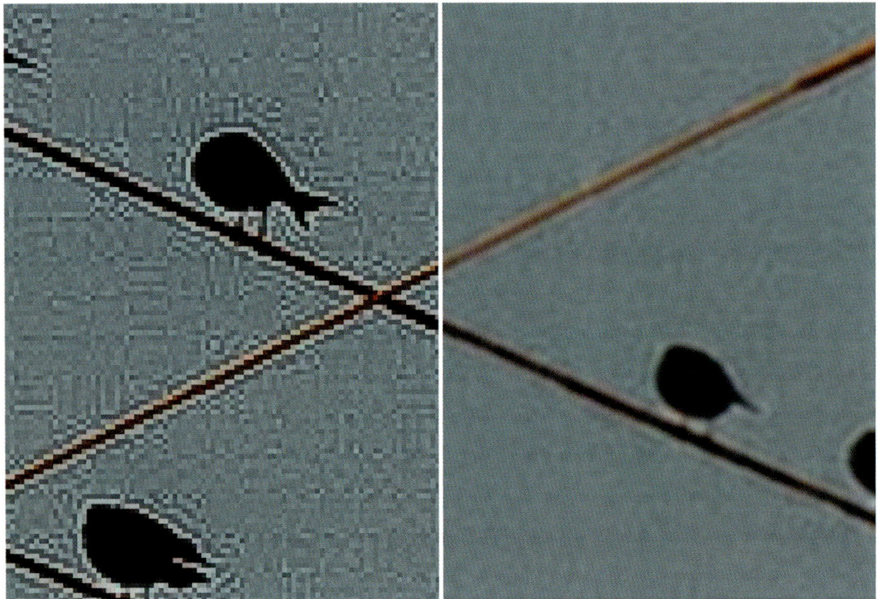

**FIGURE 5.13** In this illustration we've deliberately enlarged and oversharpened an image to create jagged edges (left). We then took that image and ran a blurring filter on it, to simulate what an anti–alias (or low–pass) filter does with jagged edges. With some blur applied, the lines smooth out and appear to be continuous. When done at the sensor level, it's a much more delicate and nuanced operation than the one illustrated here.
IMAGE © ANDY BATT, *LOW–PASS SIMULATION*, 2013.

Blooming and fringing can be dealt with easily, by using the Defringe tool, which is found in most raw processors. Moiré and rainbow noise can cause major headaches in post-processing. There are techniques for removing these problems, but they always have side effects and often aren't 100% effective.

## Moiré

*Moiré* occurs when the pattern created by the placement of photosites on the sensor are overlaid with other patterns (**Figure 5.14**). You can see this for yourself by overlaying two pieces of screen door material; by rotating them independently, you'll see interference patterns. The same thing happens with sensors, when a pattern in your scene coincides with the pattern of photosites on your sensor. Repeated patterns like herringbone fabric textures and brick walls can also cause moiré.

With a fixed subject—like a screen door—you may be able to change the interference pattern and eliminate moiré by rotating the camera slightly. If the object that's causing the problem is movable, try changing its angle. Fabric is more difficult, since it often changes direction as it moves. If it's sewn into different panels, you can end up with the same jacket having multiple orientations of the difficult pattern. You might find that you can eliminate one problem area, only to create another. The best solution is to change clothing. The second-best solution is to shoot a lot of coverage; there may be a few magic angles with minimal moiré. The last resort is to work with a retouching solution: Lightroom and Capture 1, for example, have moiré-reducing filters built in. You can also find more intensive masking and recoloring techniques.[20]

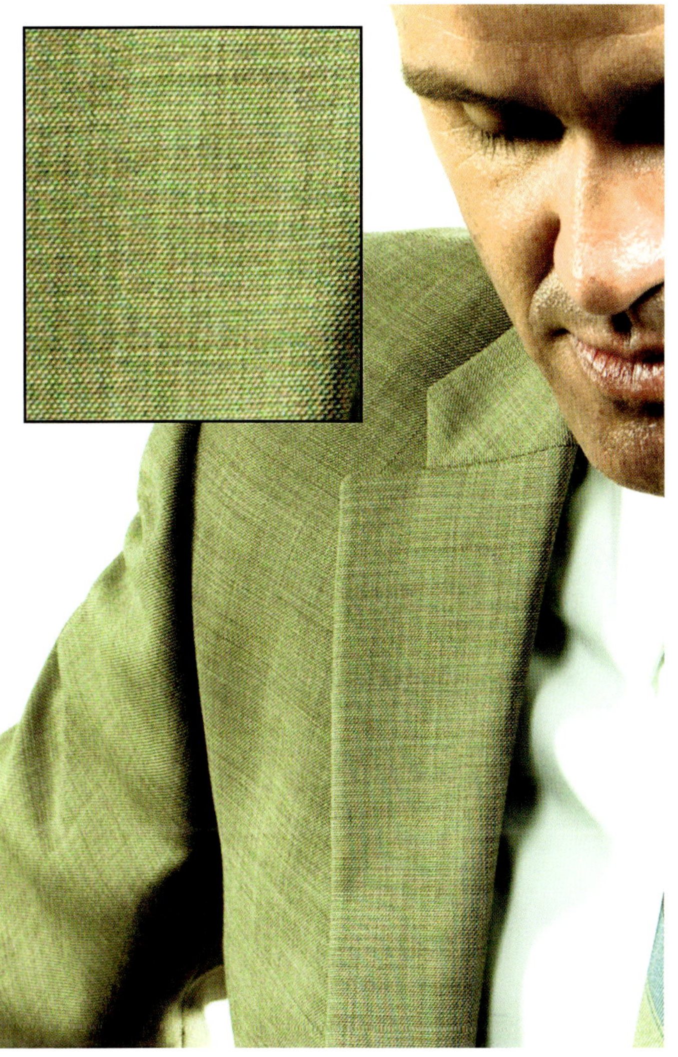

**FIGURE 5.14**
Certain patterns, especially fabrics, can create moiré with your sensor. In this image, which was shot with a CMOS sensor that had an anti-aliasing filter, we still ended up with green/magenta banding. Since fabric has multiple planes, you might not be able to eliminate the moiré by moving your camera or subject. Sometimes pulling back and changing the magnification can alter the interference. The more costly solution, in terms of money or time, is retouching. The best solution is to simply change clothing. IMAGE © ANDY BATT, *MOIRÉ SAMPLE,* 2011.

# Noise and Speed

Noise is any unwanted information in your image; anything aside from the actual image is noise. If you've ever tried to rescue a vastly underexposed image (**Figure 5.15**) or used an extremely high ISO speed, then you've seen noise. By using the lowest possible ISO speed that allows you to get the shot you want, you'll minimize the amount of noise that's inherent in the image and the amount of noise removal you'll need to do.

With ISO speeds, there's a *signal-to-noise ratio* at work. At the optimal ISO speed, this is as close to a pure signal as we can get with the sensor and all the data recorded as image data. As we increase the ISO speed, we add noise and accept a less-than-pure signal; most of the data is still image information, but some of it is noise. At the highest ISO speeds, we compromise and accept a large percentage of noise, in exchange for being able to capture images under extremely dark conditions. Many of our problems with noise come from the use of higher ISO speeds—that's the signal-to-noise ratio.

## ISO: Your Camera Is Like a One-Speed Bike

Your camera has a default ISO (aka its native speed), which is usually the lowest ISO setting available.[21] The default is the actual sensitivity of the sensor, and it's always working at this speed—even when you choose different ISO settings. By working at, or close to, the native speed whenever possible, you obtain the camera's cleanest, highest quality data.

When you increase the ISO setting, you aren't increasing the sensitivity of the sensor, you're applying *amplification* to the native speed, i.e., by setting your camera to ISO 12,500, you're telling it to take the data created at its native speed and strengthen it.

It's helpful to reach back to our music analogy again: The song you're listening to is passing through an amplifier. If you want to crank up the sound, you turn up the volume and the amplifier makes the original sound wave stronger. In a similar way, amplification allows

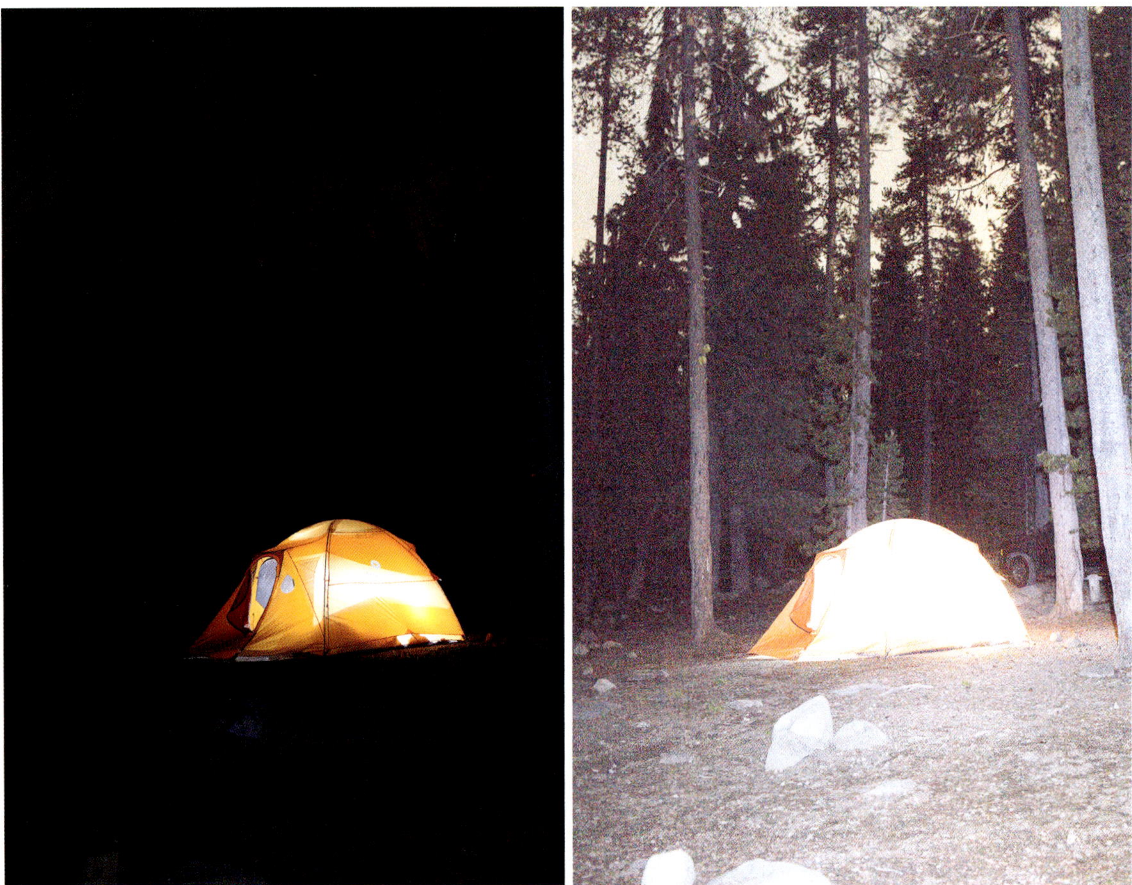

**FIGURE 5.15** Because Andy exposed for the tent (left), the dark areas surrounding it recorded very little information. When he tried to increase the exposure in post (right), the resulting image's noise was greatly amplified, since those shadow tones contain the lowest-quality, noisiest data. IMAGE © ANDY BATT, *NOISE IN THE DARK,* 2011.

photosites to create more signal with less light. Amplification can take place at either the analog stage (the voltages created by the photosites can be strengthened) or the stage when the digital information comes out of the ADC.

Let's say you're taking a photo at 1/3 sec, *f*/5.6, ISO 100. Although this gives you a good exposure, you'd rather work at 1/100th of a second, and you need the F-stop at *f*/5.6 to hold focus. There's a five-stop difference between 1/3 and 1/100 (five fewer stops of light are hitting the sensor), so you crank your camera to ISO 3200 (thus applying five stops of amplification to compensate) and take another photo. You end up with a good exposure, but you've also increased the noise in the image.

The imaging experts at DxOMark.com have this to say about base ISO speeds:

> ***The intrinsic sensitivity of a digital camera is determined by the silicon structure of the sensor itself and cannot be changed, but the ISO of the camera can be artificially increased to arbitrary values by applying a gain to the signal. The price to pay is a proportionate increase of noise and eventually, a decrease of SNR [signal-to-noise ratio] for a given output value . . . The only trick is that the gain is applied before analog/digital conversion so as to avoid quantization effects. So the fact that a camera attains ISO 10,000 is no guarantee of image quality . . .***[22]

## Noise and the "Secret Sauce"

You might think that when we shoot raw files, we're capturing pure data—but that's not necessarily true. There's quite a bit of extra circuitry between the photosites and the memory card. Within that circuitry, you'll find the manufacturer's *secret sauce*: proprietary processes that are performed on the raw data.

The resulting data that ends up on your memory card is still raw, but it's been tuned up. This secret sauce can affect things like ISO speed, noise, tonal range, improved detail, etc., but since the sauce is proprietary, it's difficult to know exactly what's going on in there. Each sensor manufacturer guards these secrets, since pushing the limits of high-ISO photography represents a real advantage to the company. Have you ever wondered about the evolution of cameras, where ISO 400 was so noisy that it wasn't usable—to new models that have ISO 6400 as a "normal" speed? It's all in the secret sauce.

### CCDs vs. CMOSs

CCD sensors generate a very low noise signal at their base ISOs (which can be as low as ISO 35). The simple explanation is that the CCD photosites gather more photons (light). More photons mean more signal, and more signal means higher-quality images.

A CMOS photosite of the same size is much more complex, so it has less available space to collect photons. At their native ISO, CMOS sensors are inherently noisier than their CCD counterparts. At higher ISO settings,[23] though, CMOS sensors have secret-sauce circuits that perform sophisticated noise-reduction techniques—the same ones that reduce the number of photons. Because they apply noise reduction at that level, the raw data CMOSs send to the ADC—at high ISO speeds—is much cleaner than the raw data from CCDs.

## Where Is that Noise Coming From?

Noise-removal tools are good—and keep getting better—but using them does have an impact on image sharpness and fine detail. It's a tradeoff. So, which things contribute to noise and how can we minimize them?

The main noise culprits are heat, bad data and errors. *Heat* comes from a variety of sources and can create both random and persistent noise patterns. *Bad data* occurs when an image is underexposed and pushed—or when it's captured at a high ISO. In extreme cases, both of these factors are at work. *Errors* arise because circuitry isn't 100% perfect; occasional errors are added to the image data due to manufacturing errors or wear and tear on the circuits. Some systems are designed to catch and remove, or actively route around, the error-prone circuits.

***Noise Sources:***

*Heat:*

- Environmental conditions around the camera, i.e., weather.
- Prolonged use of the LCD screen.
- Long exposures keep the sensor active and build heat.

*Data:*

- Underexposure requires pushing the exposure so that the shadow tones—the noisiest ones—become midtones.
- High-ISO choices use amplification to artificially boost the signal, which amplifies the amount of noise.

*Errors:*

- Inaccurate measurements and photodiode errors.
- Random photons and electrons leak into the photosites.

***When you increase your ISO speed, you also increase noise. Use the lowest possible ISO speed that allows you to get the shot you want.***

## Types of Noise

When you're trying to locate sources of noise, there are some distinctive types to look for. We're most familiar with *chroma noise,* which usually shows up as splotchy magenta and green blobs that have nothing to do with the image's colors. The amount and intensity of chroma noise climb with ISO speed—or with underexposed images that have been pushed to be brighter. Good noise-removal tools can get rid of most, if not all, of this type of noise. With raw files, the preview image is corrected (which allows you to see the improvements on screen), but the actual noise removal isn't applied to the image until it's demosaiced, during processing.

*Luminance noise* is another common issue. It appears as unwanted texture in our images and sometimes occurs as "salt and pepper" noise—small spots of black and white that appear randomly through the image. This type of noise is also corrected with noise-removal tools; just be sure to carefully apply luminance noise reduction so that you don't remove all texture. Some texture in an image is a good thing, but if you try to remove all of it in a high-ISO file, you'll end up with smearing—and irregular, unnatural, plastic-looking areas in the image.

*Fixed pattern noise* occurs as a repeated pattern and can appear in a variety of shapes. Its key characteristic is persistence. If you have fixed pattern noise, it will show up in the same location each time—in a variety of images. It's usually corrected automatically in-camera, since persistent patterns are easy to detect and remove. Any remaining fixed pattern noise can be minimized with noise-removal tools. This type of noise has a direct relationship to long exposures and increased heat at the sensor.

*Banding noise* may show up in shadow tones as continuous stripes and lines throughout the image. It's a complex problem that relates to the way data is collected from the sensor itself.[24] You'll probably only see this type of noise in the shadow tones of images that are significantly boosted in post-processing—and at higher ISOs where more amplification is used. The fix for this problem is to shoot properly exposed images, where the shadow tones don't need to be boosted.

## Hot Sensors

Heat is one of the biggest sources of noise, and CCDs are particularly susceptible to it. The problem with heat is that it generates electrons. Photosites already generate electrons from photons, even when you expose the sensor with the lens cap on (!). When electrons generated by heat are combined with those already-present electrons, the result is noisy images.

CCDs use a significant amount of power to capture an image, and more power means more heat. To reduce the amount of heat that's produced, most medium-format digital backs use a combination of active and passive cooling. You now know that when you increase the ISO on a CCD, you're amplifying the signal. Amplification requires more activity in the circuits, which means even more power and heat. We've noticed that noise becomes a significant problem with CCDs when you use ISO speeds faster than 100.

## Noise Patterns: Fixed or Random?

Both CCD and CMOS sensors are chunks of silicon with millions of tiny circuits. When the sensors are on, the electrical activity creates heat, or dark current. Dark current creates fixed pattern noise that shows up in the same place and affects the same pixels every time.

Other types of thermal noise are *random*—meaning that random pixels will suffer—and might be caused by environmental heat or the continued use of live preview. When you view a live preview image on your LCD screen, the camera keeps the sensor activated and essentially works as a video feed. This creates heat from the sensor and all its associated circuits, as well as from the LCD screen. If the camera is enclosed, or if you're working in a hot environment,[25] then all of these factors can combine and become a source of noise in your image; it's possible to have both fixed pattern noise and random noise in the same image.

## In-Camera Solutions

Some medium-format CCD cameras generate a *calibration frame*—or *black frame*—to remove heat noise.[26] After a long exposure, the camera will automatically take a second photo without opening the shutter. The internal signal processor compares the image with the black frame, and since the information on the black frame only contains information generated by heat, that information can be subtracted from the image. This process occurs after the image has been recorded; it's a quick, but not instant, process.

CMOS systems accomplish a similar function by using built-in circuits in the photosites. The built-in circuits measure the noise information and then subtract it from the signal information. They compare the values of the photosite when it's "empty" (there's no image) to when it's "full" (there is an image). The difference is a noise value, which can be subtracted from the photosite's value. All of this happens instantly, at each pixel, even at high frame rates.

# Noise Rescue: Keeping Up

Just as new cameras move forward with changing sensors and improved noise characteristics, so does raw-processing software. Whether you have a brand new camera or—especially—one that's a few generations old,[27] you stand to benefit hugely by keeping your raw-processing software up to date.[28]

The Canon 5D Mark II image in **Figure 5.16A** was processed in Lightroom three different ways: without noise reduction (NR), with NR using the 2003 process engine and with NR using the 2012 engine.[29] The 2003 process (middle image) still shows significant magenta/green splotches, irregular texture and more smearing artifacts in the noise pattern. The 2012 (right-hand image) image is much smoother, with a regular texture and no visible magenta/green shifts. **Figure 5.16B** shows the whole image processed out with the 2012 engine.

The noise standard changes quickly. As new sensors, processing engines for Lightroom and improved, alternative processing tools (like Photo Ninja) evolve, it's important to keep up with and update your noise-removal workflows. If you like, you can certainly stick with an older camera and tried-and-true software; if it worked three years ago, it'll continue to work for you now. It's not that the old tools break or wear out, it's that the benchmarks and quality levels keep climbing.

***Andy:*** When I was using my 2004 Canon 1Ds Mark II and processing the files through ACR V2,[30] there was some pretty significant noise at ISO 800. The jump from ISO 400 to 800 added a ton of noise, so going to 800 was a decision that had a lot of impact. The shots from my Canon 1Dx, processed with Lightroom 5, look amazing at ISO 800—there's so little noise. It's only when I ramp it up to ISO 6400 that I hit about same level of noise. Every time one of my cameras or software gets updated I need to test and adjust my noise workflow to keep up with the shift.

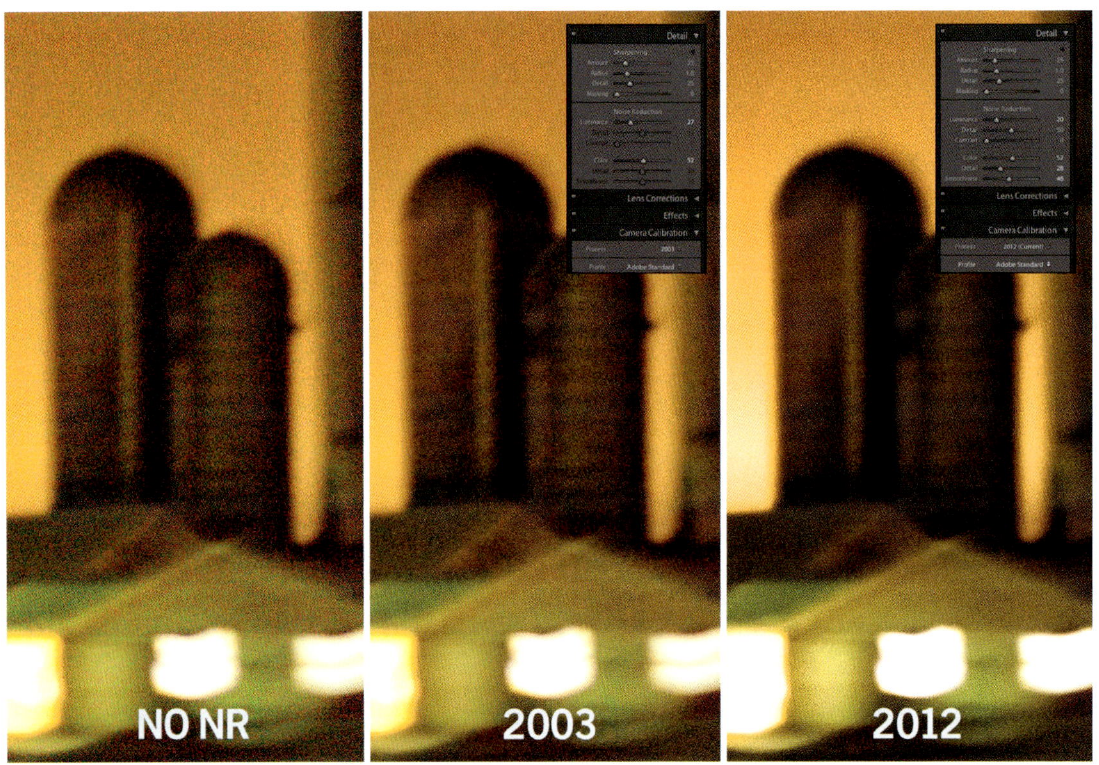


**FIGURE 5.16A** When upgrading your processing software, you retroactively improve your older files. We can see the differences in file quality between the same 5D MII file that was processed (from left to right): without noise reduction, with Lightroom 2003 noise reduction and with Lightroom 2012 noise reduction.
IMAGE © ANDY BATT, *HIGHWAY BARNS AT NIGHT—DETAIL*, 2011.

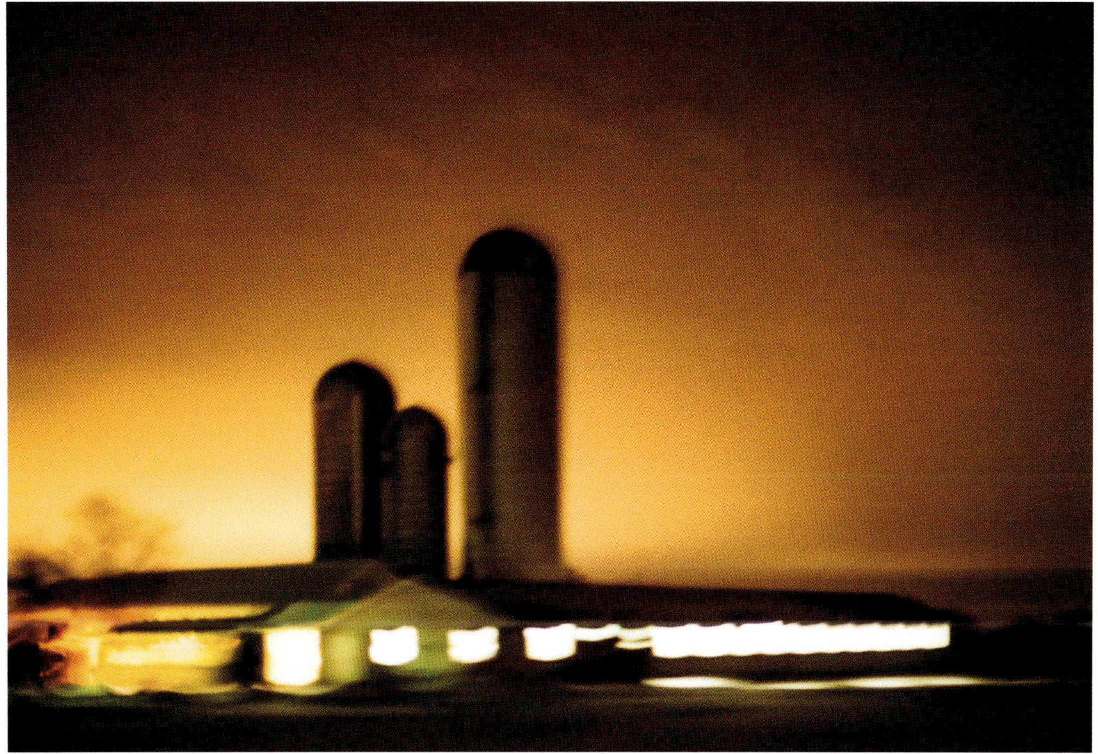

**FIGURE 5.16B** Motion blur at 1/8th and shallow DoF created the ethereal look of this glowing barn. Andy processed the file with the most current noise-removal tools to remove the objectionable chroma and luminance noise. (Shot at 50mm/1.4, 1/8th, *f*/1.4, ISO 4000.)
IMAGE © ANDY BATT, *HIGHWAY BARNS AT NIGHT*, 2011.

## FEATURED PHOTOGRAPH

### Oregon Ballet Theatre

Andy photographed Oregon Ballet Theatre's Brett Bauer and Grace Shibley dancing in his studio. This was a hybrid shoot, where he captured stills and motion footage. Through testing the latest camera and processing tools, he was able to create a hybrid workflow. Take a look at the before and after images (**Figure 5.17A**) to see noise removal at work.

***Andy:*** This was a layered shoot—we needed to capture both stills and motion simultaneously. I worked with the company's Artistic Director, Christopher Stowell, to direct the dancers' actions. I was taking still shots as well as directing two of my associates, who were capturing the high-definition motion. Since we captured stills and motion simultaneously, I couldn't use strobe lights, so we used continuous lighting instead.

There was a project a few years back when I needed to capture—at fast shutter speeds and in a high-speed series—NBA players dunking; I couldn't use strobes then, either. We ended up using 96,000 watts of tungsten lighting to get 1/1000th of a second at ISO 800. I knew we'd need about the same shutter speed to freeze the action for the ballet image. We had a limited budget, so I rented a small HMI lighting package (about 3,200 watts)[31]—which was great for the motion cameras, but really lacking in power to work at good ISO speeds and get motion-stopping shutters speeds with my still camera. I had demoed the Canon 5D Mark III recently and was impressed that it could create amazingly clean images at high ISOs.

I tested the 5D Mark III on set and was able to push the ISO all the way to 5000, while still creating amazingly clean images. We processed test images out on set with Lightroom. This allowed us to get away with a much smaller lighting package, and still achieve the high shutter speed and a good amount of DoF (**Figure 5.17B**).

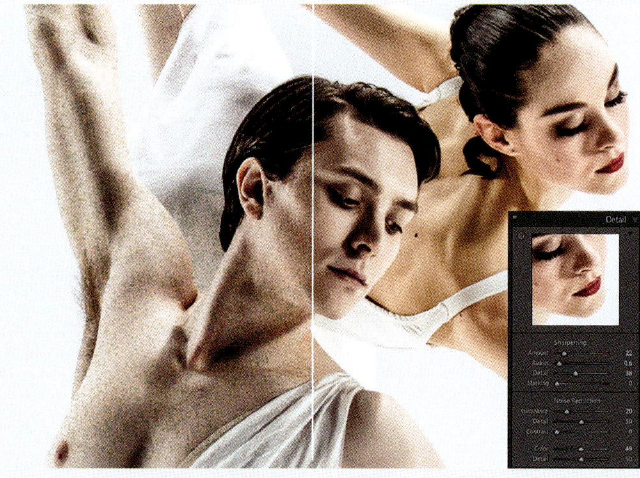


**FIGURE 5.17A** Andy shot this image with a Canon 5D Mark III, in studio at 1/1000th using continuous HMI lighting. He was able to shoot at a high shutter speed because tests at ISO 5000 showed that a clean, high-quality image could be created after noise removal in Lightroom. Here we see the image before and after noise processing—along with the Detail control panel and the sharpening and noise-sharpening settings used to process the image. In **Figure 5.17B,** we see the full image after processing. IMAGE © ANDY BATT, *OREGON BALLET THEATRE—DETAIL,* IMAGE COURTESY OF OREGON BALLET THEATRE, 2012.

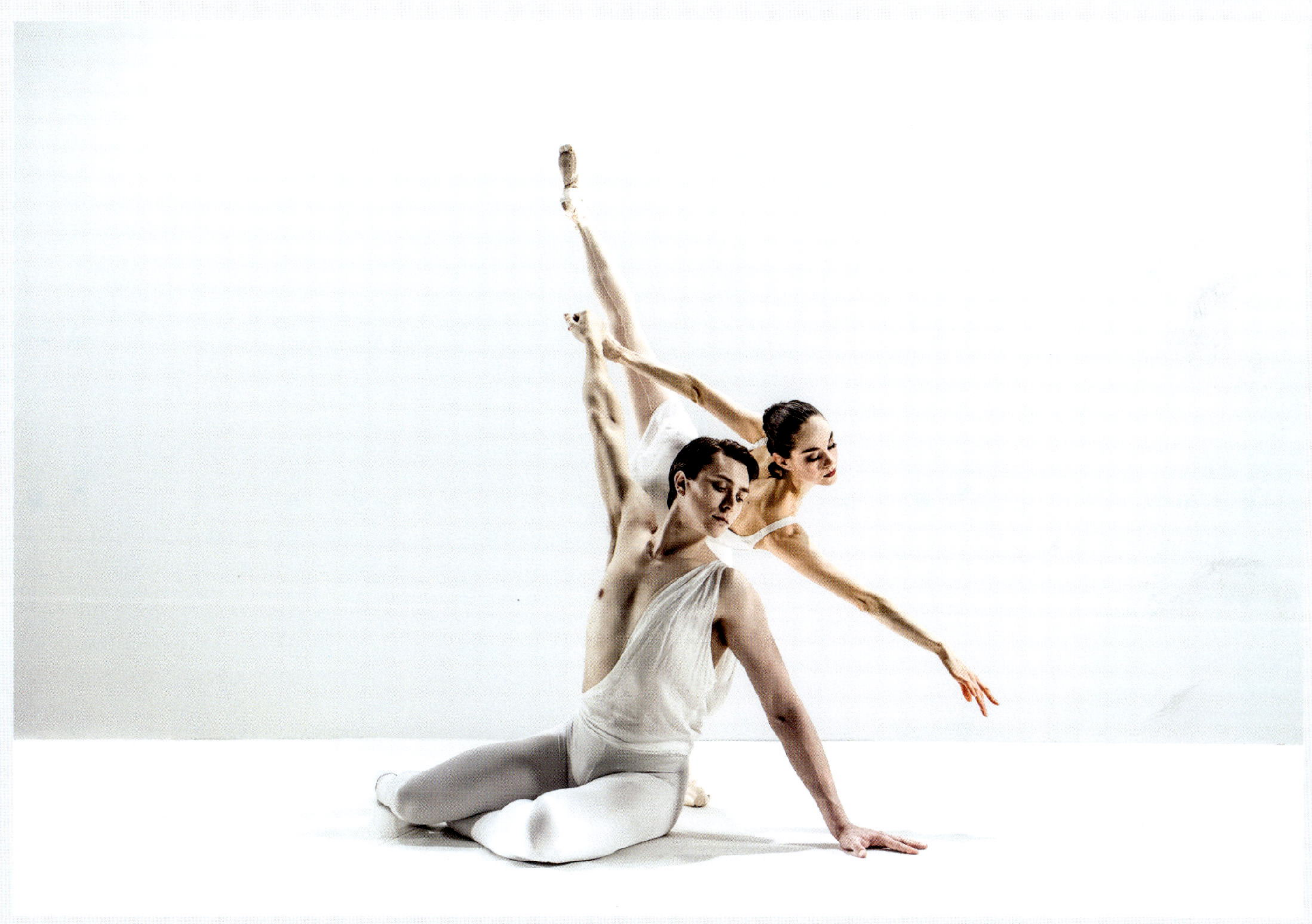

**FIGURE 5.17B** Andy photographed Grace Shibley and Brett Bauer in George Balanchine's *Apollo,* as part of Oregon Ballet Theatre's 2012–2013 Seasons.
IMAGE © ANDY BATT, *OREGON BALLET THEATRE,* IMAGE COURTESY OF OREGON BALLET THEATRE, 2012.

## Demosaicing

Once raw images are on your computer, you need to decode them—by taking the information from the Bayer pattern and creating all the missing pixel values (see *Mosaics at Work* earlier in this chapter). *Demosaicing* is the process where those missing values are interpolated. In raw-processing applications, you can move sliders around, change a curve, click a few points and export and—voilà!—you have a processed image. You know by now that there's some deep, dark science going on underneath that user interface, right? Well, we asked Jim Christian, Founder of PictureCode and author of Noise Ninja® and Photo Ninja®, to help us explain what's going on behind the curtain . . .

**FEATURED INTERVIEW**

## Jim Christian

*Author of Noise Ninja and Photo Ninja*

### Processing the Raw Data: What's Happening in There?

***Andy Batt:* Raw data comes off the chip and is stored inside of a raw file. When we open it to process the image, what steps occur "behind the scenes" to turn the 1s and 0s into an image?**

***Jim Christian:*** Imagine being asked to reconstruct a full-color image after someone has discarded the majority of the color measurements and corrupted the remaining data. In essence, that is the challenge of raw conversion.

For a color image, you need three color values—red, green and blue—for each pixel. However, most digital cameras only record one color at each pixel site in a mosaic pattern. And the data that actually does get recorded is varyingly inaccurate due to noise, quantization, nonlinearity, aliasing, optical distortion, chromatic aberration, blurring and highlight clipping. It can be quite a mess. The task of raw conversion, then, is to create a pleasing image from this incomplete, approximate data.

Note that I didn't say, "recreate the image." There is an infinite number of possible reconstructions that are consistent with the measured values, and we don't know which one is the best match for the original scene. But some are more likely than others, and some look better than others. The best we can do is to synthesize a rendering that fills in all the missing values, doesn't vary too much from the recorded measurements and is more plausible or pleasing than other renderings. (Think about this next time you hear a photographer say he wants "maximum accuracy." What does accuracy really mean in this context?)

***AB:* As the author of Photo Ninja, you've been in the trenches, creating a new raw-processing tool. Photo Ninja grew from the noise-processing work you did to create your Photoshop plugin, Noise Ninja. How did you go about building a raw processor from the ground up?**

***JC:*** This is not a trivial problem, and it is fraught with tradeoffs. Developing a state-of-the-art solution requires a broad range of applied mathematics, computer science, heuristics (i.e., black magic) and many, many hours of staring at pixels and experimenting. There is no standard formula or textbook recipe.

Moreover, it isn't really one problem. A raw conversion involves a whole suite of problems that are often interdependent, and the solution to one can impact the solution for another in a big game of mathematical whack-a-mole.

***AB:* It definitely seems like black magic! At this point in the book, our readers know that there's science behind that magic. Can you break it down into broad strokes?**

***JC:*** Sure! Here's an overview of the common steps in raw conversion. The first thing to understand is decompression. The contents of most raw files are compressed to save space. Several raw formats have adopted lossless JPEG, which is a standard predictive entropy-coding scheme, but other compression methods are in use as well. The decompression step converts the file to an array of raw pixel measurements that serve as the input for the raw conversion process.

***AB:* Predictive entropy coding?**

***JC:*** "Predictive entropy coding" is a type of compression that exploits redundancy in the data and uses fewer bits to encode the most-frequent data values and more bits to encode less-frequent values.

Photographers tend to obsess over the lossless nature of raw compression, while complaining about how much space the files consume on disk. Ironically, a significant fraction of the size of a raw file can be due to noise in the least significant bits of pixel values, especially as the bit depth of raw files has increased from 10- to 12- to 14-bits. This noisy data cannot be effectively compressed, because it's random. Raw files could probably be made meaningfully smaller—with the use of a properly designed, high-quality lossy algorithm—with immaterial impact on image quality. But marketing departments would then be forced to educate their customers as to why discarding some bits is acceptable (and conversely would have to admit that their high-bit-depth cameras are actually recording a fair amount of junk bits).

***AB:* Okay, next up is . . .?**

***JC:*** Demosaicing. Most of the current sensors only record a red, green or blue color value at each pixel in a mosaic pattern, while the final image requires all three values at each pixel. The demosaicing operation fills in the missing values. The naïve solution of simply interpolating missing values from adjacent measurements yields poor results, with lots of jaggies and color artifacts. High-quality demosaicing algorithms employ more sophisticated methods to decide the best interpolation strategy for each pixel. The "hard" case for demosaicing is when fine patterns occur at or near the sensor resolution limit, especially when the camera lacks an anti-aliasing filter. In these cases, the sensor doesn't have enough resolution to correctly sample the oscillations in the pattern, so the pattern is aliased (roughly, smeared) in a way that can make it extremely difficult to infer the correct demosaiced values—and the result is usually false colors and line segments that are oriented in the wrong direction.

In Photo Ninja we've developed some technology that can disambiguate a lot of these cases. But I still recommend that most people use cameras with anti-aliasing filters, unless they have a good reason and know how to avoid the conditions that create aliasing and moiré. Without an anti-aliasing filter, the image might look a little sharper or have a little more detail, but there is significantly more risk of demosaicing artifacts and moiré and extra post-processing work to clean it up.

***AB:* So one place to look for the "quality" of the raw processor's interpretation of the data would be areas of thin, fine detail viewed at 100%, e.g., at a 1:1 pixel view?**

***JC:*** If you were going to view images at 100% or make large prints, then of course you'd like to see fine detail rendered nicely at that level. Even at lower resolutions, what happens at 100% can have an impact. For instance, if demosaicing picks the wrong direction for a region that is more than a few pixels across, you can see false colors or artifacts even when you zoom out. That said, zooming out can forgive a lot of image-processing evils, and the reality is that a lot of images are viewed at low resolution on the web (though high-resolution display technology like Retina might change that over time).

***AB:* I've had images that appear to have blown-out white skies and specular highlights (those small, very bright areas). With raw processing, you can miraculously bring tone back in these areas. How does that work?**

***JC:*** We can restore some of this by using highlight recovery techniques. If parts of an image are overexposed, then the corresponding pixel measurements will be clipped and must be treated as missing values. Highlight recovery attempts to extrapolate the clipped values from nearby unclipped measurements. Generally speaking, small areas can be recovered more reliably than large ones, single-channel clipping can be recovered more robustly than two- or three-channel clipping and luminance (tonal values) can be recovered much more easily than color.

Luminance can be estimated from the overall levels of nearby unclipped pixel values. Color, however, requires much more elaborate analysis of the relationships of these values, and those relationships can be highly ambiguous when the burned-out region overlaps multiple image features or has color fringing along an edge.

***AB:* What about other adjustments to the "exposure" of the image?**

***JC:*** These fall under the category of tone adjustments. The overall brightness and contrast of the image needs to be established by adjusting the brightness of individual pixels. Traditionally, this was a relatively straightforward matter of mapping each pixel individually through a simple arithmetic transform or lookup table. The dynamic range of current cameras increasingly exceeds the dynamic range of computer monitors and prints. This has made it necessary to develop much more complicated algorithms for lightening shadows, compressing highlights and reducing global contrast—while preserving local contrast (detail), so that the image "fits" in the available dynamic range without looking flat or unnatural.

***AB:* Often the photographer must choose a higher ISO to get the best picture, but this means more noise. Since we rely on our software tools to make the best image in these situations, how does the raw processor handle noise? Also, will noise eventually become a non-issue as sensors improve?**

***JC:*** The noise problem is not going away any time soon. It is inherent in the physics of the image-capture process. Even if you had perfectly noise-free sensor electronics, measurable noise would still be introduced simply from the statistical randomness of photon arrivals at individual sensor sites. In well-exposed, low-ISO images or in reduced-resolution images, noise may be so low that it can be ignored. But in high-ISO images, or in the shadows of low-ISO images (especially when lightened), it can be objectionable. Moreover, I've noticed that as sensors and noise-reduction technology have improved, photographers simply push to a higher ISO, so the actual noise level that they tolerate in an image stays about the same.

Noise reduction is one of the most challenging tasks in the raw conversion pipeline, and it's an active area of research. Sophisticated (and usually computationally intensive) algorithms are necessary to strike a good balance between suppressing noise and preserving fine detail.

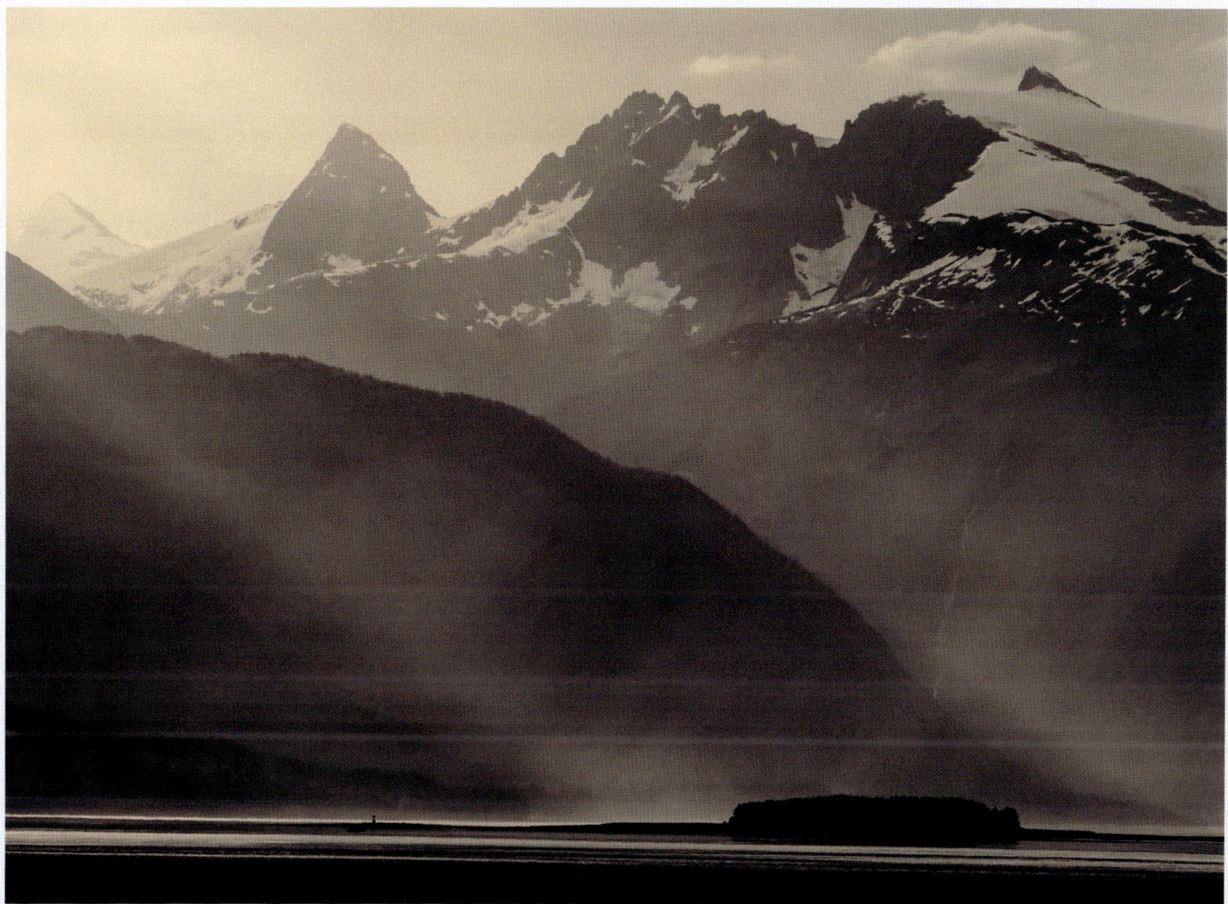

**FIGURE 5.18** This was taken on a July day, early in the morning, somewhere along the Alaska Inside Passage. Shot with a Canon 10D body and a 200mm *f*/2.8L lens, Jim processed this image in Photo Ninja, using split-toning to add warmth and a contrast boost to emphasize the light beams.
IMAGE © JIM CHRISTIAN, *EARLY MORNING—ALASKA,* 2003.

In Photo Ninja, the first thing we do is characterize the noise. Noise varies with brightness and color (for instance, dark blues are usually a lot more noisy than light greens). We scan the image looking for examples of noise and use this information to build a "noise profile" that helps the noise filter discriminate noise from detail. To remove the noise, we have to perform a delicate balancing act. On the one hand, we have to average a lot of pixels together in a region to eliminate low-frequency noise and color blobs. On the other hand, we have to minimize the blurring of fine details and texture. Suffice it to say that there is some pretty elaborate applied math that we rely on to do this. It's not perfect, but we've achieved a pretty good tradeoff for noise suppression versus detail preservation.

***AB:* Speaking of detail, most images look a little soft straight from the camera. How does a raw converter go about sharpening an image?**

***JC:*** Right, lens diffraction and the anti-aliasing filter in front of most CMOS sensors cause some blurring, even in a focused image. So, you need at least a mild, small-radius sharpening pass to compensate for this. Traditional "unsharp mask" methods fake sharpening by boosting contrast around edges. The better sharpening algorithms today use actual de-blurring methods similar to what NASA used to correct blurred images from the Hubble space telescope. They literally attempt to mathematically reverse the process that caused the blur. One difficulty is that noise reduction and sharpening can fight each other (mathematically they are practically opposites), so ideally they need to be designed to work together.

In Photo Ninja, we also have a "detail enhancement" filter that intelligently boosts local contrast. You can think of it as an unsharp mask on steroids, able to operate simultaneously at multiple radii and with a powerful engine for identifying region boundaries and preventing halos that you usually see with a traditional unsharp mask or "clarity" tools. It's one of my favorite filters. It can really make detail "pop" in a natural-looking way as long as you don't push it too far.

***AB:* To wrap up, I wanted to get your thoughts on how a raw processor can improve images taken years ago, with older digital cameras. How can a newer processing tool access "more data" than what originally seemed possible?**

***JC:*** It boils down to better algorithms and faster computers.

These are difficult, nuanced problems. As researchers and developers, our understanding has deepened as we have gained more collective experience, and the relevant technologies have evolved and improved. So, even though the data in those old (raw) files hasn't changed, our ability to interpret and optimize that data has gotten better. This process will continue in the future.

Likewise, the onward march of computing power opens up new possibilities over time. Algorithms that would have been impractically slow five or ten years ago can now be incorporated in interactive solutions. The current noise-reduction algorithm in Photo Ninja, for instance, would have been unreasonable to deploy in our original Noise Ninja product.

A number of Photo Ninja users have told me they started going through all their old images and re-converting them, because they're getting better results than what they could achieve in years past. Noise reduction, highlight recovery, adaptive tone controls—all these updated technologies are allowing them to salvage and refine old images.

So, keep your raw files! Forever!

# Noise-Removal Tools

After you do everything you can to avoid noise issues, you'll still need to do some image cleanup. We find that low-ISO images can benefit from a light touch, even if you've made good exposures and have avoided the need to rescue your images.

Lightroom, Aperture, Photo Ninja, DxO Optics and Capture 1 are all great raw processors with excellent built-in noise-reduction tools. With any of them, your goal is to remove distracting, obvious noise while preserving good detail, texture and sharpness. The secret is that your eye and opinion matter when it comes to deciding how much noise reduction is enough. Before you deliver a file to a client or send it off for printing, you'll need to view the image at 1:1 to see what the pixels look like before and after. You'll also need to make a realistic assessment of how the image will be output for its end use.

## Quick and Dirty Guide to Noise Removal

We suggest that you practice noise-removal techniques by digging through your library and finding two different images: a high-ISO image that has easily visible noise and an underexposed low-ISO image that might need to be "rescued." Your application may be different than ours, but some noise-removal basics apply to any processing software.

### General Guidelines

- Always view your NR technique at 100% pixel view; it's the only way you can really see what is and isn't working.
- Avoid removing all traces of texture, because images that are too smooth don't look natural.
- Too much noise reduction can result in a loss of fine detail and sharpness.
- An image that is noisy to begin with will always have residual texture. It will never look like it was shot at the camera's native ISO.
- Always turn NR on and off to see the before and after effects.
- Sometimes it's easier if you "go too far" with the NR tools; by backing off from a heavy-handed adjustment, you can find the sweet spot in your settings.

### The Tools

Locate the noise-removal tools in your raw processor. In Lightroom, they're under the Detail control panel in the Develop tab. The first thing to do is find the "Off" switch. In Lightroom, it's a tiny little switch on the upper left of the control panel. Alternatively, you can set the sliders (or values) to "0" to deactivate them. The Off switch is a better choice, because you really want to flip between "with" and "without" noise reduction. You also should flip back and forth between a full-screen and 1:1 (aka 100% pixel) view. (At full-screen view, you don't see the noise accurately.) It can also be useful to jump to a higher magnification for a closer look, since it really shows the effect at the pixel level.

Find the "Luminance Noise" and "Color (aka Chroma) Noise" adjustment tools. Color and Luminance are your big guns. There may be secondary levels of adjustment under each of these sliders. Start with the Luminance adjustment, which suppresses texture noise. While making the adjustment, pay attention to the edges and fine details in your image. Too much adjustment, and you'll start to soften them. If there are secondary sliders available, you can use them to fine tune the primary slider's effect on the image. In Lightroom, you can use the Luminance Detail slider to balance what's considered noise and what's considered detail. The Luminance Contrast slider modifies how the desirable texture and detail contrast are affected. In Photo Ninja, you'll find a secondary slider labeled "Residual Noise and Detail" that functions similarly; it allows you to protect some of the texture and to preserve more detail.

You'll use the *Color* adjustment to remove the splotchy green and magenta[32] patches in your images. By moving this slider, you can adjust the intensity of the correction. Pay attention to the edges and fine details in your image. If you push too hard you'll start to degrade the image. The secondary tool, *Detail*, is there to help preserve edge detail in high-noise images. The other secondary tool, *Smoothness*, gives you another adjustment to further refine and remove the chroma noise.

In each of your test images, find a spot with a lot of noise; it's usually in the shadow tones. Start with the default noise-reduction settings: Just flip the switch on and off (or whatever method works) to see the difference between "no NR" and "NR." Each image you work on will be different[33]—and each one will require some finesse to get the noise reduction right. Your eyes and experience are the best ways to judge, and the only way to gain that experience is to practice. The default settings were developed to work as a good, solid base, and they're not a bad place to start.

## Go Crazy

Now go crazy. Seriously, this is a good time to push the sliders around and go too far. By doing this, you may damage fine detail and end up making people look strange and plastic, but don't worry; these are all parametric settings, so you won't permanently damage anything. The only way to know if you've gone too far is . . . to purposefully go too far! So max those sliders out and really push the effect of each tool. Make it look bad on purpose.

Use your on/off switch to keep comparing the before and after—and then slowly back off your settings. Now that you know what ugly looks like, you can reverse the process. Search for that sweet spot where you effectively removed the noise, but preserved your edges and fine detail and kept enough texture so that it looks real. Keep checking at different magnifications and in several areas to see how the NR looks all over the image. Make sure to look over areas with critical detail; what looks great on a barn wall might look horrible on someone's face. You can always nuke the settings back to their defaults and start over.

## Add Noise!

The last step in noise reduction is to actually add noise—it's counterintuitive, but it works! In Lightroom, you can achieve this in the Effects palette. Adding a slight amount of "grain" has two beneficial effects: It can mask remaining noise that's hard to get rid of and it can actually help make the image easier to print if you have large areas of continuous color (e.g., blue sky). That small amount of grain reduces banding and actually makes the image appear smoother. The trick is to work with minimal amounts. Zoom into 100% view and add grain with the slider until you can just barely detect the change. There are other methods for adding grain; the end idea is the same for all of them.

## Visual Case Study: Using Photo Ninja for Noise Removal

It's worth exploring Photo Ninja,[34] an excellent alternative to Lightroom for removing noise. It has a similar toolset to Lightroom's toolset, but a different engine powers its processing. Photo Ninja's noise-reduction tools are particularly powerful; they allow you to apply an aggressive amount of noise reduction, while still retaining fine detail. Here's a great tip from the Photo Ninja manual:

> ***Our experience is that it is usually best to leave a little too much noise rather than too little. This usually results in a more photographic look. If too much noise is suppressed, some images can look artificial or plastic. However, it is very subject-dependent as well as a matter of taste.***

**Figure 5.19A** shows three detail versions of Andy's image of a mountain lake. It was an eight-second exposure at ISO 3200. The image has a lot of inherent noise, but there's some variation and a few midtones and highlights. Andy processed it out with both Lightroom and Photo Ninja; as a control, he also exported a version without any noise reduction or sharpening.

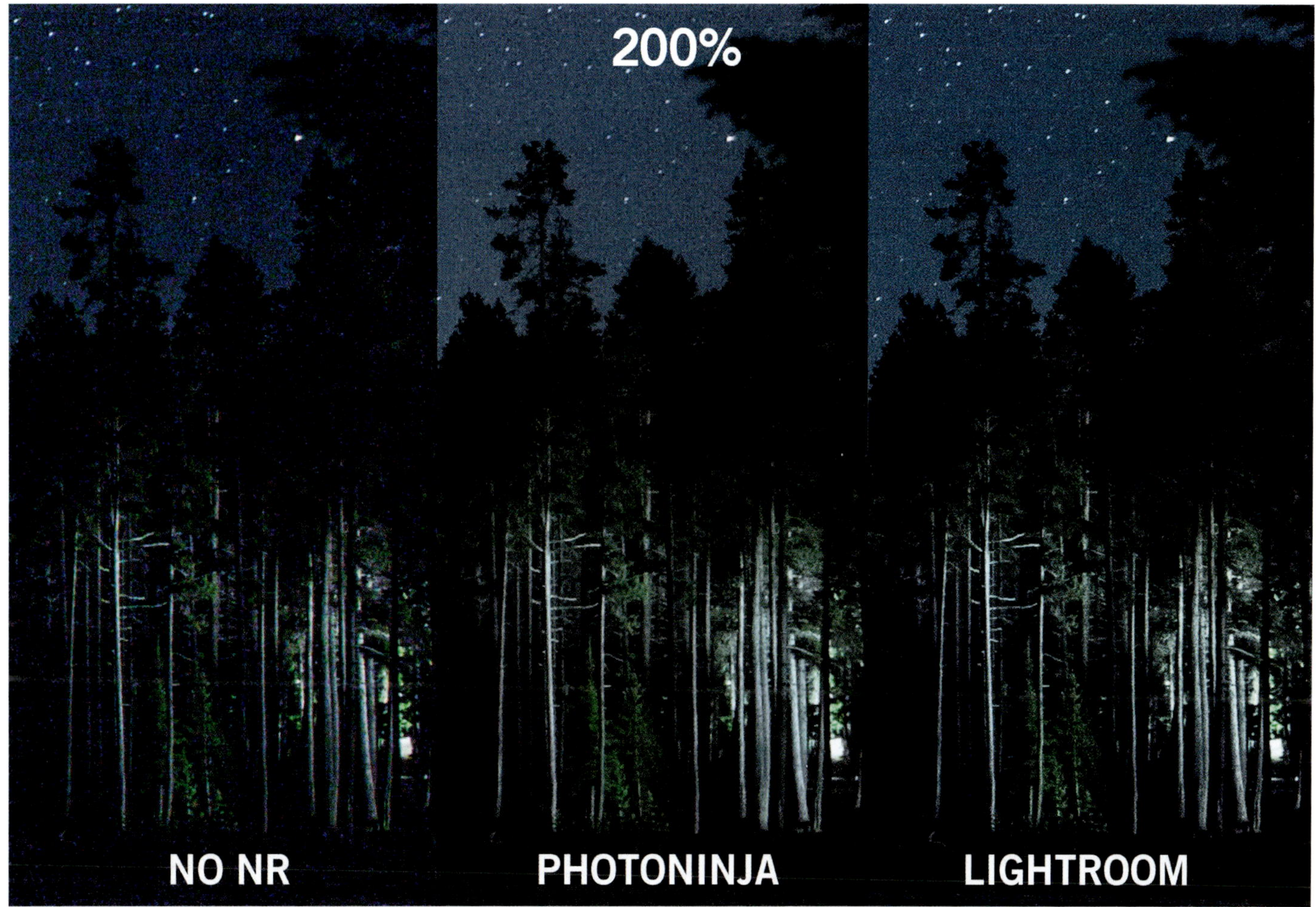


**FIGURE 5.19A** To compare the noise reduction tools in Lightroom and Photo Ninja, Andy processed out an image taken at 8 sec, *f*/2.0 at ISO 3200. For a control, he used Lightroom to create the image (left), by turning off all sharpening and NR. The middle and right-hand images were processed to their subjective best finish, using all the NR and sharpening tools available. These images show a 200% view of the pixels.
IMAGE © ANDY BATT, *FOURMILE LAKE AT NIGHT—DETAIL*, 2013.

***Andy:*** My goal was to make each version look as similar as possible in terms of color and tone, and to use the noise reduction and sharpening tools to their best advantage. The objective was to subjectively test each program's noise-reduction capabilities: Which program (in my opinion) created the best image?

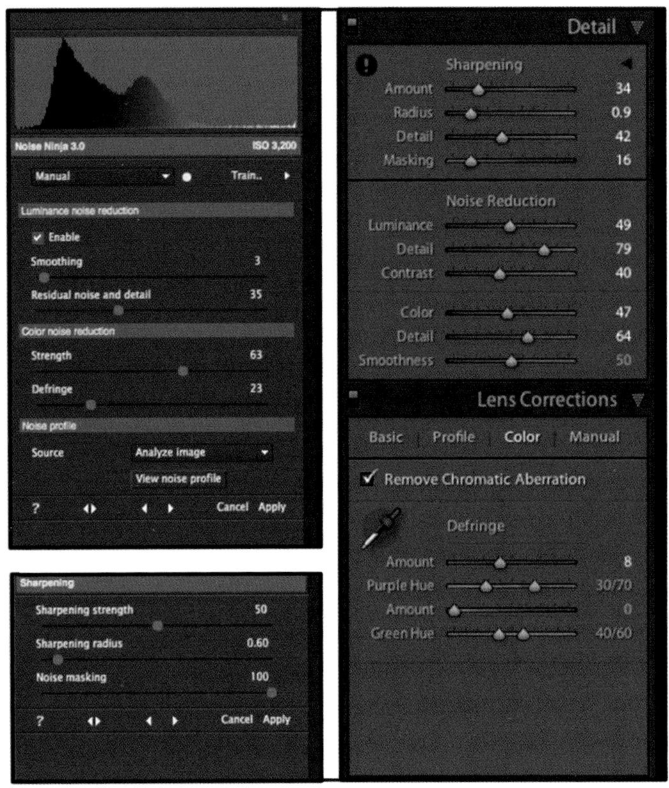


**FIGURE 5.19B** Here are the settings Andy used to process out the images in **Figure 5.19A**. The Photo Ninja NR tools are shown (left) next to the Lightroom NR tools (right).
SCREENSHOT © ANDY BATT: *PHOTO NINJA AND LIGHTROOM NOISE-REDUCTION TOOLS*, 2013.

The tool sets in both applications are similar (**Figure 5.19B**), with the notable addition of the "Analyze Image" feature in Photo Ninja. This feature looks at the data and for areas of smooth tonality where it can measure the presence of noise. It uses that "fingerprint" to create a noise-reduction profile. You can also shoot a series of test images with the purpose of building a dedicated noise profile for your camera.

*What Andy was looking for*:

- Removal of color noise
- Reduction in luminance noise (i.e., unwanted texture)
- Preservation of fine detail

## Photo Ninja Vs. Lightroom

Both applications did an admirable job. The image needed some exposure and tonal boosting, both of which raised the noise levels. You can see a "control" version (on the left side of **Figure 5.19A**) without any NR. It's close in terms of the noise removal; both processors did a great job taking out chroma and luminance noise. Photo Ninja did a better job holding onto fine detail; the thin branches and texture in the trees is a little cleaner and sharper, where Lightroom got a little soft and smeary. For smaller prints, you might not notice, but in full-size or up-rezzed prints, you'd see the difference.

## The Takeaway

You have options when it comes to processing images. There are occasions when you need a different tool in order to get the best result (**Figure 5.19C**).

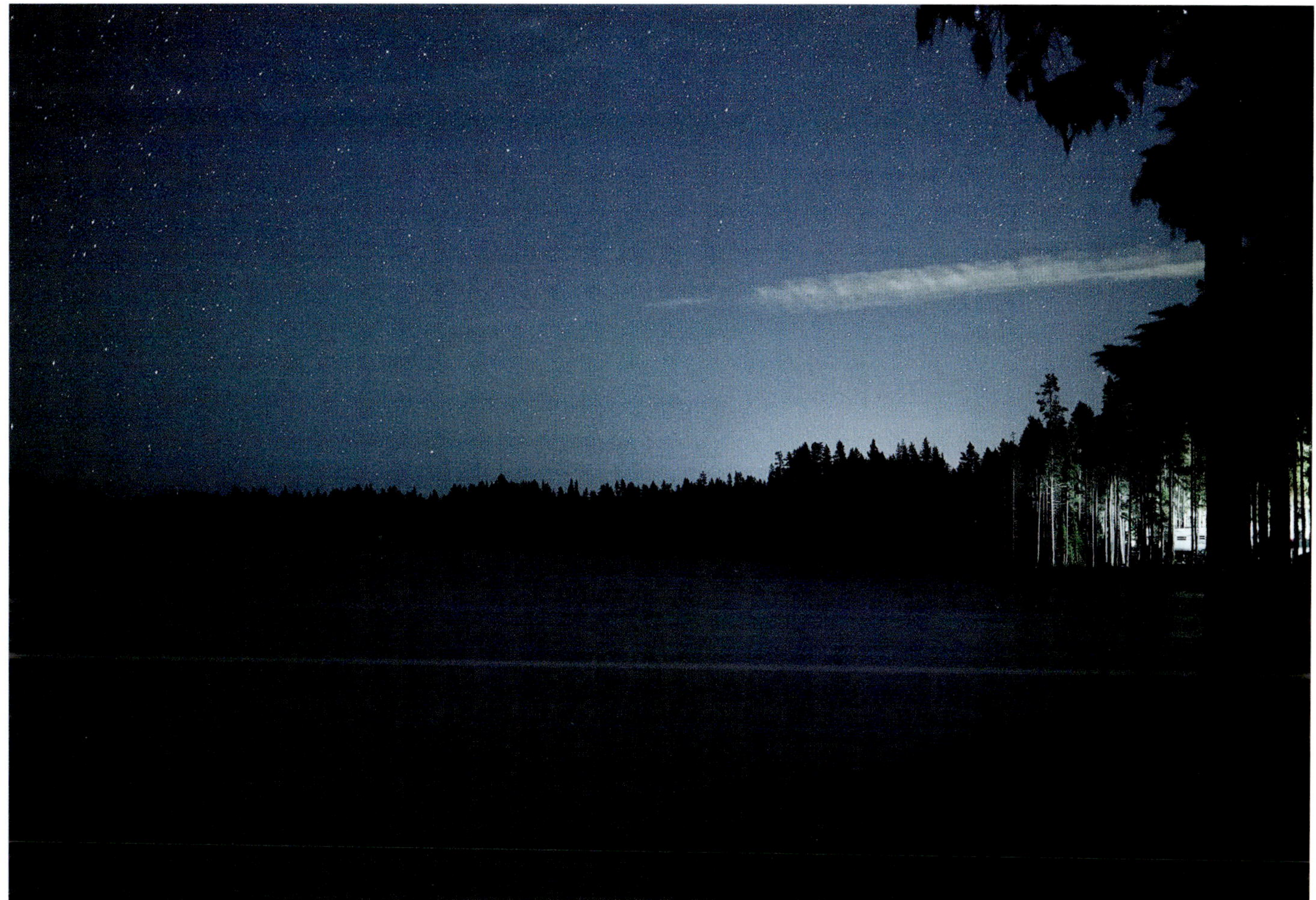

**FIGURE 5.19C** This is the full image from which the detail shot in **Figure 5.19A** was made. It was processed through Photo Ninja.
IMAGE © ANDY BATT, *FOURMILE LAKE AT NIGHT,* 2013.

## TRY THIS AT HOME

### Painted Light Portrait—a Long-Exposure Test

**For step-by-step instructions, go to: www.focalpress.com/cw/digitalimagingmasters**

Part of being a successful photographer is to know your gear, which—for this chapter—means knowing how far you can push your camera's sensor. In this exercise, you'll test your sensor by working it hard, intentionally heating it up to create some serious noise. By the time you finish, you'll be able to decide whether it's better to shoot at fast shutter speeds at high ISOs—or at long shutter speeds at low ISOs.

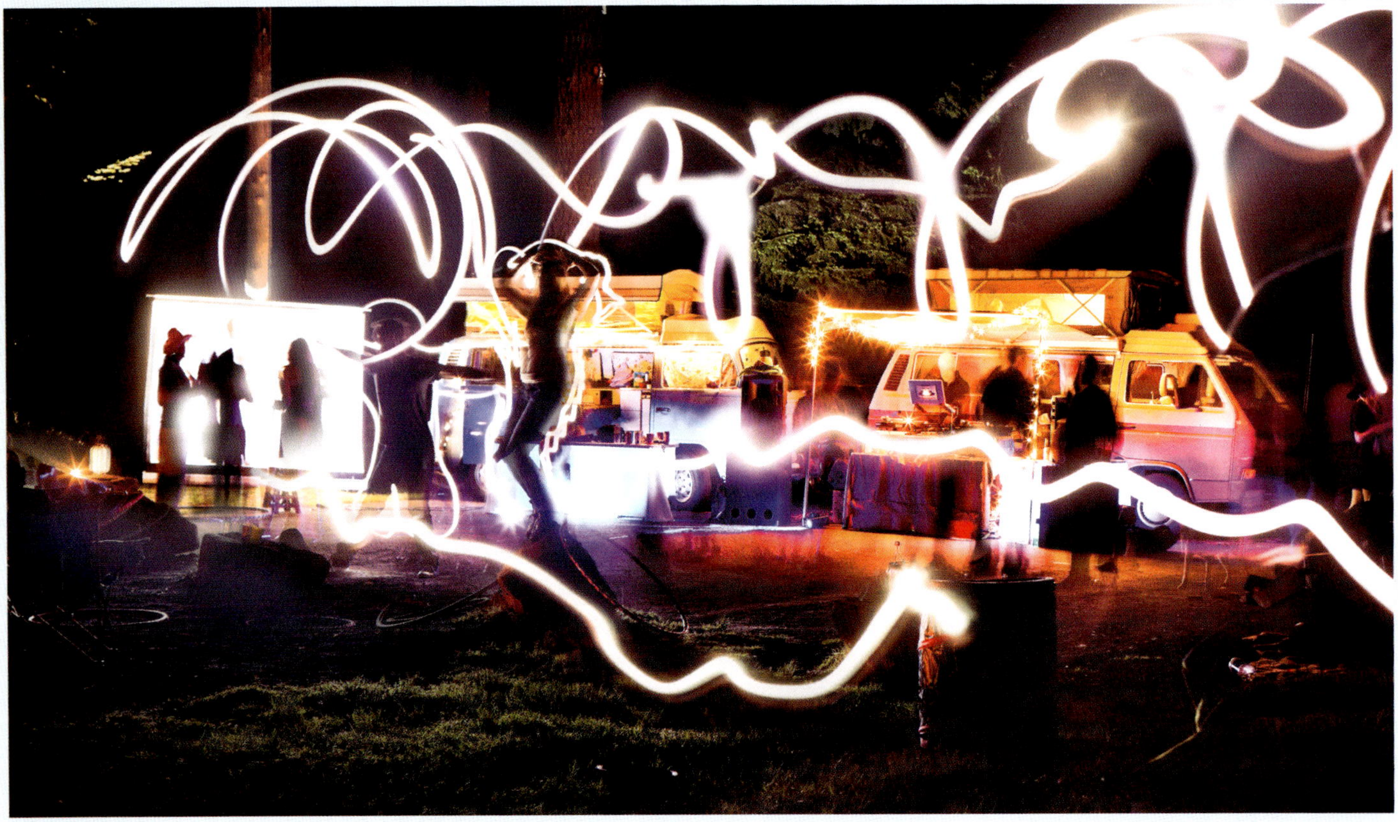

**FIGURE 5.20** Never one to leave a camera at home, Andy set up a long-exposure camera during an outdoor party and added light painting into this nighttime scene. He shot it at 8.0 sec, *f*/5.6 at ISO 1250, with a 5D MII, 50mm/1.4.
IMAGE © ANDY BATT, *TRY THIS AT HOME: DRAWING WITH FLASHLIGHTS*, 2013.

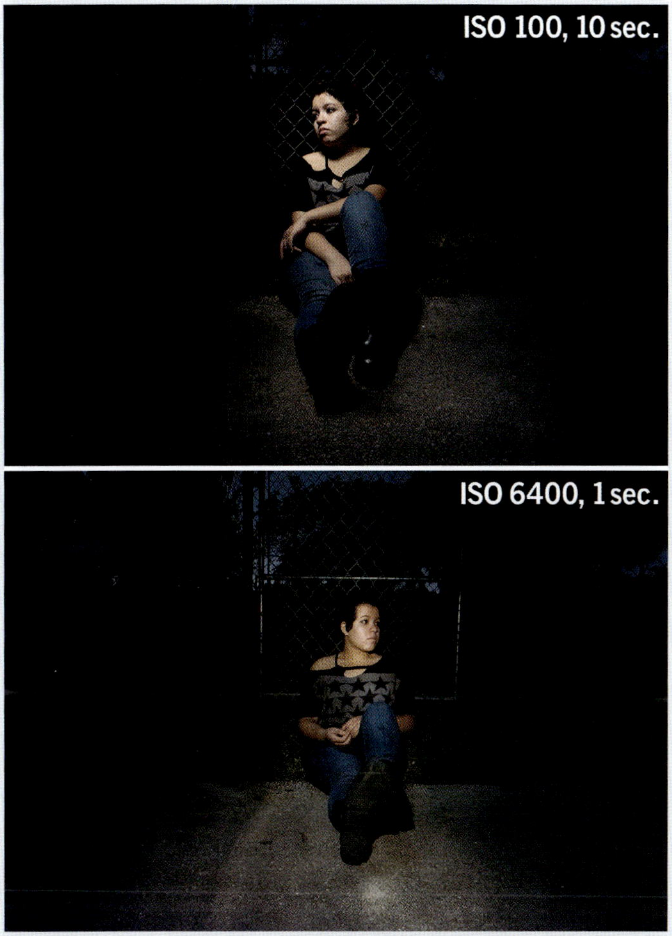

**FIGURE 5.21A** By testing ISO and exposure time, you can get a better idea of how your choices for each will affect the quality of your final image. There is no one answer; there are times when each option is the correct one.
IMAGE © ERIKA VELASQUEZ, *PAINTED LIGHT PORTRAIT*, 2013.

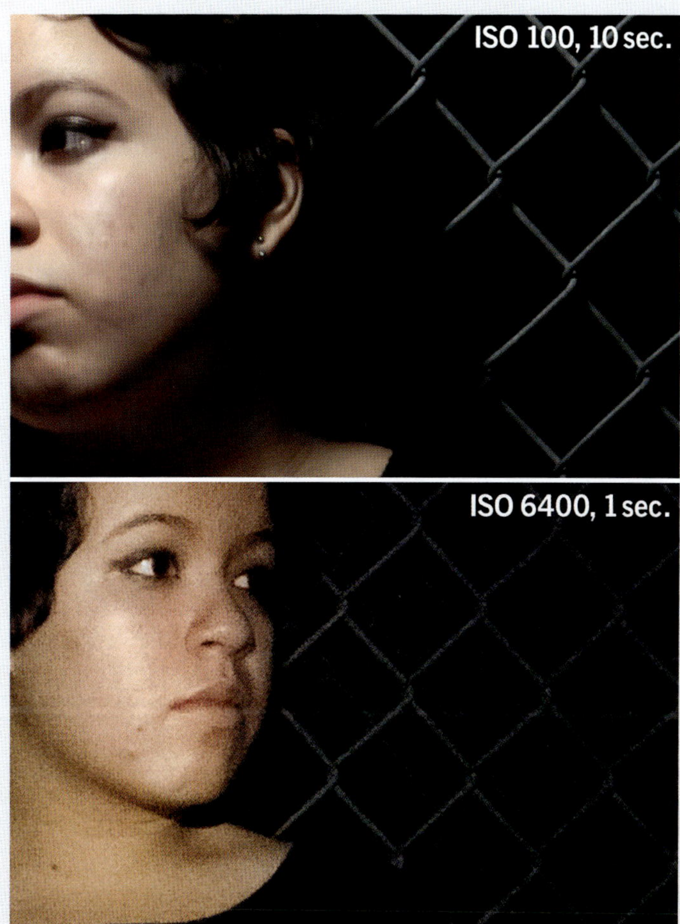


**FIGURE 5.21B** Viewing the image at 150% reveals the difference between ISO 100 and ISO 6400 in post-processed noise levels.
IMAGE © ERIKA VELASQUEZ, *PAINTED LIGHT PORTRAIT—DETAIL*, 2013.

## What Is a Camera?

There's a lot of discussion about the form factor, size and design of cameras. As with all discussions, you'll find people fervently staking out opposite positions. One person will declare "The DSLR is dead; all smart photographers who 'get it' are going to use smartphones," and at the same time someone else will declare, "Anything you can do with a smartphone camera you can do ten times better with a real camera." With this exploration, we'll explore the differences—at the sensor level—between a smartphone camera and a DSLR.

***Andy:*** Photographers can create good work with any camera, including the tiny ones built into our phones, but I wonder if some photographers are choosing convenience over quality? It's odd to me that—when choosing a tool to create art—some favor instant posting to social media over higher-quality images crafted with more control. You can use whatever camera you want—as long as you're committed to mastering it.

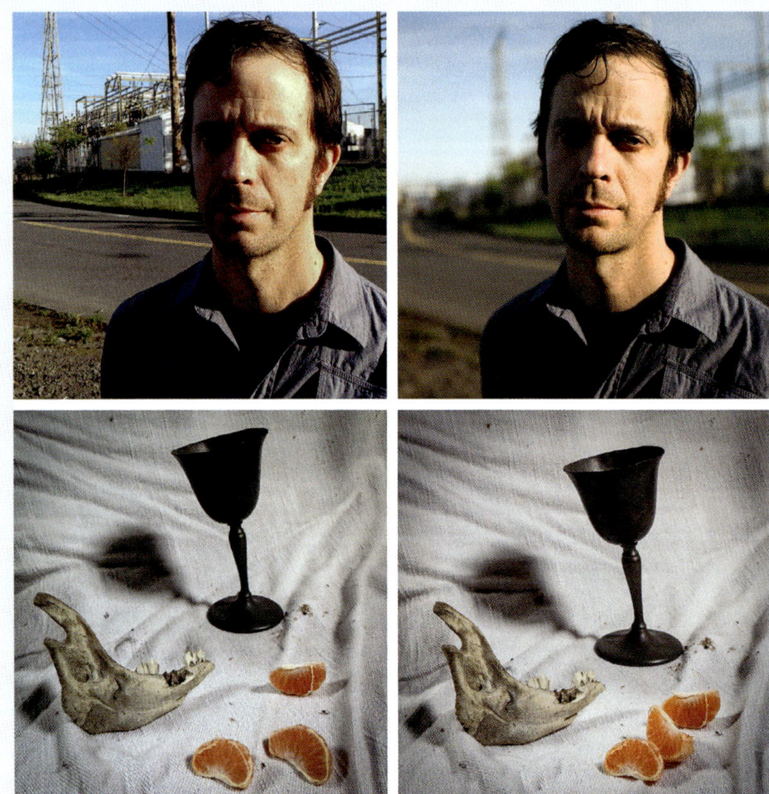

**FIGURE 5.22** It's important to understand how the camera you're using will interact with your subject. An iPhone's tiny sensor brings infinite DoF to Andy's portrait of Jed (top left). In comparison, by using a Canon 1Dx DSLR at *f*/2.8 (top right), Andy was able to drop the background significantly out of focus, separating Jed from the background, a technique that isn't possible to achieve in–camera with a smartphone.

In some cases, it's difficult to distinguish the results of a miniaturized smartphone sensor from those of a larger sensor. Can you tell which of Katrin's still lifes (bottom right and left) was shot with an iPhone and which was shot with a Sony RX100?*

*The iPhone image is the one on the left.

**Extremes**

At one extreme are 80MP digital backs with amazingly high-quality images. If you compare the quality of these images to those of other cameras, it's no contest: the 80MP is a clear winner. What's the cost of that winner? More money than it costs to buy a small car—plus a complicated workflow. (It thrives when you shoot tethered to Capture One and have a DIT on hand to manage the incoming files.)

A high-MP DLSR, like the Nikon D800E, is at another point in the discussion. It'll give you a resolution approaching that of a medium-format system, with the workflow and usability of a DSLR—and at a dramatically cheaper price. At the other end of the spectrum is a smartphone camera, with quality that varies from the 41MP Nokia phones (or are they cameras with built-in phones?) to 8MP iPhones.

**Two Sensor Sizes**

To do this Exploration, you'll need to get your hands on two cameras with distinctly different personalities. We're not looking for two DSLRs; we want a much bigger difference between the two cameras you choose. To give you a sense of how two different systems compare, we'll use as our examples an 8MP CMOS camera (iPhone 5s) and a full-frame 22.3MP CMOS DLSR (Canon 5D MIII) (**Figure 5.23**).

Let's take a look at the specifications (specs) for each camera. The smartphone camera sensor has a physical size of 2.6mm × 1.6mm, as compared to the 24mm × 36mm size of the DSLR. That's a difference of 20,669%; the Canon sensor is 207 times larger! When it comes to the number of megapixels, the percentage difference is much smaller—149%. There are a lot of photosites packed onto that tiny iPhone sensor. If we look at

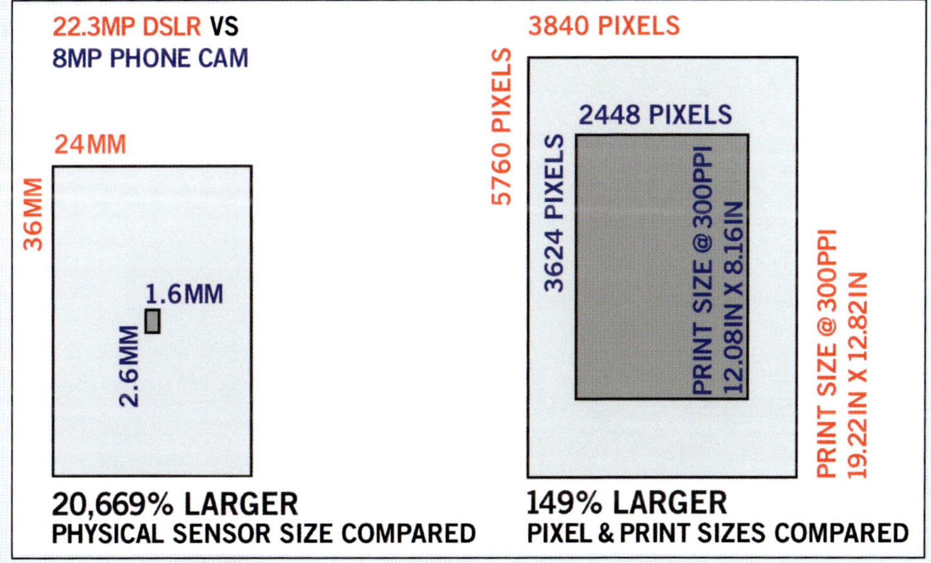


**FIGURE 5.23** When we compare sensors, two of the defining factors we look at are physical size and pixel resolution. When we know that, we can also determine how many pixels (aka photosites) are being packed into an equivalent amount of space. When we compare an 8MP sensor that's 2.6mm × 1.6mm to a 22.3MP sensor that's 36mm × 24mm, we find that its physical dimensions are 207× larger. When we compare the MPs, the difference in resolution is only 2.49× larger. We can then know that in 1mm of space the 8MP sensor is packing 1,394 pixels, and in the same space the 22.3MP sensor has only 160. Those larger photosites are going to be better able to capture more photons, have a higher signal-to-noise ratio and need less "secret sauce" to turn out good-looking pixels.

ILLUSTRATION © ANDY BATT, *SMARTPHONE CAMERA SENSOR VS. FULL-FRAME CAMERA SENSOR*, 2013.

the size of the photosites (the pixels themselves), the pixel pitch of the 8MP camera is 1.5μ (0.0015mm) vs. the 22.3MP sensor's 6.25μ (0.00625 mm). The Canon photosites are 4.7 times larger, and for every 1mm, the Canon sensor has 160 pixels vs. the iPhone's 1,394 pixels.

Part of understanding your imagery—and your sensors—is knowing your outputs. Your smartphone camera images look great on the screen, where most people look at them, but what happens when you print them? How do they compare?

**Take the Shot**

You're going to make the same photo with the two cameras you've chosen. Find a scene in a well-lit environment, so we can allow each camera to work with a clean ISO. If your smaller camera offers any quality settings, choose the largest file at the highest quality; a few smartphone cameras offer raw file formats, so choose raw if it's an option. Frame up a shot with your phone's (or other) camera first and take the shot. Then compose an image that is as similar as possible with your DSLR (or other) camera.

**Download and Re-Sample**

Bring both images into Lightroom and use every available tool to process them out as the best quality image. Export both finished images out to 300ppi, 16-bit TIFF files in ProPhoto RGB[35] at the native sizes, labeled with "_original-size" added to the filename. Make note of what the actual resolutions are for each image. With our examples, we know that the Canon is 5,760 × 3,840 pixels and the iPhone is 3,624 × 2,448 pixels.

*Downsample*: Save out a smaller version of the DSLR image, at 300ppi, 16-bit, matching the longest dimension of the smartphone camera's resolution.[36] Add "_downsampled" to the end of the filename.

*Upsample:* Save out a larger version of smartphone image, at 300ppi, 16-bit, matching the longest dimension of the DSLR's resolution. Add "_upsampled" to the end of the filename.

**Print and Compare**

You now have four images to print. We want to choose a high-quality glossy photo paper; either inkjet or chromogenic printing is fine. Print each image at the size you created. Don't let the software or your lab resize the images for you, because you want to avoid any resizing and resampling.

*Compare all four prints:*

- Which image has better tonality?
- Which image has better color?
- Which image has better fine detail?
- Which image looks better larger? Smaller?
- What's your overall comparison between these two formats?

**Bonus**: Size both images down to fit a standard 4 × 6 inch print size and make two additional prints. Is there a difference in print quality when both images are that small?

**Thoughts**

- Your choice of subject matter—and how you use time, focus and ISO—will have a dramatic effect on your results. You might want to revisit this test, changing some of the variables as you go.
- How will your two cameras compare when you're aiming for shallow DoF? How about in low-light situations and nighttime exposures?
- This Exploration isn't really about proving that a DSLR is better than a smartphone camera; it's about helping you evaluate how a camera with a small sensor succeeds and how it fails.

## Notes

1 CMOS is pronounced see-moss.

2 Phase One IQ180 back on a Hasselblad body.

3 Canon 1Dx.

4 Nikon D800.

5 Upscaling (aka "upsampling" or "up-rezzing") and downscaling (aka "downsampling" or "down-rezzing") are grouped together, because they all refer to the automatic process of resizing your image. This process is called *interpolating*. When you need to make an image larger or smaller than its original camera native size, you mathematically create or destroy pixel values, i.e., if your original file is 5,000 pixels wide and you double the size of the image, you will be at 10,000 pixels—the pixels need to come from somewhere. If you want to halve the size down to 2,500 pixels, you need to get rid of 2,500 pixels. When you upsample an image, automatic processes in your software create new pixels by sampling the neighboring pixels and creating a new fake pixel value. When you downscale an image, that process works by mathematically destroying and rebuilding the image with fewer pixels.

6 300ppi (pixels per inch) is a useful common reference point for talking about printable resolution; it's a convenient average. The problem is that 300ppi is a mythical resolution that's worshipped by designers and people who should know better. Some presses and printers use 300ppi as a working resolution, but many others use a variety of resolutions or can work with multiple resolutions, such as 233ppi, 266ppi, 355ppi, 400ppi, etc.

7 75ppi was the input resolution. The output resolution—in dpi (dots per inch)—was much higher than that.

8 MarchForth Marching Band, www.marchfourthmarchingband.com.

9 At native resolutions, most files can be easily up-rezzed 50–100% larger and printed out with very high quality.

10 FPS = frames per second, aka frame rate.

11 The photosite is the individual part of the sensor that creates a single pixel value. On sensors, then, there are equal numbers of photosites and pixels.

12 In different publications you'll see this described as a *pit*, *cavity* or *well*—you get the idea.

13 Demosaicing is the process of constructing a full-color image from a mosaic pattern of incomplete color information.

14 Binary code is the lifeblood of all things digital. The simple nature of binary code—a switch that's either on or off—allows an incredible array of complex ideas and processes to be stored digitally.

15 If it's been made in the last twenty years and didn't cost a small fortune, then it's most likely digital.

16 *Parametric* is a techie way of saying that working on raw files doesn't alter the raw data and only affects the processing instructions we give the software. Settings aren't locked in until we actually output an image.

17 It's called a low-pass filter because it's designed to keep high-frequency patterns from reaching the photosites. (Only lower frequencies are allowed through.) The types of details that cause moiré and jaggies are high-frequency information; the filter blurs these so that they become low-frequency information. The cut-off point between low and high frequency is set by the sensor designers.

18 Moiré is pronounced /mô_r(a-)/.

19 Companies like Nikon use liquid crystal low-pass filters. Pentax uses a mechanical method to either blur or not blur the image: http://www.imaging-resource.com/PRODS/pentax-k3/pentax-k3A.HTM.

20 Russell Brown's "Moiré Go Away" is a classic and still-effective technique: http://www.russellbrown.com/tips_tech.html.

21 Some cameras offer an interpolated, lower ISO that's de-amplified. For example, a camera with a native speed of ISO 100 might offer an interpolated speed of 50.

22 From DxOmark.com: http://www.dxomark.com/index.php/About/In-depth-measurements/Measurements/ISO-sensitivity.

23 This is a moving target that changes as each technology continues to improve.

24 There can be differences in the data that are gathered by the different rows and columns of photosites. The amplification that's applied to the data can cause slight variations in each grouping, creating lines and bands.

25 Shooting in 100° heat with Live Preview on will create a significant amount of heat. In extreme cases, your camera might even go into an emergency shutdown mode to cool itself down. We've heard stories of photographers who keep coolers full of ice packs on hand, just to cool down their cameras when they're working in extreme heat.

26 Significantly, Phase One and Sinar medium-format backs use this technique to remove heat noise, especially from long exposures.

27 In sensor terms, a generation is about a year's time. You'll see new sensor technology ripple throughout the whole lineup of cameras about every two years.

28 Your older raw files can be processed with new software, too, often with significantly improved results.

29 In Lightroom's Camera Calibration palette, you can choose a variety of process engines—the core software that decodes the raw file. Adobe does this mainly for legacy reasons. If you crafted an image with an older engine, you can choose to use that engine, instead of updating to the new one, which might change the look of the image.

30 ACR = Adobe Camera Raw. Version 2 came with Photoshop 8.

31 3,200 watts of HMI power is a measure of the power consumed by the lights, but not a good measure of their brightness. A very rough guide is that an HMI gives about three or four times the light output of its equivalent

tungsten hot light. So all things being equal, an 800-watt HMI would approximate a 3,000-watt tungsten light.

32 Some non-Canon cameras exhibit other colors of chroma noise.

33 Different cameras, different exposures, different subjects and different ISO settings are all huge variables.

34 See the "Featured Interview" with Jim Christian earlier in this chapter. PictureCode, www.picturecode.com.

35 The smartphone camera's native bit size is probably 8-bit, and its native color space is sRGB. Exporting the file at these settings is like putting all the data from this image into a bigger box than it needs: It won't change it or hurt it. It won't make it better, either, but it will make it consistent with your DSLR image.

36 Unless you have reversed the whole game and are using a 41MP Nokia phone and an 8MP DSLR—in which case you should reverse the downsample/upsample idea.

Six

# EXPOSURE: CONTROLLING THE LIGHT

# What Is Good Exposure?

It can vary from photographer to photographer, but at the core, images with good exposure have skin tones, textures, colors and tonalities that represent the way they are in life. From that base, you can underexpose or overexpose images to create your own interpretation of how you see the world.

## A Paradox

It's helpful to have two paradoxical ideas in your head at the same time: (1) There's a *single correct base exposure* and (2) for the same image, there can be *many correct aesthetic exposures*. Once you learn to achieve solid base exposures, you can alter them to match your aesthetic intent. You could, for instance, expose "day for night"[1] by underexposing your daylight image two stops, or drag the shutter[2] to create a nighttime image that's much brighter than it is to your eye.

To see this idea at work, try paging through a stack of fashion magazines. You'll find images that are drastically underexposed—and hauntingly beautiful; you'll also find images that are drastically overexposed (to the point of just retaining texture)—and arresting. In order to make aesthetic exposure decisions, you need a place to start. No matter what kind of work you do, it always comes back to the starting point: learning how to get a good base exposure.

Making photographs under perfect conditions is pretty easy: You compose your shot, take a meter reading, make the photo, check the histogram and you're done. The problem is that most of the time, we don't work under perfect conditions. We need to make the best of what we have at any given moment—by changing the light, moving to a different location or waiting until a different time of day to capture our shot. When we understand how to see and meter a scene, we can make better decisions while we're on a shoot.

## Good Light

Part of getting a good exposure is seeing the light. The next time you notice beautiful light, put aside any other thoughts you have running around in your head (such as subject, framing, decisive moments, etc.) and try to figure out what captured your attention. Stop taking the light for granted. Stay there awhile and spend time observing (**Figure 6.1**).

Once you begin thinking about what makes light beautiful, the world around you seems to change. You become aware that, depending on the time of day (and many other variables), light reveals different textures. It has subtle qualities as it bounces off the surfaces around you. Northern light is different from tropical light and clear mountain air is different from the air over a large city.

You might begin to hope for a nice, overcast day—which creates just enough soft fill light, takes the edge off the direct sun and allows you to shoot during parts of the day that (on a clear day) would be filled with harsh, "ugly" light. Your mind can eventually create a catalog of different sorts of light. You might even find that suddenly, it's not good enough to acknowledge beautiful light; you want to know how to capture it in your photographs.

### Why Is that Light so Beautiful?

*Whenever you see light that stops you in your tracks and makes you want to take pictures, ask yourself:*

- Where is the light coming from?
- What is its primary source?
- What are its secondary sources?
- Is it creating soft or hard shadows?
- What angle is the light coming from? Is the subject backlit, front-lit or side-lit? Even soft, overcast light always has a direction.
- If there are reflective surfaces, to what do they contribute?
- Are there small lighting differences and subtleties?

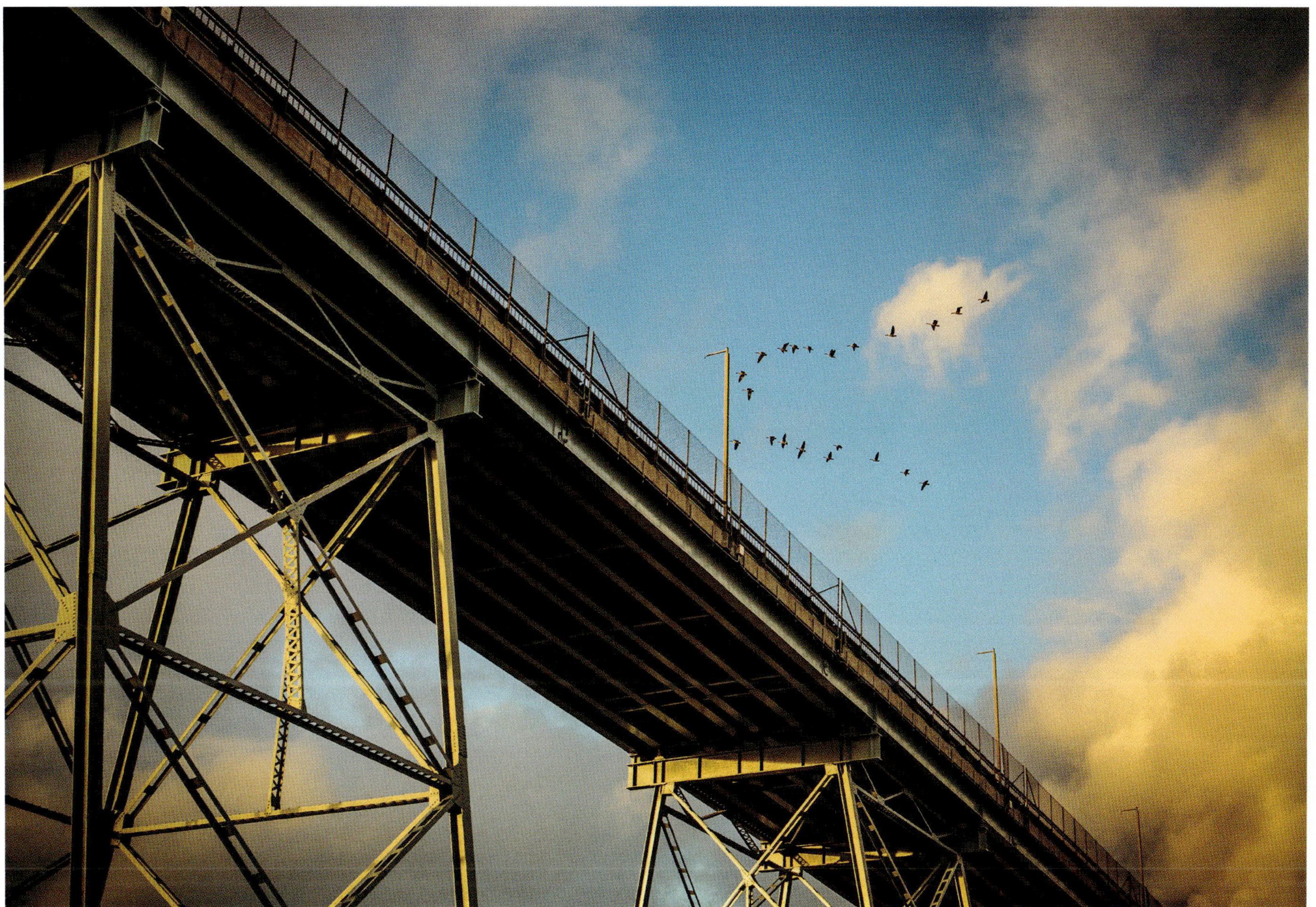

**FIGURE 6.1** Beautiful light happens. It's not something you have much control over (unless you're lighting the scene, but that's for a different book). What you can control is good exposure.
IMAGE © ANDY BATT, *LONGVIEW BRIDGE WITH BIRDS,* 2009.

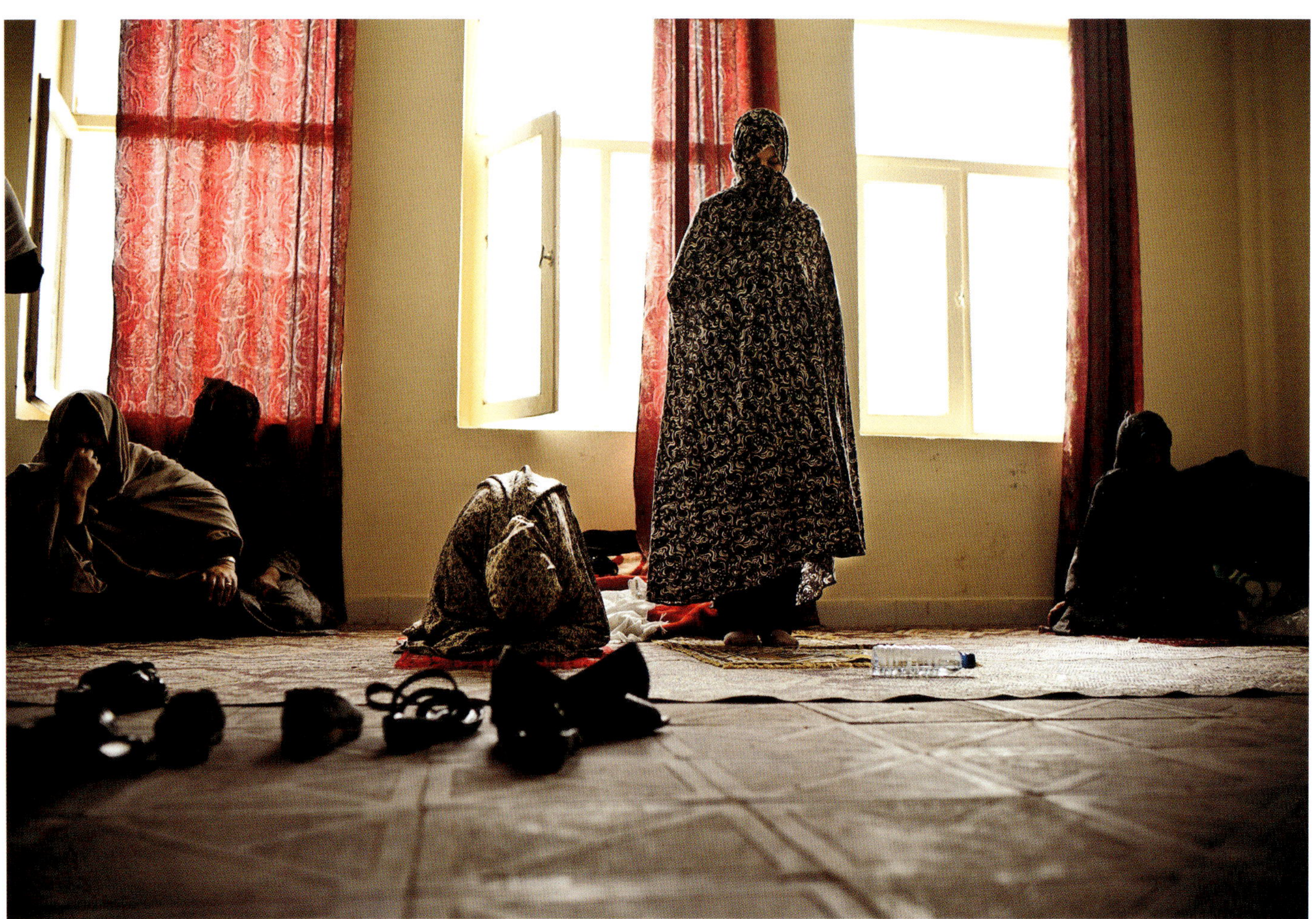

**FIGURE 6.2** In this beautifully backlit scene, students pray before class in Mercy Corps' women's vocational training center.
IMAGE BY TONI GREAVES FOR MERCY CORPS, *EDUCATION AGAINST ALL ODDS, AFGHANISTAN: PRAYER,* 2012.

## Metering: In the Beginning

To achieve good, normal exposures, we need to start with good metering practices. Suppose you see an interesting moment with great light and composition. You point your camera at the scene, and the in-camera meter takes over and spits out a reading. But what exactly is it doing? Where does that reading come from, and is it compensating for the backlight? Does it know which is the most important object in your scene?

Depending on the situation, we usually work in one of two different metering mindsets: quick or careful. We take the *quick approach* to exposure when we're in rapidly changing conditions—such as going directly from a bright, sunlit exterior to a dark interior that's lit with ancient fluorescents. You need to flex with rapidly changing lighting situations, so you might choose Aperture Priority mode to lock in a certain F-stop, knowing you'll have plenty of light for fast shutter speeds, or perhaps you'll shoot in Shutter Priority, because you need to stop action at 1/500th. Either way, it's not enough to set it and forget it. Getting good images means paying attention to what the automatics are doing, and having the experience to know if they're doing what you want them to do. In quickly changing situations you might not get a second chance.

When we have the opportunity to make images in conditions that aren't changing quickly or are under our control, we have time for a more *careful approach*. We can interpret our scene by deciding on the right time of day to make a photograph, or by using strobes or light modifiers to alter the available light. When there's time, we like to work in Manual mode, since we want to make the best decisions about shutter speed, aperture and ISO.

## Exposure: Toni Greaves

***Andy Batt:*** **What do you do to make sure you're getting a good exposure?**

***Toni Greaves:*** Usually I shoot on Aperture priority, because I'm always thinking about depth of field in my images. I frequently change the aperture and ISO—it's one of the big benefits that we have with digital, right? I go into different situations and constantly assess the light and change the ISO; or know that I want to see into more of the room, so I might extend my depth of field.

***AB:*** **What would you do if you walked into a room at noon, and half the room was bathed in hard direct light and the other half was in deep shadow? You'd have to make a very deliberate choice there.**

***TG:*** I make the choice of where I stand—because if it's a room where there's hard light and deep shadow, I am typically not going to gravitate towards shooting in a way that shows both of those things at once. I will be shooting for the light that lets me capture my subject in an interesting way. I do tend to use backlighting as a technique at times, as I think it can be quite striking (**Figure 6.2**).

## Exposure: Carli Davidson

***Andy Batt:*** **Tell us about learning to make good exposures; you can't make good photographs unless you get that right.**

***Carli Davidson:*** I have to say I had the hardest time learning this. I'd say, "Wait, what's the F-Stop and ISO—what do they mean, again?" I struggled with that forever.

***Candace Dobro:*** **I had the same experience. I think it took me ten years—I'm not joking or exaggerating—to *really* understand how to get a good exposure. What was the turning point for you?**

***Carli:*** Just being really excited about the content. I was learning photography and exploring these little moments of my life with it. I didn't need it to be perfect, because I was doing things like taking pictures with friends. In a way, it was a great exercise, because when you're shooting and don't have a Polaroid (or these days the back of the camera) to look at, you have to get a sense of your light. I had a little in-camera light meter, and that's all I ever used.

I have a good eye for the light—I think it came from shooting animals (**Figure 6.3**). They're always active, so I didn't have the time to say, "Let me make sure I'm understanding my settings properly." Working like that forces you to really know your equipment inside and out—*especially* when you have a paying job where you think to yourself, "I can't mess around anymore; I need to get this shoot right."

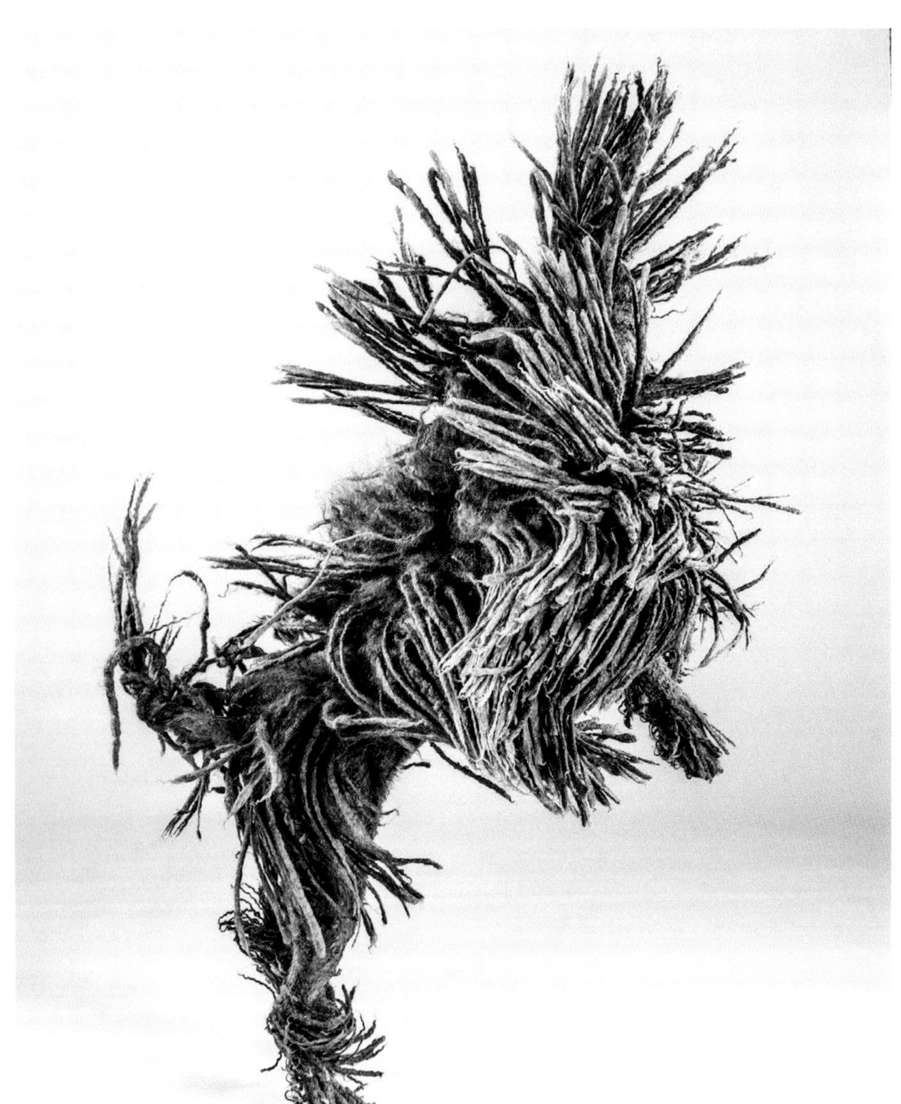

**FIGURE 6.3** This shot was captured during a shoot for the *FETCH* series, but presented a much different energy. Sometimes you find a new body of work while editing after a shoot. Carli says that working with active animals probably helped her develop a good eye for light, because it forced her to set her exposures quickly.
IMAGE © CARLI DAVIDSON, *DOG TREE*, 2012.

## Light Meters: Stewart Cohen

***Andy Batt:* Do you still use a light meter?**

***Stewart Cohen:*** No more light meter. I know that just burns your—

***AB:* No, that's cool. So how do you know you're getting good data?**

***SC:*** I just look at it. We do have a light meter that we look at sometimes for ratios. If something is super contrasty we'll use a light meter, but beyond that, I'll just look at the image and see if I've got detail everywhere. If not, I can get it there in three or four frames. I'll shoot a picture and say "Oh, that's way too hot," and then I'll shoot another one.

***AB:* So you're talking about controlling the ambient light and your strobe lights—and using test shots to get it dialed in.**

***SC:*** Yes—this is what I do: We'll have three lights up, and I'll probably have the camera locked down on a tripod. We just start looking at it. Once we get the lights in position, one by one, we'll turn them off and I'll look to see—on a 24-inch HP Dreamstime Monitor—what each light is doing . . . You've got to know what each light is doing, and you've got to understand the direction the light is coming from.

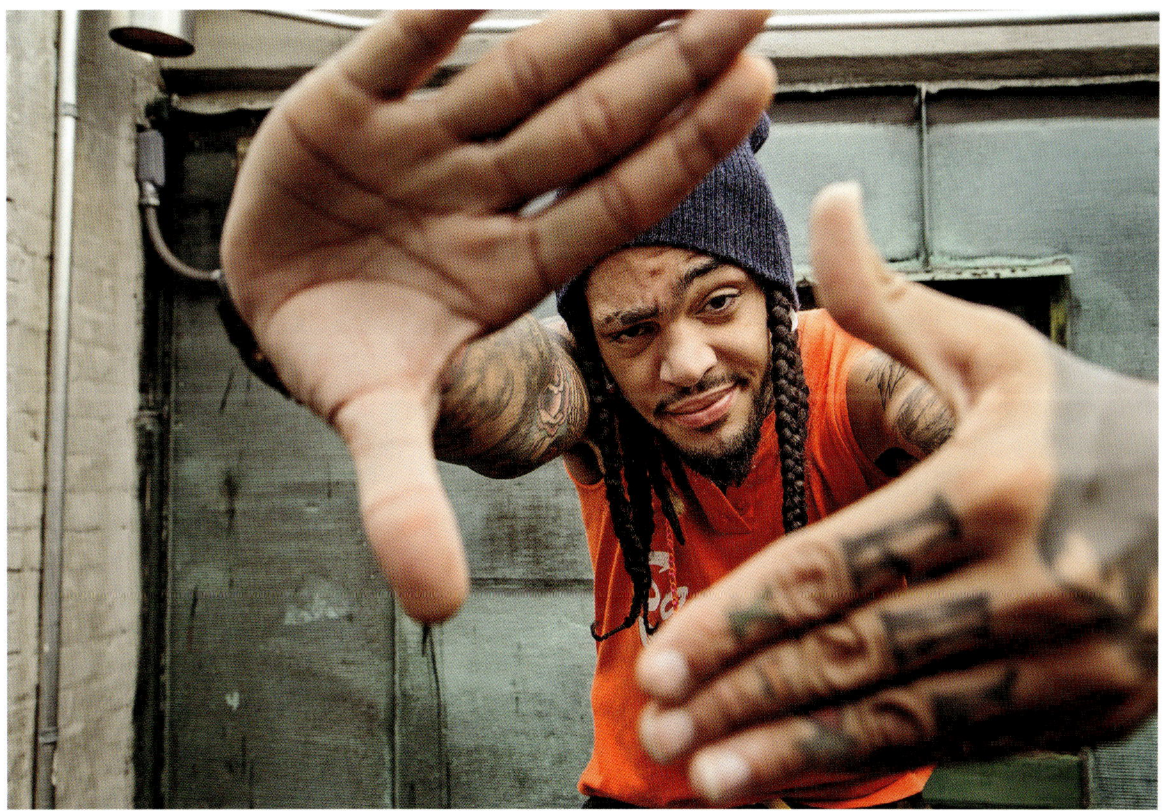

**FIGURE 6.4** Stewart shot this portrait for a Twizzlers[3] candy promotion. Although it looks like it was captured in natural daylight, he and his team lit it artificially—which requires knowledge, skill and a good exposure. Stewart used a 1Dx in Manual mode and a 24–70mm zoom lens at 1/160 sec, *f*/6.3 and ISO 400.
IMAGE © STEWART COHEN, *TRAVIE MCCOY OF GYM CLASS HEROES,* NEW YORK, NY, 2012.

# In-Camera Metering that You Control

Let's explore how to get a good exposure with a tool you already have: the in-camera meter. You've already been relying on it—even if you've been running on automatic. The in-camera meter is a great tool, and it gets even better once you know a few key pieces of information. Although there might be a few different options on your camera, there are two essential modes for the manual photographer: Matrix metering and Spot metering (**Figure 6.5**).

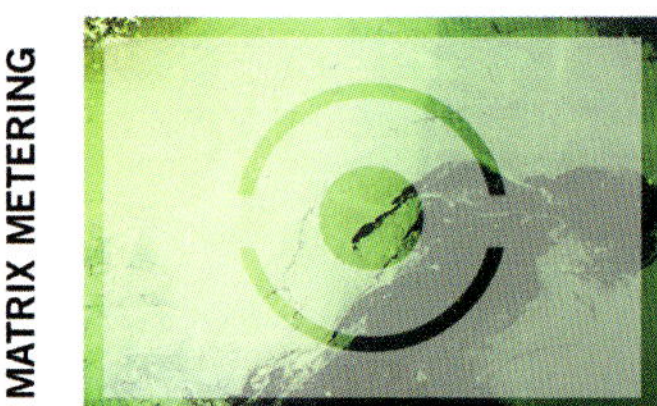

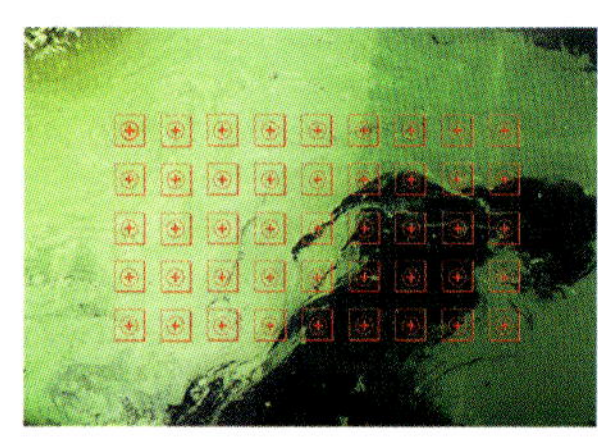
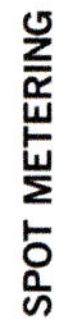

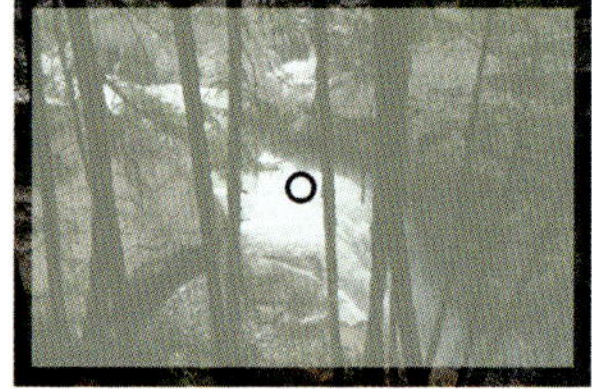
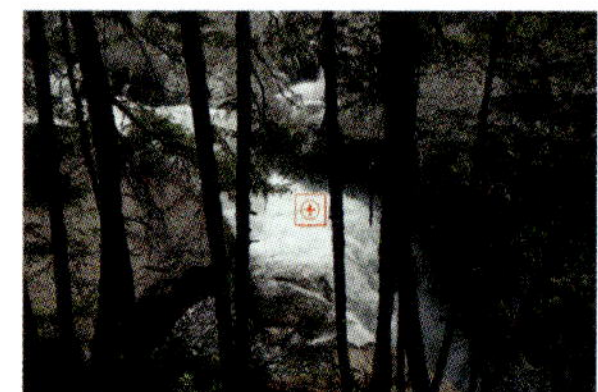

**FIGURE 6.5** When you put your meter into *Matrix* (aka averaging, pattern, evaluative, etc.) meter mode, it uses many separate points to meter from and build an exposure. In its simplest form, the camera just averages the exposure value of the points. In its more complex version, the camera compares its results to a database of other values and might shift the exposure—depending whether it thinks it's looking at a face, snow, sky, etc. In *Spot* meter mode, the camera locks out all of the "thinking" and takes a pure reading of the spot you're metering. This mode can be very useful for tricky metering situations, where your subject would be over or underexposed if the meter were reading from the entire scene.
ILLUSTRATION © ANDY BATT, *MATRIX AND SPOT METER MODES*, 2013.

## Matrix Metering

Matrix metering (also known as averaging, pattern or evaluative metering) considers the values across multiple points in an image. Some cameras are smart enough to detect colors, faces and shapes—and then use the information to alter your exposure. One of the most important things to know is that your in-camera meter is a *reflected light meter*; it simply reads the light that is reflected off of an object. When you're in Matrix mode, the meter reads the light that's reflected off all the subjects in your scene and then calculates exposure by comparing areas of different brightness to an in-camera database of patterns based on real-world scenarios.

## Key Details and Key Light

Metering is most helpful once you determine what in your scene is most important to you. For example, if a small patch of light is falling on your subject's face and he or she is surrounded by shadows or dark tones, then you need to meter that patch of light. That's your *key detail* and the light falling on it is the *key light*. It's not always the brightest or biggest light source; it's the one that's most important to you.

*To determine the key detail and key light:*

- Identify the key detail—your main area of interest.
- Locate the key light source that's illuminating your key detail.
- If you have multiple light sources, decide which one is the most important.

***Your in-camera meter is a reflected light meter; it reads the light that's reflected off of an object. When you're in Matrix mode, the meter reads the light that is reflected off all the subjects in your scene and then averages them.***

## Spot Meter Special

When the camera is in Spot meter mode, it works the same way, with one critical difference: Instead of reading multiple points and then averaging them to calculate an exposure, the meter only measures a single point—usually a 1–3° spot. As you move the camera around, the reading will change. If you point it at a black rock, you'll get a different reading than when you point it at a white one. You can use the spot meter to analyze very specific areas of an image.

***Andy:*** When I want my meter to react to the whole scene in my viewfinder, I'll leave it in Matrix mode. This works nicely for most scenes, as long as I keep an eye out for situations that can fool the meter into over- or under-exposing the image—such as someone being backlit by the sun or standing in front of a very dark background. In that case, I might switch to Spot meter, since it can give me a reading for a single part of the image.

## Spot Meter Viewing

Grab your DSLR and put it into Spot meter mode. Some cameras use the center circle as the active metering point by default, while others put the "spot" wherever the active AF point is (consult your manual for details). Pan around the shooting environment and take readings from different areas of the scene. Look for areas that are dark (shadow tones), white (highlights), have very bright reflections (specular highlights) and have "normal" midtones. Switch the metering back to Matrix, then take readings over the same areas and observe the differences.

## Exposure: Jeff Conley

***Andy Batt:*** **You come out of the classic black-and-white landscape world. Do you still run around with a spot meter?**

***Jeff Conley:*** No, now I'm using solely in-camera metering, and that was definitely an adjustment for me. Not too long ago, I realized I had been carrying around a spot meter for more than a year and hadn't been using it.

***AB:*** **So what happened when you switched to in-camera metering?**

***JC:*** I was double-checking the meter reading constantly, thinking, "I haven't arrived at this myself, so surely this can't be right!" I found that it was doing a phenomenal job; there is a lot to be said for Matrix metering. I'm still double-checking this though, and I have no problem bracketing, as well.

***AB:*** **Are you pushing your data to the right?**[4]

***JC:*** Yeah, just not too far to the right. It depends on your scene. If you're shooting something that's rich and heavy, there's no sense pushing everything to the right. You have to objectively evaluate your subject matter.

***AB:*** **Do you make active decisions about how an image will look while you're shooting, or do you tend to do that in post?**

***JC:*** I do that more in post, now, although on location I start developing a mental rough-sketch of where I see the image going. I'm looking to get the information while I'm out there. I might have a general sense of how I want the finished print to look, but I want information from the camera that I can work with—so I can use Lightroom and Photoshop to give me a negative, to then take into the darkroom.

***Candace Dobro:*** **You're making traditional negatives from your digital captures?**

***JC:*** Yes. I love the level of control you have with a digital capture, but I'll photograph, then come back and work with an image and make inkjet proof-prints on the desktop. Ultimately, when I find an image that I want to print in the darkroom, I can either make a desktop negative from my inkjet printer that I contact-print in the darkroom or—more often—I have an LVT[5] negative made, generally a 4 × 5 inch negative. I work with a lab down in Los Angeles to do that. These negatives can be enlarged optically—they're actually very beautiful negatives—so it's kind of a nice thing to be able to go with the convenience of digital capture and the instant feedback and the phenomenal level of control that you have working with digital images, but then to take that back to a negative.

I still feel very gratified working in the darkroom. I enjoy the connection with the print and I appreciate the physicality of the negative, as well. It's one thing to have images backed up in multiple variations—in the Cloud, on hard drives and all that—but it's kind of nice to hold a negative.

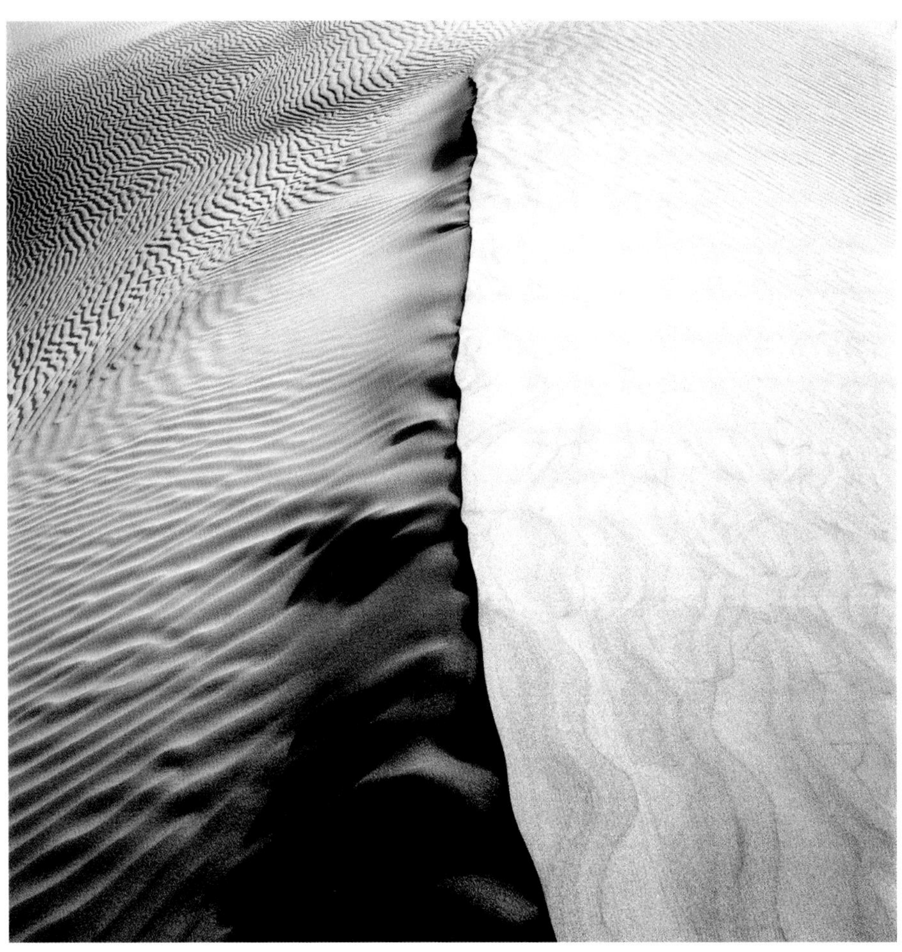

**FIGURE 6.6** With either digital or film photography, you need to make a good exposure to capture what you see. In this shot, the morning light created long, distinct shadows and highlighted the form and texture of the dune. Jeff enjoys how rapidly the dune landscape changes with the sculpting wind, forming new shapes and arrangements every day. (Captured with a Hasselblad 500CM, 50mm Zeiss lens and TMAX 100 film.)
IMAGE © JEFFREY CONLEY, *DUNE GENESIS*, DEATH VALLEY NATIONAL PARK, CALIFORNIA, 2005.

## Reflected Light: A White, Gray and Black Room

The reflected meter reads light reflecting from an object and gives you a value for it. We set the camera to what the meter is telling us, and we get a picture. That seems simple enough, and it generally works. Once you dig down a little deeper, though, it's not so simple. What do those values really mean and what is the meter actually doing?

Imagine a fairly large, square windowless room that's lit from the ceiling. All the walls are evenly lit from top to bottom, left to right. One wall is painted black, one is painted gray, one is painted white and the fourth is covered in polka dots (we don't really care about this last wall). Now, we point our camera at each wall in turn and get three different meter readings. We set the camera at 1/250th, ISO 400 and vary the aperture until the meter hits the "normal" mark.

- For the gray wall we get *f*/8.
- For the white wall we get *f*/16, which is +2 stops brighter.
- For the black wall we get *f*/2.8, which is -3 stops darker.

The same amount of light is falling onto each wall, but because the black wall is darker, less light reflects from it, and because the white wall is brighter, it reflects more light. Here comes the puzzle: If we take a picture of each wall using those settings, what will we get? The answer is: three gray walls! To test this, do the "Gray, White and Black All Over" exercise (**Figure 6.7**).

## Midtone Technology: The Gray Card

A gray card is a standardized piece of cardboard with a neutral gray surface that's designed to reflect 18% of the light that falls onto it. Its strength lies in its being a standard value. By placing a gray card into a scene, measuring the light that reflects from it and capturing it at that value, the photograph of the card will be a standard midtone gray. Your camera's meter (and handheld light meters) are calibrated to work with this standard.[6] No matter what lighting situation you put the gray card into, it will reflect 18% of the light.

By using the Spot meter mode, you can single out the gray card in a scene and easily measure the light. Why not just use Matrix metering all the time? Because, if there's a complex variety of objects and tones in a scene, then Matrix metering can be fooled.

***Andy:*** The Kodak R27[7] is a perfect gray card. I keep it in a Lindcraft pouch,[8] next to my ColorChecker[9] and WhiBal®[10] card. This card is special, because the ink is Munsell Gray #5, which is 18% and completely color neutral. I carry this gray card with me on all my shoots. It lets me quickly check my light values to make sure that my midtones are going to fall in the right spot. I couple this with my spot meter and the in-camera histogram to do quick, accurate light measurements.

## Where Should You Place the Gray Card?

Now that you have two important tools to "up" your game (spot metering and the gray card), you can walk into any situation, get an accurate meter reading for any area of an image and check the specific light values in your key details.

Be careful where you place the gray card and how you angle it for both metering and test-shot purposes. You want to situate it on the same plane as your key detail. For example, if you're taking a portrait of someone looking straight at the camera and they're lit from the front, then the gray card should point directly at the camera and be level (not pointing up or down). If the main source of light comes in from the side, then you should angle the gray card to get the full amount of key light, and then take a quick spot meter reading off the card (**Figure 6.8**).

In a scene where there's nothing but soft, even, consistent light, it's fairly easy to get an accurate reading. In many situations, though, you'll find that the light comes from many directions and has many different qualities. Choosing which area should be exposed as a midtone can be slightly tricky; you have to decide whether you want to meter the light at the front, sides or back of your subject. Once you decide that, you also need to make sure to hold the gray card correctly. By changing the angle left to right and up to down, you change the amount of light hitting the card. The rule of thumb is to angle it to simulate how the key detail is being lit.

## TRY THIS AT HOME

### Gray, White and Black All Over

**For step-by-step instructions, go to: www.focalpress.com/cw/digitalimagingmasters**

Reflected light meters measure the light coming from an object and are calibrated to make that object expose as a midtone. We assume most things we photograph are primarily made up of midtones and that metering for them will result in the correct values—but as you'll see after doing this exercise, that isn't the case.

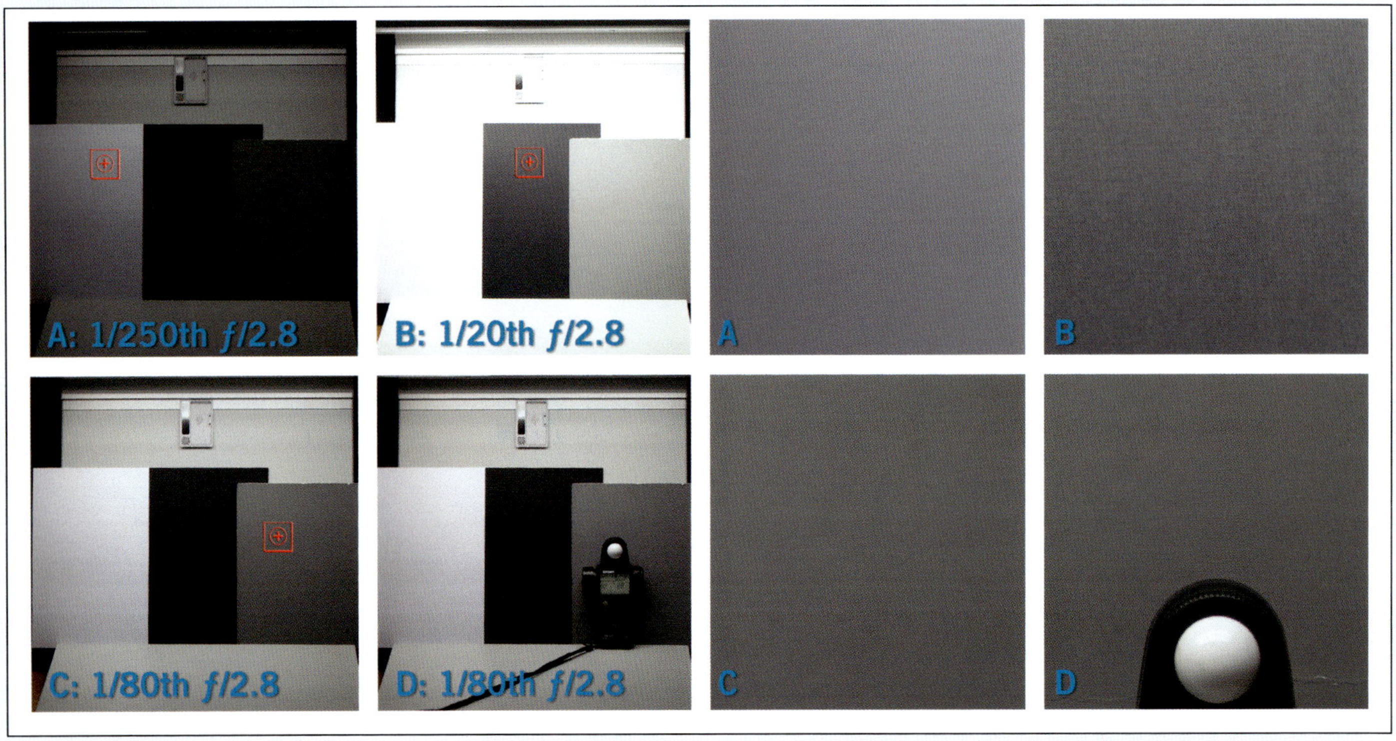

**FIGURE 6.7** Andy exposed these images based on reflected readings of each surface (red squares). We can see that both the white (A) and black (B) papers recorded as gray tones, very similar to the gray card (C and D). The gray card was a Kodak R27, which has a true neutral color value. The white and black papers are not neutral and have a slight colorcast. The meter wants to give you a midtone value for whatever you point it at. When you expose the subject at that value, you get a midtone, no matter whether the subject is white or black.
SCREENSHOT © ANDY BATT, *BORING GRAY CARDS*, 2013.

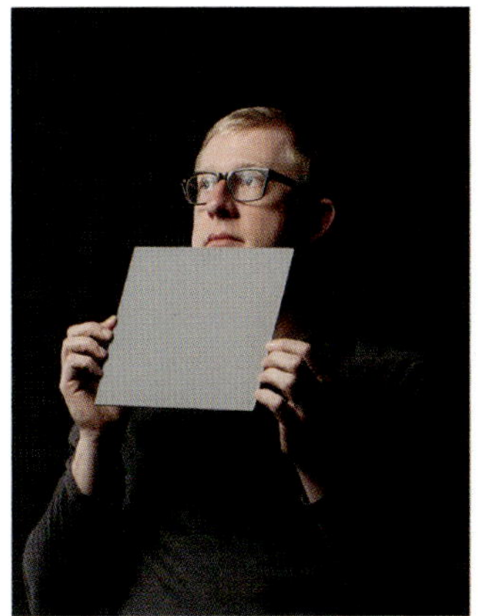

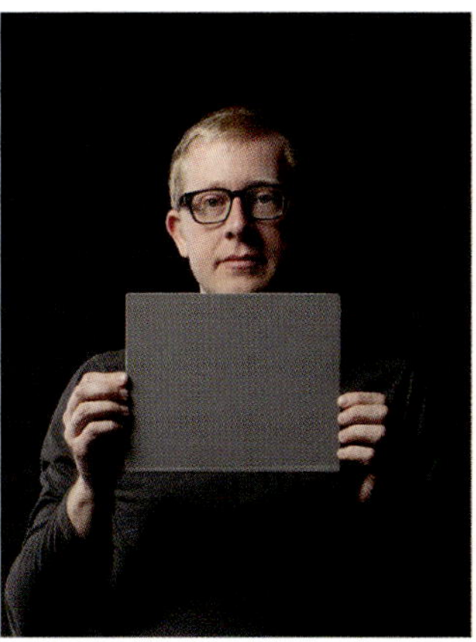

**FIGURE 6.8** On the left, Chris demonstrates how to hold a gray card to get full illumination from the light source. On the right, you can see the difference position makes.
IMAGE © ANDY BATT, *STILL LIFE WITH CHRIS,* 2013.

## Which Is the "Right" Exposure?

Take a look at the portrait in **Figure 6.9**. It was processed out with three different exposures, each at a half-stop difference, to illustrate the question: Which of these is the "right" exposure?

The image on the left is exposed at +1/2 stop for the subject's left cheek; the middle image is the "normal" exposure and the image on the right is at -1/2 stop for her right cheek. Each version of this image tells a slightly different story about the subject. If we expose for her left cheek, we open up the exposure and create a very bright image. By metering for the light on her right cheek, we create a darker, moodier image.

Obviously, you can alter the exposure later in post—that's one of the great things about shooting raw—but you need to decide on a starting exposure. The tricky thing is that the "right" one is largely a matter of opinion. By making a deliberate choice, you'll start with the strongest image as your "normal." To build your experience, experiment and test which areas to meter. Knowing which story you want to tell is a key element for learning to meter with skill.

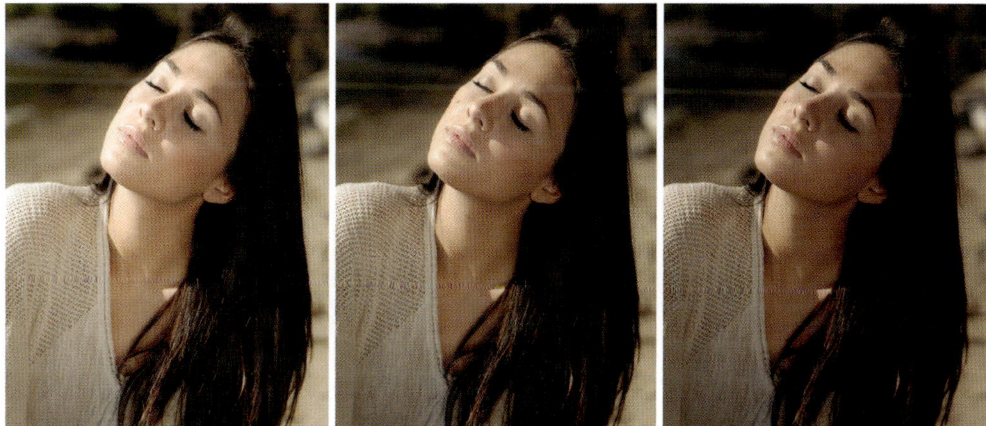

**FIGURE 6.9** Photographer Jamie Vitale exposed a simple portrait with a warm tone reflector bouncing sunlight into the fill-side of her subject's face. This is a good teaching image, because it works three different ways: balancing for the sun on her left cheek, for her right cheek or with a split value. Each shift changes the story. All three interpretations can be considered correct—it's up to the photographer to decide which is the right one.
IMAGE © JAMIE VITALE, *RACHEL'S PORTRAIT,* 2012.

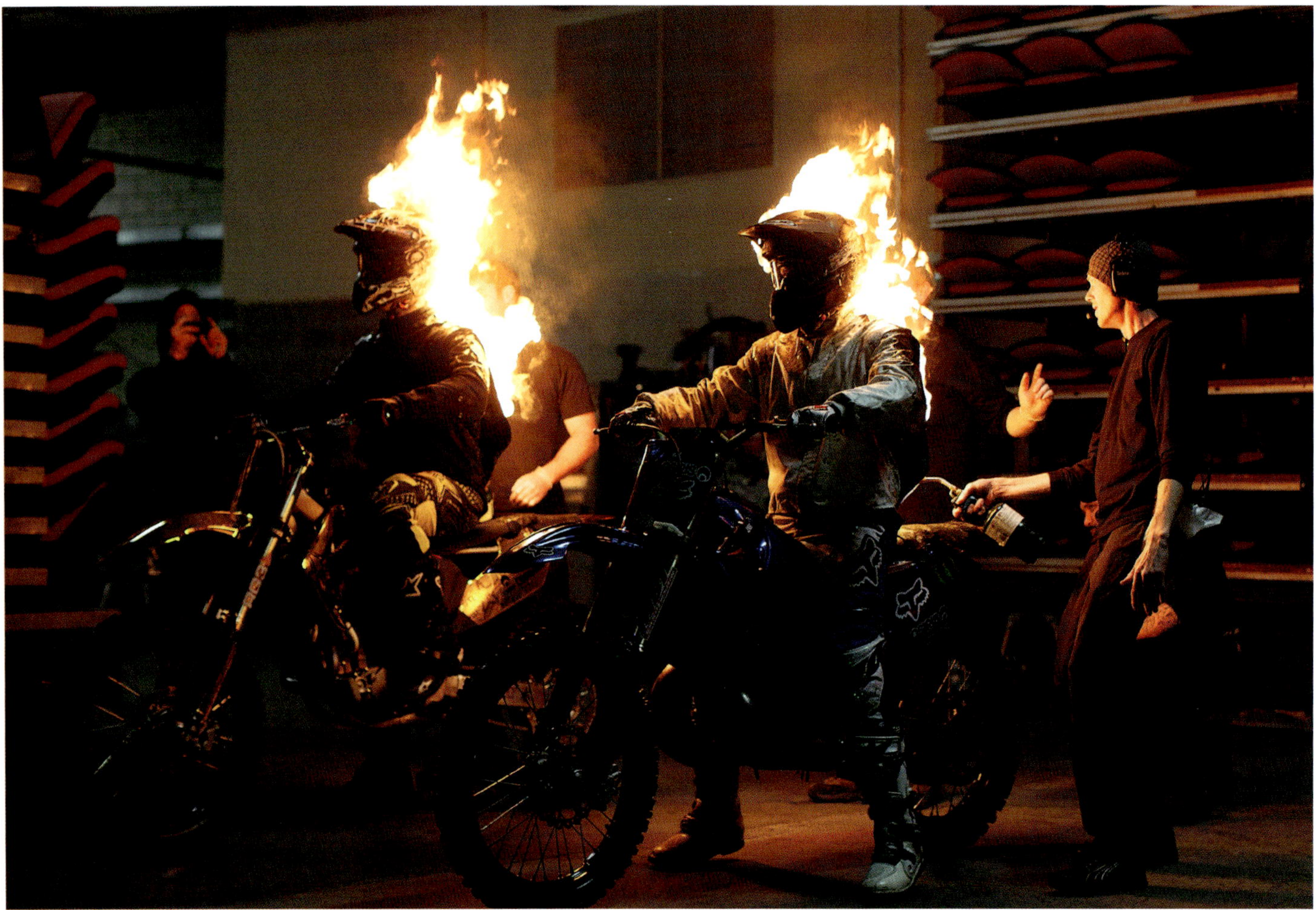

**FIGURE 6.10** Nuclear Cowboyz[11] is a post–apocalyptic motocross opera with pyrotechnics and lasers. That's a lot of goodness, all in a single stunt show. Sol looks at his images on the back of the camera to judge whether he's captured a good exposure, saying, "If you do it long enough, you become an expert."
IMAGE © SOL NEELMAN, *NUCLEAR COWBOYZ,* 2012.

## Gray Cards: Sol Neelman

***Andy Batt:* When is the last time you shot a gray card?**

***Sol Neelman:*** I haven't used a gray card since 2004. I shoot raw so I can make any changes that I need to on the computer, without affecting the original file. The one trick I do—being a Caucasian male—is to photograph my hands and use that as my exposure. Back in the day, we would photograph the pavement, because that was "gray enough." I look at the back of my camera to see if I am on—or horribly off.

***AB:* How do you know if you're on or horribly off?**

***SN:*** If you do it long enough, you become an expert. I can pick up my camera and feel very confident that I'm ready to go at any given moment.

Even if the settings are wrong, I can change them fast, and everything will make sense. That throws off a lot of newer, younger or hobbyist photographers; they simply haven't taken enough pictures yet—they need to take enough to feel like they can pick up their camera and start taking pictures without thinking.

***AB:* Do you look at the histogram?**

***SN:*** No I don't, I'm not that technical. I look at the image on the back of the camera to see if it's in line with what I imagined. I'm familiar with how it's going to look on my camera and how it usually loads up on my computer. I kind of just swing with it. With raw files, there's so much latitude that unless you're completely off, you have a lot of flexibility.

# Leveling Up to a Handheld Meter

If in-camera meters are so great, then why would you buy a handheld meter? Because if you want to know how the light is falling in a scene, a handheld meter will quickly and easily give you that information. Do you want to know the difference between the light that falls on someone's left and right cheeks? Done and done.

***Andy:*** One really nice thing about a handheld meter (**Figure 6.11**) is that its technology doesn't change. I regularly rent, buy and switch lenses, cameras, lights and locations, but my meter remains the same, which helps me create consistent and effective exposures. I use a Sekonic 758 as my main meter; it's a classic piece of equipment with a slew of great, built-in features. I use the retracted dome (a directional incident mode) most of the time, so that I can read individual light sources. When using a handheld meter, I can walk into a scene and take specific measurements to help me understand the scene's range of brightness or quickly measure and compare backlight to front light. My camera can stay on the tripod while I do the metering; I find I can work much faster that way than I can when metering through the camera.

> ***When using a handheld meter, my camera can stay on the tripod. I find I can work much faster that way than I can when metering through the camera.***
> ***—Andy Batt***

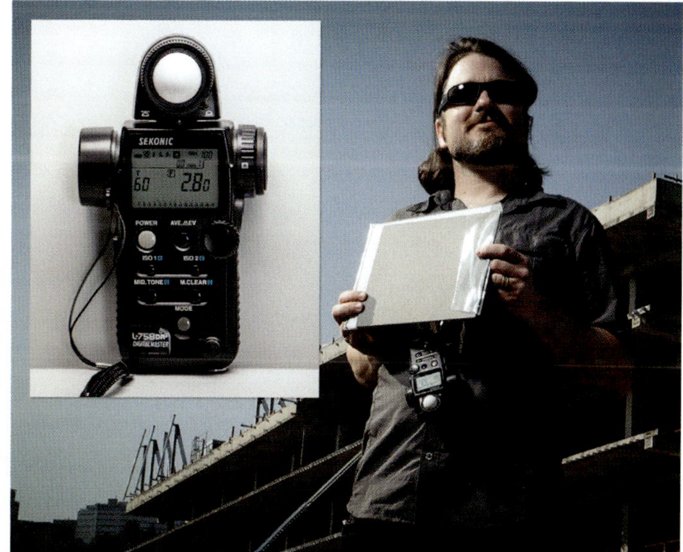


**FIGURE 6.11** There's Andy, who stepped in for a gray card test after metering with his handheld meter.
IMAGE © ANDY BATT, *SEKONIC 758 HANDHELD LIGHT METER WITH WHITE DOME*, 2013.

## The Dome: Incident Mode

The most significant difference between in-camera and handheld meters is not the electronics or customization, or even the meter's ability to create average readings; it's a white plastic dome. That dome allows you to work in a completely different way, by making it possible to read the light that falls *onto* it. Using your meter in this fashion is called Incident mode.

Loosely speaking, Incident mode refers to incident rays of light that come directly from a light source—instead of reflecting *from* a surface. The white plastic dome presents a 180° dimensional shape for light to fall onto. That way, it gathers light that comes from sources all around the meter—the front and all of the sides. All of that light is combined and a reading is created. In a way, the dome acts like the Matrix metering mode in your camera, since it reads light from multiple directions all at once.

## Using a Handheld Meter

The other big reason to use a handheld meter is to gain control—over where and what you meter—and the ability to walk around a scene to understand the range of exposures it covers. The way you use a particular handheld meter will depend on the make and model you have. There are more than a few different options out there, but the basics are all the same and with all of them, you work with the same three settings: Aperture, Shutter Speed and ISO.

With any meter, you set your working ISO speed first. Some meters allow you to set a shutter speed or an aperture value, while others only allow you to select a shutter speed. When you choose a shutter speed, point the meter and then push the "Measure" button, the meter will give you an aperture value. If you move to a different spot and measure again, you'll get a new reading.

On some meters, if you continue to hold the Measure button, the meter will read continuously as you walk around. We recommend that you always take a few readings, making very slight variations in the position of the meter. This will help you determine if there's any real variation in the light values. Small variations (like two-tenths of

## FEATURED PHOTOGRAPH

### Desert Runner

Andy made this image (**Figure 6.12**) out in the Oregon desert in 2005. He knew that he wanted to create a dramatic image—something more intense than available light could give him—of this runner without having to balance location strobes with the daylight.

***Andy:*** Here's a combination of late-afternoon sidelight and a "shiny board," made from a 4 × 4 foot piece of plywood with a bright silver coating. The light that comes off the shiny board is almost equal in exposure to the sunlight, which is a useful way of creating dramatic light without strobes. Using this technique, I was able to freeze motion at 1/1000th of a second. The dramatic light gives the image some attention-grabbing qualities, and it creates great texture and contrast in the clothing and muscles of the runner. I carefully considered the framing and locked it down on the tripod. I also pre-focused the image to the runner's mark—the ideal place for him to be in the frame—so I didn't have to rely on the autofocus system to catch a subject that was quickly moving at the camera.

I measured the exposure with a handheld incident meter that was aimed directly into the sunlight, and then directly at the shiny board. This placed the key detail and key exposure on the brightest areas of the body and created dramatic shadows across the subject's body and face. The runner had some naturally occurring sweat (we were in the desert during the summer) that created specular qualities and popped the skin tones. Once all these decisions were made, it was just a matter of having our runner sprint about twenty times so we could get the timing right—and have a selection of great positions for the client to choose from.

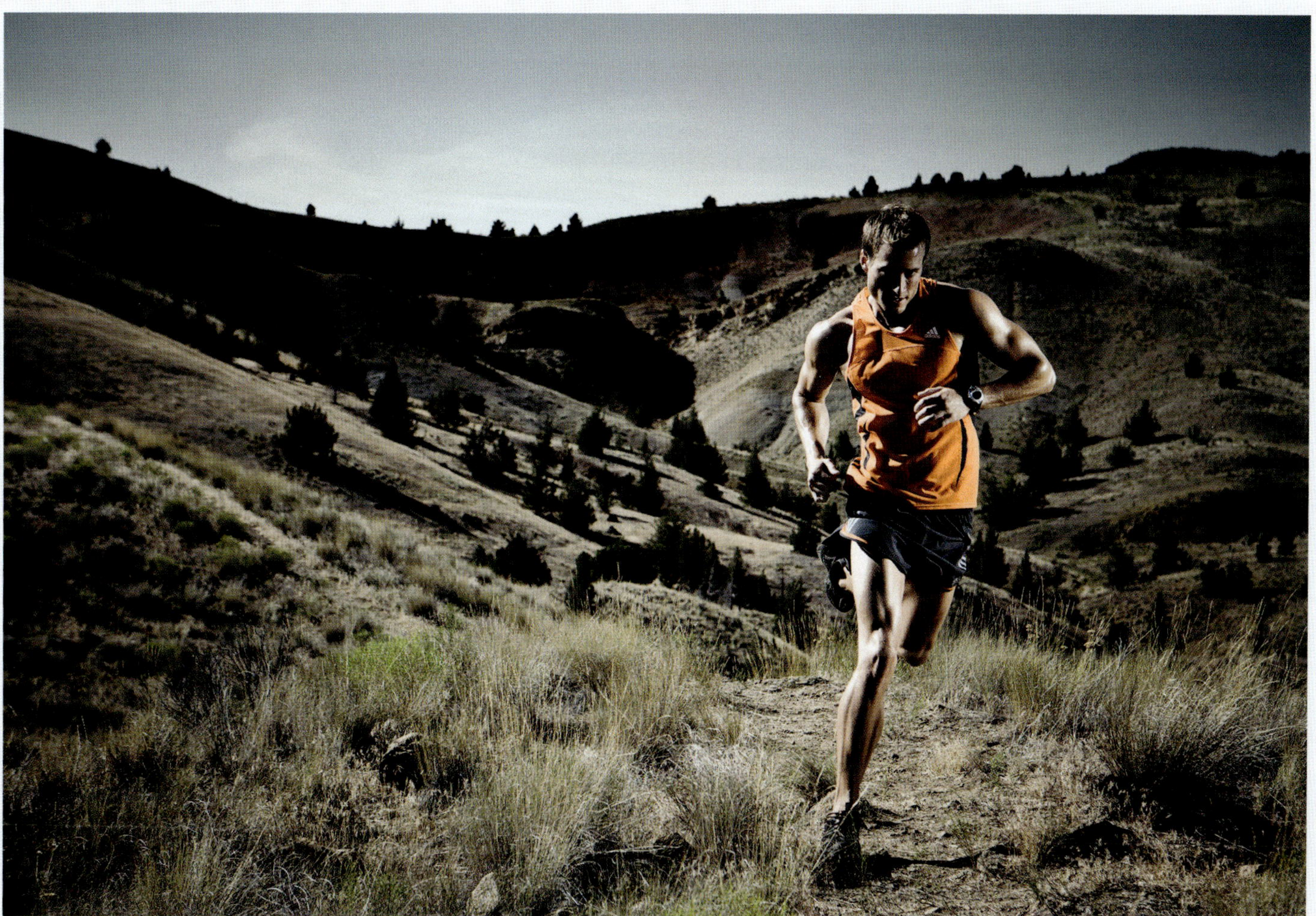

**FIGURE 6.12** By using silver reflectors and careful metering, Andy was able to create a dramatic light effect without any strobe lights.
IMAGE © ANDY BATT, *DESERT RUNNER*, 2005.

a stop) are to be expected, so don't worry about them; just make sure that moving the meter a little doesn't make the reading jump a lot.

***Andy:*** One trick I take advantage of on outdoor shoots is to use my handheld meter to monitor the rising and falling ambient light values. Once I get my camera exposure dialed in to tell my story, I'll either mount the meter somewhere or give it to my assistant. Then I'll ask them to let me know if the light values come up or down. As long as the meter is pointed in the same direction (usually straight up), it's a great way to make sure I'm consistent. At that point, I don't even need to know what the meter reads—only that it's either the same, up 1/3 stop or down 1 stop. Then I make adjustments to the overall exposure on the fly, usually by altering the ISO speed so as not to change the look of the image.

## How to Use an Incident Light Meter, in Six Easy Steps

1. Turn the meter on and engage the Ambient mode (usually the sun icon).
2. Select the ISO and shutter speeds you want to work with.
3. Place the meter right in the face of your subject. (Meters aren't always polite.)
4. Make sure the white dome is pointed directly back at your camera, so it reads read the light that's falling onto your subject.
5. Push the Measure button and get your F-stop. If necessary, adjust the shutter speed to get a different F-stop.
6. Set your camera to the combined ISO, shutter and F-stop values.

**Bonus trick**: If your subject is a human being, position the dome to point in the same direction as the subject's nose. In some cases, this will mean that the meter won't point directly at the camera. This technique allows you to average the light that falls on both sides of the face.

## Landscaping Tips

For you landscape photographers, of both the pastoral and urban decay schools, we have a handheld meter tip dedicated just to you! Remember that the light falling on you is the same as the light that's falling on your landscape, and on that field of horses or the warehouse with broken windows. If you can't get near enough to your subject to take a handheld meter reading, just look for a close-by patch of light that's similar to what you're photographing and meter off that instead.

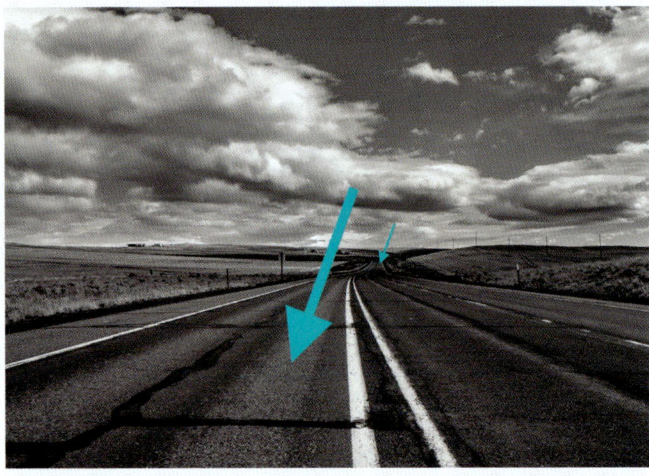

**FIGURE 6.13** The light here is the same as the light over there! If you can't get near enough to your subject to take a handheld meter reading, just look for a close–by patch of light that's similar to what you're photographing and meter off that instead. IMAGE © ANDY BATT, *DESERT HIGHWAY,* 2010

## Incident Light: A White, Gray and Black Room

Let's revisit the room with the black, gray and white walls, this time with an incident meter. We'll stand with our backs against the white wall and point the white dome away from us, towards the center of the room, where the camera is. If we do this for each wall and compare, we'll find that the reading is close to identical for each position.[12] That's because each wall has the same amount of light falling onto it. The meter is measuring the light that falls *onto* the walls instead of reflecting off them. This time, the walls will expose as black, white and gray, since the meter isn't compensating for the different tonal values.

### TRY THIS AT HOME

### Gray, White and Black All Over—Take Two

**For step-by-step instructions, go to: www.focalpress.com/cw/digitalimagingmasters**

For the last exercise, you used a reflective light meter; this time you'll use your incident meter to get a reading. The results will be different!

### Tried-and-True Tricks for Getting a Base Exposure

- **Classic**: This "Sunny 16" rule has been with us for a long time: Simply set your aperture to *f*/16 and use a shutter speed that matches your ISO speed. For example, ISO 400 would give you 1/400th. This is a very useful alignment of numbers that you can vary for other situations, such as the "Cloudy-Bright 11" or the "Overcast 8."
- **Skin tone**: You always have your hand with you, so you might as well use it. By holding your hand in the same light as your subject, you can take a reading from it and use that as a base for tricky lighting situations. To use this method effectively, you need to calibrate yourself. Take some test shots of your hand; then take some shots of your scene—using the exposure set by your hand. If your scenes are, on average, brighter than they should be, you'll need to compensate with a slightly darker exposure than your hand requires. Do the reverse for scenes that expose, on average, darker than they should.
- **Sidewalk-Asphalt-Grass**: These are three tonally useful surfaces that are often around when we're shooting, since each one has a close to midtone gray value. There's plenty of variation in each, but by taking an exposure reading from any of these surfaces, you'll have a good starting point.

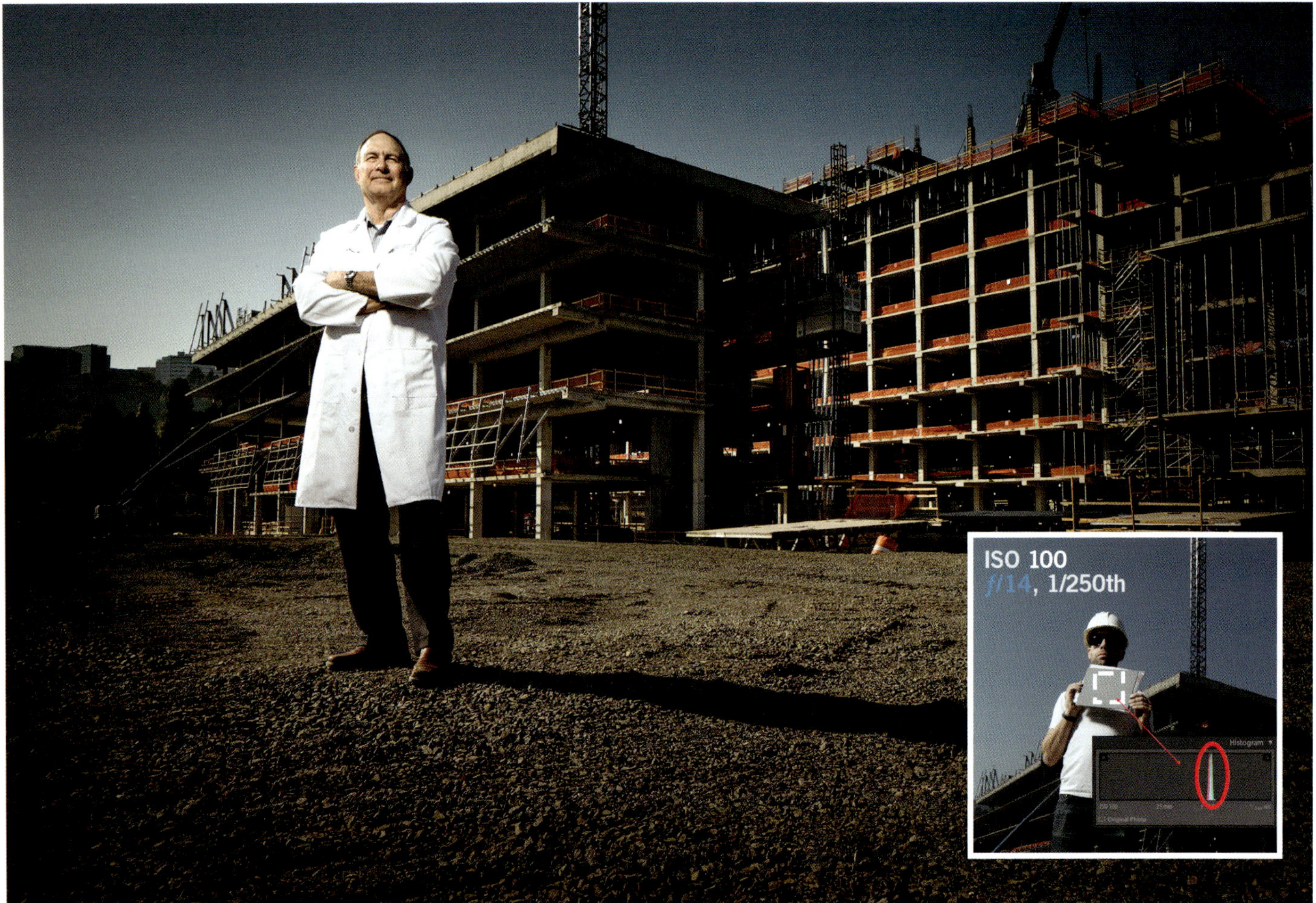


**FIGURE 6.14** Here's the Gray Card Trick in action. Andy wanted to create a dramatically lit image outside on a sunny day. That meant bringing battery–powered strobes on location and coming up with an exposure that was brighter than the daylight, but only by a stop. The full exposure on his subject was a combination of strobe light and daylight. By carefully metering and then shooting test images of a gray card, he knew he was getting ~~a good~~ exposure that accounted for both light sources.
IMAGE © ANDY BATT, *DR. JOE GRAY, OHSU,* FOR *PORTLAND MONTHLY* MAGAZINE, 2012.

## Gray Card to Meter Mismatch

The gray card is a standard. It's always the same value (18%), but it has a problem: It might not match your meter's standard. Meters are designed to deliver a midtone gray, and there's a good chance yours is designed to deliver a 12% gray value.[13] If you take a spot meter reading from a gray card and expose at that setting, there's a good chance it will be anywhere from 1/3 to 1 stop underexposed. If your 12% meter takes a reading from an 18% gray card (which is reflecting approximately a 1/2 stop more light than the meter is expecting), it will create an exposure that's 1/2 stop darker. The easy fix is to simply increase a spot-metered exposure taken with an 18% gray card by about 1/2 stop (Ctein, 2000: 33). With any kind of "smart" metering mode, like Matrix metering, this difference won't really matter, since it samples many points when calculating an exposure.

***Andy:*** I just compared Spot mode and Incident mode with my Sekonic[14] handheld meter. I placed the gray card in my Graphiclite[15] viewing booth and took an incident meter reading of *f*/8 and a spot reading of *f*/9: There was a +1/3 stop difference.

Even Kodak, maker of gray cards, says:

> ***[Reflected] meter readings of the gray card should be adjusted as follows:***
>
> - ***For subjects of normal reflectance, increase the indicated exposure by 1/2 stop.***
> - ***For light subjects, use the indicated exposure; for very light subjects, decrease exposure by 1/2 stop.***
> - ***If the subject is dark to very dark, increase the indicated exposure by 1 to 1 1/2 stops.***[16]

## The Gray Card Trick: Everybody Loves a Shortcut

By combining the gray card with the camera's histogram (or the histogram in Lightroom), we can see what a histogram of your preferred gray card exposure looks like. Once we have that in our heads, we can quickly refer to it in the field.

***Andy:*** My assistants know exactly what it means when I ask them to do the Gray Card Trick (**Figure 6.14**). Somebody grabs a gray card and runs out on set. They turn the gray card so it's aimed at the key light. I walk into the scene and take a meter reading, then a test shot.

For this project I was shooting tethered, so we could view it in Lightroom. By cropping the image to just the gray card, I could see where on the histogram the gray card data fell. On the initial test image, the values were too dark—the spike was to the left of the middle mark. I added a stop of ISO speed to increase my exposure, and the new histogram showed me that the gray card data was to the right of the halfway point (**Figure 6.14, inset**)—where I knew I was getting good skin tones. With the strobe and ambient light exposures dialed in, I was ready to make the portrait.

The "trick" part of this is that it always works. No matter what kind of camera I'm using, the environment that I'm in or how bright and shiny the image looks on the camera's screen, this method tells me what kind of exposure I'm really getting.

# Digital Exposure

To understand how exposure works, it's helpful to connect image capture with the way digital data is stored and how our cameras and software interpret that data.

## The Data Is Linear

Sensors capture data in a linear way, which is different from the way we see the world and from the way our images end up. Linear capture can be very unfriendly to shadow tones. Brighter values (midtones to the highlights) are created when many photons fall into the photosite, while dark values are created when very few photons fall into it. When there are fewer photons, there is a lower quality signal—and more opportunity for noise problems.

Our eyes give equal weight to the tones around us, while our camera sensors simply count photons, recording light values by measuring the number of photons that fall into the photosite. The brighter the value, the more photons there are. There's a finite amount of storage in a raw file, and half of it goes to the brightest stop.

***Linear capture can be very unfriendly to shadow tones . . . There's a finite amount of storage in a raw file, and half of it goes to the brightest stop.***

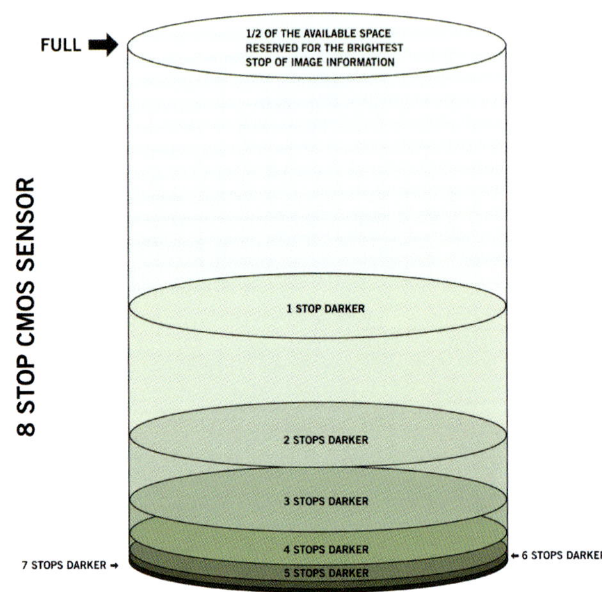


**FIGURE 6.15A** Our eyes and brains give equal weight to all the tones around us, but camera sensors simply count photons in a linear way. Think of a raw file as a cylinder that can only hold a finite amount of data. It takes a large number of photons to make up the brightest stop of information, which requires half of the total space available. The next stop down requires half that amount; the stop that follows requires half *that* amount, and so on—until we reach the darkest tones, which are recorded in the least amount of space.
ILLUSTRATION © ANDY BATT, *LINEAR CAPTURE—CYLINDER*, 2013.

That's because the difference between stops is either half the amount of photons (for 1 stop darker) or twice the number of photons (for 1 stop brighter). When these photons are turned into digital values and recorded as a raw file, the brightest stop requires half of the space available. Even if we take an image with no actual highlight tones, half of that space is reserved for them. The next darkest stop uses half the amount of storage; the next stop is halved again . . . and this repeats until we've gotten to the last stop of data. The last, darkest stop contains the fewest photons; it has the highest potential for noise and the least amount of space available for recording information (**Figures 6.15A and 6.15B**).

When we try to rescue an underexposed image and bring up tonality in the darkest areas, we find a lot of noise and not much detail—all due to linear capture. When we process out our raw images, the raw processor not only demosaics the color information to give us real color, it also alters how these tones are weighted. Each stop of tone is balanced so that the tonality looks right to our eyes.

## Push Your Exposures Around

This predicament can get us into trouble. When we're creating scenes that are deliberately full of dark tones, we end up with images that inherently have more noise. If we meter and correctly expose scenes with nearly all midtones and shadow tones, we get accurate exposures—but the tones are in the noisiest part of the capture.

To avoid this situation, we can alter the way we expose our scenes. Since the first stop of data is the sweet spot, it makes sense to use that fact to its best advantage. We call this "pushing to the right and pulling to the left."[17]

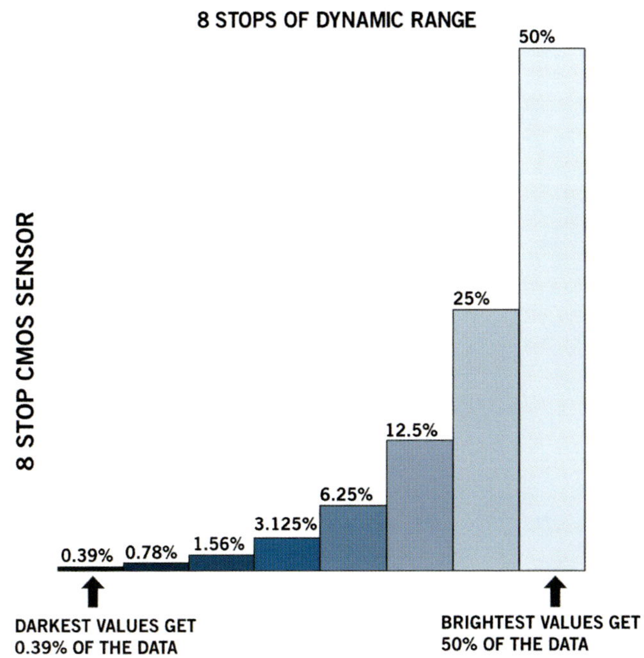


**FIGURE 6.15B** Here's a visualization of a camera that's able to record 8 stops of dynamic range (loosely defined as the number of stops of exposure that the camera can record before it clips on either end). It takes half the total space to record the brightest values. Over the 8–stop range, the available space keeps getting halved, until for the last stop—the darkest values with tone—there is only .78% of available space left to record those tones.
ILLUSTRATION © ANDY BATT, *LINEAR CAPTURE—CHART*, 2013.

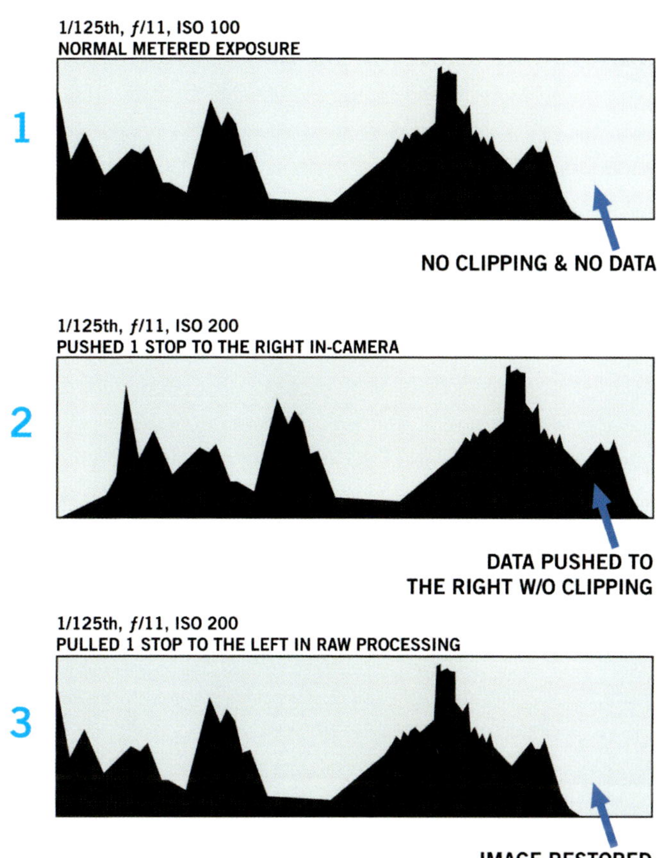


**FIGURE 6.16** By manipulating the way we capture our images, and the data, we can achieve better quality (less noise and better fine detail) in the darker tones. We can do this by pushing the image and increasing the exposure up to the point of losing detail in the highlights, capturing it there, and then reducing the exposure in post. This has the effect of capturing the original shadow tones (as in a normal exposure) at a higher fidelity.
ILLUSTRATION © ANDY BATT, *PUSH AND PULL*, 2013.

## First, the Push

Take a look at **Figure 6.16**, and you'll see three similarly shaped histograms. The first one represents a good, solid metered exposure—normal—for an image that doesn't have any bright whites or specular highlights. Everything is exposing normally, but since there's no data in the highlights section, you can choose to increase the exposure. By doing this, you'll technically overexpose the image, but because there's nothing to clip, it won't hurt anything.

Now take a look at the second histogram. By increasing the ISO speed by a stop, the image is exposed to be brighter. The entire histogram shifts to the right, but doesn't clip the data. This makes the image look overly bright on the camera's LCD, or your computer monitor, but the key is to know that you aren't clipping the data. As long as the histogram isn't hard up against the right edge, you aren't losing any detail from overexposure.

### Then, the Pull

The third histogram shows what happens when you pull the image back into the exposure at which it's supposed to be. Basically, you're recreating the original look of the image, but have upgraded the image data, since every chunk of it was moved up a level of data quality. When you pull the data back to the left, it "keeps" the improved quality, and you get an image with cleaner, higher-quality shadow tones. **Figures 6.17A and 6.17B** illustrate the push and pull effects on an image of a forest scene.

***Andy:*** Each generation of CMOS sensors gets better at removing noise at the sensor level (before the data gets encoded into the raw file); new generations of processing tools keep improving, as well. The result is that with normal exposures, the shadow tones are usually nice and clean, at higher and higher ISOs. The caveat is that if you try to make those shadow tones into midtones, the noise problems will return.

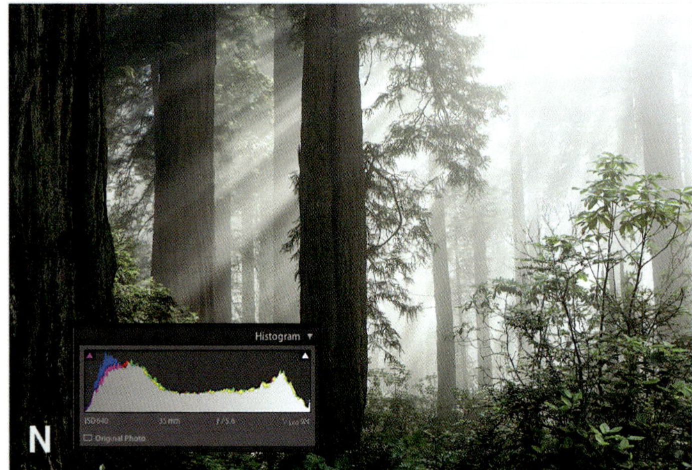


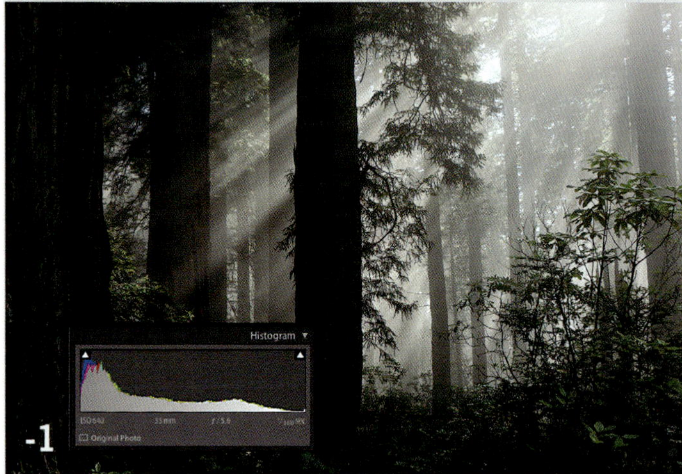


**FIGURE 6.17A** To make a moody, silhouetted image of these redwoods, the exposure on this scene can be opened up and exposed brighter (top image). The bright fog detail would hold easily, and the dark tones in the trees could be captured at a higher image quality. By adjusting the exposure slider in post by –1 stop, the image becomes more dramatic, the beams of light in the fog become more apparent, and the trees retain better detail.

IMAGE © ANDY BATT, *PUSH AND PULL—REDWOOD FOG*, 2011.

## To Clip or Not to Clip: Highlights

When you look at your histograms, especially when you're considering whether to push them to the right, it's important to know if you're blowing out the highlights—because if they're really gone, you won't be able to retrieve them. Take a look at **Figure 6.18**. The direct sunlight in this Pacific Northwest rainforest is hitting the leaves of the fern; the shiny portions of the leaves push the exposure values far above everything else in the surrounding areas.

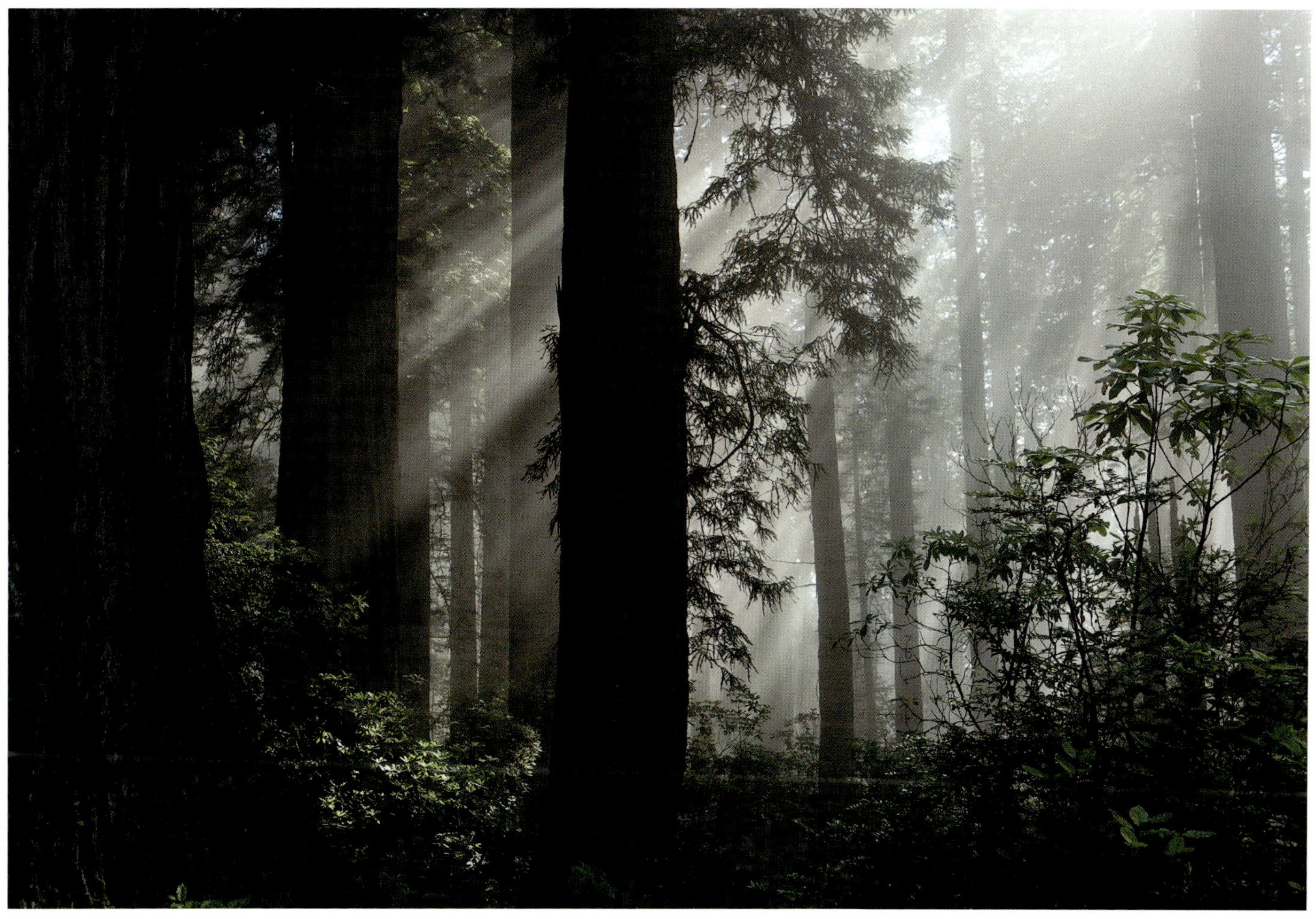

**FIGURE 6.17B** The final version of this image matches Andy's intention when taking it: a darker place in the woods with the sunlight just reaching through.
IMAGES © ANDY BATT, *REDWOOD FOG,* 2011.

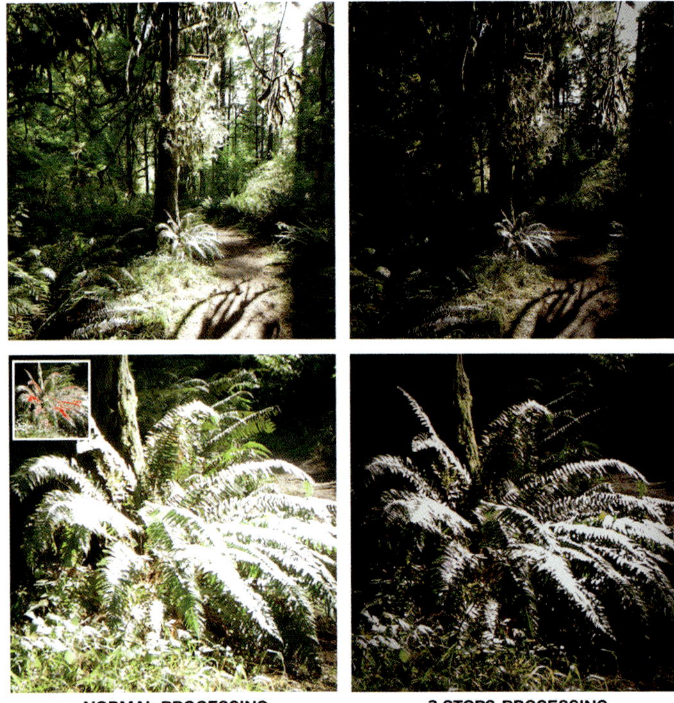


**FIGURE 6.18** In this image of a riverside forest, the patch of sunlight reflects off the waxy fern leaves, creating a specular highlight. Even when you try to underexpose your image to compensate, you'll find that specular highlights won't have tone. If you expose for specular highlights, your overall image will be far too dark.

Part of working with your camera's clipping warning is to know which kinds of highlights are clipping: Diffuse highlights usually have plenty of tone in the raw file, while specular highlights will probably be blown out.

IMAGE © ANDY BATT, *FERNS*, 2008.

## The Camera's Clipping Warning

The first tool to use when this occurs is the camera's clipping warning, which is useful—as long as you understand that it indicates clipping *way* before there's any real danger of clipping the raw data. The clipping warning bases its detection on the JPEG image that's processed out by the camera[18]—and not on the raw data itself.

The camera's clipping tool is fairly blunt: It indicates that a portion of your image is overexposed, but doesn't tell you by how much, or how it relates to the raw data. It also doesn't tell you if you're clipping in one, two or three channels (RGB). If the image is only clipping in one channel, then Lightroom (and other raw processors) do a decent job of automatically rebuilding that lost channel from the remaining data. This doesn't always work, and skin tones can be problematic; but even then, the result of recovering blown highlights usually looks better than it did before recovery.

## Lightroom's Clipping Warning

Lightroom and other raw processors have an effective clipping warning to let you know when you've pushed an adjustment too far. It's amazing how "bright" the data can get—how far to the right it can be—before it actually clips. Understanding this will help you calibrate your exposures and keep you from worrying about the flashing red danger warnings in the camera.

***Tip:*** We generally turn the camera's clipping warning off and trust the camera's histogram—and our experience.

## Specular and Diffuse Highlights

When you're staring at your scene, search out two different kinds of highlights: specular and diffuse. A *specular highlight* is a mirror-like reflection of an extremely bright light source—the sun being the most prominent example. The brightness value of a specular highlight is usually far greater than everything else around it. You can't expose for both the specular highlight and the rest of the image. A *diffuse highlight* is an area that is bright white, but still has some tone. To prevent clipping, it's a matter of getting the exposure just right. There should be tone and detail in a diffuse highlight.

If you're in Lightroom and viewing an image with both types of highlights, then try sliding the Exposure control all the way down to the left (darker), and you'll see the difference between the two different types of highlights. The diffuse ones will reduce down in tone and exposure, since they contain data that can be manipulated. The specular highlights contain no data and leave a white hole.

Check out the specular highlights of the sun on the water in **Figure 6.19A**. The good news is that viewers expect specular highlights to be bright white, so they'll accept them, because they look right. If specular highlights bother you, there's always the option later on to cheat in Photoshop[19] and give them a tiny bit of fake tone; that way, they won't show up as white holes in the final printed result.

The sun is a special case: It's a point light source, not a specular reflection. Since it's much brighter than anything else, it will usually look like a white hole in your image—at almost any exposure. At sunset, during forest fires and on heavy overcast or smoggy days, there may be enough particulate in the air to effectively reduce the sun's brightness so it's not blown out (**Figure 6.19B**).

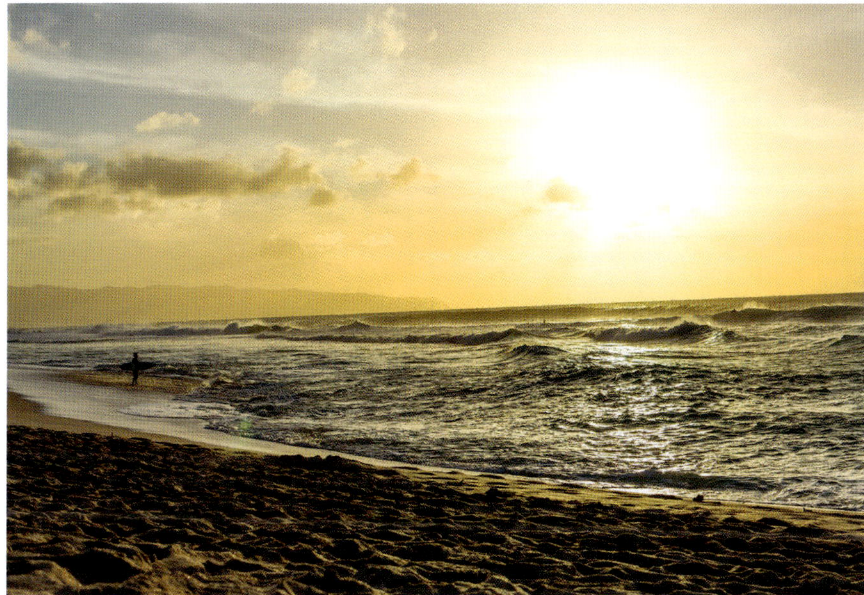

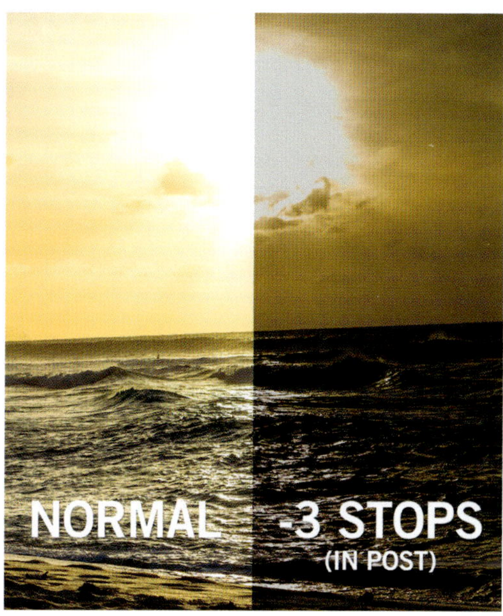


**FIGURE 6.19A** This image was exposed to create a dark image with contrast. Since the camera was pointing into the sun, it was important to get a starting exposure value that wasn't reading the sun directly into the camera. In Manual mode, Andy started with a reading from the sand and water. Knowing that he wanted a backlit feeling, he altered the exposure to darken the scene. If he had let the camera make the decision, it would have overcompensated for the sun and created a much darker image. Had he just used the base exposure from the sand and water, the sky would have blown out. (Shot in Manual mode at 1/500th, *f*/5.6 at ISO 100 with a 5D MIII and a 50mm/1.2 lens.) IMAGE © ANDY BATT, *HAWAII SURF SUNSET*, 2013.

**FIGURE 6.19B** This is a detail of **Figure 6.19A**. We can see (left) that the sun recorded as a white hole; with the high-quality sensor in the 5D MIII, there's a soft edge that keeps it from looking incorrect. The specular highlights, where the water reflects the sun, are also white holes, but they look right to our eyes. Andy dropped the exposure down –3 stops in post (right); we can see that there's no information in the sun or specular highlights in the water. Lightroom dropped the value to a light gray, but there's no real tonality. IMAGE © ANDY BATT, *HAWAII SURF SUNSET—DETAIL*, 2013.

## TRY THIS AT HOME

### Go too Far—on Purpose

**For step-by-step instructions, go to: www.focalpress.com/cw/digitalimagingmasters**

Check out this quick test for comparing your in-camera highlight warnings to your raw files. There's a difference between when your camera tells you it's overexposing and when it actually is. There's also a difference between specular clipping and diffuse detail clipping. After trying this exercise, you'll be in a much better position to judge your histograms and use the highlight warning effectively.

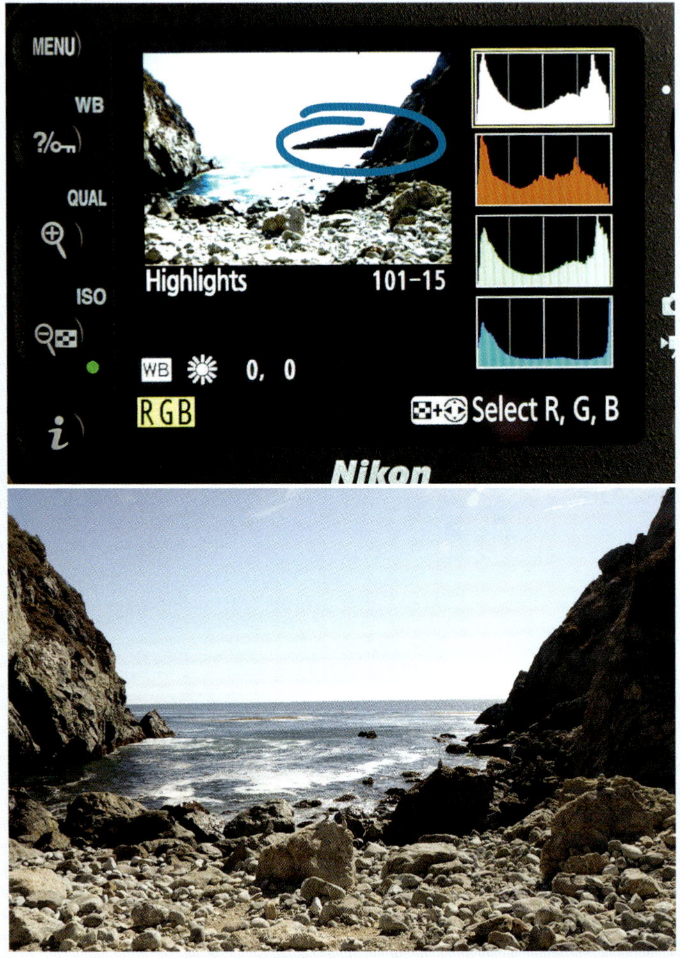


**FIGURE 6.20** In the back-of-the-camera view (top image), we see the highlight alert (circled). On this particular camera, the alert is indicated by a blinking, blacked-out area. The rest of the sky also looks clipped in the back-of-the-camera view, but when we look at the raw file (bottom image), we can see that it isn't clipped. Note that the raw file was only minimally processed; no highlight recovery or retouching was applied. The moral is, "When your camera warns of overexposure, the only way you'll know if it's telling the truth is to test it."
IMAGE © ERIKA VELASQUEZ, *CALIFORNIA OCEAN VIEW—OVEREXPOSURE ALERTS*, 2013.

## Metering Preferences: Holly Andres

***Candace Dobro*: Do you use in the in-camera light meter or histograms?**

***Holly Andres:*** I don't use a handheld light meter—I use the in-camera light meter. I also use histograms and the highlight warning to see if any highlights are blown out. Usually, I'll bracket so I can get variations in my shots. Other times, for a plate, I'll remove my subject and then bracket the space. For example, if there's a window in the shot, I might vary the exposures so that I can bring in a more properly exposed outdoor value.

# Dynamic Range

It's important to know the point at which the sensor stops capturing information and only records solid black or solid white. As sensor technology improves, the dynamic range keeps expanding, thus moving the end points of our images and capturing more detail in the shadows and highlights.

If we compared a camera with 5 stops of dynamic range to one with 8 stops, we'd find that both cameras expose their midtones similarly, and that the 8-stop camera had information at each of the ends, where the 5-stop camera had solid black or solid white—clipping with no detail.

We can find dynamic range information in the manufacturer's literature and at independent review sites. The most basic test to determine your camera's dynamic range is to photograph a step wedge—a precisely crafted and measured chart that has a range of tones from black to white. These charts are carefully photographed, and the patches are measured in the photograph to establish where the sensor stops recording information.

There is much debate about accurately measuring dynamic range, and even more debate about interpreting the results. What's a "usable" level of shadow detail? Is it where you have "good" information or "any" information? Who defines "good"? The term "any" can be problematic, since it might not indicate a useful dynamic range to the photographer who ends up using the camera.

## Rocks and Tones

Take a look at **Figure 6.21A**, which shows a lava-tube cave in Northern California. The areas circled in blue are lit by the sun, and the green-circled areas look into the inky shadows of a cave. It's a very high-contrast image. It's definitely outside the tonal range of a 5D MII to capture detail in the darkest shadows *and* hold tonality in the brightest highlights within the same image.

Image A was taken at fifteen seconds, Image B at eight seconds, Image C at four seconds and Image D at two seconds. In Image A, the white rock is clipped to full white, and while there is technically tone in the shadows, it's of a low quality (**Figure 6.21A, top left, inset**). There's some tonality in the blue circle of Image C, but it's not until Image D—3 stops darker—that the rock has good tonality. In Image D, the cave darkness has crept outwards, and the black tones are solid black with no detail.

If we try to fix Image A in post-processing, we end up with the top image in **Figure 6.21B**. In this version, Andy recovered highlights, reduced exposure and opened up the shadows. The resulting image has gray "holes" and its colors have shifted unnaturally.

If we try to fix Image C, which has tonality in the highlights, we can do a much better job of expanding the image (**Figure 6.21B, bottom**). The key is that we can only expand an image using data we've already captured. We can't add dynamic range that's not present to begin with—no matter which processing tools we have.

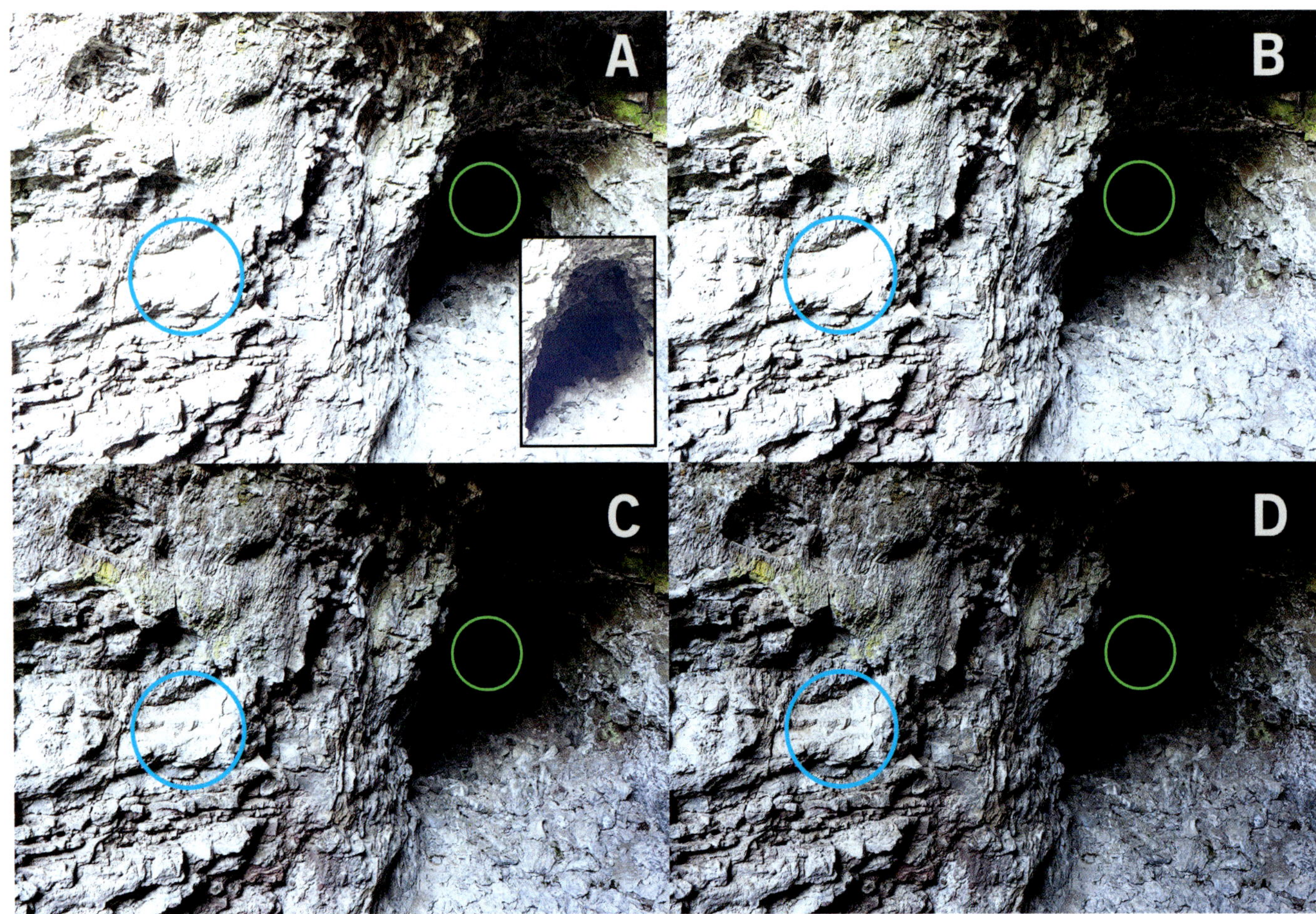


**FIGURE 6.21A** This image of the mouth of Bear Foot Cave has a dynamic range outside that of the 5D MII's sensor, so it can't capture the brightly lit rocks and the dark recesses of the cave in the same image. The values in this bracket are: A) 15 sec, B) 8 sec, C) 4 sec and D) 2 sec, all at *f*/11, 1/160th, Manual mode.
IMAGE © ANDY BATT, *GRID: BEAR FOOT CAVE, LAVA BEDS NATIONAL MONUMENT*, 2011.

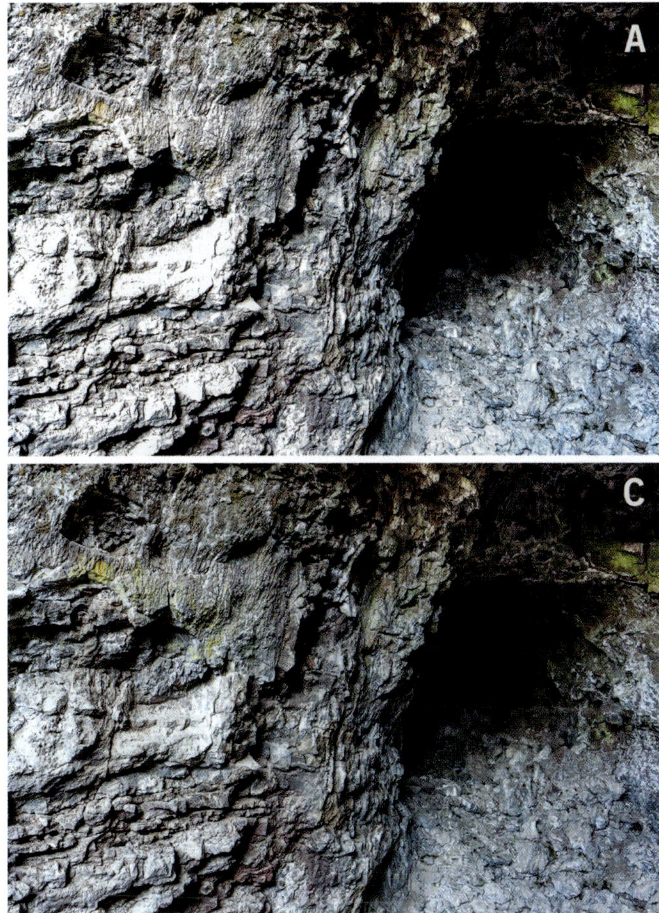


**FIGURE 6.21B** If we try to fix Image A (from **Figure 6.21A)** in post-processing, we end up with the top image in this illustration. Andy recovered highlights, reduced exposure and opened up the shadows, but the resulting image has gray "holes," and its colors have shifted unnaturally. If we try to fix Image C (from **Figure 6.21A**), which has tonality in the highlights, we can do a much better job of expanding the image (bottom of this illustration). The key is that we can only expand an image using data we've already captured. We can't add dynamic range that's not present to begin with—no matter which processing tools we have.
IMAGE © ANDY BATT, *BEAR FOOT CAVE, LAVA BEDS NATIONAL MONUMENT,* 2011.

## TRY THIS AT HOME

### Gray Cards at High Noon: Your Camera's Dynamic Range

**For step-by-step instructions, go to: www.focalpress.com/cw/digitalimagingmasters**

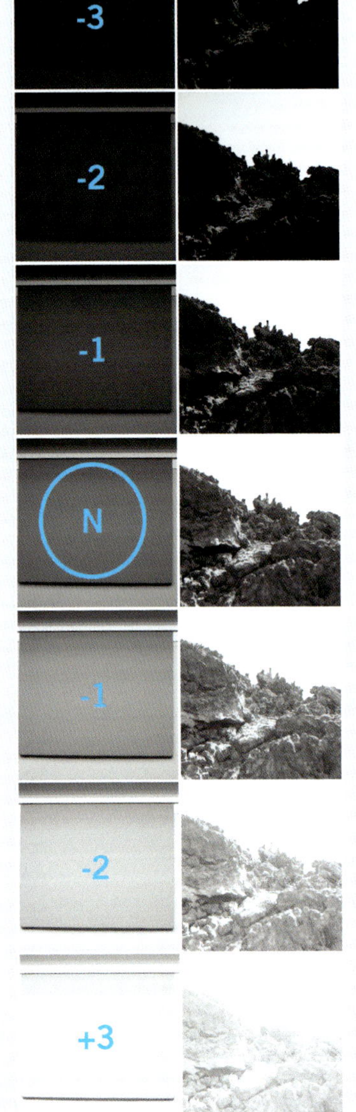


This two-part exercise is a useful way to test your camera's dynamic range. You'll be using a stalwart standby—the gray card—to create a multiple-value step chart.[20]

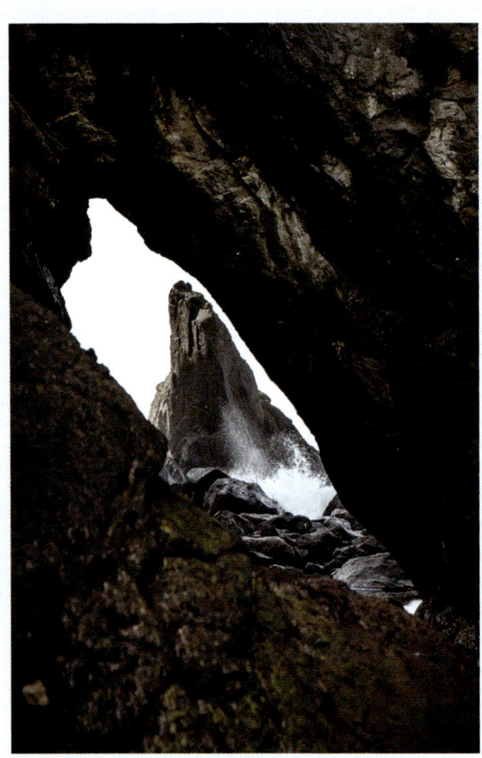

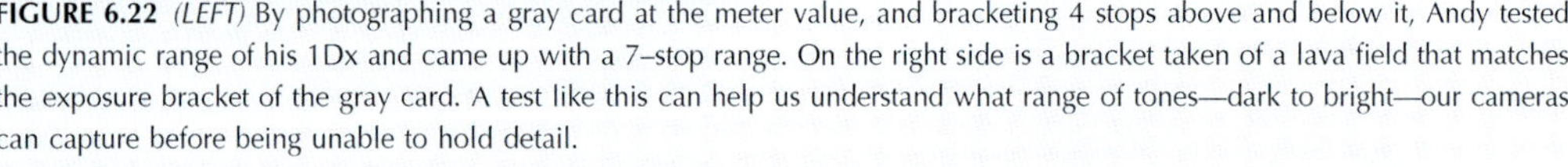

**FIGURE 6.22** *(LEFT)* By photographing a gray card at the meter value, and bracketing 4 stops above and below it, Andy tested the dynamic range of his 1Dx and came up with a 7–stop range. On the right side is a bracket taken of a lava field that matches the exposure bracket of the gray card. A test like this can help us understand what range of tones—dark to bright—our cameras can capture before being unable to hold detail.
ILLUSTRATION © ANDY BATT, *GRAY CARD DYNAMIC RANGE TEST*, 2013.

**FIGURE 6.23** *(ABOVE)* Making this high–contrast image required Andy to make a decision about which tones to meter for. It was an overcast day with bright white skies—which meant soft, forgiving light on the rocks, but a huge difference in tonal value between the white sky and the dark lava rock.

Andy could have chosen to photograph this scene three different ways: by holding the sky values, opening up the rock values or trying to find a balance between the two. He decided that part of the beauty of the image was opening up and exposing for the rocks, to show their textures and subtle tones. Quickly metering off the rock face gave him his exposure, which he modified with a high shutter speed to freeze the spray of the water hitting the rocks. (Shot at 1/500th, *f*/8 at ISO 640 on a 5D MII with a 50mm/1.4 lens.)
IMAGE © ANDY BATT, *WESTWIND OCEAN ARCH*, 2012.

# Jodie Steen

*Co-Author of* Camera & Craft *and Owner of 127 Productions, Inc.*[21]

***Andy Batt:* When measuring exposure, what's the practical difference between using a light meter and software?**

***Jodie Steen:*** Once you take a reading with a light meter, the answer to your exposure question is clear: You click a button and get a definitive answer. For the amount of light falling on the scene, your exposure is, for example, *f/*8 and 7/10ths. You set your camera to that F-stop, and you have a perfectly exposed image.

When metering with software, you have many more tools to judge exposure, but at no point does the software tell you at what aperture and shutter speed to set your camera. You must make this decision based on the tools available. There's more information, which can lead to making a more informed decision; it could also lead to confusion. Often the monitor (or LCD screen) further confuses issues. Since we photographers are visual people, we tend to judge exposure by relying on what we see on screen. This, however, can lead to terribly exposed photos.

***AB:* How can you use software to get an accurate exposure? What other tools do you need?**

***JS:*** The top three tools that most digital capture applications offer are the histogram, spot meter and over- and under-exposure alarms. The histogram is a great way to see how much information you have in your image; it helps you to see specific tonal ranges. Exposure alarms can be helpful when you want to hold detail in highlights and shadows; they provide an excellent warning when you're over- or under-exposing and your data is out of range.

The digital spot meter[22] can be the most useful tool of all. I use this along with an X-Rite 24-patch ColorChecker to judge accurate exposure. I'll have someone place the checker in the most important area of the frame—or ask my subject to hold it. I take a test photo—I'm usually shooting tethered so that I have instant access to the image. With the Spot Meter tool, I'll select a patch on the ColorChecker and take a reading. It's important to choose to measure for either input or output values[23]—there's a big difference between them.

***AB:* It's useful to mention that how this is done really depends on the raw-processing software. Lightroom, for example, uses the Eyedropper tool, measures in percentages and uses a version of ProPhoto RGB as its working color space—these would be its input values. To get to an output value, you need to create a soft-proof version of the image and specify the color space you want to use—Adobe98, for example.**

***JS:*** Right—those input values are the RGB raw values[24] and can vary, depending on what the internal working space is. The RGB output values are set to match the output color space—Adobe RGB (1998), for example. The number values of the output space are going to be different than the input—for the same patch on the ColorChecker (**Figure 6.24**). When I'm doing my test shots, I want to get the most important tones to hit properly—they're the middle gray, white and black, in that order. I'll shoot a test and measure each of the patches. If I get the right values for those patches, I know that I have a proper exposure. My goal is to have values at or close to 244 for the white patch (A4), 120 for middle gray (D4) and 52 for black (F4). If I don't get those values, I'll adjust my lighting and test again.

***AB:* One thing that's important to mention about ColorCheckers —and that photographers who aren't accustomed to using them might interpret the wrong way—is that the white and black patches represent white and black *with tone*; they aren't supposed to be bright white or solid black. You don't try to make those patches look like bright white and dark black; you just want to use them as exposure references so that you have measured values in the three main areas of exposure: highlights, midtones and shadow tones.**

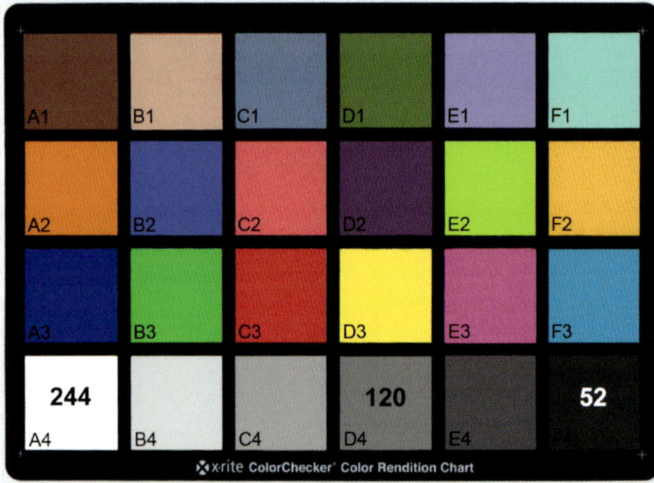


**FIGURE 6.24** Jodie uses a traditional ColorChecker to evaluate her exposure. First she takes a test image with the ColorChecker placed in an area where it's getting full exposure of the key light. By using the Eyedropper/Spot Meter tool in her raw processor, she can measure the Adobe RGB (1998) values for the gray/D4, white/A4 and black/F4 patches. If they closely match her desired values (244, 120, 52), then she has a good exposure. If they're off, she'll make adjustments to the exposure and perform another test. This works well because it's an objective measure of exposure; the monitor, camera LCD and histogram aren't being evaluated subjectively by eye. Jodie might adjust her final exposure to be brighter or darker for aesthetic reasons, but this method gives her an excellent starting point.
IMAGE © TOM ASHE AND JODIE STEEN: *X-RITE, MACBETH COLOR CHECKER,* 2013.

**This leads to a related question: What's the difference between an "accurate exposure" and an "aesthetic exposure"? How do they relate to raw processing?**

***JS:*** There is a measured "right" and "wrong" when it comes to accurate exposure—the numbers are supposed to be a set value. Aesthetic exposure breaks those rules. Perhaps the photographer intentionally wants to underexpose an image, to create a darker mood, for example. Or perhaps when shooting a portrait, the photographer chooses to overexpose slightly, to make the skin appear brighter. The key here is to make these decisions intentionally and expose the image in that way. Not only is the aesthetic of the image firmly in place, but also, there will be enough latitude in the file to make any necessary minor tweaks. Although the raw-processing tools make it easy to slide the Exposure slider and change the image, an intentionally exposed shot inevitably creates a better quality image.

***AB:* How do we take these software metering techniques out of the studio and into the world of untethered DSLR shooting?**

***JS:*** It's not practical to hook up a computer and use all the raw software tools to check an image exposure while shooting on location with a DSLR. This is where basic photography knowledge really comes in handy. Get to know your F-stops and shutter speeds and how they relate to each other. I still use a handheld light meter for all shooting, whether on location or in the studio. I think it's still a good idea to shoot a 24-patch color checker on location, because it acts as a guide. You can see if your exposure changed from shot to shot when you're back in a controlled environment, and then use the software to make corrections as necessary.

## Histograms and Image Archetypes

There are certain types of images—and histograms—we see repeatedly. Recognizing these image types will help you understand your scene. To do that, we need to know a little more about how the data is being represented in those histograms.

### The Basics

Your histograms stretch left to right, with the darkest tones on the far left and the brightest ones on the far right. The vertical scale is a little trickier; it's a dynamic representation of the total number of pixels in an image. This is where the weight of each pixel is shown in comparison to the whole. Check out **Figure 6.25A:** There are lots of dark tones in this image, and the left side of the histogram is full of data (**Figure 6.25B**). The right side of the histogram shows just a

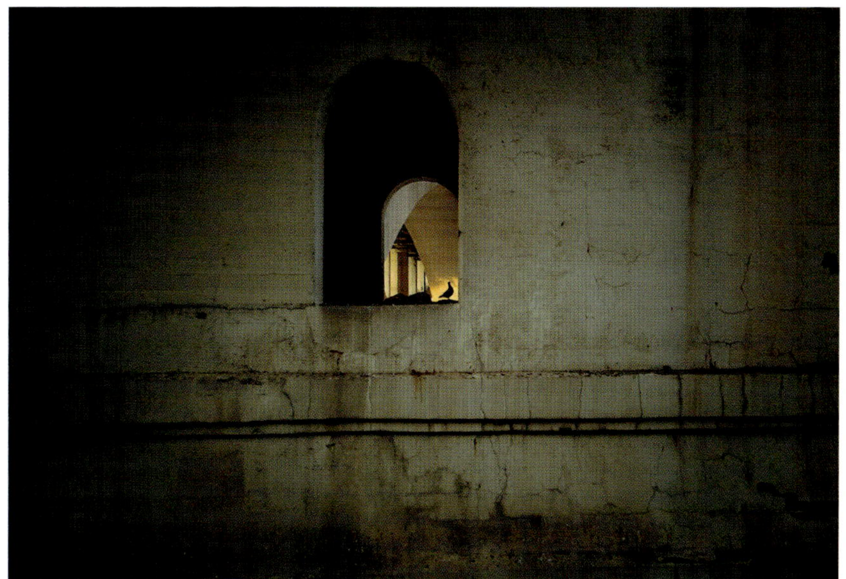

**FIGURE 6.25A** This portrait of a pigeon in an archway is a fairly low-key image, with lots of dark tones representing the majority of the image. We need to be especially aware of the most important tones—the ones representing the key light and key detail of the scene. In this case, they barely register on the histogram because proportionally, they have little volume, i.e., there are very few pixels used for those tones in comparison to the quantities used to express the rest of the image. See **Figure 6.25B** for what happens when we crop to just show the key area. (Shot at 1/200th, *f*/8 at ISO 800 on a 5D MII with a 35mm/1.4 lens.)
IMAGE © ANDY BATT, *PORTRAIT OF ARCH AND BIRD*, 2009.

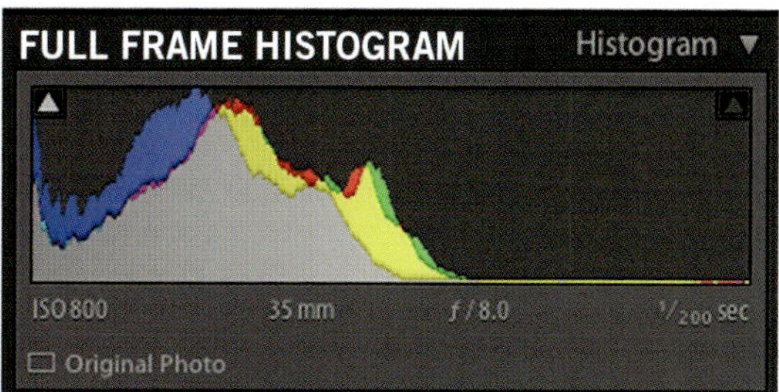


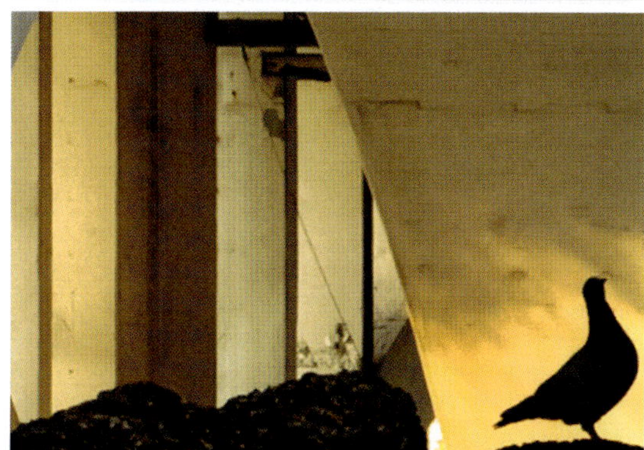

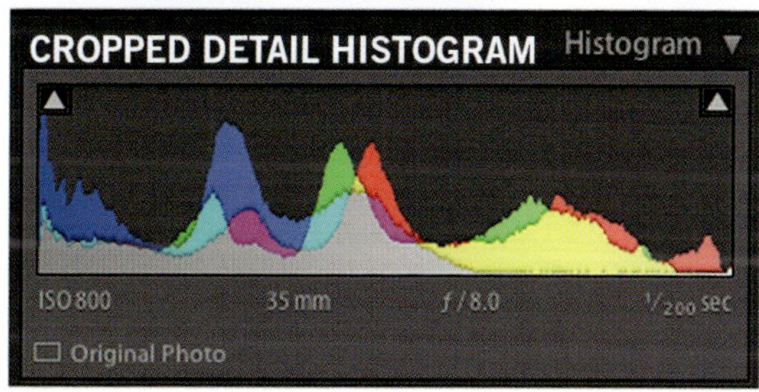


**FIGURE 6.25B** This is a detail shot of **Figure 6.25A.** Compare the histogram for the full image (top) with the histogram of the cropped version (bottom). By restricting the histogram to this area, the vertical axis of the histogram is recalculated. Proportionally, those bright tones now make up a much greater part of the image, so they have more visual weight in the histogram. When you're evaluating histograms, be aware that key data might be "hiding" because of this proportional weighting.
IMAGE © ANDY BATT, *PORTRAIT OF ARCH AND BIRD—DETAIL*, 2009.

few values, relative to the amount of dark tones. If we crop into this image and build a new histogram for the cropped version, suddenly the histogram is full of midtones and highlights. This may seem counterintuitive, since we removed a lot of information, but it makes sense when you understand that *the histogram relates only to the total number of pixels in use.*

This is handy to know, for a few reasons: If a certain area of the image is important to us, we might need to adjust how we view its histogram. If we're tethering the camera, we can quickly crop into the image in Lightroom and see the histogram for the important part of the image. If we're working with just a camera, we can either zoom in or walk in and take a detail photo to see how the important values look. If we don't have that luxury, then we can use our experience to recognize that the full-image histogram might not be giving us the most important information.

It's useful to recognize how the data relates to each of the following image types. Try to make connections between the way an image looks and the way its data looks; it'll help you read a scene and judge exposure.

## Full-Range Images

A full tonal-range image has a histogram with significant data in the shadows, midtones and highlights. There shouldn't be any clipping at either the shadow or highlight side. The shape of the histogram will vary, depending on colors and tonal differences in the subject (**Figure 6.26**).

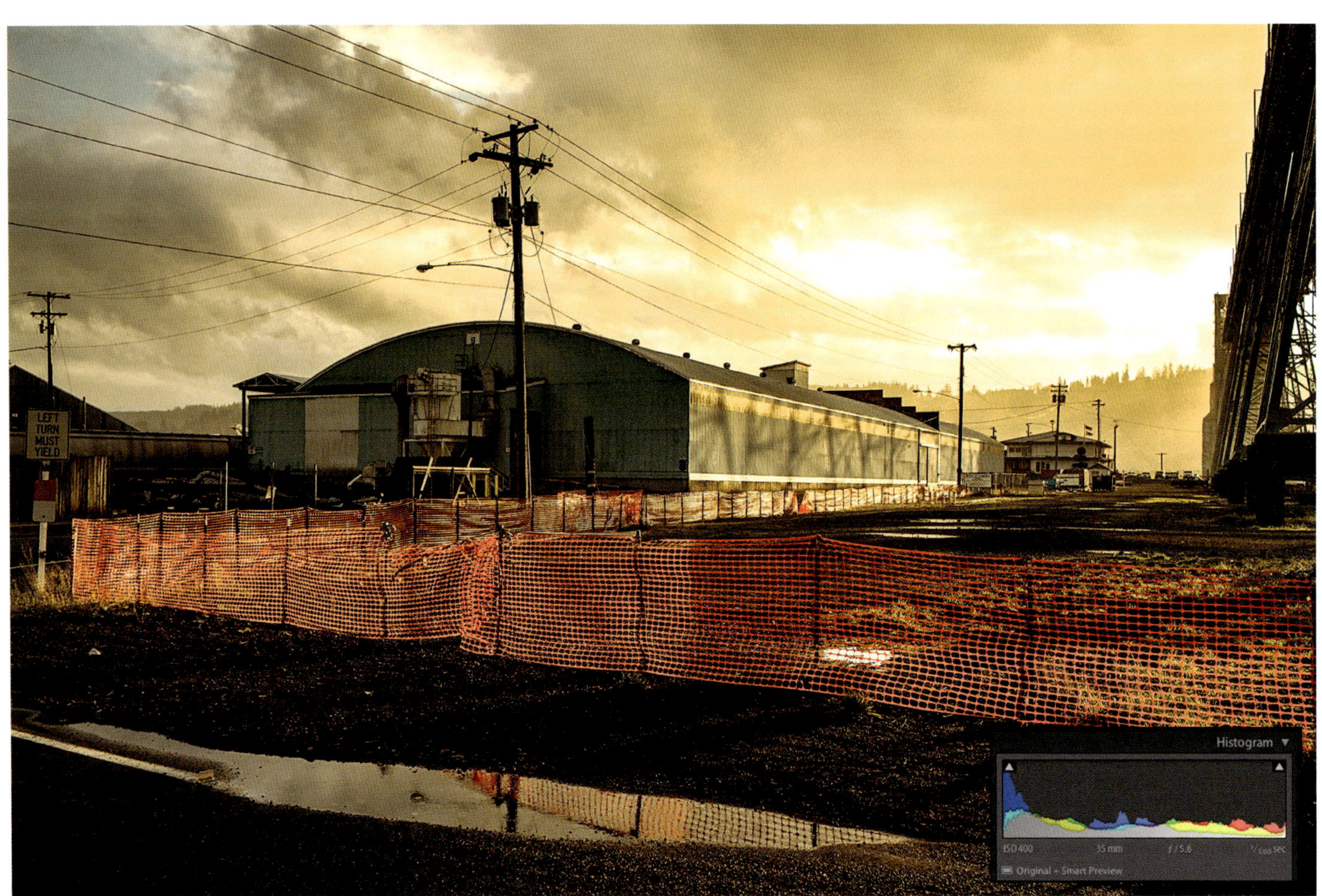


**FIGURE 6.26** Dramatic light and a heavy cloud cover combine to create a beautiful urban landscape. In this full-range image you can find tonal detail in all areas: There are significant shadow tones, highlights, and midtones. (Shot at 1/500th , *f*/5.6 at ISO 400 on a 1Ds MIII with a 35mm/1.4 lens.)
IMAGE © ANDY BATT, *LONGVIEW, WASHINGTON,* 2009.

## High-Key Images

Think of high-key images as having many bright tones. This could be bright colors, but could just as easily be whites and light grays. The majority of the data shows up on the right-hand side of the histogram. Dark tones or shadows might be present, but they'll be in the minority—although they may still be important to the image (**Figure 6.27**).

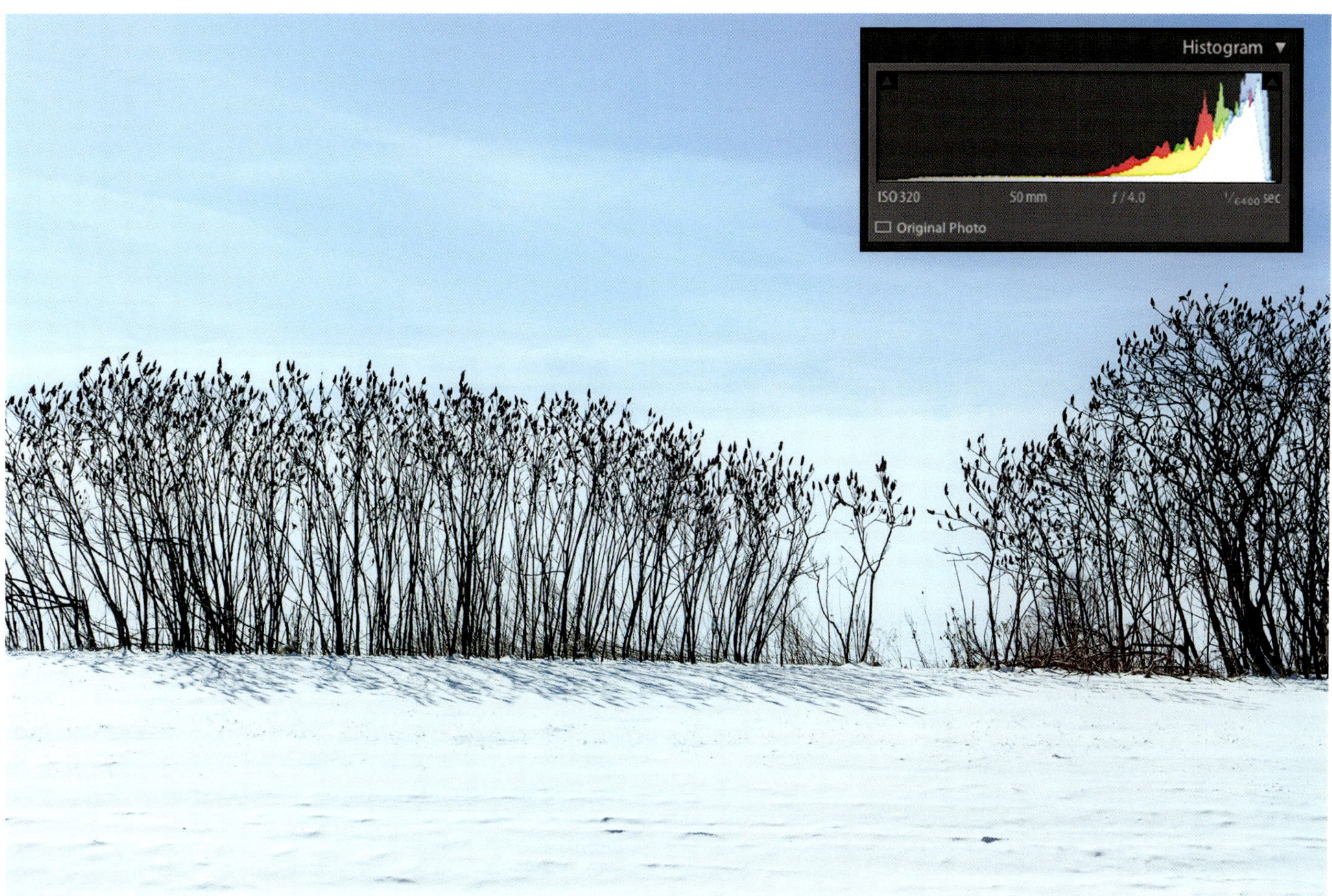


**FIGURE 6.27** Andy shot this high-key image out of a car window while traveling to Rochester, NY. You can see that the majority of the data is in the highlights. There's important data in the darker tones—the bare branches of the road side plantings—but their proportion to the snow and sky are minimal. (Shot at 1/6400th, *f*/4.0 at ISO 320 on a 5D MII with a 50mm/1.4 lens.)
IMAGE © ANDY BATT, *I-95 TREELINE,* 2011.

## Low-Key Images

Low-key images are filled with dark tones. They're not underexposed; the subjects are dark because you consciously make them that way. With these images, the majority of data is on the left side of the histogram. There can be highlights or bright tones as well, and although they usually appear in small data quantities, they can be significant to the image (**Figure 6.28**).

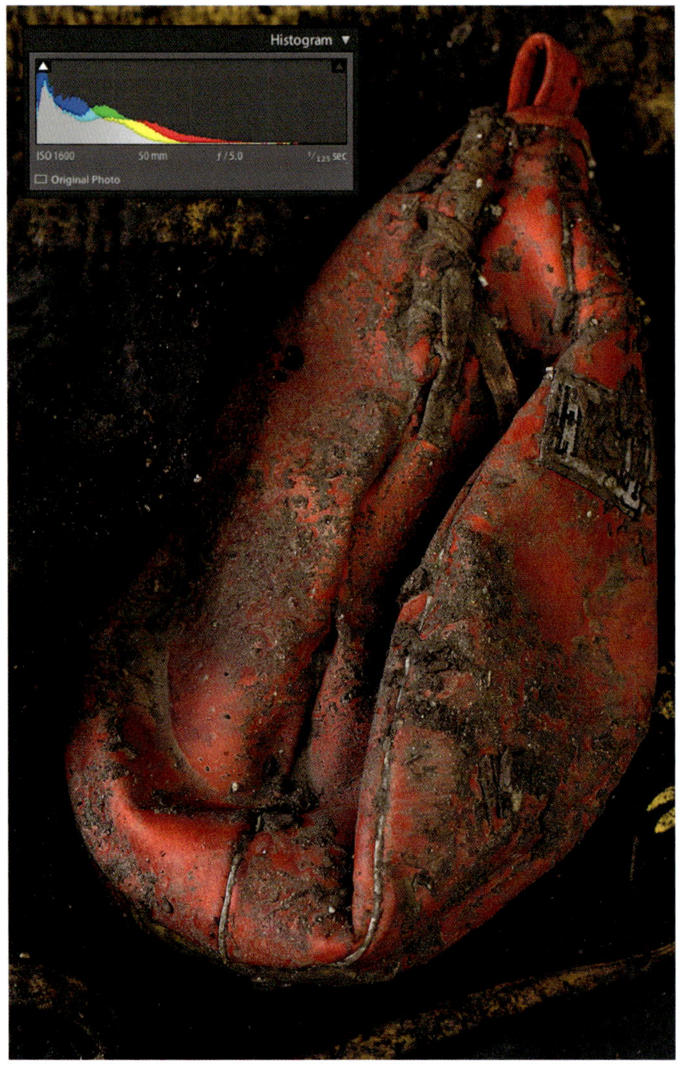


**FIGURE 6.28** Photographer Colin Murphy created this moody low-key photograph of an object found after a flood. There are no bright tones in this image—everything is a mid or darker tone, deliberately. This is a great example of how tonal range can contribute a great deal of emotion to a shot. Since there's a big empty area in the histogram, you might be tempted to think that the image wasn't exposed properly. In this case, however, the photographer's knowledge of data—in relation to his subject—helped him react correctly and create an accurate exposure. Colin used a Nikon D3100, 50mm, 1/125th at *f*/5.0.
IMAGE © COLIN MURPHY, *BOXING GLOVE AFTER THE FLOOD*, 2012.

## High-Contrast Images

High-contrast images show information in the dark and bright tones, but little in the midtone area. Depending on the image—and the photographer's decision of how to expose the scene—there might be deliberate clipping to solid black, solid white or both (**Figure 6.29**).

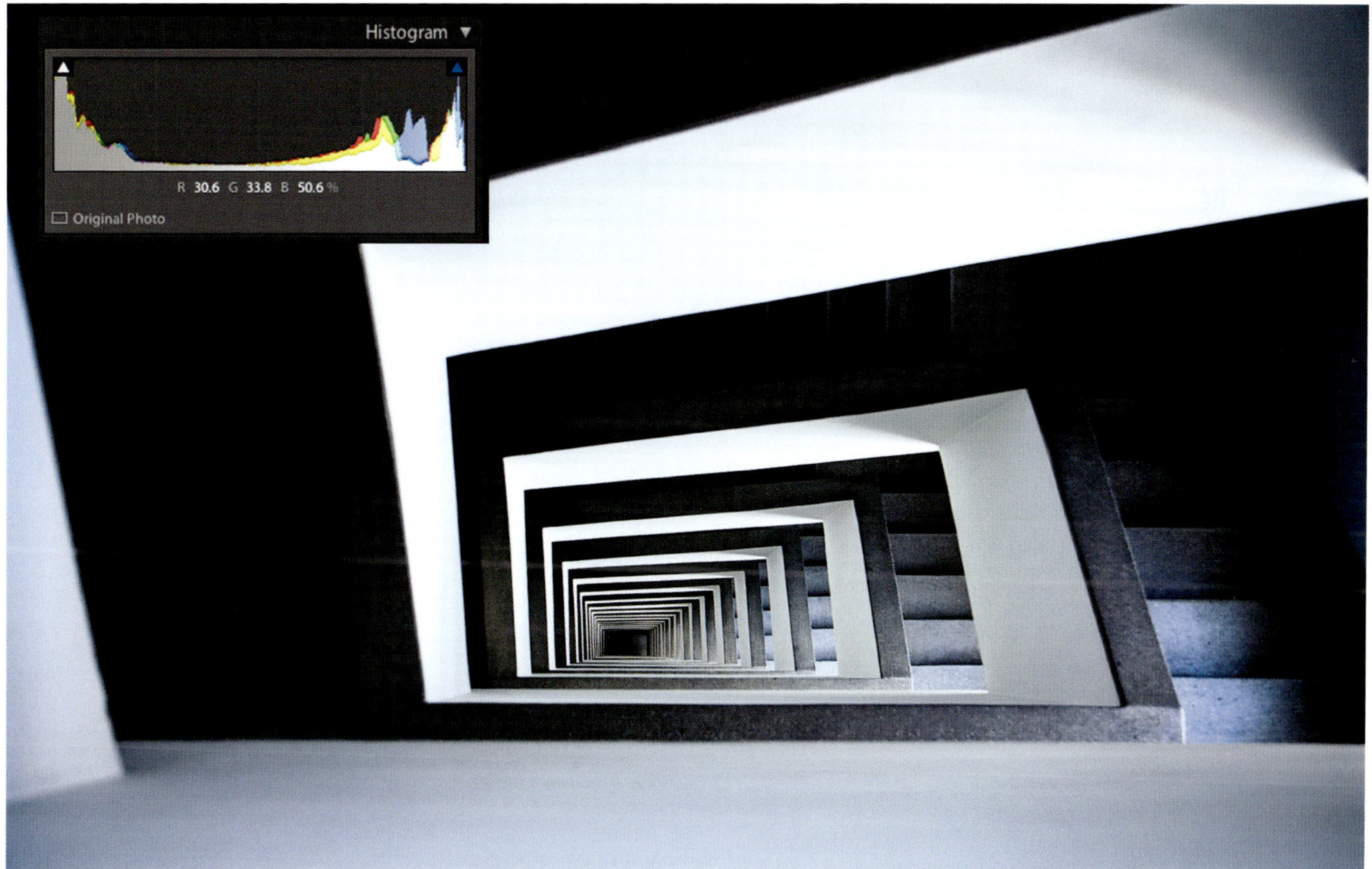


**FIGURE 6.29** This image is a little vertiginous—and the high-contrast striping of the stairwell keeps your eyes spiraling downward. The histogram shows that the two biggest areas of data are in the shadow tones and highlights, with parts of the image clipping at both ends. (Shot at *f*/4.0, 1/40th at ISO 400 on a 1Ds MII with a 16–35mm zoom at 32mm.)

IMAGE © ANDY BATT, *SQUARE SPIRAL—RIO DE JANEIRO,* 2006.

## Low-Contrast Images

Low-contrast images have a very short tonal range that's well within the dynamic range of the camera. Usually the data is centered at around the 50% mark of the histogram and will have few—if any—deep shadows or bright highlights. A portrait or landscape taken on an overcast day (**Figure 6.30**) would fit right into this category and might be a good candidate for the "push to the right and pull to the left" process (see *Push Your Exposures Around* earlier in this chapter).

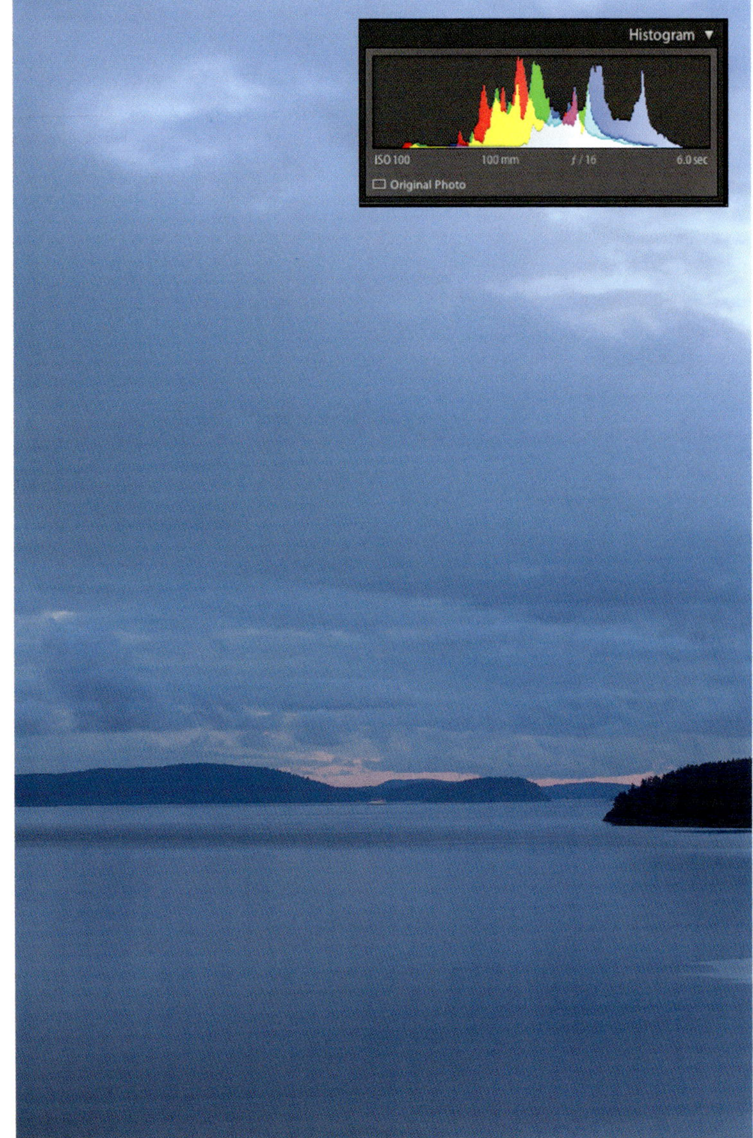


**FIGURE 6.30** This quiet view of the inter-island waterways in the San Juan Islands is a good example of a low-contrast image; the majority of its histogram data is in the midtones. The obvious visual highlights and shadow tones—the pink band at the horizon and the dark island to the right—are barely there in the 3/4 and 2/4 tones. This shot was exposed at *f*/16, 6 sec at ISO 100 on a 1Ds MIII with a 100mm/2.8 lens.
IMAGE © ANDY BATT, *ORCAS ISLAND VIEW*, 2010.

# Camera Neutrality: Picture Styles and Raw Data

One of the ways we interact with our images on a day-to-day basis is by looking at the back of the camera. We know that the camera's LCD screen is not a reliable tool, so we use histograms as a way of understanding our images. The histogram tells us exposure information, dynamic range, where our midtones are and whether we can push and/or pull the image. It's a very useful tool. The problem is that it might not be giving us a truly accurate idea of our images, and in some cases it might be outright wrong.

What you see on the camera's screen is not a raw image—it's a JPEG that's been processed from the raw data. We can't see raw data on the camera's LCD screen, because it hasn't been demosaiced. Your camera uses a recipe to process the raw data (with most DSLR cameras, it uses whichever Picture Style setting is selected[25]) and the in-camera histogram is built from the processed image.

## Picture Styles: Toni Greaves

***Andy Batt:*** **Do you trust the picture on the back of the camera or look at the histograms?**

***Toni Greaves:*** I may look at the picture on the back of the camera to get an initial hint of what's happening with the lighting. I'll do a test shot, but I don't really look at the histograms. Given that I'm usually working in a documentary style though, things are changing constantly, so it doesn't really work to stop and check images. In fact, it's often counter to getting the shots I want. In my particular photographic discipline, it's also quite frowned upon (it's called "chimping" to look at the back of the camera in the midst of shooting). I can see using histograms for other styles of work, though.

***AB:*** **They can be very valuable, and at the same time you shouldn't trust them—at least not all the way. You just need some tricks, and a little training. Do you know what Picture Styles are?**

***TG:*** I don't really use them, but yes.

***AB:*** **The dirty little secret is that whatever Picture Style you have dialed in is what the camera will process the raw data with to create the preview JPEG that's on the back of your screen. The histogram that you're viewing is from that JPEG—from the Picture Style.**

***Candace Dobro:*** **What's the problem with that?**

***AB:*** **If you have an extreme Picture Style—maybe you've played with the Vivid setting and have an image that looks super saturated and super contrasty—you're getting a histogram from that style. That histogram will look different than what you get from the raw file when you process it.**

**To make this [system] more useful, we can choose a Picture Style that makes our camera histogram look more like the raw histogram. I've found that choosing "Neutral" and reducing the contrast and saturation[26] gives me a useful histogram.**

***CD:*** **The histogram that you get on your LCD from the camera won't match your raw file in Lightroom. It's a disconnect—if you set your camera the way Andy is suggesting, then your pictures will look flatter in the LCD screen, but will be a lot closer to the histogram that you get when you're processing. It's very cool.**

**Andy's settings:**

- Start with Neutral as the Picture Style.
- Set the contrast down two marks.
- Set the saturation down two marks.

*My in-camera evaluations improved immediately after I switched to Andy's settings! Seeing the images in their neutral state helped me determine whether I was getting what I wanted out of my exposures.*

*—Candace Dobro*

## TRY THIS AT HOME

### Change the Photo by Not Doing Anything

**For step-by-step instructions, go to: www.focalpress.com/cw/digitalimagingmasters**

The mission for this exercise is to shoot the same scene five times—switching only the Picture Styles (Canon) or Picture Control (Nikon)—and to carefully observe the LCD image and histogram for changes.

**FIGURE 6.32A** In this grid of images, we can compare the raw file version with the JPEGs—which were photographed on the back of the camera to show the range of visual shifts and histogram shifts, both caused by the change in Picture Styles. The camera was set to capture Adobe RGB colors, but the camera itself shows histograms for sRGB. Take a look at the spike of red data in the raw file's histogram and compare it with the others. Notice that the data in the "Landscape" style pushes the red data off the edge and into clipping, where in the raw file it clearly is not.
IMAGE © ANDY BATT, *BACK-OF-THE-CAMERA GRID—VW PETE'S ORANGE WHEEL*, 2013.

**FIGURE 6.32B** In this second grid of images, we can compare the raw file version with the JPEGs as they are in Lightroom, shown as native Adobe RGB files. Compare the "Landscape" style in this grid to the grid in **Figure 6.32A** to see the difference in where the red data sits.
IMAGE © ANDY BATT, *LIGHTROOM GRID—VW PETE'S ORANGE WHEEL*, 2013.

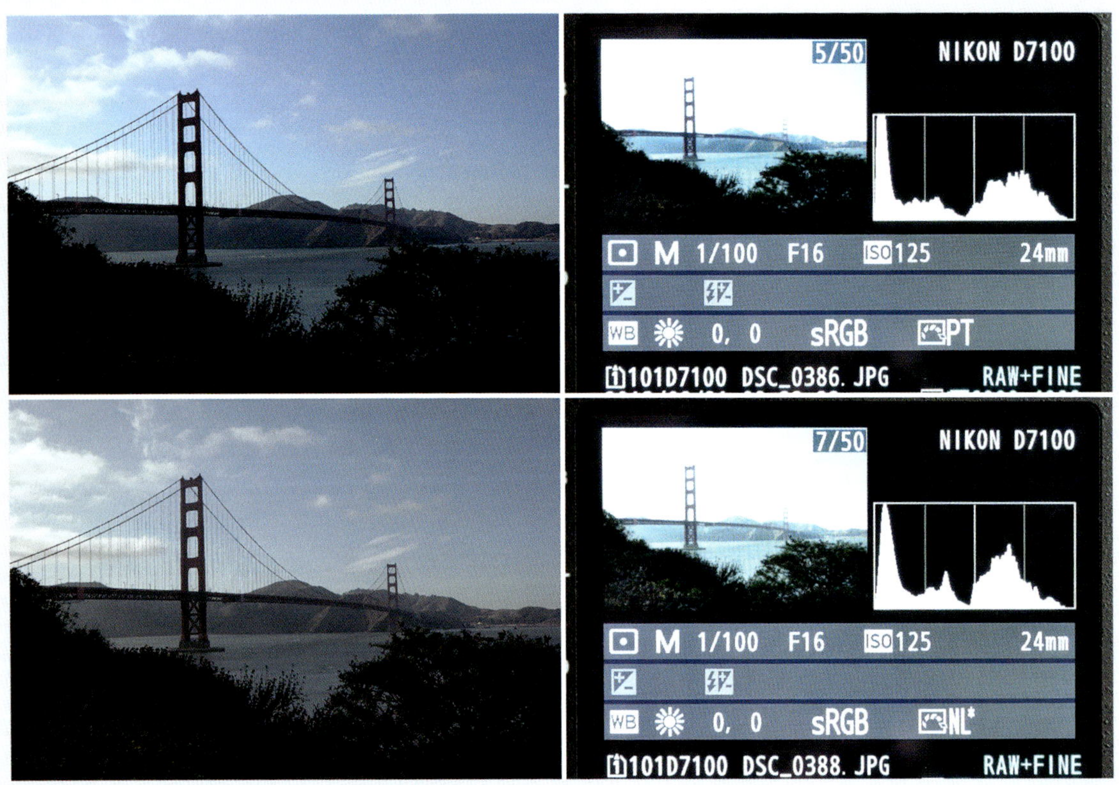


**FIGURE 6.31** By simply changing the Picture Control (Nikon) and nothing else, Erika created two shots with different histograms. The raw data is exactly the same in both of these images.
IMAGE © ERIKA VELASQUEZ, *GOLDEN GATE BRIDGE—PICTURE CONTROL*, 2013.

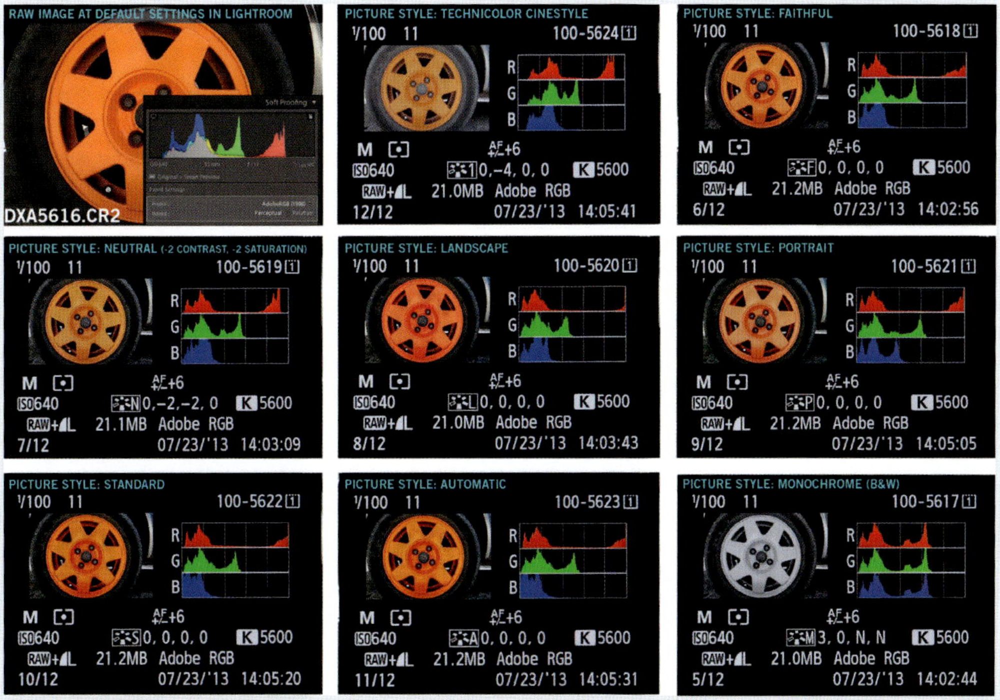

RAW IMAGE AT DEFAULT SETTINGS IN LIGHTROOM

DXA5616.CR2

PICTURE STYLE: TECHNICOLOR CINESTYLE

1/100 11 100-5624

M AF+6

ISO640 1,0,–4, 0, 0 K 5600

RAW+L 21.0MB Adobe RGB

12/12 07/23/'13 14:05:41

PICTURE STYLE: FAITHFUL

1/100 11 100-5618

M AF+6

ISO640 F 0, 0, 0, 0 K 5600

RAW+L 21.2MB Adobe RGB

6/12 07/23/'13 14:02:56

PICTURE STYLE: NEUTRAL (-2 CONTRAST, -2 SATURATION)

1/100 11 100-5619

M AF+6

ISO640 N 0,–2,–2, 0 K 5600

RAW+L 21.1MB Adobe RGB

7/12 07/23/'13 14:03:09

PICTURE STYLE: LANDSCAPE

1/100 11 100-5620

M AF+6

ISO640 L 0, 0, 0, 0 K 5600

RAW+L 21.0MB Adobe RGB

8/12 07/23/'13 14:03:43

PICTURE STYLE: PORTRAIT

1/100 11 100-5621

M AF+6

ISO640 P 0, 0, 0, 0 K 5600

RAW+L 21.2MB Adobe RGB

9/12 07/23/'13 14:05:05

PICTURE STYLE: STANDARD

1/100 11 100-5622

M AF+6

ISO640 S 0, 0, 0, 0 K 5600

RAW+L 21.2MB Adobe RGB

10/12 07/23/'13 14:05:20

PICTURE STYLE: AUTOMATIC

1/100 11 100-5623

M AF+6

ISO640 A 0, 0, 0, 0 K 5600

RAW+L 21.2MB Adobe RGB

11/12 07/23/'13 14:05:31

PICTURE STYLE: MONOCHROME (B&W)

1/100 11 100-5617

M AF+6

ISO640 M 3, 0, N, N K 5600

RAW+L 21.0MB Adobe RGB

5/12 07/23/'13 14:02:44

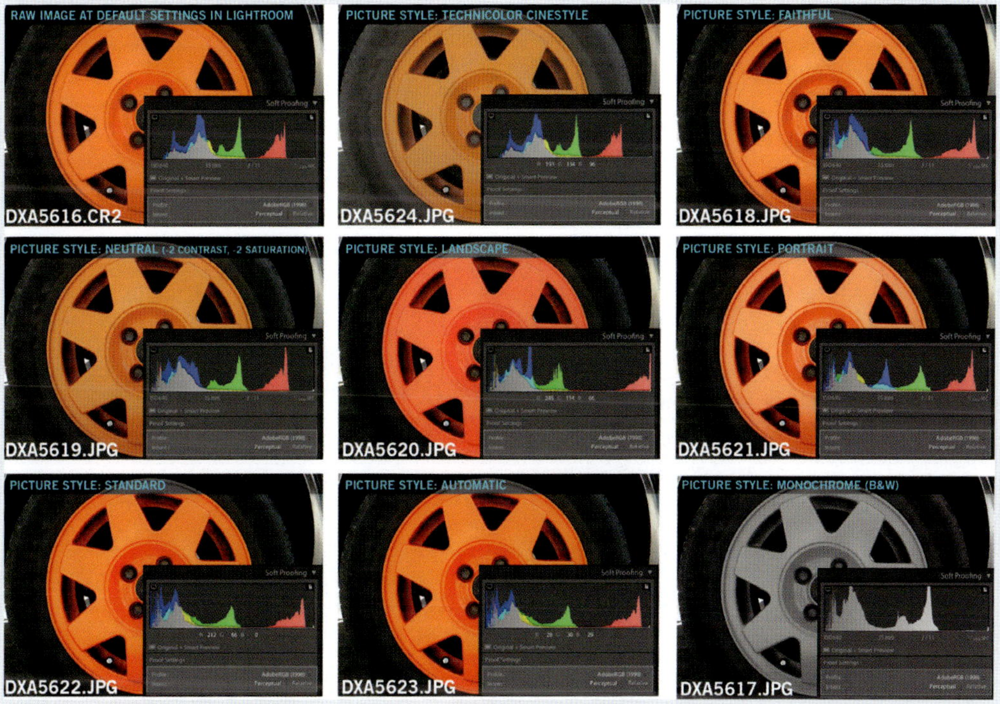

RAW IMAGE AT DEFAULT SETTINGS IN LIGHTROOM

DXA5616.CR2

PICTURE STYLE: TECHNICOLOR CINESTYLE

DXA5624.JPG

PICTURE STYLE: FAITHFUL

DXA5618.JPG

PICTURE STYLE: NEUTRAL (-2 CONTRAST, -2 SATURATION)

DXA5619.JPG

PICTURE STYLE: LANDSCAPE

DXA5620.JPG

PICTURE STYLE: PORTRAIT

DXA5621.JPG

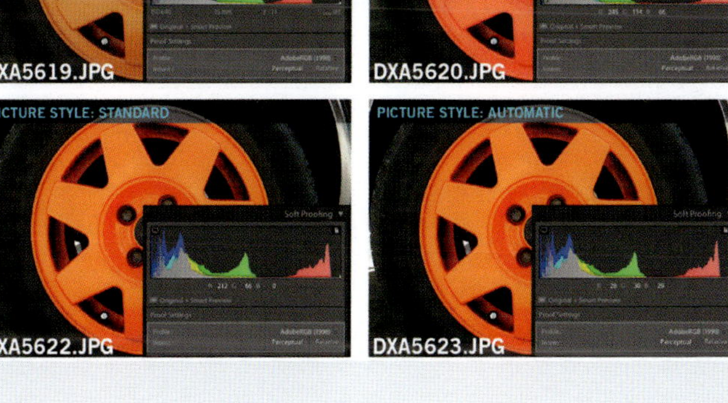


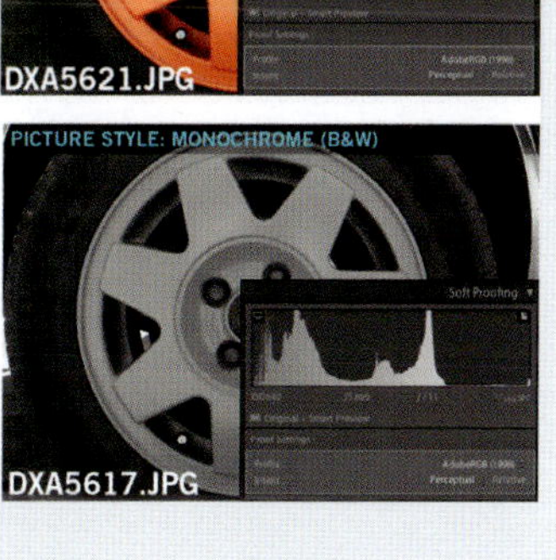

***AB:*** **The caveat to keep in mind is that the way the LCD looks—the color, tonality, etc.—will probably not look like your color-managed, calibrated and profiled monitor. This isn't that big a deal, since you aren't making critical color decisions on the back of your camera. It's just good to know so you don't go chasing your tail, trying to make them match.**

***TG:*** This answers my frustration with my images in Lightroom—I would feel like I was shooting a certain way, but then I'd get the images into Lightroom and think, "Huh?". So when you have the Picture Style at its default or any other setting, what the camera is actually shooting is the same . . . it's just showing a different-looking image on the back of the camera?

***AB:*** **Right! The *raw file* is the same, no matter what Picture Style you choose.**

## sRGB and Adobe98: JPEGs and the Raw File

There's one more factor at work in this scenario, and that's color space. Most cameras allow you to choose an output color space of either sRGB or Adobe98; this has no effect on raw files, but it does change the JPEGs the camera creates. Adobe98 is a bigger color space, and the histograms from an image in that color space vs. sRGB will be different. It's important to know that the image on your camera's LCD is being displayed in sRGB and that the histogram you see on your camera is also an sRGB histogram—even if you've set Adobe98 as the output space.

Take a look at **Figure 6.32C**, where we compare histograms from the same JPEG image: At the top is the in-camera histogram, in the middle is the JPEG opened up in its native Adobe98 RGB space and at the bottom is the image after being converted to sRGB. There's a striking similarity between the camera's histogram and the converted one.

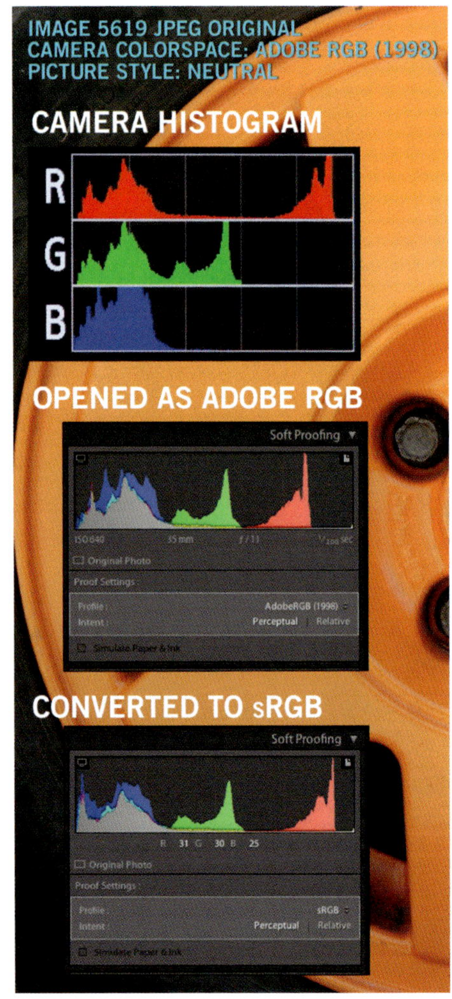


**FIGURE 6.32C** All of these are histograms of the JPEG original, shot with the "Neutral" Picture Style. From top to bottom we have the camera's histogram, the native Adobe RGB (1998) JPEG, and that same JPEG converted to sRGB. The camera's LCD screen is an sRGB device, and the histogram of the preview image that we see on the camera is being shown to us in sRGB. For viewing purposes, sRGB is fine, the problem lies with the histogram. Since we are getting sRGB histogram data, which is a much smaller color space (less possible color data), we aren't getting an accurate representation of the raw data. If we are making a decision about exposure, it's important to get as accurate an idea about our data as possible.
IMAGE © ANDY BATT, *SRGB VS. ADOBE98—VW PETE'S ORANGE WHEEL*, 2013.

### Why Does This Matter?

It matters because the camera's LCD seems to indicate that the red channel is pushed much further over to the right. There's also a very fine line of red data on the right-hand side that seems to be clipped.

Now compare the grids in **Figures 6.32A and 6.32B**: For the same original Adobe98 RGB JPEG images, you get two different sets of histograms. When we compare everything to the raw file version at its default setting in Lightroom, we see two important things:

1. The histogram in the raw file is most similar to the Neutral image's Adobe98 histogram.
2. The histogram for the same image, viewed on the back of the camera (**Figure 6.32A**), moves the red channel data significantly to the right.

Based on the sRGB data, you might make a different decision about your exposure settings. For a more extreme example, compare the Landscape Picture Style—in both the Adobe98 RGB (**Figure 6.32B**) and the sRGB versions (**Figure 6.32A**): The red data is clipped—and the clipping occurs because of the way the camera processes the raw data, not because the raw data is clipping.

### The Takeaway

When we choose the best possible Picture Style, we enable the camera's histogram to give us the best possible data to work with—but even then, we need to know that there's a significant difference between what we see on the camera's LCD and what we get from the raw file.

## Correcting Exposures

We spend lots of time and effort trying to capture good—if not great—exposures in-camera. The reality is that we don't always get it right, so we rely on a few, key raw-processing tools to get us through the occasional bump in the road.

### To Capture Good Exposures In-Camera

1. **Avoid problems**: Check your settings and light levels with paranoid levels of attention. The easiest fix—by far—is to train yourself not to have the problem in the first place.
2. **Have insurance**: Shooting raw files at the lowest ISO possible gives us plenty of flexibility in post.
3. **Know your tools**: Lightroom, Photo Ninja, Capture 1, Aperture (and many others) all have great built-in exposure tools. Get familiar with them *before* you have a problem.

### Basic Processing Tools to Fix Bumps in the Road

**Exposure Slider**: Usually expressed in "stops," this is roughly equivalent to a stop of exposure in-camera. It's really useful at times, e.g., when you meter at ISO 400, but expose at ISO 100. Depending on the kind of image you capture and how far you need to push or pull it, you can usually work a range of +/–2 stops to rescue your image. Primarily, this tool tweaks your midtones, but it also affects the white and black points.

**Highlight Recovery**: This is a separate tool that's built to go after those difficult, blown-out highlights. It isolates the highlight data so you can work on it without greatly affecting the rest of the exposure.

**Shadow or Fill Light**: This tool is built to open up the crushed blacks. If you have decent data in that area, you can make quite a few adjustments to reduce contrast and stretch your dynamic range. If you have bad data, though, all you'll end up doing is showing off the noise in your image.

**White Point**: With this tool, you can adjust the area where the brightest data clips to pure white. The White Point tool also works in combination with the Highlight Recovery tool.

**Black Point**: This tool allows you to adjust your images in the areas where the darkest data clips to pure black. It also works in combination with the Shadow tool.

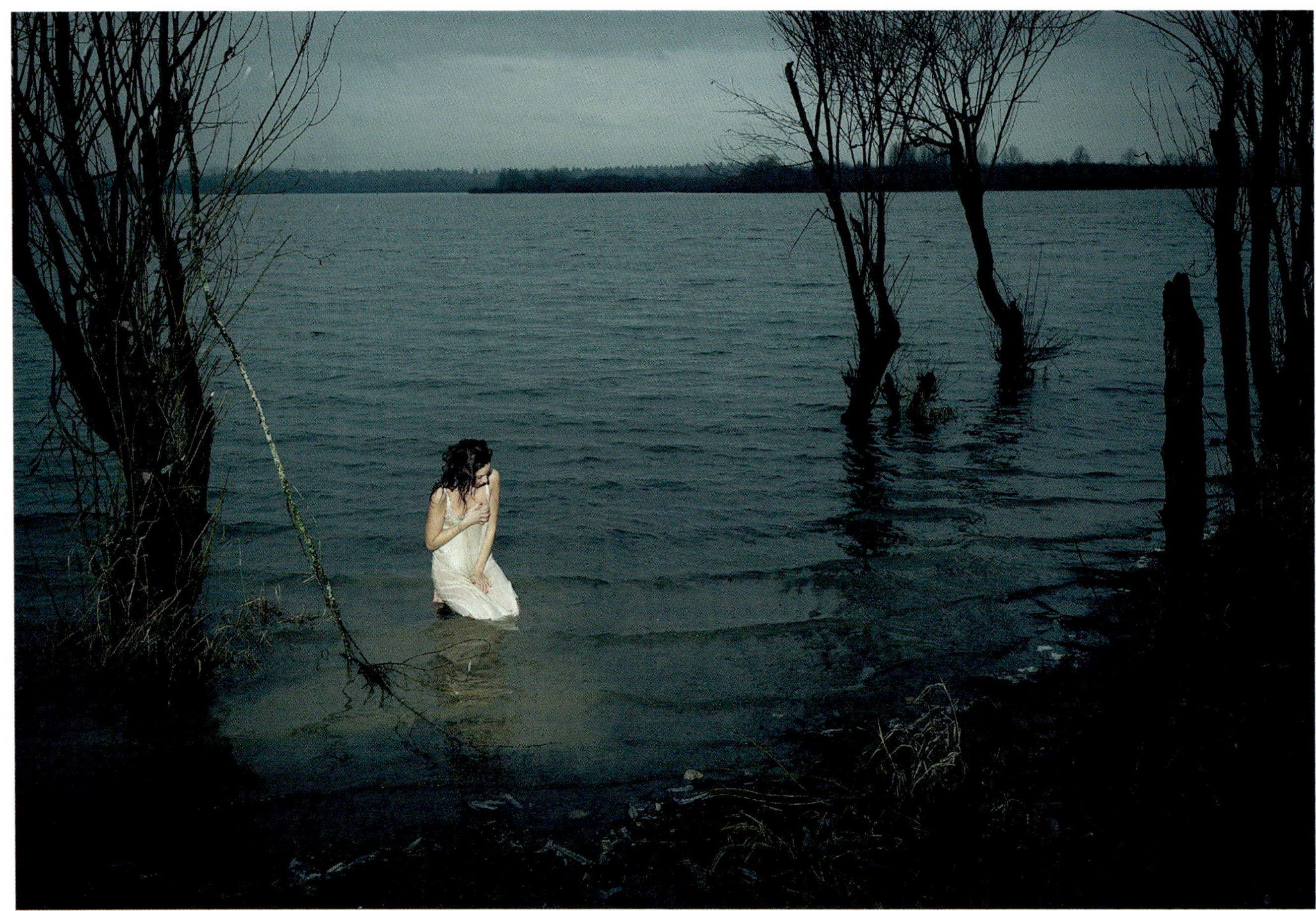

**FIGURE 6.33** This image was shot on a cold, gray winter day. Andy knew there was extremely limited time to create the story, since he wanted to keep his heroine from freezing to death.
IMAGE © ANDY BATT, *LAKE GIRL*, 2009.

## Exposure in the End

We know that you probably won't use a gray card every time you shoot—it's not like you can hand a football player a gray card and ask him to wait while you do a quick spot meter. We do want to encourage you to use *some* tools, so you can figure out how to expose a complex scene without going into bracket-flail mode. We love gray cards, because they provide a known value—when used with your light meter and to give you a reference subject for test shots. Grabbing a test shot with a gray card enables you to check out your exposure values in Lightroom, which comes in handy when you're doing a test shoot in preparation for an important gig.

With any metering technique or camera mode, your goal is to establish a good base exposure; from there it's up to you to decide how to expose a scene. You can start exploring ways to interpret exposure—how to measure and see the individual sources of light; how to decide what the key detail and key light are and how to make creative decisions in interpreting your scene. With practice, you'll gain a working knowledge of how exposure, histograms and camera settings are interrelated. You'll also understand the connection between your scene, exposure, data and the final image. All of these things are key to informing your photography. Remember, you—not the meter, gray card or camera—are the photographer.

***Andy:*** The key light on *Lake Girl* (**Figure 6.33**) was created with a single strobe head. I wanted her exposure to be roughly a stop over the ambient light so the world around her would be dark. We were lighting pale skin and a pale dress, and I wanted a bright exposure on her, but needed to be careful with clipping since we weren't going to get many shots with her in the water. By carefully metering the strobe and ambient light values, I set the final exposure before she ever got into the water.

## EXPLORATIONS

### Connect the Skin Tones to the Midtones

Each person you photograph has his or her own unique skin tone. In an ideal situation, you'd search out a range of skin tones and test them all in the same light at the same time. For now, though, we'll use one person's skintone to help you build a predictable relationship between your camera, a gray card, midtones and skintones.

**Gear**: A camera, a tripod and a gray card
**Subject**: At least one good friend who's willing to let you get up close
**Lens**: You'll need to fill up the frame with your subject's face. You can choose either a longer lens and photograph from farther away, or a shorter lens and photograph very close to your subject. Either way, you want to create a composition that is mostly face, with a simple background.
**Light**: Soft, indirect, overcast, open shade. For this Exploration, you want even light with minimal shadows and contrast.

#### Set Up and Shoot

Put your friend on a stool, apple box or any other place where she or he can sit comfortably. Orient the subject so the face is evenly lit by the indirect light. Grab your handheld incident meter, point it straight back at the camera and take a reading. If you're using an in-camera meter, then have your subject hold the gray card right in front of his or her face. Tip up the card slightly to make sure you're getting good light on it. Take an in-camera spot meter reading off the card. In your notebook, write down this exposure.

You want to begin with an exposure that has room to go four stops above and below, so try starting with a shutter speed of 1/250th. The light should remain consistent throughout the whole series; make sure it doesn't change while you shoot.

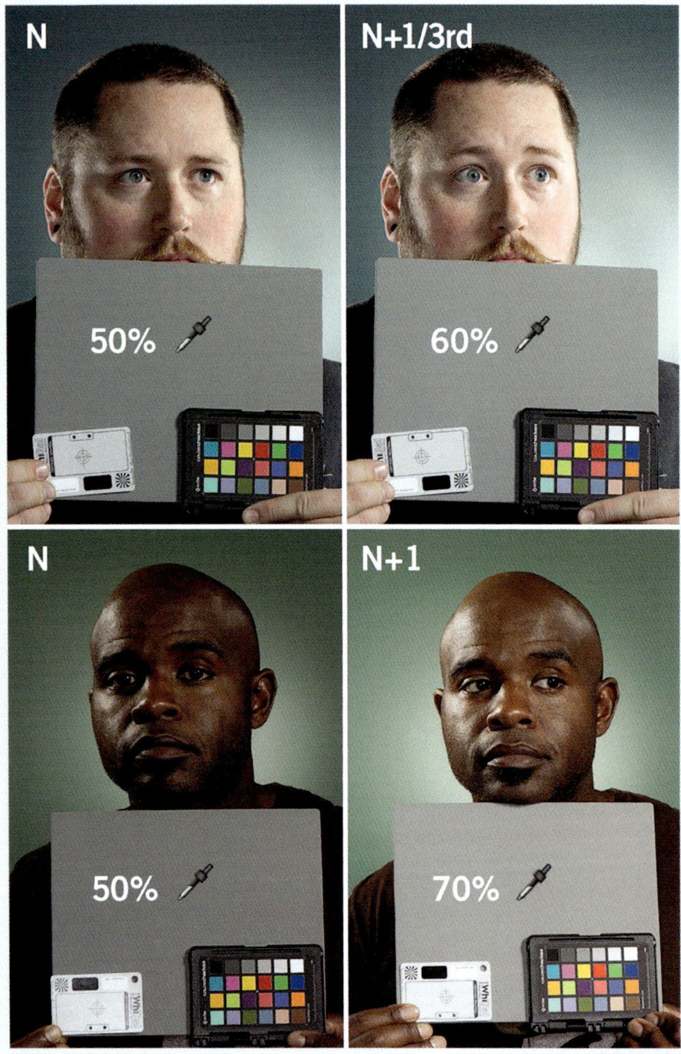


**FIGURE 6.34** By using your gray card or light meter, you can establish a base exposure, but you may need to adjust your final exposure to get good final results. With Galvin (top) and Chris (bottom) we had two different skin tones to test. The images on the left were shot at the metered normal exposure and give us approximately a 50% value in Lightroom from the gray card. For the top image, a +1/3 stop increase in exposure created good skin tones. In the bottom image, a +1 stop increase in exposure was needed to get a good skin tone.
IMAGE © ANDY BATT, *SKINTONE TEST*, 2013.

For each exposure, take a photo of your friend with and without the gray card.

### Ingest and Evaluate

Ingest all your images into Lightroom (or whatever you use) and pair them up so that you can check out the gray card and the matching skin tone. Find the images you took at the metered exposure (the one you wrote down) and look at their numeric values with the Eyedropper/Spot Meter tool. If you're in Lightroom, you should be getting about a 50% value (50R, 50G, 50B)[27] when you click and neutral balance on the gray card.[28] If you're not roughly there, then double-check your notes, exposures and the position of the gray card (to make sure it's not pointed incorrectly). Also check the ambient light, since any change in the ambient exposure could also account for the difference.

When you look at the portrait you took at the metered value, does it look "real" and "correct" to you?[29] This will be a judgement call on your part. If the portrait doesn't look right, then go shopping through the brighter and darker images until you find the one you consider "correct." Make note of the exposure and how it compares to the metered exposure. Andy finds that with his camera, he needs to dial in at +2/3 over meter (as in: we want ⅔ more light) to achieve good skin tones.

### The Takeaway

You now have a solid reference for exposing skin tones the way you like them. The type and quality of the skin and the direction of the light all come into play. So does the camera/lens combination you're using. Try repeating this exercise with different people, different lighting scenarios and/or different cameras and lenses to find out if you can discover a constant adjustment you'd like to make.

## Notes

1 "Day for night" is a concept from filmmaking for those times when you need to make it look like nighttime, but can only shoot during the day. Besides reducing the exposure, there are many other elements to consider if you want to fool your viewer.

2 Drag the shutter = slow the shutter speed.

3 © The Hershey Company.

4 See *Push Your Exposures Around* later in this chapter for more information.

5 Light Valve Technology—a film recorder for creating film outputs from digital files.

6 Except when it's not. Some meter manufacturers use a slightly different percentage than 18% to calibrate their meters. They do this with the hope of hedging the meter's measurements to make sure you get a good exposure, even if it's not a precisely accurate one.

7 The R27 is different than a white balance card. Various white balance cards use different gray tones and are usually lighter than the Kodak R27. We'll discuss this more in the next chapter.

8 Lindcraft pouch, Filmtools, Inc., http://www.filmtools.com/catalogsearch/result/?q=lindcraft+pouch.

9 MacBeth ColorChecker®, X-Rite, Inc., http://xritephoto.com/ph_product_overview.aspx?ID=1192.

10 WhiBal® White Balance Reference, Michael Tapes Design, http://michaeltapesdesign.com/whibal.html.

11 Nuclear Cowboyz, www.nuclearcowboyz.com.

12 Roughly, because depending on the size of the imaginary room, the meter readings may be influenced by the opposite walls. A white wall behind the camera will reflect some light and a black wall behind the camera will absorb some light.

13 See, for example, David R. Spielman, "The ANSI PH3.49–1971 Specification and the Myth of the 18% Light Meter Calibration," http://www.dspielman.com/Gray_Card/ANSI_PH3_49_1971.PDF, 2001; Richard Hess, "Why the 18% Gray Card is a problem," http://www.richardhess.com/photo/18no.htm, 1998; and Thomas Hogan, "Meters Don't See 18% Gray," http://www.bythom.com/graycards.htm, 2003.

14 Sekonic, www.sekonic.com.

15 Graphiclite®, GTI Graphic Technology, Inc., www.gtilite.com.

16 This quote is from the exposure instructions that are packaged with the Kodak R27 Gray Card.

17 Another way of putting this is to "expose to the right," which also works—but we prefer the push-pull notion, since it's a two-part process.

18 The camera still creates a JPEG on the fly, even if you're shooting Raw Only. For more info, see *Camera Neutrality: Picture Styles and Raw Data* later in this chapter.

19 You could add fake tone by using a masked Levels adjustment to force the specular highlight to a very light gray—a value of 242 instead of 255, for example. You could also hire a retoucher to help.

20 This exercise is based on an excellent article, "How to determine the best exposure for a specific photograph with film and digital capture," written by Alain Briot for *The Luminous Landscape*, http://www.luminous-landscape.com/columns/determining-exposure.shtml, 2004.

21 127 Productions, Inc. is a consulting company that creates color management and workflow solutions for the professional photography and graphics industries, www.127productions.com.

22 This software spot meter works likes a real spot meter in that you're getting a point reading of a specific place in the image. Different raw processors have different tools and names for this, e.g., in Lightroom, the WB Eyedropper doubles as a spot meter tool, since it gives you numeric data readouts for whatever spot you're hovering over.

23 Some applications approach this differently.

24 Raw values come from the internal working color space of the raw processing engine of the application. Lightroom, for example, uses a modified version of ProPhoto RGB.

25 Even if your camera doesn't have a "Picture Styles"-type menu, it's still processing out the raw data on the fly, and using some recipe when it displays an image on screen.

26 That's two clicks each for Canon.

27 For other applications, the numbers will be different, since they depend on the working space. The spike should still show up at about the halfway mark in the histogram. If you're having trouble isolating the histogram data, you can crop the image temporarily to include just the gray card. That should remove all the other tones.

28 You can do this because that Kodak R27 is a special kind of gray card. Check out *Chapter 7* for more information.

29 You should be using a good quality monitor to judge this. Laptop monitors aren't up to the task of high quality assessments. Any monitor should be calibrated and profiled, and any "Auto Brightness" settings should be shut off. If you don't have a good setup, then your judgements for tests like this can be based on the wrong information.

# YOUR COLOR IN CONTROL

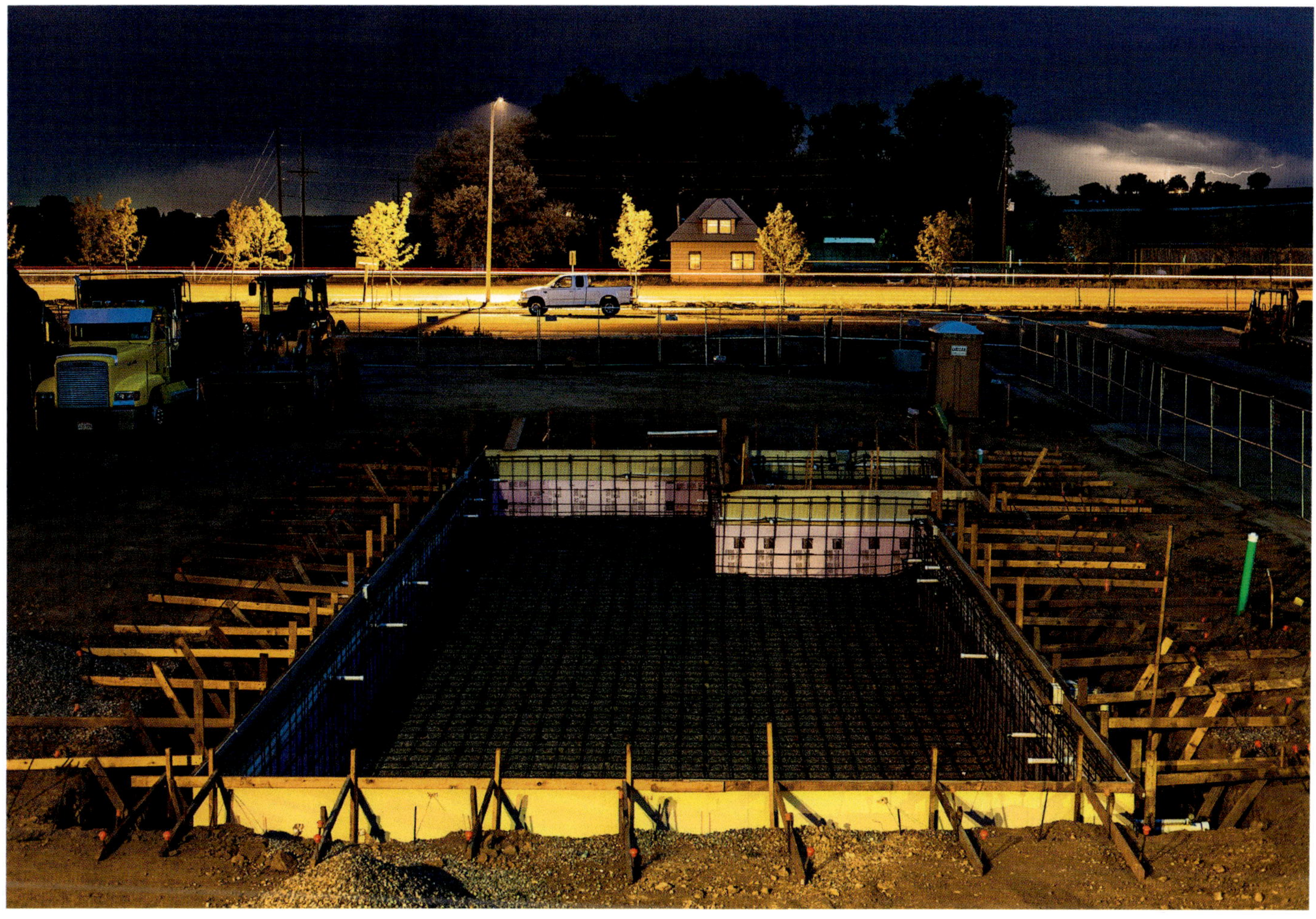

**FIGURE 7.1** Nighttime shows a whole range of colors that our eyes filter out, from the yellow–orange of sodium vapor streetlights to the purple blacks of storm clouds. IMAGE © ANDY BATT, *NIGHTTIME IN COLORADO,* 2006.

## Color Is a Choice

Whether you decide to control it or let it control you, color has a great influence on your work. In the foreword to one of Andy's favorite books about color, *If It's Purple, Someone's Gonna Die,*[1] the author Patti Bellantoni says, "It's a sneaky business, this thing called color. It's right there in front of you, but more times than not you don't notice what it's doing." Color is a big part of the photographic language, and every time you capture an image, you make decisions about it that will play directly to your viewers' emotions and instincts.

Some photographers strive towards neutrality and prefer to reproduce color so that the light source they're photographing is precisely matched to the color temperature and color balance of their camera. Journalistic photographers might decide to deliver final images with neutral color or to reproduce a scene the way they remember it. For photographic illustrators, color has a lot to do with the stories they want to tell and the experiences they want their viewers to have.

Colors have coded meanings: We accept the notion that moonlight is blue, even though it's not. Red can be deliberately added to a photograph to provoke a strong or aggressive response. You can subtly alter the color temperature of an image by either cooling or warming it—or you can make more dramatic adjustments to create unreal images. Any time you manipulate color, you influence the story you tell, whether your intent is to preserve a faithful rendition of a scene or create an intensely artificial image.

This idea applies to black-and-white imagery, as well. When you decide to remove color, you're deliberately choosing to tell your story with tone and contrast instead. Further, if you decide to crush the blacks and blow out the whites, you'll communicate a very different meaning than if you had used a color version of the image.

There's a great definition of color in the classic book, *Real World Color Management* (Fraser, Murphy & Bunting, 2005: 5):

> *Color is an event that occurs among three participants: a light source, an object and an observer. The color event is a sensation evoked in the observer by the wavelengths of light produced by the light source and modified by the object. If any of these three things changes, the color event is different—in plain English, we see a different color.*

## Your Camera Has No Color

To understand color, you need to understand that raw files aren't actually in color. They're the result of photons being passed through a colored filter and recorded by your sensor, and a raw image isn't really an image until you process it and apply color. Your camera doesn't know what the colors in the scene look like. If you process a raw file in Photo Ninja, Aperture, Lightroom and Capture One, you'll get four different interpretations of the colors in the image. The four interpretations might get close, but each application uses its own methodology to change the 0s and 1s into color information, so they won't be the same.

## Pleasing or Accurate?

Wrap your brain around this: *Pleasing color* is not always accurate color. An image that may be emotionally satisfying to you probably doesn't contain the most accurate color rendition of the subjects in your image. Instead, it has a tone or palette that feels right; it represents the mood or feeling you remember or want it to have (**Figure 7.2**). We can make color-accurate images, but depending on your goal, accuracy might not be your first choice.

Color expert Tom Ashe writes:[2]

> *In different types and applications of photography we want to render our images in various ways, weighing different priorities. In some cases, like fine art reproduction, catalog photography and product photography, we want to render our images to have accurate color—meaning colors that match the original scene or objects in the scene as closely as possible. In other types of photography, like portraiture, landscapes and Instagram images, we don't necessarily hold as much importance to the absolute accuracy of colors. In these cases we are more concerned with rendering our images to have aesthetically pleasing colors that we and our viewers will respond well to.*

Out in the real world, "perfect" light rarely happens, and that's a good thing. We want our world to be made up of many different colors of light; it makes things interesting. The time of day (morning, noon, afternoon), the sources (moonlight, tungsten bulbs, fluorescent tubes), the weather (overcast or blue sky), the natural modifiers (amber waves of grain, light filtered through green leaves)—and even the

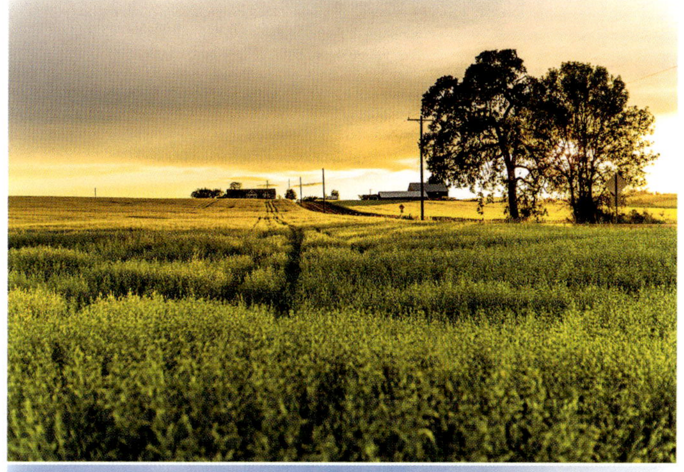

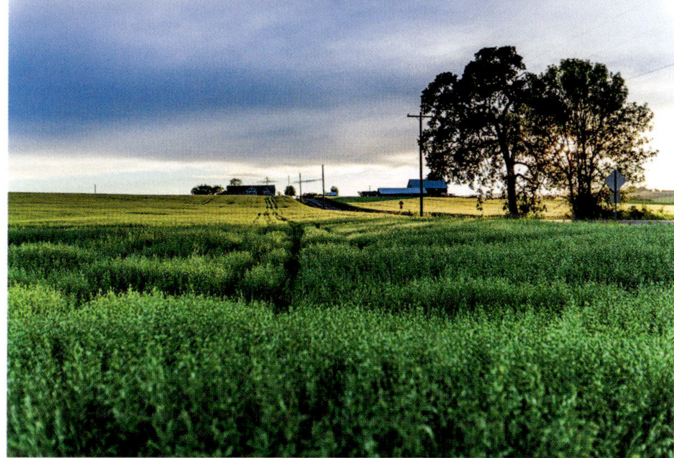

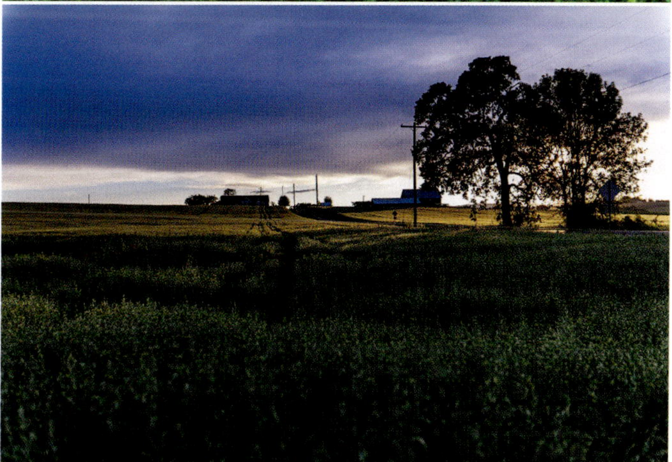

latitude you're in—all create exciting palettes of color. The color qualities we often like most are a result of all these variations. In our work to create aesthetically pleasing images, we seek to heighten and reinforce these differences.

*Accurate color* is absolutely neutral; it's measured for accuracy and nothing is interpreted. When might we want to use it? Accurate color is great for precise catalog photography, art reproduction and forensic documentation. These are circumstances when you want the information to be as close to perfect as it can get.

Most of our work, and likely, most of your work as well, will fall between these two ideas. To move along this continuum, you don't need the advice of a celestial voice beaming down at you; you just need to know what your goals are and what kind of story you want to tell.

## Processing Raw Color: Jim Christian

***Andy Batt:*** **One of the biggest benefits of capturing raw files is the ability to adjust their color in post-production. Since the camera doesn't really know what the scene is supposed to look like (or how you want it to look), how does a raw processor handle this process?**

***Jim Christian:*** The human visual system includes a mechanism called "color constancy" that enables us to see a white object as white, even when it's illuminated with a significant colorcast. Camera sensors, however, don't have this mechanism, so they will record white as some other color when the light source isn't neutral. (For instance, tungsten light has a red cast and deep shade has a blue cast.) Of course, other colors are also affected, but it is more obvious for whites and grays. In addition, the green channel of a camera sensor is usually more sensitive than the red and blue channels, so even in a neutrally lit scene, a white object will be recorded with unbalanced red, green and blue values. The white balance operation in raw conversion multiplies the individual red, green and blue channels by scaling factors to remove the colorcast.

**FIGURE 7.2** Is this an early morning, late afternoon or mid–day scene? Andy used color as a powerful tool to interpret the landscape three different ways.
IMAGE © ANDY BATT, *OREGON FARM FIELD,* 2005.

Even after white balancing, the colors in a raw image will look "off," unless we apply additional color correction. This is because the spectral response of a camera sensor is different from the response of the human visual system, so the camera "sees" colors and color relationships that are skewed and distorted, as compared to the perception of a human observer. The color correction step applies a mathematical transform to the pixel values to bring the color relationships into correspondence with human perception.

Together, white balancing and color correction yield "accurate" color in a clinical colorimetric sense; however, the real significance of corrected color is that it is canonical—in a known, standardized state—so subsequent processing can yield consistent, predictable results.

***AB:* We can process a file to get the best, most accurate image possible—but that's not always the goal, right?**

***JC:*** You're talking about *accurate versus pleasing color*. While many photographers will claim they desire accurate color, in truth they want pleasing color. They want the image to look the way they perceived it, which is often different from the mathematically "accurate" colors. Colorimetrically accurate images usually look dull or "flat." Partly, this is because images are often viewed under reduced brightness levels as compared to the original scene, and so the human visual system perceives saturation differently as a result. In addition, subjective factors (aesthetics, culture) can bias the perception of color. Generally, people want to see healthy skin tones, vibrant foliage, deep skies and rich earth tones—more than is mathematically prescribed by accurate color correction.

***AB:* And if we want to push the blue of a sky deeper or make the green trees less intense, how is that handled?**

***JC:*** I call that "color enhancement," which I distinguish from "color correction," because it has a different objective: to take the corrected colors and make them look more pleasing. So, whereas color correction is mostly objective, color enhancement is subjective. It also tends to involve more interaction from the user. Under the hood, the technology is similar to color correction—an assortment of mathematical transforms and/or lookup tables—though there can be other processes at work to handle selective adjustments.

## Taking Color's Temperature

You work with color temperature every time you pick up your camera; you even interact with it when you leave your camera on AWB. By understanding the warm-to-cool (yellow-to-blue) and green-to-magenta scales, you can control them—and your images' color.

### Lord Kelvin

It's useful to understand how your camera and raw-processing software handle this information, which leads us to Lord Kelvin and his scale. William Thomson, Baron Kelvin of Largs[3], was a scientific pioneer in the fields of physics, natural philosophy, electromagnetism, and—most important for us—thermodynamics. Lord Kelvin developed the idea of an absolute zero, the temperature where all activity stops, even down to the atomic level. With this benchmark, it's possible to plot the temperature of many things, including light.

In theory, if you had a perfect black-body radiator (imagine a square of absolute darkness that would absorb any heat you threw at it with 100% efficiency) and heated it up in a super-oven capable of reaching any temperature you wanted, you could heat it to 2500K (Kelvin), and it would glow just like a household tungsten light. If you heated it to 5500K, it would be the same color as an idealized sunny day. In this way, you could theoretically apply the right amount of heat to conjure any color in the visible spectrum. For photography, we work with a range from roughly 1700K (the color temperature of warm, reddish flames) to +20,000K (the color temperature of an intensely blue sky).

# The Standards: 3200K and 5500K

We photographers orient ourselves to two specific standards: 3200K and 5500K. Although some of this stems from the tradition of film photography,[4] it's still relevant today. Professional tungsten lights[5] have a bulb inside them that contains a heavy-duty filament made of tungsten wire. When current is passed through that wire, it heats up to 3200K and emits a powerful beam of full-spectrum light. This is a standard used by almost every manufacturer of movie and photography lighting.

In contrast, household light bulbs are usually warmer and can be from 2000K to 3000K. We use 5500K as our standard for daylight, but that's really an approximation. Real daylight is tricky, since it depends on local atmospheric conditions (pollution, clouds, etc.), the position of the sun with the earth (is it overhead or low on the horizon?) and the mix of direct sunlight with skylight.

## Sunlight, Skylight and Daylight

If we could take a color meter into space and measure the pure sunlight, we'd find that it's approximately 6500K. When sunlight moves through our atmosphere, atmospheric particles scatter the blue light, which gets reflected down to the earth as intense blue light—skylight—that can have a value as high as 20,000K. The warmer light continues directly onward to earth as sunlight.

Daylight—which is a blend of sunlight and skylight—can range anywhere from 4000K to 8000K (Stroebel, Compton, Current & Zakia, 1986: 209). The time of day (sun position) and atmospheric conditions determine where in that range the color temperature will be.

*Although we use the term 5500K to mean "daylight," the color temperature of light changes throughout the day and is directly affected by weather conditions:*

- During most of a normal day (from about two hours after sunrise until about two hours before sunset), daylight—direct sunlight with a bright blue sky above—will average 5000K to 6000K.
- The cloudier it is, the cooler the color will be (and the higher its color temperature). A light, overcast day will average around 6500K. The particulate in the clouds acts as a filter.
- If you're under an open-blue sky, but the sun is blocked (in the open shade of a large building or if the sun is covered by a particularly dense cloud), then the light will be extremely blue (as high as 20,000K), since most of the illumination is coming from skylight.
- The lower the angle of the light, the warmer it will be (and the lower its color temperature). This occurs because the sunlight travels a much longer distance through the atmosphere, which scatters even more of the blue light and results in a warmer light at sunset and sunrise.

Once you begin to understand how the Kelvin numbers relate to the light around you, it becomes second nature to make some educated guesses. Just as you can predict a starting exposure after shooting thousands of images in similar conditions, you can make solid guesses as to the Kelvin temperature of the light surrounding you. This will help you more accurately match your settings or deliberately warm and cool your images.

## Does It Look Backwards to You?

Have you ever looked at Lightroom's interface for setting WB (**Figure 7.3**)? It's backwards! The higher numbers—7500K—are warmer (redder), while the lower numbers—2850K—are cooler (bluer). The color temperature bar in Lightroom represents the effect the setting has, not the temperature of the source. The Lightroom color temperature bar is really a filter bar; it indicates the kind of *effect* that's applied to your image. By sliding the indicator to the right, you add warmth. By sliding it to the left, you add coolness.

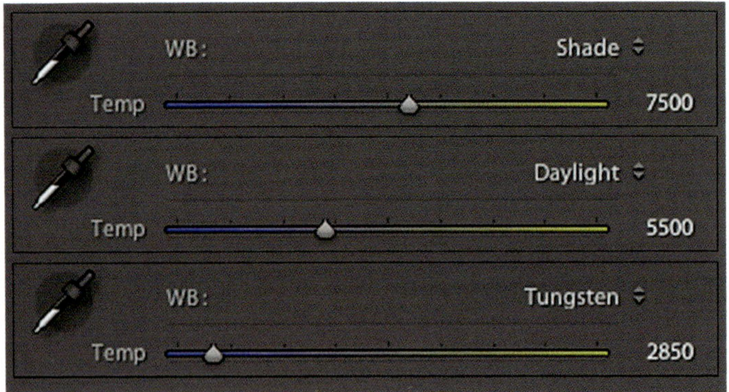


**FIGURE 7.3** Lightroom does it backwards—on purpose—to simplify the process of adjusting WB. Lightroom's color temperature guide shows us the *effect* of the adjustment, not the original source.
SCREENSHOT © ANDY BATT, *LIGHTROOM TEMPERATURE BARS*, 2013.

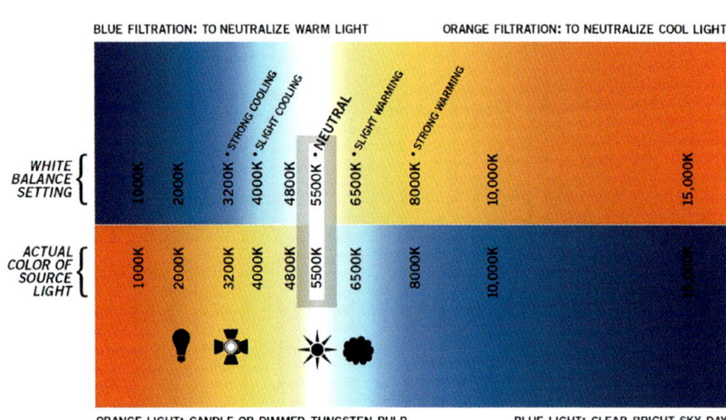


**FIGURE 7.4** The bottom bar in this illustration shows the approximate color temperature of the light sources we commonly see. The top bar shows the shift from neutral: If you shoot under a 5500K source (the rule of thumb for daylight on a clear, sunny day) with your camera set to 5500K (or the Daylight icon), you'll end up with a fairly neutral image. By moving your Lightroom WB setting to a higher number, you can add warmth. By moving it to a lower number, you can add coolness. Compare this illustration to the one in **Figure 7.7**, which shows a tungsten source.
ILLUSTRATION © ANDY BATT, *DAYLIGHT COLOR BALANCE*, 2013.

The Lightroom bar uses daylight as its standard. When the light source and the WB setting match, you end up with neutral color. Lightroom assumes that most of your work will be shot at the daylight setting, so the neutral area is right at 5500K.

### *Example 1*

Take a look at **Figure 7.4.** The bottom part of the illustration shows the color temperature of the light source: household light bulbs clocking in at around 2000K,[6] pro-tungsten lights at 3200K, daylight at 5500K and overcast light at 6500K. The top color bar shows the *effect* the different Lightroom WB settings will have on the image when the light source stays consistent at 5500K. **Figures 7.5 and 7.6** show an image Andy shot with a 5500K source—then processed at three different color temperatures.

### *Example 2*

Now check out the second version of the color chart (**Figure 7.7**), which represents a 3200K tungsten light source. The bottom bar doesn't change, since it represents the actual color temperature of the light source—but the top bar shifts, since it shows the *effects* different Lightroom WB settings will have when the light source stays consistent at 3200K. In this scenario, a choice of a 3200K WB setting will result in a neutral image, while a choice of a 5500K WB setting will result in a warm one (**Figures 7.7 and 7.8**). Notice that the same 5500K WB setting in the raw processor gives different visual results with a 3200K light source (**Figures 7.7 and 7.8**) than it does with a 5500K light source (**Figures 7.4 and 7.5**).

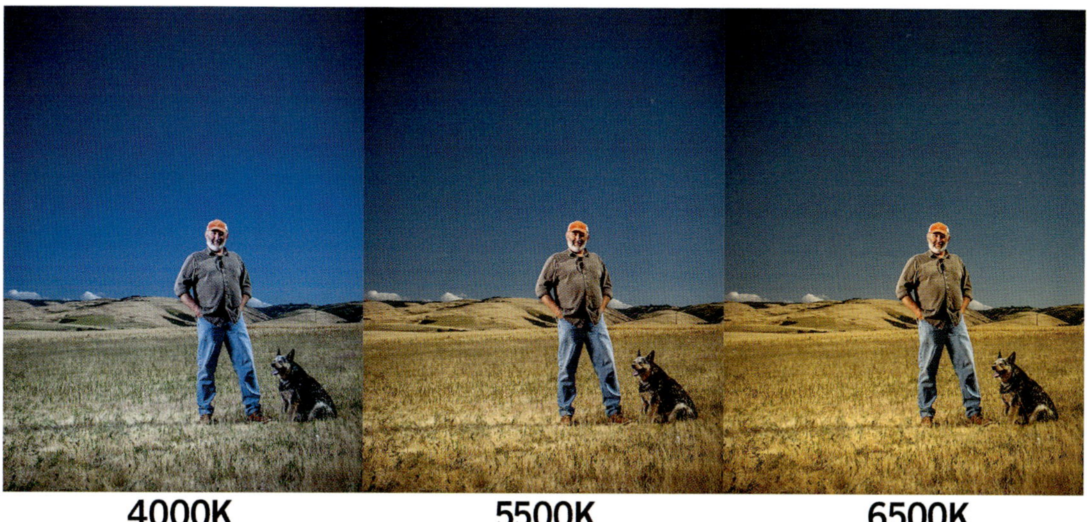


**FIGURE 7.5** This comparison shows the same photo (shot with a 5500 light source) processed out at three different color temperatures: 4000K, 5500K and 6500K.
IMAGE © ANDY BATT, *COMPARISON OF JIM LAVADOUR PORTRAIT AT THREE DIFFERENT COLOR TEMPERATURES*, 2011.

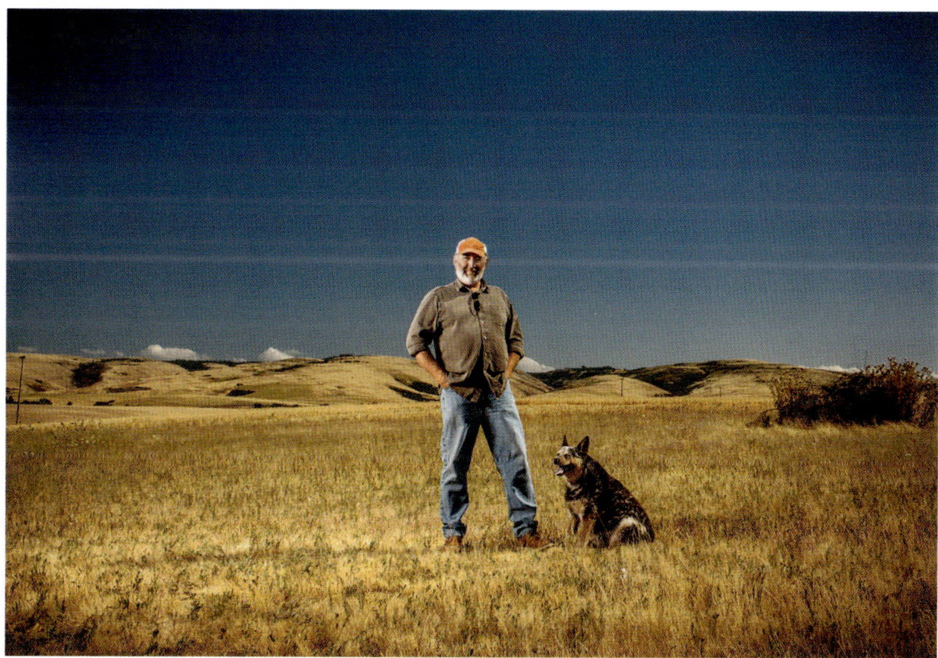

**FIGURE 7.6** Andy photographed artist Jim Lavadour as part of a series for the Oregon Cultural Trust. He wanted to create an image of Jim in the landscape that influences his work, and to capture the feeling of warmth that radiates from the landscape. Processing the image out at 6500K—a warmer WB setting than the 5500K light sources—gave him the look he wanted.
IMAGE ©ANDY BATT, *ARTIST JIM LAVADOUR, EASTERN OREGON*, 2011.

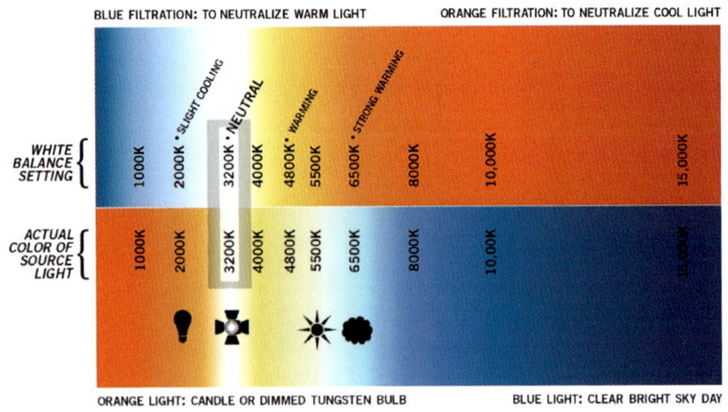

**FIGURE 7.7** The bottom bar is the same as the one in **Figure 7.4**, but since we're using a 3200K source as our standard (instead of 5500K), the top bar shifts accordingly to indicate the different effects the Lightroom WB numbers have. Instead of 5500K resulting in a neutral image, here it creates a warm image, because the tungsten light source is already warm.
ILLUSTRATION © ANDY BATT, *TUNGSTEN COLOR BALANCE*, 2013.

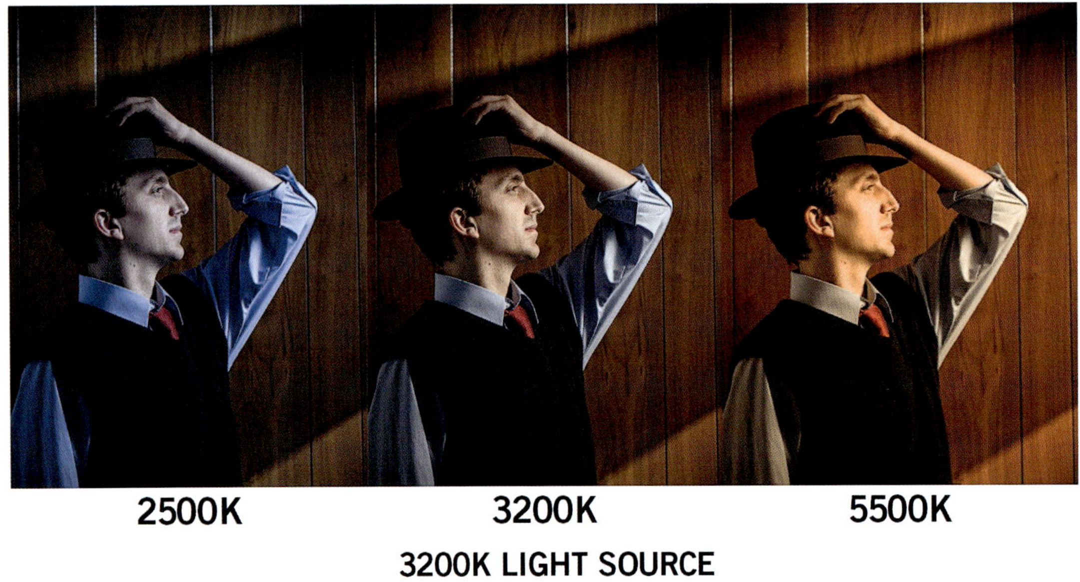


**FIGURE 7.8** This time, the light source is a from a 2,000-watt Fresnel Light—a 3200K tungsten source. Andy processed out the same photo at three different color temperatures: 2500K, 3200K and 5500K.
IMAGE © ANDY BATT, *COMPARISON OF PORTRAIT AT THREE DIFFERENT COLOR TEMPERATURES*, 2008.

## Why Are the Numbers Different?

The goal for each raw-processing application is to show an accurate rendition of the white balance for that image. The Kelvin numbers displayed are internally consistent; you can depend on them while working inside of the application. When you compare those numbers in different applications, however, you run into problems, because the applications approximate those numbers and each one uses its own method to calculate them (**Figure 7.9**).

Photo Ninja author Jim Christian gives us a little insight into the process of decoding WB values:

> ***Kelvin numbers [in raw-processing applications] are usually only an approximation. There is no standard procedure for measuring and characterizing illuminants such that white balance scaling factors from different systems can be correlated to accurate color temperature values.***
>
> ***Every processing pipeline is different, and there is no standard procedure for constructing color correction profiles . . . this doesn't affect the ability to achieve an effective white balance but it can make it difficult to compare precisely across [raw-processing applications] . . .***

Your takeaway? Just don't try to compare the numeric values in different raw processors.[7]

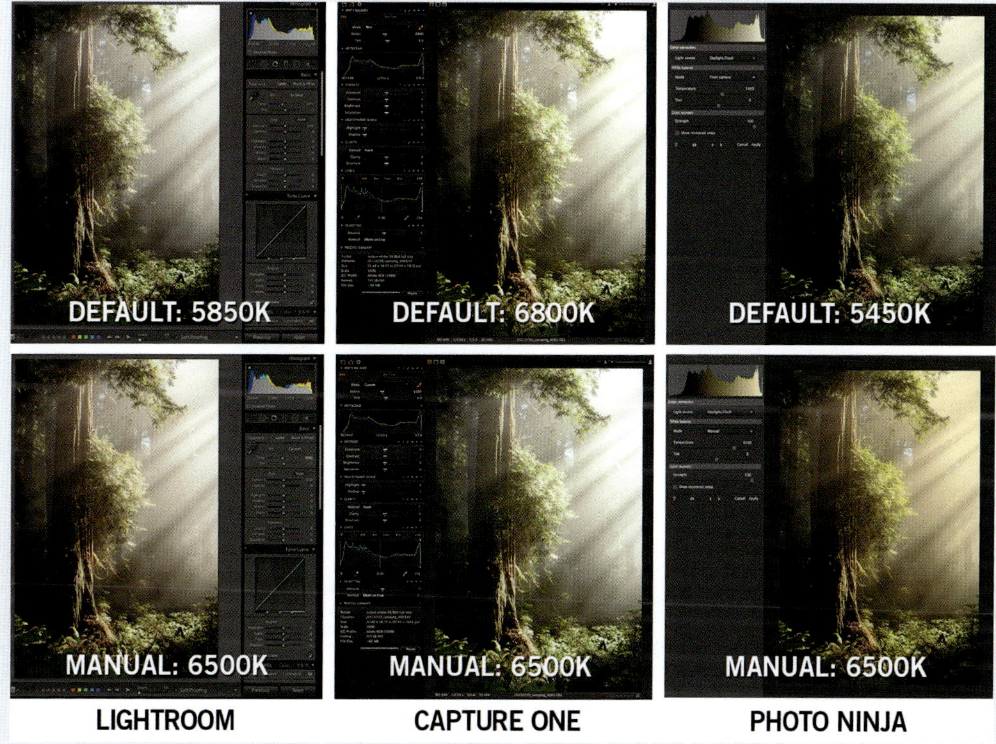


**FIGURE 7.9** By using the same raw file in three different raw processors, we can see how the default Kelvin values differ. At the default settings, we get different visual results, and each processor reports a different numeric value. When we set the same numeric values we also get three different visual results.
IMAGE © ANDY BATT, *WHITE BALANCE COMPARISON–REDWOODS*, 2011.

## Tint It!

There's another color balance issue to deal with, and that's tint. Tint shifts the green-to-magenta balance of an image. Since many light sources include colors that shift into these tones, we need to compensate for them by shifting the WB of the image along this axis.

Most cameras have an internal WB and Tint adjustment that goes beyond picking an icon or WB number. Since the back of your camera isn't a great place to make subtle color correction judgements, we generally make these corrections in our raw-processing application. Just because we don't want to deal with these tools in-camera doesn't mean they're unimportant!

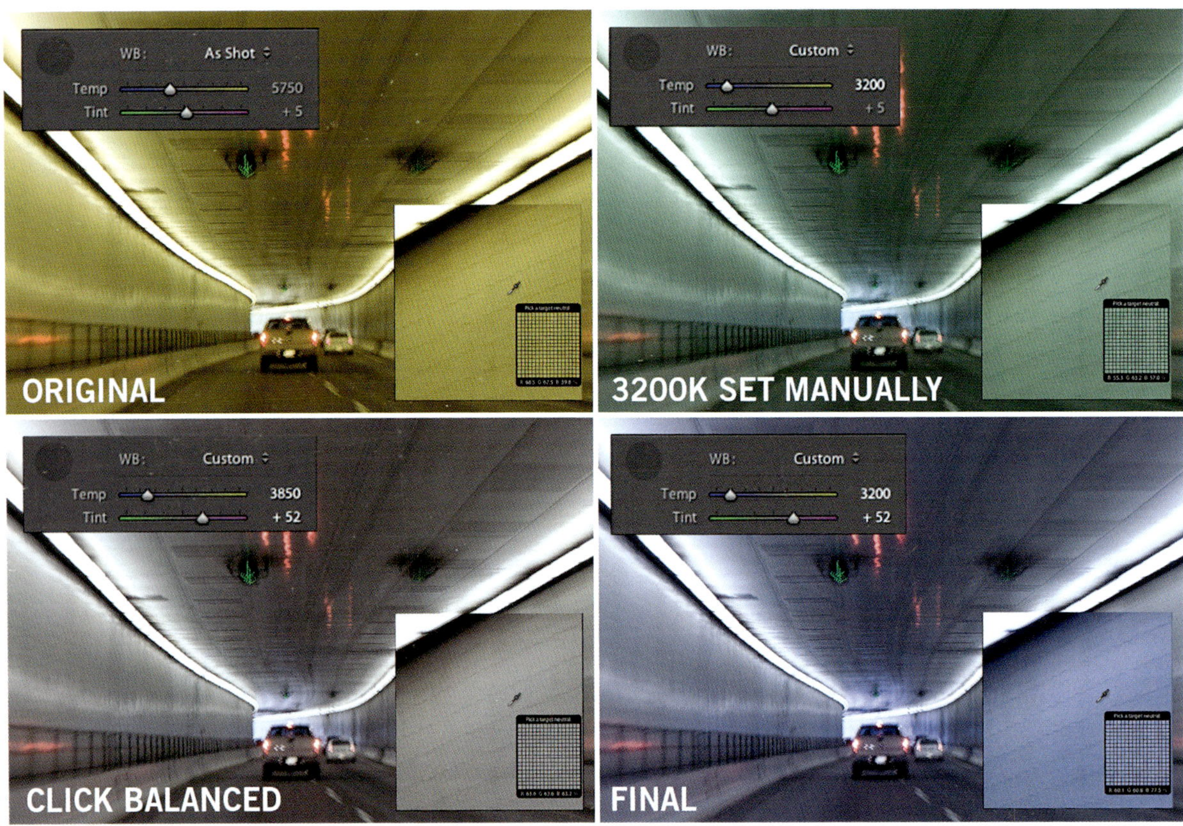


**FIGURE 7.10** Andy took this shot using a slow shutter while driving through a tunnel in Colorado. The camera's WB was set in-camera to 5750K and resulted in a yellowish image (upper left). If we simply set the WB to 3200K (upper right), it removes the yellow cast, but leaves the green tint caused by the lights. Click balancing on the tile wall neutralizes the image (lower left). By adjusting the WB slider to 3200K after click balancing (lower right), a blue cast was purposefully added to the image.
SCREENSHOT © ANDY BATT, *REMOVE THE GREEN: DETAIL OF TUNNEL IN COLORADO*, 2006.

## Two Axes: Warm-to-Cool and Green-to-Magenta

Color-balanced light sources work on two axes: the warm-to-cool axis and the green-to-magenta axis. We've already established a solid connection with the warm-to-cool axis, so let's talk about tint, which deals with the green-to-magenta axis. More often than not, you'll need to add some magenta to balance out the green tints. These can stem from outdoor sources, such as daylight filtering through green leaves, and also from lights—such as fluorescents or sodium vapors—that use excited gas as their energy sources. These lights can spike so high, in comparison to other colors, that they add a green cast.

The easiest way to deal with a green cast is to perform a click balance in your raw processor. We'll give more detailed info on click balancing later in this chapter, but for now, all you need to know is that clicking with the Eyedropper tool on a spot that is neutral in your image will restore the warm/cool balance and remove the magenta/green cast. It's important to realize that not everything that looks white or gray is actually neutral; gray concrete, for example, can have many different casts. A neutral balance card, like the WhiBal®, is the only thing that will be a truly neutral surface. You can still click balance on that gray concrete, but just realize that if you do, you'll be working in the "aesthetically pleasing" rather than the "accurate color" arena.

Click balancing will also get rid of any warmth or coolness—either from the WB you chose in-camera, or from a look you've created in Lightroom. Remember that by choosing "As Shot," you can restore both the color temperature and color tint back to the original setting. Take a look at **Figure 7.10** for a step-by-step explanation.

## Color Balance: Bruce Ely

***Andy Batt:*** **Do you use Auto White Balance (AWB)?**

***Bruce Ely:*** It really varies, depending on the situation. If I anticipate going from one light to a different one, then absolutely, I will put it on Auto. I shoot at the Rose Garden [in Portland, Oregon] with the NBA team all the time. I know the color temperature of the environment so it's a preset on my camera. I put it on and don't even think about it. Sometimes, I'll use the daylight setting.

***AB:*** **When you process a raw file, how do you set your color?**

***BE:*** I just make the picture look like what I remember it looking like. There's zero trickery. I set the white; I set the black; I lighten and darken a little bit to make it look like it did when I took it.

***AB:*** **What you *remember* it was like. Your impressions are at work here.**

***BE:*** Yes, but that's minimal. There are different levels of acceptability; people who push those boundaries get into trouble. I've always played it safe; in my career I just try to capture good pictures. I'm less art, more documentary—and I enjoy that.

### AWB Can Be Fooled

Some of you will be AWB holdouts, because it's a convenient setting and works well enough, often enough. As with any other automatic process, though, it's a good idea to understand what's going on beneath the hood.

*Beware; the AWB portion of your camera's "brain" is fallible:*

- **Is it really white?** Your camera looks for areas that it thinks are neutral and sets the WB from that spot. The problem is the neutral area might not be neutral—it might be warm gray, cool gray or have a colorcast.
- **External camera sensors**: Some cameras have a built-in color meter that reads the light falling on the camera. The problem? The subject you're photographing might not be in the same light as your camera. This could happen, for example, if you were standing in the deep shade while you photographed something in the bright daylight.
- **Color fields**: If you're photographing a scene that has a large field of color—and no neutral for the camera to analyze—then the AWB might be fooled into creating an image with a colorcast.

## Mired Shifts

Understanding mired shifts helps us get a handle on how the color of light changes across our working spectrum, from candle flames to the deepest shade on a blue-sky day. The essential thing to know is that small shifts in the Kelvin value at lower color temperatures (i.e., 2000K–3000K) translate to much larger visual changes than they do at higher color temperatures (7000K–8000K; **Figure 7.11**).

> ***For the same change in numeric Kelvin value, cool colors shift slowly, while warmer colors shift quickly.***

Mired stands for "micro reciprocal degree," but "mired" is way easier to pronounce. Mired values give us an alternate way of looking at color temperature values, but you aren't likely to find them on your camera, in Lightroom or in a normal conversation. You *will* find them if you want to add filters to light sources, e.g., putting a full-blue conversion filter onto a tungsten light source to make it function as a daylight source.

The formula is pretty simple: The mired value is equal to 1,000,000 divided by the Kelvin value. So the mired value for 5500K is 1,000,000/5500 = 182. You don't need to memorize this formula—it probably won't come up at your next cocktail party.

A 350K change between 3200K and 2850K (the difference between Canon and Lightroom's tungsten default) has a significant visual change—and the mired value between them is 38 points. Compare that to the 300K difference between 5500K and 5200K (the difference between Canon and Lightroom's daylight default). This difference would be barely noticeable, since the mired value difference is only 10 points.

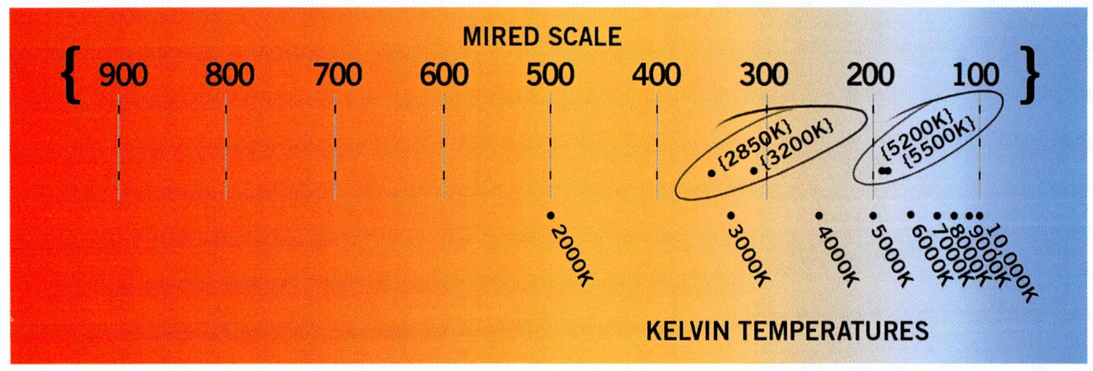


**FIGURE 7.11** Mired values are a way of looking at color so that the numeric differences between points are relative to the amount of effect the change has. This color bar is plotted on the mired scale. Notice how bunched up the cooler values are: There's very little space between 5200K and 5500K. (As you can see, the dots marking these values are actually touching.) The difference is 300K—but only 10 mired points. Now check out the warmer values: There's a much bigger gap between 2850K and 3200K. At 350K, there's almost the same Kelvin difference as the previous example, but the mired difference is 38.
ILLUSTRATION © ANDY BATT, *MIRED SCALE WITH KELVIN NUMBERS*, 2013.

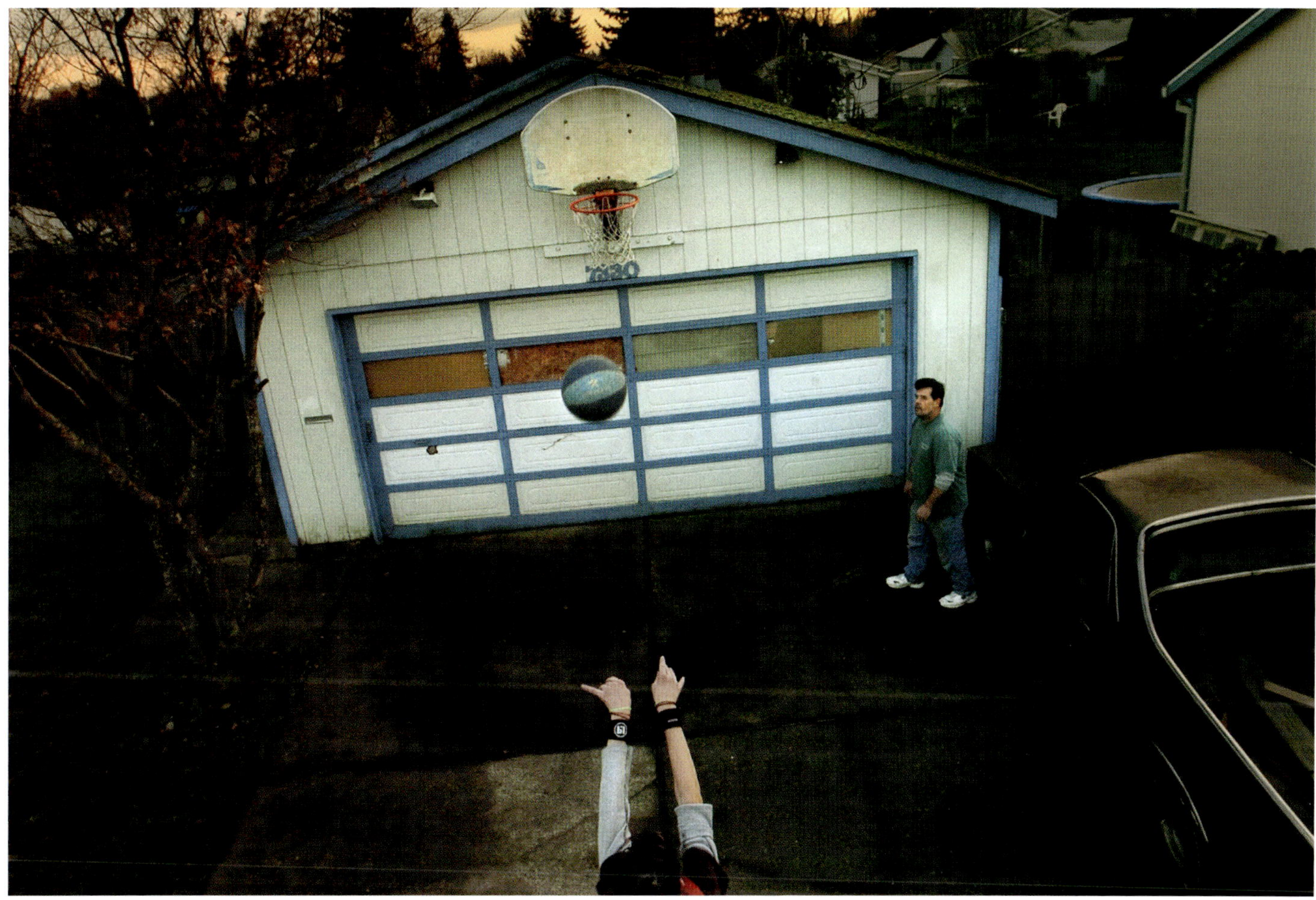

**FIGURE 7.12** Desperately wanting to make the basketball team at school, Mike Luckenbaugh practices his shot at home after the first day of tryouts. Scott Luckenbaugh, right, and his son Mike have a bet on who will break the last piece of glass from the garage door. When Bruce processes raw files, he sets the white and black, then lightens and darkens his images to make the scenes look like they did when he captured them.
IMAGE BY BRUCE ELY, *THE GAMES WE PLAY—TAKING A SHOT*, © AND COURTESY OF *THE OREGONIAN*, 2004.

## TRY THIS AT HOME

### Shift Your Image

**For step-by-step instructions, go to: www.focalpress.com/cw/digitalimagingmasters**

For the "Make the Wrong WB Choice" exercise in *Chapter 1*, we explored the notion of flip-flopping the "right" color setting to create dramatic changes. In this exercise, we'll see how adding warmth or coolness in small, bracketed increments can create more subtle changes.

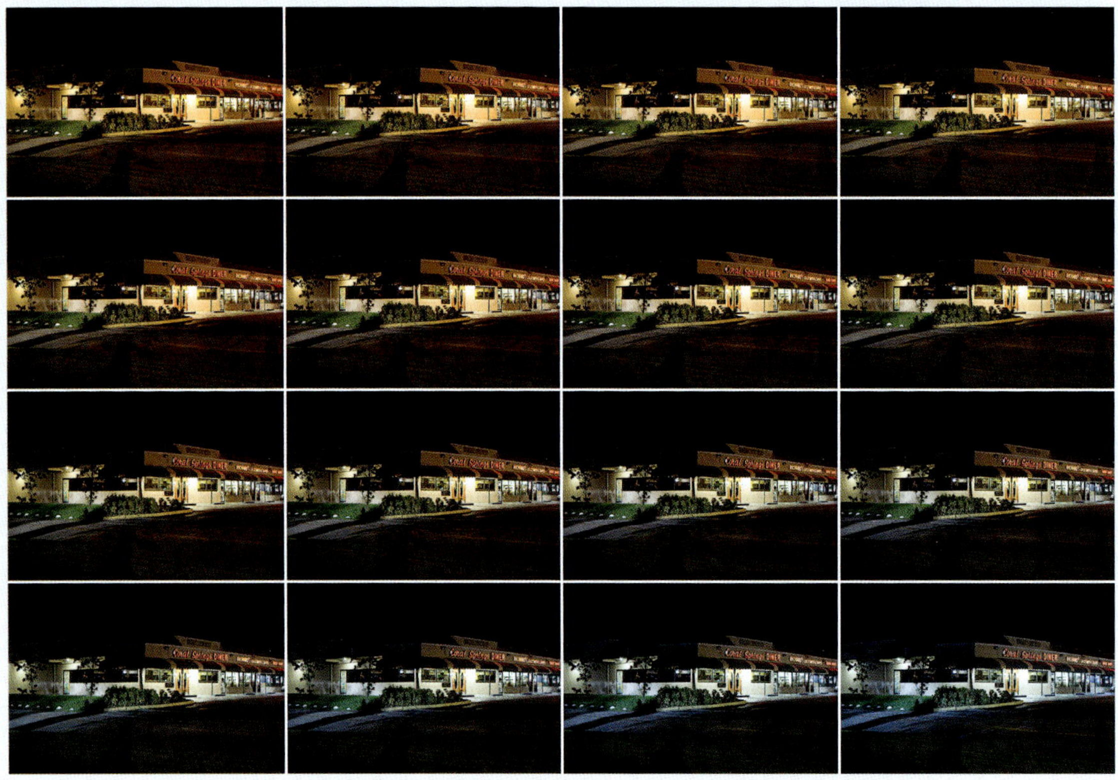

**FIGURE 7.13** By changing the WB in 100K intervals—from 3500K to 2000K—we can see the colors shift in the various light sources. IMAGE © ERIKA VELASQUEZ, *CORAL SPRINGS DINER—COLOR SHIFT*, 2013.

## Balanced Icons

We've circled back around to those handy icons your camera provides as shortcuts, and this time, we're going to apply Kelvin values to them so you know exactly what color temperature you're using. First, though, we're going to do some testing. The chart in **Figure 7.14** shows how four of the most useful icons—tungsten, daylight, cloudy and shade—link to the Kelvin temperatures used in Lightroom, Canon and Nikon.

By looking at the tungsten section, we can see that all three companies chose a different definition for tungsten. If you used the light bulb icon on your Nikon camera, the "as shot" reading in Lightroom would be 3000K; if you were to choose the Lightroom preset for tungsten it would switch to 2850K; and if you were to photograph the same scene with your Canon camera, it would come into Lightroom "as shot" at 3200K. The confusing part is that none of these is wrong. Lightroom believes that most photographers working in tungsten light will be doing so with household lamps—think documentary work. Canon sticks with settings that correlate with professional light sources and Nikon splits the difference so that it doesn't commit to either side.

Remember, it's not the icon that counts, it's the actual light source. Once you know about these defaults, you can keep using the icons, or you can switch to the direct Kelvin settings in-camera. We prefer to manually set our color to the numeric Kelvin setting; that way, we control the color we think tungsten should be.

| | LIGHTROOM (PRESETS) | CANON (PRESETS) | NIKON (PRESETS) |
|---|---|---|---|
| TUNGSTEN | 2850K (HOUSEHOLD BULBS) | 3200K (PROFESSIONAL BULBS) | 3000K |
| DAYLIGHT | 5500K | 5200K | 5200K |
| CLOUDY/OVERCAST | 6500K | 6000K | 6000K |
| OPEN SHADE | 7500K | 7000K | 8000K |

**FIGURE 7.14** The trick to using the WB icons in your camera is to know which color temperatures they refer to. Just because they use the same icon or title doesn't mean that they use the same numbers! Take a look at the tungsten setting: Lightroom uses 2850K, which is a good starting point for household 60-watt light bulbs. Canon uses 3200K, the standard for professional tungsten lighting, and Nikon tries to split the difference with 3000K. All three settings are identified by the same icon, but the results are different.
ILLUSTRATION © ANDY BATT, *KELVIN'S ICONS*, 2013.

## Neutral Color—How Do We Get There?

Even if your goal is to make an aesthetic image—i.e., using creative color over accurate color—it's useful to start with a neutral image. How can you know what "neutral" is for a particular image? If you choose AWB, then your camera will hunt for bright tones and hope they're neutral. If you use one of the WB icons, then your camera will make an educated guess to match the setting to the color. You can set a numeric Kelvin value—or refine the match even further by using a color meter[8] to measure the actual color temperature in your scene.

The best way, though, to get neutral color is to photograph a true neutral card (**Figure 7.15**) and use your raw-processing software to read it. Then, you can set a combination color temperature and tint adjustment. To get a super-clean, neutral image you'll need a true neutral reference. Enter the neutral card zone . . .

### Neutral Cards

A neutral card helps you understand the color in your scene, because it's an object that has been created, measured and proved to have no color. One of Andy's favorites is the WhiBal® card from Michael Tapes Design. This solid plastic card is a bright gray tone (brighter than a

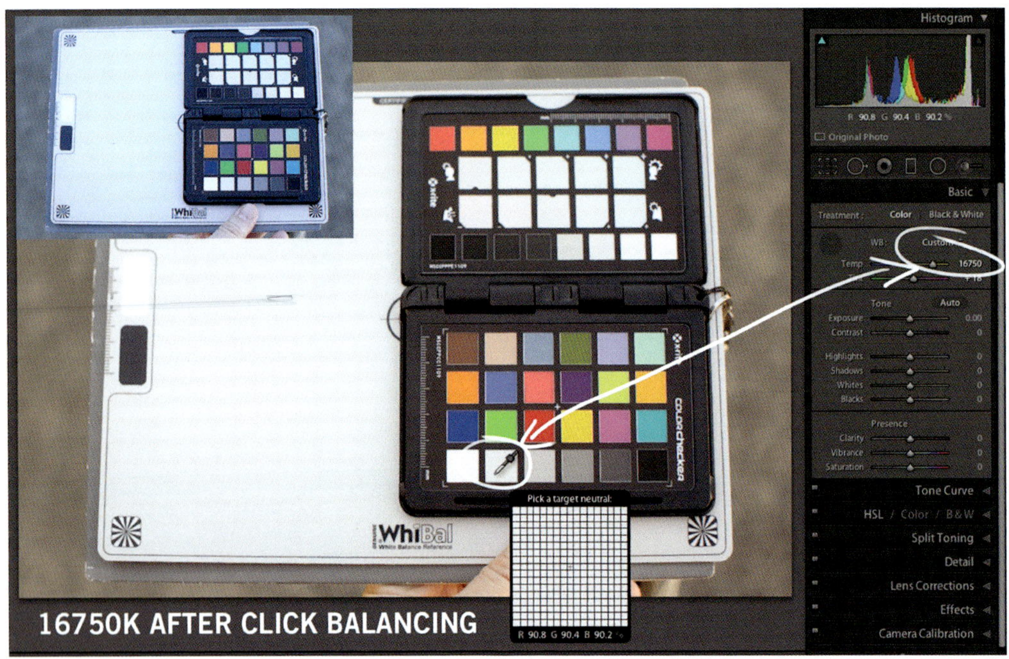


**FIGURE 7.15** When you click Lightroom's Eyedropper tool (aka WB tool) on a WhiBal card—or the gray B4 patch on an X-Rite ColorChecker—Lightroom balances the image and gives you a color temperature readout and a tint setting.
SCREENSHOT © ANDY BATT, *CLICK KELVIN*, 2013.

gray card) and has been calibrated with a spectrophotometer to ensure that it's neutral. WhiBal cards are durable, made of the same material all the way through, easy to clean and—if you scratch one, it's not a big deal. Andy has beaten his up quite a bit, and it keeps on working.

With a good exposure, a WhiBal card will give you a bright tone with full detail, and since its information is up in the far right side of the histogram, you know it's in the "best" part of the data. To use a neutral card, you place it in an area of key light and/or key detail in your scene and shoot a test image. Pay particular attention to the way you angle the card; there will be a difference between the shadow side and the bright side of your image. *Bonus tip:* in tricky lighting situations—where there may be variations in color—Andy often takes a few shots with his neutral card in a variety of locations, so he can have options in post. For example, he'll place it in the shadows, in the direct sun and anywhere else he thinks might be useful to record the color of the light.

## Click or Custom?

So, how can we use this amazingly neutral card to improve our images? There are two ways: click balancing, which takes place during post-processing, and custom balancing, which takes place in-camera. With both methods, you're telling the software or camera, "Here's a neutral object. Please read it and balance my color to it." It's a handy method, since it balances both your Kelvin numbers and your magenta/green tint.

## Custom WB In-Camera

Here's how it works: The custom WB icon in your camera looks like a square sitting on two triangles. Choose this icon and take a photo of a neutral card in your key light. Fill the majority of the frame with the card and take a photo at a good normal exposure. You want that card's values to show up in the highlight section of the histogram. Find the "set custom WB" command in your camera's menu.[9] After running that command, the camera should prompt you to select the photo you just took. The camera's onboard image-processing monkey will grab that image, set the WB based on the neutral card and store it in the slot reserved for that funky icon.

Some cameras allow you to save multiple custom WB settings, which is handy if you're jumping around in an environment with different light sources. Once you've set a custom WB, you can use it whenever you shoot photos in the same light.

Keep in mind that light changes frequently, so the custom WB you set outside at 2:00 p.m. might not work at 6:00 p.m. Even for indoor environments, the lights will shift if there are any windows—or if any of the light sources switch on or off. Just remember to set a new custom WB setting each time you notice the light changing or whenever you shift locations.

## Click Balancing In-Camera

Click balancing is very similar, and easy—as long as you take a neutral card image every time the light or location changes. Just hand the card to your model, place it next to your still life or hit the self-timer and walk into your landscape with the card. As long as the card is placed in the same key light as your subject, is reasonably in focus and is at least a few hundred pixels in size, you should be able to get a good reading from the card.

Once you're back in your raw-processing application, you can grab the WB tool, hover it over the image of the card and click it. Blam! You've just neutral balanced your image (**Figure 7.15**). The bonus is that you'll get a Kelvin readout in Lightroom (or whatever application you're using) for the light source in your scene. If you pay attention to these readouts, you'll build up experience points for judging the color temperature by eye.

### All Gray Cards Are Not Neutral

Cheaply made 18% cards are not color neutral or color stable. For color balancing, they aren't accurate to begin with and will probably shift over time. The Kodak R27 Gray Card is an option for neutral balancing, since it's a true, neutral Munsell gray (X-Rite, 2007), a reliable color standard; but a purpose-built neutral card, like the WhiBal, is easier to use when judging for color neutrality. The Kodak card is a midtone gray, and the tones are noisier than they are on the WhiBal. At low ISOs this isn't a big deal, but at high ISOs, the amount of color noise makes getting a neutral balance trickier, since it adds artificial colors.

# Creative Color—Stop Worrying!

We use neutral balance cards to get rid of colorcasts. For jobs that require accurate color as the end goal, e.g., art reproduction, then we're all set—but if our goal is creative color, then we're in the realm of aesthetic choice. How do we know what's good or bad? When it comes to creative color, the best tools are our eyes and our brains. Color tools give us a foundation, and it's up to us to build upon it.

One of the biggest problems we face when processing images is that there are too many choices: We have to decide whether to set the color temperature to be neutral, warm or cool; if the image will look better with a slight hint of magenta or green; and which other color adjustments to apply. We need to learn the best ways to tweak the Hue, Saturation and Luminance controls in Lightroom and whether we would push the reds towards orange or the blues towards green. There are a host of creative color choices we can make in this process! How should we go about it?

## TRY THIS AT HOME

### Colors Spin You Right Around

**For step-by-step instructions, go to: www.focalpress.com/cw/digitalimagingmasters**

An old-school technique for exploring color options is the "color ring-around." [10] To get started, you'll choose an image you want to experiment with and tweak it to a good neutral state. Then you'll create a series of color options and arrange them around the neutral version, increasing the intensity of the effect with each "ring" that circles the original (**Figure 7.16**). This technique is easy to do and can reveal the potential of an image (**Figure 7.17**).

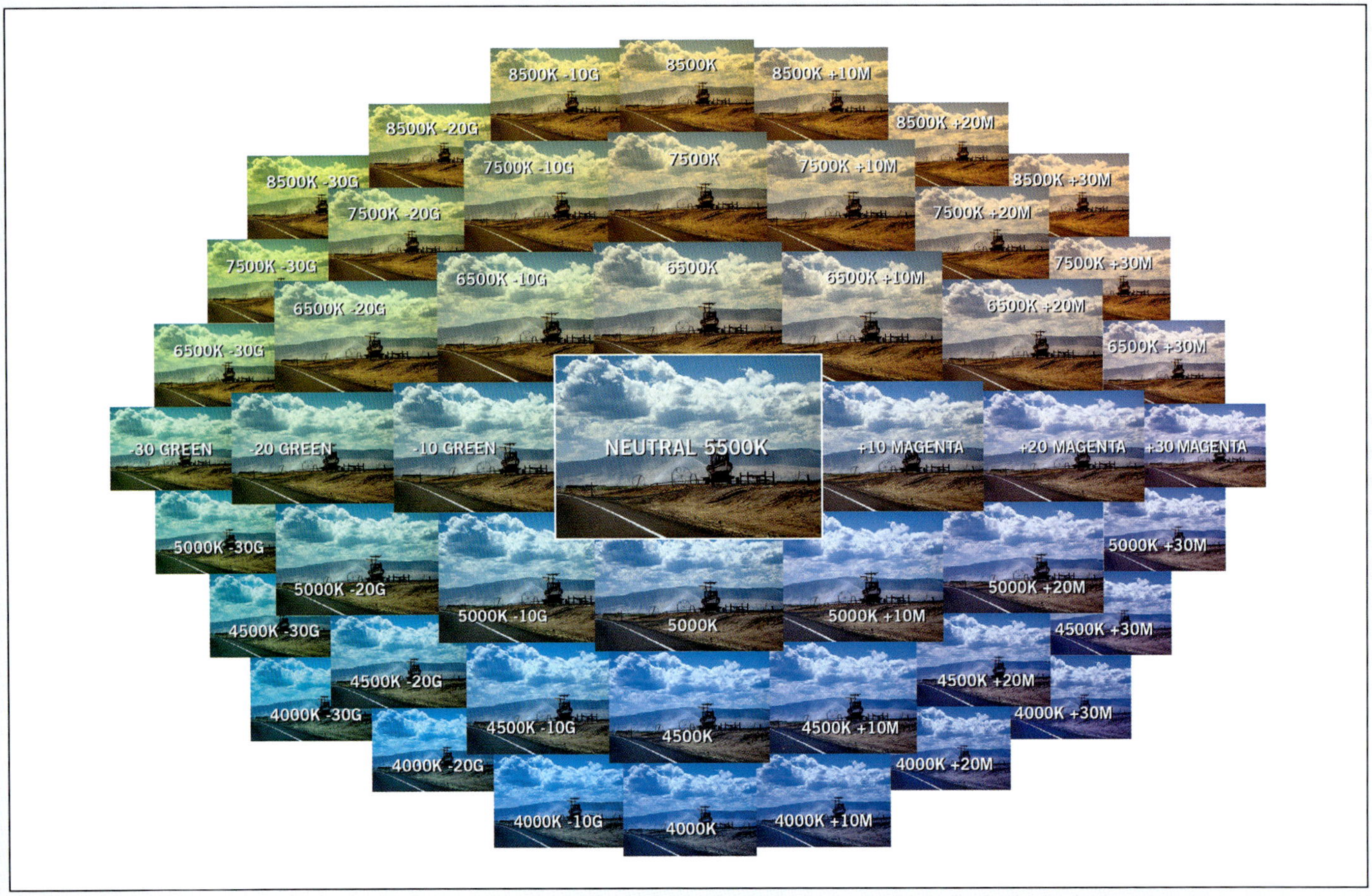

**FIGURE 7.16** Andy created loads of Virtual Copies in Lightroom to give us a peek into the world of color options. He shifted the Kelvin values from a neutralized starting point (center image at 5500K) by 1000K points to the warm side: 6500K, 7500K and 8500K. He shifted another set to the cool side, but this time with 500K intervals, since tungsten values shift faster: 5000K, 4500K and 4000K. He also performed a Green Tint shift with three –10 intervals and a Magenta Tint shift in three +10 intervals, at 5500K. Then, just to see what it would look like, he created additional sets that combined warm color temperatures with green shifts, warm temperatures with magenta shifts, cool temperatures with greens shifts and cool temperatures with magenta shifts.

The hardest part was putting them all together in Photoshop to create the illustration. Andy used Lightroom's Survey mode to move the various images around to see how they compared.

IMAGE © ANDY BATT, *COLORS SPIN AROUND*, 2013.

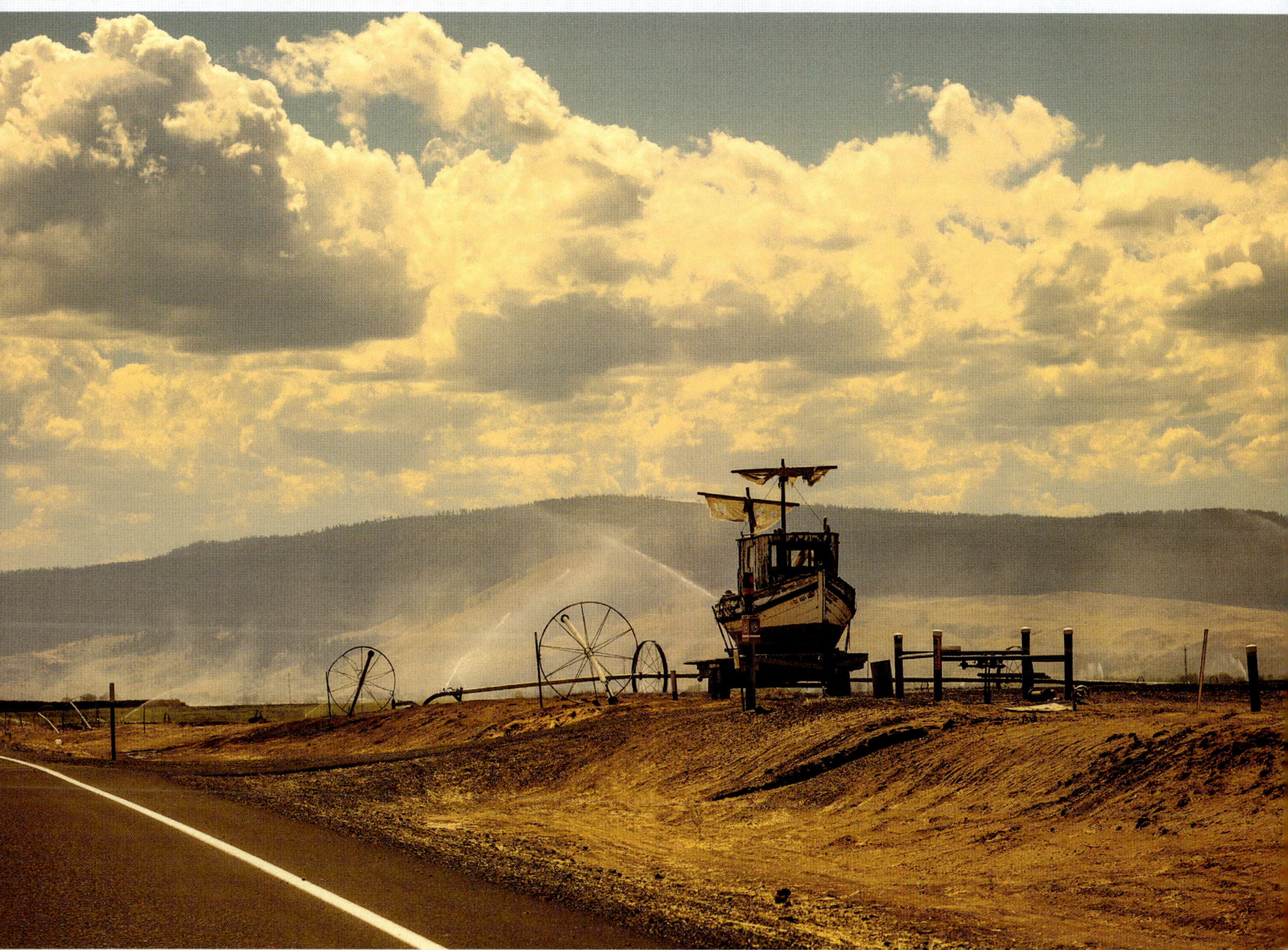

**FIGURE 7.17** By exploring the image using the ring–around in **Figure 7.16**, Andy chose the 8500K, +10 magenta version for his final image. He found that pushing the color temperature up and adding magenta gave the image a sense of the hot desert that felt right for the subject matter. After applying a slight desaturation and a bit more vignetting, he was happy with the shot.
IMAGE © ANDY BATT, *DESERT BOAT*, 2011.

First, remember that we're in charge of this process and we decide what's right and what's wrong. Second, recognize that it takes experience, and that we can build it up by making active color decisions. Third, experiment. It helps that we're working with raw images, because they provide a safety net; you can always go back and try again if you aren't satisfied with the changes you've made. The trick is to avoid being paralyzed by all the choices. Try to stop worrying so much about getting it right. When it comes to creative color, "right" is whatever you choose.

## Enter the Dragon: Color Management

Maybe you've been ignoring this topic, because it seemed too technical, sprawling and difficult to understand—or perhaps you hoped someone else would figure it out for you, so you could sit back and let the automated software, printers, monitors and widgets take over and do their thing.

In this section, we're going to introduce some concepts to acquaint you with color management, but if you're serious about the topic, we recommend that you read *Color Management & Quality Output,* another book in *The Digital Imaging Masters Series.* You'll hear from Tom Ashe, the author of the book, later on in this chapter.

Color management covers a broad territory. It's a chain that begins when raw data is processed off your sensor and ends with the final image—whether it's printed in magazines, shown on the web or hung as fine art. This chain includes multiple devices, software and inks. The happy news is that color-management tools continue to improve over time. Each generation offers monitors that are better able to display colors, printers that can self-calibrate and software tools that—when properly employed—enable the entire chain to communicate more effectively.

## FEATURED PHOTOGRAPH

### Charlie's Story

Andy photographed this project for the United Way. Part of the project was to deliberately use color to tell the story of a character named Charlie.[11]

***Andy:*** Here's the story: Charlie lost his job and started spiraling downwards. By getting help from United Way, he was able to rise and succeed. The project was to create an animation of still images, so all of the shots were made with the intent of being animated. We wanted the early images to have a desaturated, cool-blue quality and to become warmer and richer as Charlie rose above his circumstances. I put together an image grid (**Figure 7.18**) to showcase Charlie's arrest, the lowest point in the story. Compare the blue-green version to the neutral-balanced one. There's something more intensely miserable about those blue-green tones.

At the shoot, we photographed a neutral card in each scene so we could purposefully click balance the images and make our color corrections based on that starting point. For this scene, our neutral card image was click balanced to 5700K and +13 Magenta; we ended up at 3426K with a tint setting of –54 Green.

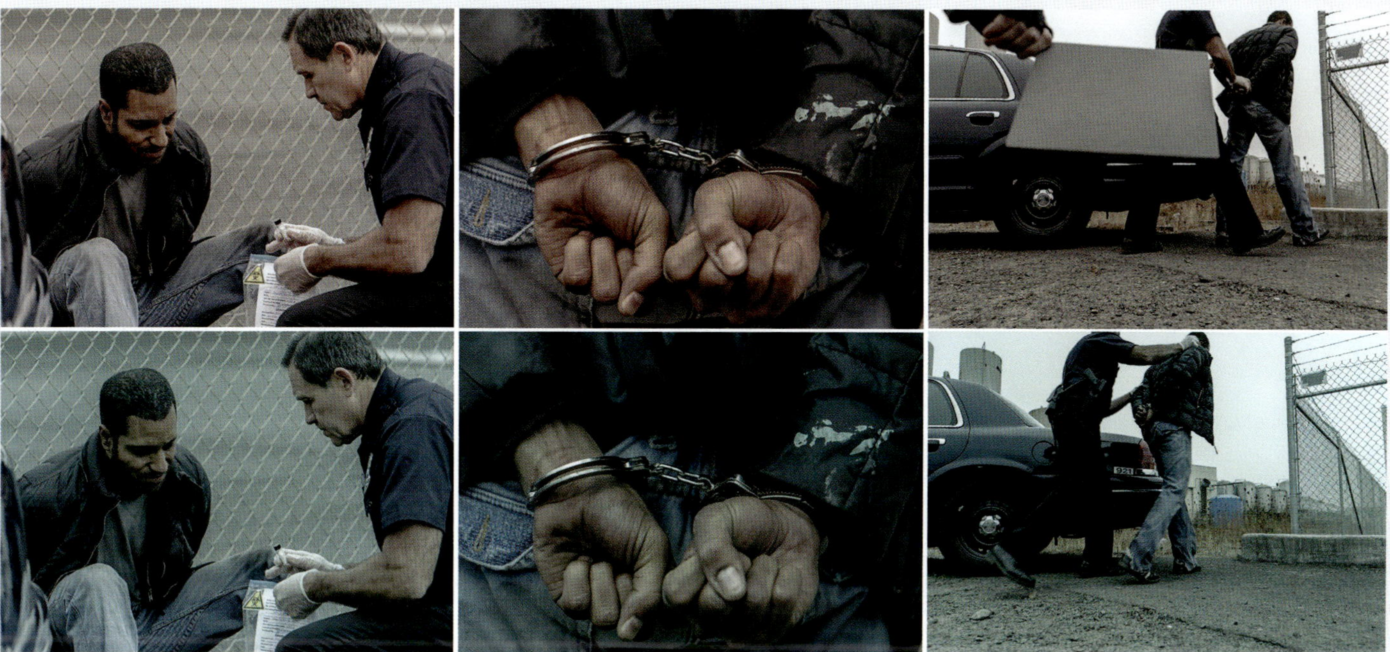

**FIGURE 7.18** We wanted these images to have a de–saturated, cool–blue quality to express the lowest point in Charlie's story. Compare the way the blue–green version (bottom grid) communicates misery with the neutral–balanced version (top grid). We ended up using a color temperature of 3426K with a tint setting of –54 Green.
IMAGE © ANDY BATT, *IMAGE GRID: CHARLIE'S STORY (FOR UNITED WAY)*, 2012.

## Color-Space Crash Course

We think of color spaces as containers; each independent *color space* is a different-sized container. Of the standard working spaces, sRGB is the smallest, ProPhoto is the largest and Adobe RGB (1998) is somewhere in between (**Figure 7.19**)—plus, there are other smaller and larger color spaces than these. When a raw image is processed, all of its color information gets placed into one of these containers. If the container is too small, the excess color information is either cut off or converted, depending on the software that's doing the work.

ProPhotoRGB, Adobe RGB (1998) and sRGB are all *independent* color spaces. Unlike *monitor* color spaces, which only describe the way a particular monitor handles color, these color spaces are independent of any particular device and are used more universally. In an effort to achieve "successful" color[13] on a consistent basis, some device manufacturers adopt independent color spaces as their working space.

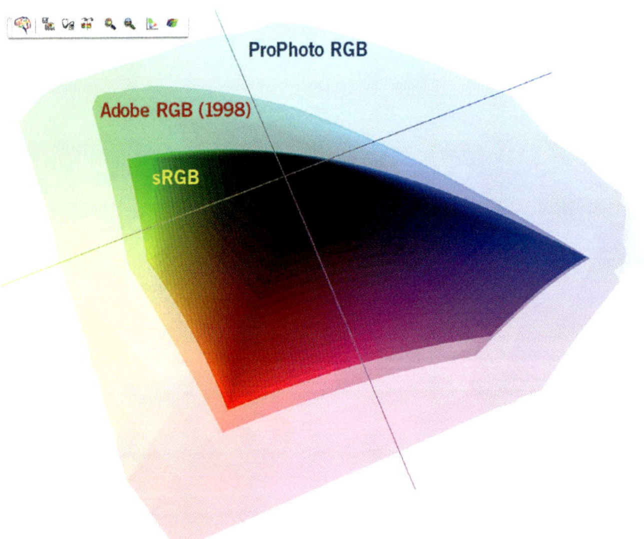


**FIGURE 7.19** In this illustration, created with CHROMiX ColorThink,[12] you can see three standard "containers" for color. These types of color spaces are independent of any particular device and are designed to contain a possible range of colors. Because raw files can have far more colors than the sRGB color space contains, we use ProPhoto RGB as our standard working color space, once our images are in Photoshop. As a bonus, Lightroom uses a modified version of ProPhoto RGB as its internal working space.
ILLUSTRATION © ANDY BATT, *STANDARD WORKING COLOR SPACES*, 2013.

## Protect and Preserve Your Color

When an image is in its raw form, it doesn't occupy any color space. As soon as it's demosaiced and created as a viewable image, then it's in a working color space—like sRGB, ProPhoto RGB or Adobe98 RGB. The working space is an independent, standard space (container) that holds color information. The actual color information that describes the image is what is "put into" the container.

Take a look at the image in **Figure 7.20** and the graphs in **Figure 7.21** to get a sense of what happens when the container is too small. The image of the tree has very strong greens and yellows. As a raw image, all those greens are available to us. If we exported the image out as an sRGB TIFF, we would run into a problem, since many of those colors lie outside the sRGB container. Depending on the software and methodology used, those greens would either be clipped off or remapped to (the more limited) greens that are *inside* the sRGB space. If we processed this image into ProPhoto RGB, a much larger color space, we could preserve a lot more of the green and yellow colors.

The graphs in **Figure 7.21** show the tree image's color data as colored circles inside a wireframe outline. The top graph shows the sRGB space, with colors extending well outside the wireframe. The bottom graph shows ProPhoto RGB; its wireframe holds all of the green and yellow colors the sRGB frame leaves behind.

### Which Color Space?

We suggest using *ProPhoto RGB* as your standard working space, because of its ability to preserve as much color information as possible —including colors that you might not be able to see on your monitor. Why would you want to preserve those? Because some current printers can utilize those colors, and you want to preserve your data for future improvements.

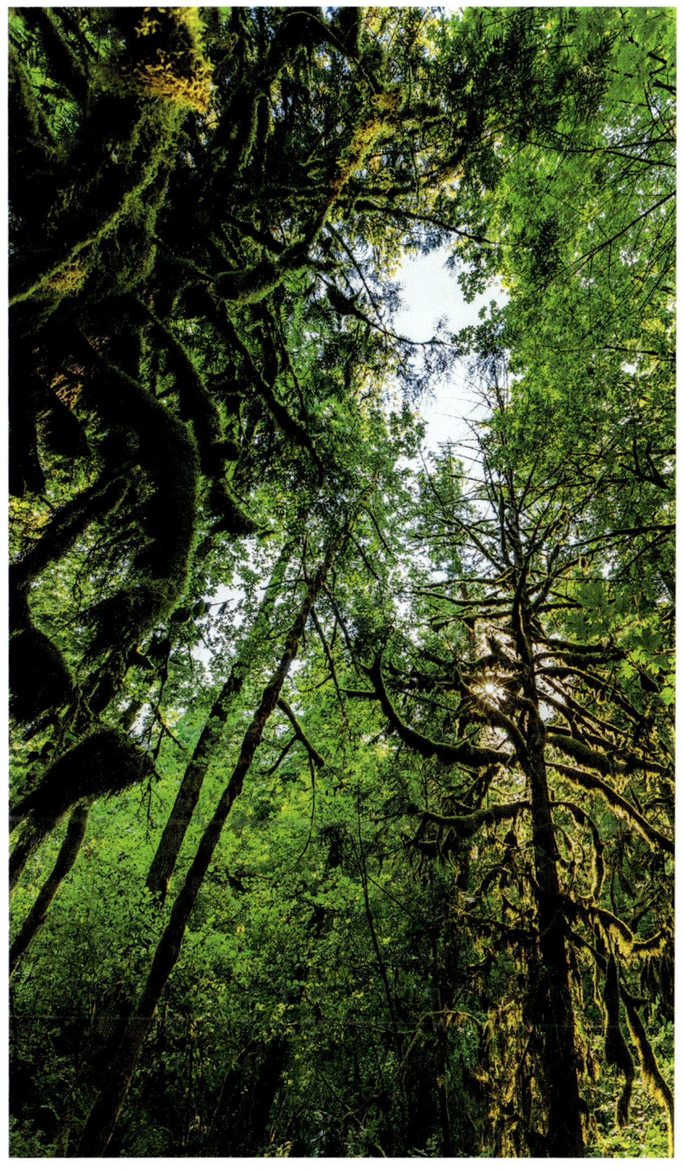

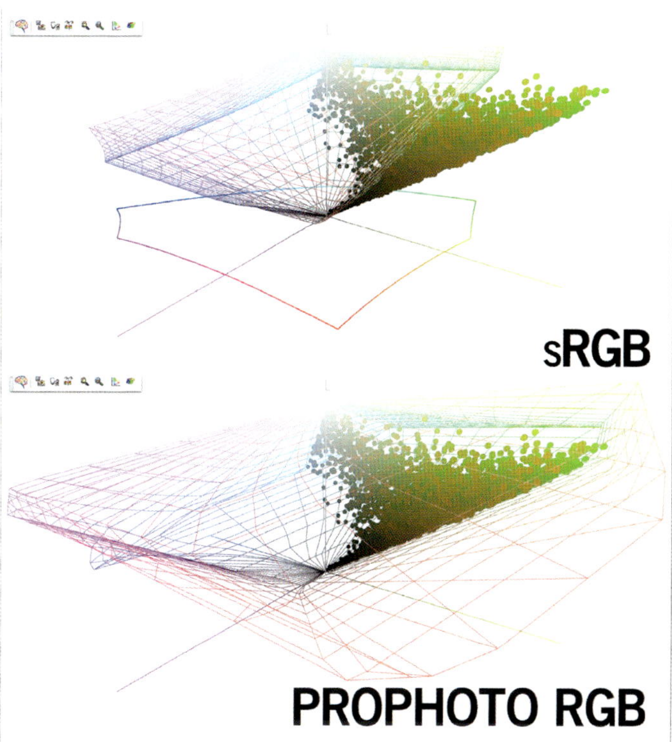


**FIGURE 7.21** *(ABOVE) COLORTHINK GRAPH OF MOSSY TREES, PROPHOTO AND sRGB,* COLORTHINK COURTESY OF CHROMIX, 2013.

**FIGURE 7.20** *(LEFT)* IMAGE © ANDY BATT, *MOSSY TREES,* 2010.

This image of a mossy tree (**Figure 7.20**) contains a lot of green/yellow image data. Andy processed it out of Lightroom as a ProPhoto RGB image to preserve that data. He created two graphs (**Figure 7.21**) with CHROMiX ColorThink to show how the color information in the image relates to the sRGB and ProPhoto RGB color spaces. You can see the amount of data that would be clipped off if he used the sRGB space and that the data is easily contained inside the ProPhoto RGB space.

We're not saying that you can't work successfully with sRGB, because there are many monitors and printers that use sRGB as a standard since it's the lowest common denominator of the color space options. It's important to know, however, that you can increase your options for better color by using a color space that will preserve all of the color data in your images.

It makes sense to use *sRGB* as a delivery space when you're delivering images that will be used solely online or that will go to a printing press that's optimized for sRGB. Adobe RGB (1998) is also a common standard; it's larger than sRGB, but smaller than ProPhoto RGB and has become a working standard in the photography industry. *Adobe RGB (1998)* is useful for specific purposes, such as delivery to Adobe RGB (1998)-optimized printers or by retouchers who use it as their preferred working space.

# Applied Color Management: Jodie Steen, Owner of 127 Productions, Inc.

Color can seem like a mystery. When the image you're viewing on your display doesn't match the printed page, it can cause frustration, wasted hours and wasted money on materials. With so many profiles to worry about—monitors, working spaces and printer profiles—it's no wonder that the complexity of color management can feel intimidating.

## How Can You Trust What You See on Your Monitor?

One of the most common questions I hear is, "How can I trust what I'm seeing on my monitor?" Proper calibration[14] is the key, and luckily, it isn't too expensive or difficult to achieve. All you need is some color-management hardware, software and a little bit of how-to knowledge.

### Calibration Tools

We have two different tools for *monitor calibration*: a colorimeter and a spectrophotometer. The *colorimeter* is the more common and less expensive option. It measures emissive light only—light that comes out of your display. A *spectrophotometer* can measure emissive or reflective light and can also be used to make printer profiles by reading color values from a printed test page. Each brand of colorimeter will come with its own calibration software, but each works similarly. It measures a series of specific colors with known values that flash on the monitor and compares the difference between the measured and known values. The software uses these values to *calibrate the display* and *generate a profile.*

### Calibration Software

There are a few notable differences in calibration software. Some software will allow you to set specific settings for color temperature, brightness and contrast, while others offer more basic presets. (We'll explain more about settings in just a moment.) Some software, such as X-Rite's i1Profiler,[15] includes a verification option. That means you can read another series of color patches and check to see if your monitor profile is valid. Genius! Now you can tell that the profile you just built is working properly, and you can even track the results over time. Let's assume you've run out and gotten your calibration unit and you're ready to do your first calibration.

*Before you start the software, there are a few things to do:*

- Reset your monitor to the factory default. Most monitors have a "Reset All" function in the monitor's menu system. This brings it back to a known state. Some monitors—such as Apple monitors—do not have this option.
- Next, if there is an Auto Brightness function on your display, disable it. If it's left on, then the monitor may change during the calibration process, which can cause an invalid profile.
- Temporarily disable your screensaver; if it comes on during a calibration, it will create an invalid profile or error.
- Finally, turn down the lights. Some devices can be influenced by ambient light.

### Launch the Software

Now we're ready to launch the software. You'll find lots of options for how to calibrate. Which one is correct? The answer is that there is no "right" or "wrong." These options exist because different settings help achieve different goals. Most software programs will ask you to make three main decisions: color temperature, brightness and gamma.

### Color Temperature

For *color temperature*, most photographers will want to stay between 5500K and 6500K. The lower the number, the warmer your display will appear. Selecting a lower number is useful if you're matching a warmer stock of paper and trying to get the best screen-to-print match; 6500K has long been accepted as a standard, as it's based on daylight temperature.

I find that 6000K is a good general number if you aren't trying to match anything in particular. 6500K is a bluer temperature that's a good match for bluer paper stocks[16] such as premium glossy. Most retouchers will calibrate their displays to 5700K, as it matches proofing paper well and isn't too warm or too cool.

*For your own display, ask yourself what your goals are:*

- Am I trying to match my print output? If so, take into consideration how warm or cool your paper stock is when deciding on a color temperature.
- *Do I need a general-purpose setting for web and prints?* If so, try between 5700K and 6000K.

### Monitor Brightness

Next, the calibration software will ask how bright you want your display. This is expressed in candelas, or cd/m$^2$ (candelas per meter squared). Here's the secret: The goal is to match the amount of light that's hitting your print to the amount of light that's coming out of your display. This will give the best density match from the screen to the print.

It would be great if there were an easy tool to measure the amount of light, so you could plug that number into the calibration software, but for now it's more of a trial-and-error approach. A good starting point is 160. If you're working in a dark environment, you may want to try a lower number. If you're working in a very bright environment, like outside on location on a bright sunny day, then try a higher number. Again, there is no right or wrong answer here, so try experimenting with the guidelines for your own environment. In our experience, most monitors will perform well at 100–160cd/m$^2$.

### Gamma and Gamut

Gamma is the next option: we typically select 2.2, and if there is an option for gamut, we select "Monitor Native." A deeper discussion on these points can be found in Tom Ashe's color management book, but for this discussion we'll simply say that these are the most common settings to use for calibration.

### Let the Software Run

Now we let the software run, always following any specific instructions it gives us. The resulting profile can be saved at the end of the measurement and is automatically applied at the system level. If your software offers a *verification* option, we strongly suggest taking advantage of this feature. It will tell you how close your monitor is to your intended target, and you can decide from there if the profile is acceptable. You can even track your monitor's performance over time, which gives valuable insight if your monitor is starting to fail.

## How Can You Get Your Prints to Look Like the Images on Your Monitor?

The second most common question is, "How can I get my print to look like the image on my monitor?" No matter what printer you're using, the key to getting great-looking prints is to use the correct *printer profile,* which is specific to the printer, ink, resolution and paper. Think of a profile as a snapshot of what your printer is capable of accomplishing with a specific paper. Profiles come from the printer manufacturer, the paper companies, RIP software[17] and from making custom profiles with a spectrophotometer.

### Using Profiles

*However you get the profile, the key is to:*

- Work in your working space, e.g., ProPhoto RGB.
- Convert the image to the printer (aka output) profile in the print dialog.
- Turn off color management in the printer driver.

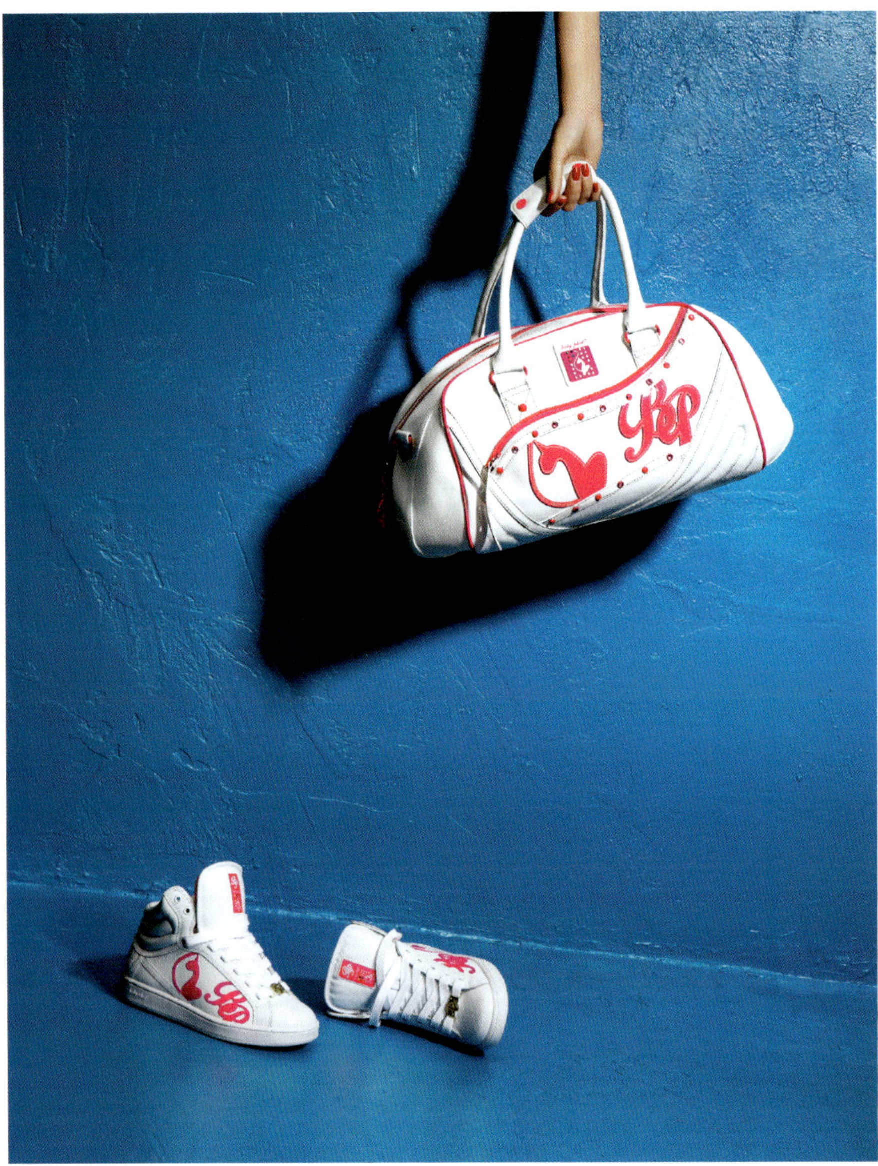

**FIGURE 7.22** A critical aspect of this photo, originally shot for a Baby Phat accessories campaign, was to achieve vibrant and accurate color. Jodie (Mastromatteo) and her husband Joshua (Steen) used a Leaf digital back and a calibrated Eizo display on set, then sent the image to a retouching house for final color correction.
IMAGE © MASTROMATTEO + STEEN, *POOL*, 2008.

Do your retouching and processing in your normal working space.[18] In the Print Dialog box, select the correct output profile for your printer and paper—note that this means you don't need to convert your image to the printer profile in your image-editing application. Finally, when the Printer Dialog box pops up, select the option for No Color Management. If you select any other option, such as "Epson Standard" or "Vivid," then color management will be applied twice (once by you in the image-editing application, when you selected the printer profile, and once again by the printer driver), guaranteeing disastrous results. Because these options are different in different image-editing applications and printer drivers, you will need to read the manufacturer's specific guidelines. But the good news is that the concept is the same no matter what printer or paper you're using.

## How Can You Get Even Better Results?

So now let's assume that you've calibrated your display and it looks fantastic. You're printing with printer profiles and things are looking way better. Your color settings are correct and you're using your color-management system with confidence. It's possible to use your color-management system correctly—and still get results that aren't quite perfect. The last question that people inevitably ask is, "How can I get even better results?"

### Monitor Choice

How do you get that last 10% of color matching nirvana? It has to do with your monitor choice. All displays (monitors) are not created equal. A good calibration system will not compensate for a display's inherent limitations. For example, different monitors have different gamuts. A newer, high-end graphics display will cover nearly all of Adobe RGB 1998, while older, less expensive displays or laptops will cover significantly less than that.

Practically speaking, if you're using a smaller-gamut monitor, you may not be seeing all the colors that actually exist in your image. This makes matching a print really difficult! High-end graphics displays, such as Eizo's CG line,[19] offer a few more bells and whistles that help achieve color nirvana. Brightness and color uniformity mean that across the entire screen, the image will be consistent. This isn't true for less expensive LCD monitors, where you may find "hot spots" that are brighter, or areas that are visibly different in color. Another thing to look for in a display is smooth gradations. Some graphics displays are factory adjusted for smooth gradations and gray balance across the monitor. Less expensive monitors may show breaks or banding and may also reveal a magenta-to-green cast that appears in the grays. To test this out, after you calibrate your display, create a new document in Photoshop and use the gradient tool to make a simple black-to-white gradation. What do you see? If you see magenta and green, then the monitor isn't capable of showing a perfectly neutral gray at all tonalities.

### Printing Systems

Just as different displays will give you different results, so too will your choice of printing system. The gamut of your inkjet printer is one factor in how closely you can print your images; newer printers offer eleven or twelve inks and have the largest gamuts available. The greater the gamut, the more colors you can possibly print, so this gets you one step closer to reproducing your image as you see it on screen. Using a custom profile for your exact paper and printer can help to reproduce your image more closely, as well.

### RIPs

Often for the best results, a RIP[20] (raster image processor) will be brought into the color management mix. A RIP is a piece of software that drives the printer instead of using the printer manufacturer's driver. A RIP offers more sophisticated handling of color, plus loads of other printing features—such as layout tools and the ability to add crop marks to images and to print multiple images on one page (aka "nesting"). Different RIPs have different functions; some are aimed at proofing, others at production and still others at fine art printing. A custom profile created through a RIP can offer the best output.

### Viewing Color Accurately

It never fails to amaze me to see just how different a print looks under different lighting conditions. I think this is the most underestimated factor in color workflow: light. The best way to view prints is under a D50 light made for viewing color accurately. There's an international standard for viewing conditions (ISO 3664:2009), and many manufacturers make products that meet this standard (GTI and Just Normlict are a couple).

The best screen-to-print match is achieved with a *dimmable viewing box*. This allows you to match the perceived brightness coming from your display to the amount of light hitting your print. If a viewing station isn't in the budget, consider buying *new bulbs with a high CRI* (color rendering index) rating. Every bulb has this rating marked on the box, and the higher the number, the better the job it does at rendering color. A rating of 90 or higher is required for viewing color; however, just because a bulb has a rating of 90 or above does not mean it matches the stricter ISO standard for viewing color.

## ICC Profiles

When you begin to work with color management, you'll find that working color spaces, printer profiles and monitor profiles are all ICC profiles. They are all used for different parts of color management, but are unified by the file type ".icc."

An ICC profile is a container that's used to hold all of the color information about a particular input device, working space, output device or color space. It accurately describes the color, and does so by the standards issued by the *International Color Consortium* (ICC). Think of it as a trading card: It tells you the player's name, position and all the stats you'd ever want to know. These cards are used to describe things like printers, monitors and working spaces. Since all the players in the color-management system use ICC trading cards, it's easy for any software or hardware to work together.

## An Acceptable Level of "Good"

There's a dirty secret when it comes to good color: Even when you use one of the many methods to measure, calibrate and create "good" and accurate color, your images will still look different, depending where you view them—from monitor to monitor, in various magazines, as fine art prints or on billboards. They might not look different to anyone besides you, but you'll know deep down that the shade of green is too yellow in one publication and too blue in the next.

Assuming you've done all the right things already—what can you do about this problem? You can relax. Let go a little. Color management technology has come a long way, and it's now possible to get very close results across the spectrum. By doing your part and adopting a good color-management system, you can know you're achieving the best possible color on your end. Are you the only person who will ever see the difference? Would it take a spectrophotometer and lab-quality lighting to prove to someone that there is a difference? If your images still look good—even if they're a slightly different version of good—then you can relax.

## Camera Profiles: Tom Ashe, Author of *Color Management & Quality Output*

***Andy Batt:* Tom, can you talk about camera-specific ICC profiles? We see them in Lightroom, and in some applications, like X-Rite's ColorChecker Passport software, you create them. How do they fit into color management?**

***Tom Ashe:*** There are two types of digital camera profiles. *Input ICC profiles* can be assigned in Adobe Photoshop and other ICC-compliant applications, like Phase One's Capture One. The other type is a *DNG profile*; you can select this kind in the Lightroom Develop Module or Adobe Camera Raw's Camera Calibration section.

### How Are They the Same?

Both types of digital camera profiles are built by taking a capture of a color target, like the X-Rite Classic 24-patch ColorChecker or the X-Rite ColorChecker SG, with your digital camera. In building either type of profile, the image of the ColorChecker is then brought into a software package to compare the image of the ColorChecker with its known colors. From this comparison, the software is able to analyze how the camera sees color with this lens and ISO setting, and, most importantly, under the specific light source(s).

### How Are They Different?

1. The Input ICC profiles for digital cameras only work with image files that are no longer RAW—images that have been processed (interpolated) to have full red, green and blue (RGB) values, like TIFFs. DNG Profiles only work with RAW or DNG files that have not been processed to RGB yet.
2. When assigned to an image in Photoshop or Capture One, *ICC digital camera profiles* will make the application reinterpret the meaning of the RGB numbers in the file, so that the colors and tones of the image of the ColorChecker match the colors of the original ColorChecker. At the same time, this forces all the colors and tones (lightness/darkness/contrast) of the images shot with this camera and under the same lighting to more closely match the colors and tones of the original scene. These can be big changes in appearance. On the other hand, the changes from selecting a *DNG profile in Adobe Camera Raw or Lightroom* are much subtler. These profiles only change the rendering of the colors—but not the tone (lightness/darkness/contrast)—making the reds more magenta, skin tones warmer or the blues more saturated, so that they match the colors of the ColorChecker more closely.

## EXPLORATIONS

### Auggie's Spot

In a single location, the color, texture and shape of light changes every day. It can change with the angle of the sun, the weather, the pollution in the air—and even with the seasons. When we walk into a location, we see the light as it is at that instant. It's hard to know what it might look like at sunrise or sunset without being there at those times.

A place that seems dull and un-photogenic during the harsh light of high noon might take on an all-new meaning when there are dark clouds overhead and a beam of western sunset light illuminating it. There's a scene in the 1995 film *Smoke*[21] that features Harvey Keitel as "Auggie" coming clean about why he can't take a vacation—why he's never left Brooklyn: He's been taking the same photograph over and over every day, for over ten years. Here's an excerpt from the script:

***Paul:*** (Astonished) They're all the same.

***Auggie:*** (Smiling proudly) That's right. More than four thousand pictures of the same place. The corner of Third Street and Seventh Avenue at eight o'clock in the morning. Four thousand straight days in all kinds of weather. (Pause) That's why I can never take a vacation. I've got to be in my spot every morning. Every morning in the same spot at the same time.

***Paul:*** (At a loss. Turns a page, then another page) I've never seen anything like it.

***Auggie:*** It's my project. What you'd call my life's work ... They're all the same, but each one is different from every other one. You've got your bright mornings and your dark mornings. You've got your summer light and your autumn light. You've got your weekdays and your weekends. You've got your people in overcoats and galoshes, and you've got your people in shorts and T-shirts. Sometimes the same

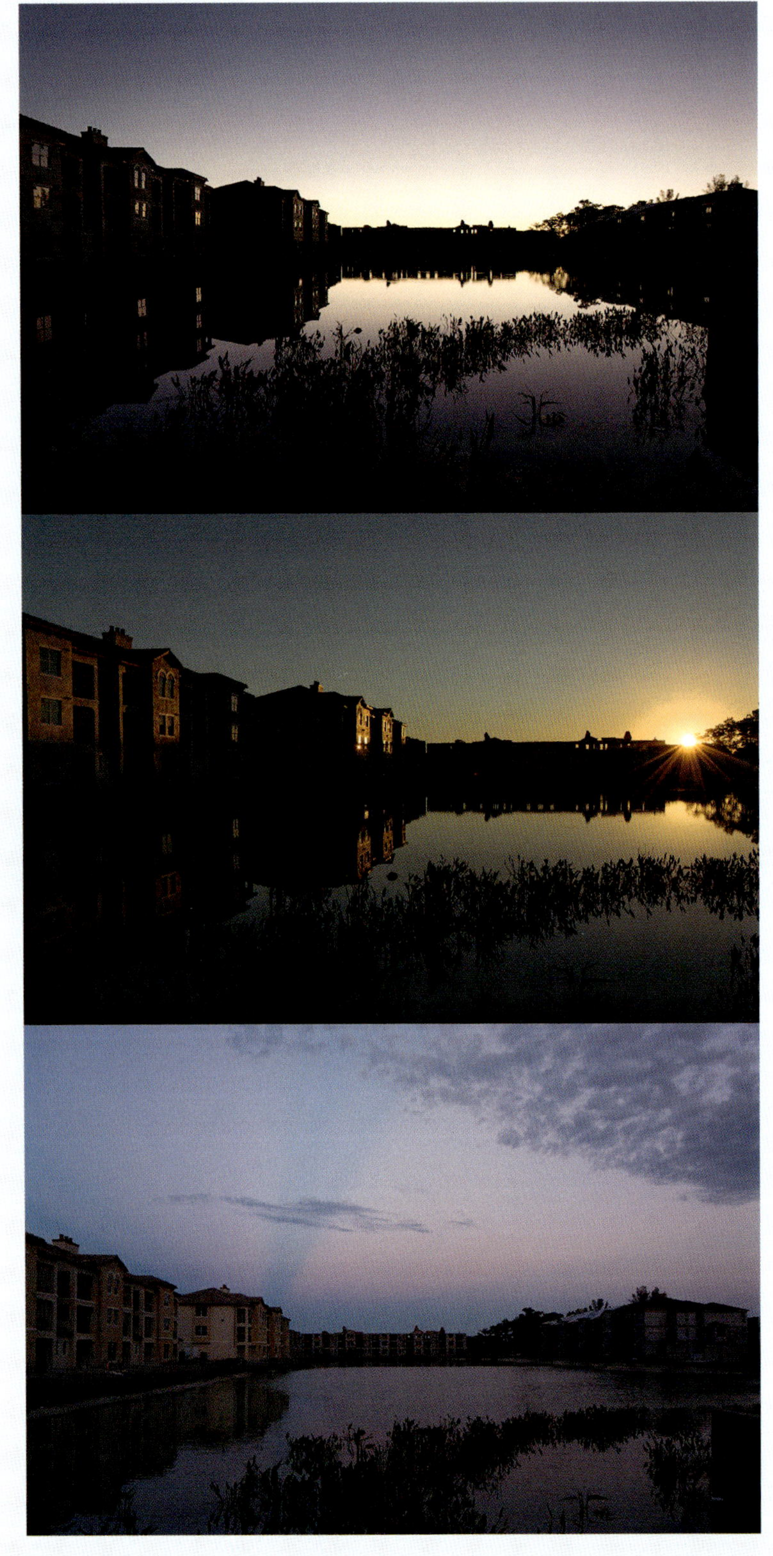

people, sometimes different ones. And sometimes the different ones become the same, and the same ones disappear. The earth revolves around the sun, and every day the light from the sun hits the earth at a different angle.

### *Inspiration*

Take this as an inspiration, not an assignment. We wholeheartedly endorse vacations—still, there's something compelling about seeing a familiar place in a new way. You can create a unique look at a place by photographing it over and over again. As Auggie says, "You've got your bright mornings and your dark mornings. You've got your summer light and your autumn light." We want you to find those changes—to let the colors and light shift and show you a new way of seeing.

### *Make Some Choices*

Find a place that you can photograph on a repeated basis. You'll want to observe the subtle and dramatic shifts in light and color over time. Choose 5500K (or the daylight icon) and stick with it for the entire assignment. If you match the light to the WB, you'll end up neutralizing your images—and the point of this exercise is to keep all those color shifts, not remove them.

### Option 1: A Day in the Life

1. You'll need a specialized piece of gear for this one: an *intervalometer*. This gadget lets you set a time interval and will automatically take a photograph for you at that interval. For example, if you set it for 60 seconds and wait for an hour, you'll have 60 photos. If you set it for once an hour and wait for the day to pass, you'll have 24 photos at the end of a day.
2. Pick a location where the light will be different at various times of the day; one that looks north or south would probably work best. Set up a tripod so that your framing will be the same for every shot.
3. Choose an interval—we suggest every 10 minutes. You'll be running this Exploration for at least 12 hours—from predawn to twilight. Make sure that your memory card can handle the total number of shots. If you want to shoot an image every minute, you'll end up with 720 photos in 12 hours. If you shoot an image every 10 seconds, you'll end up with 4,320 photos.
4. For the best single image quality: if you want to let this run by itself, then use automatic ISO mode. This allows you to dial in a set shutter speed and aperture and has the camera alter the ISO as needed. Think carefully, though—you don't want to pick a setting that won't work well throughout the day.

### Option 2: A Week in the Life

In this version, you'll be coming back to your location for a week—so make sure you can access it and that nobody is going to park a huge truck right in front of your view. A north or south view will probably give you a good range of light and color. You'll want to return back to this spot as often as you can, but especially when there are different types of light, times of day and changes in weather. You want variety in your image, but repetition in your framing.

- *Mark it:* You probably won't be able to lock down a tripod at this location, so consider some chalk marks, grease pencils, colored golf tees or other markers to help you set up your equipment at the same spot each time you visit. Document the height, focus point and camera angle as best you can.

**FIGURE 7.23** By using 5500K as a standard, Erika allowed the color of daylight to shift, transforming her chosen location at different times of a single day. If she had neutralized the color in every image, she would have removed what makes it beautiful.
IMAGE © ERIKA VELASQUEZ, *FLORIDA AT 5500K—3 IMAGES*, 2013.

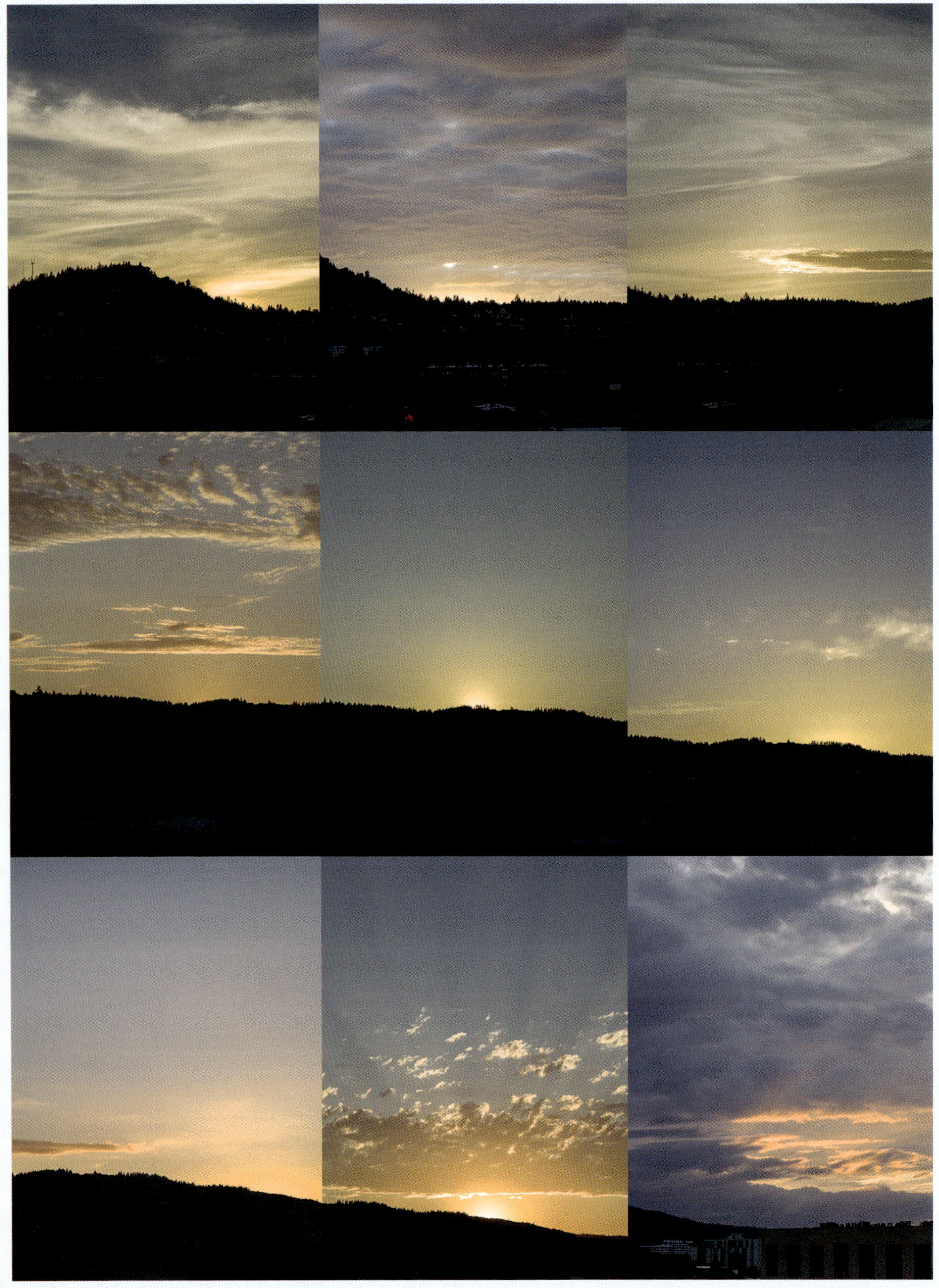

- *Choose an aperture to lock in your DoF* while you vary the shutter speed and ISO to maintain those settings. That way each image will have the same focus and appearance.

### *The Results Are In*

Once you've downloaded your media card and have the images arrayed in front of you, then start editing. Remember that you purposefully preset your WB at 5500K, so don't change this or let any automated processes neutralize your images. Add a 1-star for anything that stands out—an image that's especially cool or warm. If you ran this Exploration through the night, see what kinds of color shifts occurred. The point of this exercise is twofold: to see the same location revealed to you in different ways and to understand that every location's personality is changeable.

### *Print and Share*

Build a collection of your favorite 15+ images and print them out. Make them as big or small as you like, with the idea of displaying them all together on a single page, or as a single framed piece. Invite a friend over, have them look at your images and tell them to slow down, because although each image is the same—as Auggie says, "each one is different from every other one."

**FIGURE 7.24** Tom tracked the progression of the sun as it traveled and set at a slightly different location each night over a period of months, resulting in an appealing assortment of tones and colors.
IMAGE © TOM HASSLER, *SUNSETS FROM THE DECK*, 2013.

## Notes

1 Patti is a fellow Focal Press author and former School of Visual Arts (SVA) teacher.

2 This quote is from an email exchange between Tom and Andy.

3 University of Glasgow History, http://www.universitystory.gla.ac.uk/biography/?id=WH0025&type=P.

4 In the pre-digital age, we had only these two choices of film stock. If you wanted to photograph with other color temperatures, you'd choose the closest one and add filters to your lens to balance the color of your scene.

5 Think of those big, keg-shaped lights you see on movie sets.

6 Household tungsten bulbs run all over the place in color temperature; that's why even if you choose the "light bulb" setting, tungsten light often looks warm, instead of neutral.

7 The exception is when you're using Adobe Camera Raw (ACR) and Lightroom, which use the same processing engine and have consistent numbers—as long as their versions are in line with one other.

8 Color meters look very similar to light meters, and are used in a very similar manner. Instead of an exposure value, a color meter gives you a Kelvin reading and a Green/Magenta reading of the light.

9 Refer to your camera manual for directions. The process for setting a custom WB should be similar from camera to camera, but there may be differences.

10 We used to use this technique in the color darkroom to preview color options when printing.

11 Thanks to Craig Opfer—and all the gang at Magneto Advertising—for this project; to Nartan, the most excellent actor who helped out United Way by playing Charlie; and to Jerry, who played Narcotics Cop #1.

12 CHROMiX ColorThink, CHROMiX, www.chromix.com/colorthink/.

13 "Successful" color doesn't mean that it's better, more accurate or more beautiful; it means that it suits the user's needs. Device manufacturers base their choice of color space on different variables, depending on their users. For example, a printer might be more successful if it uses a small color space—such as sRGB—if it wants to appeal to customers that don't calibrate their monitors.

14 Monitor calibration refers to the use of specialized software and hardware to adjust your monitor so you can trust what you're seeing.

15 i1Profiler (i1Publish), X-Rite, http://www.xrite.com/product_overview.aspx?ID=1397.

16 Many photo papers add a bluing agent to enhance the appearance of brightness in the print. It's "invisible"—you don't perceive the paper as being blue.

17 RIP = Raster Image Processor. RIP software takes over all the jobs associated with printing and provides much greater color control over the printer itself.

18 In Photoshop, you choose your working space. In Lightroom, you use the default internal space—a modified version of ProPhoto RGB—or use soft-proofing to work in another space, such as Adobe RGB (1998).

19 Eizo®, EIZO Corporation, http://www.eizo.com/global/solutions/graphics/index.html.

20 RIP is pronounced "rip," as in "to tear a piece of paper."

21 Screenplay by Paul Auster, *Smoke*, Miramax Films, 1995. Produced by Hisami Kuroiwa, Harvey Weinstein and Bob Weinstein; directed by Wayne Wang and Paul Auster; features Harvey Keitel as Auggie and William Hurt as Paul.

Eight

# PRE-PRO/ SHOOT/DELIVER: INTERVIEWS WITH THE PROS

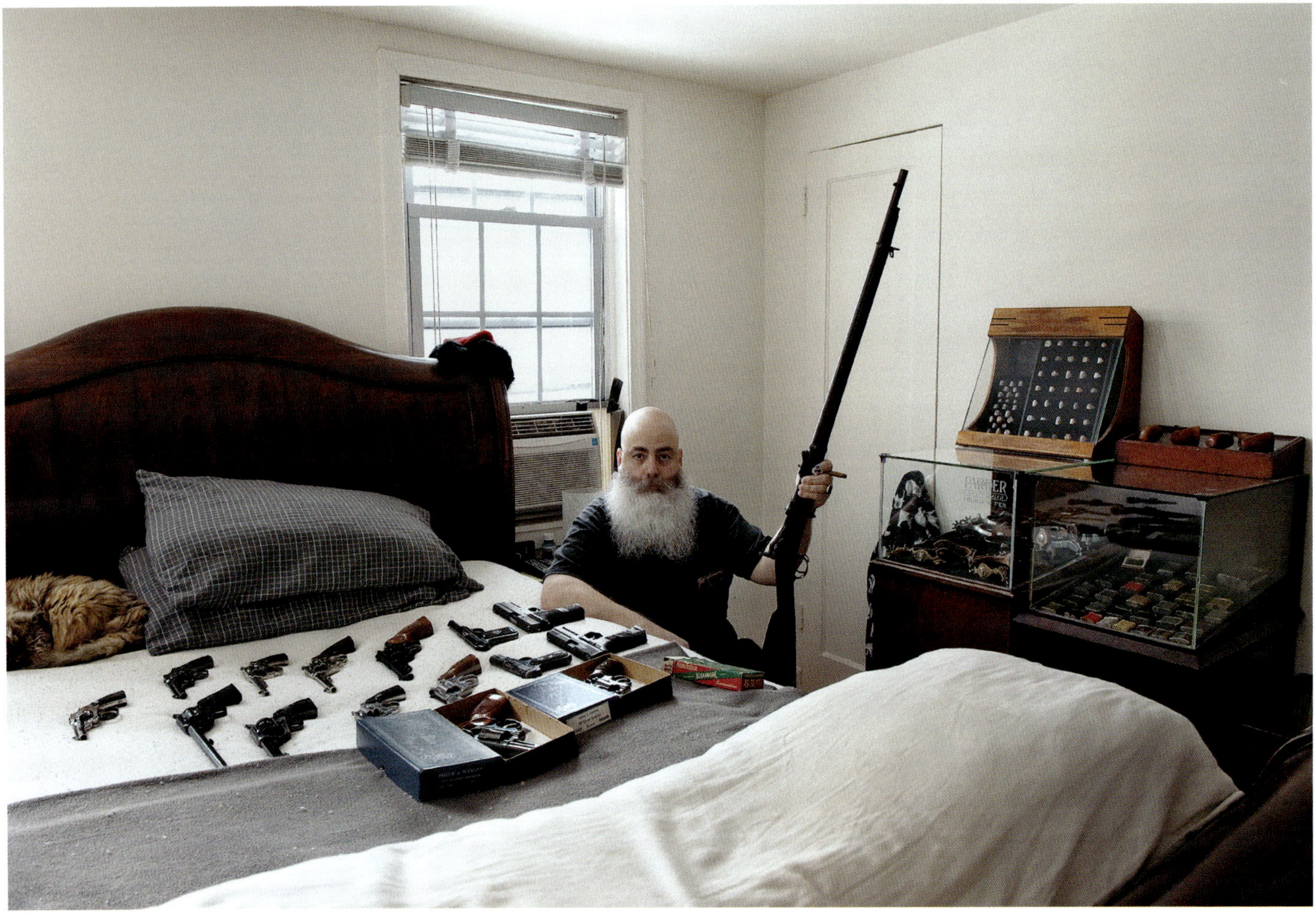

**FIGURE 8.1** For the project *As Close as One Can Get,* Candace photographs subjects in their personal living spaces, along with a variety of objects they select and arrange themselves. She spends hours on each shoot, talking and collaborating to create unguarded moments.
IMAGE © CANDACE DOBRO, *STEVEN,* 2010.

In the previous chapters, we covered everything from T-stops to photosites and lens physics to handheld meters—all in pursuit of learning to overcome technical limitations, continue the lifelong process of mastering gear and understand what goes into making an image.

We thought it would be useful to shift direction now, with a soup-to-nuts view of how the pros work through a project. In this chapter, we talk with our experts about preparing for projects and about the specialists that help them get the job done; then we talk about the shoot and the delivery of a project. This is where we bring together all of the technical skills we've explored and apply them to real-life situations.

## Pre-Production: Andy Batt

***Candace Dobro:*** **How do you define pre-production?**

***Andy Batt:*** It's the work you do before the work. The details are hard to pin down—every project is unique. There are similar things we do for many projects, like setting up a location studio to create portraits of celebrity athletes; there are also one-of-a-kind productions, like the Indy car job I've already talked about.

***CD:*** **When does a project start for you?**

***AB:*** If we're talking about a commercial advertising project, it usually starts when an art producer or art buyer emails us, because they have something coming up and want to know our availability. The email might also come from a client we've been marketing to directly or someone who's found us through our other marketing efforts. The first thing they all want to know is, "Are you available and how much will it cost?"

***CD:*** **What's the first thing *you* want to know?**

***AB:*** I want to know what they're after—besides all the basics, like how many shots or where we'll be shooting. I want to know the kind of story they want to tell. Do they want a hard and gritty portrait of an athlete or an action shot of someone flying through the air? Part of that initial contact is to find out exactly who the end client is and what the scale of the job will be.

Building an estimate is one of the things that helps us understand the project. It's on the accounting side, but for me, it's also a creative exercise. When I build the estimate, I try to pre-visualize the way I'm going to create the photographs. We have as many questions for our clients as they have for us. This process helps all of us understand the scope of the job.

***CD:*** **Does all of this take place before the job is awarded?**

***AB:*** Oh, yeah! A lot of work is done before the job ever gets awarded. We're asked to commit to a price, and to do that, we have to fully understand what we're being asked to do.

***CD:*** **Let's say you've just been awarded the job—what happens next?**

***AB:*** We go over the creative aspects of the job with the Art Director or Creative Director—or sometimes with an entire creative team. Advertising jobs are moving targets. The scope and requirements shift around, so there's a lot of due diligence to make sure we're all on the same page.

We spend time understanding the kind of final output the client wants. It's always useful to know how big the images will be and where they'll be printed. There's a difference between a high-resolution display print for a corporate office and an outdoor 30-sheet poster.[1] You might think the outdoor board would require a higher-res camera, but it's the opposite.

Large prints that will be viewed fairly close-up—maybe six feet away—require high-resolution files. Those outdoor boards work well with DSLR files, since they're typically printed at around 75ppi. I shot a campaign for Portland's Habitat for Humanity (**Figures 8.2A and 8.2B**) using a Canon 1Ds Mark III, and the files were 5,616 × 3,744 pixels. One of the smaller final sizes was 48 × 14 feet. Since those images were designed to be seen from a hundred feet away, they looked amazing.

***CD:*** **Does that type of information determine how you approach a project, right from the start?**

***AB:*** Sure, everything ripples. If I need to shoot with an 80MP medium-format system instead of my DSLR, then I'll need to shoot at a much deeper F-stop to hold more focus—and to hold more focus, I'll need more light, which means that the lighting budget needs to be increased.

Knowing the parameters is part of the creative discussion. When the client says, "Okay, you have the job," then it's time to roll up our sleeves. We figure out which techniques we'll use to make the creative vision happen.

***CD:*** **Can you tell us about a specific job?**

***AB:*** For the Verizon project I talked about in *Chapter Four* (**Figure 4.11**), I photographed Will Power, Verizon's primary Indy car driver, and the #12 Penske car.[2] It was a big job with a fairly long pre-production phase.

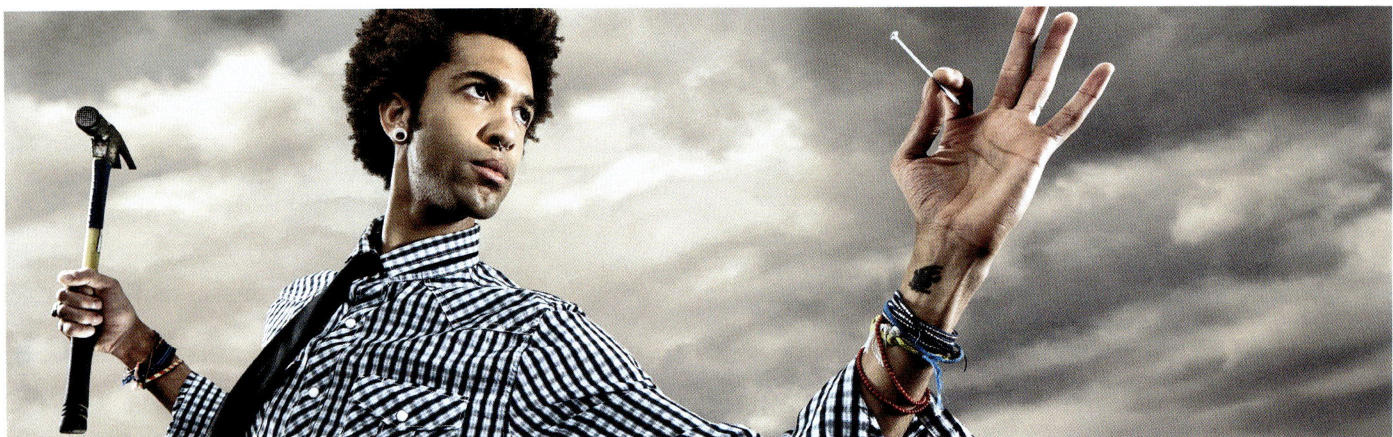

**FIGURE 8.2A** The original image, shot with a Canon 1Ds Mark III (with a Zeiss 21mm lens at 1/160th, *f*/9), had a native file size of 5,616 × 3,744 pixels.
IMAGE © ANDY BATT, *HAMMER BOY*—COURTESY OF PORTLAND HABITAT FOR HUMANITY, 2011.

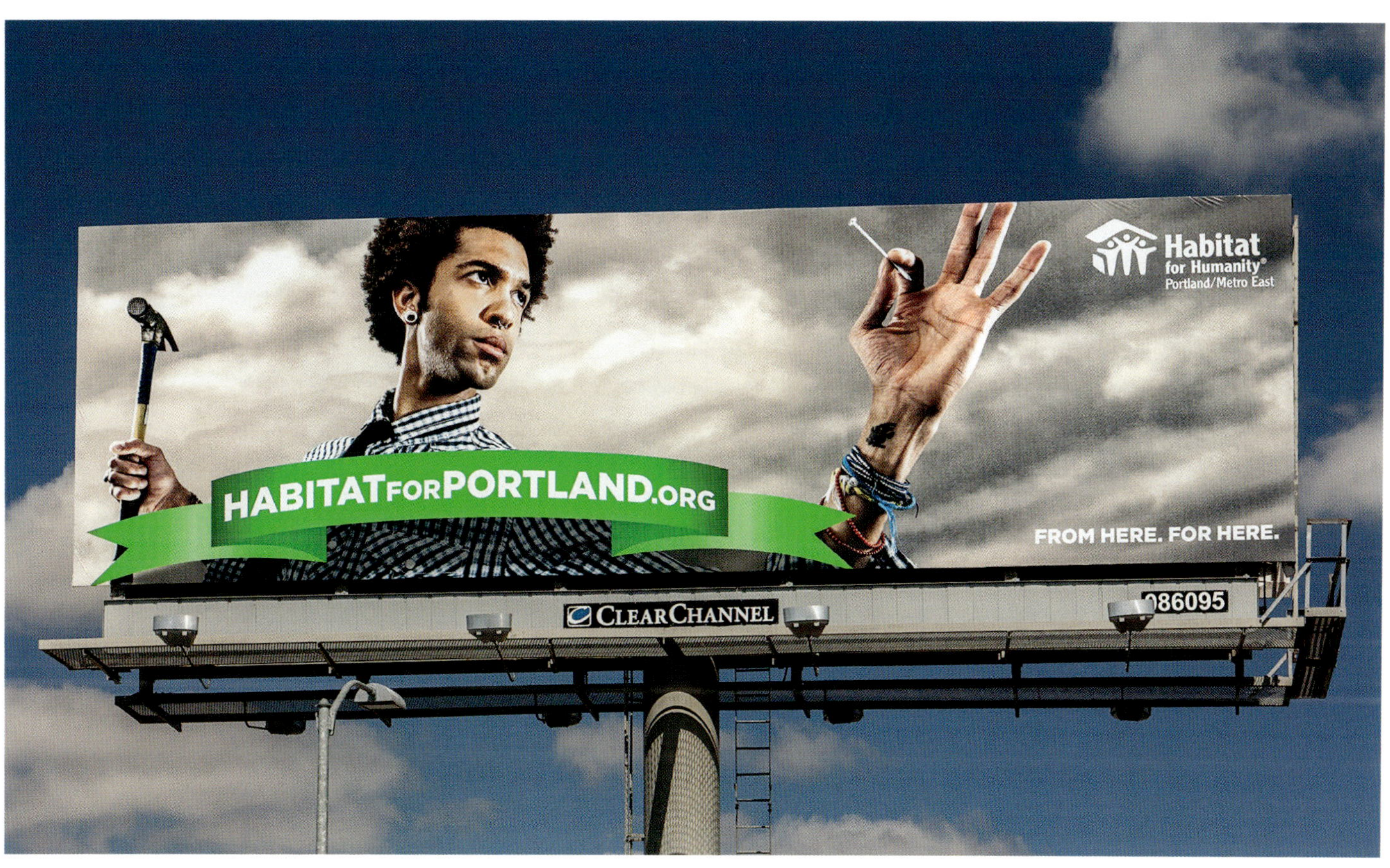


**FIGURE 8.2B** This image was output at 48 × 14 feet on an outdoor board.
IMAGE © ANDY BATT, *HAMMER BOY*—COURTESY OF PORTLAND HABITAT FOR HUMANITY, 2011.

At the beginning, we put together a treatment—a presentation—outlining my ideas from a creative and technical standpoint. From there, we needed to put together the estimate, which was tough, because we had to figure out the whole job on paper, first.

For example, I wanted to attach multiple cameras on the Indy cars themselves and photograph them from a chase vehicle as they sped around the track. This meant putting together a big camera package—bodies, lenses, remote triggers, batteries, etc.—plus a grip team to get the cameras safely attached to the cars and a professional chase vehicle with a driver. We also needed to figure out how many days we'd need in pre-pro (pre-production) to test all the gear and get the cameras dialed in and how many rigging days to get the cars rigged up.

***CD:* Who was working with you at that point?**

***AB:*** We have a great in-town crew that I hire on a project-by-project basis. For this one, I brought in my DIT and first assistant for pre-pro; we spent several days getting ready for the shoot here in Portland. Then I hired two more photo assistants and a PA (production assistant) locally in North Carolina. I also hired Bruce Ely [one of our photo experts] to shoot additional coverage, some overhead views. In North Carolina we hired a great local rigging team and chase truck that were with us for our test day and shoot days.

***CD:* What pre-pro did you do in Portland?**

***AB:*** We picked up all of our rental cameras and lenses and made sure they were set identically—all those little things that photographers do so their cameras are set up the way they like them. We calibrated the autofocus system in each camera to the specific lens that would be mounted, and we labeled the cameras and lenses to make it easy to build them up on shoot day. We also made sure that the clock-time on all the cameras was the same. You try to avoid all the small things that can cause big headaches later on.

We brainstormed: What kinds of shots could we dream up? What gear would it take to do them? How long would each one take? What kinds of problems might we run into? By the first day of this shoot, we already had our game plan (**Figure 8.3**).

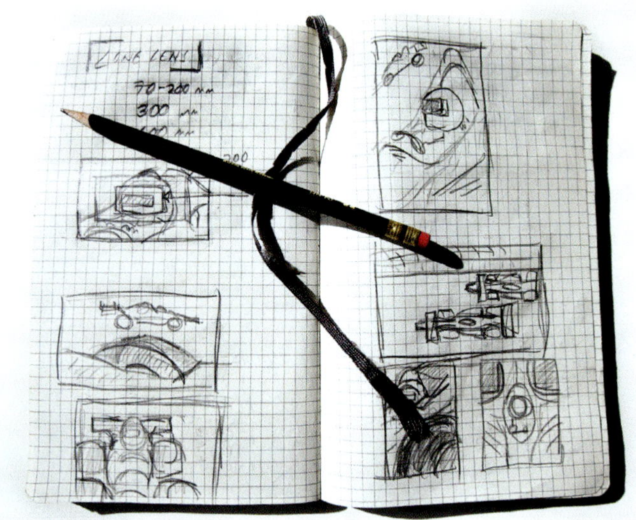

**FIGURE 8.3** Here's a page from Andy's sketchbook—some concept drawings for camera angles on the Verizon Indy car project.
IMAGE © ANDY BATT, *INDY CAR SKETCHES*, 2013.

***CD:* And when you arrived in North Carolina . . .?**

***AB:*** Even with all the pre-pro work we do ahead of time, we still needed to unpack the gear, get things dialed in and find the rhythm of the shoot. That very first shot helps determine everything else we're going to do, so it takes more time. Once we have that rhythm, everybody hits their stride, and the rest of the shots go more quickly (**Figure 8.4**).

***CD:* This type of photo shoot is very different from a solo photographer's shoot.**

***AB:*** Yes, the scale is much bigger—but there's a lot of overlap between big jobs and small ones. You still have clients, a creative brief or shot list (something that guides what you're doing), cameras and subjects. If it's an all-day shoot, you still have to feed somebody lunch, even if it's just you.

There are many jobs where an assistant and I show up with a camera bag and some bounce cards to shoot an editorial portrait. In

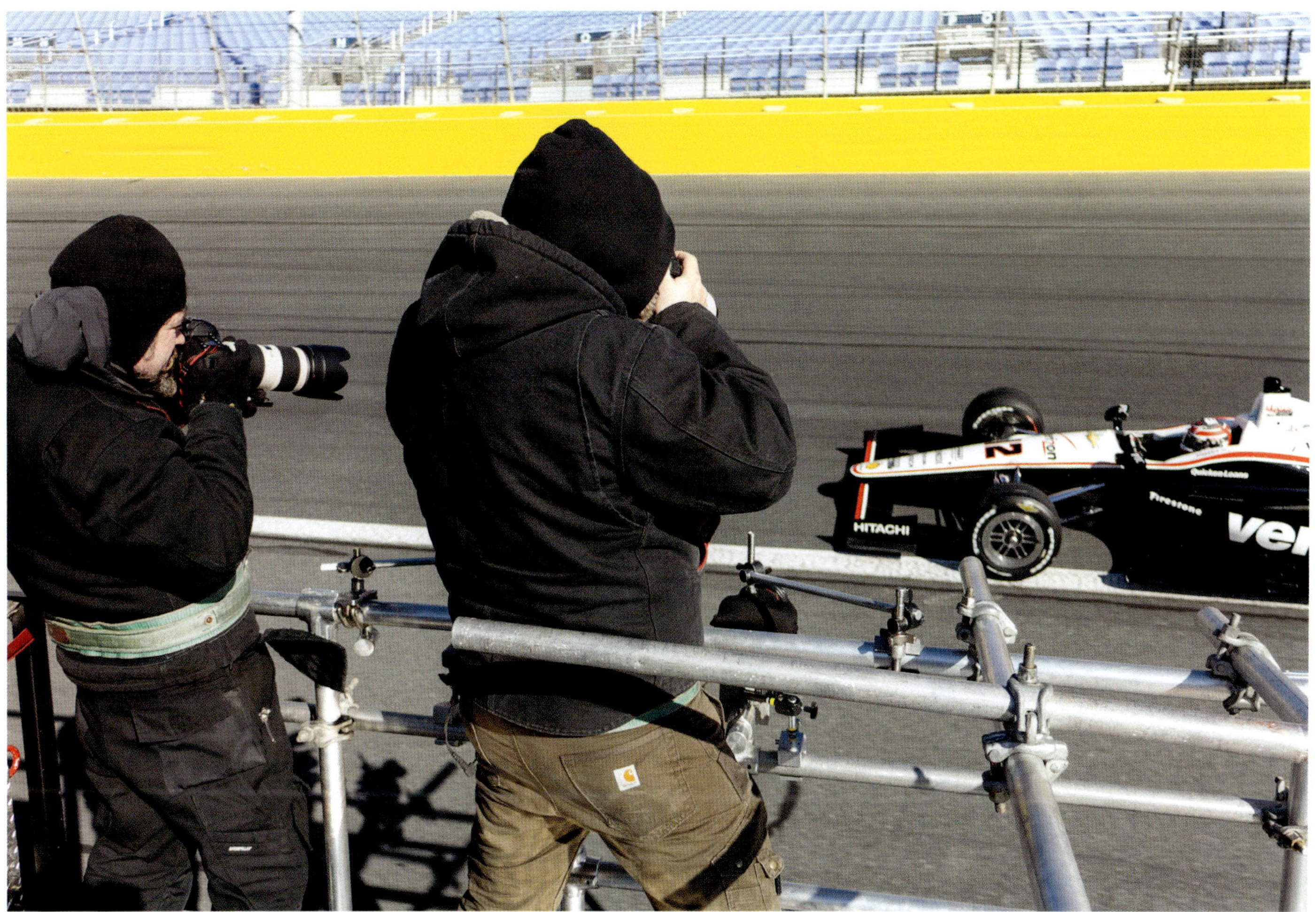


**FIGURE 8.4** Andy is standing on the left side of the image—and going 70mph on a 24° incline.
IMAGE © BRUCE ELY, *BEHIND THE SCENES ON THE VERIZON INDY CAR SHOOT*, 2013.

those cases, the process is much the same, just on a much smaller scale. For example, I always try to tech scout the location before the shoot. I want to know what the location looks like at the time of day I'll be shooting it. That way, I can know where to take the shot and see if there's any additional equipment I'll need.

***CD:*** **How do you deal with rain, if you're supposed to be shooting outdoors?**

***AB:*** We always have a contingency plan. Sometimes it's just waiting it out and grabbing the shot during a break in the rain. On one job we had, it was raining when we needed to get a shot on a deck. Luckily, it was a light rain, so we put a pop-up canopy over the deck, someone held an umbrella over me and we got the shot. That pop-up canopy was on the truck because we'd discussed it during pre-production. Other times, we reschedule the shoot. It's always best to discuss this with your client way before the shoot. Reshoots always cost something extra, even if you waive any weather-day fees.

***CD:* Let's talk about creative direction; who comes up with the ideas you shoot—you or the client?**

***AB:*** On some jobs, I execute a layout or idea that's someone else's concept, but there's still room for me to be creative—any idea is an interpretation. My clients hire me for that interpretation. On other jobs, I have a free hand to create—to base my shots on their brief, without following a specific layout or shot idea.

With the Indy car job, I had free rein to create interesting images. I worked with two creatives who gave feedback while we shot and made sure I stayed on message. I like having agency creatives on my jobs; it can be a very collaborative experience. It's also important to know that I'm delivering photos to match their expectations.

Editorial assignments tend to be looser. You get to do what you want to do, but even with these types of assignments, I still have extensive conversations to find out what the story is. I want to know the tone of the story or idea they want to illustrate. A magazine's photo editor might tell me that it's a serious story and that they need a dramatic image, rather than saying, "Make it look specifically like this." There's always some kind of guidance—I actually prefer to have creative structure.

***CD:* Without structure, it's difficult to know if the images you come up with will be anything like what the client needs or expects.**

***AB:*** The way I create is to react to something, even if it's just a basic concept, like a dramatic portrait. I need that piece of sand to build a pearl around. My creativity doesn't spontaneously burst into existence; it has to be inspired by something.

## Pre-Production: Holly Andres

***Andy Batt:* Can you tell us about pre-production for your fine art photographs? You work with models, locations, wardrobe and props, and everything in your images appears to be carefully considered.**

***Holly Andres:*** It's almost like preparing for a short film. They're period pieces that reside in a different time period, so I spend a lot of time in thrift shops, which are a fertile place for my creativity. Often, I'll find an object that triggers a memory or is visually compelling, and then I craft a narrative around it (**Figure 8.5**). My garage has a surplus of props, clothing, fabrics and furniture—things I use to art-direct my space.

It's a laborious part of my process. Some of my work is like an installation, where I repaint the walls; other times I design custom wallpaper on my computer, print it out and hang it.

***Candace Dobro:* Do you create these projects in your house?**

***HA:*** Yes, and afterwards I'll clean up the scenes in Photoshop. I spend a lot of time thinking about what goes into a shot before I even whip out the camera.

When I'm doing editorial work, I try to spend as much time researching the subject as I can. I did a project for *Runner's World* on Steve Prefontaine. I was marginally familiar with him, but I had some time to really delve into his story and kind of fell in love with him before the shoot even started. I frequently ask if it's possible for me to read the story first, so that I can best match the tone of the piece.

***AB:* There's magic to being on editorial assignments—they're different than commercial assignments. Are they something you want to do more of?**

***HA:*** Editorial work is so much fun. First of all, the subject has to be newsworthy for it to run in something like *The New York Times Magazine*, so that means I get to connect with someone who has a miraculous story. It's such a creative workout; it's like being a student: "Here's your assignment: How are you going to solve it creatively; how

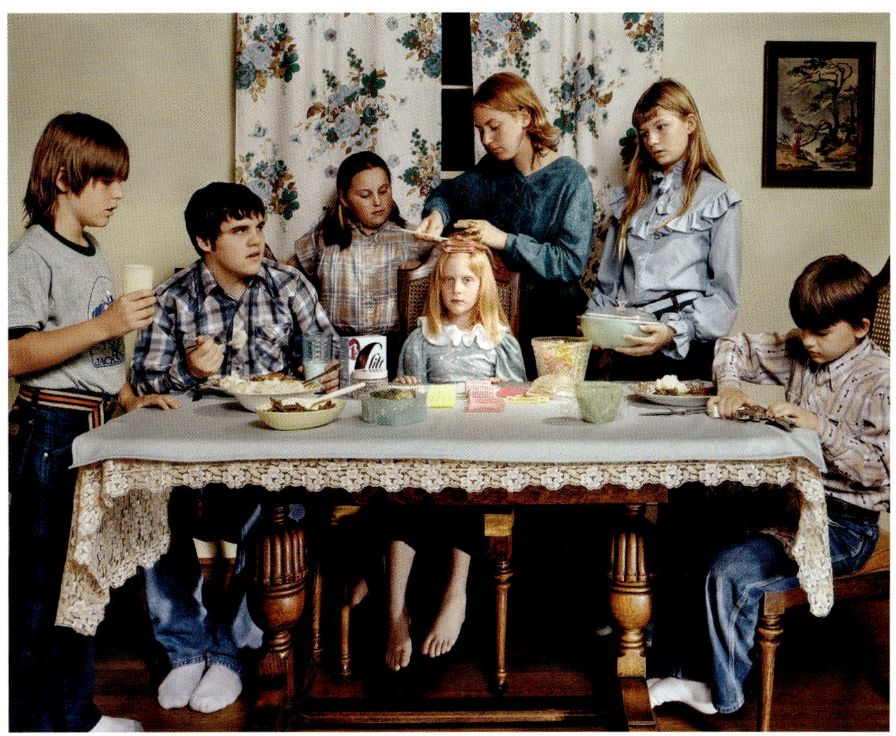

**FIGURE 8.5** Holly spends a lot of time in thrift shops, collecting objects to art-direct her photographs.
IMAGE © HOLLY ANDRES, *FIONA I*, FROM *STORIES FROM A SHORT STREET*, 2006.

are you going to use the camera to best illustrate the tone of this piece or best represent this subject?"

I just did a project for *The New York Times Magazine* on Mariel Hemingway (see **Figure 9.19** in the next chapter). Because she invests so much of her time to better herself as a person, meeting her was life-transforming. I can say that of most of the assignments I've done. I just love it. The compensation isn't very high for editorial work. That's the only bummer.

***AB:*** **I found a reference to a $125 flat day rate from *Fortune* magazine in 1952. Applying a Consumer Price Index inflation rate to that figure gives us a rate of $1,103.19 in 2013 dollars—but photographers on average get only $500 per day for editorial work.**

***HA:*** Yes, the day rate for *The New York Times Magazine* is $500. You can, of course, recoup some of the expenses. They pay for the crew and for gear rental.

> ***Editorial work is so much fun; I think of it as a creative workout, "Here's your assignment: How are you going to solve it creatively; how are you going to use the camera to best illustrate the tone of this piece?"***

## Pre-Production: Sol Neelman

***Andy Batt:* What do you do to prepare for a job?**

***Sol Neelman:*** I usually take a nap; I like to be well rested. I consider myself like a pro athlete who always sleeps before game day. My Think Tank® backpack is full of gear, and I'm ready to go at any point.

***AB:* What research do you do to find Weird Sports?**

***SN:*** I have a list of over 400 Weird Sports (**Figure 8.6**) on a database; my calendar is ridiculous. I know what's happening around the Weird Sports world, so if I see something that just happened, I'll put it in the calendar for next year—hopefully there is a next year and I'll be alive and ready to take pictures. If the stars align, I try to make it happen.

I found out about Chuck Wagon Racing last year and marked it on my calendar. I'm free that weekend, so it looks like I'm going to Arkansas. There are Deaf Olympics (Deaflympics) in Bulgaria, River Soccer in the UK, World Mountain-Bike Bog Snorkeling in Wales next week and a German bike race that looks kind of silly.

***Candace Dobro:* How do you decide which ones to go to?**

***SN:*** I go for things that have lots of low-hanging fruit—lots of visuals. If I'm going to fly somewhere, I don't want the event to last five seconds and be over. Chuck Wagon Racing lasts three days. If I cannot come

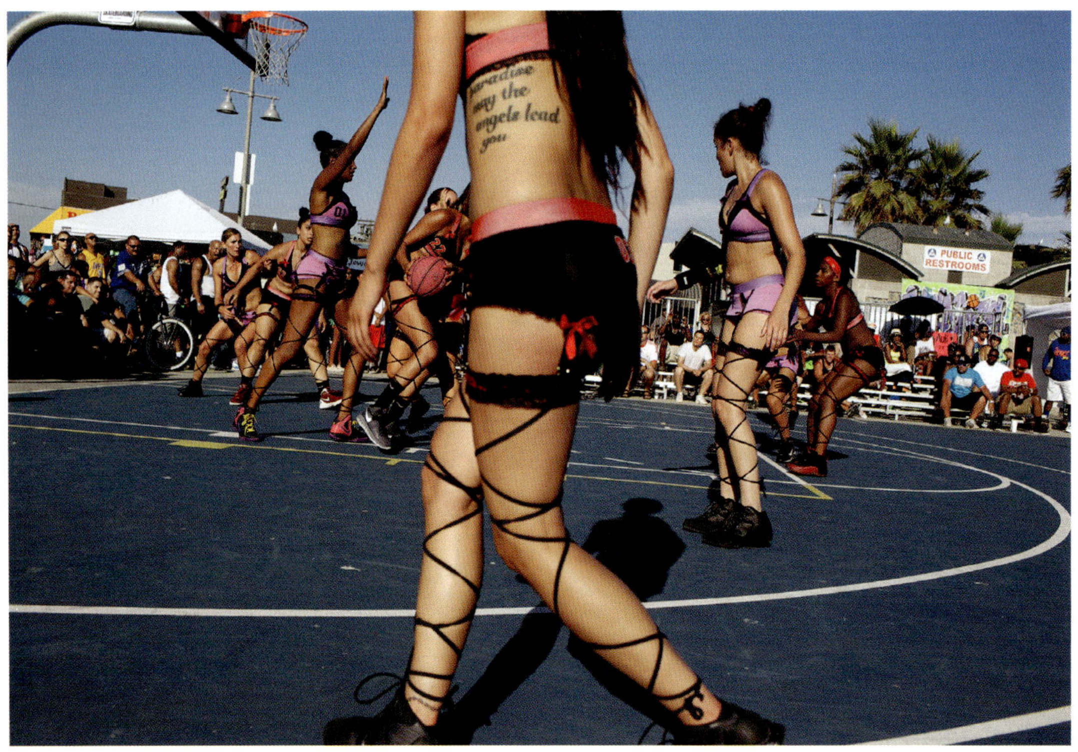


**FIGURE 8.6** Besides the players, Lingerie Basketball[3] requires only two basic things: lingerie and a basketball.
IMAGE © SOL NEELMAN, *LINGERIE BASKETBALL*, PRINTED IN *MARIE CLAIRE*, 2013.

back with a decent Chuck Wagon picture in three days, then I should find another project.

***CD:* What's a Chuck Wagon Race?**

***SN:*** It's like a Wild West horse race.

***CD:* What do they do? Whoever gets to the end first wins—if they don't fall over and die?**

***SN:*** We'll find out; I'll let you know.

***AB:* What about editorial assignments; how are those different for you?**

***SN:*** I usually call people up and introduce myself. Sometimes people are nervous about being photographed and I tell them it will be painless, that we'll have a good time. There was one woman I shot when I was working at newspapers. I called her up and said, "I work at *The Oregonian*. My name is Sol—I'm going to come out and take your photograph on your goat farm." She said, "I'm really unattractive and not at all photogenic." I told her, "I doubt that's true; we're going to have a good time. At the end, you'll be laughing, trust me." I showed up and she was fine—she was photogenic. I took some pictures and at the end, she was laughing.

## Pre-Production: Stewart Cohen

***Andy Batt:* Let's say you just got a phone call that you got the job. What happens now?**

***Stewart Cohen:*** I learned when I started doing TV—which was years ago—that it was all about great pre-production. With stills, pre-production often gets glossed over and isn't taken seriously—depending on the size of the job. I think the more you put into pre-pro, the better your shoot's going to be, so from the second we get a job, we'll sit down, go over the scope of the project and decide what we need to do.

Pre-production is about making a giant list of the things you think you'll need for the job, and then going down the list and making sure you have them. We'll research what we're trying to do, and sometimes we'll find "scrap" for research in the style we're looking to shoot in.

*Pre-production is about making a giant list of what you think you're going to need going into the job, and then going down the list, making sure you have everything.*

***Candace Dobro:* What's scrap?**[4]

***SC:*** It's when you go through magazines and search websites to find images with different looks and feels. We've been pulling scrap for years. If we're shooting someone—like a woman at a computer—we'll go through and cull every picture we can find of a woman at a computer, just to see what other people have done. We do this to get ideas. Many times, the clients will have done that work for us.

***AB:* What's next?**

***SC:*** We have a checklist; our producer will break it down. If we're shooting out of town, we might use a local producer as well. If we need a location, we'll hire a scout. We'll cast. We find the best crew, assistants, stylists, prop people, hair/makeup people, etc. (**Figure 8.7**). You make a list of what you need, and then decide who will find it. For instance, our assistants will find assistants through the assistant underground. We rely on word of mouth a lot.

Make sure you find the best crew for your job—that's really key—and make sure they work within your budget. Be very upfront with them about your budget; make sure they agree to it. On any kind of important agreement, get it in writing.

***AB:* That's something I think we all learn the hard way—get everything in writing. What about casting; how do you handle that?**

***SC:*** When it comes to casting, the request might be, "We need a 30-something young family." Well, what color are they? What's their socioeconomic level? What type of house do they live in? Tell me a little bit about who these people are. This is the time to ask questions and to get specific. If they say, "We want the family to dress casually," do they mean jeans, shorts or khakis?

***CD:* If you don't ask specific questions, who knows what might get missed? What else is important?**

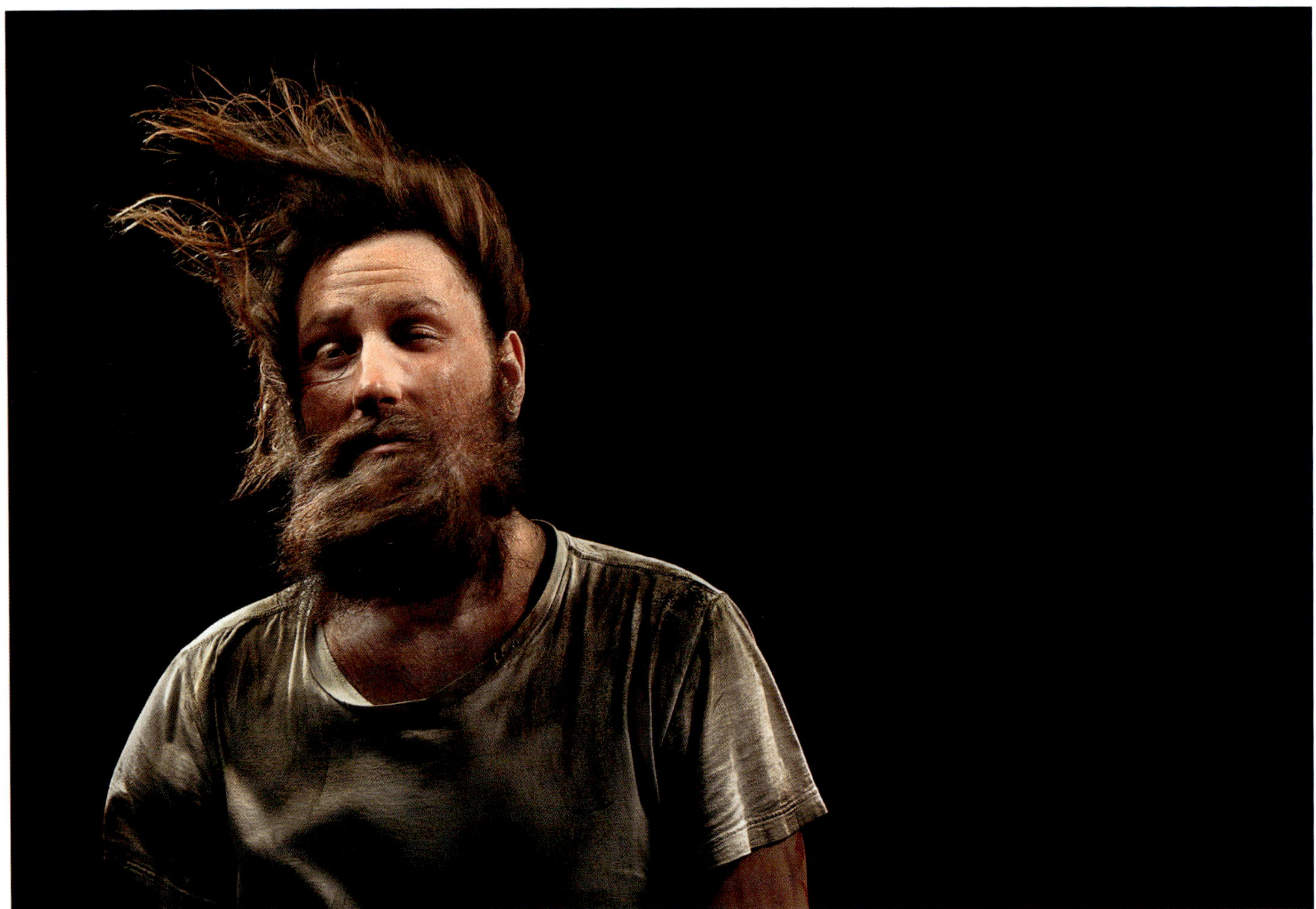

**FIGURE 8.7** It's important to find a good crew, a good stylist and a good hair/makeup person. Stewart starts by making a list of what he needs, and then decides who will find it.
IMAGE © STEWART COHEN, *SHOT FOR VORNADO® FANS CAMPAIGN*, 2011.

***SC:*** Pre-production is the time to ask questions. When the crew doesn't ask questions, I sense there's a problem. If a wardrobe stylist says, "Oh yeah, I got it," then I want to know if she's *really* got it—if she knows what she's looking for. Where is she shopping? What is she going to get? At the end of it all, if something gets messed up, the whole job has my name on it. I'm not totally neurotic—I'm really easygoing, but at the same time, the job has one's reputation attached to it, so it has to look good. You are only as good as your last shoot.

***AB:* Do you ever do test shoots, and if so, are they for jobs, or just to try things out?**

***SC:*** Yes, we shoot tests all the time, sometimes to get ready for a specific job. We just went out and shot a high-school football game to prep for a Gatorade project. I go all-out on test shoots for something new. We once got a line on a skincare project that was all nudes, and I didn't have many of them. I really wanted the job, so we went out and shot a portfolio in the same style as the brief. It's amazing how fast you can shoot a whole portfolio of nudes when your mind is set on it. If we're trying to do something crazy, I'll usually get the guys to set it up and try stuff. I'm always shooting and trying new ways of doing things.

## Working with a Crew: Andy Batt

***Candace Dobro:* Your shoots can involve photo assistants, DITs, wardrobe stylists, makeup artists, hair stylists, prop stylists, craft services, etc. Can you describe your cast of characters?**

***Andy Batt:*** The projects vary in scope and size, and my crew shifts right along with them. We've been working with some of my crew for years, but we hire some for the first time in cities we travel to for shoots. Therese, our producer, and I are involved with every job.

A smaller job usually has a *DIT (Digital Imaging Technician)* and a *photo assistant*. My DIT handles all things related to image data, and my photo assistant handles cameras and lights. On a really small job, it will just be my DIT (who is also a great photo assistant) and me. On bigger jobs, it's a matter of expansion. Instead of having one assistant who handles cameras, grip and lights, I might have three, each dedicated to one of those tasks.

If the job gets even bigger, then each of those three has a second assistant to work directly with them. That way, I have people who know what their jobs are and things get done efficiently. Most of my jobs are slightly informal; we expect everyone to pitch in and work across departments on occasion, especially if we're trying to move quickly out of a location. All my crew are great about that—many of them are also cross-trained and can fill other roles as necessary.

The rest of the crew fills out, according to the needs of the job. The Verizon project had a big shot list and took place at multiple locations, with multiple models, in a single day. Each scene needed wardrobe and props. For that job, we had a sizable crew. Our first hire was our *location scout*, who found our locations and helped us get permits for them. On our pre-production and shoot days, we had a lead *wardrobe stylist*, with three assistants; a lead *prop stylist* with one assistant; a *makeup artist*; a *hair stylist* and a *production assistant (PA)*[5]—plus four photo assistants[6] and a DIT.

That might seem like a lot of people, but when you're trying to get a big shot list done in a short amount of time—and it involves multiple locations, multiple models and set dressing—it's the way you need to go.

***CD:* You described the different roles assistants can have—can you expand on that?**

***AB:*** My DIT is one of the key people on set. Generally, anything involving images falls to him: tethering, downloading, backing up, on-set editing, JPEG processing and working with clients to make selects. Whenever I'm worried about making a backup or adding metadata, it means part of my attention is not on making images. He handles all of that stuff so I can concentrate on making the images.

***Whenever I'm worried about making a backup or adding metadata, it means part of my attention is not on making images. My DIT is on set so I can concentrate on making the images.***

My first assistant's job changes according to the project, but on any job, it's the production assistant's responsibility to take the camera bag into his or her world. The PA hands me cameras that are ready-to-roll (based on our metering and testing), and when I'm done shooting, I hand the camera off. The PA takes care of charging batteries, keeping all the glass clean, etc., and works with the DIT to handle the transfer of CF cards. My first [assistant] will help me set and adjust the lighting, and then tear it all down when we're done. On a bigger job, I'll have other assistants to handle the build-up and teardown, and my first [assistant] will manage those assistants.

The assistant's job includes: calling the rental house to put our orders in; scoping all the rental gear to make sure we get what we ordered and that it all works; keeping an eye out on set to make sure the lights are working; dressing the cables and keeping the set safe for civilians; and keeping our gear safe from weather, theft and breakage.

When I have a team of people working towards a goal, everything moves faster. If I'm working with my regular crew, I'll give them detailed instructions and know they can build lighting and get the tests done, while I'm busy working with the styling team or consulting with the clients.

***CD:* How many regulars do you have, and are they all cross-trained?**

***AB:*** I have six people that I consider regulars; they're all able to handle just about any task I throw at them. The DIT is one of my most key people. DITs need to be trained about the way I do things, and they must be able to think on their feet and bring new ideas into our workflow. A DIT has a lot of responsibility, since the whole job rests in his or her hands.

***CD:* What might you ask of the DIT that's specific to your way of doing things?**

***AB:*** I like to use particular software, workflows, naming conventions and folder structure; it's not that the individual pieces are that difficult, but it takes some skill and training to consistently follow through on a good workflow. I also want my DIT to react quickly. That's a good measuring stick: It's not about how well they do under normal circumstances, but what happens when things get crazy.

***CD:* If you don't have a DIT, then how do manage your workflow or download images?**

***AB:*** I try not to be in that situation. If I'm walking around street shooting, I don't bring a DIT with me—that'd be weird. I do many low-budget gigs, where the small amount of budget goes towards hiring a DIT or assistant. Those are usually jobs I want to get a portfolio image out of, so it's worth the peace of mind to have a DIT. I can tech for myself, but that takes energy away from making the image.

***CD:* For photographers who usually shoot solo, can you describe what it feels like to work with a crew? What kinds of responsibilities do you have as you're operating in the center of it all?**

***AB:*** Some days it's exhilarating. I feel the energy of the shoot when everyone is collaborating (**Figure 8.8**), the shots are coming together, my clients are happy and I like the work we're producing. Other times it's exhausting, because I'm putting out fires and trying to see two moves ahead—and I've been burning hard for a few days. Actually it's always exhausting, but on the fun jobs, I don't realize I'm exhausted until I fall into bed.

I'm a creative person, and I'm also the director. I have to make decisions about fun stuff, but I also have to shoulder the responsibility—it's my name on the door.

## Working with a Crew: Holly Andres

***Andy Batt:* Do you work with stylists on your commercial shoots?**

***Holly Andres:*** I like to do my own styling (except for makeup and hair, because my strengths or interests don't really lie there). I've been working on some bigger projects where there are more and more people collaborating with me.

***AB:* At a certain point you have to give up some of the control.**

***HA:*** Yeah you do; it's true, I often find myself thinking, "Get out of the frame, get out of the frame—I'm ready to take the picture!" As a fine artist I did all the styling—although I've *always* worked with a photo assistant.

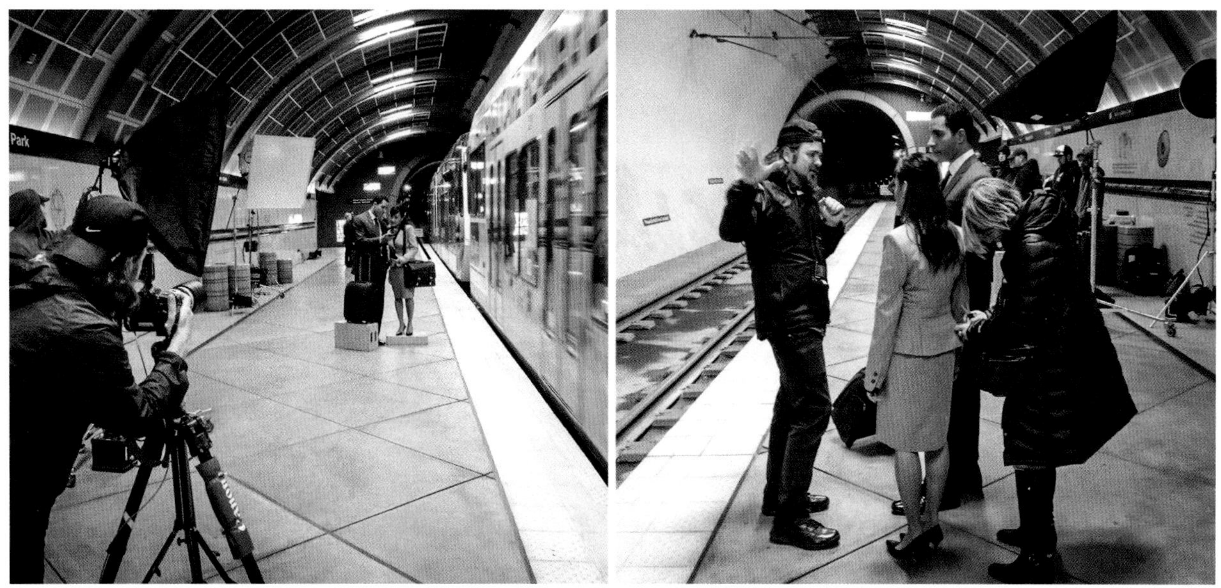

**FIGURE 8.8** Here's Andy in the tunnels, working with models and crew for an HP shoot.
IMAGE © THERESE GIETLER, *BEHIND THE SCENES ON HP,* 2013.

***Candace Dobro:*** **What do your assistants do for you?**

***HA:*** I make sure to work with assistants whose technical skill level surpasses my own. I want to spend as much time thinking in the creative realm as possible, not being distracted by a bunch of technical variables. Often I'll have someone on a light, dialing it up and down or moving it back and forth. I always work with an assistant or two; that's my preference.

I just worked on a project photographing the band Pink Martini—and between the fifteen-piece band, art directors, publicity managers, hot-air balloon technicians, stylists, caterers and my assistants, there were over sixty people involved (**Figure 8.9**).

***AB:*** **It's nice to delegate some of the responsibilities a little, isn't it?**

***HA:*** Oh my gosh, of course—it's such a luxury when my only job is to get the shot. I don't have to worry about all of these other variables.

***AB:*** **What do you look for in an assistant?**

***HA:*** First and foremost, I like to work with assistants I feel comfortable around. If I haven't worked with an assistant before, I'll usually have a little powwow with him or her beforehand. I tell them I'm really kind and patient, I'm fun to work with and I'm creative, but I have an artist's mind and can be pretty absentminded sometimes. Of course, it's really, really nice to have help moving the equipment.

***It's such a luxury when my only job is to get the shot. I don't have to worry about all of these other variables.***

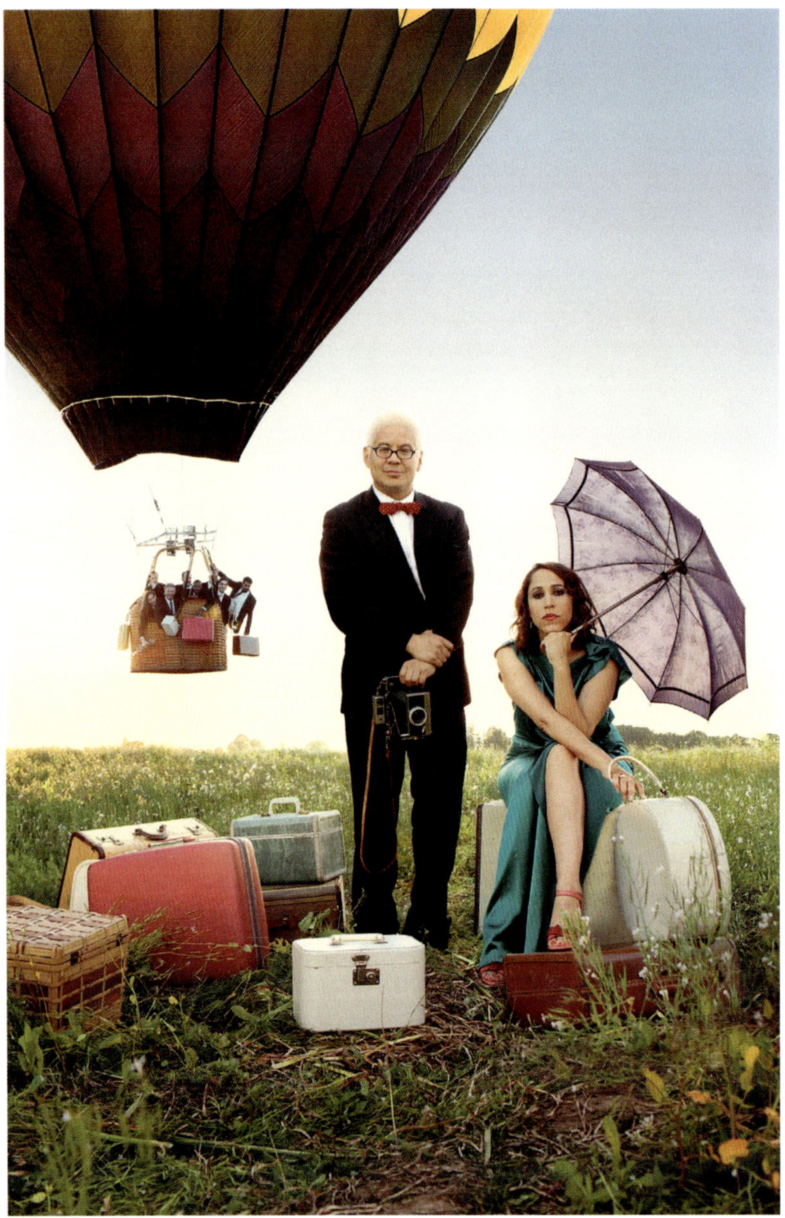

**FIGURE 8.9** Working with a small army of people allowed Holly to create this complex image. IMAGE © HOLLY ANDRES, *PINK MARTINI,* 2013.

## Working with a Crew: Stewart Cohen

***Andy Batt:* What are your thoughts about working with crew?**

***Stewart Cohen:*** Working with crew is really important (**Figure 8.10**). I've always been collaborative; I think including people in the process is really important. You need to treat them with respect, because they bring their expertise. I get many comments from my crews that they love working with us, because it's so chill and because I don't raise my voice. I asked them, "What are you talking about?" and they said you wouldn't believe the number of egomaniac *!@*#!s out there.

I need them as much as they need me. I want a stylist to bring something I didn't ask for; I want a hair and makeup person to put a model's hair in something cool that I didn't ask for. I want an assistant to say, "What if we do this?" I'll say, "Good idea"—and sometimes I'll do it, even if I know he's wrong, just to see what it looks like.

***CD:* That must make your set a fun place to work. It changes the environment—for everyone.**

***SC:*** Yes, but when push comes to shove, people learn that you've got to work fast. Working with crew is about setting expectations and communicating. We need to tell them, "Here's what we're trying to accomplish today. This is the number of setups. Any input is great, but this is what we've got to do."

***CD:* What runs through your head when you first walk onto a set? You want to make sure that whatever you do, however you speak, gives a particular message about the way you want to work. When you walk through that door, how do you establish a scene and get things to go the way you want them to go?**

***SC:*** If we hired a big, local crew, the first thing I'll do is walk in and say good morning to everyone and introduce myself. I try to gather

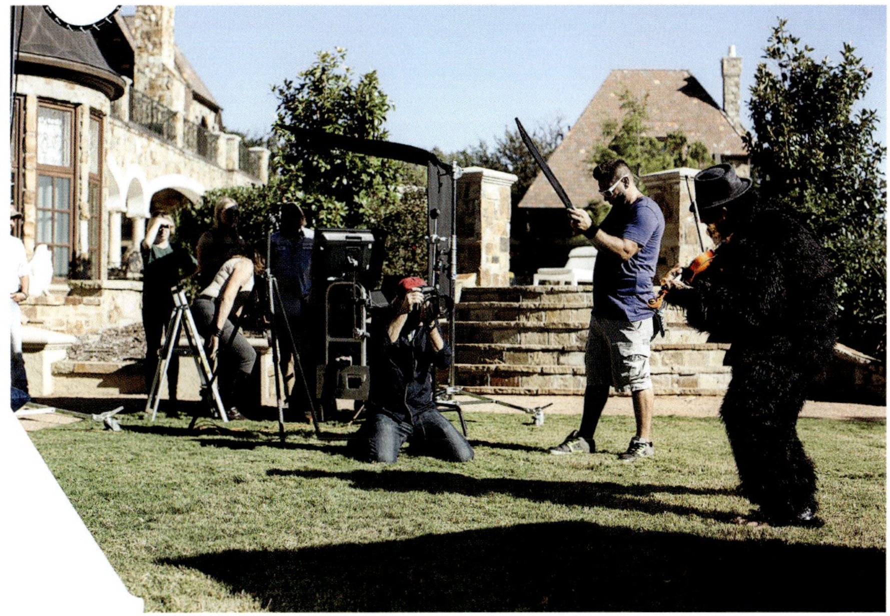

**FIGURE 8.10** Stewart shot this production still on location in Texas, while photographing a violinist in a gorilla suit for Perennials Fabrics.
IMAGE © STEWART COHEN, *BEHIND-THE-SCENES CREW*, 2013.

everyone around and make introductions, give a quick spiel like, "I'm happy you guys are here with us, thank you so much for coming. This is what we're doing today, this is what I know and this is what I don't know." We like to keep it light-hearted—it's all about the people.

Whether we're doing a portrait of a famous person or a lifestyle shot of some homeless guys, the vibe that's on the set is the vibe they're going to give back. You have to be conscious about that. If it's tense behind the camera, people feel it. If there's tension between the agency and the client, I feel it. It's my role to keep everybody loose and happy.

A lot of people in our business have big egos, which is cool, because to be a creator, you need a big ego—but you also want things to run smoothly and be fun. When you become a *prima donna*, there may be no tomorrow—you'll do this job, but it'll be the last time you'll ever hear from those people.

If your clients don't come back when the job is right, then you're not going to have a long career. It's a lot easier to maintain existing clients than it is to completely nurture new clients with every job.

> *If you don't have clients come back, then you're not going to have a long career. It's a lot easier to maintain existing clients than it is to completely nurture new clients for every job.*

## Working with a Crew: Sol Neelman

***Andy Batt:*** **Do you ever need people to help you out on assignments or personal projects?**

***Sol Neelman:*** I need to bring a shrink and a masseuse! Generally I don't, since I'm not hired for many big production jobs, though I would like to be. I did a big one for Nike last year, and they had everything. It was a movie shoot and was kind of fun. If I have an assistant, that's a luxury. I'm used to working on my own; that's what I bring to my projects.

**FEATURED INTERVIEW**

## Therese Gietler

*Producer*

***Andy Batt:*** **Can you define what a producer does?**

***Therese Gietler:*** When a producer is on the job, the photographer doesn't have to figure out what time the model and crew should show up, what the crew should eat for lunch and where the model releases are. All the photographer wants to do on the day of the shoot is take pictures, and that's all he or she should be doing—because it takes every ounce of attention, creativity and energy to be engaged in doing that job. You shouldn't be distracted by all the other details.

> ***When a producer is on the job, the photographer doesn't have to figure out what time the model and crew should show up, what the crew should eat for lunch and where the model releases are. All the photographer wants to do on the day of the shoot is take pictures, and that's all he or she should be doing—because it takes every ounce of attention, creativity and energy to be engaged in doing that job.***

Let's say there's an editorial job, and all you need is one picture of somebody in a hospital. There are still a whole bunch of details to deal with: When are you going to schedule the shoot; do you have the hospital's permission; where are you going to park your car; can you bring gear in? A producer takes care of all these things—either ahead of time or on the job—so the photographer can do his or her job (**Figure 8.11**).

I've had assistants come to me during a job and ask, "What do you do, anyway? It doesn't look like you do anything."

PRODUCTION CHECKLIST

| | |
|---|---|
| **PRODUCTION CREW** | **TALENT** |
| Producer | Casting Fee |
| Production Assistant | Casting Director |
| Digital Tech | Casting Facility |
| Camera Assistant | Talent |
| Lighting Assistant | Extras |
| Grip Assistant | Animal Trainer |
| | Animal Talent |
| **RENTAL** | |
| Camera | **STYLING DEPARTMENT** |
| Lighting | Hair Stylist |
| Digital | Makeup Stylist |
| Grip Van | Grooming Stylist |
| Walkie Talkies | Grooming Assistant |
| Generators | Wardrobe Stylist |
| Special Effects | Wardrobe Assistant |
| | |
| **PRODUCTION EXPENSES** | **ART DEPARTMENT** |
| Production Expenses | Art Department Lead |
| Messengers/Overnight Air | Art Assistant |
| Catering | Set Dressing Props |
| Craft/Working Meals | Model Making |
| Insurance | |
| | **PROPS/WARDROBE** |
| **TRAVEL** | Prop Rental/Purchase |
| Airfare | Prop Transportation |
| Luggage Fees | Wardrobe Rental/Purchase |
| Lodging | Wardrobe Transportation |
| Car Rental/Transportation/ Expenses | |
| Per Diems | **LOCATIONS** |
| | Location File Pull |
| **POST PRODUCTION** | Location Scout |
| Hard Drives | Scout Expenses |
| Image Delivery | Motorhome Rental |
| Retouching | Motorhome Expenses |
| Archiving | Expendables |
| | Location Fees/Permits |
| | Parking/Barricades/Closures |
| | Security |
| | Studio Rental |
| | Studio Manager |
| | Building Materials |
| | Floor Surface |

**FIGURE 8.11** With every project, there's an immense list of details that need going over. This is a partial list of common production crew and line items. The full list is about six pages long and covers everything.
CHART © ANDY BATT, *PRODUCTION CHECKLIST*, 2013.

I say, "If I've done my job right and no problems crop up, then on the day of the shoot, I don't have anything to do and I'm there for fun." There are always problems, though. Photo shoots are not perfect; things always go wrong and all the problems come to me—not to Andy. The first hour of a big production is the hardest for me, every single time. I calm down after that, but that first hour we're at a location, everybody wants to know where to park their cars, where to set up their tables, etc., and all of that comes to me.

***AB:* When does a job start for you?**

***TG:*** My job starts with the first phone call from the client when they ask for an *estimate*. Much of the pre-production happens during the estimate phase. That's when I get a lot of things lined up, regardless of whether the job is or isn't awarded to us.

***Candace Dobro:* Things like . . .**

***TG:*** The first thing I do after someone describes the job is to sit down with the *calendar* (**Figure 8.12**) and put in "hold" dates. If it's a one-day shoot, I put down the shoot day. The day before that is a pre-production day. I put down a day for tech scouting, lighting tests and pre-lights, and the day before that is for getting the gear together. The day after the shoot is a "wrap" day. I look at it all on the calendar first. A one-day shoot can take five days of pre- and post-production.

***AB:* How do you know how many days the shoots are going to be?**

***TG:*** The client talks to me about the job and we go back and forth about how much time it might take, how much time we want it to take and the type of budget they have. We consider Andy's input as well, although we tend to ignore him at that point; I know he hates that.

***AB:* Once the job's been awarded—and the budget is worked out and we have a good idea of what we're doing—what other logistical things do you need to line up before a day of photography begins?**

***TG:*** The calendar needs to be set and approved by the client. From that point, I hire and book all the *crew*. In order of protocol, there's the DIT, which is the Digital Tech, first assistant, second assistant, third assistant and fourth assistant. I break those jobs down to camera and lighting assistants and production assistants (PAs). PAs are the bottom of the barrel in terms of protocol, because they're the ones that run errands, sit with gear when it's being left behind and schlep things back and forth the most. They're also the least experienced.

***AB:* That's part of the way they gain experience. It's a great way to learn how this business works.**

***TG:*** Next in line are the *stylists*, meaning hair stylists, and their assistants. Sometimes there's a hair stylist and a makeup stylist; other times there's one person who does both hair and makeup; I call them "groomers." The number of stylists I hire depends on how many people we have to photograph. There's always a lead and assistants underneath them, so I don't have to manage their assistants for them.

Then there are wardrobe stylists. They sometimes shop for wardrobe, or they manage the wardrobe that subjects bring with them. They steam the clothes and put them together in outfits. They're on set to make sure that the models' collars look good, their shirts are buttoned properly and that belts are buckled. On one of our jobs, we didn't have a wardrobe stylist, and these football players all left their buckles wide open—every single one of them—and not one of us noticed! That's why you hire wardrobe stylists; you think you're not going to need them, but their eyes are looking at clothing, and it's really important. You know those baseball caps with the hologram stickers on them? I almost peeled off all the stickers, because I thought, "That's what you do, we don't need the stickers." Well apparently, those baseball hats are cool because of the stickers. I didn't know that; that's what wardrobe stylists are for.

Sometimes we have to *build a set*, or if we're on location and are in a house, we have to take out all the furniture and put in our own, because a house is never perfect. You can never find a house with just the right stuff in it; you always end up having to bring your own. It takes three days of pre-production for them to go shop for the furniture and then hours and hours ahead of time to do the set dressing. It's very time-consuming.

***CD:* I'm tired just thinking about it.**

***TG:*** Location scouting is a really important thing we didn't talk about before. The *location scout* goes and finds a variety of locations for us to work in. Houses are the hardest, because everybody has an idea of what they want: "I want a rustic house, a modern house or a suburban house." What does a "suburban house" mean to you?

***AB:* Part of our job is to fulfill the client's requests before we ever do an actual day of photography. What's your advice for photographers who are getting their first few jobs?**

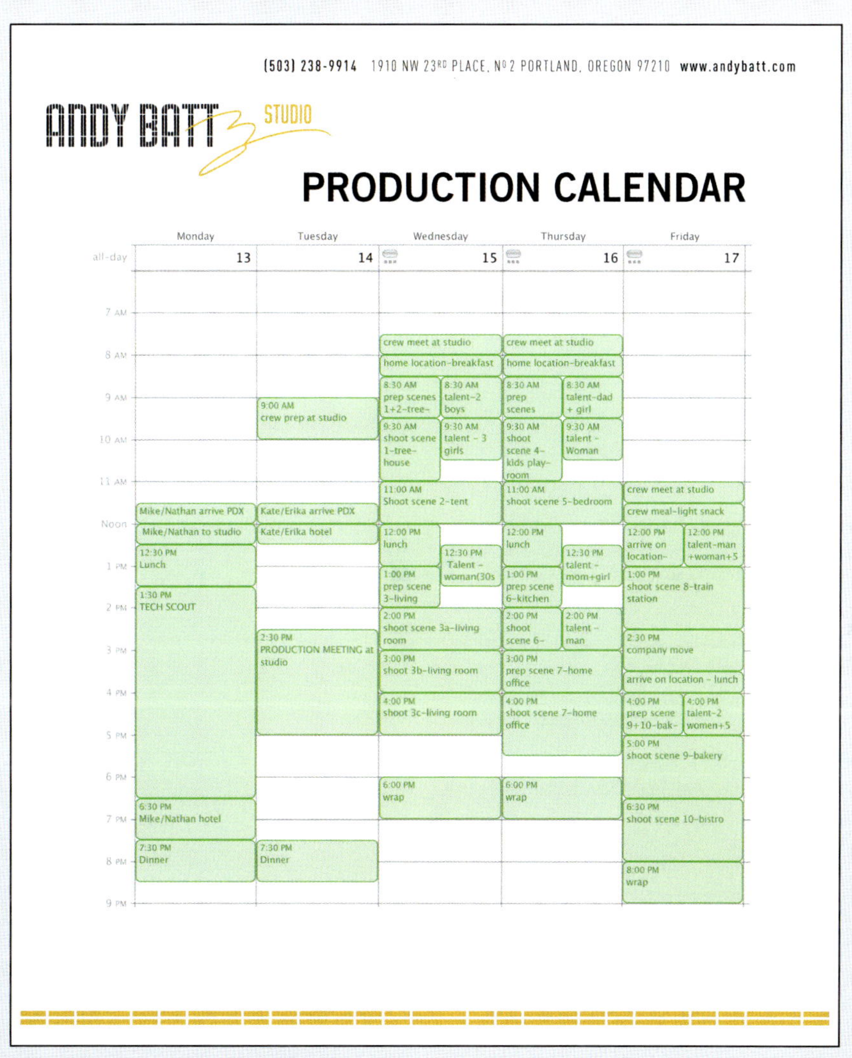


**FIGURE 8.12** All shoots revolve around the calendar. A successful job is a matter of being aware of the schedule and taking control.
ILLUSTRATION © THERESE GIETLER, *PRODUCTION CALENDAR*, 2013.

***TG:*** My first suggestion is to not try to do it all yourself. It's very tempting to feel like you're capable of doing it all yourself, but it will stretch you thin. The best thing you can do is surround yourself with people that are more experienced than you are. That means having a good network of people you can turn to. How do you get that network? By joining trade organizations like ASMP,[7] APA,[8] WPPI[9] and PPA[10]—and by joining local photo clubs. In the beginning, you may not have a budget to pay everybody much, but it's really important to learn about your strengths ahead of time and find people that can do the rest.

***AB:* We advocate photo assistants quite a bit, because we both came up through that system. Can you talk about how and why we hire assistants and what it's like to be one?**

***TG:*** One of the main reasons we hire assistants is to carry gear, because Andy has already damaged his back.

***AB:* What are some reasons to be an assistant?**

***TG:*** What better way is there than on-the-job training to learn so many things? It gives you an opportunity to figure out what works best for you. Do you like working with natural light, strobes or HMIs? You get to learn from photographers that specialize in all different ways of working.

It's also a great learning experience to watch them deal with clients. Assisting is definitely a job for people who can be seen and not heard. The best way to learn is to just step back and watch what happens during emergencies and during good jobs. How do the photographers handle problems?

Our crew is very well versed to deal with problems on set so that the client never knows. I sometimes don't even know when problems are happening. I'll usually pick up on it, but it's never spoken.

***CD:* That's a very impressive thing to hear, because you want there to be a sense on set that you're controlling everything and that the clients are in good hands. Can you tell one story?**

***TG:*** We were on a job shooting video and stills, and Andy handed off the card that he'd just shot to the assistant. The assistant dropped the card, picked it up, got it confused with the fresh card and handed the wrong one to Andy. Andy formatted it and looked up at the assistant, saying, "Are you sure this is the right card?" The look on his face . . . Both of those cards got taken out and they just went away—and Andy kept shooting. I caught wind of the assistants on the phone asking, "How do we get this information back?" They were calling one of their friends up in Seattle to recover this card, but it was all done quietly. The clients—to this day—never knew that happened.

***CD:* I guess the information was recovered?**

***TG:*** Yes—Andy and his crew worked very hard to recover that data. There was a postmortem on that job about ways we could avoid that ever happening again.

***CD:* Photography is not for the weak at heart.**

***TG:*** No, because most often, you can't redo your mistakes. If you do have to redo something, it's got to come out of your own pocket, because it's your mistake.

***CD:* What qualities do you look for in an assistant? Think of your favorite ones; what made them so great?**

***TG:*** After years of hiring assistants, I look for great personalities, people who are fun to be with. Good photo assistants listen well, admit when they don't know something, never assume that they know best and are punctual. They also know how to

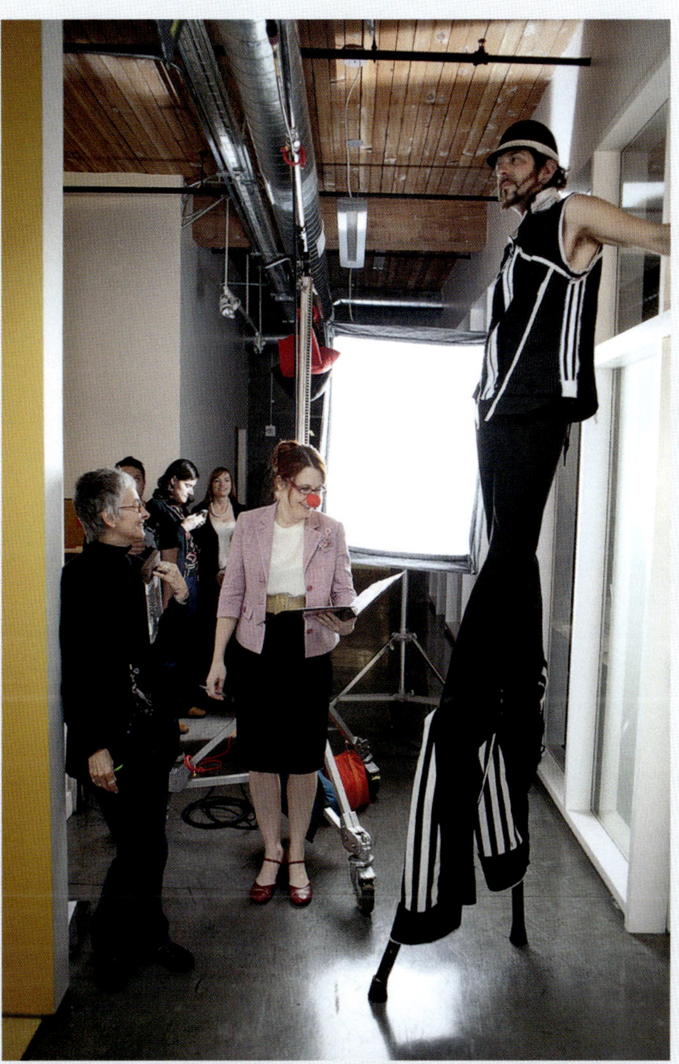

keep their mouths shut. I know it sounds awful, but seriously, you can't have a yakkity yak on set.

They don't have to be great photographers. Interestingly, a lot of assistants don't come with portfolios anymore. It's not about the work; it's about being able to get along with the person. Having a good work ethic and their not "knowing best" are what's important.

***Good photo assistants listen well, admit when they don't know something, never assume that they know best and are punctual. They also know how to keep their mouths shut. I know it sounds awful, but seriously, you can't have a yakkity yak on set.***

***CD:* An open attitude is hugely important.**

***TG:*** We create a family on our jobs. Most assistants feel that camaraderie and want to be part of it.

***AB:* What is "protocol," and what is it for?**

***TG:*** *Protocol* is about understanding your place within the structure of the job—knowing your place on the totem pole. In our structure, for instance, the photographer, director and producer are all at the top of the totem pole and the heads of each department are the next ones down. Then come the head of the photo assistants, the head of the styling crews and the head of the set department. Protocol becomes important when you have questions or problems, because it helps you go to the right person for answers.

**FIGURE 8.13** In addition to Therese's skills as a producer, she's also a fine art photographer and accomplished bookbinder. This diverse skillset is part of what makes her a good producer—it's a job that's never the same twice. Sometimes being a producer means standing in front of the camera, wearing a clown nose. Therese had a cameo in *Stella's Flight*, the short film she produced. It was shot by Andy and directed/written by Courtenay Hameister.
IMAGE © TOM HASSLER, *BEHIND THE SCENES ON* STELLA'S FLIGHT, 2010.

Little problems don't go to Andy, they go to his assistants, because they'll know how to handle them or know to either bring them to me or to Andy. Most of the problems on set should come to me [not Andy], unless they're directly photo-related.

***CD:* It's like triage at a hospital.**

***TG:*** Completely.

***CD:* Yours is a very service-oriented job. You grease the gears between all the different parts so that everything goes smoothly and people feel as genial as possible.**

***TG:*** Absolutely—and knowing when to bring down a little bit of the law when it's needed. Because we maintain a very relaxed atmosphere on our sets, sometimes people get carried away with having fun, and that can affect our productivity. I have a few small techniques: One of them is to call "Quiet on the set," and everybody knows what that means, which is "Shut up, and start paying attention." Quiet on the set is a nice way of saying it so that my clients don't think we're goofing off.

***CD:* For you, there are no divas; everyone works together to get the job done** (Figure 8.13)**. You don't need someone with a big ego or an outsized personality to get in the way of the work.**

***TG:*** I work hard to hire people who aren't given to drama. Once we land a job and are shooting, our goal is to make the client so happy that they want to come back again. Our eyes are always on the next prize.

## The Shoot: Andy Batt

***Candace Dobro:* When, in your mind, does the actual shoot begin?**

***Andy Batt:*** If you're asking about when the cameras come out—when I begin doing what we all think of as photography—I'd say it happens when the pre-light starts. Some shoots have a pre-light day (or days), and others have a pre-light hour. Some shoots have no pre-light at all; you just have to jump in and start working.

The pre-light is when you get to work out all the kinks in your lighting or test different ideas. Even if you aren't doing any lighting, you might use the pre-light as a "tech scout," where you visit the location at the same time of day you'll be shooting it and grab some test shots of your assistant.

If we're doing a studio job with a high-profile celebrity, we'll hire a stand-in—with the same build, skin tone and hair color as the celebrity—to work with us on the pre-light day. The studio is a blank slate; we need to build up the set from scratch. We figure out what kind of light looks good on any celebrities before they show up. On the shoot day, the celebrity will walk in and find everything dialed in and ready. With a couple of quick adjustments, we'll be up and shooting.

On a smaller-scale shoot, we'll spend a few hours getting ready, testing the lights with one of my assistants standing in. We want to achieve the lighting we're looking for before our subject shows up (**Figure 8.14A**).

***CD:* You've told us some stories about the Verizon Indy car shoot. Can you describe your pre-light day for that job?**

***AB:*** We were shooting at the Charlotte Motor Speedway in North Carolina. It was January—and it was sunny, but really cold and windy. On that shoot, we had a full rigging day so we could build up our camera-mounts, walk the track and see what the light was like. We got up very early, headed to the garage at the speedway and introduced ourselves to the Penske racecar team and our rigging crew.

There were many logistics to work out on this project. For example, we had to figure out where we could (and couldn't) mount the cameras. We were working with these guys for the first time and

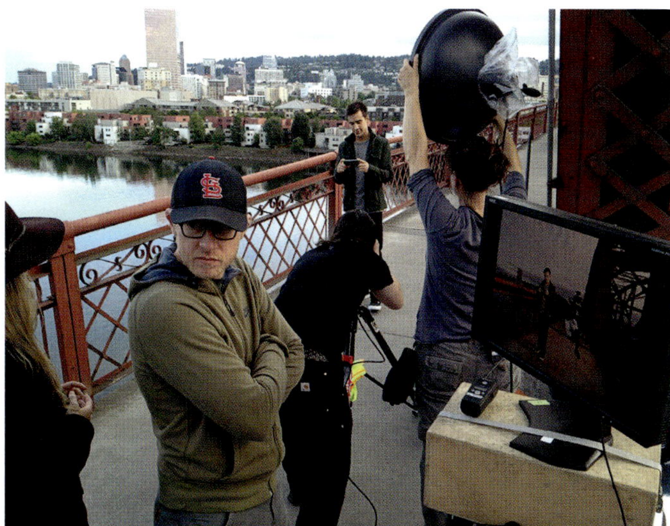

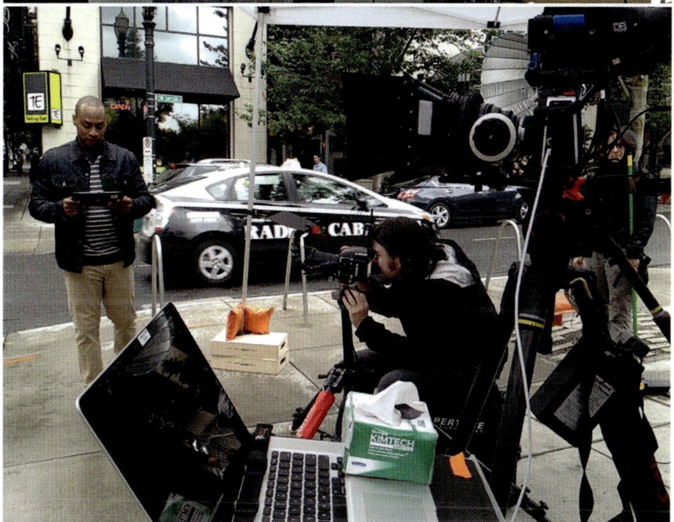


**FIGURE 8.14A** Some shoots require moving quickly with a large crew and a lot of equipment.
IMAGE © THERESE GIETLER, *BEHIND THE SCENES—PHOTOGRAPHING NFL PLAYERS FOR A VERIZON PROJECT*, 2013.

that takes a little longer. Once everyone was on the same page—after we went over our shot ideas and got some of the groundwork done—things clicked and we made good progress.

Jobs on this scale involve lots of preparation, so it's important to schedule in extra days as a buffer. Despite all your careful planning, sometimes there's a crucial tool or idea that becomes obvious only after you get to the location. Those buffer days give you time to figure out an alternate way of doing things; occasionally, someone has to run and get equipment or something.

***CD:* At what other locations have you shot projects?**

***AB:*** We've been inside the (former) Home Depot Center Stadium in LA, on the beach in Rio de Janeiro and recently, in a cornfield in Iowa. We shoot in many different places—which is one of my favorite things about this business—but they may not always be glamorous. The beach in Rio was certainly more glamorous than the cornfield in Iowa, and both of those were amazing compared to some of the dark alleys and freeway underpasses I've shot in. Still, they're all really cool places, visually speaking, and resulted in good, creative work. I appreciate the novelty of going anywhere different, seeing anything new—whether it's Middle America or South America. As long as I get to do good work, then it doesn't matter where I go (**Figure 8.14B**).

### Andy's Philosophy on Travel

*I appreciate the novelty of going anywhere different, seeing anything new—whether it's Middle America or South America. As long as I get to do good work, then it doesn't matter where I go.*

***CD:* It sounds like you like your job.**

***AB:*** Yeah, I do. Shoot days are pretty great.

***CD:* How much control do you typically have over the environment you work in?**

***AB:*** It depends on the job. If I'm standing in a cornfield, then I have zero control over the thunderstorm that's about to happen. In a studio

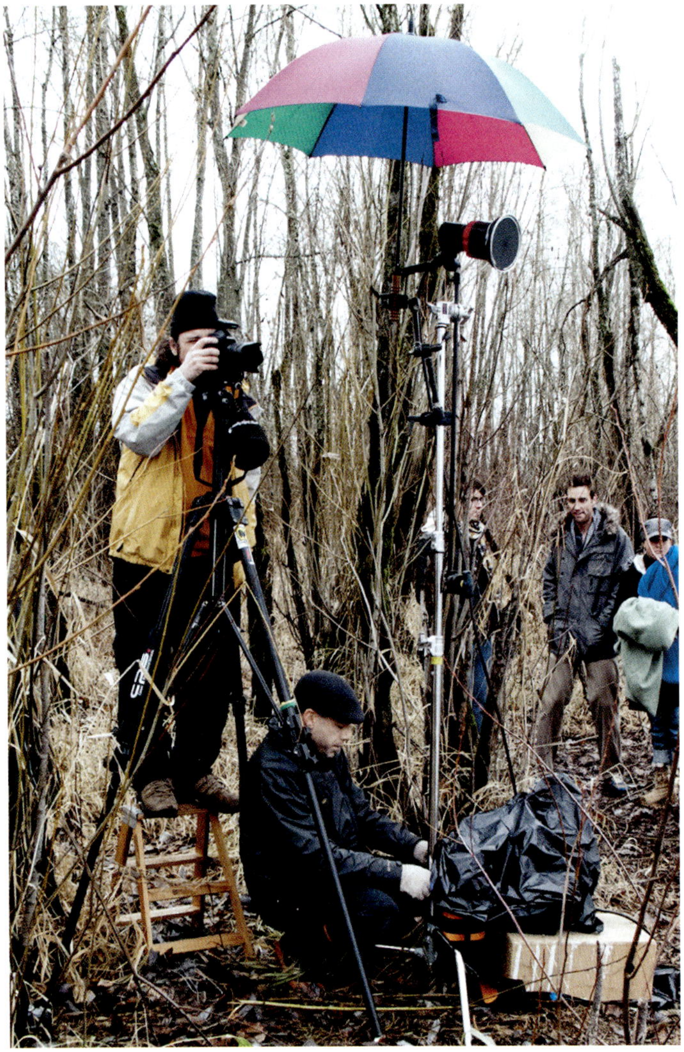

**FIGURE 8.14B** Here's Andy, working in the rain on *Lake Girl*. See **Figure 6.33** for the final shot.
IMAGE © THERESE GIETLER, *BEHIND THE SCENES ON* LAKE GIRL, 2009.

situation, though, I have nothing but control. Even in a daylight studio, you can control the time of day to work and you can choose a north-light studio as opposed to a west-light studio. You can also gain control by doing a tech scout—by understanding what it's actually like to be at a particular location at a particular time of day.

***CD:* Who does the *tech scout*?**

***AB:*** Sometimes I do it; sometimes I have one of my trusted assistants do it. If it's a very technical job, I'll definitely do the tech scout, because I need to get my boots on the ground, take a look around, figure out angles and light and see the location with my own eyes. If it's a matter of timing when I'm flying into a location right before a shoot, I might have a local assistant do a quick tech scout, report back and show me some test images.

***CD:* Do you ever do test shoots in your lab? I know you admire Gregory Heisler's notion of the studio as a lab.**

***AB:*** I love that idea from Gregory. He does nothing but location work. He has a studio solely so he can pre-visualize and test what he's going to do on location. The idea of studio-as-lab is a fantastic one. We do lots of test shoots in the studio—sometimes to figure out a new technique or try out new equipment. Other times it's about testing for an upcoming job, if we need to work out something tricky.

***CD:* What do you get out of these *test shoots*?**

***AB:*** It depends if I'm testing for creative purposes or to see what a specific piece of equipment will do. If I'm working on something creative, then the goal is a portfolio piece; otherwise, it's to get to know the ins and outs of my gear. Testing expands my technical knowledge of the gear, so my tools are ready when I need them. A lot of my testing is to learn, "What happens if I do this?" (**See Figure 8.15.**)

***CD:* Can you describe one of those tests?**

***AB:*** Recently I did a project where I was going to do studio action shots, but only had a limited amount of time with some NFL players. I needed to figure out how to get twice as many shots—using a medium-format camera. Those high-MP backs are slow [as compared

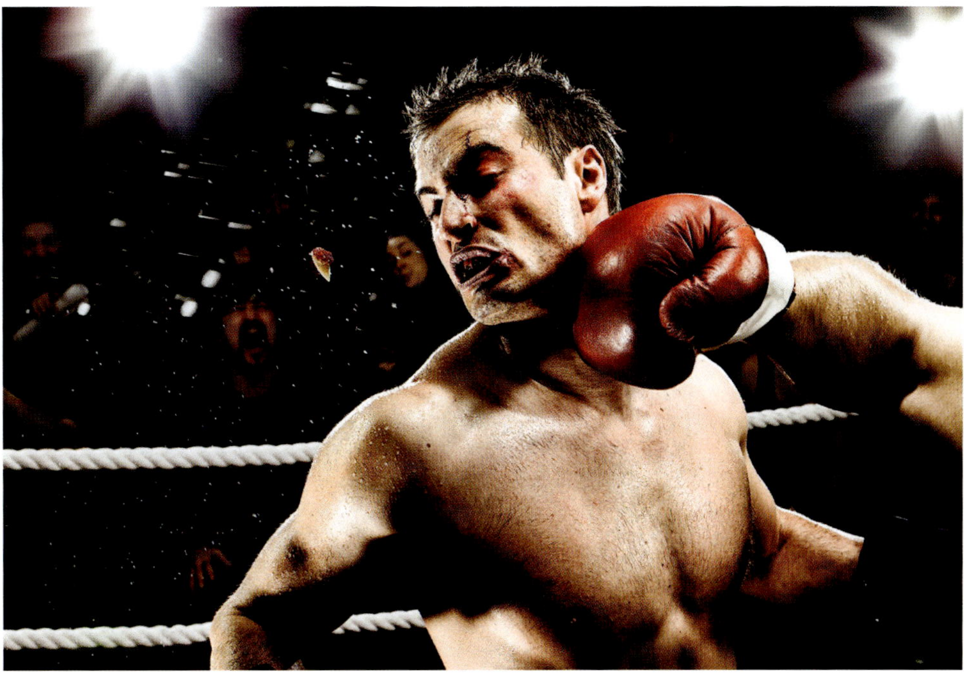

**FIGURE 8.15** Andy wanted to see if he could fake a boxing ring in his studio. This entire shot was created there, in a single image. Except for the flying tooth and the flying sweat, everything else is real. I photographed the tooth on set, along with the blast of sweat on set, so that it was all lit in the same setup.
IMAGE ©ANDY BATT, *BOXING TOOTH*, 2008.

to DSLRs]; they cycle so slowly that essentially, they don't have a frame rate.

We ended up using two cameras, with the second one slaved to the first and split by a few microseconds. The first camera would fire, and a tiny beat later, the second one would fire. One of my assistants was on the B camera, keeping it framed up and focused on the football player—but he didn't have to fire it. For every action, we captured two image options. All of that was tested in my studio before the shoot day.

***CD:* Let's talk about how you approach your subjects. Some photographers interact with their subjects, while others direct them or prefer to remain "invisible" while observing them. What's your style?**

***AB:*** I tend to work very directly with the people I photograph. My goal is to help them be comfortable. I want them to feel like I'm just a normal guy, because that's who I am. I keep a pretty low-key profile—I don't have a big ego on set. I'm in charge, and everyone knows the buck stops with me, but it's not the "Andy Show," with me at the center of attention. The people I'm photographing are at that center, whether they're real people, models or famous athletes.

Even if my subjects are super-famous, I treat them like normal people. No fan boy stuff is allowed on my set. Nobody is allowed to ask for autographs or ask "fan" questions—unless the person we're photographing offers directly. We make sure that celebrities have fun and feel important, but not at the expense of making it feel like a PR event.

***CD:* Do you find that people respond well to you?**

***AB:*** Yeah—I get good results. It's hard to know how it all works though, because I can't step outside of myself and watch. I really don't know any other way to do it—or how somebody else would do it. I try to have empathy for my subjects as they sit on the other side of the camera; I want them to feel comfortable—and confident that I know what I'm doing (**Figure 8.16**).

I also want them to know that I'm there to work with them and make them look good. There are people who think they don't photograph well and don't like having their picture taken. I always tell them, "That's because you haven't had anyone take a good photograph of you!" If they believe that they can be photographed well, then they will be. It's up to me to help them feel good about the process.

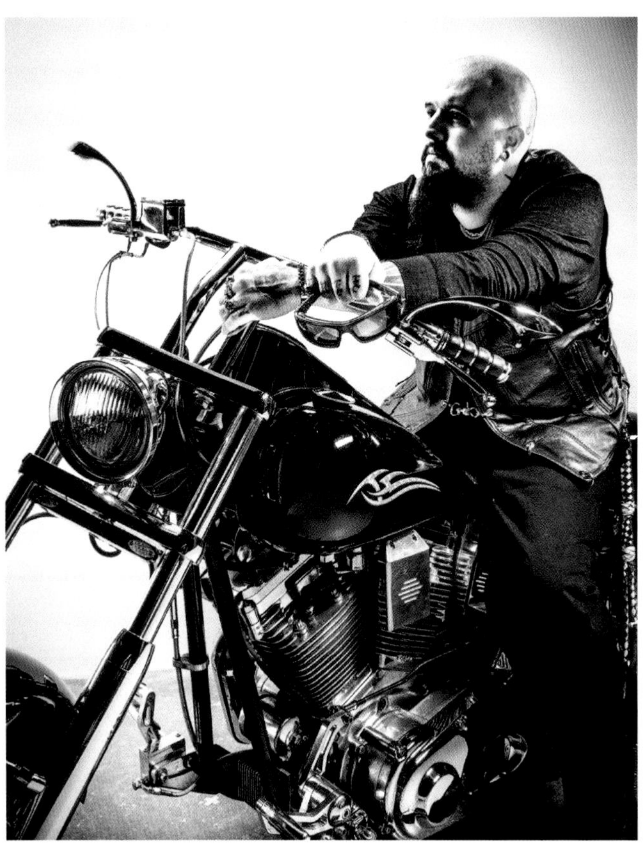

**FIGURE 8.16** This was Cory's first time being in front of a camera. We hired him for a motorcycle sunglasses campaign. He took direction really well and proved to be a great first-time model.
IMAGE © ANDY BATT, *WILEY X SUNGLASSES SHOOT,* 2011.

It doesn't always work; some people have it fixed in their head that they don't photograph well, but if I can get people to relax and enjoy themselves a little bit, if I can figure out what they don't like about being photographed, then sometimes I can get them to come around. Once they relax and start being themselves, I usually get a good photo.

***CD:* What's your state of mind when you're shooting? I remember your telling me that you sometimes forget to eat!**

***AB:*** When I'm working, I throw myself body and mind into the project. The more people there are, the more protocols and layers of crew there are. Generally, I work with a small group, but on big productions, eight different people all want my decision about something.

It's my job to make sure that we are staying true to the "big idea"—my interpretation of whatever story we're telling. I make sure everybody carries out this mission. It's easy to get into a mindset where the rest of the world falls away and I'm just focused on the job. I constantly make sure I'm creating images that are artistic and that make the client happy.

***CD:* Did you always approach your jobs in this way, or has it changed as you've gained experience?**

***AB:*** The intensity has always been there, but I'm definitely not the same photographer I was ten years ago. And I'm glad I'm not. For me, there's constant growth; I'm happy adopting new behaviors and figuring out ways to improve. It's not a standstill kind of thing. I'd like to be able to honestly say—every couple of years—that I have improved dramatically.

***CD:* It's really important, especially in this industry, not to get stale.**

***AB:*** Definitely.

## Good Recovery: Bruce Ely

***Andy Batt:* Can you tell us about making that image of the girls' synchronized swimming team** (Figure 8.17)**?**

***Bruce Ely:*** It's kind of a funny story [about getting the shot, even when things go wrong].

***AB:* That's what professionals do, though. Problems happen with every photographer; the professionals are the ones that roll with it and come up with the shot, anyway.**

***BE:*** I wanted to go shoot this, even though I'd never shot synchronized swimming before. I had a little ewa-marine bag[11] for shooting underwater. I had called the coach; she was really nice and said, "Yeah, come by the pool, we'll be here." It was about a twenty-minute drive from my house. Practice was only going to last an hour that day, so I got there right as they were getting started. I was ready to jump into the pool—I had my camera all set up and just needed to change into my swimsuit: "Uh, oh," I realized, "I forgot my swimsuit."

I looked at my clock and thought, "Do I have time to go back home? When I get back, there'll be fifteen minutes left for practice." [I decided to do it.] I got into the water with ten, maybe fifteen minutes of practice left. I don't know if you've ever shot with [your camera in an ewa-marine bag], but it's kind of tricky, because you can't move the dials and you can't see through it very well.

I was swimming underwater and holding my breath—I think I only went underwater and successfully shot two series of pictures before they were done. I got that picture, and it's still one of my favorites. If I had shot the whole practice, maybe I would have been tired by the time that moment happened.

***AB:* You got the shot. It always comes down to that, with any subject—whether you have hours or minutes.**

***BE:*** That's how my life and career have gone; I just kind of roll with it.

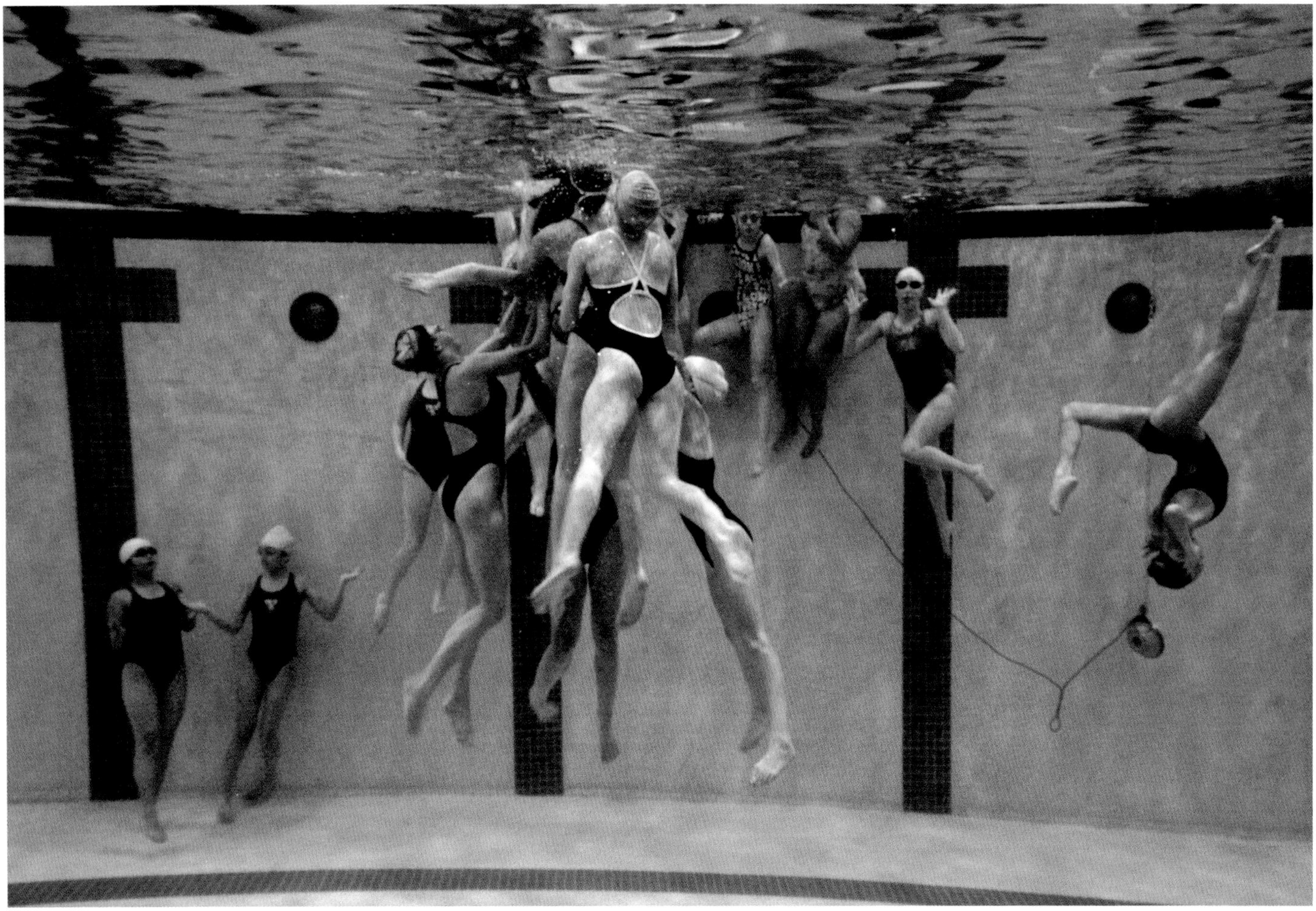

**FIGURE 8.17** Bruce's ability to work effectively under pressure is the backstory for this image. He says that an editor once described his photographic strength as "an ability to walk into nearly any chaotic scene, break it down and find a defining moment that tells the story." His style is pretty simple: to capture a moment and take people places they can't go.
IMAGE © BRUCE ELY / *THE OREGONIAN, TUALATIN HILLS SYNCHRO CLUB*, 2010.

## House as Studio: Holly Andres

***Candace Dobro:* What is your studio like?**

***Holly Andres:*** Well, it's not a studio; it's my house. It looks a lot like my photographs do, because the things in my photographs are things that I live with; there's a particular aesthetic that I like to photograph and be around. I love working from home. I've had lots of opportunities to work in an out-of-home studio space, but I have two cats that I like having near me—and I like the fact that last night I worked until 1:00 a.m. and slept until 10:00 a.m. It's such a way of life for me and is really all I want to do (**Figure 8.18**).

***CD:* Is it awful when you have to go out on a shoot, or are you okay with that?**

***HA:*** No, no, no, I like going out and shooting! It breaks things up. I just got back from an incredibly demanding shoot schedule and was feeling overworked. Now I'm ponying up to the computer, and that feels good.

***CD:* I work at home, too. If you're a certain kind of person, it just fits.**

***HA:*** Yeah, I'm pretty self-directed and motivated. If anything, my challenge is to be less obsessive and spend less time thinking about my work.

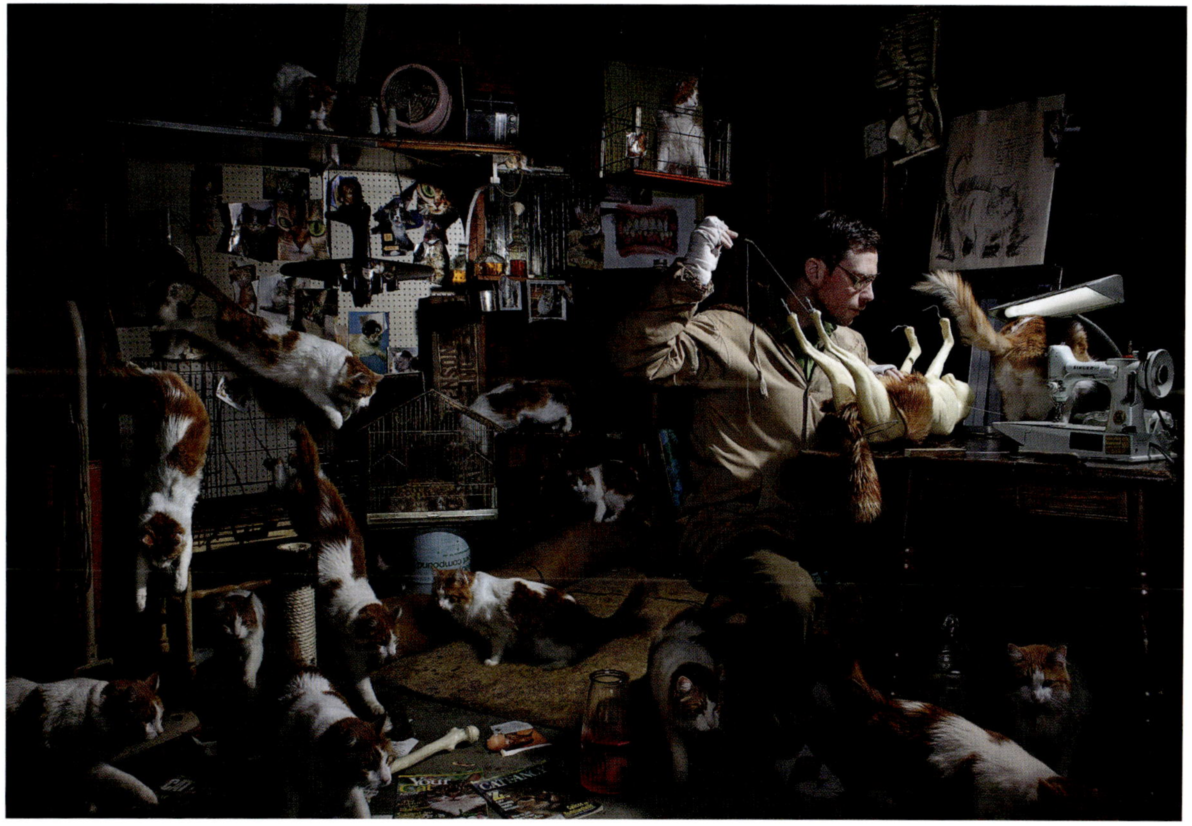

**FIGURE 8.18** This image is one of many projects for which Holly used her house as studio and stage.
IMAGE © HOLLY ANDRES, *THE CAT WHISPERER*, 2011.

## Location Work: Toni Greaves

***Andy Batt:*** **You can only carry so much on one of your trips; how do you decide what to put in your bag?**

***Toni Greaves:*** When I do assignments, people often comment about how little gear I have. I usually just have a camera backpack, one personal luggage bag and my waist pack. I hate tripods—I've carried them before, but almost always regret being stuck carting a tripod around.

If there's an unusual situation—or for reasons of safety—I'll take my little waist pack, so I don't have to walk around schlepping my big 53-pound backpack. I just take out whatever I think I need for the day. One reason for that is convenience, but there are situations where it's just not okay to walk into a family's home with a massive backpack. It's a matter of trying to fit into the environment you're invited into. Being there with a ton of gear just makes it a lot more difficult, at least in the way that I like to work.

I try to minimize my presence. I'm already an intrusion, so I just try to intrude as little as possible. I'm more about the moment and the situation than the technicalities of it. I'd rather have beautiful, natural moments than have all the lenses with me that I might want.

*I try to minimize my presence. I'm already an intrusion, so I just try to intrude as little as possible.*

***Candace Dobro:*** **What else is in that bag?**

***TG:*** Two camera bodies and four lenses, which are all Canon L-Series: Usually I choose to carry the 35mm, the 50mm, the 24–105mm and the 16–35mm. Sometimes also the 135mm.

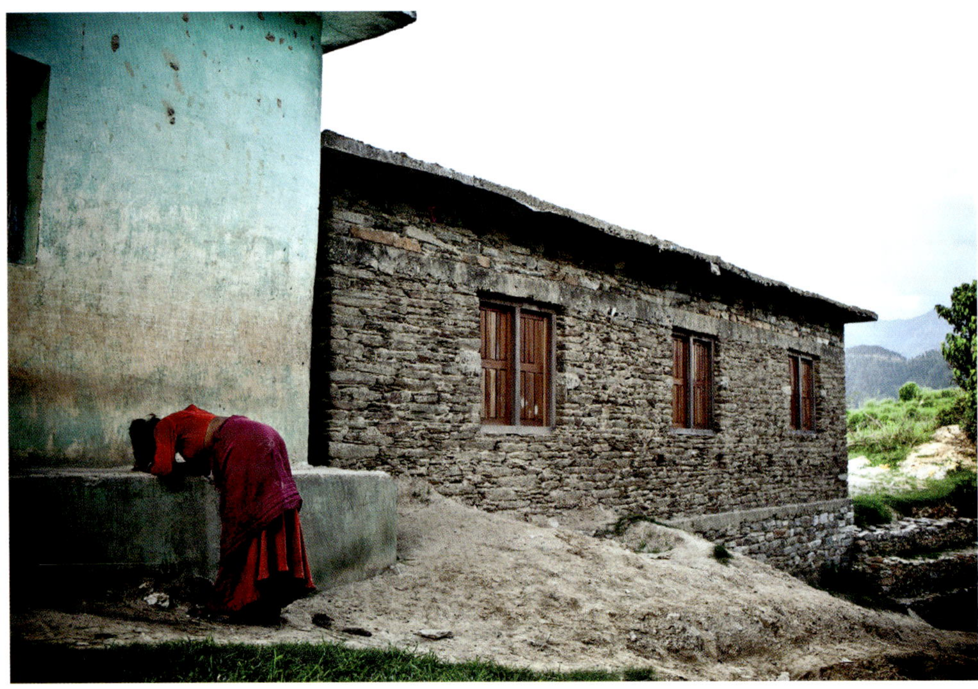

**FIGURE 8.19** Given the difficulties with her first birth, when she almost died, Maheshwori is terrified that the same thing will happen again. Each year, more than 6,000 women in Nepal die during childbirth. Most of them give birth at home, without the help of a skilled—or even trained—attendant.
IMAGE BY TONI GREAVES/GETTY IMAGES, *BIRTH IN RURAL NEPAL, THE MOST DANGEROUS DAY: MAHESHWORI BEFORE GIVING BIRTH,* © BILL & MELINDA GATES FOUNDATION, 2009.

***AB:*** **Besides deciding what to put into the kit, what else do you think about to get ready for a shoot?**

***TG:*** I'm researching and learning as much as I can about the subject within the time that I have available, because for me, so much of it is about relationships. I need to understand the situation; I need to understand the people—and I need to know all of that before going into a place. I can't show up being ignorant; how would I get access, and how would I know what the story might be? I need to have a general sense of what's going on—to inform the decisions about the gear I'm taking, the kinds of things I might want to shoot, and the way I shoot the images.

Even more important than anything technical is my ability to interact with the people. (Of course, if the technical stuff isn't working, you don't even get pictures.) I need to be accepted by them; they need to be comfortable with me in order for me to get the kinds of photos I want to take. A huge part of it is human interaction; it's also one of the things I like. I like learning about people who are often from very different worlds than I am, and I enjoy the challenge of figuring out these scenarios on the fly (**Figure 8.19**).

***CD:*** **Can you describe your thoughts as you determine which moment to capture?**

***TG:*** There ends up being a rhythm. I'm currently working on a long-term project in India about a family. I was there in 2012 for my second visit with them. I intended to go for three weeks, but ended up staying for five. That's a long time. Early on, they were getting used to me again, and I was getting used to what was happening—to the patterns of life, where to stand. You end up finding the pattern of things: "*This* is happening at 8:00 at night over here but *that* is happening at 8:00 at night over there." So some evenings you shoot one thing, and other evenings you shoot the other.

For shorter-term projects, like the one I shot in Afghanistan for Mercy Corps, I just looked for the most beautiful scenarios, being aware of the storytelling aspect of things. In that situation, the most action was happening in the kitchen where the sisters were cooking, so that was the place to be. The story was about a young woman who is receiving training through Mercy Corps' programs. It became a little day-in-the-life story about her, so anything she was doing was what I needed to be taking pictures of. Without even thinking about it, I gravitate towards whatever is most interesting, *always* being mindful of the interaction and being as unobtrusive as possible.

For me, people being comfortable and okay with my presence takes priority over any photos. I think this is one of the reasons I've been successful doing this type of work, because I'll go home without any pictures before I'll damage the relationship. I care about the people very, very much. People know I'm not there to take advantage or to misrepresent them. I've been told that comes through in my interactions, and it brings a level of trust.

## The Shoot: Stewart Cohen

***Andy Batt:*** **Tell us about working in front of the camera, about directing your work.**

***Stewart Cohen:*** One of things with lifestyle photography is that you're directing people and trying to capture a moment and an emotion (**Figure 8.20**).

***AB:*** **Is giving direction to talent—models, actors or even "real people"—a learned skill?**

***SC:*** I think it's innate, but it's also something you learn over the years. I used to be more intimidated by it, but today I just encourage the talent to be part of the process. I can ask people questions, when I'm behind a camera, that I would *never* ask in a million years normally—and they totally open up. The invisible barrier just goes away.

> *I can ask people questions, when I'm behind a camera, that I would never ask in a million years normally—and they totally open up. The invisible barrier just goes away.*

***Candace Dobro:*** **There's a divide between photographers that are comfortable taking pictures of people and photographers that aren't.**

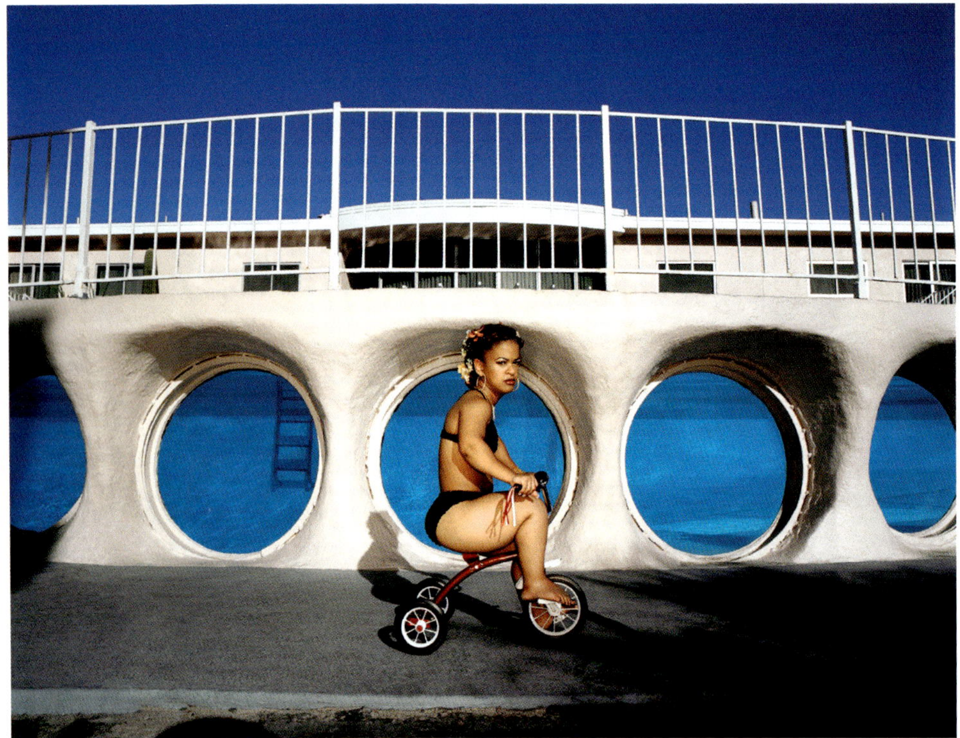

**FIGURE 8.20** Stewart encourages his models to be part of his process. To become more comfortable approaching your subjects, he advises that you "just put yourself in the other person's shoes."
IMAGE © STEWART COHEN, *GLASS POOL INN, LAS VEGAS*, 2003.

**How can somebody who has to shoot people—and isn't comfortable with it—approach their subjects?**

***SC:*** Just put yourself in the other person's shoes. I went back to film school five years after I started shooting and took a class called "Acting for Directors." It was the hardest thing I ever did. You see what it's like to sit on set with all these lights and people; you have no idea what they're saying about you. They're pointing at your face, pointing at your hair, then they say, "Now, perform!"

I'll say to guys that have worked here for a while, "Hey, shoot this portrait." I'll watch, and soon it becomes dead quiet. I'm thinking, "Dude, this person is sitting there, totally self-conscious. Engage them somehow." That might be the thing to tell your readers: Engage your subjects; understand what it feels like to be sitting on that side of the camera. I still have my guys photograph me once a year or something. It's not comfortable.

## The End of the Shoot: Andy Batt

***Candace Dobro:* We've talked about when the shoot begins. When is it over?**

***Andy Batt:*** The photography part is over when all the gear is put away and the lights go off. For the subjects and clients, though, it ends when the last shot, the *"Martini Shot,"* is done. There's always some celebrating—we usually take a group photo and sometimes have a beer—but the crew still has a lot of work to do.

***CD:* Okay, what's a Martini Shot?**

***AB:*** It's a filmmaking term. The Martini Shot is the last shot of the movie.[12] Traditionally, it's the last shot, when the whole job wraps up, although some people apply the concept to the last shot of any day of photography.

***CD:* I kind of liked the idea of everyone having Martinis.**

***AB:*** Me too! Once you're done with the last shot, you *can* go have martinis—but even after the Martini Shot is done, there's still equipment to put away, and we have to make backups and apply metadata. If we've been shooting cards, there might still be a stack of them to download.

If the job has a pressing deadline, the clients might sit down and make selects right away. Often we'll need to create a JPEG drive immediately so the Art Director can take it away to edit from. We might upload images to Dropbox[13] for offsite clients to look at.

With most jobs, I'll stay until the equipment is packed up and ready to travel. If we're out on location in the Portland area, the shoot doesn't end until we've gone back to the studio, dropped off the equipment, set the burglar alarm and are driving away.

There are rare occasions when I have enough crew—with a few really good department heads—when I'll walk away after the wrap. I'll go back to the hotel and crash, because it's exhausting being "on" for ten to twelve hours: You're operating; you're working; you're smiling and keeping everybody going and motivated. You put a lot of your own energy into getting the work done, so when it actually ends, you realize that you've been running on empty, and you're exhausted.

***CD:* When you're outside the Portland area, do you usually travel home the same day, or do you wait until the next day?**

AB: If I can avoid same-day travel, I do. It's not a fun thing to work your butt off, wrap out the shoot, prep for airplane travel, drive to the airport, sit in the airport, get on the plane and then fly home. That's an exhausting day for everybody, so I try not to do it. Then again, that's my world—which is very different from Bruce Ely or Toni Greave's worlds of journalistic and documentary photography. They're able to do their work carrying around a camera bag, and their days are very different from mine.

***CD:* I was amazed when Bruce told us he knows newspaper people who do three different shoots in the same day, day after day.**

***AB:*** Yeah, it's pretty different. Journalists get their assignments and might need to be in one place in the morning, find a way to make a great shot at noon, then be at an event at the end of the day. Sometimes the events they cover are intense journalistic stories that need research and planning—and sometimes it's a hotdog-eating contest that needs a fun shot for the lifestyle page. There are so many different ways to be a photographer.

***CD:* How hands-on are you with the creation of final images; for instance, do you have in-house retouchers, or do you always hire Craig (Ferroggiaro)?**

***AB:*** I have me—for smaller projects. For larger commercial gigs, I usually hire Craig.

***CD:* You do your own retouching? I didn't know that.**

***AB:*** Yeah, if it's for an editorial job. Editorial budgets are very small, and usually the projects aren't gigantic. I don't do what I consider "retouching." I process images. I do style work, applying a look and feel. Occasionally, I'll do small retouches and take out dust—or do some slight skin retouching to clean blemishes. I don't do massive retouching or replace body parts. I don't enjoy knocking out[14] images and layering them together; that doesn't appeal to me.

***CD:* When might you hire Craig to do your retouching?**

***AB:*** When it's time to replace body parts or blend multiple images! If it's a big project, I'll generally have Craig work on it. He's my go-to guy for anything that involves "real retouching." I've also hired him to do simpler stuff, when the project has an ultra-fast turnaround and I'm off to another shoot. I trust him to make the images look like mine and to work with my clients. Craig's skillset runs the gamut from heavy retouching and body-part assembly to processing the raw files, developing great looks for my work and delivering files to the client's specifications.

***CD:*** **What things are important for photographers to know when working with a retoucher?**

***AB:*** Language is a very big thing. It's important to communicate clearly upfront and to make sure everybody's talking about the same thing. For instance, what does a "round" of color mean? Everybody needs to agree. What's light retouching? What's heavy retouching? What's included in the price? You should have a good, open talk with your retoucher about every project, and to do that, you need to understand how to talk about the technical side of your work.

## What Photographers Can Do to Help Their Retouchers: Craig Ferroggiaro

***Andy Batt:*** **What's your top-ten list of things that photographers can do—or not do—to make the retoucher's life happier and the end product better?**

***Craig Ferroggiaro:*** The number one thing is to talk to the retoucher about what you're going to do before you do it. For a real-world example, let's say I have a client (an ad agency) that I know very well and a photographer I've worked with. The photographer is going to shoot women's purses and jewelry sitting on a car seat. It's supposed to look casual, so ahead of time they consult with me and say, "Here's the project we're doing; do you have any thoughts about it?"

***Candace Dobro:*** **Do they actually do that—communicate with you beforehand?**

***CF:*** They should. In this case, I'd suggest that they lock down the camera [on a tripod, so it won't move], if they can, and take a shot.

They would shoot plates[15] without any jewelry there, because inevitably, the client will want the jewelry swapped out. If they're shooting it on a striped seat or something, it's going to be incredibly time-consuming to remove the jewelry in Photoshop. That's a simple example of why you would talk to a retoucher ahead of time. Other things could be more—much more—complex. Now I'm thinking of jobs that Andy has done here (**Figures 8.21A and 8.21B**).

***AB:*** **You can use me for an example. What have I done wrong, Craig?**

***CF:*** No, no, you talk ahead of time; you're very good about that. How about the meeting we had before the Verizon job? We said, "Okay, we need a football player in one part of it, we need a background, and then we need consumers over in the corner. What's the best way to shoot this?" Talking about that in a meeting ahead of time, ideally with the client, is great. Just having that conversation is huge. Hopefully, it's been good for you, Andy when we've discussed these things.

***AB:*** **It always clarifies what I do have to do—and sometimes what I *don't* have to do. It can free me up when you tell me, "Oh, don't worry about that, that will be fine." Sometimes, because we talked, I don't have to worry about creating an asset I thought I had to create, so it definitely helps.**

***CD:*** **What would you say to photographers who are thinking, "I'm supposed to be able to do all this stuff by myself, but it's hard to develop those skills *and* all the other ones"? At what point in photographers' careers might they consider hiring a retoucher?**

***CF:*** As early as possible. If anything, working with a retoucher would get you on the right track. He or she could tell you how you would process an image and how you would retouch something—and what something looks like when it's retouched well.

***CD:*** **What *does* an image look like when it's retouched well?**

***CF:*** It looks completely natural, like nothing has been altered at all, generally. A lot of people don't know that it's bad to blow out the sky

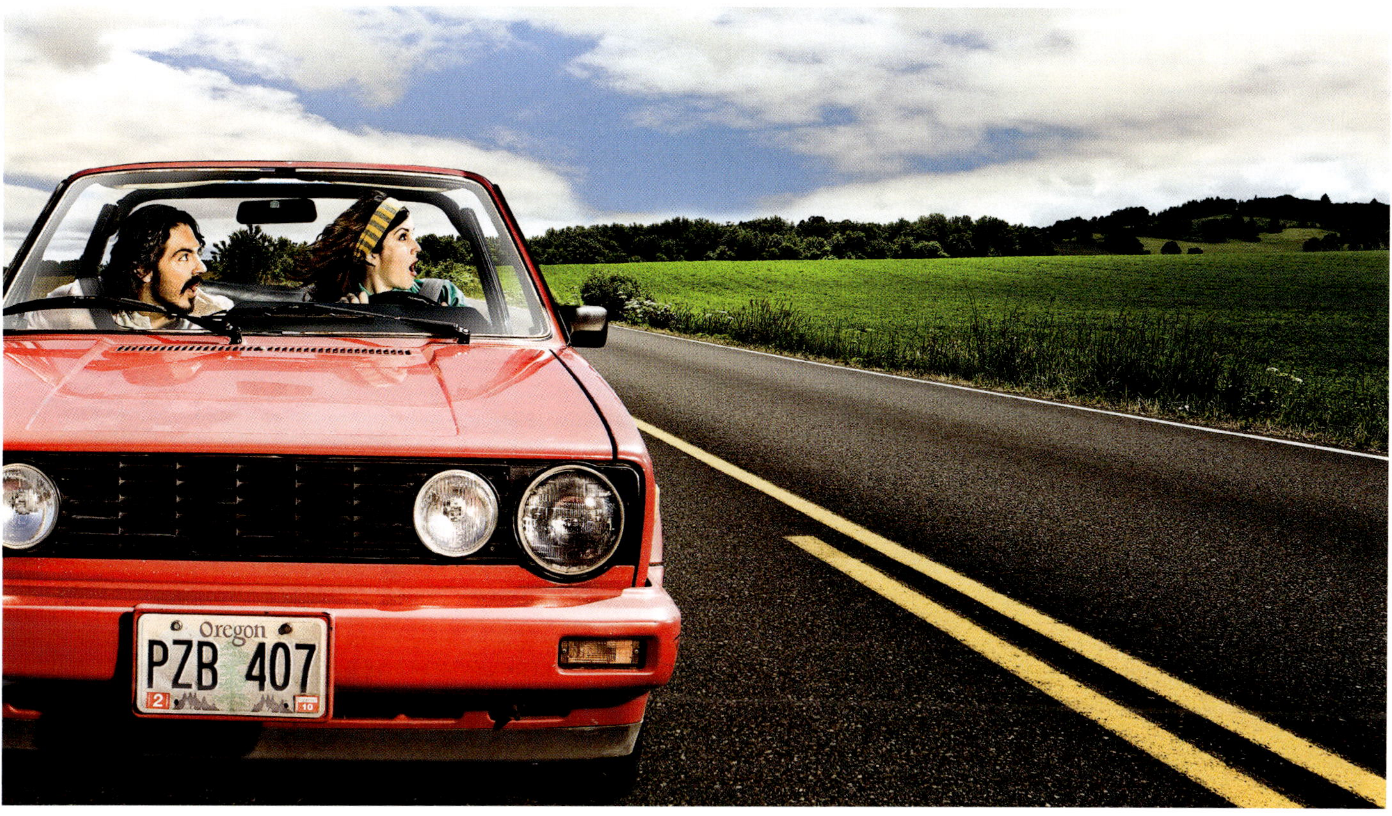


**FIGURE 8.21A** Craig composited this image together for a Powerball lottery outdoor board campaign. The models are looking at the giant LED numbers on the board that show the current dollar amount of the jackpot.

***Andy:*** We were after a very saturated and crisp look, so we needed to add lighting to our subjects. Since we couldn't exactly shut down a country highway (unless we had a bigger budget, a flagging crew and a guarantee of good weather), we photographed the VW and our models in an empty parking lot, which we lit with a combination of strobes and high overhead sunlight. We had multiple images in this campaign and needed different roads and terrain—so we spent a day driving 500 miles around various parts of Oregon taking shots of the road.

IMAGE © ANDY BATT, *POWERBALL BOARD,* 2008.

in certain situations. It's bad because—even if you plan to put a different sky in later—it won't work if the image is blown out where it wraps around your subject. You've lost it at that point.

I don't know any professional photographers—or even retouchers—that don't work without a team. A retoucher is just another person on your team, the same as a producer. You would drive yourself crazy if you had to produce, right?

*When a photo is retouched well, it looks completely natural, like nothing has been altered at all. It's very difficult to see good retouching.*

***AB:* We all started by walking around taking pictures—then it grew from there. We think, "I'm going to do it all, because I have to." It's hard at first to wrap your head around the notion that it's a team effort and that there are ways of maintaining creative control without being the one who takes care of every single thing.**

***CF:*** The only photographers I know that work alone are fine art photographers. There are no commercial photographers to speak of—and if there are, there shouldn't be—that work alone.

***AB:* There are some that have in-house retouching.**

***CF:*** Yes, and that's fine. Maybe it's just you and an assistant, and your assistant is also your retoucher. Plenty of studios are set up that way.

***CD:* If the first big thing we can do to help retouchers is to communicate clearly, then what's the second thing?**

***CF:*** Communication is number one and number two is shooting plates.

***AB:* Tell us what a plate is and why it's so important.**

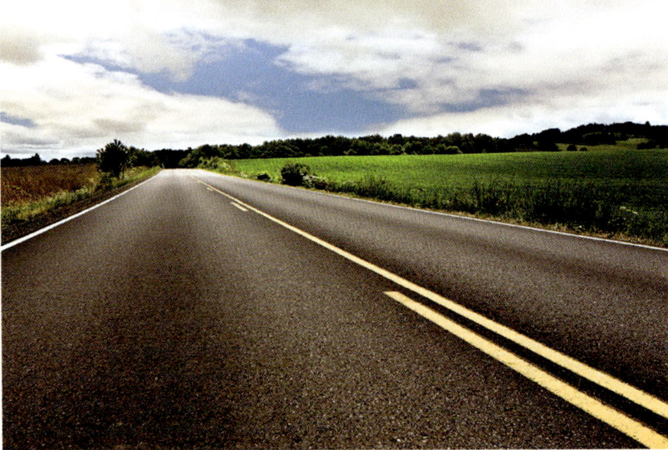

**FIGURE 8.21B** The image in **Figure 8.21A** was composited from two main images, both shot with the same camera, lens, aperture and relative position.
IMAGE © ANDY BATT, *POWERBALL BOARD—BREAKDOWN*, 2008.

***CF:*** A plate (**Figure 8.21B**) is, by my definition, a shot of the surroundings in which you're shooting—whether it's a studio, a tabletop, an office or the great outdoors—without anything (equipment, flashes, people) in it.

***CD:* Do plates have to be shot under the same lighting you're using for the final shot?**

***CF:*** Ideally yes, but that's not even necessary. More important than the lighting are the objects in the general scene. I would recommend that a photographer (either before or after they're shooting and with their flashes and equipment gone) shoot some plates of other things around that room.

The other objects in the room are valuable to a retoucher, because if we have them, we can use them. It's very normal for a client to have everything looking great, and then to have their client—some corporation—come back and say, "We like this so much, we want it to be a double page!" So, what do you do with the second half of the page? If you even have some elements that were in the room, you could somehow blend them in. Your clients will love you if you shoot those plates, because the retoucher can work with them.

***AB:*** **If you don't understand the importance of plates, it's difficult to schedule the time to get them, and it's hard to explain to your client why there's still work to be done after the main shot has been captured. Sometimes you have to fight for the time to shoot plates—but you need to do it, because in retouching there's almost always a need for this stuff.**

***CF:*** It's like insurance, really. You're tempted to go without it, because it's easier, but you don't want to get caught without it. That's what it comes down to.

***AB:*** **Is there a usual turnaround time?**

***CF:*** It's completely dependent on the image I'm working on. On the short end, it would be a couple of hours; on the long end, from start to actual finish, it could take two weeks or more. From start to first round, it's usually not more than a few days, on average.

***AB:*** **What's the best way for photographers to communicate the changes they want to make?**

***CF:*** Open your image in any program that lets you mark it up. Then, mark it up, for example, by circling a book in the background of the image saying something like, "Remove the title." You could also circle an area that you want lightened or darkened. The retoucher will make those changes and then send the image back. You (the client) will either approve it or make another round, where you can make more comments. That markup will go back and forth until the image is done. Some images can be finished in one round, but I would say the average is probably four or five rounds.

## File Delivery: Andy Batt

**Candace Dobro: How do you deliver files to your commercial clients?**

***Andy Batt:*** However they want them. These days, it's hard to know what clients are going do with the images. I think that most of the time, my clients really don't know the answer, so if they want Adobe98, 8-bit files at 300ppi, that's what I send them. The flip side is that image reproduction has gotten a lot more consistent, and a good press can achieve good-looking color—as long as somebody who has experience is in charge of it.

When I do small projects for clients who don't understand any of this stuff (for example, musicians, comedians, actors and people who need to have images for themselves), I'll give them sRGB files, because that's a fairly bulletproof format. It's a color space with a tiny gamut that's smaller than anything it could ever be printed on, so it has the advantage of reproducing well, no matter where it appears. It just won't ever look as good as it possibly could.

***CD:*** **For people who are just viewing their imagery on their monitors, isn't sRGB the way to go?**

***AB:*** Nope, not anymore. More and more monitors are defaulting to wide-gamuts. At least at the higher-end, we see more screens that can show us almost all the colors available in the Adobe RGB (1998) color space. sRGB was born out of the need to standardize the color space of older monitor technology.

Tech stuff ripples outward and downward, so you know that at a certain point, it'll be just as cost-effective to make an Adobe98 monitor as it is to make an sRGB monitor, and then it will become the new standard. If that happens, then sRGB will diminish. It all depends on your point of view. If you want everybody on the entire planet to be able to look at your images, no matter what, then maybe you need to use sRGB, even though it limits your images.

## File Delivery: Stewart Cohen

***Andy Batt:*** **The shoot is over once the lights are wrapped up and the trucks are loaded, but what about the job—when does the job actually end?**

***Stewart Cohen:*** It never really ends, if your goal is to keep clients happy, but a project ends after final delivery of all the completed assets. We finish the day on set, and then of course, we spend all our profit on a giant dinner for everybody.

Then we get to business wrapping. We do the edit. Our DIT organizes and copies the files while we're wrapping up. We have multiple drives and we split them up into different guys' backpacks. We usually have two or three copies of the job; they're locked up in safes or we carry them with us. The stylist is wrapping, everyone is wrapping—and the producer is collecting invoices.

The other thing we do is to get an advance on *every* job. I make it a point to pay all the crew out of the advance. My crew is all over the world and they never—I mean *never*—wait to get paid, because I feel that, when push comes to shove, I need these people. When I call them three weeks from now and have a job the next day, and they have a hold[16] (with someone else), I want them to take *my* job.

***Candace Dobro:*** **How did you come to this arrangement—out of experience?**

***SC:*** I feel that a photo assistant making $250 or $300 a day doesn't have the luxury of waiting 30 days to get a check. They're working for us, and I think the best way to spread goodwill is to pay them immediately. While they're wrapping the job, the producer is collecting invoices, looking at the spreadsheet and making sure we're on budget. Some clients demand backup[17] for props, wardrobe, hotels—everything. We have to collect, copy, actualize and turn in a book that has all the receipts.

I'll do an edit and mark my selects. We'll upload (usually through WeTransfer[18] or something) JPEGs of each shot for the Art Director to see. When we get back to the studio, we archive all the files on our big RAID and start going through it, doing the selection process. Sometimes agencies do their own retouching; a lot of times we do it. We stay with the job as long as they want us with the job. Some agencies want all the files, so they say bye-bye. Sometimes we take it all the way through to the end.

We just had a job where, after it was wrapped, the client didn't ask for backup. We delivered and everybody was happy; they loved the pictures. About two months later, they said, "We want to see all the receipts for the clothing." You know what? You've got to do it; you don't have a choice. Paperwork and bookkeeping are really important, and you need to be buttoned up. Don't forget that sometimes you're dealing with a couple of hundred thousand dollars. You're the guardian of those people's money, and they have every right to know where it all went.

***CD:*** **It gives you an incentive to work efficiently.**

***SC:*** One of my goals is to always under-promise and over-deliver. That's what keeps people coming back. If they're looking for three shots—and that's listed in the estimate—we'll shoot eight. I do that because I want them to say, "These are great—hey, we would like to license a couple more." That's why we under-promise and over-deliver, because it leaves that door open.

***CD:*** **It's good business.**

***SC:*** Ninety-three percent of business is relationships.

## FEATURED INTERVIEW

# Therese Gietler

*Producer*

***Candace Dobro:*** **What is it like the minute you step onto the set the first day of a shoot?**

***Therese Gietler:*** It's controlled chaos. There's this supercharged energy that I need to direct. I like to be the first one on the set. I'm a bit of a control freak, so I like it done my way—it's not the only way, it's just how I like it done. I want the table set up a certain way, I want the craft service (the food, the snacks, the beverages) to look a certain way. I typically get there an hour before any clients arrive. I want my clients to come in and feel, "Not only is everything in control, but wow, this is nice!"

***CD:*** **What time does a typical shoot begin?**

***TG:*** I would say around 8:00. Clients will show up anytime between 7:30 and 8:30 in the morning. Everyone is coming to me with questions. I'm getting hit from all sides, and decisions have to be made. If you can't make decisions you cannot be a producer.

***Andy Batt:*** **So, we've gotten through the chaos of the morning . . .**

***TG:*** The next thing that happens after my clients arrive is that I get them settled. Sometimes, it's just one person, but on bigger jobs, it can be up to ten people. You've got your art director, the creative director, at least two account managers, the agency producer and then the actual client.

***CD:*** **You need to have enough food for all of them . . .**

***TG:*** Right, exactly. It's also about the level of the food on the set, how fancy it's going to get. I like to have food on set that nobody else has ever had before.

***CD:*** **It sets the tone.**

**Wednesday scene 2: Kids bedroom/playroom - Airprint**

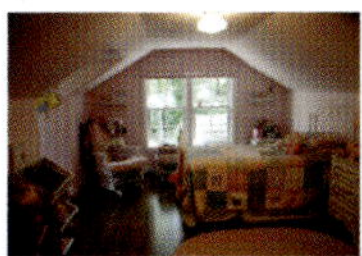

**Scenario:**

Father and daughter printing a drawing she made on her tablet. Quality time after school/work.

**Props:**

Photosmart 6520 (In scene), Slate7, iPad

Legos, toys (dolls, stuffed animals), large full-color world map on wall, wooden kids table and chairs*

**Call outs:**

Dad - Olive

Girl (4-6) - Olive

**Wardrobe:**

DAD: Casual, loose work attire, light blue buttoned shirt, rolled up sleeves, khaki slacks DAUGHTER: yellow & orange ruffled skirt, long sleeve shirt, orange and white shoes, yellow plastic hair clip

**Thursday scene 6: Bedroom - Airprint**

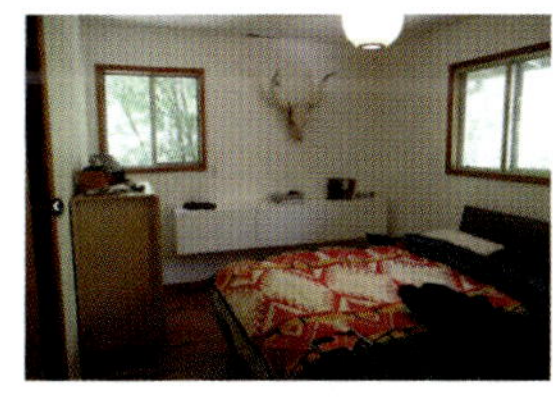

**Scenario:**

Woman sending image from her mobile device to the printer in the bedroom using her wi-fi connection.

Printing a home décor inspiration

**Props:**

ENVY 120 (in scene), BlackBerry Z10, Galaxy S4, iPhone

Home décor magazines, white bedding

**Call outs:**

Mom (35-39) - White

**Wardrobe:**

Casual and comfortable, long sleeve patterned t-shirt (make sure the neck is tight enough due to the camera angle), dark grey sweats

**FIGURE 8.22A** This is a sample shot list for an HP project Andy did.
ILLUSTRATION © THERESE GIETLER, *HP SHOT GUIDE,* 2013.

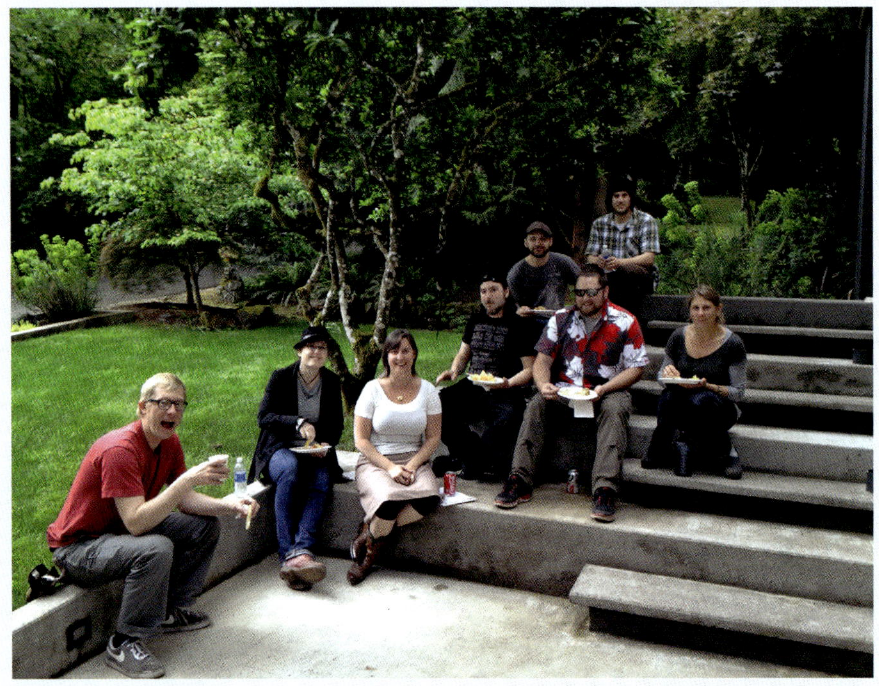

**FIGURE 8.22B** Always feed your crew, and always give them the best possible meal you can. It's amazing how well a group of people can sustain themselves if they're taken care of. The cost of a good meal is more than paid back by hard work and team effort.
IMAGE © ABS CREW, *HP SHOOT*, 2013.

***TG:*** It does. Everybody sees a lot of money going towards the photography, so they want to feel pampered—and that's my job. Once Andy begins shooting, I calm down a little bit and the reality of the schedule comes in. I have to start letting Andy know what time it is and if he's on schedule or not.

***CD:* Do you use a prepared shot list?**

***TG:*** Most of the time we do, and the day is scheduled around the *shot list* (**Figure 8.22A**). If there are big problems—things I need Andy to be aware of—I go up to him myself and put a bug in his ear about whatever's going on.

***CD:* What happens next?**

***TG:*** My next job is getting us to *lunch* (**Figure 8.22B**). On bigger jobs, I've hired a caterer to bring it in. If it's a smaller job, I'll have a PA get the lunch order from everybody and pick it up—and have it laid out on the table so we can all sit down and enjoy lunch.

***CD:* That's a great thing to think about—even for a one-person photo-studio—because you can emulate that. You don't have to have a caterer, you don't have to have a producer, and you can still make sure that whomever you're working with is fed a good lunch, and that you take a break to relax a little in the middle of the shoot.**

***TG:*** That's important, because those are the things they're going to remember. People remember being cared for.

***CD:* Now, take us to the wrap—what's the end of a shoot like?**

***TG:*** Once *wrap* is called, I like to have—depending on the job, obviously—a bottle of champagne go off, boom! We have a little celebratory drink, or a beer or something (**Figure 8.22C**). The agency folks and the clients usually leave right after that. That's when wrap happens. It's another chaos moment, but all the players know their job at that point.

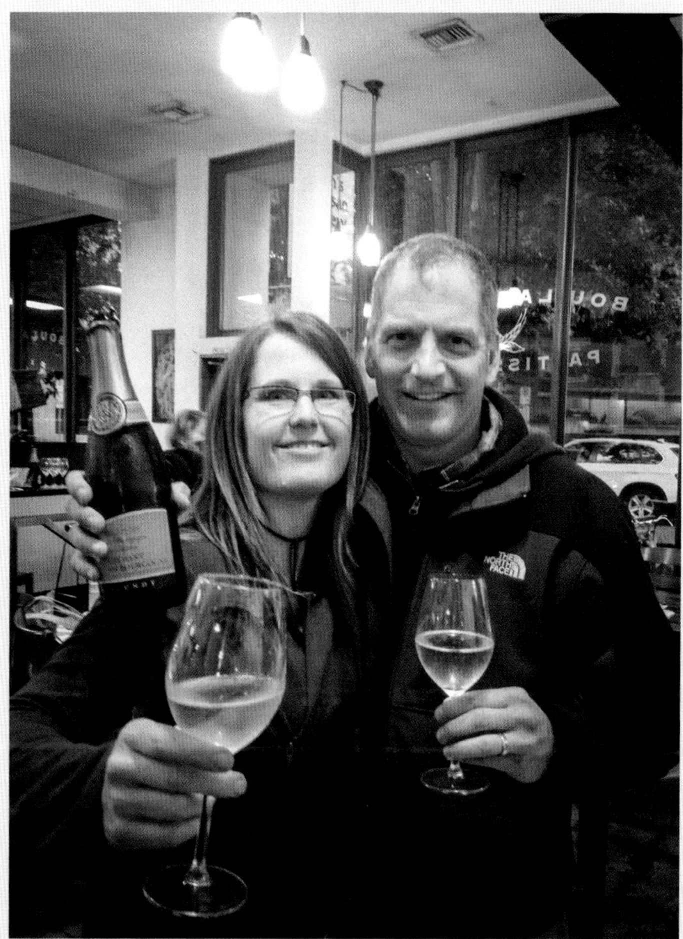

**FIGURE 8.22C** That's a wrap!
IMAGE © ABS CREW, *HP SHOOT*, 2013.

It's remarkable how quickly these people disappear. They get their jobs done and are out the door like nobody's business. I'm pretty much yelling behind them, "Invoice me tomorrow. I need my invoices people; I'm not paying you without them."

The photo team typically takes the longest. Everybody has to go back to somewhere—the studio to drop off gear, or back to the hotel. Wrap happens mostly on its own; I make sure things aren't left behind, that the people from whom we rented the location are taken care of and that there's no garbage left behind. It's like the cleanup after a good party.

***AB:* For photographers who are just starting to do commercial shoots (working on a smaller scale) and want to hire a producer—what can they do to make your job easier?**

***TG:*** Let me do my job. Get out of my way and let me do it. If they're new, then they should lean on me—and my experience—to get things done.

***CD:* Does your job stop when the photography stops?**

***TG:*** No, it doesn't. Once the job is done, I go back to the office and collect all the invoices. Depending on which agency we're working with, I might have to hand in all the receipts.

***AB:* Your job still goes on for a while, until the project is delivered. After the photographer has shot, it's not done. You're still working with clients.**

***TG:*** That's very true and easy to forget, because we work with such good people, like Craig [Ferroggiaro], our retoucher. I do have to watch that budget all the way to the end, because retouching can—and often does—go over what was budgeted. It can go on for months, really.

***CD:* I remember talking to Andy after one of your shoots, and he told me you were both recovering. It wasn't just an hour later, it was a number of *days* after the shoot, and you were still charged up. What's that like?**

***TG:*** You end up putting in so much energy and so much of your brain power into that moment. It might be a day of photography or a week of photography, but you work so hard towards the shoot, and that's all you'll think about. The whole rest of your life is on hold while you're doing this job. You don't see your friends, you don't make phone calls—and then suddenly, the job is over. There's a little hiccup, a moment of, "Well, now what?" Everybody's going home, and this family that you created for a week is not there the next day. I feel kind of lonely; it's just Andy and me again. It's almost like a post-shoot depression.

> ***You work so hard towards the shoot and that's all you think about it. The whole rest of your life is on hold while you're doing this job. You don't see your friends, you don't make phone calls—and then suddenly, the job is over.***

***CD:* Yeah, it's a letdown.**

***TG:*** Once we're done with the shoot, I get to thinking, "How could I have done it better?" All the self-doubt hits you like a wave for a minute—until you start seeing the pictures in post-production and think, "Oh, that was cool, that's awesome!" It's an emotional rollercoaster.

***AB:* The end of a big shoot is always intense. Okay, last question: If you had to pick one mistake or pitfall that you could tell an up-and-coming photographer about—what would it be?**

***TG:*** The mistake we made—and the mistake I think everybody is going to make—is assuming "I don't have to do my time. Other photographers have to do their time, but I am going to skip over that." Very few photographers are going to become the next big star without putting in years of work. We all have to go through it. We all struggle; you're not going to skip it. I thought I was going to skip it. I know Andy, you thought you were going to skip it . . .

***AB:* I was *hoping* to skip it . . .**

***CD:* That's a great piece of wisdom. No matter how smart and talented you are, it takes really hard work to be successful.**

***TG:*** And being persistent and hardheaded about it: "I'm going to do this! I know I am going to do it!" You have to ignore all the writing on the wall that you're not going to survive this—because then, you do.

## EXPLORATIONS

### The Other Side of the Camera

> ***Just put yourself in the other person's shoes . . . I have my guys photograph me once a year or something; it's not a comfortable process. You have to know what it feels like to be on the other side of the camera. It'll make you a better photographer.***
>
> ***—Stewart Cohen***

You'll need a fellow photographer for this one, since it's an exercise built for two. If you're used to being on the "safe" side of the camera (looking through the viewfinder)—then steel yourself. You're going to the other side to have your portrait taken.

**Set Up**

Pick a location with soft, even light. Early morning, late afternoon, an overcast day or the light from a north-facing window will all work well; these types of light look good on anyone—including you.

- Grab your light meter (or use the in-camera one) and establish a good exposure at a shallow DoF ($f$2.8–4.0 is a good range).
- Make sure you're working in Manual mode with a shutter speed that's fast enough to handhold. Match that to a good ISO setting.
- Pick a lens you'd like to work with—something in the 50–135mm range is traditional, but feel free to change it up.
- Take a couple of test shots to nail the exposure. Check the histogram for good values.
- Check your exposure throughout this test; your light levels may go up or down.
- Now, hand over the camera!

**The "Before" Test: Silence**

Have your partner photograph you for 15 minutes, taking at least 50 photos. The trick is that they aren't allowed to talk to you. They can take any kind of portrait they like, but they can't give you any direction. Once your 15 minutes are up, trade places (no talking!) and photograph your partner for 15 minutes, taking at least 50 photos.

**The "After" Test: Patter**

Switch places again. Check your exposure values to make sure the light hasn't changed. This time, they should talk to you—about anything—as long as they talk to you the entire time. Play this out for 15 minutes (again, taking at least 50 photos), and then switch places. Now it's your turn to keep up a running patter and photograph your partner. The key is to talk about anything that gets a reaction: Tell bad jokes, make small talk or share something personal. If you're talking, you're engaging your subject.

**Take Notes**

- How comfortable was it to be photographed in silence?
- How comfortable was it to photograph someone without talking to them?
- How did it change when you were each able to engage verbally?
- How hard was it to talk to someone non-stop for 15 minutes?
- Which session felt like it passed slowly—and quickly?
- Which session felt better—as subject and as photographer?

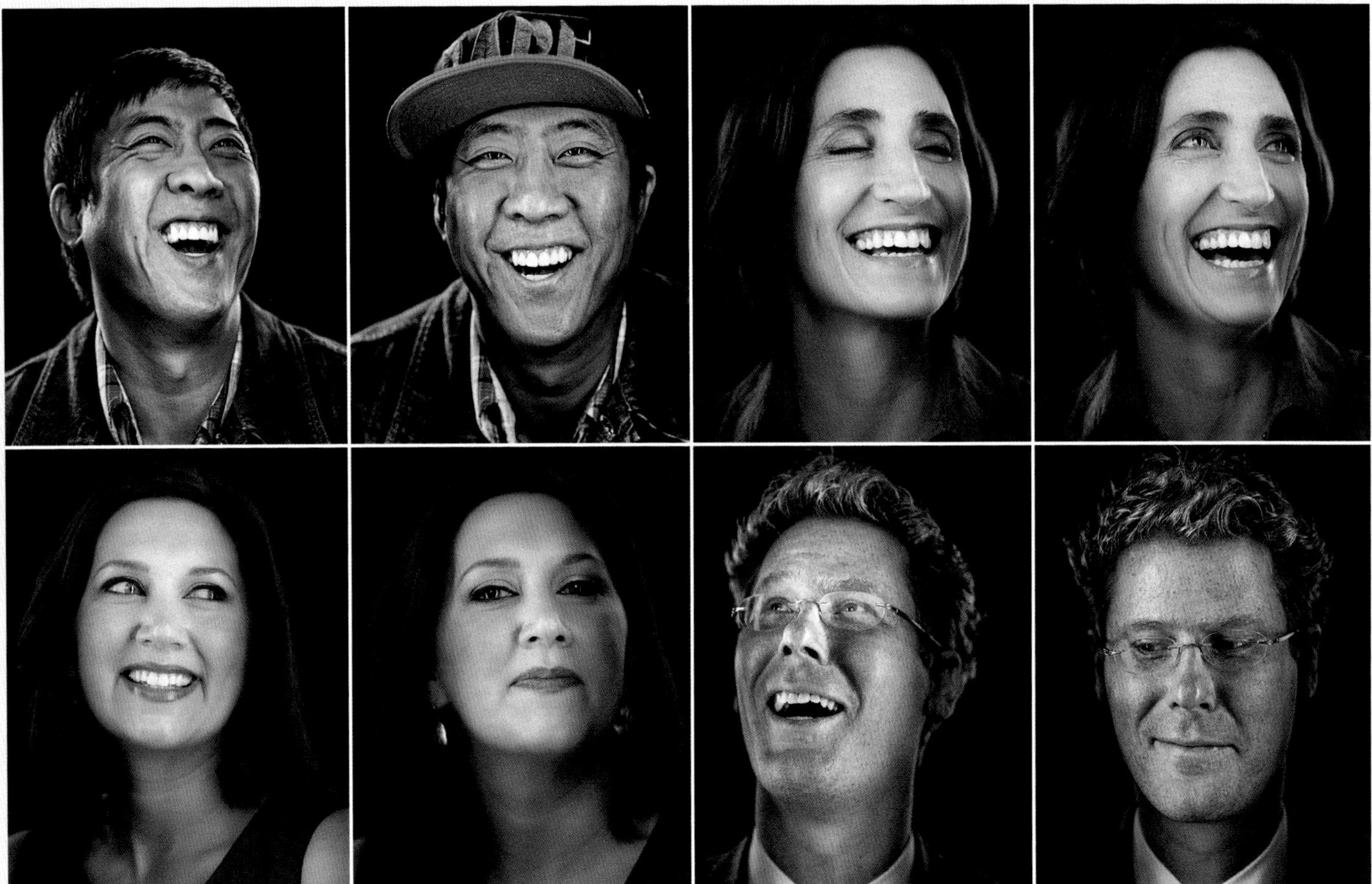

**FIGURE 8.23** Andy photographed a series of portraits for an editorial about non–traditional, but influential people in Portland. The goal was to have a very specific lighting style, but to create an environment that allowed the subjects to relax and be themselves.
IMAGE © ANDY BATT, *PORTLAND POWER PLAYERS,* FOR *PORTLAND MONTHLY* MAGAZINE, 2011.

**Download and Analyze**

Ingest your images into Lightroom. Use the Collections feature to divide your shoot into four groups. Take turns rating the images, getting it down to three images from each of the four groups.

- *First pass:* Have your partner select the images of you from both sessions; then select the images of your partner. Choose a convention, such as the green Color label, to mark the selections.
- *Second pass:* Now pick your own images (this is not optional; you have to!) then have your partner select his or her own images. Choose a second color (blue) for any new selects, and a third color (red) for any images you both selected.
- *Compare:* Compare all of the portraits. Which session resulted in a better image of you? Of your partner?

We're willing to bet that—in the majority of circumstances—the talking session resulted in better portraits, and that both the subject and the photographer had a better time making them. Most likely, neither of you will remember what you talked about; it's the act of communicating that's important.

## Notes

1 What we call a billboard is known inside the marketing world as a "30-sheet poster," which is a roughly 23 × 10 feet outdoor sign.

2 Team Penske, www.teampenske.com.

3 Lingerie Basketball, LLC, www.lingeriebasketball.com.

4 Scrap is also referred to as "tearsheets" (as in to tear apart) or "tears."

5 A production assistant (aka gopher, runner, guy/girl Friday) is a crewmember with a general—rather than photo-specific—skillset.

6 A photo assistant is a crewmember with specific, photo-oriented skills. Photo assistants might be dedicated to particular parts of a job.

7 American Society of Media Photographers, www.asmp.org.

8 American Photographic Artists, www.apanational.org.

9 Wedding and Portrait Photographers International, Emerald Expositions, www.wppionline.com.

10 Professional Photographers of America, www.ppa.com.

11 Ewa®-marine, ewa-marine GmbH, www.ewa-marine.com.

12 According to Dave Knox, author of *Strike the Baby and Kill the Blonde*, the martini is the last shot because "the next shot after that is 'out of a glass'" (2005: 126).

13 You can use Dropbox, www.dropbox.com, or any Cloud-based file service.

14 Knocking out is when you cut a person or object out of their background to combine them with another image—or to place them against a clean, white background.

15 A plate is, by Craig's definition, a shot of the surroundings in which you're shooting—whether it's a studio, a table top, an office or the great outdoors—without anything in it: no equipment, no flashes, no people.

16 A crewmember is on "hold" when a photographer is trying to land a job. The hold switches to a "booked" status when the job is awarded.

17 Backup, in this context, refers to copies of all the receipts that back up the amount of money that's charged as expenses.

18 WeTransfer, WeTransfer BV, www.wetransfer.com.

Nine

# GUEST PHOTOGRAPHERS: PHOTOS AND ADVICE

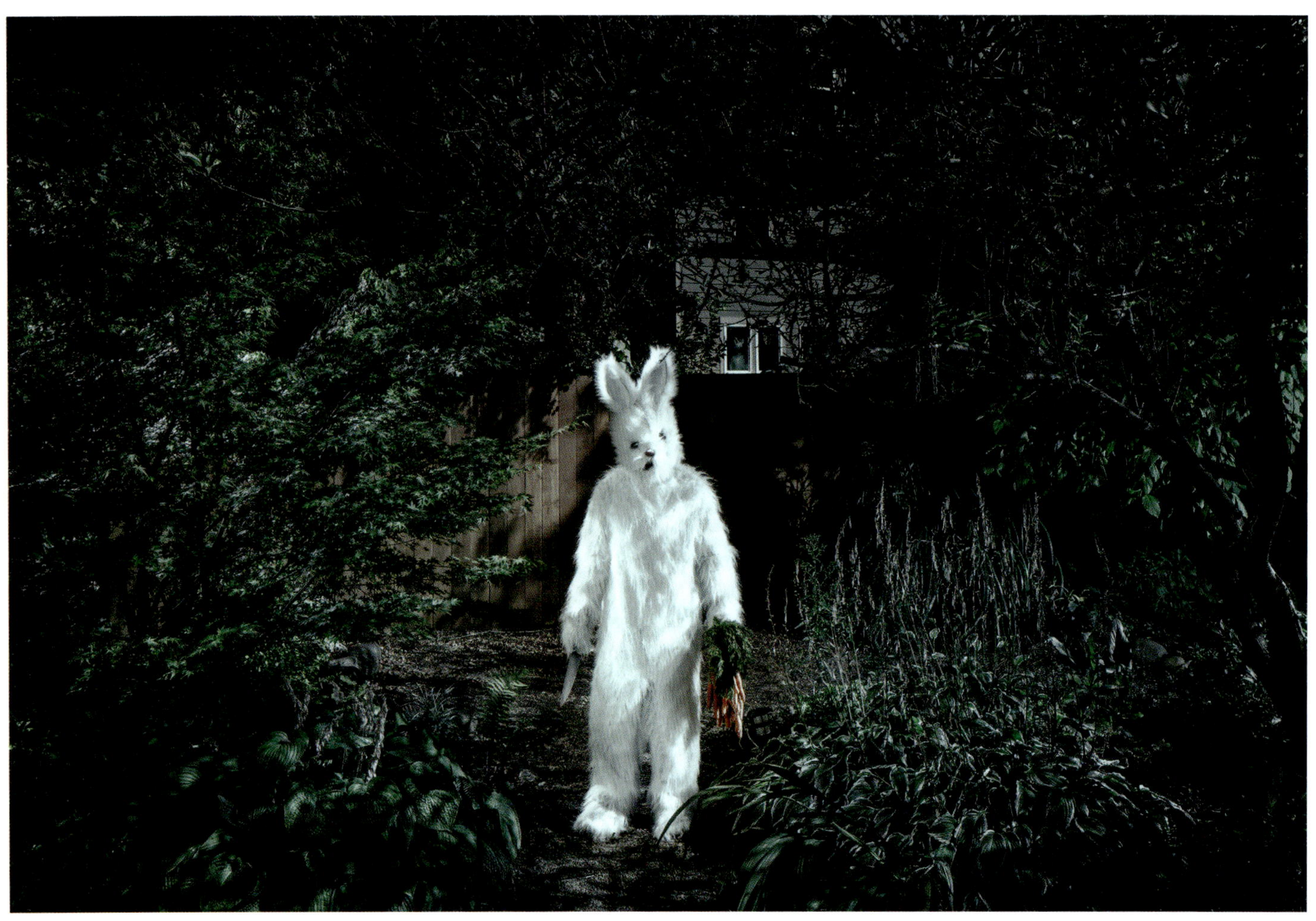

**FIGURE 9.1**
IMAGE © ANDY BATT, *BUNNY IN THE GARDEN*, 2010.

The best way to end any book about photography is with great photography; so, we invited each of our photo experts to provide us with two of their favorite images—images that inspire, affect or stand out, images we can (and do!) have conversations about. We also asked them to share their photographic advice, including tips and experience that might help in our quest to make better images.

Our guest photographers work in singular ways to create images that are uniquely theirs. All of them use craft—and cameras—to realize their ideas. Some of them use the camera as a tool for reacting, drawing their images from the friction between their own experience and what's happening around them. They seek out the truth and use their cameras as documentary tools. Others invent their work. Out of what seems to be thin air, their images emerge from the mind's eye, and the camera is the tool that brings them to life.

All of us—the reactors and inventors, the portraitists and journalists, the fine artists and documentarians—seek to create meaning by communicating an elusive essence, a "decisive moment."[1] We couldn't put it better than John Szarkowski did (Eggleston, 2002: 6):

> ***It is not easy for the photographer to compete with the clever originality of mindless, mechanized cameras, but the photographer can add intelligence. By means of photography one can in a minute reject as unsatisfactory ninety-nine configurations of facts and elect as right the hundredth. The choice is based on tradition and intuition—knowledge and ego—as it is in any art, but the ease of execution and the richness of the possibilities in photography both serve to put a premium on good intuition. The photographer's problem is perhaps too complex to be dealt with rationally. This is why photographers prowl with such restless uncertainty about their motif, ignoring many potentially interesting records while they look for something else.***

## Stewart Cohen

### *Director/Photographer*

***Stewart Cohen:*** I shot El Tigre, The Black Tiger (**Figure 9.2**), in Monterrey, Mexico while shooting a personal project on Lucha Libre.[2] We were invited to a party by some people we met at a taquería after a wrestling match; then we stumbled upon this scene and put El Tigre into it—at 3:00 a.m. We didn't prop this shot; I have no idea why Sponge Bob (the piñata) was still intact. The entire party had moved out to the street, and this room was so great that I asked El Tigre to sit in the scene.

***Andy Batt:*** When you shared this image with me, I figured it was one of your usual (and fascinating) setup shots. You're adept at creating great combinations of interesting people in interesting places, and I was surprised to hear that this was real! Since when does anyone just stumble across a scene like this, with a Luchador in tow? Photographers need to be ready, because sometimes the world just gives you a gift.

***Candace Dobro:*** It's amazing that this shot wasn't set up. I would have sworn that a stylist had something to do with those beautiful complementary colors. It's a great example of color theory at work—just look at the way the turquoise of the walls and the orange of the subject's suit play off each other.

***AB:*** There's a strange and wonderful formality in this composition; it's a balanced image, shot straight on, but with heavy asymmetry. The Luchador—The Black Tiger—has such weight. Your eye keeps landing on him, but is forced to keep traveling around the image.

Strobe light has a deliberate quality that reinforces the formality, and the Luchador pushes back against it. He's not looking at the camera, and he's holding a paper cup. It's like he's waiting for the room to fill up so he can take a whack at the piñata.

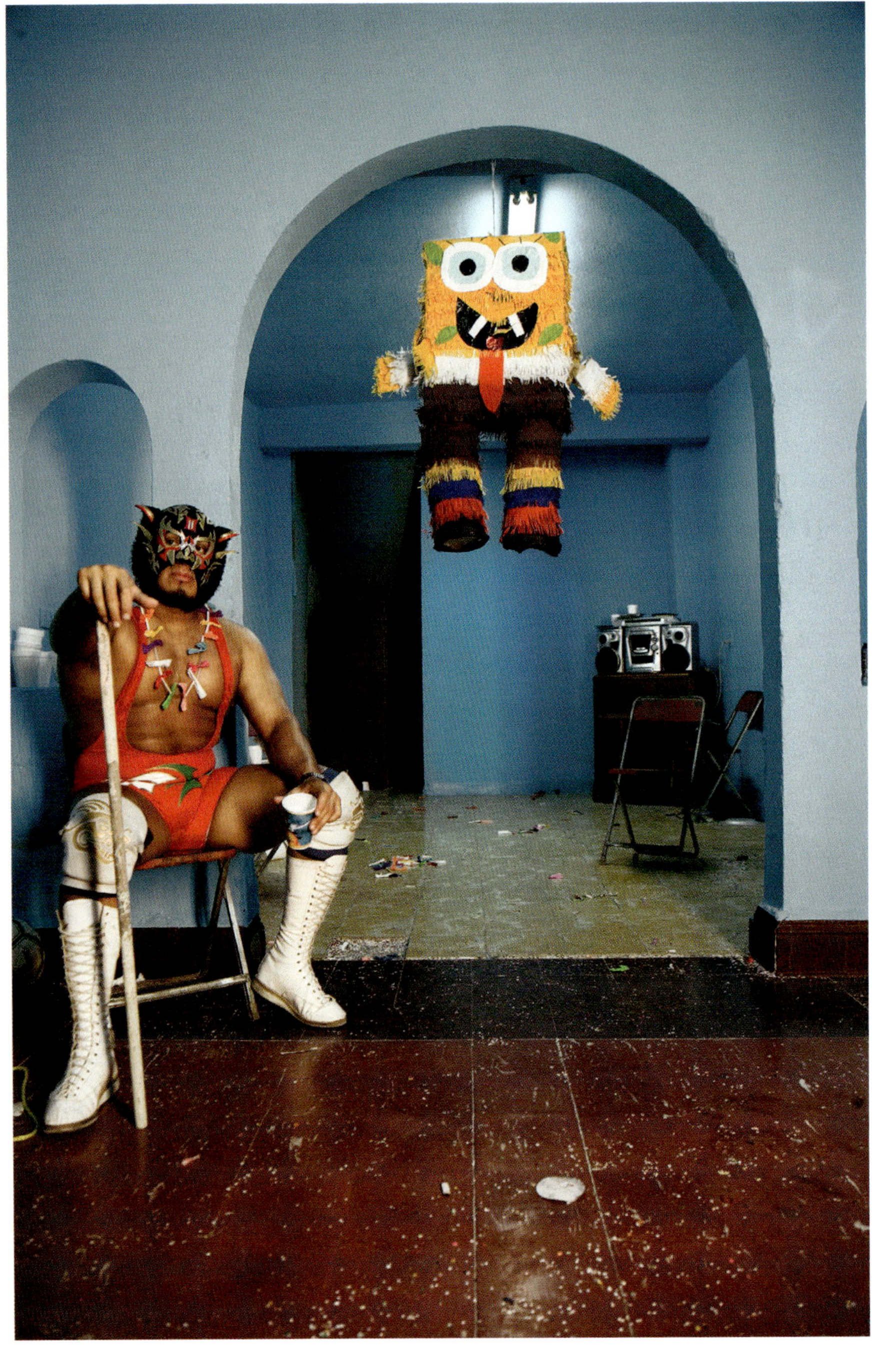

**FIGURE 9.2** This was shot with a 24–105mm zoom (at 24mm) on a Canon 1Ds Mark II with a manual exposure of 1/40th @ *f*/4.5, ISO 800. The slow shutter speed enabled Stewart to drag in the existing room light behind the piñata and sync his camera with the strobes.
IMAGE © STEWART COHEN, *PORTRAIT OF THE BLACK TIGER*, 2006.

***CD:*** The framing is masterful, and you chose a great combination of lens and camera distance to achieve a perfectly balanced canvas. The Luchador takes up so much space in his environment; he seems larger than life—especially his calves and feet. Those white boots leap out of the foreground, and the lens distortion from the 24mm adds to the effect. The image does have a wonderful formality; I find it very beautiful. Even though El Tigre's face isn't visible, his body language communicates how imposing a figure he is. He's almost confrontational, as though he and the photographer are facing off.

***AB:*** Stewart, how long did it take to set up your lights and shoot this image?

***SC:*** When I saw this shot, I sent my assistants running out to the truck to grab a quick simple lighting setup, probably a Profoto with a medium box. We'd been shooting at the wrestling match earlier that night, so we had strobes with us. The whole shoot probably took about thirty minutes from start to finish. It was just one light, so it was pretty simple. It's really cool to me how something that happened so fast became such an iconic image.

***AB:*** You just need the idea—plus travel time, concept time . . . and a lifetime of experience.

***SC:*** The image of Camp Bosworth[3] (**Figure 9.3**) was shot in Marfa, Texas. Camp is dressed in a custom-made suit that his wife, Buck, bought for him from one of the many artists in Marfa. The guns are made of Balsa wood, which is what he uses to make his art.

***AB:*** When I asked you about this image, you thought it was a good visual metaphor for your work: stylized, fun and well-produced images that are framed loosely. The loose compositions balance out the sometimes over-the-top nature of your subjects. When I survey your portfolio,[4] I see this idea played out over and over. It's a studied nonchalance.

The vertical lines in Camp's portrait are keeled over just a little; the giant neon horseshoe is obscured; elements bleed off the edges of image. We not only want to know more about this pastiche cowboy (Where did he get his giant guns?), but also, we suspect that there's a bigger, weirder world outside the frame—if only we could convince you to back up and show us.

***CD:*** Studied nonchalance; I like that. Look at the way the horseshoe and the arched window-frame echo each other and cradle the cowboy. It makes him jump out at you. Having the subject in the center of the frame is unconventional, but it works. Again, I'm struck by your use of color. The palette is almost monochromatic—an interesting choice, and so different from the previous photo.

***AB:*** This image works because all the elements reinforce each other: A giant horseshoe sits on the ground, Camp holds the cartoon guns like a character in a long-lost Saturday morning show and the Texas-sized cowboy hat and crazy bespoke suit full of embroidered goodness belong there with them. Each element is strong, but the total of all the parts is way more than the sum.

***CD:*** This portrait brings to mind the things you told us about interacting with your subjects. You can see how comfortable the cowboy is; you can feel the exuberance in his actions. What was this photo used for?

***SC:*** I photographed Camp for a magazine that my rep (at the time) was putting out. I went to Marfa because it's an artists' community. I thought there would be a lot to shoot there, but went without knowing *what* I'd shoot. I photographed a bunch of artists that day; Camp was the last. This shoot was another one that happened fast—probably twenty minutes. I lit it with a ring light and shot directly to card—I kept it simple.

***AB:*** Do you think it's different for photographers who are starting out today from when you were starting out?

***SC:*** I wish I were starting today; that would be awesome! In some ways it's easier now. For the young photographer who's smart and aggressive, it's an open door today. You have access to people all over the world. When I started, you really had to work on your local market first—it was years before you got national work.

***AB:*** Is it too easy?

***SC:*** Well, all of a sudden we're bidding against photographers that have a website with only five decent pictures on it. They're bidding

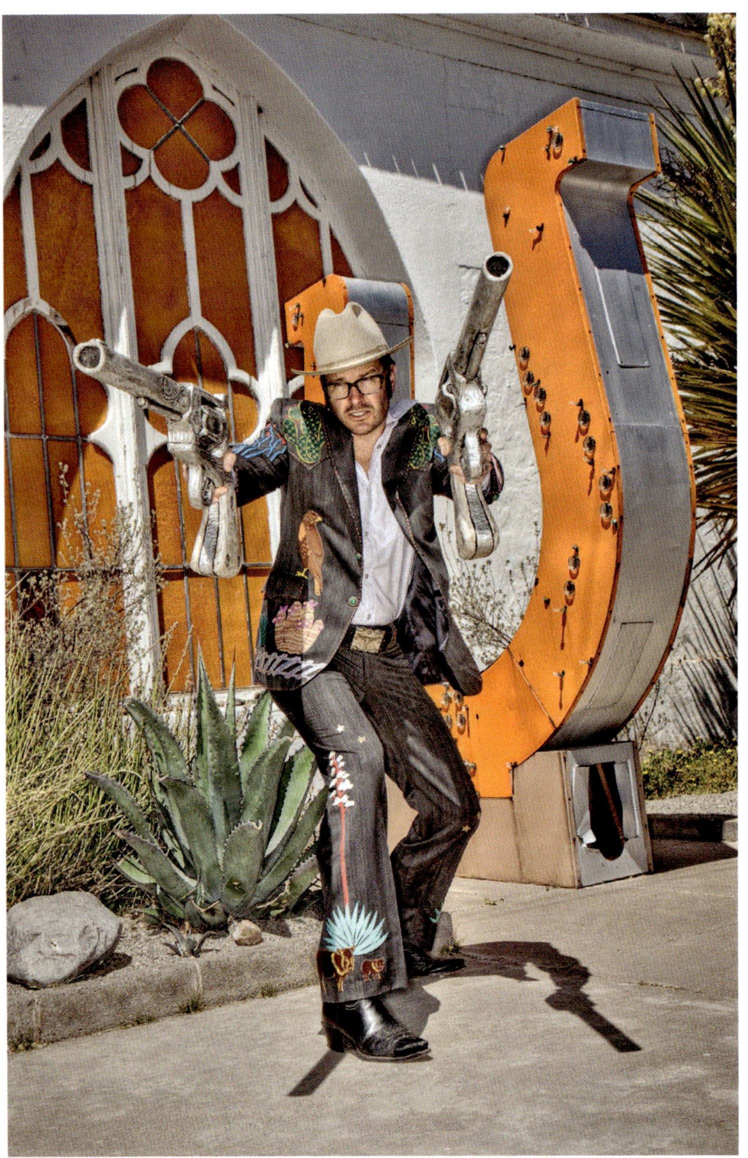

**FIGURE 9.3** Stewart captured Camp at 40mm (with a 24–105mm zoom) on a Canon 1Ds Mark III, with a manual exposure of 1/250th at *f*/8, ISO 100. A shutter speed of 1/250th is the edge of where that camera can sync with the ring light strobe that was used to fill in the shadows and create an up–lit look. The sun is coming from overhead: This is a high–noon photograph if ever there was one.
IMAGE © STEWART COHEN, *CAMP BOSWORTH, MARFA, TEXAS*, 2009.

on jobs they really shouldn't be bidding on—with art directors or clients that really don't know the difference, either.

***CD:*** Would you do anything different if you were starting out today?

***SC:*** I would do the same thing I'm doing right now. I look at every day like it's a new start, because I don't take much for granted. We still take advantage of traditional print marketing, as well as social media like LinkedIn, Facebook,Tumblr, Twitter, Instagram, a half-dozen paid online portfolio sites, etc. The key is that you need to find an audience that wants to hire you. Nothing has changed. When I started, you needed to find a following that wanted to hire you, as well.

Finding your following today is different. It might be a little bit easier, but one could also be lazier. You might not think to get on the phone, to get out of the office, to go knock on doors. People starting out today don't jump on planes to go meet people. I believe that's the lost art: in-person communication. If young photographers can learn that, they can leverage social media with traditional, old-school ideas. That could make them very successful, very quickly.

> ***I believe that's the lost art: in-person communication. If young photographers can learn that, they can leverage social media with traditional, old-school ideas. This could make them very successful, very quickly.***

## Sol Neelman

### *Commercial, Editorial and "Weird Sports" Photographer*

***Andy Batt:*** You can't control a moment like this (**Figure 9.4**). Your subjects are in motion, falling down in the mud, caring not one bit about the photographer who's trying to find the shot. That image only happens for the photographer who's ready and in control of the equipment. You can also control the composition by finding the spot, the framing and . . . ready, set, wait! You're rewarded—not every time, but often enough.

This would be a great image, even if it only included the mist, the mud and the people scrambling over the obstacles—but to get this perfect moment with the woman screaming and her pink hair flying up in the air like a Troll doll?[5] You have to be good, and you have to be ready.

This isn't a created image—it's a received image. It was fleeting: there for a moment, then gone.

***Candace Dobro:*** Anyone who has ever tried—unsuccessfully—to shoot sports (yes, that would be me!) can appreciate how much experience it takes to capture a shot as pristine as this one. Sol chose the perfect combination of camera settings to arrive at an exposure that stopped the action and a DoF that lures the eye straight to the subject. I love the crisp detail, the way it reveals the distinct textures of hair, fabric and mud.

***AB:*** Here's a simple shot (**Figure 9.5**) that took a lot of experience and a trained eye. This is life—not a situation where you can ask people to go back and do it again so you can try a different angle. You frame up the shot with your camera dialed in, and you use all your attention, so you're ready when the moment arrives.

***CD:*** You're very low-key, Sol. When you talk about your work, people might think you're just out there to have a good time—but there's nothing casual about the concentration required to create work like yours.

***AB:*** You told us you love to shoot sports with a wide lens, because you get "messy frames." Tell us how this is a messy image, besides the fact that you were about to get covered in mud.

***Sol Neelman:*** Messy to me means having lots of junk in a photo. That junk is information, and those imperfections make the photo priceless. In this image, there's a red plastic security line, a guy with a super-clean, green trucker hat and folks wearing bright yellow shirts. All of that's distracting—but it's part of the reason why it works. It feels real and random. If I were ever to stage a scene, I'd never think to include those perfect imperfections. They help place the moment I captured. I want people to feel like they're standing right next to me (without needing to get covered in red Georgia clay).

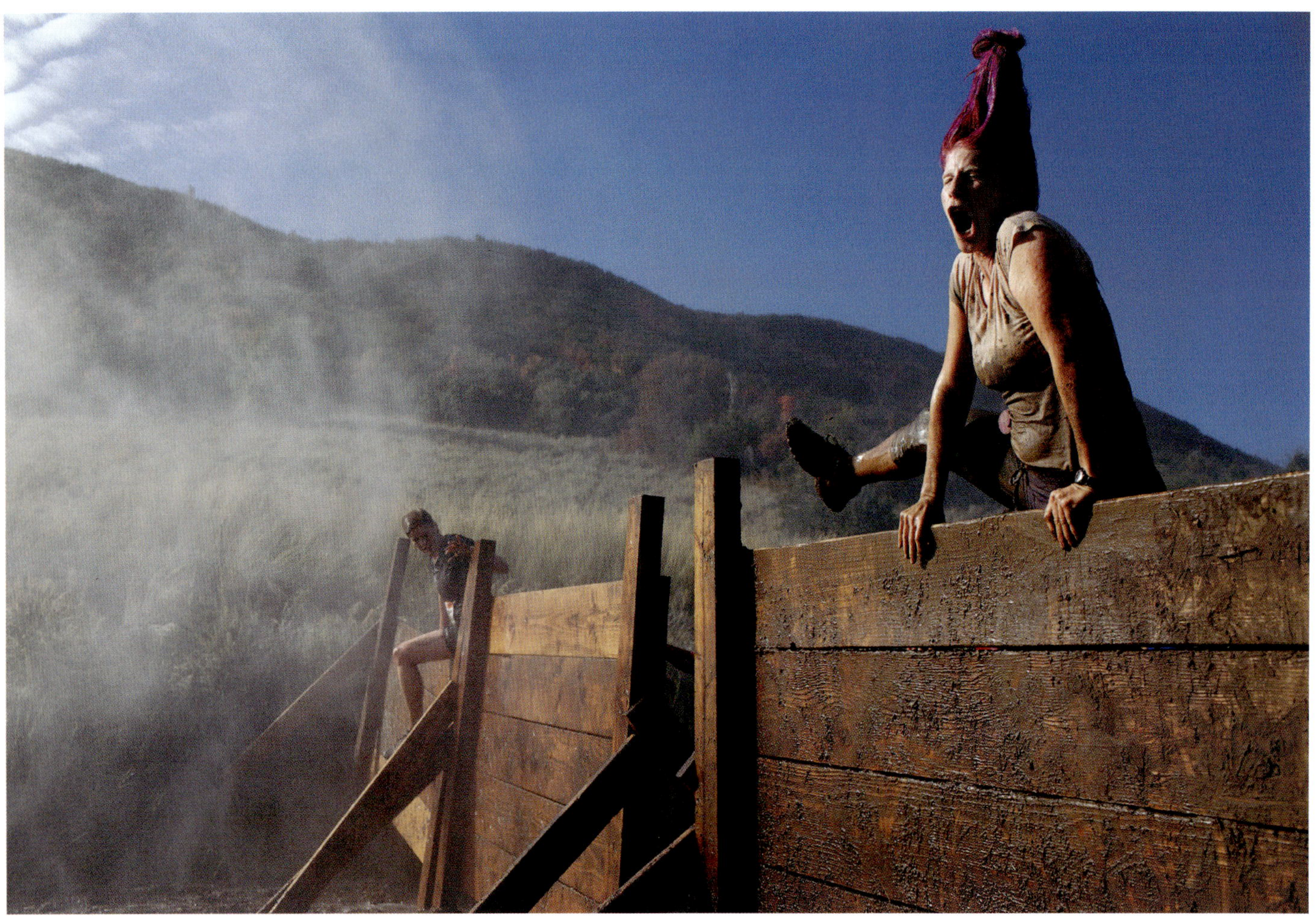

**FIGURE 9.4** Sol shot this image using a Canon 1Ds Mark III with a 35mm, *f*/1.4 lens bolted onto it. A 1/1000th of a second at ISO 320 stopped the action, and by setting the aperture to *f*/6.3 with this lens, Sol achieved plenty of DoF.
IMAGE © SOL NEELMAN, *DIRTY DASH*, PRINTED IN *MARIE CLAIRE*, 2013.

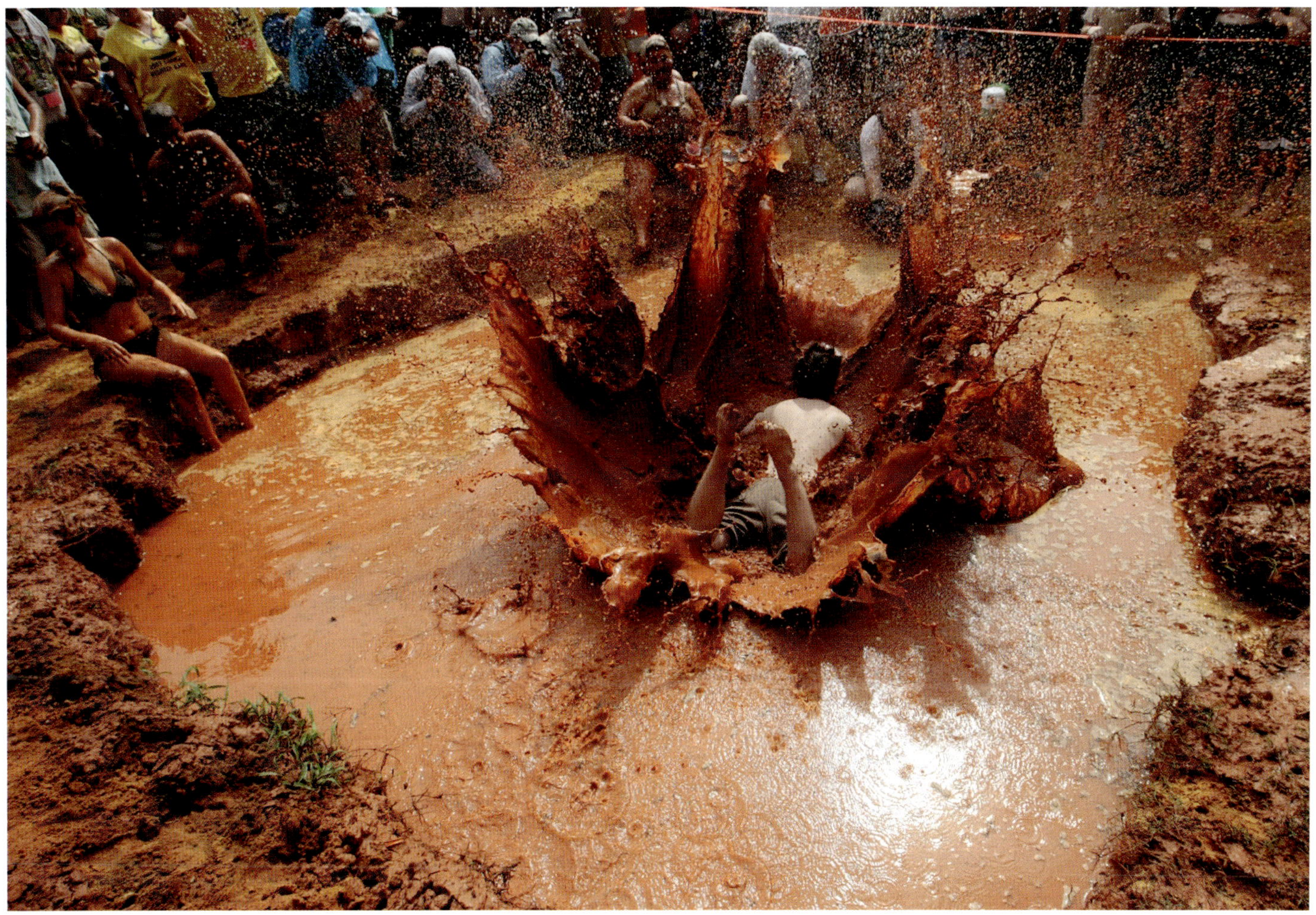

**FIGURE 9.5** A 1/1000th of a second exposure at ISO 400 "froze" the mud mid–splash.
IMAGE © SOL NEELMAN, *REDNECK GAMES,* ORIGINALLY PRINTED IN *NATIONAL GEOGRAPHIC* MAGAZINE, 2008.

> ***If I were ever to stage a scene, I'd never think to include those perfect imperfections. They help place the moment I captured.***

***AB:*** It's a perfectly frozen moment—another great example of knowing your gear and being ready in the right place: You got the shot right at the peak, with a huge splash, but 1/1000th of a second before he's engulfed by the mud. His back is clean—that's part of what makes this shot for me. There's a visual tension between this clean guy and the utter mess of the mud puddle; it's the moment before it all changes, before he becomes coated in red mud like the woman sitting to his left. In a weird way, it reminds me of those perfect pour shots, those images that illustrated liquor ads or something—it's not a usual sports shot.

***SN:*** For me, there's only one rule in photography: There are no rules. Back in the day, my editors and colleagues tried to get me to follow the rules: Shoot cleaner photos, make images with a quicker read, use more long lenses. There was a certain point when I realized that I don't want a quick read in my images—I want that messy frame. Several years ago, Rob Finch, a talented friend and colleague at *The Oregonian*, told me that he spent fifteen minutes looking at one of my wide-angle photos. That floored me. He said that there was so much for him to discover in that single image that he couldn't take his eyes off it. That helped set the bar for me.

***AB:*** If you were going to give advice to an up-and-coming photographer —or, to put it another way, if you had to give advice to a younger version of yourself—what would it be?

***SN:*** The number-one thing is to define what you love to photograph and shoot it recklessly for the rest of your life—until you find other things that you want to photograph. Weird Sports are funny, because when the book came out (Neelman, 2011), I received a lot of attention—which was flattering—and my images have now been published in a bunch of places. Nobody wanted my images before the book was published. I broke even with the book project itself (but not with all the costs to produce the images). That's not why I do it. I do it because I love it; it makes me laugh. I'm going to photograph Chuck Wagon Racing next weekend in Arkansas—I love it!

Everyone has their own path and their own way of shooting. I try to embrace mine—I don't think it's very intelligent or sophisticated. I've been a photographer for over fifteen years (I'm 43 years old) and I'm still trying to grow, but I'm also comfortable with who I am as a photographer and what I bring. The challenge of being a paid photographer is to find clients who appreciate what I have to offer, instead of people who are looking for a style I'm not strong at.

At least for newspaper photographers, there's this huge pressure (understandably) to please the newspaper. If I were talking to a younger me, I would say, "Treat the newspaper like a client—make sure the client is happy—but take pictures for yourself, as well." At the time, I was trying to make pictures that I was happy with and to force them down the throat of a client who didn't want them. I've taken plenty of ad pictures as a freelance photographer, and as long as the client is happy, I'm ecstatic . . . then I go make pictures for myself.

## Kim Campbell

### *Portrait Photographer*

***Andy Batt:*** There's a coral snake in your playful work. And a meat cleaver. And a tied-up child. And more sinister stuff. It's easy to have your brain fooled with a first glance at this image (**Figure 9.6**) from your *Childhood Gravity Games* series. There's the deliberate use of primary yellow and the weightless feeling of children flying through the air—but there's also something darker going on. I see this as a meditation on childhood. Growing up is fun and games, but at times, it's about finding yourself in a perilous situation. There are questions here, and open-ended moments that aren't resolved.

This is a montage—a work created in Photoshop—but it's not about Photoshop. It's about using tools and techniques to build an image that was designed and thought out *before* it was ever captured or layered together in post.

***Candace Dobro***: Your work *is* incredibly playful—and inventive. You were evidently born to photograph children. There's a genuine sense of whimsy, spontaneity and fun in your portraiture; no wonder children are comfortable sitting (and moving) for you.

***AB:*** What motivated you when you were creating this image—and the rest of the series?

***Kim Campbell:*** Turning ideas into reality is one of my favorite pastimes. With the *Childhood Gravity Games,* I wanted to create a series of images that convey a playful feeling of buoyancy. I did several test shoots to dial in my lighting and camera placement, all within the controlled environment of my studio. This is where I get to be more creative. I get to thinking, "Wow, this has evolved from test shooting with a couple of kids." For this series, I decided to shoot it all from a bird's-eye perspective, so I mounted the camera on the ceiling. I tried different backgrounds underneath the subjects. I tried different fabrics, different colors, until I decided that I was going to use black—black floating in space. I took over a thousand images to create the *Childhood Gravity Games*; I had a huge library of poses, actions and brilliant defiances of gravity.

I had to work through some technical ideas to do the series: I kept asking myself, "Where's my light coming from?" I wanted to make sure I wasn't just taking a kid and twisting him around in the computer. I pose them correctly *when I'm shooting*, so the light's always coming from the right direction. If you look at the light source, it's coming from one side, so if I was making a kid look like she was diving down to the bottom of the frame, I wouldn't just spin her around in Photoshop, I would make sure that I shot her like that.

When I rigged the camera to the ceiling of my studio, I used a wireless shutter release and a monitor connected to the camera, so I could see the images as I took them. In the beginning, I went up and down a ladder to pose my models. Near the end, I could just stand by the side and know what I was getting. It was a fun process to try a totally different way of shooting. I spent a lot of time on the computer, masking and manipulating.

This kind of setup would have really intimidated me earlier in my career; now I relish figuring out how to bring images like this to life. I'm producing images that not everyone can; I'm crafting my unique role in the portrait and fine art photography marketplace.

> ***I create images that not everyone can; I create my own, unique role in the portrait and fine art photography marketplace.***

***AB:*** *Hollow* (**Figure 9.7**) is such a strong image. Using a skull as a prop is a double-edged sword: It's so iconic and brings with it such strong associations that it can easily overpower the image, or even turn on itself and work against the image. The skull in *Hollow* does none of that; instead, our fascination with the skull—with icons of death in general—is balanced against what appears to be a young, innocent girl. I say, "Appears," since we never see her face. Is that the worn fingernail polish of a 12-year-old or an 18-year-old girl? Is it a girl? The subject feels feminine, but we can't be sure.

***CD:*** It's a study in white, and since the image is so spare, we're encouraged to rest our eyes and contemplate all of these things—the feelings, the symbolism, the mystery.

***AB:*** This is such a beautiful image. It's simple, but there's a lot going on. Can you tell us more about it?

***KC:*** In 1997, I lost two people whom I cared deeply about. Both deaths were unexpected and hit me like a sledgehammer. My first fine art series came from this experience: I photographed a young woman who had an androgynous look and oversized wings in an abandoned warehouse. She allowed me to bring darkness into the light and was game to try anything I asked, which gave me the opportunity to bring some of my feelings into a visual reality. That series is entitled the *Angel Archives.* I still have several of these images hanging in my home, so I encounter them daily. The ones that draw me in are the simplest ones.

Death, loss, and the unknown are concepts I still like to touch on in my work. This image, *Hollow,* is a great example of how my work has evolved over time. I've been experimenting with bones in photos over the years. I want to know how I can take a skull and use it in an image, in a transformative way.

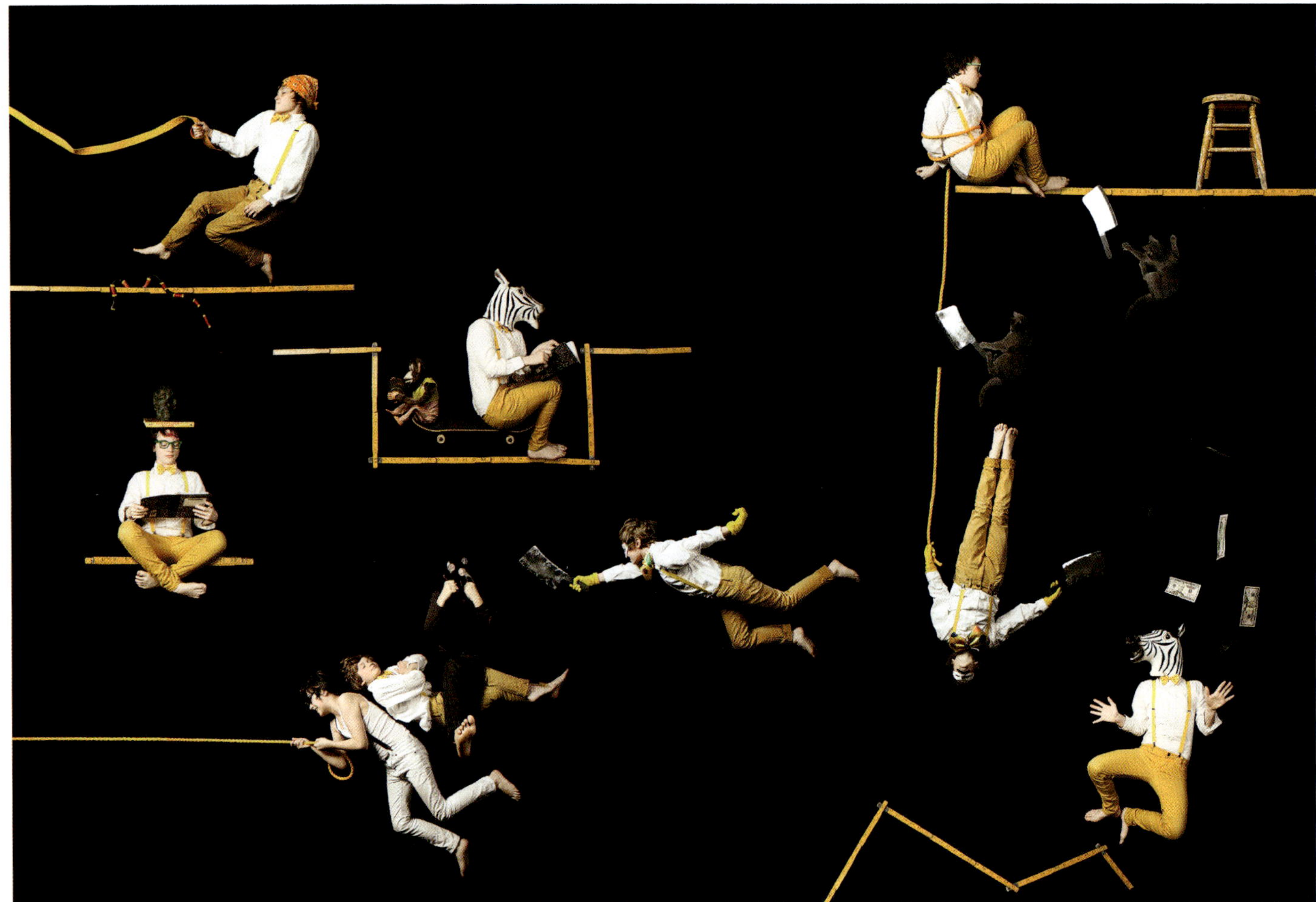

**FIGURE 9.6** Kim wanted to shoot from a bird's–eye perspective, so she mounted the camera on the ceiling of her studio. She used a wireless shutter release and a monitor connected to the camera for easy, instant viewing.
IMAGE © KIM CAMPBELL, *CHILDHOOD GRAVITY GAMES—YELLOW*, 2013.

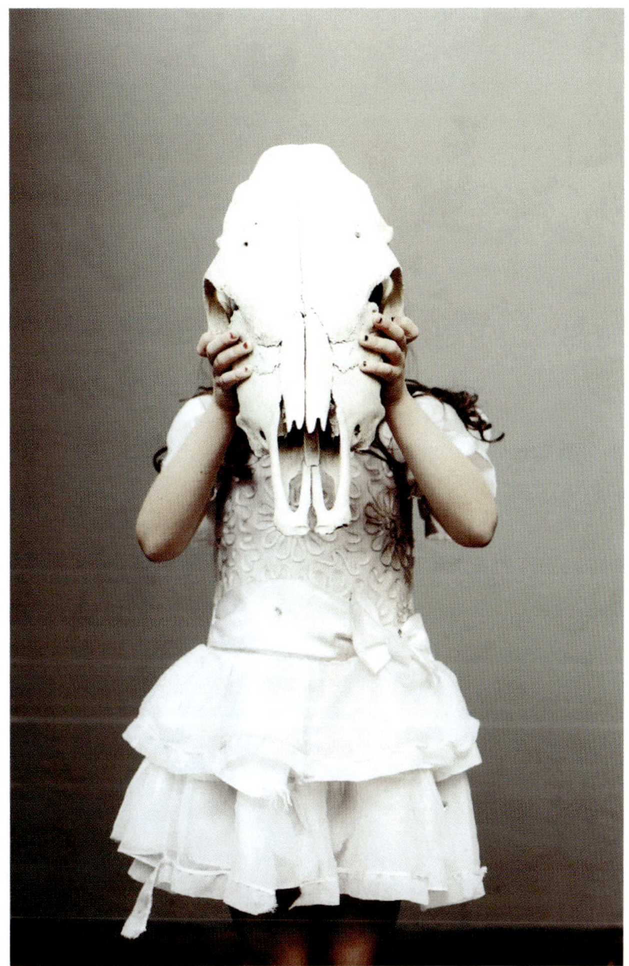

**FIGURE 9.7** Kim says that because kids aged 5–12 have little inhibition, "They're creative, so they add to my own creative process . . . they're great inspiration."
IMAGE © KIM CAMPBELL, *HOLLOW,* 2010.

I have several photos with this model and found that the placement of the skull over her face is incredibly powerful. The way the hollow eye sockets of the bleached cow skull line up near her face, the ragged clothes, the mismatched and deteriorating fingernail polish—all lend themselves to the strangeness of the photo. It is simple and powerful at the same time. To me, if I can evoke feeling from the viewer, it always feels like a success.

*If I can evoke feeling from the viewer, it always feels like a success.*

***AB:*** If you could go back in time, what would be the one piece of advice you'd give the younger version of yourself?

***KC***: You've got to be in there—and be at the top of your game—to make a living at it. So I would say that focusing to find your own voice is really the key. I think I was able to do that, because my husband and I come from a fine art background, so we didn't go through the traditional portrait-photographer training route. We just created pictures that moved us or interested us, which was a little different approach in the portrait-photography field. Because of that, our photos never looked like everybody else's, and I think that's one of the reasons we have such a good niche—and that our photos are recognizable. We just created something that looks unique. It stands by itself.

## Jeff Conley

### *Landscape and Nature Photographer*

***Andy Batt:*** You used formal composition and a time-honored landscape-photography technique—softly blurred water—to create a unique image (**Figure 9.8**). The landscape image has been photographed over and over, so it's always amazing to see your work. You find compositions that are hidden in front of the rest of us.

Layered simplicity is at work here: The composition is clean, iconic and classic, but there are layers upon layers of nuance. The water isn't blurry, but it's not sharp, either. It's ethereal. The boulders appear to rise from the ocean. We have no sense of depth or distance—all we know is that there are seven otherworldly objects either rising above or sinking below the waves. The horizon line is distinct, separating sea from atmosphere, but the image could be upside down: The clouds and sea share qualities that make you question gravity.

***Candace Dobro:*** You're so right, Andy; the division between the elements is almost mystical—as though they exist in a fantastical world.

***AB:*** Jeff, where did you find such uniquely wonderful objects?

***Jeff Conley:*** This photograph was made in Moeraki—on the east coast of the south Island of New Zealand—with a Hasselblad 500CM, 180mm Zeiss lens and a Hasselblad CFV50 digital back.

Along this stretch of coastline are these wonderful, captivating, spherical boulders. I arrived on the beach in the early afternoon and explored the area thoroughly, finding a cluster of boulders that I liked very much. I established some framing and perspective options that appealed to me, and then left to explore some other areas.

I returned about two hours prior to sunset, because I felt the lighting on the boulders would get interesting closer to sundown—and also because the tide would be coming in. In the final image, the movement of the water and the slight movement of the clouds isolate the boulders and let them stand out as the focal point. Landscape photography is often about allowing a scene to unfold on its own terms and sometimes requires tenacious patience and planning.

***CD:*** It's satisfying to hear how thoroughly you explored the site; it really does take patience and planning to create beautiful landscape photography. These qualities are so apparent in your work—you simply can't get results like this by taking impulsive snapshots.

**FIGURE 9.8** Here's a great illustration of the core photographic toolset: carefully considered framing, the use of shutter speed to communicate the passage of time and good exposure that reveals texture and detail in the dark crevices of the boulders.
IMAGE © JEFFREY CONLEY, *SEVEN ROUND BOULDERS,* NEW ZEALAND, 2011.

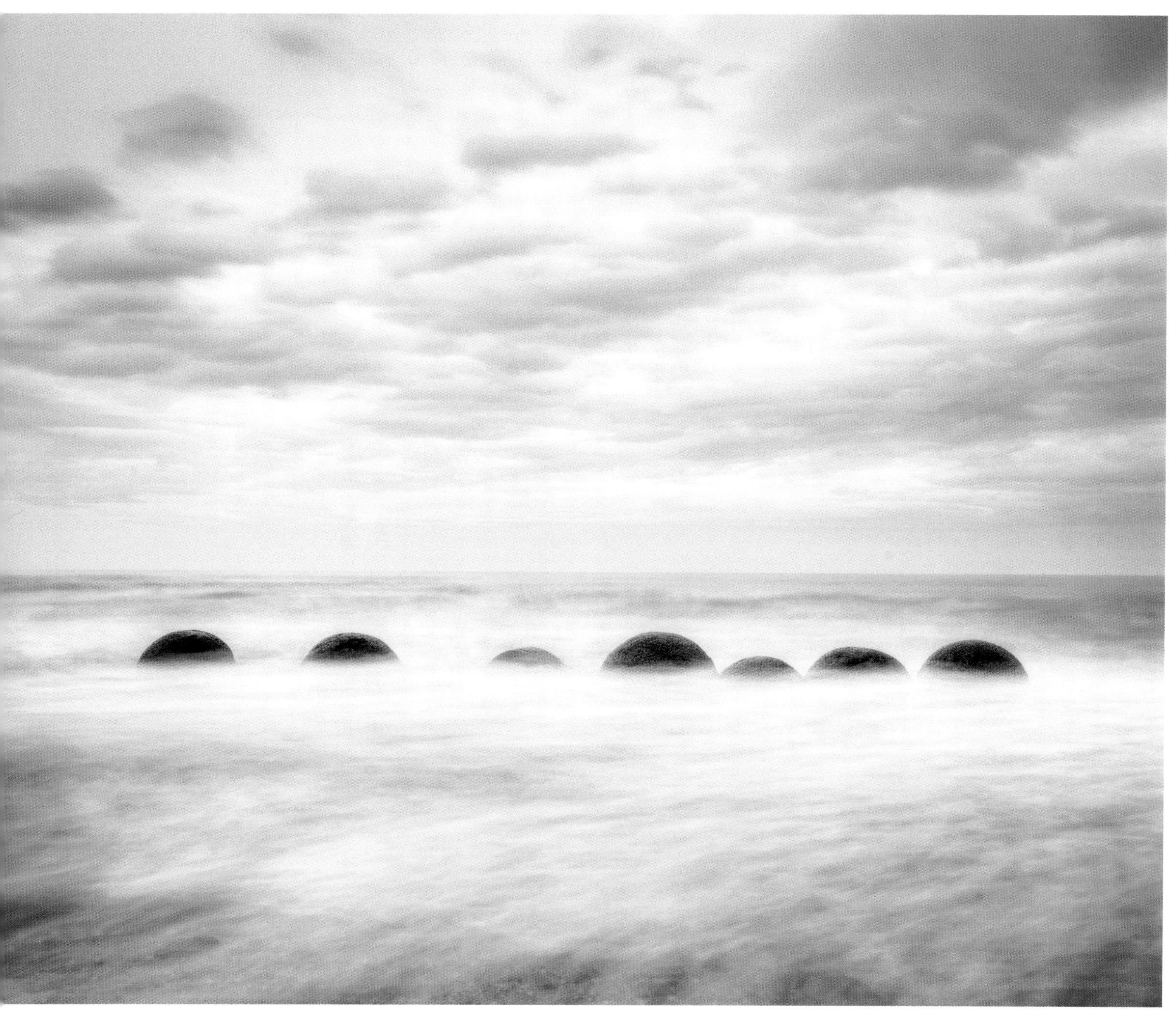

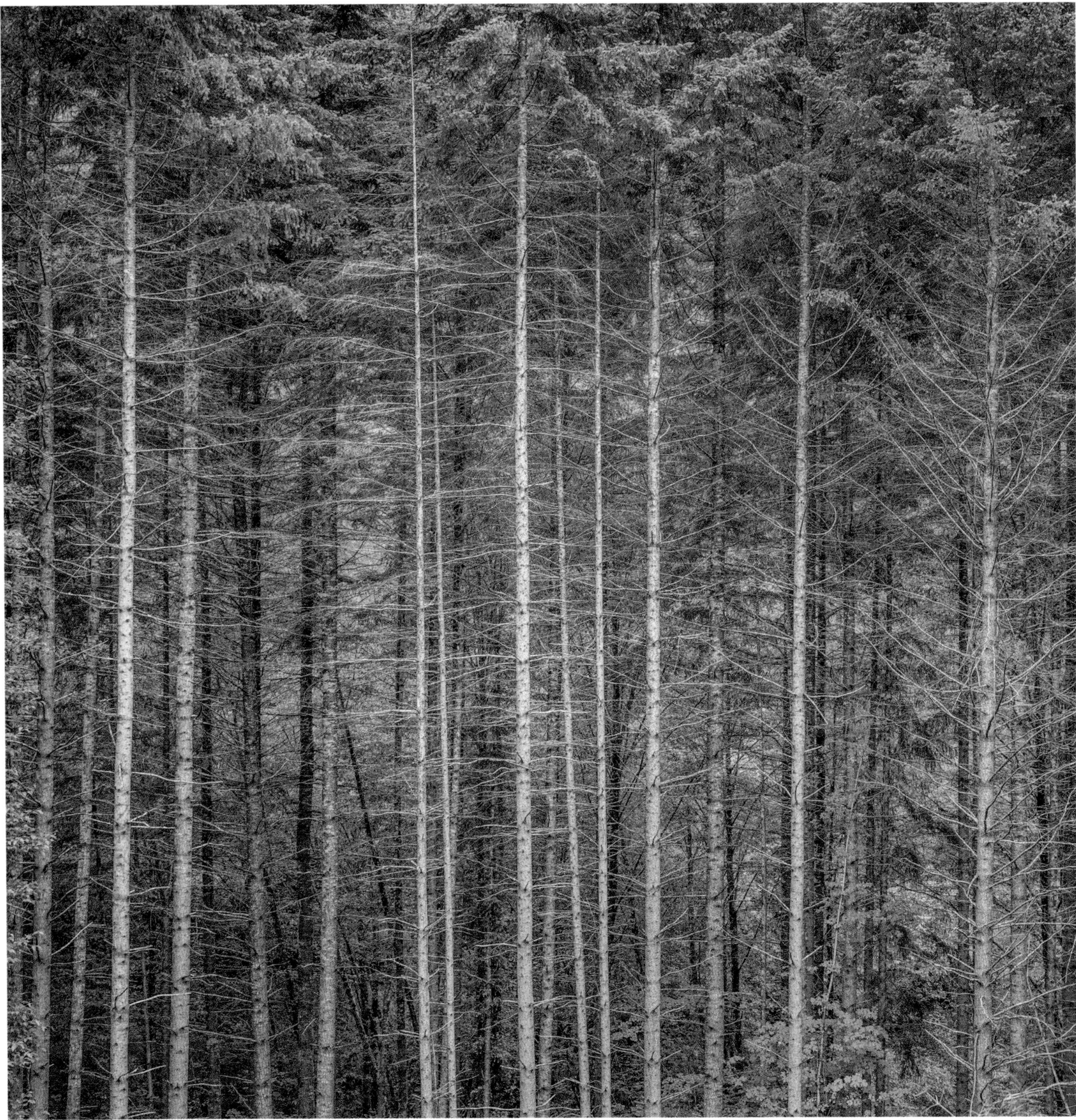

***Landscape photography is often about allowing a scene to unfold on its own terms and sometimes requires tenacious patience and planning.***

***AB:*** This image (**Figure 9.9**) is defined by texture and pattern; the fine detail is amazing. On screen it's phenomenal; I can only imagine what it looks like on a gallery wall. I could be looking at trees—or at the bronchiole and alveoli in a microscopic view of a lung. Again, there's simple complexity, or maybe it's complex simplicity. At first glance this seems to be a flat image—shallow, all on one plane. When I keep staring at it, I become aware of the depth. There are pale tree trunks in the front, and dark shadows haunt the background. The tree limbs are impossibly thin; there's a shock of leaf at the top of the image. It's an abstraction, full of texture—and at the same time, it's a definitive image of a forest.

Behind this image (figuratively) is where we find you at work. You're able to see a stand of trees and translate your mental impression of them into an image. You understand how the tones will translate into black and white and what the detail will look like printed on a large scale. This is a learned process.

***CD:*** Your work is all about the final print. How does that end product come into play?

***JC:*** Recently, I've been experimenting with stitching together multiple images, which allows me to make very large prints that contain extremely rich detail. I'm striving to achieve a level of detail close to what you'd get from large-format contact prints made from film negatives. With this process, I can extend the resolution of my current camera system (a 36MP Nikon D800) far beyond its single-frame capability. There are many challenges when shooting images to stitch; for example, I need to have a relatively static scene with little or no movement in it. I've also found that I need to have consistent lighting conditions. It's important to avoid variations in exposure throughout the many frames required.

***AB***: If you could send one key piece of photography advice back in time to a younger version of yourself, what would it be?

***JC***: To be honest—we've joked about "M&P," right, Andy?

***CD:*** You're talking about an extremely technical class you both took at RIT called "Materials and Processes."

***JC***: Yes. It was a highly technical class, and I had this attitude that, "They don't really understand; they're not bringing the instruction back to the creative side of photography," which has always been the most provocative thing for me about photography. I didn't get enough out of that class, and I regret that. I think I could've gotten more out of my education at RIT, so my advice would be: Pay attention more!

***AB***: And if you were giving advice to a young, upcoming photographer?

***JC***: Photograph what you want to photograph; follow your own vision. It's what I've done, for better or for worse. I've tried to be true to my own interest in photography. It is quite a challenge, though, from a financial perspective, trying to live a somewhat conventional life with a very unconventional livelihood in the arts. There's a paradox there, but I think it's important to live the life you want to live and to be able to shoot the things you want to shoot. It's important to produce photographs on your own terms. That's really vital.

***CD:*** What personality traits do you need to make that happen?

***JC***: A strong work ethic, combined with a confidence in one's vision; a feeling that you have something to add to the visual conversation. I suppose I'm alluding to the elusive element of "drive" that makes someone go.

***AB***: Photographers are good at being stubborn—or maybe it's patience.

**FIGURE 9.9** This photograph is comprised of 12 individual images that were stitched together. To capture it, Jeff used a 105mm lens with a Nodal Ninja multi-row panorama head. It can be successfully printed at 33 × 33 inches at 360ppi and has a real resolution of 141.1MP. Stitching enables Jeff to make very large, richly detailed prints.
IMAGE © JEFFREY CONLEY, *FOREST VIEW—JULY 2, 2013.*

***JC***: Yeah, maybe a little bit of ignorance in there, too, which you need in order to follow your own path. Being patient is important, because getting into the fine art end of things is a very difficult row to hoe. It's taken me a very long time to make contacts and develop relationships with galleries. They've given me the time to work—and to have a client base large enough so that they can actually market my work. That's taken the last fifteen to eighteen years. It's been very slow progress, but it has happened.

***CD:*** Do you think it's still possible in today's world to have a life like that?

***JC***: I go back and forth. I look at photographers who are self-representing artists that can now potentially make a living by promoting and selling their work directly from their websites—versus the old paradigm of partnering with the gallery that amplifies your work and gets it out into the broader art scene.

There's a compelling argument for both sides, but I think there's a sense of validation—especially from an art collector's point of view—that comes from working with brick-and-mortar galleries. Putting your physical work in front of people is a very difficult experience to replicate electronically. I think that the gallery paradigm will evolve, moving forward, because this new way—where artists can show work online and build an audience through social networking—is kind of intriguing.

***AB***: I always think there's value in being the opposite of whatever is the mass trend. So, if we're in a world of screens and instant gratification and a forget-about-it-in-thirty-minutes mentality, there's something to be said for building a beautiful print, hanging it in a real place and getting it in front of real people.

***JC***: I do believe that with the evolution of digital technology, people will look at darkroom work or traditional darkroom prints—gelatin-silver prints, platinum prints—as being something handmade and quaint. As recently as ten to fifteen years ago, making darkroom prints was considered a highly technical medium, more technical than other works on paper. Now, because technology is changing so much, it's come to the point where darkroom work is quaint, almost akin to basket weaving.

***AB***: It might be better for you, as a fine artist. Twenty years ago, there was still a massive rejection (in the fine art world) of the idea that photography was serious art. Anything you could make identical copies of didn't count. Because most things are inkjet-printed today, the silver gelatin print is now defined as an art process, and not a commercial one. This re-establishes its value as a work of art—an actual physical thing that's worth money and consideration.

***JC***: Yeah, I think so as well.

## Craig Ferroggiaro

### *Fine Art Photographer and Retoucher*

***Andy Batt:*** Adding a wash of faded blues and browns is a technique that links directly to the tradition of hand-colored images and immediately conjures a nostalgic feeling in me. Much of the original hand-colored photographs were done before color photography was commonplace. The goal of the artists who made them was to create lifelike color, to add back to the black-and-white photograph the things that were missing. As the technique evolved, it became an artistic, expressionistic tool. It was no longer about the realism of the scene, but about creating a compelling image.

Fast forward to now: We see this image (**Figure 9.10**) as an artistic interpretation, but we also feel the weight of time. The beautifully composed landscape has been turned into something stronger, through skillful retouching.

***Candace Dobro:*** Craig, can you tell us how you made this image? Where did the idea come from?

***Craig Ferroggiaro:*** I started by creating a black-and-white image from the raw file. I used a Photoshop technique that I developed to tint it. The idea came out of my analog days. I had always enjoyed working with Marshall's Photo Oils, hand-tinting black-and-white photographs. They have a unique look that I wanted to recreate with my digital images.

My first attempt was to hand-color digital prints using colored pencils, powdered pastels, watercolors, oils and other mediums. Most

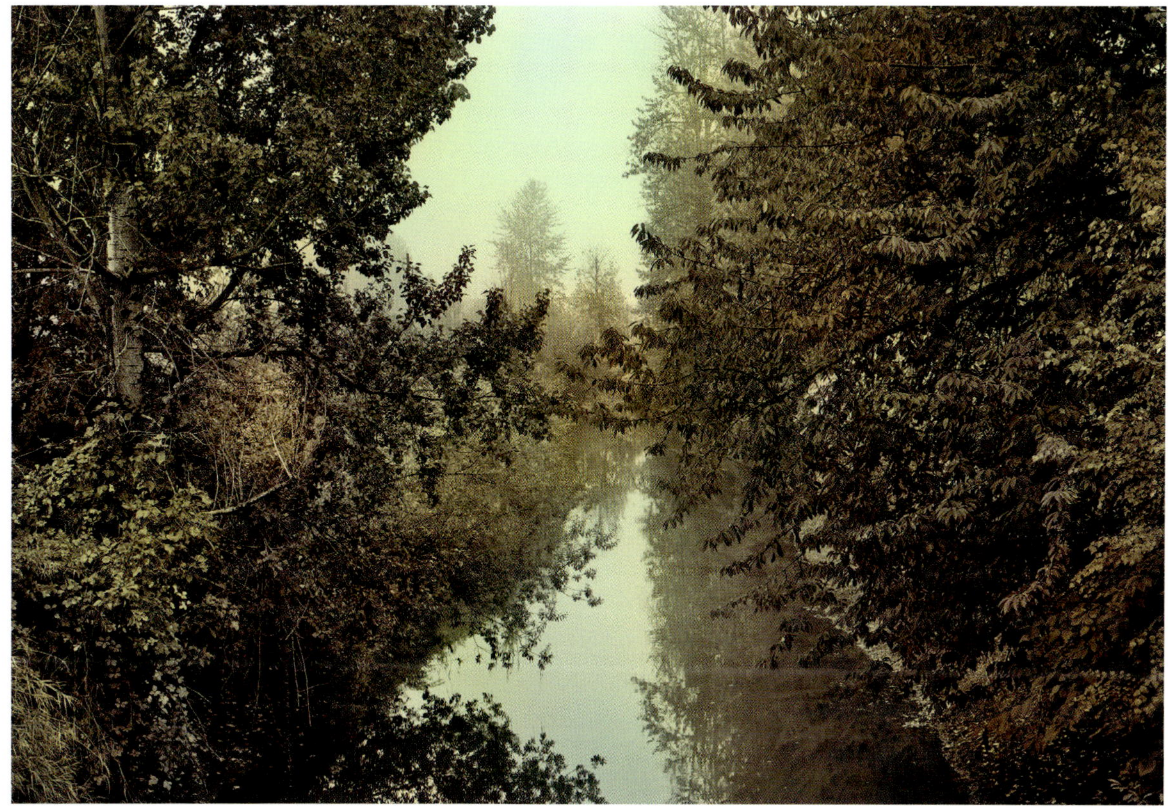

**FIGURE 9.10** Craig created this shot with the original 12.8MP Canon 5D and the EF 50mm *f*/1.4. This is an instance of buying and using good technology—and not feeling compelled to upgrade to the latest and greatest. The camera is a tool. Why upgrade if it still performs the work you ask of it and is capable of creating amazing images? Even with a camera that was released in 2005, you can still take advantage of newer and better processing algorithms.
IMAGE © CRAIG FERROGGIARO, *COLUMBIA RIVER SLOUGH*, 2008.

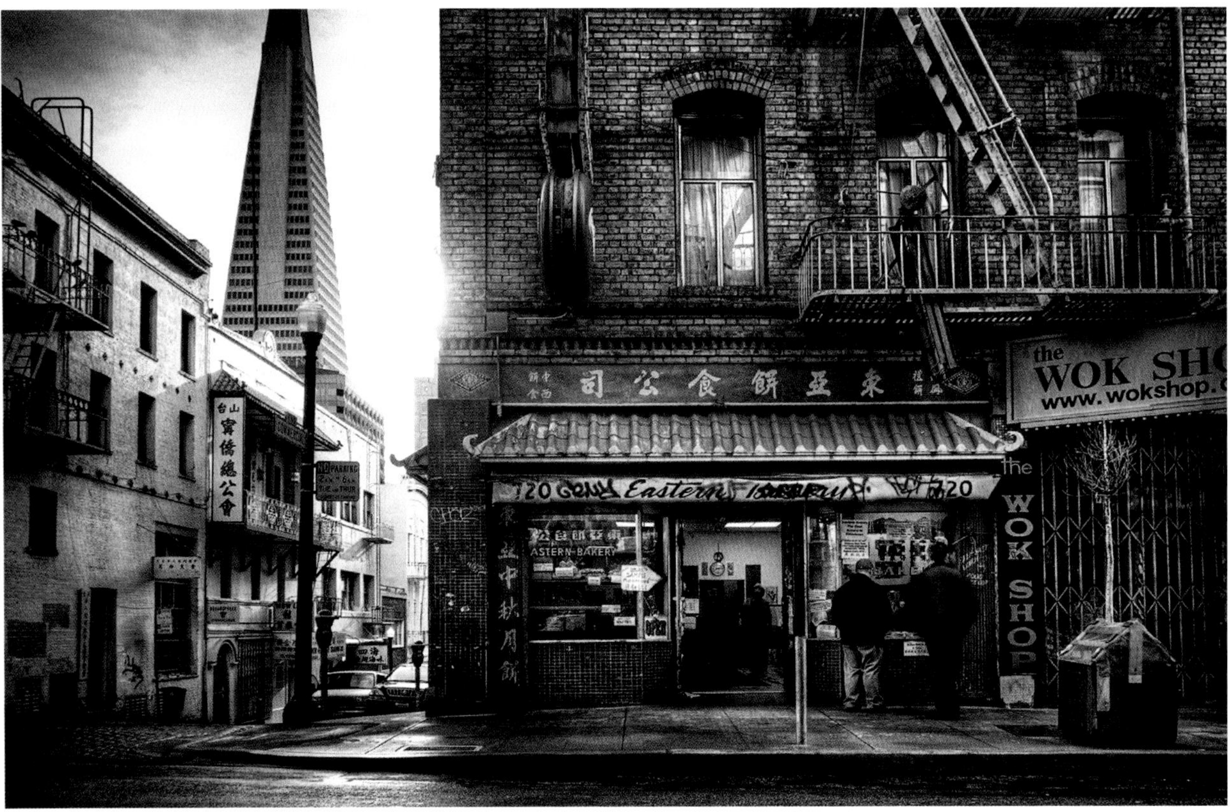


**FIGURE 9.11** Craig made this image using an 8MP consumer Canon Rebel XT. It just goes to shows you that it doesn't matter what kind of camera you use. What matters is how well you understand it and how well you use it.
IMAGE © CRAIG FERROGGIARO, *GRANT STREET*, 2005.

of these just wrecked the prints! None of the techniques had the same feel as Marshall's Photo Oils, so I decided to recreate the look using digital tools. I had attempted to come up with a digital technique for this before, but the process I created was tedious, and not very creative. Trying again, I pushed through and came up with a Photoshop-based technique that looked right—and was enjoyable. This was the first time I'd considered the idea that my artistic process needed to deliver the results and had to be engaging. I needed to enjoy working on my images.

***CD:*** I wish we could share a larger version of this image, because it exemplifies how clean a file can be when it's handled with skill and care. Really, Craig, every leaf is discernible, and the gradation of tone is gradual and lovely. The way you handled the color is very delicate and subtle; it evokes a sense of mystery and otherworldliness.

***AB:*** This image (**Figure 9.11**) is more than a street shot; it's an urban landscape. There are two men window-shopping: Do they know each other, or are they strangers? There's a person looking right at the camera, hidden in the back of the store. We always want to know about the people in an image; without the human presence, this photograph would lack an important story-building element.

Look at the contrast between graffiti tags and the Chinese and English signage. We also see a contrast between the old brick building and the new architecture of the Transamerica Pyramid. Notice the shadows and the sun blooming around the edge of the building and skipping off the wet sidewalk. There's so much rich detail here; it's a story about texture. The light transforms the street; it reveals and hides at the same time and has an uncanny ability to make the mundane special.

***CD:*** Craig, tell us how you made this photograph; did you use any special techniques?

***CF:*** This is one of my favorite images—it's an HDR image, but it doesn't look like what people expect an HDR image to be. Before this, most of what I was making was the traditional over-processed HDR look. I was shooting into the sun and bracketing and blending many different exposures. I discovered that I didn't want to make an image that had more information than I could see with my own eyes—to me that's when things start to look fake. To increase dynamic range in a way that feels real to me, I found that I only needed three exposures: normal, 2-stops over and 2-stops under. I also use a technique of blending the composite HDR image with the original base exposure to intentionally cut down some of the HDR look.

I was walking through San Francisco's Chinatown when I came upon this scene. I set up the camera on my tripod and started clicking away as the sun rose over the buildings, keeping my version of HDR exposure in mind. I didn't think much of the shot while I was photographing it. When I got back to my computer, I started to play with the exposures. With some time and effort, I created this image.

***AB:*** Do you have any advice—whether it comes out of your retouching work or your experience as a photographer—which you want to pass on to our readers?

***CF:*** Try to find that balance of the technical and the artistic. You have to have both. I think we all tend to gravitate towards one or the other; it's normal for us to latch onto something and go for it. It's rare to see images that are very creative and proficiently executed and technically great. That's a good goal to have. With my landscape photography, that's one thing I really work on: not getting lost in either realm.

***AB:*** Successful photography is a perfect blend of those two factors; it exists in the nexus between those two realms. I think that's what separates a good photographer from everybody else who has a camera.

***CF:*** I agree. There's a lot of talk about both the technical and creative sides. It's a real challenge to keep both things in the forefront of your mind. It's easy to get out on the beach and say, "Okay, I screwed this up last time, so I have to make sure to overexpose, because the sun is shining into my camera." And then you take the most boring, perfectly technically executed image ever. You see those all over the web.

***AB:*** They're pretty, but they often lack meaning.

***CF:*** I listened to a talk by Edward Burtynsky,[6] who is an amazing photographer and as accomplished as you could ever get. He explained how he loved landscape photography, but that all he was doing was making what he called "calendar" images. He could never get away from it.

He wanted to do landscapes, and he kept making these calendar photos over and over again. His change came about when he was able to go shoot in a mine, or maybe a quarry, and with that subject matter, he was able to break away from what he had been doing. He had the technical dialed in, but he couldn't quite get the subject matter down—until he found that change.

***CD:*** He needed a little nudge to match his skill with his subject, right?

***CF:*** Yeah, that's the challenge. I say good luck with that; that's where the 10,000 hours come in. In my opinion, you can spend your 10,000 hours on that one subject alone: how to balance the technical with the artistic.

## Toni Greaves

### *Documentary Photographer/Photojournalist*

***Andy Batt:*** This image (**Figure 9.12**) has everything. Before we ever read the caption, we know we're sharing something intimate and personal. The light is incredible. It's all real (a true documentary image), but it feels cinematic—almost as if Toni directed a beam of light to issue forth and illuminate the moment. The composition has such balance. It's the essence of using the entire frame.

***Candace Dobro:*** Toni, this really is a magical photograph. It's so still and monumental, almost like a classical painting—with chiaroscuro, drapery and sculpted forms. The connection between the women is palpable. They're so entirely focused on the business at hand that we viewers don't sense your presence. You told us that you try to become "invisible" when you're shooting. Whatever you did to hide yourself worked!

***Toni Greaves:*** Well, in that situation all I was doing was silently sitting pressed against a wall about five or six feet away. I had been moving about the room a little before then, too. The thing about becoming "invisible" simply has a lot to do with the way you move around people and the way you relate to them. Also, one's own comfort level in a situation directly affects the comfort level others have with your being there. After developing a level of trust and comfort, I just try to never break the situation, so although the subjects know I'm there, they can get back into their realm and ignore me.

***AB:*** Toni, here you captured another intimate moment (**Figure 9.13**). This time, we know we're on a plane or helicopter. We know that the only people that get medical transport like this have a serious problem. We're seeing through the eyes of someone—you—who has managed to become part of the scene, but who has disappeared and faded back. The person attending looks confident, calm and collected. We see competence, not panic. This is not TV.

***CD:*** It's striking how successfully you've captured two vastly different medical situations and remained true to the environmental realities of each. If I'd been presented with both of these photographs without knowing who shot them, I wouldn't have guessed the same photographer had taken them. You're able to faithfully report what you see—and to understand and empathize with any subject—no matter what the situation is. Wow.

***TG:*** Thank you! That's what I love about this kind of photography. I get to engage in so many varied situations, and I'm quite comfortable in pretty much any realm. This photo was taken in a helicopter, and I was strapped in and unable to move. There really were no corners for me to crouch down and tuck myself away in, but I had spent a teeny bit of time with both the medic and patient before we took off. The patient needed to remain anonymous, and she needed to believe that I would honor that request, so sometimes trust has to be built very quickly.

***AB:*** If you could go back to the beginning of your career, what kind of advice would you give yourself as a young up-and-coming photographer?

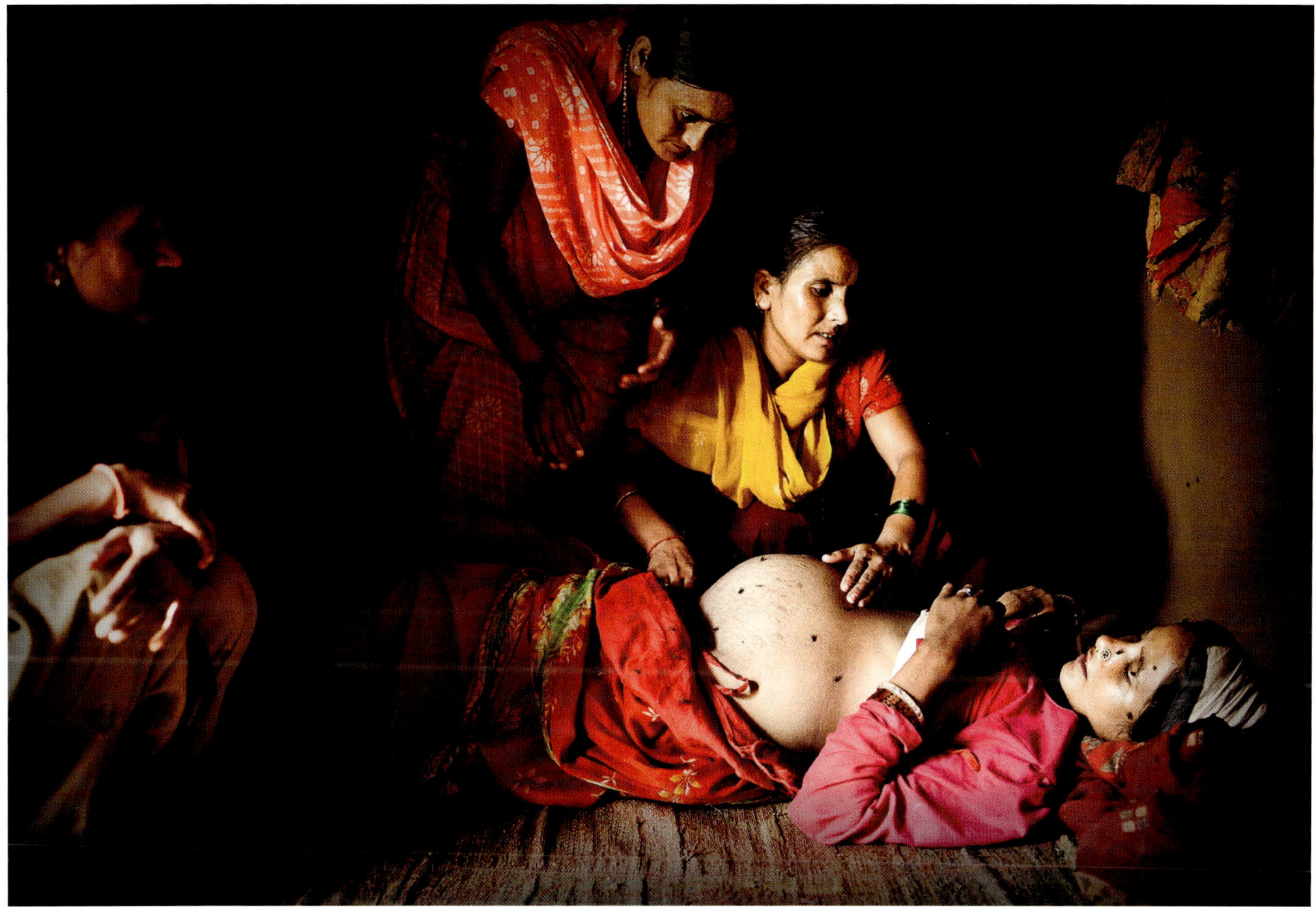

**FIGURE 9.12** Women in Nepal, considered to be unclean while menstruating or giving birth, are often expected to give birth in the cowshed. Maheshwari is fortunate to be able to deliver her second child in the local health clinic, with the help of a birth attendant. The attendant visits her at home to check on her pregnancy.
IMAGE BY TONI GREAVES/GETTY IMAGES, *BIRTH IN RURAL NEPAL, THE MOST DANGEROUS DAY: THE CHECK–UP,* © BILL & MELINDA GATES FOUNDATION, 2009.

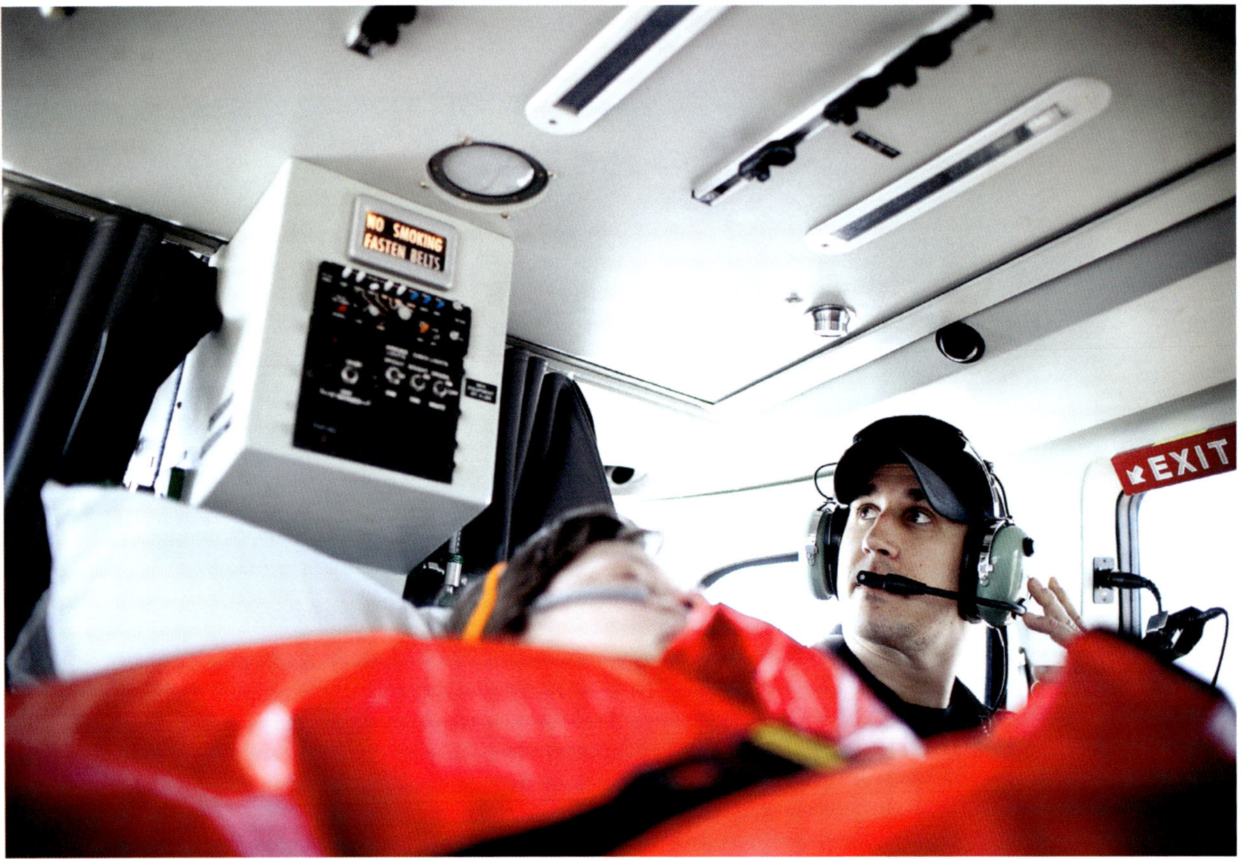


**FIGURE 9.13** Toni shot documentary-style images in dozens of scenarios for Cleveland Clinic's Brand Book and Annual Report. The photographs are part of the hospital's large image library, which is used for a variety of purposes.
IMAGE BY TONI GREAVES/GETTY IMAGES, *CLEVELAND CLINIC CRITICAL CARE TRANSPORT,* 2011.

***TG:*** The first thing that comes to mind is: don't have so much self-doubt.

***AB:*** What do you mean by that?

***TG:*** I used to have a lot of anxiety about what I was doing in my work. Somehow, I just figured it out, and I don't worry so much anymore.

What else? I would say really, really focus on the stories—the story and the longer term. I've always done this to a certain degree, but I'm more aware of it now.

When you're working on a long-term project, in the world that we live in now, there's this constant pressure to get your work out there. People want to see pictures. They'll say, "Oh show me this, show me that!" For my project on the nuns, I had gotten some of the work out there early on and had some initial success, but I ended up continuing shooting.

My strategy now is: don't do it. Hold off. You'll make a much bigger impact by holding onto the images until you've *finished* the project; then get it out there as a complete body of work. If you just trickle work out before you're finished, it ends up feeling like old news by the time you have something more substantial.

I started a project in 2012 that may be a ten- to twenty-year project. I have two other projects in process (that I began in 2009) that I'm still working on. For my personal work, I'm more interested in the longer-term vision of my stories these days. Of course, it takes a lot of patience to keep working on a project for years, and not just push something out quickly. But that's also the reason for its success: The shooting will invariably get stronger over time, and the story gets deeper and richer with time.

There are all kinds of reasons that pressure you to get images out quickly. I've even read about photographers who say they do it to get initial feedback. But you know what? When they put images out quickly, they're not necessarily the strongest images. They're already creating an impression about that project and about the work they're doing. I very deliberately wait. People say—because I've mentioned this India project to them—"I want to see pictures." I tell them, "Whenever it's ready. It's not fully baked, yet."

***CD:*** Do you have any additional advice to people who are passionate about a project and want fulfillment and recognition so they can make a living?

***TG:*** You just have to focus on doing very, very good work. That—and have personal projects. I have conversations with photographers who bellyache about what's not working for them in the industry—but they're just relying on trying to get assignments. They're not really pushing to work on projects for themselves. There's a documentary photographer named David Alan Harvey,[7] who's part of Magnum. He said—and I've thought of this ever since I heard it while I was in school—"Everything good that ever happened to me came because of personal projects." Working on the personal project—where you can really immerse yourself and thrive and create something exceptional—is a starting point; and then the rest will happen. You can't set out to win awards and get notoriety.

***CD:*** People *do* set out to do that, though.

***TG:*** Well, right. I don't believe they succeed if they set out *just* to do that. If they set out to do exceptional work, then that will often be the result—but it all comes from their really good work. I find it quite curious, because people comment on my work and will say, "Oh, you know how to put your work together, you know how to present your work." . . . like that's the thing alone that makes it successful. Well okay, I do know how to present my work. But probably the work I'm doing is also very good. It starts with doing really good work.

There's a Steve Martin quote: "Nobody ever takes note of [my advice], because it's not the answer they wanted to hear. What they want to hear is 'Here's how you get an agent, here's how you write a script,' . . . but I always say, '*Be so good they can't ignore you.*'"

If you begin at that point (and do the hard work that comes after that), then success will be a byproduct and—even if you don't become successful, you'll be happy, because you've done really good work, right?

## Carli Davidson

### *Animal Photographer*

***Andy Batt:*** The image in **Figure 9.14** seems like a simple snapshot at first glance. It's not about a big moment, or stylized and set dressed, or of a particularly beautiful place; it's just normal. It's a parking garage. And it's a photograph of a dog in a wheeled prosthetic, going about his dog business. We want to know why: What's the story behind this dog? And then we're invested in knowing more.

There's subtle stuff at play here. The simple perspective lines from the yellow paint also seem to serve as a highlight—a warning of sorts—about the story of the pup. Our eyes are brought down to see the world from dog level. Carli, the dog doesn't seem to notice you at all. He has serious business elsewhere.

***Candace Dobro:*** Your empathy for animals is very apparent in this shot. You bent down to capture the world from the dog's point of view, and it's very appealing and touching, without being saccharine. I already care about this dog and want to know his story . . .

***Carli Davidson:*** I had wanted to work with special-needs pets. I was at the coast a few years ago and saw this awesome German shepherd with a similar chair—he was playing fetch with his owner, but I never went over and asked them about it. Later on, I was driving in Portland and saw Little Man Rue walking with his owner and I just pulled over, went up to her and introduced myself. (I'm not shy.)

I ended up spending a bit of time with Little Man Rue and his owner, doing documentary work, like this, and studio work. I like to explore my subjects in different styles. Little Man Rue has a great life: He travels with his owner every day and is doted on by all the staff at work. He does require a lot of work, making sure he doesn't get sores from the harness; he needs special doggy shoes, and he eats a raw-food diet. To me, this shot is about human and animal companionship—how owners will go above and beyond for that relationship.

***AB:*** **Figure 9.15** shows an image of Mane, the world's most mellow Dogue de Bordeaux. I've met Mane—he's super friendly and is an amazing (dog) model. There are so many fun things going on in this image; it's about how we anthropomorphize our pets and what delights and entertains us. Plus he's really funny-looking. When you combine dogs and "funny" with strong photographic technique, you get Carli's *SHAKE* series. This image is also about revealing shapes and textures and stopping time to show us something we can't see with our naked eyes.

***Candace:*** Is there anyone who doesn't love your *SHAKE* images? They are thoroughly absorbing and fascinating. Can you share some of your thoughts about the project, and about this shot in particular?

***Carli:*** The funny thing is that I photograph Mane all the time, and he's the same breed as my own dog, Norbert. Norbert hates having his photo taken, but Mane loves it. I can count on Mane to be super mellow and not affected by anything. I did photograph Norbert for the book, but it took a lot of patience; I have animal-behavior training and needed to use it with him. Mane is owned by Amanda Giese, who runs Panda Paws Rescue, in Vancouver, Washington. Mane helps out as a surrogate mom for new puppies!

The shot here is part of the *SHAKE* series. I used a specific strobe technique to capture Mane in mid-shake, and the lighting is also very purposeful. I didn't just turn the lights on—I wanted to bring out the definition and texture in the skin and fur to create a dimensional effect. And I had to do this in a big area, because my subjects need to move around. Part of what made this body of work successful was getting a camera that could keep up with the way I wanted to work. I used a Nikon D4 for most of *SHAKE*. It was a big upgrade in sensor, frame rate and focus and image quality, and it allowed me to be more flexible—and get better results.

***AB:*** What do you think is the best advice to give a photographer who's trying to "make it"?

***Carli:*** The only way I learned was by shooting, and by doing it constantly. It's one of those things that if you stop when you're halfway through learning, you're just going to forget.

Put your camera on Manual, give yourself a weekly allotment of photos and shoot five hundred shots a week—no less than that. I don't

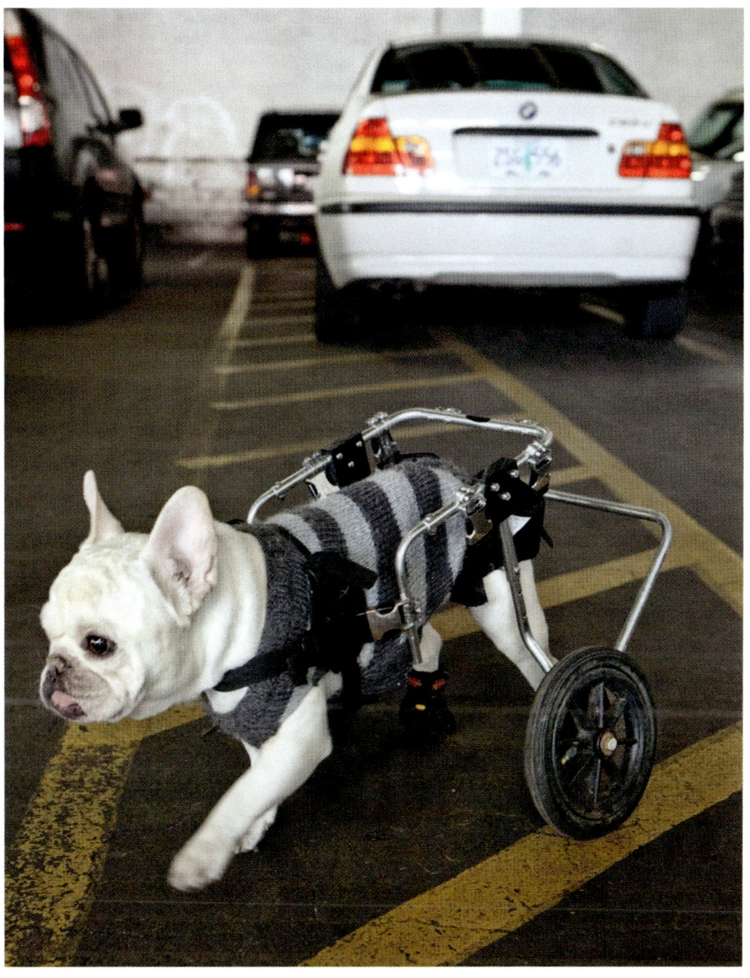

**FIGURE 9.14** Carli had always wanted to work with special-needs pets. She captured Little Man Rue in Portland, Oregon.
IMAGE © CARLI DAVIDSON, *LITTLE MAN RUE*—FROM THE *INVINCIBLE* SERIES, 2010.

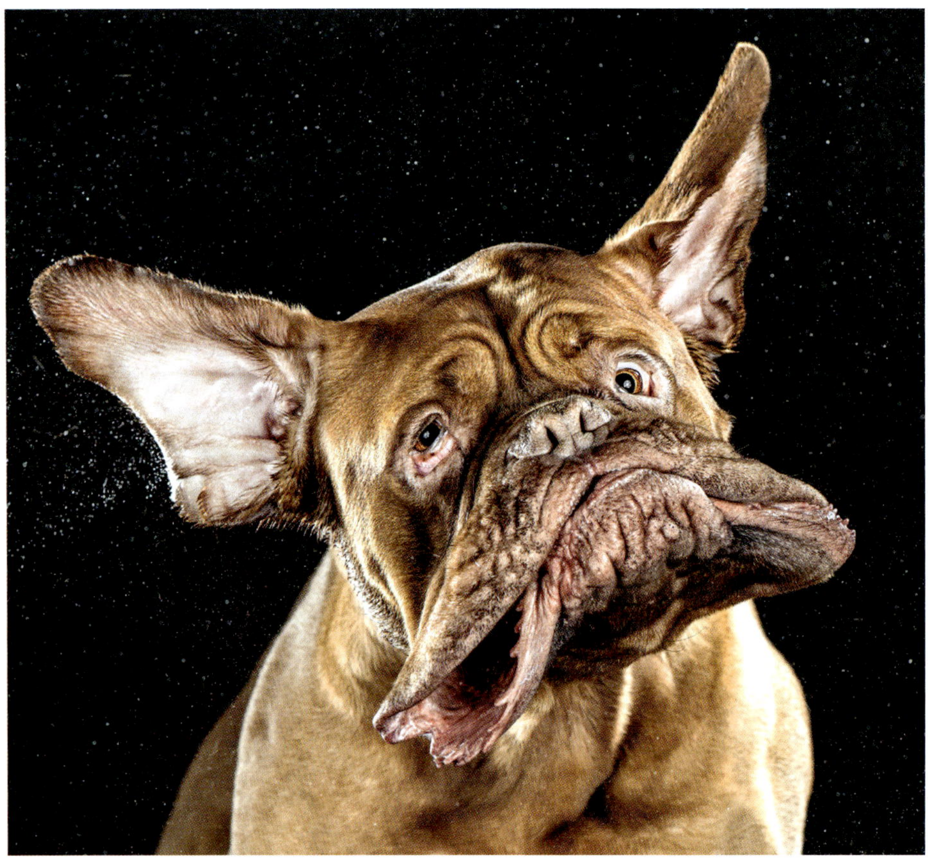

**FIGURE 9.15** Mane, the world's most mellow Dogue de Bordeaux, loves having his photo taken.
IMAGE © CARLI DAVIDSON, *MANE*—FROM THE *SHAKE* SERIES, 2013.

care if you're sitting in your room playing with all the different settings on your camera and taking a picture of your wall. Give yourself a weekly shot number. That's a really good exercise to play with, because then you have people taking the same shot twelve times in different settings, and they can start *seeing*. I'm a very visual learner, so if I'm reading a camera instruction and it doesn't stick with me, I have to do it.

***AB:*** You mentioned something earlier about giving yourself exercises. Do you do this frequently?

***Carli:*** I actually do—absolutely. When I started really focusing on doing portraits of animals, I was shooting at least three times a week. I was just finding anything I could, and people were hiring me for gigs or whatever. I just don't feel there's a reason to *not* be shooting. If you're a photographer and you're into the subject matter and what you're doing, then it's rewarding to shoot a few times a week. I shoot pretty constantly; I take pictures of my dog and cat when I'm at home, because I can.

***AB:*** One of the things I'll do—if I'm going on a trip that's not for a job—is to grab a camera and pick one lens. I only bring that lens—and then yell and curse the whole time, because I've chosen the wrong one. I keep seeing pictures that would be great with a different lens, but force myself to work with that one, because it makes me move around or compose different kinds of shots.

***Carli:*** For the sake of our backs, we should only use one lens. I often throw a 50mm on my camera, because it's very light and small. If I'm going somewhere on a whim I'll say, "I'm going to have to think with a 50mm lens, and that's just the way it's got to be." It does challenge you. And I love it—except for those moments when I see this amazing shot, and I don't have what I want. I think a lot of photographers challenge themselves to keep things fresh.

It's like shooting with a cell phone for Instagram. It's not a technical way to work, but I see people taking brilliant shots that are just about the way they look at everyday objects—and that makes them so fascinating. Many of these people are never going to be photographers, and I look at their shots and think, "This is brilliant; I wouldn't have thought about that!"

I challenge myself to try to take a shot with my cell phone every day. It's an exercise in framing for me: How do you get an idea or a story across in a single shot?

***Candace:*** Do you have any other words of wisdom?

***Carli:*** We were talking about how important it is to test and try equipment, and not to be afraid. That's a great and really valid point that will help people learn. Often you're not looking for the good idea—it just happens.

## Bruce Ely

### *Newspaper Photojournalist*

***Andy Batt:*** This shot (**Figure 9.16**) involves the waiting game. It's about watching a crowd and looking for the people that are going to do something interesting. Once you find them, you camp out—camera up to your eye—waiting for that moment to happen, and then quickly, instinctively frame and reframe as the shot changes. These two guys aren't just here for the body paint and attention; they're invested in the turmoil of the game. We can feel their raw emotion and fan mania. They're framed in by hands—pointing, clapping, fists clenched.

***Candace Dobro:*** Bruce, I'm in awe that you're able to create shots like this. The atmosphere must have been completely frenetic, yet you distilled a clear moment that almost feels choreographed: The expressions are perfectly frozen, and nobody's limbs are in the way of the main subject, which is beautifully framed by a halo of dark tones. How did you accomplish that?

***Bruce Ely:*** I concentrate on the faces and reactions, waiting for things to fall into place. It's about hoping, not controlling. As a photojournalist I can't say, "Move your hand to the left or the right." I just have to get myself in the right place, hoping the image will come together.

***AB:*** Night shots are hard, because the amount of exposure our eyes need to see is out of whack with what our cameras need to stop a moment in its tracks. What looks bright and well lit becomes a sea of darkness when you try to pull a good shutter speed and F-stop. We grasp at the higher ISO values in these conditions, knowing we're making a deal with the devil: "If you'll let us get a shot that's not blurry from slow shutters or shallow DoF, then we'll let you put as much noise into the image as you like."

Knowing about your output helps; newsprint is only capable of limited color depth and fine detail and is a lower quality as compared to a glossy magazine. Newsprint's saving grace is that you can get away with a *lot* of noise and softening of fine detail.

***AB:*** The composition is the first thing I notice with the shot in **Figure 9.17**. It has a nice balance of symmetrical and asymmetrical elements. The players are centered and the camera is shooting slightly upwards at them—for the "heroic" angle. They're mirroring each other too, with their uniforms, helmets held to the outside and each with his right leg in mid-step.

The background has the dark weight of the buildings on the right and the emotional and compositional weight of an American flag at half-mast on the left. There's a figure under the flagpole, waiting (or so it seems) for these players. The light tells us it's late afternoon, which sets the stage, subtly giving us a clue that this is after the game, not before.

The fascinating thing for me is that there is so much emotion—although we don't know if the subjects won or lost their game. They could be consoling each other over a major loss or basking in the glow of victory. Either way, we feel the connection between them, and we feel that moment after the game—even though we can't see their faces. There are no eyes, no smiles or tears; there's just body language, light and composition.

***CD:*** I love that you shot your subjects' backs; it was such a sensitive choice to make. We don't need to see their faces, because their bodies—and the environment—express it all.

***BE:*** I was on the field and saw them walking away, so I shot from where I was standing. It wasn't preplanned; I just reacted to what was in front of me.

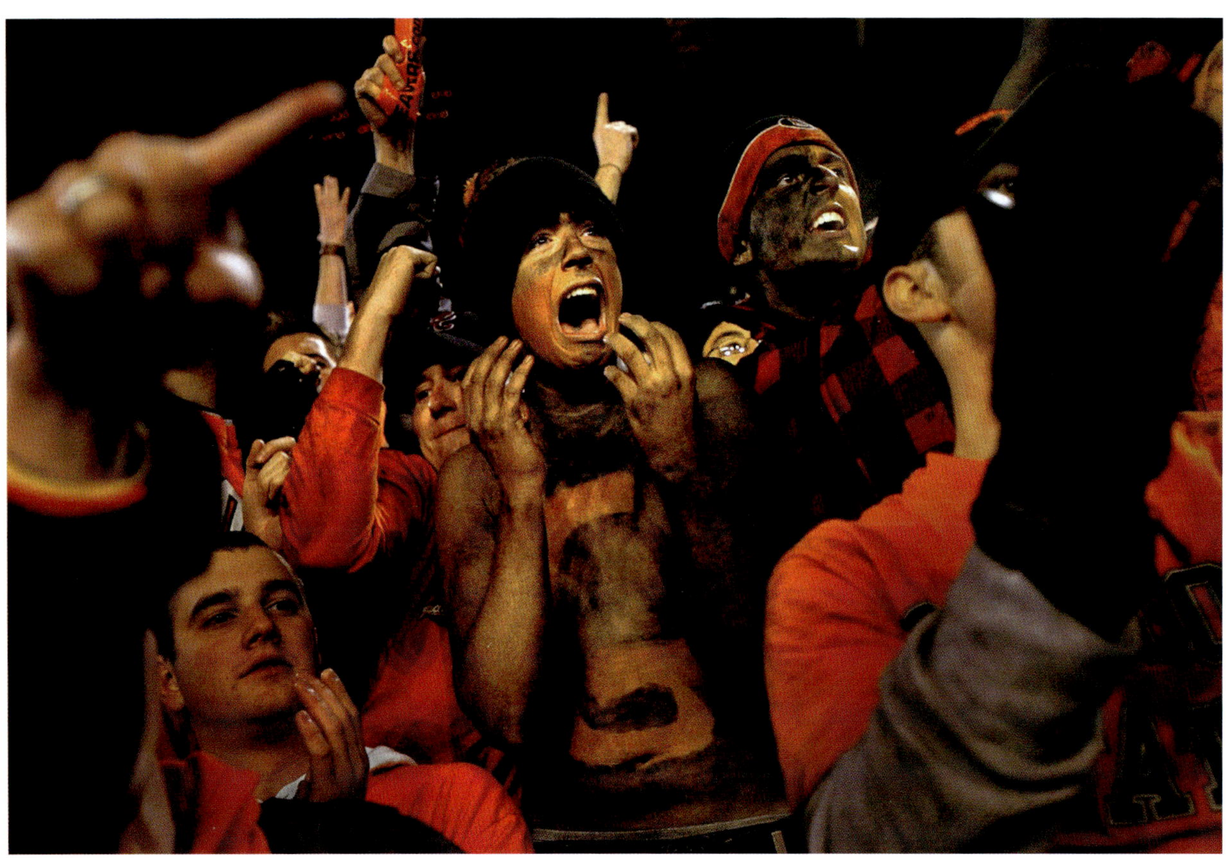

**FIGURE 9.16** Oregon State fans erupt into cheers as their quarterback scores in the final quarter of the annual matchup with Oregon in the Civil War football game. IMAGE BY BRUCE ELY, *OREGON STATE FOOTBALL—CIVIL WAR GAME,* © AND COURTESY OF *THE OREGONIAN,* 2004.

***CD:*** When I look at this image, I find myself constructing a story: It's a perfect fall day and the high-school football team just lost. The light is glowing, the grass is green and, despite their loss, the players have their whole lives ahead of them . . .

***BE:*** Out in Burnt River there are only two local kids on the football team; the rest are exchange students from China, Germany—all over the place. They were literally learning how to play football, and this shot was taken after their first game. The team had been turning the ball over and playing poorly, and they were out of shape—but having fun. Both teams agreed that they'd end the game early, at the end of the third quarter. The flag's at half-mast because it was September 11.

***AB:*** You shot this at *f*/2.8 with Aperture Priority. There was plenty of light, since the camera was exposing 1/1328 sec at ISO 100—so having that falloff was a deliberate choice. It gives the image a nice quality, dropping the focus in the background down just enough to create a distinct transition from sharp to soft.

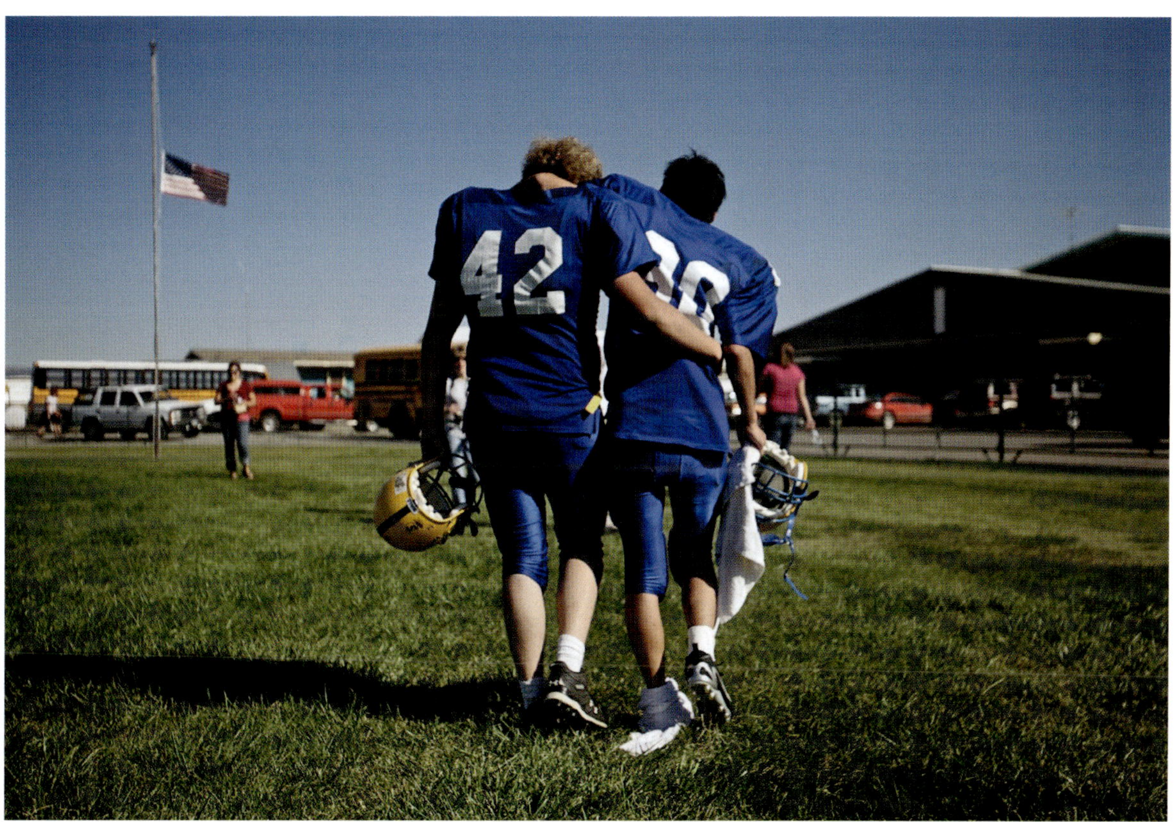


**FIGURE 9.17** This image was made with a Canon 1D Mark III and a 35mm lens. The smaller (APS-H CMOS) sensor cropped into the image circle and gave Bruce an angle-of-view equivalent to a 45mm lens on a full-frame camera.
IMAGE BY BRUCE ELY, *BURNT RIVER*, © AND COURTESY OF *THE OREGONIAN*, 2009.

There would be a very different feeling if the image were sharp all the way through. This way, the football players are visually isolated—from the bus, the parents, and even from the American flag. The visual isolation also serves to create a narrative: We feel the camaraderie between the players, we feel their exhaustion and we feel that they're in their own post-game world.

***AB***: You often talk to journalism students. Is there anything you tell them—or wish somebody had told you when you were starting out?

***BE:*** We told one of my interns at the newspapers to stop worrying about new equipment—to just use whatever she has, because it doesn't really matter, not anymore. When digital first started, yeah, it mattered, but everything is good enough right now. There isn't a bad camera out there. Any camera is going to give you the ability to do what you want. As a student, the last thing you need to obsess about is equipment. You need to learn how to be a better journalist and just learn to take pictures. The ability to use the equipment is a different subject.

***AB***: Break that down a little bit for us, because that's a good point —the difference between the equipment itself and the ability to use it.

***BE:*** I gave that advice to the intern, because she was obsessing over what camera to get: "Do I get this camera or do I get this camera? This one has more megapixels . . ." I said, "Don't worry about that; just get one that's reasonably priced. By the time you buy it, there's going to be a newer, cheaper, better one. Get the camera and just go out and shoot pictures. Instead of sitting at the computer and looking at cameras, spend your time learning to use it."

It's interesting that these cameras do the same thing as they did a hundred or fifty years ago. There is an aperture and there is a shutter and there is a button you push to take the picture. All of these digital cameras come with a bunch of bells and whistles and give you a little bit more ability to do things, but really, they're no different than they were back when there was film. Obviously, the post-processing is much different.

***CD:*** I assume you're differentiating between DSLRs and other cameras.

***BE:*** I'm not sure I would.

***AB:*** There are journalists who go into war zones and carry nothing but point-and-shoots, because they can keep a very low profile that way. They don't look like they're worth shooting.

***BE:*** If people see you with a big camera, a 1D Mark IV or whatever, they actually act differently. With a big camera, you're a photographer, versus that guy [with a point-and-shoot], who's a tourist. A little point-and-shoot isn't intimidating to people. So no, I wouldn't stop an intern who wanted to get a point-and-shoot.

***CD***: Well, that's interesting! As a journalist, you don't have to blow images up to a large size. It would be a different story if you did.

***BE:*** Right.

***AB***: I advise my students to buy the cheapest camera that does what they need—and to put the money into a better lens, which is one of the limiting factors. You can ruin a perfectly good photograph with a really cheap lens. If you're going to spend money, then spend it on the lens; you'll keep it for a long time, and a good lens will hold its value.

***BE:*** Right, lenses are getting better, but they're not changing that much right now. That's good advice.

I don't think the newspaper world is full of heavily technical minds. There are exceptions, obviously; a few who obsess whether the right exposure is *f*/4.0, *f*/5.0 or *f*/5.6, you know. Newsprint is forgiving, and if pictures are underexposed or overexposed, they'll print and seem as if they were right on.

## Holly Andres

### *Fine Art and Editorial Photographer*

***Andy Batt***: In this wonderful photo (**Figure 9.18**), Holly captured Camas Davis, founder of the Portland Meat Collective, for *The New York Times Magazine*. It's beautifully framed and lit; you can see all the gears turning in this image: There's a symmetrical composition with Camas balanced in the window, between the curtains at the head and center of the table, flanked by her students—and the layout of the butchered pig is very precisely done. But there's a great asymmetry here: The students are active in the frame; they're very relaxed, and each one has a different personality and position. The one student looking directly into the camera breaks the formality of the image, balancing out the body language of Camas, whose pose reminds me a little of *American Gothic*.

***Candace Dobro***: And of Norman Rockwell's iconic *Freedom from Want* painting. What a spot-on contemporary take on an American classic.

***Holly Andres***: It's actually a direct reference to that painting!

***AB:*** It's also a great example of an editorial photograph that's not documentary. There's truth in the image, but it's really an illustration that was designed to counterpoint the story in the magazine.

***CD:*** The composition is so carefully considered. I love the way the patterns and colors of the oilcloth and apron play off each other. The hair and makeup are perfect, too: They're natural, but not a hair is out of place to distract the viewer's gaze. Can you tell us about the team that helped create this shot? Also, the expression on each face is perfect. Is this a single shot, or a composite of multiple images?

***HA:*** Thank you for saying so, because this was actually a relatively quick shot. The subjects were students that had just learned to butcher this pig, and because the meat could only be unrefrigerated for a short period of time, we had to shoot fast. Fortunately, I was able to set up a table and hang curtains within the classroom while they were working. I had just one assistant, and my lights were dialed and ready to go by the time the students and their pig assembled in front of my lens. Since it was an assignment for *The New York Times Magazine,* it had to be a "straight" shot, no altering or compositing was done. I was intentionally paying homage to Norman Rockwell's iconic Thanksgiving painting, and so I used that as a reference while directing my subjects and framing the portrait.

***AB:*** This was shot with a Canon 5D Mark II—in camera years, it's outdated, but in terms of usefulness and ability to create amazing images, it's as current and relevant as anything else. The sensor produces beautiful images at a size that is perfect for any kind of magazine work. The 1/60th-second exposure exposed the windows correctly. It also allowed plenty of ambient fill light to balance out the key strobe light that was coming in from the left. An aperture of *f*/9 at 62mm held the DoF throughout the entire image.

***AB:*** You spent a lot of time with Mariel Hemingway (**Figure 9.19**) to create a level of trust and capture a moment of freedom. This is one of those images that looks simpler than it is. There's beautiful sunlight coming through the trees, Mariel is smiling and moving acrobatically at the apex of her jump from the trampoline—which is deliberately framed out of the shot, heightening the feeling of being weightless. The light falling on Mariel is clean and simple, and photographing her against the white sky gives us a very clean image—plus the light wraps around her body, giving her a subtle glow.

***CD:*** The carefree and relaxed quality of this shot is astonishing. It was worth every minute of the time you spent to connect with your subject and produce such a splendid instant in time.

***AB:*** Above all else, we come away from this image with a childlike sense of being happy, which connects powerfully to the text, which is about Mariel's distinctive lifestyle and her choices to be happy.

***CD:*** There's such a golden quality to this image. What did you do to make it happen?

***HA:*** I photographed during the "Golden Hour," when the sun was low in the sky. The summertime light of Calabasas, California, is especially heavenly. I popped a bit of frontal fill light with a large soft box on Mariel while she jumped, but primarily relied on natural light.

When I was a kid, my mom shot—with a point-and-shoot camera—a photo of my older brother jumping on a trampoline on his graduation day. I recall thinking the snapshots were magical. In his blue cap and gown, he appeared to be soaring high in the sky. When I saw Mariel's trampoline, I recalled that moment and revisited it for inspiration.

***AB:*** What words of wisdom do you have for people who want to improve their photography?

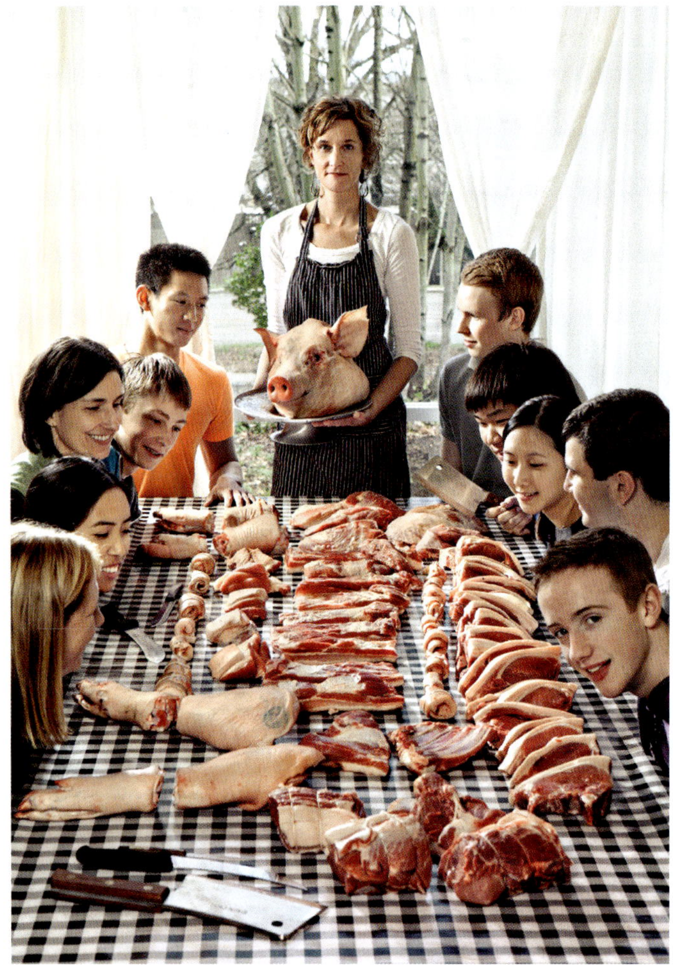

**FIGURE 9.18** Holly photographed Camas Davis, founder of the Portland Meat Collective, for this assignment. The students at the table had just learned to butcher a pig.
IMAGE © HOLLY ANDRES, *THE PROPER WAY TO EAT A PIG*, FOR *THE NEW YORK TIMES MAGAZINE*, 2013.

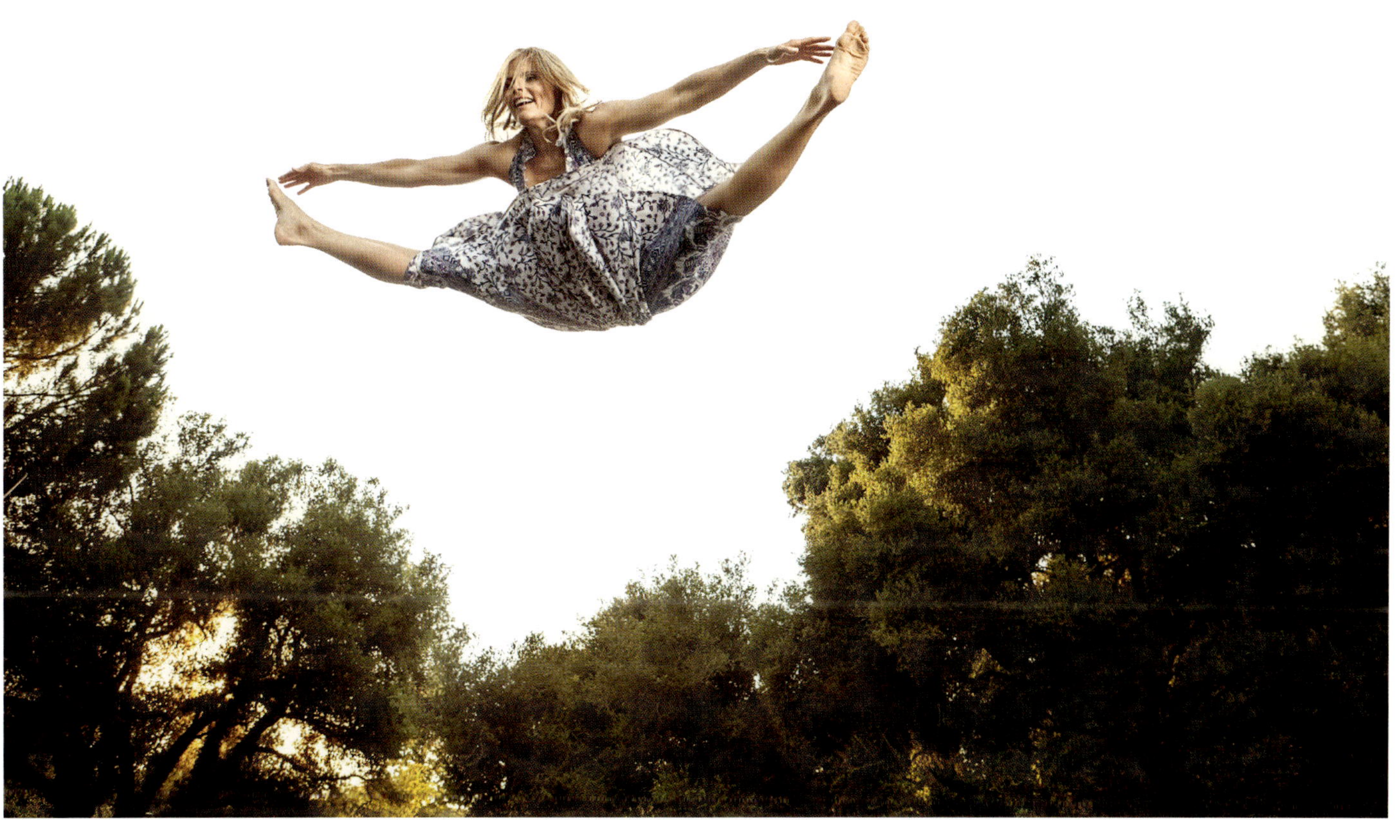

**FIGURE 9.19** Shot at the "Golden Hour," Holly created this image to illustrate a story about Mariel Hemingway's lifestyle.
IMAGE © HOLLY ANDRES, *MARIEL HEMINGWAY, THE IMPORTANCE OF NOT BEING ERNEST,* FOR *THE NEW YORK TIMES MAGAZINE,* 2013.

***HA:*** Just shoot tenaciously—shoot and shoot. Also, when you're not behind a camera, think of your mind's eye as the viewfinder. I think it's a more delightful way of experiencing the world, to see things with more beauty and wonder or irony—and I think it makes you a better photographer. I was talking to Corey Arnold[8] a while ago (actually when I first met him), and he asked, "Have you been shooting a lot lately?" and I said, "Well, in my head," and I really meant that. For example, as I'm talking to you right now, I want to position my head in such a way to artfully frame you between those elements on the wall.

***AB:*** I prefer to be artfully framed.

***HA:*** And oftentimes, I'll hear a shutter go off in my head when I see something beautiful. Of course, now we have iPhones and Instagram, so that's a whole other way of sharing that expression.

***CD:*** That's a great explanation, and so poetic! Andy and I have talked about the Zen place we're in when we look through the viewfinder; it changes your brain, something happens.

***HA:*** I think it makes you a better photographer if you try to perceive the world through the "lens" of a camera.

## Andy Batt, Candace Dobro and Jodie Steen: Parting Words

Here we are at the end of the book. Before we say goodbye, we'd like to point you towards the *Bibliography*, which includes books we recommend for further exploration into the wide world of photography, as well as references cited in this book. In addition, we hope you'll visit the *Camera & Craft* website: **www.focalpress.com/cw/digitalimagingmasters**, where you can find more information about this book—and its authors and guest photographers.

Our journey began with the idea that creativity can be fueled by craftsmanship, and we explored some of the things that make photography work. Now that you've read through the book and practiced some of the *Explorations* and *Try This at Home* exercises, we hope you've occasionally experienced that Zen-like presence we talked about when you lift the camera to your eye—and that you'll be aware of a new, cyborg-like connection between your camera and your body. Be deliberate with your actions. With practice, you'll reach the level where you can instinctively apply the things you've learned so that you can work more creatively.

You've become acquainted with our guest photographers and tech experts and have some insight into the various ways they use their skills to make images that matter. The tools we use unite us all, but the images we create are unique. That's the amazing thing about photography; there's infinite room for creative perspective. Once we master our tools, we can set about the lifelong business of mastering our creativity.

## Look Back to Move Forward

- **Chapter 1, Prerequisite: Photo 101**—A modern camera is a technological marvel, but unless you understand how to control time, focus, exposure and color, it will be more in control of your images than you are. How might your technical choices affect the aesthetics of your images?
- **Chapter 2, It's Your Viewfinder: Interviews with the Pros**—The viewfinder is our intimate connection to the image before it's been created and gives us the opportunity to make choices and changes. How did our photo experts influence your thinking about using this essential tool?
- **Chapter 3, Your Digital Skeleton**—Without good workflow, you have digital chaos. Even if things seem okay, small problems can ripple forward to become big ones over time. What one key step you can take right away to improve your workflow?
- **Chapter 4, Creative Control: Using Your Lens**—Your lens choice has an immediate and dramatic effect on your images. What do you want your next lens to do for you that your current lenses can't do?
- **Chapter 5, Light Becomes the Image**—Understanding technology basics means making better choices that will lead to better images. How in control are you over image noise?
- **Chapter 6, Exposure: Controlling the Light**—Exposure is a rabbit hole: Once you understand what a good exposure is—according to your meter—how will you make the right aesthetic choice?
- **Chapter 7, Your Color in Control**—Your camera has no opinion about what good color is. Left to its own devices, it can attempt to make neutral color, but how can *you* make better color in your images?
- **Chapter 8, Pre-Pro/Shoot/Deliver: Interviews with the Pros**—There are as many different ways to "do photography" as there are photographers. The anecdotes and advice in this chapter apply to you, no matter what your style and subject are. How can you take a "big idea" and scale it to fit your needs? What steps can you take to improve your shoot, before you ever pick up the camera?
- **Chapter 9, Guest Photographers: Photos and Advice**—Our guest photographers apply the knowledge in this book in their own ways. They need to make all the same photographic decisions you do, but they have their own voices and styles. How can you use their ideas to help find your voice?

## EXPLORATIONS

## Greatest Hits

This last Exploration is our version of the book's Greatest Hits. Here are a few "games" we like to play to keep our photo senses fresh.

### The Exposure Game

Most of the photographers we know play this game—with strobe lights or ambient light. After spending years metering and figuring out exposures, you develop a sense of exposure values. You can hone this instinct by taking a guess and then metering to the situation. This is more than just a party trick—it's a way to understand your scene at a higher level.

Make your guess, and then take a meter reading. Look at that field drenched in late-afternoon light and throw down your best guess: *f*/4 at 1/500th, ISO 800 for someone lit directly by the sun, *f*2.8 at 1/100th, ISO 800 for someone backlit by the sun. Never stop playing this game; eventually, you'll be right more often than you're wrong.

### The Lens-View Game

Develop your lens-view instincts by learning to think like a lens. You'll make better lens choices if you can sense what your lens view will be before you put it on the camera. You'll also have an easier time deciding which lenses to take and which ones to leave back in the studio.

Bring a wide, normal and long lens with you (or a variable prime), and find an interesting scene and subject. Before picking up the camera, predict how each lens will interpret the scene. Now take a photograph with each lens option and see how your predictions play out. By practicing this game, you'll spend less time trying out different focal lengths when you're shooting.

### The Game of Choices

Even though Andy's not a big fan of hard-and-fast rules, he thinks creativity can be fueled by boundaries and restrictions. Sometimes, it's hard to be creative when there's nothing to react to. The easiest way to add that spark is to make a choice: Impose a restriction on your image-making, something that forces you to work a certain way. You can make a game out of any restriction; the key is to stick with your arbitrary choice and work through or around it, without abandoning it. It almost doesn't matter what choice you make, as long as you make one.

*Here are some ideas to get you going:*

1. Pick an ISO speed that seems opposite to your situation, and stick with it. If you have plenty of daylight, then choose ISO 800. This will force you to work at higher shutter speeds or deeper apertures.
2. Pick a single focal length and shoot with only that lens all day. If you find yourself wishing for a different lens, find a creative solution with the lens you have.
3. Pick a specific aperture, based on its DoF. Create images with that DoF firmly in mind, making sure that you use it to a creative advantage.
4. Pick a specific shutter speed, based on either freezing time or blurring it. Whichever direction you choose, create images that have a reason to be frozen at 1/8000th or blurred at 1/4th. Show your viewers that you worked this way intentionally.
5. Pick a white balance—warm, cool, blue . . . anything but straight-up neutral. Remember while shooting that your scene is affected by that choice. Make images that are informed by the white balance.

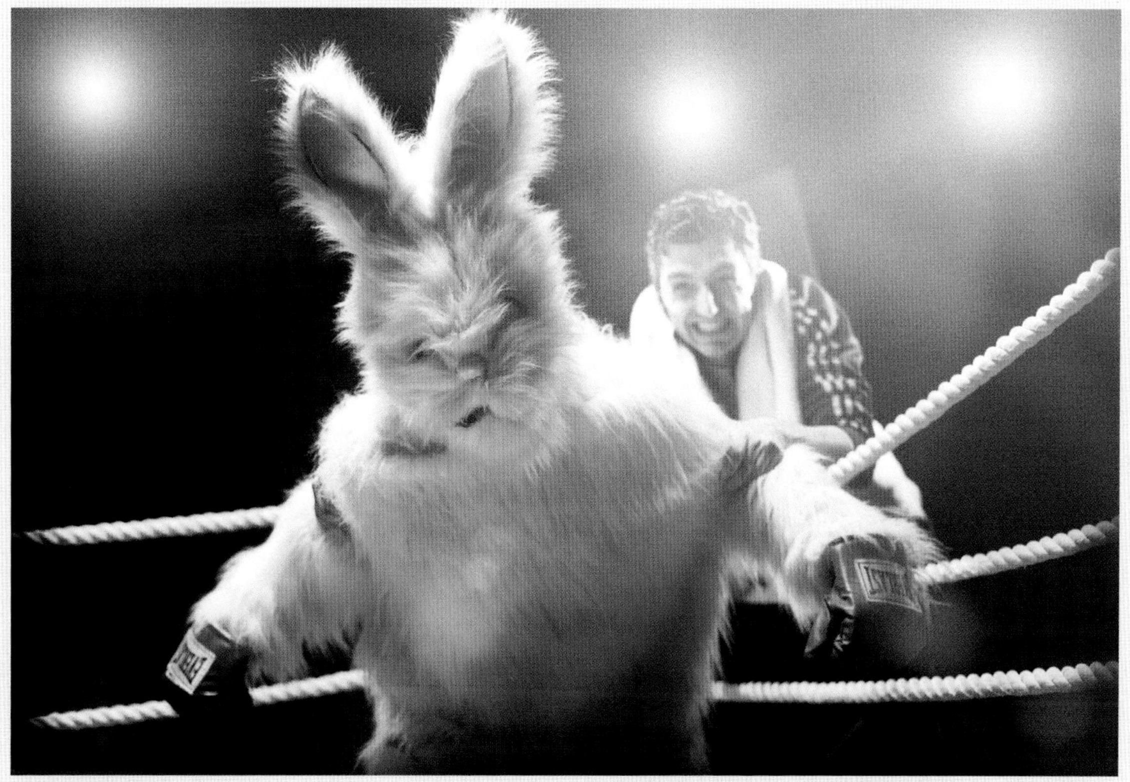

**FIGURE 9.20** That's all, folks.
IMAGE © ANDY BATT, *RAGING BUNNY*, 2011.

*Pick up your camera—and go make some great photos!*

*—Andy, Candace and Jodie*

## Notes

1 The *decisive moment* is a term that's associated with the photography of Henri Cartier Bresson, but it has implications for all photographers. To see Bresson's work, check out his page on Magnum Photos's website: http://www.magnumphotos.com/C.aspx?VP3=CMS3&VF=MAGO31_10_VForm&ERID=24KL53ZMYN.

2 Lucha Libre is a form of professional wrestling in Mexico. The participants, Luchadores, wear ritual masks.

3 Camp Bosworth is an artist who constructs narratives through his wood-working practice: www.campbosworth.com.

4 Stewart Cohen Pictures, www.stewartcohen.com.

5 Troll dolls were a popular toy in the 1960s, http://disco90s.com/troll-doll/.

6 Edward Burtynsky is a well-known Canadian photographer, http://www.edwardburtynsky.com.

7 David Alan Harvey, Magnum Photos, http://www.magnumphotos.com/C.aspx?VP3=CMS3&VF=MAGO31_10_VForm&ERID=24KL53ZJCV.

8 Corey Arnold is a photographer and commercial fisherman, www.coreyfishes.com.

# Bibliography


Adams, A. (1980). *The Camera: The New Ansel Adams Photography Series / Book 1*. Boston: Little, Brown and Company.

Adams, A. (1981). *The Negative: The New Ansel Adams Photography Series / Book 2*. Boston: Little, Brown and Company.

Adams, A. (1983). *The Print: The New Ansel Adams Photography Series / Book 3*. Boston: Little, Brown and Company.

Angier, R. (2007). *Train Your Gaze: A Practical and Theoretical Introduction to Portrait Photography*. Lausanne: AVA Publishing.

Ashe, T. P. (2013). *Color Management & Quality Output: Working with Color from Camera to Display to Print*. Burlington, MA: Focal Press.

Assouline, P. (2013). *Henri Cartier-Bresson: A Biography*. London: Thames & Hudson.

Bayer, B. (1975). *Color Imaging Array*. US Patent 3,971,065, filed March 5, 1975, and issued July 20, 1976. Retrieved from http://www.google.co.uk/patents/US3971065

Bellantoni, P. (2005). *If It's Purple, Someone's Gonna Die*. Burlington, MA: Focal Press.

Bloch, C. (2007). *The HDRI Handbook: High Dynamic Range Imaging for Photographers and CG Artists*. Santa Barbara: Rocky Nook Inc.

Brown, B. (2012). *Cinematography Theory and Practice: Image Making for Cinematographers and Directors* (2nd ed.). Burlington, MA: Focal Press.

Canon Inc. Lens Products Group. (2008). *EF Lens Work III: The Eyes of EOS*, (11th ed.). Tokyo: Canon.

Clarke, A. C. (1967). *Profiles of the Future: An Inquiry into the Limits of the Possible*. New York: Bantam Books.

Ctein. (2000). *Post Exposure: Advanced Techniques for the Photographic Printer*, (2nd ed.). Woburn, MA: Focal Press.

Davidson, C. (2013). *Shake*. New York: Harper Design.

Eggleston, W. (2002). *William Eggleston's Guide*, (2nd ed.). New York: The Museum of Modern Art.

Eismann, K., Duggan, S., & Grey, T. (2011). *Real World Digital Photography*, (3rd ed.). Berkeley: Peachpit Press.

Evening, M. (2010). *Adobe Photoshop Lightroom 3 Book: The Complete Guide for Photographers*. Berkeley: Peachpit Press.

Faris Belt, A. (2012). *The Elements of Photography: Understanding and Creating Sophisticated Images*, (2nd ed.). Burlington, MA: Focal Press.

Fraser, B., Murphy, C., & Bunting, F. (2005). *Real World Color Management*, (2nd ed.). Berkeley: Peachpit Press.

Gerber, M. E., (1995). *The EMyth Revisited*. New York: HarperCollins.

Gulbins, J. & Steinmueller, U. (2011). *The Digital Photography Workflow Handbook: From Import to Output*. Santa Barbara: Rocky Nook Inc.

Hagen, C. (1977). An Interview with Garry Winogrand. *Afterimage, 5*(6), 8–15.

Hunter, F., Biver, S., & Fuqua, R. (2012). *Light Science & Magic: An Introduction to Photographic Lighting*, (4th ed.). Amsterdam: Focal Press, 2012.

Johnson, C. S., Jr. (2010). *Science for the Curious Photographer: An Introduction to the Science of Photography*. Natick, MA: A K Peters LTD.

Knox, D. (2005). *Strike the Baby and Kill the Blonde: An Insider's Guide to Film Slang*. New York: Three Rivers Press.

Kobré, K. (2008). *Photojournalism: The Professionals' Approach*. Amsterdam: Focal Press.

Krough, P. (2009). *The DAM Book: Digital Asset Management for Photographers*, (2nd ed.). Sebastopol: O'Reilly Media, Inc.

La Grange, A. (2005). *Basic Critical Theory for Photographers*. Amsterdam: Focal Press.

McNally, J. (2009). *The Hot Shoe Diaries: Big Light From Small Flashes*. Berkeley: New Riders.

Mearian, L. (2013). SSDs Do Die, as Linus Torvalds Just Discovered, *Computerworld*, September 12, 2013. Retrieved from http://www.computerworld.com/s/article/9242367/SSDs_i_do_i_die_as_Linus_Torvalds_just_discovered?taxonomyId=234&pageNumber=1

Meola, E. (2013). *India: In Word and Image*, (Revised, Expanded and Updated). New York: Welcome Books.

Neelman, S. (2011). *Weird Sports*. Heidelberg: Kehrer Verlag.

Rosenblum, N. (1997). *A World History of Photography*, (3rd ed.). New York: Abbeville Press Publishers.

Russotti, P., & Anderson, R. (2010). *Digital Photography Best Practices and Workflow Handbook: A Guide to Staying Ahead of the Workflow Curve.* Burlington, MA: Focal Press.

Scheier, R. L. (2007). Study: Hard Drive Failure Rates Much Higher Than Makers Estimate, *Computerworld*, March 2, 2007. Retrieved from http://www.pcworld.com/article/129558/article.html

Schewe, J. (2013). *The Digital Negative: Raw Image Processing in Lightroom, Camera Raw and Photoshop.* Berkeley: Peachpit Press.

Shahani, C. J., Basil Manns, B. & Youket, M. (2005). Longevity of CD Media: Research at the Library of Congress. Washington DC: Preservation Research and Testing Division, Library of Congress. Retrieved from http://www.loc.gov/preservation/resources/rt/studyofCDlongevity.pdf

Strobel, L. & Zakia, R. (1993). *The Focal Encyclopedia of Photography* (3rd ed.). Stoneham, MA: Butterworth-Heinemann.

Stroebel, L., Compton, J., Current, I. & Zakia, R. (1986). *Photographic Materials and Processes.* Boston: Focal Press.

Szarkowski, J. (2012). *Winogrand: Figments from the Real World*, (5th printing). New York: The Museum of Modern Art.

Wilson, L. (2003). *Avedon at Work in the American West.* Austin: University of Texas Press.

X-Rite. (2007). Defining Color: Systems for Precise Color Validation [Munsell Color], Retrieved from http://www.xrite.com/documents/literature/en/L10-315_Defining_Color_Munsell_en.pdf

# Index

F



G



H



I



J



K



L